Religious Diversity in Muslim-majority States in Southeast Asia

The **Institute of Southeast Asian Studies (ISEAS)** was established as an autonomous organization in 1968. It is a regional centre dedicated to the study of socio-political, security and economic trends and developments in Southeast Asia and its wider geostrategic and economic environment. The Institute's research programmes are the Regional Economic Studies (RES, including ASEAN and APEC), Regional Strategic and Political Studies (RSPS), and Regional Social and Cultural Studies (RSCS).

ISEAS Publishing, an established academic press, has issued more than 2,000 books and journals. It is the largest scholarly publisher of research about Southeast Asia from within the region. ISEAS Publishing works with many other academic and trade publishers and distributors to disseminate important research and analyses from and about Southeast Asia to the rest of the world.

Religious Diversity in Muslim-majority States in Southeast Asia

Areas of Toleration and Conflict

EDITED BY

BERNHARD PLATZDASCH
JOHAN SARAVANAMUTTU

INSTITUTE OF SOUTHEAST ASIAN STUDIES
Singapore

First published in Singapore in 2014 by
ISEAS Publishing
Institute of Southeast Asian Studies
30 Heng Mui Keng Terrace, Pasir Panjang
Singapore 119614

E-mail: publish@iseas.edu.sg   • Website: bookshop.iseas.edu.sg

All rights reserved. No part of this publication may be reproduced, stored in a retrieval system, or transmitted in any form or by any means, electronic, mechanical, photocopying, recording or otherwise, without the prior permission of the Institute of Southeast Asian Studies.

© 2014 Institute of Southeast Asian Studies, Singapore

The responsibility for facts and opinions in this publication rests exclusively with the authors and their interpretations do not necessarily reflect the views or the policy of the publisher or its supporters.

ISEAS Library Cataloguing-in-Publication Data

Religious diversity in Muslim-majority states in Southeast Asia : areas of toleration and conflict / edited by Bernhard Platzdasch and Johan Saravanamuttu.
1. Religious pluralism—Indonesia.
2. Islam—Indonesia.
3. Religious tolerance—Indonesia.
4. Religious pluralism—Malaysia.
5. Islam—Malaysia.
6. Religious tolerance—Malaysia.
7. Islam—Relations.
I. Platzdasch, Bernhard.
II. Saravanamuttu, Johan.
BL2112 R381   2014

ISBN 978-981-4519-64-9 (soft cover)
ISBN 978-981-4519-65-6 (E-book PDF)

Typeset by International Typesetters Pte Ltd
Printed in Singapore by Markono Print Media Pte Ltd

CONTENTS

Acknowledgments ix

Glossary xi

About the Contributors xxv

INDONESIA

1. Introduction 3
   Bernhard Platzdasch

2. NU and Muhammadiyah: Majority Views on Religious Minorities in Indonesia 16
   Robin Bush and Budhy Munawar-Rachman

3. Islam, Religious Minorities, and the Challenge of the Blasphemy Laws: A Close Look at the Current Liberal Muslim Discourse 51
   Supriyanto Abdi

4. Reading Ahmadiyah and Discourses on Freedom of Religion in Indonesia 75
   Andy Fuller

5. Sanctions against Popstars ... and Politicians? Indonesia's 2008 Pornography Law and Its Aftermath 89
   Helen Pausacker

6. The Inter-religious Harmony Forum, the Ombudsman, and the State: Resolving Church Permit Disputes in Indonesia? 113
   Melissa Crouch

7.	In Each Other's Shadow: Building Pentecostal Churches in Muslim Java *En-Chieh Chao*	133
8.	Christian–Muslim Relations in Post-Conflict Ambon, Moluccas: *Adat*, Religion, and Beyond *Birgit Bräuchler*	154
9.	Chinese Muslim Cultural Identities: Possibilities and Limitations of Cosmopolitan Islam in Indonesia *Hew Wai Weng*	173
10.	Majority and Minority: Preserving Animist and Mystical Practices in Far East Java *Nicholas Herriman*	196
11.	An *Abangan*-like Group in a *Santri* Island: The Religious Identity of the *Blater* *Yanwar Pribadi*	214

MALAYSIA

12.	Introduction *Johan Saravanamuttu*	237
13.	Islamic Praxis and Theory: Negotiating Orthodoxy in Contemporary Malaysia *Gerhard Hoffstaedter*	253
14.	Religious Pluralism and Cosmopolitanism at the City Crossroads *Yeoh Seng Guan*	268
15.	The Christian Response to State-led Islamization in Malaysia *Chong Eu Choong*	290
16.	The Politics of Buddhist Organizations in Malaysia *Tan Lee Ooi*	321
17.	Hindraf as a Response to Islamization in Malaysia *Arunajeet Kaur*	341

18.	"Deviant" Muslims: The Plight of Shias in Contemporary Malaysia *Norshahril Saat*	359
19.	Being Christians in Muslim-majority Malaysia: The Kelabit and Lun Bawang Experiences in Sarawak *Poline Bala*	379
20.	Everyday Religiosity and the Ambiguation of Development in East Malaysia: Reflections on a Dam-Construction and Resettlement Project *Liana Chua*	400

Index   419

ACKNOWLEDGMENTS

This book project began about two years ago with the idea of commissioning writers for a volume on the theme of religious minorities in Muslim Southeast Asia. We thought that such a volume would be very appropriate and valuable for ISEAS to publish since no substantial book-length work existed on such a topic in the literature. The issue of religious tolerance in Muslim-majority Southeast Asia has certainly been becoming highly significant. Hardly a week would pass in Indonesia and Malaysia, the two Muslim-majority states of Southeast Asia, without some controversy emerging about non-Muslim minorities. While much work exists on Islam in the two countries, the work on how Islam has impacted on religious minorities was rather sparse. Through a call for papers on the ISEAS webpage and through our own expertise on the subject, we put together a team of scholars to write this collection of empirical case studies on the subject.

The editors would like to thank Mr Tan Chin Tiong (Director of ISEAS), Dr Ooi Kee Beng (Deputy Director), Mrs Triena Ong (former Head of Publications), Mr Ng Kok Kiong (current Head of Publications), Ms Sheryl Sin Bing Peng and the rest of the team for their encouragement and support in making this book possible. We want to thank all the authors for their commendable efforts and their reliability in meeting deadlines and in correspondence. Finally, our thanks go to two anonymous readers who gave us valuable comments on an earlier version of the manuscript. All responsibility for inadvertent omissions or errors naturally rests on the editors.

Bernhard Platzdasch
Johan Saravanamuttu

GLOSSARY

INDONESIA

abangan	nominal, less strict, (Javanese) Muslims
adat	customary practice or laws
agama	religion
ahl al-kitab	denoting the scripture-based religions of the Muslim, Jewish, and Christian communities, acknowledged and, according to Islam, completed by the Qur'an as the final revelation
ahl as-Sunnah	Sunnis (or Sunnites): the largest denomination of Islam
Ahmadiyah	a controversial minority Muslim sect
aliran sesat	deviant sect
al-Mahdi	the prophesied redeemer of Islam
al-Masih	Messiah
AKKBB	Aliansi Kebangsaan untuk Kebebasan Beragama dan Berkeyakinan (National Alliance for Freedom of Religion and Faith), coalition promoting religious freedom and tolerance
angpao	red envelope with money, a present given during Chinese New Year
Ansor	the young men's branch of NU
azan	call to prayer

bahasa gaul	social talk, the slang used by Indonesian youth
Bahtsul Masail	a body within NU that debates classical texts and issues "*fatwa*" like decisions on NU policy and stance on social and religious issues
bajingan or *badjingan*	a common term for scoundrel in Madura and East Java and a more derogatory term sometimes used for *blater*
Banser	the paramilitary wing of Ansor
bangsat or *bhangsat*	a word that is sometimes used to refer to *blater* today
BAPPN	Badan Anti Pornografi dan Pornoaksi Nasional (National Anti-Pornography and Porno-actions Agency)
bay'at	a pledge of allegiance
bedug	a drum calling to prayer
bhubuwan	the amount of money given to the host of a *remo*
bid'ah	"improper" innovations
Blambangan	the realm which was centred in contemporary Banyuwangi, from the fourteenth to the nineteenth century.
blater	local strongmen in Madura
budaya	culture
carok or *tjarok*	a distinctive fight in Madura using sharp weapons, mostly but not exclusively sickles to regain one's honour
dakwah	invitation to faith, religious preaching, Islamic outreach
dai	preacher, agent of the call to faith
doa	recital of prayers
DPR	Dewan Perwakilan Rakyat (Peoples' Representative Council, parliament)

dukun	shamans, healers, and fortune-tellers
ELSAM	Lembaga Studi dan Advokasi Masyarakat (Institute for Study and Community Advocacy)
fatwa	religious opinion given by Islamic scholars and authorities
FORGAPP	Forum Gerakan Anti Pronografi dan Pornoaksi (Forum for the Anti Pornography and Porno-action Movement)
forum externum	external manifestations of freedom of religion or belief
forum internum	internal aspects of freedom of religion or belief
FUI	Forum Umat Islam (Forum of Believers)
FUII	Forum Umat Islam Indonesia (Indonesian Ulama Forum)
FPI	Front Pembela Islam (Islamic Defenders' Front), Islamic vigilante group formed in 1999 to combat immoral behavior in Indonesian society
garis keras	hardline (Muslims)
GBI	Gereja Bethel Indonesia (Indonesian Bethel Church)
GKJ	Gereja Kristen Jawa (Javanese Christian Church)
Golkar	the ruling government party during the New Order (1966–98)
gombor	traditional Madurese black-coloured trousers
hadith	sayings of the Prophet Muhammad
halal	lawful or 'permitted' according to Islamic principles
halal-bihalal	a gathering for mutual forgiveness to celebrate Idul Fitri
haram	unlawful or 'prohibited' according to Islamic principles and law
Hizbut Tahrir	Liberation party; founded in Jerusalem in 1953 with central aim of reviving the caliphate; the Indonesian branch was active from 1982

Hokkien	a Chinese dialect originated from the Fujian province in China
hukum	law
ICCPR	International Covenant on Civil and Political Rights
ICIP	International Centre for Islam and Pluralism
Idul Fitri	religious festival marking the end of the fasting month
imlek	Hokkien term for Chinese New Year
Islam Hatuhaha	a local variant of Islam in the Moluccas with peculiarities such as holding a weekly prayer on Friday instead of the obligatory five daily prayers and the calculation of Muslim festivals such as Idul Fitri by *adat* elders
jago or *jagoan*	local strongmen in nineteenth-century Java
JIL	Jaringan Islam Liberal (Liberal Islam Network)
jawara	local strongmen in Banten
jilbab	head covering, headscarf
jubah	long and loose dress, which hides the whole body shape
juru kunci	custodians of graveyards
kabah	cubicle shrine in the Great Mosque of Mecca
kebatinan	syncretism, syncretist beliefs, and sects
kerapan sapi	Madurese bull racing
khaul	annual celebrations on the death anniversaries of religious leaders
kiai dukun	*kiai* who also acts as shaman, healer, and fortune-teller
klebun	Madurese village heads
klenteng	Chinese temple
koko	Hokkien term for older brother

koko shirt	a collarless shirt, commonly worn by male Indonesian Muslims
Kowani	Kongres Wanita Indonesia (Indonesian Women's Congress)
KUHAP	Hukum Acara Pidana (Code of Criminal Procedures)
LAIM	Lembaga Antar-Iman Maluku (Moluccan Interfaith Council)
LPPI	Lembaga Penelitian dan Pengkajian Islam (Institute for the Study and Teaching of Islam)
mazhab	(medieval) school of law in Islam
maksiat	sin (i.e., un-Islamic deed and thought)
maw'izah hasanah	good learning
masjid	mosque
mengharamkan	"the prohibiting of"
MIAI	Majelis Islam A'laa Indonesia (Supreme Council of Indonesian Muslims); formed in 1937
MK	Mahkamah Konstitusi (Constitutional Court)
MONAS	Monumen Nasional (National Monument)
MMI	Majelis Mujahidin Indonesia (Council of Indonesian Muhajideen), Islamist grouping established in 2000 in Yogyakarta
Muhammadiyah	largest modernist Muslim organization in Indonesia, established in 1912
MUI	Majelis Ulama Indonesia (Indonesia Ulama Council)
mujadalah	discussion and civilized debate
murtad	someone who is considered to have left Islam
napel	giving money to the dancer(s) in *remo* by putting it on the dancer's chest
ngompang	the *blater*'s act of giving more money to the host (a fellow *blater*, who was himself a guest at an earlier occasion) in *remo* than he received from him before

ngaji (as a noun)	*pengajian*; religious instruction; any meeting of people in which the participants recognize the purpose to be religious but which is not among the rituals prescribed in traditionalist Islam
ngaji (as a verb)	to partake in formalized group Islamic instruction
NGO	non-governmental organization
NU	Nahdlatul Ulama, largest traditionalist-orthodox Muslim organization in Indonesia, est. 1926
nyareh Taretan or *nyareh Kancah*	means of establishing new fraternities or fortifying old brotherhoods in *remo*
odheng	traditional Madurese head accessories
ormas	*organisasi masyarakat*, community-based organization
osing	the predominant ethnic group in Banyuwangi
PAN	Partai Amanat Nasional (National Mandate Party)
Pancasila	the Five Moral Principles that make up Indonesia's national doctrine
pasarean	sacred burial grounds
PBHI	Perhimpunan Bantuan Hukum Indonesia (Indonesian Legal Aid Association)
PBNU	Pengurus Besar Nahdlatul Ulama (Executive Board of NU)
pesa'an	traditional Madurese black-coloured shirts
PKS	Partai Keadilan Sejahtera (Prosperity and Justice Party), largest Islamist party in Indonesia
patkwa	Chinese eight-sided diagram, symbolizing luck and prosperity
peci	rimless cap, commonly worn by male Indonesian Muslims
pela	traditional village alliances
pembauran	intermingling, blending

pengajian	Islamic study session
pesantren	Islamic boarding school
PITI	Persatuan Islam Tionghoa Indonesia (Indonesian Chinese Muslim Association)
PPP	Partai Persatuan Pembangunan (Unity Development Party), Islamist party
preman	thug, gangster, term commonly used in Jakarta
pryayi	the aristocratic, bureaucracy-based mystical and Hindu religious adherence identified by Geertz in 1950s Pare.
qigong	Chinese breathing exercise
Qur'an	God's word revealed to the Prophet Muhammad, the supreme source of Islam
Ramadan	Islamic fasting month
rakaat	prostrations during prayer
reformasi	political, social, and economic reform — refers to the period immediately preceding and for several years following Soeharto's fall in May 1998
remo	a feast characteristic to the *blater* community
rokat	Madurese rituals to ask protection from the spirits of their ancestors, to avoid calamities as well as to get blessings
RMS	Republik Maluku Selatan (Republic of the South Moluccas)
sabung ayam	cock fighting
sakera	typical Madurese red and white striped t-shirt
sandur or *sandhor*	Madurese dancing performed in *remo*, in Java called *tayub*
santri	pupils or followers of a *kiai*
sesat	deviant
syariah (*shari'a*)	Islamic law

Shiism (Sy'ia, Sy'iah, Shia)	one of the two major branches of Islam, regarding Ali, the son-in-law of Muhammad, as the Prophet's legitimate successor
sholat	ritual prayers performed five times daily
silaturahim	friendship, good relationship
siwalima	referring to a cultural dichotomization of Moluccan society (*siwa* and *lima*) that, however, can only exist in its unity
SKB	Surat Keputusan Bersama (Joint Ministerial Decree)
syahadat	oath
syiar	preaching
syirik	idolatry, polytheism
tandhak	dancers in *remo*
taraweh	non-obligatory evening prayers during fasting month
tayub	traditional Central and East Javanese art performance whose dancers are called *tledhek, taledhek, ledhek,* or *tandak*. An integral part of spirit shrine ritual associated with the annual *bersih desa* (spirit shrine ritual) festivity
Tionghoa	Hokkien term for Chinese people
umat, ummah	Muslim community
UUD	Undang-Undang Dasar, the national constitution of Indonesia
walisongo	the nine saints popularly credited for spreading Islam in Java
waria	transgender people
YHMCHI	Yayasan Haji Muhammad Cheng Hoo Indonesia (Muhammad Cheng Hoo Foundation)
YLBHI	Yayasan Lembaga Bantuan Hukum Indonesia (Indonesian Legal Aid Foundation)
ziarah	pilgrimage to the graves of saints

MALAYSIA

ABIM	Angkatan Belia Islam Malaysia (Malaysian Youth Islamic Movement)
Allah	Muslim name for God, a term also used by Christians and Sikhs in Malaysia
ACCIN	Allied Coordinating Committee of Islamic NGOs
ASWJ	*Ahlus Sunnah Wal Jamaah.* The official Sunni-Shafi'i school of Islam practised in Malaysia prescribed by the Malaysian Department of Islamic Advancement Malaysia
azan	Muslim call to prayer
Bahasa Malaysia	The national language of Malaysia, sharing a linguistic root of Malay with Bahasa Indonesia
Bahasa Indonesia	The national language of Indonesia.
Barisan Nasional	National Front, which was originally made up of the political parties United Malays National Organization (UMNO), Malaysian Chinese Association (MCA), and the Malaysian Indian Congress (MIC) when it was named Parti Perikatan (Alliance Party)
Baitullah	House of Allah
bomoh	shaman, traditional healer
Bumiputera	A Malaysian term meaning 'sons of the soil' referring to the Malays, indigenous peoples of Peninsular Malaysia and the natives of Sarawak and Sabah
CCM	Council of Churches Malaysia, the national body that represents mainline Protestant churches in Malaysia.
CFC	Christian Federation of Malaysia
dakwah	Islamic missionary activity
Dhammic socialism	Synthesis of a Buddhist worldview and Western egalitarian political idealism encouraging Buddhists to be actively engaged in worldly affairs to fight for a just world

Darul Arqam	House of Arqam, a group considered deviant by the Malaysian government and Malaysian Islamic authorities
halal	permissible in Islam
haram	forbidden in Islam
Hindraf	Hindu Rights Action Force
ijtihad	individual reasoning (in Islamic jurisprudence)
Kaabah	The large stone structure in Mecca which is circumambulated by Muslims during the pilgrimage
Kaedah-Kadeah Hukum Sebat	Caning methods sanctioned by *hudud* law
kafir	Unbeliever or non-believer in the eyes of Muslims
hudud	The class of punishments under *Syariah* fixed for theft, robbery, illicit sex, alcohol consumption and apostasy
haj	Pilgrimage to Mecca, one of the five pillars of faith for Muslims
IFC	Inter-Faith Commission
IIUM	International Islamic University of Malaysia
ISA	Internal Security Act. The ISA was repealed and replaced by Security Offences (Special Measures) Act 2012 on 18 June 2012
Islam Hadhari	Civilizational Islam
JAIS	Jabatan Agama Islam Selangor (Islamic Department of Selangor)
JAKIM	Jabatan Kemajuan Islam Malaysia (Malaysian Department of Islamic Advancement Malaysia)
JAWI	Jabatan Agama Wilayah Perseketuan (Islamic Department of Federal Territory)
kaum muda	modernists
kaum tua	traditionalists

Ketuanan Melayu	Malaya supremacy or Malay lordship
khalwat	Term used in Malaysia to mean the compromising proximity of single men and women, chargeable as an offence for Muslims.
malu	embarrassment, shame
MBA	Malaysian Buddhist Association
MCCBCHST	Malaysian Consultative Council for Buddhism, Christianity, Hinduism, Sikhism and Taoism
Parti Keadilan Rakyat	People's Justice Party
Persatuan Ulama Malaysia	Association of Islamic Scholars Malaysia
PAS	Parti Islam Se-Malaysia (Islamic Party of Malaysia)
PERKIM	Pertubuhan Kebajikan Islam se-Malaysia (Malaysian Islamic Welfare Organization)
Malay	Constitutionally defined as those who practise Malay customs (*adat*), habitually speak the Malay language and are adherents of Islam
kampung	Malay village/neighbourhood
Kelabit	The Kelabit inhabit the highlands of Central Borneo in the state of Sarawak, East Malaysia, and are also known as the Highlanders
Lun Bawang	Formerly identified as Murut, the Lun Bawang community are closely related to the Kelabit people and considered to be earlier settlers of the highland regions of northeastern part of Sarawak
Majlis Kebangsaan Bagi Hal Ehwal Ugama Islam	Malaysian National Council of Islamic Affairs
MBA	Malaysian Buddhist Association
Menteri Besar	Malay term for chief executive of the state government, equivalent to chief minister

nasyid	Islamic devotional music
NECF	National Evangelical Christian Fellowship, the national body that represents Evangelical (independent Protestant) churches in Malaysia.
OIC	Organization of Islamic Conference
Pakatan Rakyat	People's Alliance, the political coalition made up of opposition parties that were formed in 2008. The major parties in this coalition are Parti Keadilan Rakyat/People's Justice Party (PKR), Democratic Action Party (DAP) and the Islamic Party of Malaysia (PAS)
PEMBELA	Muslim Organizations in Defence of Islam
pondok	Islamic boarding school
Puzhao Buddhist Vihara Puzhao	A multi-purpose Buddhist training, education, research and cultivation centre built by YBAM
qisas	Offenses that involve bodily injury or loss of life punishable by death and imprisonment but which can be compensated by money or property
shahadah	Islamic declaration of faith
sheik	Arabic honorific
Shiism (Sy'ia, Sy'iah, Shia)	Followers of Ali, who regarded him as the legitimate successor to the Prophet Muhammad
Sijil Farid	A certificate stating that inheritance is distributed in accordance to Islamic law in Malaysia
solat	Prayer as defined in Islam
Sunnah	Teachings, sayings, and practices of the Prophet Muhammad
syariah (shari'a)	Islamic law
Tabligh groups	Islamic missionary groups springing from the Deobandi movement, Tabligh Jumaat, of the Indian subcontinent

taqlid	imitation
tariqa	Sufi order/brotherhood
ummah	community of Muslim believers
UMNO	United Malays National Organization
ustad (*ustaz*)	religious teacher (Islam)
Wesak Day	(Vesak or Vesakha) Day is a holy day for Buddhists in Sri Lanka and Southeast Asian countries. It encompasses the day of the birth, enlightenment, and passing away of Gautama Buddha in Theravada traditions
YBAM	Young Buddhist Association of Malaysia
Yang Di Pertuan Agong	The Paramount Ruler or King in Malaysia
zakat	Donation of a proportion of one's earnings, one of the five pillars of faith for Muslims
zinah	Sex outside of wedlock or adultery as defined in Islam

ABOUT THE CONTRIBUTORS

Bernhard Platzdasch is the former Assistant Director (Projects) at the Centre for Research on Islamic and Malay Affairs (RIMA) in Singapore. He previously worked at the Institute of Southeast Asian Studies (ISEAS) in Singapore. His Ph.D. was published as *Islamism in Indonesia: Politics in the Emerging Democracy* (2009). He is co-editor of the book *The Malay Heritage of Singapore* (2011) and the author of numerous articles on the topics of politics and Islam in Indonesia. He also worked as a freelance consultant for Oxford Analytica.

Johan Saravanamuttu is Visiting Senior Research Fellow at the Institute of Southeast Asian Studies, Singapore and was formerly professor of political science at Universiti Sains Malaysia (USM) in Penang where he served as Dean of the School of Social Sciences (1994–96). He recently authored *Malaysia's Foreign Policy, the First 50 Years: Alignment, Neutralism, Islamism* (2010) and edited *Islam and Politics in Southeast Asia* (2010). He also co-edited *New Politics in Malaysia* (2003).

Robin Bush is Senior Research Fellow at the Asia Research Institute (ARI), NUS, Singapore. Her research interests revolve around the interfaces between Islam, politics, and development, particularly in Indonesia and Southeast Asia. She is pursuing two research projects at ARI — the first is an updated and in-depth examination of NU and Muhammadiyah, Indonesia's largest mass-based Muslim organizations, and the second is contributing to the cluster's overall project on Religion and Development in Asia. Prior to joining ARI in December 2011, Dr Bush spent eleven years at The Asia Foundation's Indonesia office — directing its programmes on Islam for the first six years, and then as Deputy and Country Representative for the last five years. Her book is entitled

Nahdlatul Ulama and the Struggle for Power in Islam and Politics in Indonesia (2009), and she is the author of numerous other articles on Islam in Indonesia.

Budhy Munawar-Rachman leads religion-related programming at The Asia Foundation, Jakarta. He was Director at The Paramadina Center for Islamic Studies (1994–2005), and prior to that was the Director of The Institute for the Religious and Philosophical Studies (LSAF, 1992–95). In 2004–05 he founded the Project on Pluralism and Religious Tolerance, The Center for Spirituality and Leadership (CSL) to promote the late Nurcholish Madjid's thought on Islam and religious pluralism. He holds a doctorate in philosophy from STF Driyarkara. He teaches Islamic Studies and Religious Studies at Paramadina University, The Driyarkara School of Philosophy (STF Driyarkara) and the University of Indonesia. He has written more than fifty books, including *Pluralist Islam* (2000), *Interfaith Theology* (co-author, 2003), *Reading Nurcholish Madjid* (2008), and *Reorientation of Islamic Reform: Secularism, Liberalism, and Pluralism* (2010).

Andy Fuller is a researcher and writer with interests in urban cultures, literature and Islamic thought. He has had post-doctoral fellowships at KITLV (Leiden, 2011), IIAS (Leiden, 2012) and the University of Macau (2012). He has published in academic and general journals and include "Going to Guluk-Guluk" (*RIMA*, vol. 45, 2012), "States of Violence" (*Warscapes*, July 2012), "Writing Jakarta in Seno Gumira Ajidarma's *Kentut Kosmopolitan*" (ARI NUS Working Paper No. 160, 2011) and "Asian Urbanisms and Mallness in Recording the Future" (ARI NUS Working Paper No. 183, 2012). His book *Sastra dan Politik: Membaca Karya-karya Seno Gumira Ajidarma* was published in 2011. A collection of Fuller's translations of Afrizal Malna's poems was published in 2013.

Helen Pausacker is Deputy Director of the Centre for Indonesian Law, Islam and Society (CILIS), a principal research assistant at CILIS and the Asian Law Centre, Melbourne Law School and an editor for the *Australian Journal of Asian Law* at the University of Melbourne. Helen received her Ph.D. from the University of Melbourne in 2013. Her BA (Hons) thesis (1975) discussed Indonesia's 1974 Marriage Bill and the debate between Islamic and other groups that surrounded it. Helen edited *Inside Indonesia*'s issue on "Freedom of Religion" (no. 89, April–June 2007) and co-edited *Chinese Indonesians: Remembering, Distorting, Forgetting* (2005) with Tim Lindsey.

Helen has also researched *wayang* (shadow puppetry) and her publications about *wayang* include the book, *Behind the Shadows: Understanding a Wayang Performance* (1996).

Melissa Crouch is a Research Fellow at the Centre for Asian Legal Studies, the Law Faculty, the National University of Singapore. She has previously been a Research Fellow at the International Institute of Asian Studies (Leiden), and the Centre for Islamic Law and Society and the Asian Law Centre at the Melbourne Law School, the University of Melbourne. Melissa is the author of *Law and Religion in Indonesia: Conflict and the Courts in West Java* (2013). She is also the co-editor of a volume on *Law, Society and Transition in Myanmar* (forthcoming, September 2014). Her current research is on constitutionalism and the process of law reform in Myanmar, and also on Muslims and the state in Myanmar.

Hew Wai Weng is Research Fellow at the Zentrum Moderner Orient, Berlin and currently working on a research entitled, "Sites of Inclusion and Exclusion: New Muslims Places in Urban Malaysia and Indonesia". He graduated from the Australian National University, where he submitted his Ph.D. thesis, "Negotiating Ethnicity and Religiosity: Chinese Muslim Identities in Post-New Order Indonesia". He was also a postdoctoral fellow at the International Institute for Asian Studies, Leiden. He is the author of *Identiti Cina Muslim di Malaysia: Persempadanan, Perundingan dan Kacukan Budaya* [Chinese Muslim Identities in Malaysia: Boundary-making, Identity Negotiation and Cultural Hybridity] (2014).

En-Chieh Chao is a Postdoctoral Research Fellow at the Center for Social Sciences and Humanities at Academia Sinica. She received her Ph.D. degree in anthropology from Boston University in January 2013. She is currently working on a book project titled *The Companionship of Religious Others: Women, Islam, and Pentecostalism in Indonesia*, a study on how inter-religious relations and new gender norms reshape self-identifies and Javanese society. Her research interests include anthropology of religion, identity politics, Southeast Asia, as well as Muslim–Christian relations across the globe. More recently, she has been investigating the intersection between scientific and religious discourses regarding medical practices among Muslims and Buddhists in Asia.

Birgit Bräuchler is lecturer and researcher of social and cultural anthropology at the University of Frankfurt. Her main research interests are media and cyberanthropology, conflict and peace studies, cultural rights and the revival of tradition. She is the author of *Cyberidentitiesat War. Der Molukkenkonflikt im Internet* (transcript, 2005), editor of *Reconciling Indonesia* (2009), co-editor of *Theorising Media and Practice* (2010) and has published several book chapters and articles in peer-reviewed journals. An English language edition of *Cyberidentites at War* has been published in 2013 (Berghahn). Her current research is on the cultural dimension of reconciliation in Indonesia.

Nicholas Herriman is Senior Lecturer in Anthropology at La Trobe University, Australia. His doctoral thesis was based on over a year's fieldwork in Indonesia, studying the killings of "sorcerers" and what they tell us about state-society relations. It was awarded Best Thesis by the Australian Anthropological Society in 2008. His book *The Entangled State* (Yale Southeast Asia Studies, 2012), which was translated into Indonesian as *Negara vs Santet* (Obor, 2013), revises the image of an overbearing state in Indonesia. A further monograph entitled "Witch Hunt and Conspiracy" (Monash University, forthcoming) presents new insights into an outbreak of sorcerer killings in East Java in 1998.

Supriyanto Abdi is currently completing his Ph.D. thesis at the Asia Institute of the University of Melbourne, examining Muslim intellectual debates on state-religion relations and religious freedom in post-New Order Indonesia. He obtained a Master degree of Contemporary Asian Analysis from the same university in 2005 and worked for several years as a researcher at the Centre for Human Rights Studies of the Islamic University of Indonesia in Yogyakarta.

Yanwar Pribadi teaches at State Institute for Islamic Studies (IAIN) "Sultan Maulana Hasanuddin" Banten, Serang, Indonesia and is a researcher at Laboratorium Bantenologi at the same university. He obtained his Ph.D. in 2013 from Leiden University. His recent publications include "Strongmen and Religious Leaders in Java: Their Dynamic Relationship in Search of Power", *Al-Jamiah Journal of Islamic Studies* 49, no. 1 (2011); "Kiai in Madura: Their Roles in Local Politics in Indonesia", *American Journal of Islamic Social Sciences* 29, no. 3, Special Issue Muslims and Political Change (2012); and "Another Side of Islam in Banten: The Socio-Political Roles of Jawara During the New Order Era 1966–1998", *Journal of Indonesian Islam* 7, no. 2 (2013).

Gerhard Hoffstaedter is lecturer in Anthropology in the School of Science at the University of Queensland, Australia, researching religion, ethnicity and the state, international development and refugees in Southeast Asia. He has published widely on Malaysian identity politics, focusing on ethnicity and Islam, in edited volumes and journals, such as *Ethnicities, Contemporary Islam and Asian Ethnicity*. His first monograph *Modern Muslim Identities: Negotiating Religion and Ethnicity in Malaysia* was published in 2011.

Yeoh Seng Guan is Senior Lecturer at the School of Arts and Social Sciences, Monash University (Sunway Campus). He is an urban anthropologist who researches primarily on the interfaces between cities, religion, media and civil society in Southeast Asia. He also produces ethnographic documentaries. Recent publications include "Holy Water and Material Religion in a Pilgrimage Shrine in Malaysia", in *The Spirit of Things: Materiality in an Age of Religious Pluralism in Southeast Asia*, edited by Julius Bautista and Antony Reid (2012) and "Malaysian Figures of Modernity", in *Figures of Southeast Asian Modernity*, edited by Joshua Barker, Eric Harm and Johan Linquist (2013) and *The Other Kuala Lumpur: Living in the Shadows of a Globalising Southeast Asian City* (2014). He is editor of *Media, Culture and Society in Malaysia* (2010).

Chong Eu Choong is a Senior Lecturer at Citizenship Values Education Unit, School of Education, Taylor's University, Selangor, Malaysia. He obtained his Ph.D. in political science in 2010 at the Science University Malaysia (USM). He has published "Strengthening Democracy in Malaysia: The Need for a Vibrant Public Sphere", in *The Bible and the Ballot: Reflections on Christian Political Engagement in Malaysia Today*, edited by Joshua Woo and Soo-Inn Tan (2011) and "Delving into the Whirlwind: Some Explanatory Notes on Everyday Life and Gender", *Akademika 63* (July 2003).

Tan Lee Ooi is a lecturer in Mass Communication Department in KDU College Penang, Malaysia. He completed his Ph.D. at the National University of Singapore. He is the author of *Dinamik Ruang Siber dalam Gerakan Reformasi di Malaysia* [The Dynamics of Cyberspace during the Reformasi Movement in Malaysia] published by National University Press of Malaysia. He was previously a journalist and has written on current issues for newspapers and the online media.

Norshahril Saat is a doctoral candidate at the Department of Political and Social Change, School of International, Political, and Strategic Studies, College of Asia and the Pacific, Australian National University (ANU). Before pursuing his Ph.D. studies, he was research associate at ISEAS (2010–11). He is a recipient of the Islamic Religious Council of Singapore (MUIS) Post-graduate Scholarship 2011. He was also a recipient of the Tun Dato Sir Cheng Lock Tan M.A. scholarship (ISEAS) and the National University of Singapore MA scholarship. He recently published "Islamising Malayness: Ulama, Authority and Discourse", *Contemporary Islam: Dynamics of Muslim Life*, vol. 6, no. 2 (2012).

Arunajeet Kaur was most recently a Fellow at the Institute of Southeast Asian Studies (ISEAS), Singapore. She completed her doctoral dissertation at the Australian National University entitled, "From Independence to Hindraf: The Malaysian Indian Community and the Negotiation for Minority Rights". She has also recently co-authored a book, *The Migration of Indian Human Capita: The Ebb and Flow of Indian Professionals in Southeast Asia* (2011).

Poline Bala is Senior Lecturer at the Department of Anthropology and Sociology, Faculty of Social Sciences, University Malaysia Sarawak (UNIMAS). She graduated with an M.A. in Asian Studies at Cornell University and received her Ph.D. in Social Anthropology from University of Cambridge, UK. She has published *Changing Borders and Identities in the Kelabit Highlands: Anthropological Reflections on Growing Up in a Kelabit Village near the International Border* (2002), and "Interethnic Ties along the Kalimantan-Sarawak Border in Highlands Borneo: The Kelabit and Lun Berian case in the Kelabit-Kerayan Highlands", *Borneo Research Bulletin*, vol. 23 (2001).

Liana Chua is Lecturer in Anthropology at Brunel University, London. She works on Christianity, ethnic citizenship, resettlement, and conservation in Sarawak, and has broader research and teaching interests in materiality, museology, and ethnographic photography. She is the author of *The Christianity of Culture: Conversion, Ethnic Citizenship, and the Matter of Religion in Malaysian Borneo* (2012), and co-editor of a number of books, including *Southeast Asian Perspectives on Power* (2012).

INDONESIA

1

INTRODUCTION

Bernhard Platzdasch

In August 2012, a crowd of Sunni Muslims (Islam's largest denomination) attacked a community of minority Shiite Muslims in the Sampang regency on the island of Madura, part of East Java. They burned down dozens of houses belonging to Shiite members and killed two people. Views of what caused the violence differed greatly. Government officials declared the attacks to be rooted in a "family conflict"; human rights activists held that the attack was carefully planned in advance and that a deep-seated mistrust towards members of the Sy'ia community concerning their religious beliefs was at the root of the Sy'ia–Sunni violence.[1] They asserted that the violence was triggered by a group that had intended to stop a number of Shiite students from returning to their boarding school in the town of Bangil, East Java, after spending the holidays marking the end of the fasting month of Ramadan at home. After the Shiite students had reported the threats to the local police, around 1,000 attackers burned down their village.[2]

The assault evoked memories of a similar incident in late 2011, when the home and *pesantren* (local boarding school) of a Madurese Shiite leader by the name of Tajul Muluk were destroyed. Tajul had been facing accusations of preaching that Islam's holy book, the Qur'an, was not God's original scripture and that its true and final version would only be revealed to the Mahdi, the prophesied redeemer of Islam at the end of times. In response to the charges, the local branch of the Indonesian Ulama Council (Majelis Ulama Indonesia [MUI]) released a *fatwa* (legal ruling) declaring Tajul's teachings to be "deviant". The local district court subsequently charged

Tajil with "defamation of religion", which carries a maximum sentence of five years in prison.

These two incidents took place against a backdrop of increasing religious segregation and intolerance in Indonesia. Various surveys suggest that an increasing number of people harbour feelings of resentment and suspicion towards people of different religious convictions, in particular if these happen to live in the same neighbourhood. The most recent survey (at the time of writing), publicized in October 2012, put that share at 67.8 per cent.[3]

Indonesian officials' responses to the Madura assaults followed those of other cases of inter-religious conflict. Minister of Religious Affairs, Suryadharma Ali, condemned the violence whilst calling on Shiites to convert to Sunni Islam in order to avoid persecution. Minister of Home Affairs, Gamawan Fauzi, suggested relocating the victims of the attacks to the mainland of East Java to prevent similar conflicts in the future. Mutawakkil Alallah, a local leader of the Nahdlatul Ulama (NU), Indonesia's largest Muslim organization, said: "Shiism is against human rights and they [Shiites] despise Islam. ... Banning them is not the solution, but we want Shiites to abstain from worshiping publicly." And further: "If they do not enter the public sphere and keep [their religious activity] within their own home, they will be safer."[4] At the same time, to various extent many of the main Muslim organizations issued counter-statements distancing themselves from accusations of blasphemy by individual representatives, thereby pointing to deep divisions within both these groups and Indonesian Muslim society in general.

DIVERSE MAJORITY, HYBRID IDENTITIES

An overwhelming majority of Southeast Asian Muslims (96 per cent) live in Indonesia and Malaysia.[5] Indonesian Islam is formally homogeneous in its religious outlook with about 86 per cent of Muslims being Sunnites of the Shafi'i legal school (*mazhab*), yet both Islam and Indonesian society in general are characterized by a profusion of belief patterns, cultures, and languages.[6] The remaining religions are made up of Protestants (6 per cent), Catholics (3.5 per cent), Hindus (1.8 per cent), Buddhists (1 per cent), and around 0.6 per cent whose religious beliefs are not clearly defined but effectively consist of indigenous, syncretic and animist beliefs and sects (*kebatinan* or *aliran kebatinan*). Indonesian citizens are required to declare themselves as a follower of one of the six officially acknowledged religions (*agama*) in their ID cards.

It is a scholarly truism that Indonesian Islam is highly varied in outlook and practice. It embraces and incorporates a wide array of domestic and foreign influences, from the localized and district-bound to the pan-Islamic, from ecumenist to *jihadist* readings. By comparison, Islam's role in politics has historically been smaller in Indonesia than in Malaysia. As Fealy (2005, p. 153) writes: "In Malaysia, Islamisation has resulted in greater Islamism and legalism; in Indonesia it has had more pluralistic and liberal manifestations." What is more, with a Muslim population of a comparatively small 60 per cent Malaysia is statistically the more diverse country, yet "it is the least tolerant of any state towards its majority population, legally allowing no Malay at all to be other than a Sunni Muslim" (Reid 2011). This intimate association between an ethnicity and a particular creed is absent in Indonesia.

Notably argued by Olivier Roy, literal and conservative expressions of faith are flourishing, pointing to a disassociation between communities of various faiths and their socio-cultural identities. Religions break away from their cultural roots — a *deculturation* process in which individuals consciously abandon a particular culture or certain cultural characteristics (Roy 2010).

Any study on religious diversity in today's Indonesia and Malaysia is set against the background that Muslims in these countries have become more self-consciously Islamic in the last twenty-five years or so — an Islamization that is both momentous and ongoing (Ricklefs 2008; Ricklefs 2012). This process went along with a widening and fortification of religious observance; it was accompanied by "a strong political will for increased public expression of Islam" (Bush 2012) and with the "[e]stablishment of dogmatic forms of religion on the rise" (Reid 2011). It has resulted in the historical Southeast Asian trademark of religious and cultural diversity being juxtaposed against and challenged by a contrary trend towards religious conservatism and mutual religious exclusivism, an increasing appeal of "pure" belief models, and the resulting scepticism for local accommodations towards religious scripture and apprehension towards inter-religious mingling (Reid 2011). According to Roy (2010):

> What we see today is the militant reformation of religion in a secularized space that has given religion its autonomy and therefore the conditions for its expansion. Secularization and globalization have forced religions to break away from culture. It was instrumental for establishing "a system of religions that are competitive and mutually exclusive".

"Indonesia today can be aptly described as bi-polar", write Robin Bush and Budhy Munawar-Rahman in chapter 2. This can be understood as a general observation of the country's dual position as a stable democracy and regional economic hub on one hand yet plagued by unrelenting woes such as the seemingly ubiquitous corruption in all levels of society and pervasive legal uncertainty. Yet "bi-polar" also aptly captures Indonesia's uneasy fluctuation between a traditional devotion to pluralist religious ideals and a tendency towards religious bigotry and state meddling in religious affairs.

The picture appears to be paradoxical in more than one regard. Islam's popularity and appeal is on a continuous rise; Islamic politics, however, is not — in fact, measured by popular support for Islamist parties (i.e., parties adopting Islam as party ideology), it is on the decline. The popular vote for Islamist parties dropped from 21 per cent in the 2004 general elections to 16.5 per cent in 2009 and thus back to the level of the Islamist share in the first post-New Order democratic polls in 1999. If one adds the vote of Indonesia's Islam-oriented parties (parties that are linked to large Islamic organizations but have not adopted Islam as party ideology), the 2009 result looks even worse, with a decline from about 36 per cent in 1999 and roughly 37.5 per cent in 2004 to 29 per cent in 2009.

The Soeharto government (1966–98) had endorsed Islamic cultural expressions whilst keeping a tight grip on its political aspirations. In Malaysia, by contrast, both the Malay-nationalist UMNO (United Malays National Organization) and the Islamist PAS (Parti Islam Se-Malaysia), made the promotion of Islam and its intrinsic connection with Malay identity a key agenda, at times outdoing each other in their claim for Islamic authenticity (Fealy 2005). This distinction appears to be gradually recoiling. Many Indonesian Muslim voters today perceive religious interests as adequately represented by non-Islamist and by nationalist parties. Islamist parties have lost a good share of their distinctiveness as mainstream, and supposedly "secular" parties have increasingly adopted pro-Islamic agendas in their party platforms. These parties have increasingly moved towards a pro-Islamic ideological middle ground in recent years by assuming a strong economically nationalist cum Islamic identity (Platzdasch 2009*a* and *b*).[7] Traditionally, proponents of a formalist and legalistic role of Islam have regarded Islam's history in the modern Indonesian state with a sense of victimization which colours their position towards religious minorities, especially Christians (Platzdasch 2009*b*, chapter 2). As Bush (2012, p. 189) summarizes this multifaceted dynamic between the ongoing pro-Islamic drift on one side and pluralist traditions on the other: "Religion is obviously an issue on which feelings run deep, and the Muslim community has often felt that it has not received the political recognition it is due. At the same time, Indonesians of all religions are strongly proud of, and committed to, the pluralist nature of their society...."

STATE INFRINGEMENT: "PROPER" AND "IMPROPER" RELIGION

Even in 1945, the architects of the then-infant Indonesian Republic appeared deeply aware of the latent precariousness of the combustible religious and ethnic mixes of its peoples. Its legal foundation came about after intense debate and ideological quarrel, settling on a constitution that "kept *sui generis* religion at bay of the political system or defined it in neutral terms" (Kersten 2011). This, Kersten highlights, did not equal a banning of religion from the public sphere but rather sought to exercise control and circumscribe the parameters in which religions and beliefs would be allowed to operate. Hence, as Steinberg (2006, p. 14) points out, and stressing the contrast to the largely secularized public spheres of much of the western world, Indonesia "continue[s] to draw upon religious institutions and authority to shape their several cultures, societies and governmental structures".[8] In Indonesia, state infringement in defining what is religion and what is not indeed dates back to independence. To a large extent, it has been carried out through the Ministry of Religious Affairs, which has largely been acting as a Ministry of Islamic Affairs since the 1970s. From then on, the Indonesian state has been reinforcing an official, majoritarian, version of what religion, including Islam, constitutes and what the acceptable doctrinal boundaries of religious beliefs are.

Indonesia's constitution recognizes six religions (classified as *agama*): Islam, Protestantism, Catholicism, Hinduism, Buddhism, and Confucianism, the latter only added by a presidential decree in 2000. Unlike in Malaysia, Islam does not formally have a special status in the constitution yet the first principle of the Pancasila — "the belief in the One All-Powerful God" — is an avowal to monotheism and as such was a concession to Islamic majority sentiment in the early days of the Republic.[9] Older religions centring on spirit worship, syncretic, and mystical belief systems (*kebatinan*) are officially deemed inferior and undeserving of the *agama* label. They are thus given lesser official treatment, and they have "not being institutionalized in the modern sector" (Picard and Raillon 2011; Kersten 2011). Being officially part of the six recognized faiths — mostly Islam and Christianity — adherents of these beliefs thus exist essentially as administrative phantoms of a veiled religious identity. Those customs and practices linked to the beliefs that preceded the arrival of the world religions are captured in the term *adat*. Although intrinsically linked to syncretism and local beliefs, *adat* managed to sustain a more positive connotation that those beliefs themselves were able to manage.

Progressively more throughout the last decade, Indonesian lawmakers and the government have appeared susceptible to the insistence that "beliefs" are dangerous to the establishment of a "proper", officially acknowledged, form of "religion". In Indonesia in reality this only affects Islam. These "beliefs" remain under the domain of the Ministry of Education and Cultures unlike the official religions, which operate under the Ministry of Religious Affairs. Agnosticism and, especially, atheism remain officially non-existent, partly because of the officially cultivated and widely cited association with communism, partly because of the similarly cultivated, romanticized depiction of the Indonesian populace as a "religious peoples" (*umat beragama*). This rests on a thinly veiled model adopted from the Islamic heartland where pre-Islamic indigenous religious communities were not part of the "people of the book" (*ahl al-kitab*) and thus had little or no rights in the Muslim-dominated society they lived in. Altogether, in Indonesia there are, as Reid notes, "no congenial precedents" for today's non-conformist main offshoots of "proper" religions. Examples are the Islamic Ahmadiyah sect, Shiism, or the Jehovah's Witnesses, which are not being recognized as separate Muslim or, respectively, Christian, communities (Reid 2011).

TOLERATION AND CONFLICT

State patronage of Islam stresses the boundaries of religious faith and promotes a set of fundamental convictions that all Muslims should have in common. It sanctions the moral and historical supremacy of a murkily defined majority-Islam. It is also endorsing a mindset that "mainstream" Muslims are under threat and that they must be protected from "improper" religious readings. It sets political incentives for conservative agendas perceived as convenient resources for political moblization and support. This is, referring to Roy and the *deculturation* of religion, contributing to a gap between the believer and the non-believer as individuals in religious communities no longer believe in sharing either religious practice or common values; it has contributed to stereotypization and segregation along religious fault lines, thereby aiding social disturbances and legal injustice.

Mob violence such as in the cases outlined at the beginning of this introduction has often been left unpunished, creating disdain of Indonesia's dearly held claim to be not merely a religiously tolerant but a lawful society (*negara hukum*). Over the last five years or so, Indonesia's legal and constitutional impasses regarding religious freedom have become more apparent and increasingly the topic of academic debate. This debate has highlighted the inherent contradictions and omissions of Indonesia's 1945 constitution, challenging common wisdom that the country protected and guaranteed full religious freedom (Crouch 2011; Platzdasch 2011). Indonesia has made headlines for attacks against minority Islamic groups (particularly Ahmadis and Shiites) and the jaundiced eye of government officials for Islamist groups and their agendas including the forced closure of churches, especially in the province of West Java and in the larger Jakarta area. External criticism over these matters often reveals considerable levels of national sensitivity and, among parts of both the Muslim and nationalist sections, a feeling of cultural defeat. Overall, Indonesia has frequently been making international headlines for wrong reasons. Inter-religious conflicts and a mixture of failure and unwillingness by government officials to respond adequately are eagerly picked up by the foreign press, eclipsing achievements in other areas and damaging the country politically and economically.

The chapters in the Indonesia section of the volume demonstrate that a state-sanctioned form of Islam and the state's interference into religious matters has impacted on the lives of non-Muslim as well as on Islamic minorities (in other countries, a similar role is being played by a particular ethnic or linguistic section of the population). Some of these writings at the same time show the remarkably enduring diversity of beliefs and practices, which contrast with the more singularly purifying discourses amidst the solidification of a legal-bureaucratic Islam in Malaysia. They thus present case studies of smooth as well as of antagonistic spheres of coexistence. They cover the stance of Indonesia's two largest Muslim organizations — NU and Muhammadiyah — on religious pluralism and tolerance; internal Islamic doctrinal discourses and legal and constitutional impasses for full religious freedom in Indonesia. They deal with Muslim and Christian rivalries over public space, specifically, inter-religious disputes over obtaining permission to build places of worship, and the potential significance of local customs (*adat*) to rise above inter-religious conflicts, using the case of the Moluccas. Other chapters explore the rich diversity of Indonesia's Muslim community itself, with one chapter discussing the doctrinal bearings of the Chinese Muslim minority. Other contributions debate opposing views on the question of religious freedom on the basis of the precarious situation of the Islamic Ahmadiyah sect, the persistence and idiosyncrasies of minority syncretist forms of Islam in the far east of Java and on the island of Madura, northeast of Java.

Chapters 2 and 3 deal with the inherent plurality of Indonesian Islam and critically examine Indonesia's dedication to full religious freedom, inter-religious tolerance, and Islamic moderation. In chapter 2, Bush and Munawar-Rahman establish the track records of Indonesia's two largest Islamic social movements, the traditionalist-orthodox NU (est. 1926) and the modernist-reformist Muhammadiyah (1912) with regard to attitudes towards both Islamic and non-Islamic minorities. NU and Muhammadiyah are of particular significance since they, Bush and Munawar-Rahman highlight, "have tremendous authority" in the country. Both organizations are often being classified as main proponents of a mainstream Islam in a country "beset by increasing contradictions and polarisation". The authors therefore argue that a predictable moderate voice from NU and Muhammadiyah was indispensable. They present a positive "historical record" arguing that both organizations have traditionally sought to "avoid the extremes of any interpretation or debate". They also, however, detect a discrepancy between NU's internal discourse, described as a centre of "progressive" Islamic thought and its external action, as "one rarely sees [NU] using its political and social clout to advocate strongly for minority rights or religious freedom...". They portray Muhammadiyah as inherently more coherent in its positions on religious minorities yet "more conservative on issues of pluralism and religious freedom". As examples for NU's and Muhammadiyah's stance on religious minorities, Bush and Munawar-Rahman examine positions over quarrels on the construction of churches and the status of Shiites and Ahmadis.

Supriyanto Abdi's chapter probes further into the constitutional legal framework for religious freedom in Indonesia, especially Law No. 1/PNPS/1965 on the "Prevention of Desecration of Religion and/or Blasphemy", which is sometimes seen as a main obstacle to full religious freedom in Indonesia. The Law prohibits and criminalizes religious interpretations or practices that are considered non-standard and deviating from the core tenets of six religions adhered in Indonesia. The author then portrays the liberal Muslim support for some of the core principles in international human rights discourse on the right of freedom of religion or belief such as the principle of equality or non-discrimination and the principle of state neutrality. In an increasingly competitive "market of ideas" and a religiously conservative and uncooperative state, he argues, the broader appeal of liberal Muslims' views on religious freedom, however, remains limited.

The manner in which Islam is invoked in the discourses on Ahmadiyah and freedom of religion is the subject of Andy Fuller's chapter. He draws on material from the mainstream liberal media as well as from texts that seek to condemn liberal thought. Fuller detects a "polyvocality" in contemporary discourses on Islam in Indonesia amidst a "negotiation and re-negotiation of Islamic thought" process in which the state, law, and Islamic authority cross paths. Reminiscent of various other chapters in the volume that highlight the ambiguities in Indonesian society and politics today, Fuller sees this polyvocality as indicating richness, yet the discourses also appear to be mutually exclusive.

Chapter 5 by Helen Pausaker examines the moral panic about Indonesia's infamous Pornography Law from 2008. Boosted by *deculturation*, Muslims have increasingly voiced the uniqueness of various values, such as sexual modesty, to their religion, and perceived as a communal duty, not an individual one (Roy 2010). The bill drew support from both Islamist and nationalist groups and parties and was opposed by an alliance of religious minorities, liberal Muslims as well as many secular and leftist intellectuals and artists. Pausaker argues that the pressure that resulted in the implementation of the bill "shows the increasing influence by conservative Muslim groups, following the decline of authoritarian social control in post-Soeharto Indonesia". The Yudhoyono government has allowed bodies such as MUI to assume a greater political role and has consulted their leaders for advice on religious matters. Many of MUI's *fatwas* are reissues of older edicts without having had a comparable political significance in the past. Significantly, Pausaker demonstrates the political rationale behind the bill as cases prosecuted under the law only targeted particular individuals regarded as "soft targets", leaving other persons and the underground pornographic market untouched.

The conflicts between religious communities over building places of worship are the topic of Melissa Crouch's chapter. Crouch concentrates on the province of West Java (and especially the city of Bogor) where difficulties have been the most severe in recent years. She examines the role and effectiveness of the two main bodies involved in these matters: the Inter-religious Harmony Forum, largely responsible for issuing permit applications for constructions at the regional level, and the Ombudsman, which has the authority to deal with public complaints against the regional government. Crouch illustrates the high level of intricacy of these issues by particularly investigating the Bogor Church Permit Case. She shows that the Harmony Forum has worsened the strain between the religious communities through its anti-Christian stance. While legal challenges to the Forum's recommendations might in other cases stand a good chance for success, she further shows that favourable court decisions often do not result in action on the ground if there is a potent political opposition to them.

A fitting following entry to the discussion of the previous chapter, En-Chieh Chao highlights an intriguing dialectic in her contribution: parallel to the shift of the traditional forms of Islam towards more conservative forms of religiosity, previous members of mainstream churches have been flocking to puritan expressions of the Christian faith which makes Pentecostalism the fastest growing religion in the world today.

The author made the Central Javanese city of Salatiga her case study. Salatiga goes by the moniker "a Christian city", due to its comparatively high number of Christians (21 per cent). Chao's research centres around competition over the religious identity of the city with many Muslims feeling marginalized by the Christian population despite the former's numerical dominance. She describes "miracle discourses" as central to the Pentecostals' claim that their existence in the Salatiga community rested on divine legitimacy. She sets these discourses against the "perennial worries of Muslim leaders" regarding the Christian mission and concludes that "peaceful co-existence will demand constant renegotiations".

In her chapter on post-war Ambon in Indonesia's far eastern Maluku Islands, Birgit Bräuchler writes that she intends "to deconstruct the simplified image of a harmonious traditional past versus religious strife that neglects the diverse and complex processes of negotiation", in which the conflict lines of religion and *adat* continue to interact and compete against a background of daily interaction of people from different religious communities. She writes about continuing "high expectations towards the integrative character of *adat*" as a shared tradition of its inhabitants, illustrated by a detailed depiction of a traditional village union in Ambon. But Braeuchler also emphasizes the contradictions and exclusivist potentials of *adat* itself, "a fact that is not sufficiently taken into account". She writes that inter-religious relationships in Ambon were in the past based on passive tolerance and that inter-religious dialogue was missing. This, she argues, made it easier for religion to become the mobilizing force for violence in a culture where daily needs, *adat*, and religion coexist and simultaneously compete with each other.

The concluding three chapters present studies of the plurality and diversity in Islam itself. In his study on "Chinese Muslim Cultural Identities", Hew Wai Weng deals with the underlying theme of what Roy (2010) calls *inculturation* (as compared to *deculturation*), seen as an undertaking to reconcile a religious belief with traditionally non-Islamic cultural elements, in Hew's case "Chinese culture". Hew points to the inclusion of Chinese converts in various Muslim organizations, the popularity of Chinese Muslim preachers in Indonesia and highly symptomatic developments such as the celebration of the Chinese New Year in mosques. He sees in these phenomena evidence of Islam's tolerance towards different expressions of culture. By accounts of the views and teachings of various Chinese Muslim notables, he at the same time demonstrates that Chinese Muslim cultures are overall "tending towards religious conservatism" whilst embracing some forms of what the author calls "cosmopolitan Islam".

The continued existence of a small cluster of villages adhering (seemingly in contrast to larger overall trends) to a mythical and animist folk religion amidst a community and a region (Banyuwangi in East Java) that is overwhelmingly following the traditionalist-orthodox NU's brand of Islam is the topic of Nicholas Herriman's chapter. The author highlights conformity to what he terms "NU Islam" as the principal feature of the region and describes its pre-eminent characteristics. Herriman's account of this "conformity" is more a conformity to a notion and ideal (that of "NU Islam") rather than a standardized adherence to a particular doctrine. It is one of mutual toleration amongst the majority NU Islam and between that majority and the minority (the village animists), with purifying campaigns of what he calls "Middle Eastern style puritans" amongst the villagers constituting a potential source for future conflict.

The final chapter by Yanwar Pribadi covers a community on the periphery of this volume's topic in a sense that its members represent most blatantly a gap between cultural and religious markers. His chapter deals with the *blater*, a distinct subset of people home to the island of Madura. Pribadi describes *blater* as "feared local strongmen with a high position in society and who are held in awe by the local population". *Blater* are often employed in private security services. They enjoy access to local political and religious leaders, especially *kiai* (Islamic scholars and leaders) with whom they establish "mutually beneficial relationships". *Blater* follow a lifestyle that one would normally describe as "un-Islamic". Yet a considerable number of *blater* claim to have a background in local *pesantren* (Islamic boarding schools); and they observe a variety of *quasi*-religious rituals, which Pribadi describes in considerable detail. Their self-perception is that of being "mystical-syncretist Muslims", and as such they are both an integral part and markedly diverge from the majority orthodox Muslims of their shared homeland.

Notes

1. The activists came, among others, from Indonesia's Setara Institute Bhinneka Tunggal Ika National Alliance Forum (ANBTI).
2. "Two Dead in Sunni-Shiite Mayhem in Madura", *Jakarta Post*, 27 August 2012; Sumanto Al Qurtuby, "A Camouflage for Religious Violence", *Jakarta Globe*, 2 September 2012.
3. The survey was conducted amongst people with a senior high school or lower grade. "Survey Reveals Rising Religious Intolerance in Indonesia", *Jakarta Globe*, 22 October 2012.
4. "Attacks on Shiites Stemmed from Family Conflict: Government", *Jakarta Globe*, 28 August 2012.
5. Indonesia has a population of about 230 million and is the world's largest Muslim country.
6. The Sjafi'i school is the dominating Muslim law school in Muslim Southeast Asia. The other schools are the Hanafi, Hanbali, and Maliki.
7. Paradoxically, it is often the secular-nationalist parties that have supported the application of *shari'ah* by-laws on a local level. This is despite that religious matters are under the authority of the central government. This is unlike in the federal state of Malaysia where federal courts can apply their own *shari'ah* laws.
8. Malaysia even presents a stronger case in point.
9. The remaining principles are humanitarianism, nationalism, democracy, and social justice.

References

Al Qurtuby, Sumanto. "A Camouflage for Religious Violence". *Jakarta Globe*, 2 September 2012.
"Attacks on Shiites Stemmed from Family Conflict: Government". *Jakarta Globe*, 28 August 2012.
Bush, Robin. "Islam and Constitutionalism in Indonesia". In *Legitimacy, Legal Development and Change: Law and Modernization Reconsidered*, edited by David K. Linnan. Farnham: Ashgate, 2012.
Crouch, Melissa. "Law and Religion in Indonesia: The Blasphemy Law and the Constitutional Court". *Asian Journal of Comparative Law* 7, no. 1 (May 2012).

Fealy, Greg. "Islamisation and Politics in Southeast Asia: The Contrasting Cases of Malaysia and Indonesia". In *Islam in World Politics*, edited by Nelly Lahoud and Anthony H. Johns. New York: Routledge, 2005.

Kersten, Carool. "Urbanization, Civil Society and Religious Pluralism in Indonesia and Turkey". Paper presented at the Placing Religious Pluralism in Asian Global Cities conference, Singapore, 5–6 May 2011.

Picard, Michel, and Remy Madinier. "Preface: The Politics of Agama in Java and Bali". In *The Politics of Religion in Indonesia: Syncretism, Orthodoxy, and Religious Contention in Java and Bali*, edited by Picard and Madinier. New York: Routledge, 2011.

Platzdasch, Bernhard. "Down But Not Out: Islamic Parties Did Not Do Well but Islamic Politics Are Going Mainstream". *Inside Indonesia*, July–September 2009*a*.

———. *Islamism in Indonesia: Politics in The Emerging Democracy*. Singapore: Institute of Southeast Asian Studies, 2009*b*.

———. "Religious Freedom in Indonesia: The Case of the Ahmadiyah". ISEAS Working Paper on Politics and Security Series no. 2, 2011. Available at <http://web1.iseas.edu.sg/wp-content/uploads/2010/11/Religious-Freedom-in-Indonesia1.pdf>.

Reid, Anthony. "Many but One: The Paradox of Religious Pluralism in Southeast Asia's History". Paper presented at the Placing Religious Pluralism in Asian Global Cities conference, Singapore, 5–6 May 2011.

Ricklefs, Merle C. "Religion, Politics and Social Dynamics in Java: Historical and Contemporary Rhymes". In *Expressing Islam: Religious Life and Politics in Indonesia*, edited by Greg Fealy and Sally White. Indonesia Update Series, The Australian National University; Singapore: Institute of Southeast Asian Studies, 2008.

———. *Islamization and Its Opponents in Java: A Political, Social, Cultural and Religious History, c. 1930 to the Present*. Singapore: National University of Singapore Press, 2012.

Roy, Olivier. *Holy Ignorance: When Religion and Culture part ways*. Columbia: Hurst, Columbia University Press, 2010.

Steinberg, David Joel. "Secularism Neutralized in the Malay World". In *Religion and Religiosity in the Philippines and Indonesia: Essays on State, Society, and Public Creeds*, edited by Theodore Friend. Washington, D.C.: SAIS, 2006.

"Survey Reveals Rising Religious Intolerance in Indonesia". *Jakarta Globe*, 22 October 2012.

"Two Dead in Sunni-Shiite Mayhem in Madura". *Jakarta Post*, 27 August 2012.

2

NU AND MUHAMMADIYAH
Majority Views on Religious Minorities in Indonesia

Robin Bush and Budhy Munawar-Rachman

INTRODUCTION

Indonesia today can aptly be described as bipolar. It is the rising star of the international finance and business communities in Asia, with growth and other macroeconomic indicators attracting ever-increasing investment and attendant international clout. On the other hand, twin dark clouds of corruption and the tenuous status of religious minorities hang over the bright horizon in ominous contrast. In this chapter, we look at the factors underlying the increasing precariousness of religious minorities in Indonesia, we make a case for why the stance of Nahdlatul Ulama (NU) and Muhammadiyah matter, and we examine both official and non-official positions of the two mass-based organizations on both Islamic and non-Islamic minorities in Indonesia. We conclude that Indonesian society is becoming increasingly polarized, and that as such, NU and Muhammadiyah's mission of occupying a "middle path" is increasingly important. The two organizations navigate the terrain of the "middle path" differently due to their contrasting structure and internal culture; however, they are both important players in the ongoing discourse on religious freedom in Indonesia.

There is no question that the problem of its treatment of religious minorities is threatening Indonesia's status as the "golden-haired boy" of democratic reform which is often touted by international observers and Ministry of Foreign Affairs officials alike.[1] Recent violent attacks against Shi'a minorities in East Java, Hindu minorities in Sumatra, the forced closure of churches in Bekasi and Bogor, and the brutal murders of three Ahmadis in Cikeusik, West Java, have called into question whether the Indonesian state has the ability to provide the most basic level of security to its citizens, much less fulfil rights to freedom of worship accorded by the 1945 Constitution. Although Islam is the religion of the vast majority of Indonesia's citizens (88 per cent), there are significant Protestant (6 per cent), Catholic (3 per cent), and Hindu (3 per cent) minorities, in addition to followers of Buddhism, Confucianism, and other beliefs.[2] In Indonesia's recent history, mainstream Muslim leaders have been amongst the advocates for religious minority rights in Indonesia; however, a combination of lack of state ability or will to protect these rights, and increasing society-level intolerance has resulted in their erosion in recent years. Polling data from the Centre for the Study of Islam and Society indicate that between 2001 and 2010, proxy indicators of intolerance such as the percentage of Muslims who reject the building of a church in their neighbourhood, or who refuse to have non-Muslim teachers in their children's schools, have steadily risen.[3] In 2010, the Setara Institute counted 200 cases of violations of religious rights, which rose to 244 cases in 2011.[4] In its 2010 report, Setara also indicated that the primary non-state perpetrators of violence against religious minorities were hardline groups like the Islamic Defenders' Front (FPI).[5]

One should not, however, come to the straightforward conclusion that Indonesia is increasingly coming under the influence of a conservative Islamist agenda. There is a vigorous debate among scholars and activists both inside and outside Indonesia as to whether Indonesian Islam is "radicalizing", one indicator of which would be the intolerance of religious minorities. Saiful Mujani and Bill Liddle find declining support for "Islamist values" in the surveys of LSI (Indonesian Survey Institute) conducted from 2005 to 2008.[6] They also make a strong argument on the basis of survey data and the electoral record that Muslim parties have lost ground to secular parties, and that as such, Indonesia "is becoming a secular democracy".[7] They would likely see the violence against religious minorities not as reflecting majority views among Muslims, but rather being the actions of a vocal and well-connected minority. Other scholars, however, argue that Indonesia's "secular parties" (generally understood to include Partai Demokrat, Golkar, and PDIP at a minimum) have only gained ground because they have accommodated an Islamist agenda, and that an examination of legislation passed and policy issued by the executive over the past five years would indicate that Islam in Indonesia is in fact increasingly (1) conservative and (2) influential.[8] Merle Ricklefs, writing in 2007 about trends across the sweep of history from the early nineteenth century in Indonesia argues in effect that both sides of this debate are correct:

> ... I could make a case for increasing strength and influence on the part of Islam that is puritan, inflexible ... intolerant of other cultures and faiths ... or even willing to use violence. I think that I could as easily show that the forces opposed to such versions of Islam are strengthening .... So we are observing renewed polarisation of Javanese society along the lines of religious identity, as occurred between c. 1850 and 1965.[9]

The battle for religious identity, and national identity, and the interplay between the two, is at the heart of many of the recent acts of intolerance against religious minorities. These current eruptions are indicative of movements in Indonesian national psyche taking place over many decades. Robert Hefner argues that over the last 50 years, the "*abangan*" and other varieties of "non-mainstream" Islamic identity have been gradually eradicated, and an institutionalized, "religionized" Islam has become dominant in Indonesia.[10] Hefner claims that in the mid-twentieth century, more than two-thirds of Javanese considered themselves to be *abangan* — but that over time *abangan* and other local, "non-standard" public religious traditions "have been displaced, not just by "Islam", but by an Islam organized in a more standardized, textual, and de-territorialized form as 'religion' (*agama*)".[11] The consolidation of the authority of the Ministry of Religious Affairs (MoRA) and the state's role in defining Islamic identity has played a central role in this process.

As Masdar Hilmy has argued, "by and large, the crux of the problem faced by the country in terms of freedom of religion is interpretation: which and whose doctrines to represent the 'true' Islam".[12] The question of who gets to define Islam relates not only to intra-religious conflict or the question of authenticity, but also to inter-religious conflict and non-Muslim minorities. Hilmy has outlined clearly that the problem is not one of regulation — Indonesia's 1945 Constitution clearly states that "the state guarantees the freedom of each citizen to believe his/her own religion and to observe according to his/her religion and belief" which is further solidified by Law No. 39/1999 in which Article 22 reiterates the freedom of Indonesian citizens to worship according to their own belief.[13] Complications arise, however, because both the Constitution and Law 39, while protecting freedom of belief, also include language restricting these freedoms "for the purpose of guaranteeing admission and respect of human rights and freedom of others, ethics, public order and national interest" — Law 39/1999, Article 73.[14]

This classical dilemma of an individual's freedom impinging on the rights and freedoms of another — and the role of state and religious authorities in determining where the lines of justice are drawn within society is at the heart of the law on defamation of religion, also known as the "Blasphemy Law" (Law No. 1/PNPS/1965), which was the basis for the Joint Ministerial Decree restricting activities of Ahmadiyah in 2008.[15] In 2010, a group of human rights activists brought the law to the Constitutional Court for judicial review, arguing that it restricted freedom of religion; the Court's decision upheld the law, in a move that was widely read as regression for religious freedom.[16] The most contentious element of the law is in the first article: "… every individual is prohibited from intentionally, in public … conveying an interpretation of a certain religion … where such interpretation and activities deviate from the basic tenets of the religion."[17] As Bagir eloquently explains, "by mentioning 'deviation', the law imagines that there is (could be) a fixed body of orthodoxy that establishes the truths (including of interpretations) of a religion's teachings (the deviation from which is considered a criminal offence …)."[18] It is this question of who has the right to define orthodoxy, and to both determine and reflect to a regulatory apparatus the norms and values of a religious belief system, that brings us to the role, and the importance of the NU and Muhammadiyah regarding religious freedom in Indonesia.

WHY DO NU AND MUHAMMADIYAH MATTER?

Nahdlatul Ulama, established in 1926 and claiming a membership of approximately 40 million people, and Muhammadiyah, established in 1912 and claiming a membership of approximately 25 million people, are the largest mass-based Muslim organizations in Indonesia (and the world) and represent the majority of mainstream Muslim thought and practice in the world's largest Muslim-majority nation.[19] The two organizations have a reach and presence that stretches from Jakarta down to the village level throughout the country, through a network of branch offices at provincial, district, and sub-district levels. In addition, both organizations boast thousands of schools and clinics, hundreds of universities and hospitals, and a vast number of women's, students, and NGO affiliate groups. Due to the sheer scale of their presence throughout the country, both organizations are politically powerful and have been important political players historically. While this is changing somewhat, there is no doubt that the two organizations are still deeply influential, and highly representative of mainstream Muslim views within society.

Recent survey data from The Asia Foundation and LSI (Indonesian Survey Institute) shows that no less than 57 per cent of the respondents of a nationwide, random-sampled statistical survey identified themselves as being affiliated with either NU (49 per cent) or Muhammadiyah (7.9 per cent).[20] Furthermore, although the survey indicates a declining role for *ulama* or religious authorities' influence in the political domain, it shows that religious leaders associated with these two organizations are still highly influential on socio-religious issues, with 44 per cent of the public consulting religious leaders on social or religious issues.[21]

When it comes to issues of religious minorities, the influence of NU and Muhammadiyah is vast and plays out in multiple arenas. At a discourse level, the leadership of these two organizations is able to dominate the public production of Muslim thought on this and other issues. For example, as Martin van Bruinessen explains, during the late New Order, the "liberal, tolerant, and open-minded discourse of ... Nurcholish Madjid and Abdurrahman Wahid was almost hegemonic ..." and he goes on to note that after their demise in the post-Soeharto era there has been a turn towards conservatism in the public Muslim discourse.[22] In fact, Ufen has argued that the influence of NU and Muhammadiyah in structuring the discourse on Islam is so great that in some ways it "limit[s] the ability of the state and political parties to set the agenda and mobilize Islam in certain ways".[23] In a more structural sense, NU and Muhammadiyah leaders occupy key positions throughout the Ministry of Religious Affairs, which, as mentioned earlier, is the primary government body defining, policing, and regulating religious practice in Indonesia. At a local level, where often the enactment of state control and/or protection of minorities take place, NU and Muhammadiyah play an important role both as representatives of "Muslim majority" because often local government and law enforcement heads are affiliated with these organizations. Recent research examining why some churches are given permits to build houses of worship and others are not concluded that the second most influential factor (the first being support from local government and police) is support from religious elites in the area surrounding the church, and the third most important factor is successful dialogue with the Muslim community in the area.[24] Both of these factors relate to the role of NU and Muhammadiyah leadership at the local level.

Sunny Tanuwidjaja has made a convincing argument that, rather than being on the decline, as some scholars believe, Islam in fact plays a central role in Indonesian politics.[25] "Herein lies the paradox and the puzzle. ... Despite the minority status of Islamic political parties in the Indonesian parliament, over the past few years a significant number of laws have been passed ... that promote an Islamic or religiously conservative agenda."[26] Tanuwidjaja has argued that not only is religious conservatism on the rise (an assertion which he backs up with polling data) but also that it is so strong that elites across all parties have to accommodate this agenda.[27] If this is the case, the role of NU and Muhammadiyah is even more crucial — their leadership sets the discourse on Islam, both establishes and reflects the majority Muslim opinion on a wide range of issues, occupies decision-making positions both within the bureaucracy and across all major parties, and is a recognized authority on Islamic orthodoxy — or what is "true" and what is "deviant".

NU AND MUHAMMADIYAH POSITIONS ON RELIGIOUS MINORITIES — HISTORICAL RECORD

The two primary features of NU and Muhammadiyah's positions on religious minorities and religious freedom over the last several decades are "moderation" and significant internal variation. When we use the term "moderation" we do not use it in the ideological, often western construct of the "moderate Muslim".[28] Rather, we refer to the classical term *tawassuth*, most often translated into English as "moderation", or following the "central path" which is a central tenet of primarily NU but is also the Muhammadiyah creed.[29] What is meant by this is that both organizations seek to avoid the extremes of any interpretation or debate, and seek to accommodate the centrist position on the issue. Thinkers from both organizations will often draw on the Qur'anic reference to Muslims as "*ummat-an wasathan*" and Islam as "*al-dîn al-wasath*" (Qur'an 2, p. 143) which means "followers or religion of the middle path".[30] KH Said Aqil, currently the head of NU and himself an expert in Islamic doctrine, interprets this to mean that, "We can receive all groups within Islam, such that there are no divisions between those who are within the brotherhood of Islam."[31] This "moderation" plays out in the sense that both NU and

Muhammadiyah will usually take a middle-of-the-road position between what they see as the extremes of liberalism within Islam and Islamism, including issues of religious freedom. So, for example, both NU and Muhammadiyah rejected — and foiled — the attempt of some Islamist groups to integrate Shari'a into Constitutional revisions in 2002; on the other hand, both also supported the decision of the Constitutional Court to uphold the "Blasphemy Law", which activists felt was a regression for human rights.[32]

Historically, NU has often been more outspoken in defence of religious minorities than has Muhammadiyah — which is for a complex mixture of theological and political reasons.[33] The role of Abdurrahman Wahid (head of NU from 1984 to 1999), a leading proponent of religious freedom, was key to the development of an NGO subculture within NU that strongly advocated for minority rights both within NU circles and at a national policy level during the 1990s and 2000s.[34] LKIS (Lembaga Kajian Islam dan Sosial; Institute for the Study of Islam and Society), an NGO closely affiliated with NU's Yogyakarta branch, conducted seminars and study groups drawing on the classical Islamic doctrine of *al-kullîyât al-khamsah*, argue for five basic human rights, including the right to religious freedom.[35] P3M (Perhimpunan Pengembangan Pesantren dan Masyarakat; Association for the Development of Pesantren and Society), comprised of activists from both NU and Muhammadiyah, worked in the late 1990s and early 2000s within *pesantren* circles, promoting a discourse of tolerance and human rights drawn from classical *fiqh*.[36] Also in the early 2000s, Muhammadiyah's IRM (Ikatan Remaja Muhammadiyah; Union of Muhammadiyah Youth) sponsored a programme of GRATK (Gerakan Aktif-Tanpa Kekerasan; Movement of Active Non-Violence) in which they brought together youth from Hindu, Buddhist, Christian, and Muslim circles to study the great anti-violence activists of history and formulate their own anti-violence projects.[37]

Although these activities bloomed in the *reformasi* period just prior to and after Soeharto's downfall, both NU and Muhammadiyah were marked by strong internal divisions around ideological issues related to liberal democratic values. By the mid-2000s, some observers noted the growing dominance of more conservative voices in both organizations which was in keeping with nationwide trends at the time.[38] In 2004 and 2005, both NU and Muhammadiyah held their national congresses (held every five years), and in both there was what van Bruinessen calls a "purge" of liberal leadership.[39] In Muhammadiyah, Din Syamsuddin replaced Syafi'i Ma'arif, long known for his support for democracy-related activism within the organization, and at NU's 31st Muktamar (national congress), the "socially and religiously conservative" Hasyim Muzadi was re-elected at least partially on a platform of "anti-liberalism" in which he backed an official edict of the *bahth-u 'l masâ'il* (NU's *fatwa*-making body) that the Liberal Islam Network (Jaringan Islam Liberal or JIL) was not in keeping with the core values of NU.[40]

In 2005, the Majelis Ulama Indonesia (MUI; Indonesian Ulama Council) issued a series of *fatwa* that caused a great deal of controversy in the general public domain in Indonesia, but which also underscored the internal divisions within NU and Muhammadiyah along ideological lines. One of these was a *fatwa* against secularism, pluralism, and liberalism (referred to by the acronym SIPILIS in typical Indonesian humour).[41] Another was a *fatwa* declaring inter-faith prayer meetings to be *haram* (forbidden), and yet another was the anti-Ahmadiyah *fatwa* mentioned earlier.[42] KH Ma'ruf Amin, a senior and long-standing NU leader (Vice-Chair of the Syuriah, NU's religious council, in the 1970s and currently a member of the Mustasyar, NU's advisory board), was the Chairman of MUI's Fatwa Commission at the time, and he strongly supported these *fatwa*.[43] Immediately upon the release of *fatwa*, however, KH Masdar Mas'udi, the then secretary of the Syuriah and speaking in a representational capacity, wrote a public refutation of these fatwa, especially the anti-liberal *fatwa*, and even appeared in a public forum debating these issues directly with KH Ma'ruf Amin.[44] On the Muhammadiyah side, Din Syamsuddin, who had been Secretary General of MUI since 2000, was elected to be Chairman of Muhammadiyah in the same month (July 2005) that the MUI *fatwas* were issued. Syamsuddin's positions on these issues have been observed to adapt to his audience, but he played a leading role in explaining and defending these *fatwas* to those within Muhammadiyah who disagreed with its contents.[45] Interestingly, while Gillespie sees Syamsuddin's election as Chairman of Muhammadiyah in 2005 as evidence of the organization's shift in a more conservative direction,[46] Feillard and Madinier have argued that at the time he often took the middle ground between "conservatives and liberals" and that being elected Chairman of Muhammadiyah appeared to have a moderating effect on him.[47]

Essentially while one can see movement in a conservative direction within both organizations in the middle of the 2000s, in retrospect we can also identify that that movement reflects nationwide trends — as indicated by the MUI *fatwas* of 2005, by the fact that *shari'ah* related legislation peaked in 2003,[48] by the political momentum enjoyed at the time by Islamist groups such as MMI, Hizbut Tahrir, and so on. However, even at the time, there was considerable internal opposition to this rightward shift by activists and intellectuals within both organizations. Boy Pradana describes the heated debate taking place within Muhammadiyah at this time, centring around issues of minority rights, religious freedom, and pluralism.[49] By the time of the 2010 Muhammadiyah Muktamar (National Congress), after five years of Din Syamsuddin's leadership, external and internal observers alike noted that Muhammadiyah appeared to have shifted towards a more liberal position, especially on these ideological issues.[50] One indicator of this "progressive" shift was the official record of the proceedings, and decisions made at the 2010 Muktamar emphasized the crucial role of Muhammadiyah in engaging in inter-faith dialogue.[51] Similar debates and movements were taking place within NU in the last half of the decade, and by the time of the 2010 NU Muktamar, observers noting the appointment of some long-standing advocates for liberal values to the Board posited that "the trend towards a more fundamentalist and anti-liberal version of traditionalist Islam appears to be reversed".[52] For example, the appointment of senior activists such as the former head of LKIS, Imam Aziz, as a *Ketua* (one of sixteen senior-most leadership positions on the central board) of PBNU, and former Lakpesdam NU official Imdadun Rahmat as Vice Secretary General of PBNU was cause for optimism in activist/intellectual circles, as both men had been leaders in the civil society/democracy movement within NU since the 1990s.[53] And, as van Bruinessen notes, even the victory of Said Aqil over Hasyim Muzadi as Chairman of PBNU was seen as a positive development for those concerned with minority rights.[54]

NU AND MUHAMMADIYAH — CONTEMPORARY VIEWS ON RELIGIOUS MINORITIES

In order to look more deeply into these shifts in ideological views and to gain more insight into the current position of both NU and Muhammadiyah on religious freedom and minority rights, we have chosen to delve further into three main issues — all of which are points of contention in the Indonesian public discourse today — the status of the Ahmadiyah, the status of the Syi'ah, and conflicts over the building of churches.

The first two issues relate closely to the question of how one defines "Islam", and who has the authority to do so — as such, we first examine NU and Muhammadiyah responses to efforts to regulate and define "Islam" and religious freedom. Individuals within NU and Muhammadiyah have both made very progressive contributions to the discourse on religious freedom and engaged in debates over the "Blasphemy Law". Here again, however, one sees a picture of strong contrasts and divisions within both organizations. A group called the Religious Freedom Advocacy Team brought the "Blasphemy Law" (Law No. 1/PNPS/1965) to the Constitutional Court for judicial review on the grounds that rather than protecting minority rights, it was often used to restrict religious minorities. Among other human rights activists, the Religious Freedom Advocacy Team included Abdurrahman Wahid, former head of NU; Siti Musdah Mulia, affiliated with NU women's movement; KH. Maman Imanul Haq, human rights activist affiliated with NU; and M. Dawam Raharjo, a prominent Muhammadiyah intellectual. In a staunch opposition to the judicial review of this law were (among others) Din Syamsuddin, Chairman of Muhammadiyah; Hasyim Muzadi, the then-Chairman of NU; Suryadharma Ali, Minister of Religion and a NU leader; and KH Ma'ruf Amin, mentioned above.[55] The polemic in the public arena but especially within religious circles around this court case was heated — for example, Hasyim Muzadi at one point said that the activists calling for judicial review of the law were "atheists riding on the democracy movement".[56]

While the official position of both NU and Muhammadiyah at the time was that Law No. 1/PNPS/1965 was needed in order to maintain harmony both within religions and among followers of different religions, activists and intellectuals from both organizations have spoken out strongly against the danger of regulating belief. Abdul Moqsith Ghazali, a prominent NU intellectual, believes that the term "defamation of religion" used in the law and also used in the Indonesian Criminal Code (KUHP) verse 165a is "extremely damaging" to the efforts to promote human rights and religious freedom in Indonesia.[57] "If one examines carefully the logical consequences of the verse 165a of the Criminal Code, and Law No. 1/PNPS/1965, it is very clear that they are in contradiction with the constitution — because both of these legal instruments can be and are used to undermine the rights of citizens to belief and to religious practices — as such they must both be eliminated."[58] Meanwhile Bahtiar Effendy, Dean of the Political Science Faculty at the State Islamic University in Jakarta and former Muhammadiyah Board Member, draws the connection between ineffective rule of law and violence. "It's clear that [religion-related] violence occurs among other things because those who perpetrate violence are not apprehended. They don't feel that the state has forbidden their actions. When they conduct violent acts, they should be punished according to the law."[59] However, as mentioned earlier, in 2010 the Constitutional Court upheld the "Blasphemy Law", reinforcing the state-sanction on "orthodox" or "standardized" Islam and tacit approval for the exclusion of those falling outside of those boundaries.

AHMADIYAH

The connection between state sanction (or lack thereof) and violence is probably nowhere more clear than in a recent outbreak of violence against Ahmadis in Indonesia in February 2011, when three Ahmadis were brutally murdered in full public view by a mob of around 1,500 people in Cikeusik, West Java. The case has become a totem not just for minority rights in Indonesia, but also for the inability or unwillingness of the security and justice sector to protect all citizens, as the murders took place with police officials standing by, and perpetrators were subsequently sentenced to only three to six months in jail. Prior to this incident, most analysts of the Ahmadiyah issue in Indonesia look to the MUI Fatwa of 2005 against Ahmadiyah, or the subsequent Joint Ministerial Decree of 2008 — both of which were followed by outbreaks of violence against Ahmadiyah.[60] In fact, the anti-Ahmadiyah sentiment within both NU and Muhammadiyah, has much longer historical roots — Muhammadiyah issued a *fatwa* declaring Ahmadiyah to be a deviant sect in 1930,[61] long before the first MUI *fatwa* against Ahmadiyah in 1980, and NU took pains to ensure that Ahmadiyah was excluded from the MIAI (Al-Madjlisoel-Islamil-A'laa Indonesia; Great Islamic Council of Indonesia) in the early 1940s[62] and followed up with its own anti-Ahmadiyah *fatwa* in August 1995.[63] Furthermore, these views appear to have broad support in both organizations to this date. Jeremy Menchik collected survey data in 2010 from branch leaders of both NU and Muhammadiyah; the results indicate that 80 per cent of Muhammadiyah and 67 per cent of NU respondents say Ahmadiyah should not be allowed to build houses of worship in Jakarta, and 75 per cent of Muhammadiyah and 59 per cent of NU leaders reject the possibility of an Ahmadi becoming mayor in Jakarta.[64] Intolerance of Ahmadiyah is thus historically rooted and currently widespread throughout the majority of NU and Muhammadiyah membership. In both cases, it serves to reinforce the role of both organizations as the arbiter of mainstream Islamic belief and practice in the Indonesian context.

In more recent years, however, NU's official position has included an explicit rejection of violence against the minority sect. When a spate of violent attacks against Ahmadis took place immediately after the 2005 MUI Fatwa was issued, senior NU leaders met in Bogor and issued a formal statement, while NU did view Ahmadiyah as a deviant sect, and not Muslim, it also prevailed upon the public not to be "anarchist towards Ahmadiyah" and left the issue of whether or not to ban Ahmadiyah up to the government. The statement went on to decry the activities of Ahmadis in NU areas, but at the same time called upon its members to use "peaceful and polite" approaches in their dealings with Ahmadiyah.[65] Notably, this statement was signed by KH Ma'ruf Amin, KH Said Agil Siradj (current head of NU), KH Masdar Mas'udi, and HM Rozy Munir — showing a rare example of solidarity among the quite conservative (Amin) to quite liberal (Mas'udi) elements of the NU Board.

The government took three years to take a formal stance on Ahmadiyah, but in June 2008 the Joint Ministerial Decree was issued, which significantly restricted Ahmadiyah activities, but stopped short of banning them altogether.[66] The Central Board of NU (PBNU) was fully in support of this position, and Slamet Effendy Yusuf, senior board member and also head of the Interfaith Relations section of MUI, further argued that "the best solution would be for Ahmadiyah to declare itself not Muslim in order to avoid further conflict. The violence that has occurred thus far in society has taken place because Ahmadiyah members are not adhering to the Joint Ministerial Statement."[67] A similar view blaming the victims was issued by the Minister of Religion, Suryadharma Ali, who declared that "it is best for Ahmadiyah to be banned, because clearly they have deviated from the teachings of Islam, and resistance to them will continue to be seen within society. If they are not banned, the problems will spiral out of control", he stated ominously.[68] Meanwhile Hasyim Muzadi, then head of NU, declared "if Ahmadiyah would declare themselves to be followers of their own religion, and not Muslim, then they would be in the position of enjoying the freedom of religion that all Indonesian citizens enjoy."[69] In Muzadi's view, the Ahmadiyah issue is not one of the freedom of religion but rather one of the defamation of religion.[70]

NU intellectual Moqsith Ghazali, on the other hand, begs to differ.

> In Indonesia, this is a relatively new situation. The government appears unsure of itself — it is not responding firmly and appropriately when faced with Ahmadiyah invoking the symbols of Islam and provoking anti-Ahmadiyah groups. But if this case is brought to court, the legal

instruments that will be deployed in deciding on this case are the defamation law and the Criminal Code. However, if you ask what is meant by "defamation", the judge will not ask the Supreme Court for a response, but rather will consult with MUI. The MUI will immediately state that Ahmadiyah have acted in defamation of Islam, and so the judge will rule against Ahmadiyah. Yet the MUI is not a part of the hierarchy of legal institutions that are meant to be ruling on these issues.[71]

Meanwhile, Muhammadiyah also supported the Joint Ministerial Decree and underscored the importance of dialog with the Ahmadiyah community to encourage them to join "mainstream Islam".[72] Din Syamsuddin, head of Muhammadiyah, issued an official statement reiterating that Muhammadiyah appreciated and accepted the decision of the government in the Joint Ministerial Decree, but that Muhammadiyah would not be involved in the movement to ban Ahmadiyah. "We defer to the government to take firm action based on the constitution, because the issue of the existence of a particular group is a state matter."[73]

However, as we know the Ahmadiyah issue did not end with the issuance of the Joint Ministerial Decree. Minor attacks and discrimination took place in ensuing years, culminating most recently and dramatically with the aforementioned murders of three Ahmadis at Cikeusik in February 2011 (captured graphically on cellphone recordings that were circulated widely on the internet and broadcast on local television stations). The response of NU and Muhammadiyah officials to this most flagrant violation of basic citizen's rights — the right to security — on the part of the state was predictably mixed. Immediately following the murders, Minister of Home Affairs Gamawan Fauzi invited NU and Muhammadiyah leaders to discuss the problem. The two organizations were represented by their heads, KH Said Aqil Siradj (NU) and Din Syamsuddin (Muhammadiyah), and by the Secretary General of NU Masudi Syuhud, the Vice Chair of NU As'ad Said, the Secretary of NU's Syuriah Malik Madani, the Secretary General of Muhammadiyah Agung Danarto, and the head of Muhammadiyah's Majelis Tarjih (religious council) Syamsul Anwar.[74] These NU and Muhammadiyah leaders were unanimous in their position that Ahmadiyah was a deviant sect, their position had not changed on this, and it was the responsibility of the government to handle this matter.[75] The government's response was to blame the victims again — the Minister of Religion, Suryadarma Ali issued statements indicating that it was the Ahmadis' own fault that they were killed, and the courts then sentenced the perpetrators to three to six months in length for the cold-blooded, premeditated, and witnessed murder of three people.[76] It was such a clear travesty of justice that Din Syamsuddin himself issued a statement that this verdict brought shame upon Islam.[77]

The internal diversity of opinion within NU and Muhammadiyah on the issue of Ahmadiyah is not limited to the usual "liberal/activists" versus "conservative/central board" divide, but is further complicated by the decentralized power structure of these organizations, especially of NU. In Kuningan, West Java, the District Branch of NU (PCNU) did not adhere to PBNU (central board) policies of eschewing violence towards Ahmadiyah, but they were actively involved in provoking and allowing attacks on an Ahmadiyah mosque in December 2007.[78] PBNU officials summoned the District Branch NU head HR Mahmud Silahuddin to Jakarta for a reprimand. Furthermore, the head of the youth wing of NU, GP Ansor, also disagreed with the District Branch of NU with regard to sanctioning violence against Ahmadiyah — resulting in threats from the District Branch to disband that Ansor Chapter and disbar its head.[79] In response to the attacks on the Ahmadiyah mosque, the heads of the five chapters of Ansor in that province (Ansor Cirebon [city], Ansor Cirebon [district], Ansor Indramayu, Ansor Majalengka, and Ansor Kuningan) came together to issue a press release protesting the violence, and promising to deploy 50,000 Banser "troops" to protect Ahmadiyah communities. It was in response to this action that the PCNU (district branch of NU) Kuningan demanded that the head of Ansor be disbarred.[80]

On the other hand, in East Java, we see the national/local diversity within NU playing out in a different way. In East Java, Banser (the "paramilitary" wing of Ansor) did often protect Ahmadiyah communities — one notes that there have not been any incidents of Ahmadiyah mosque burning or destruction in East Java. At the same time, however, they deployed the tacit threat of their "paramilitary" strength to restrict Ahmadiyah activities. After the Cikeusik incident, several local governments took it upon themselves to ban Ahmadiyah in their province/district — one of these was the Governor of East Java.[81] The head of the East Java chapter of Banser, Mujib Syaddzili immediately made a statement indicating that Ahmadiyah communities must comply with the Governor's edict, and that Banser would assist with "socializing" this edict in various Ahmadiyah communities in East Java.[82] Furthermore, when the East Java chapter of Ahmadiyah rejected the Governor's edict on the grounds that it was unconstitutional and threatened to take him to court, Syaddzili said effectively, "Let him take the case to court. But if he tries to mobilize the masses to support his position, Banser will be at the front lines to stop him."[83]

With regard to Ahmadiyah, there appears to be strong consensus throughout most of Muhammadiyah and NU that it is a deviant sect, and does not adhere to the tenets of orthodox Islam. The internal variance in position comes with regard to the sanctioning of violence to restrict Ahmadiyah activities, or to eradicate them from a particular community. Here, we see localized dynamics coming to the fore, in which in some cases elements of NU ally themselves with conservative anti-Ahmadiyah groups even in opposition to the official PBNU/central board positions. This kind of variance is not seen as much within Muhammadiyah — in part because there is likely to be less variation of opinion, especially with regard to Ahmadiyah, but also because the structure of Muhammadiyah is more hierarchical and allows for less autonomy than does the structure and nature of NU.

SYI'AH

In another recent case of persecution of religious minorities in Indonesia, a *pesantren*, mosque, and homes of a Shi'ite group in Sampang, Madura were attacked in December 2011, and earlier in the year violence against Shi'ites took place in Pasuruan, and Bondowoso, East Java. In this case we see, again, significant internal variance in positions and views on the matter, especially within NU.[84]

In the Sampang case, on 29 December, a group of approximately 500 people who claimed to be from an *"Ahlus Sunnah Wal Jamaah"* (Sunni) group attacked and burned down the Shi'ite Misbahul Huda *pesantren* complex. A total of 360 Shi'ite residents were relocated to the Sports Stadium of Sampang, and the following day the local government, local parliament, police, MUI of Sampang, MUI of East Java, and NU's Sampang branch convened a meeting which concluded that the conflict was caused by defamation of religion. This meeting was followed by another between the MUI of Sampang and the District NU branch of Sampang, which further concluded that the violence did not happen because of "radical" activities on the part of the Sunni mob, but rather because of the social unrest caused by the "defamation of religion" conducted by the Shi'ite leader, Ustadz Tajul Muluk. The local government ultimately decided that the solution was to conduct an inventory of the local Shi'ite population and classify individual Shi'ites as "fanatic" or "non-fanatic". Those classified as "fanatic" would then be transmigrated to another location. The Vice Governor of East Java, long-time senior NU leader Saefullah Yusuf, agreed with this solution, and offered an area in East Java, outside of Madura, for the relocated Shi'ites. Meanwhile, the local government did not provide support or protection to the displaced Shi'ite citizens whose residences had been burned down, and they continued to experience threats and acts of terror.[85] No legal action was taken against the mob.

Interestingly, in this case, not only was NU divided, but also MUI itself was divided — MUI Sampang and East Java branches issued statements that Shi'ites are deviant and cannot be considered Muslim, while KH Mar'uf Amin, national-level head of MUI, issued counter-statements that MUI does in fact recognize Shi'ites as being bona fide Muslims.[86] The same tension and contradiction, took place within NU with the head of NU's Sampang district branch, KH Muhaimin Abdul Bari, declaring Shi'ites to be deviant, and the head of NU, KH Said Aqil Siradj, and indeed other members of the Central Board of NU, declaring very strongly that Shi'ites are not deviant. Siradj invoked the curriculum of his alma mater in Saudi Arabia, the University Ummul Quro, saying "even the strict Wahhabis don't call Shi'ites heretics", and he called on the Ministry of Religion Suryadharma Ali to apologize for stating that Shi'ites are heretics.[87] The head of NU's Syuriah (religious council) East Java branch, Habib Achmad Zein Alkaf, accused Siradj of betraying NU by defending the Shi'ites.[88] A delegation of the East Java Branch of NU then visited PBNU in order to deliver their *fatwa* that in fact Shi'ites are heretics — the meeting which was apparently attended by senior NU officials was not attended by Siradj due to "traffic delays".[89] Hidayatullah.com reported subsequently that Siradj had quietly signed in October 2011 a Memorandum of Understanding (MOU) with Universitas al-Mustafa al-'Alamiyah, Qom, Iran, to work together on research and cultural activities — as soon as this was brought to light by Cholil Nafis, the Vice Chair of the *Baḥth-u 'l-masâ'il* (*fatwa* committee) of PBNU, the Syuri'ah immediately cancelled the MOU without consultation with PBNU.[90]

Such conflicts within NU are not new — even in Abdurrahman Wahid's (Gus Dur) era, he created controversy by saying NU beliefs and practices were actually not so different from those of the Shi'ites.[91] Furthermore, the position of PBNU, as expounded by its spokesman Sultan Fatoni, was that, just as in the era of Gus Dur when there were faith-related conflicts, NU members were told (*diberi pemahaman*) that these were not really faith-related conflicts, but rather social conflict wrapped up in a religious guise — and that the same is true in the case of the Shi'ite conflict in East Java. As such, he reiterated, it is the job of NU's Board to maintain tolerance and avoid such conflicts.[92]

Muhammadiyah's Central Board, like NU's, recognizes Shi'ism as a bone fide stream of Islam. According to Din Syamsuddin, head of Muhammadiyah, "there is not a huge difference between the two main schools of Islam, Sunni and Shi'a. Both Sunnism and Shi'ism acknowledge the same God and Prophet."[93] He believes it would be useful for the Muslim community to engage in an internal dialogue to discuss how to deal with differences among Muslims, in particular between Shi'ites and Sunnis.[94] Dr Zulkifli, lecturer at the State Islamic University in Jakarta, has argued that the difference between Shi'ism and Sunnism is similar to the differences between NU and Muhammadiyah — in both cases, he says, the differences should not be emphasized, or conflict will emerge.[95]

Again, as with the case of Ahmadiyah, levels of tolerance that one finds at the central level of both NU and Muhammadiyah on issues of orthodoxy and mainstream Islam, may have variance at the local level. The decentralized nature of NU as an organization lends itself to this variance taking expression more visibly than within Muhammadiyah.

BUILDING OF CHURCHES

The problem of conflict and violation of religious freedom related to the building of houses of worship is a long-standing and multifaceted one, which is addressed elsewhere in this volume, as well as in other recent scholarship.[96] Both NU and Muhammadiyah have a strong history and record of protection of the right of Christians to worship and build houses of worship. For example, when a suicide bomber detonated a bomb outside a church in Solo, Central Java, on 25 September 2011 (killing only himself, but wounding eleven others), both Said Aqil and Din Syamsuddin were quick to make strong public statements denouncing the violence.[97] This is in keeping with clear concerns about, and public opposition to, radicalization and Islamist violence on the part of both organizations.[98] Also, ever since six churches in the Jakarta area were bombed during Christmas celebrations of 2000, leaders of both NU and Muhammadiyah have made strong efforts to ensure safety of Christians at Christmas. For example, in December 2006 Din Syamsuddin held a meeting of the ICRP (Indonesian Community for Religion and Peace — of which he was then chairman) at the Muhammadiyah headquarters in Jakarta. There he offered up Muhammadiyah offices, schools, and buildings across the country to be used by Christians for Christmas celebrations in the event that their churches were closed or they did not feel safe there.[99] Abdurrahman Wahid (Gus Dur, then head of NU) went a step further and penned an article in December of 2003, in which he drew on the classical *fiqh* to argue that Muslims were permitted to join in non-Muslim religious services, as long as they did not take part in the actual worship rituals.[100] This was a fairly controversial position, even within NU, but it has been upheld by Gus Dur's family and other like-minded NU leaders to date — Gus Dur's daughter Innaya Wahid, along with the head of Fatayat NU (NU's women's group) and the head of Ansor NU (NU's young men's group) attended the 2011 Christmas Services held by the Yasmin Church of Bogor, out of solidarity for the embattled church.[101] Furthermore, it has become a tradition for Ansor and in particular its "paramilitary" unit Banser to deploy its members to protect churches during the Christmas season. The head of the Jakarta branch of Ansor, Nusron Wahid, deployed 1,200 Banser members to protect 49 churches in the region during Christmas 2011.[102]

Another example of progressive thought within NU with regard to protection of churches and church-goers comes from the tradition of Bahtsul Masail, usually described as NU's "*fatwa*-making body", which examines the classical scriptures (*kitab kuning*) for responses to a problem or issue, debates the matter, and then issues a kind of "*fatwa*" or NU position on the matter. In August 2010, an NU-affiliated NGO called Rumah Kitab (Home of Scriptures) convened a discussion on the issue of church-burnings and closures which had become increasingly frequent in the West Java/Bekasi area. Rumah Kitab was based in Bekasi and founded by an NU leader from Cirebon, KH Dr Affandi Muchtar, who was also a Ministry of Religious Affairs official. The group examined the scriptures and debated the issue, and issued the following edict — Muslims are forbidden (*haram*) to damage houses of worship belonging to other religions. Furthermore, if the refusal to give permission to build a house of worship will cause more disadvantage than advantage, this refusal of permission is also forbidden (*haram*).[103] Muhammadiyah leadership has also been actively involved in seeking solutions to church-related conflict, especially in the Jakarta-Bekasi-Bogor area. Ahmad Syafi'i Mufid, the head of FKUB Jakarta and a Muhammadiyah member, has successfully mediated several instances of church-related conflicts, resulting in positive outcomes for the churches — including in the cases of GKI Kebayoran, GKI Taman Aries, Gereja Maria Karmel, Gereja Maria Vianney, and Gereja Katolik St. Gabriel.[104]

On the other hand, at the community level, one often finds opposition within NU and Muhammadiyah to the building of churches in their own neighbourhoods. One often sees banners flying in particular neighbourhoods, rejecting plans to build a church there — such as the banner erected by the South Jakarta branch of NU, opposing the establishment of a church in Gandaria City Mall. Most local NU and Muhammadiyah leaders, when queried as to the reasons for their opposition, insist that it is purely because these churches do not have a licence to build a church. By invoking this reason, NU and Muhammadiyah are aligning themselves with the official response usually given by the Minister of Religion, Suryadharma Ali, as well as Islamist groups, when conflict around church-building breaks out — the church congregation is in the wrong because they do not have the proper licence. This superficial response ignores (or intentionally whitewashes) the underlying realities that church communities often have difficulty obtaining licences because of the way that the approval process is structured.[105]

The ongoing conflict related to the building and closure of churches reflects the broader trends of increasing intolerance and disharmony across religions, mentioned earlier in this article — however, the issue of churches seems to be particularly problematic for the majority of Indonesian Muslims.[106] In an LSI (Indonesia Survey Circle) survey conducted in December 2010, a significant majority of respondents (75.6 per cent) had no problem having a neighbour of a different religion — however, only 52 per cent of the respondents would agree to the building of a house of worship of a different religion in their neighbourhood.[107] Similar, but even more striking results are found when NU and Muhammadiyah communities are surveyed. In The Asia Foundation/Lembaga Survey, Indonesia survey on NU and Muhammadiyah, a series of questions was asked to gain insight into views within the two organizations on issues of pluralism, tolerance, and religious minorities. The survey results show high levels of support for "democracy" as a general concept — 89 per cent of Muhammadiyah members and 76 per cent of NU members believe that "democracy is the best form of government for a country such as ours".[108] And, when asked standard proxy questions for tolerance, such as views on a non-Muslim teaching in state schools, or moving into the neighbourhood, both organizations show average-to-high levels of tolerance, commensurate with national averages in similar polls (see Figure 2.1). However — levels of intolerance spike when the question of building houses of worship arises — 76 per cent of

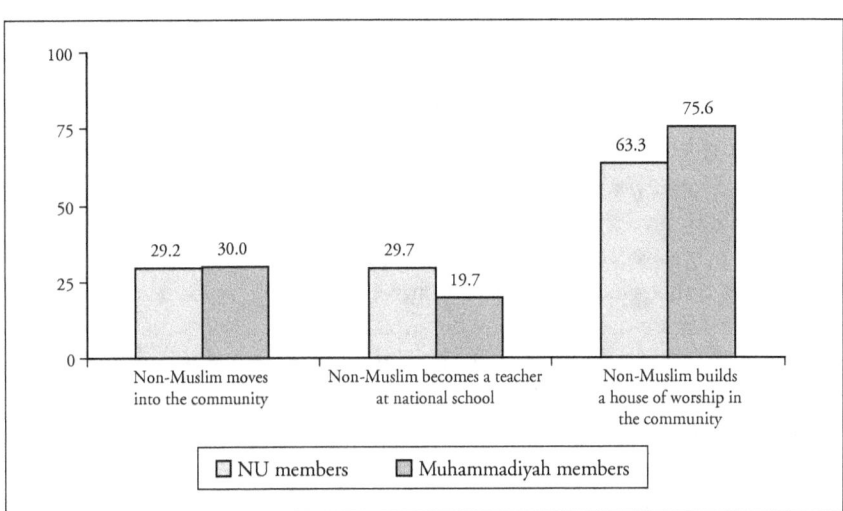

Figure 2.1
Socio-religious Tolerance, by Per Cent of Those That "Object" or "Strongly Object" to the Following Scenarios

Source: Asia Foundation/Lembaga Survey Indonesia, 2011.

Muhammadiyah and 63 per cent of NU respondents object to having a non-Muslim house of worship in their neighbourhood.

When these results were presented to the leadership of NU and Muhammadiyah, they reacted with surprise and concern at the extent of the intolerance reflected within their own communities. KH Masdar Mas'udi, Vice Chair of the Syuriah of NU, convened a closed door roundtable of the Syuriah in order to discuss the implications of these results for NU and to discuss ways to increase tolerance within their own communities. Similarly, Secretary of the Board of Muhammadiyah, Abdul Mu'thi, built on these results to conduct further research on levels and the nature of intolerance within Muhammadiyah and then to apply that research to the development of curriculum within Muhammadiyah schools.[109]

In addition to these immediate actions, actors within both Muhammadiyah and NU are continuing to conduct pluralism-related educational activities and trainings within both organizations. PP Ma'arif NU, an NU institute that conducts education-related activities, and Majlis Pendidikan Dasar dan Menengah Muhammadiyah (Muhammadiyah Council for Basic and Secondary Education) as well as the Ma'arif Institute of Muhammadiyah, an NGO established by former Muhammadiyah chair Syafi'i Ma'arif, have actively developed curriculum and materials to be used in NU and Muhammadiyah schools, that teach pluralism, tolerance, and harmonious relations amongst religions.[110]

CONCLUSIONS

Post-*reformasi* Indonesia is beset by increasing contradictions and polarization — at once praised for being a model of democracy in the region, the darling of investors and international business advisors, yet weighed down by pervasive corruption and beginning to see regression on fundamental freedoms guaranteed to all citizens. In such a context, two large, mainstream, mass-based Muslim organizations whose mission is in fact to occupy the "middle path" amidst bewildering extremes, may be precisely what Indonesia needs. NU and Muhammadiyah navigate this centrist course in different ways due to their varying internal structure and culture.

Nahdlatul Ulama continues to have within its ranks among the most "progressive" Muslim thinkers in the country on issues of inter-faith relations and religious freedom.[111] However, while some of these intellectuals sit in decision-making positions on the PBNU, one rarely sees PBNU using its political and social clout to advocate strongly for minority rights or religious freedom, beyond participating in public inter-faith forums of the kind often sponsored by the Ministry of Foreign Affairs and foreign donors. The exception to this relative passivism is seen when intolerance bleeds over into violence — then one can see PBNU responding more aggressively. The very visible statements made by KH Said Aqil urging the government to disband "radical organizations that use violence and stir up unrest" (referring to without naming the FPI) and urging the country to beware of "radical Islam" are a somewhat rare example of this.[112] Similarly, when local branches take positions allowing or even encouraging violence against minorities, we see PBNU reacting to pull their cadres back into line, as in the case of the Shi'a in East Java and the Ahmadiyah in Kuningan. But even with these calls to disband the FPI, one sees a markedly different line coming from PBNU to that coming from the branch office. In a statement released by the East Java branch of Ansor and Banser, the Deputy Chairman Hendro Tri Subiyantoro called for the government to disband FPI and offered the services of Ansor to assist in this process, saying, "East Java Ansor and Banser will use peaceful methods. However, if those organizations push back with violence, Ansor and Banser will not retreat. It's like what people say, 'you get what you give'."[113] This veiled threat to halt violence with the use of violence is clearly at odds with the position of PBNU which calls for FPI to be disbanded on the grounds of its usage of violence. Nevertheless, it is precisely NU's internal diversity and relatively loose internal controls that provide the opportunities for human rights advocates within the organization to speak out with relative freedom — this is a great strength of the organization. This has allowed NU thinkers to be among the few really grappling intellectually with the limits of religious freedom as interpreted by the legislative and judicial system in Indonesia, in which a central "orthodoxy" is given the right and authority to define belief.

Muhammadiyah, with its stricter hierarchy and organizational structure has greater coherence to its public messaging, which lends it credence and weight when it does put its clout on the line on social issues. However, it also tends to be more conservative on issues of pluralism and religious freedom, in keeping with reformist/modernist Muslim doctrine on these matters. However, shifts described earlier at its latest national congress in 2010 provide opportunities for minority rights activists within its ranks. At the 2010 Muhammadiyah national congress, M. Dawam Rahardjo issued scathing criticisms of Muhammadiyah for losing its "modernity" and ignoring the contemporary struggles and realities of religious minorities — in response to that, fifteen young Muhammadiyah intellectuals took his words as a rallying cry to advocate for internal renewal of thought within Muhammadiyah on these issues.[114]

One can then find hope and opportunity in the different strengths that these organizations bring to the discourse and activism on religious freedom in Indonesia. These opportunities do remain limited and often at the level of the individual, however, the larger potential that these vast and influential organizations has remained unrealized. In a struggle in which an "orthodoxy" is invoked in order to define and limit what is or is not a particular religion, NU and Muhammadiyah have tremendous authority.[115] One has, however, not yet seen either organization, as institutions, drawing upon that authority in the interests of religious minorities.

Notes

[1] Endy Bayuni, "Indonesia Loses Its Bragging Rights", <Transitions.Foreignpolicy.com>, 12 March 2012, available at <http://transitions.foreignpolicy.com/posts/2012/01/11/indonesia_loses_bragging_rights> (accessed 15 March 2012).

2. "International Religious Freedom Report 2010", U.S. State Department, November 2010, available at <http://www.state.gov/j/drl/rls/irf/2010/148869.htm> (accessed 27 February 2012).
3. "Indonesia: 'Christianisation' and Intolerance", International Crisis Group Policy Briefing, Asia Briefing No. 114, 24 November 2010.
4. Agus Triyono, "Activists Question Indonesia President's Silence over Religious Violence", *Jakarta Globe*, 5 February 2012, available at <http://www.thejakartaglobe.com/home/activists-question-indonesia-presidents-silence-over-religious-violence/496019> (accessed 7 February 2012).
5. "Indonesia, a Bad Year for Religious Rights", *Jakarta Globe*, 26 December 2011, available at <http://www.setara-institute.org/en/content/indonesia-bad-year-religious-rights> (accessed 29 February 2012); also see Kondisi Kebebasan Beragama/Berkeyakinan di Indonesia 2010 [Status of Freedom of Religion/Belief in Indonesia 2010], Setara Institute Report, February 2011, available at <http://www.setara-institute.org/en/content/kondisi-kebebasan-beragamaberkeyakinan-di-indonesia-2010>.
6. S. Mujani and W. Liddle, "Muslim Indonesia's Secular Democracy", *Asian Survey* 49, no. 4 (July/August 2009): 588.
7. Ibid., p. 576.
8. B. Platzdasch, *Islamism in Indonesia: Politics in the Emerging Democracy* (Singapore: Institute of Southeast Asian Studies, 2009), pp. 331–41, and S. Tanuwidjaja, "Political Islam and Islamic Parties in Indonesia: Critically Assessing the Evidence of Islam's Political Decline", *Contemporary Southeast Asia: A Journal of International and Strategic Affairs* 32, no. 1 (April 2010): 29–49.
9. M.C. Ricklefs, "Religion, Politics and Social Dynamics in Java: Historical and Contemporary Rhymes", in *Expressing Islam: Religious Life and Politics in Indonesia*, edited by G. Fealy and S. White (Singapore: Institute of Southeast Asian Studies, 2008), pp. 115–36.
10. R. Hefner, "Where Have All the Abangan Gone? Religionization and the Decline of Non-Standard Islam in Contemporary Indonesia", in *The Politics of Religion in Indonesia: Syncretism, Orthodoxy, and Religious Contention in Java and Bali*, edited by M. Picard and R. Madinier (London: Routledge, 2011), pp. 71–90.
11. Ibid., p. 72.
12. M. Hilmy, "The Politics of Negotiating the Authenticity: Problems and Challenges of Regulating Freedom of Religion in Indonesia", paper presented at the Law and Religious Pluralism in Contemporary Asia conference (Singapore: Asia Research Institute, National University of Singapore, 17–18 December 2011), p. 5.
13. Ibid., pp. 1–2.
14. Ibid., p. 3.

15 Z.A. Bagir, "Defamation of Religion in Post-Reformasi Indonesia: New Legal Issues in the Old Politics of Religion", paper presented at the Law and Religious Pluralism in Contemporary Asia conference (Singapore: Asia Research Institute, National University of Singapore, 17–18 December 2011); and Bernhard Platzdasch, "Religious Freedom in Indonesia: The Case of the Ahmadiyah", ISEAS Working Paper, Politics and Security Series No. 2 (2011), p. 21, available at <http://web1.iseas.edu.sg/wp-content/uploads/2010/11/Religious-Freedom-in-Indonesia1.pdf>. See also, Ismail Hasani, ed., *Putusan Uji Materi Undang-undang No. 1/PNPS/1965 tentang Pencegahan Penyalahgunaan dan/atau Penodaan Agama terhadap Undang-undang Dasar 1945 di Mahkamah Konstitusi* (Jakarta: Publikasi Setara Institute, 2010). This book contains the complete decision of the Constitutional Court No. 140/PUU-VII/2009 upholding Law No. 1/PNPS/1965, as well as many of the arguments made in favour of the judicial review by Bonar Tigor Naipospos (Setara Institute), Usman Hamid (KONTRAS), Zainal Abidin Bagir (CRCS UGM), dan Amicus Brief (ARTICLE 19).

16 Bagir, "Defamation of Religion", p. 2.
17 Ibid.
18 Ibid., p. 7.
19 For background on NU, see Robin Bush, *Nahdlatul Ulama and the Struggle for Power within Islam and Politics in Indonesia* (Singapore: Institute of Southeast Asian Studies Press, 2009); Greg Fealy, "Ulama and Politics in Indonesia: A History of Nahdlatul Ulama, 1952–1967", Ph.D. dissertation, Monash University, Clayton, 1996; Andree Feillard, *NU vis-à-vis Negara* (Yogyakarta: LKIS Press, 1999); and Ali Haidar, *Nahdatul Ulama dan Islam di Indonesia* (Jakarta: Penerbit Gramedia, 1998). For background on Muhammadiyah, see Mohammad Damami, *Akar Gerakan Muhammadiyah* (Yogya: Fajar Pustaka Baru, 2000); Sirajuddin Syamsudin. "Religion and Politics in Islam: The Case of Muhammadiyah in Indonesia's New Order", Ph.D. dissertation, University of California, LA, 1991; and Mitsuo Nakamura, *Crescent Arises over the Banyan Tree: A Study of the Muhammadiyah Movement in a Central Javanese Town* (Yogyakarta: Gajah Mada University Press, 1983).
20 R. Bush, "NU and Muhammadiyah: Changing Political Roles and Spheres of Influence", paper presented at the Muslim Religious Authority in Contemporary Asia conference (Singapore: Asia Research Institute, National University of Singapore, 24–25 November 2011), p. 4. While the survey puts Muhammadiyah at only 7.9 per cent of the population, its influence is still significant, as many senior-level bureaucrats, especially within the Ministries of Education and Health, come from a Muhammadiyah background.
21 Ibid., p. 7.

22 M. van Bruinessen, "New Leadership, New Policies?", in *Inside Indonesia*, 16 June 2010, available at <http://www.insideindonesia.org/weekly-articles-100-apr-june-2010/new-leadership-new-policies> (accessed 16 January 2012).
23 Andreas Ufen, "Mobilising Political Islam: Indonesia and Malaysia Compared", *Commonwealth and Comparative Politics* 47, no. 3 (2009): 310.
24 Ihsan Ali-Fauzi, Samsu Rizal Panggabean, Nathanael Gratias Sumaktoyo, Anick H.T., Husni Mubarak, Testriono, dan Siti Nurhayat, eds., *Kontroversi Gereja di Jakarta* (Yogyakarta: Gajah Mada University, Centre for Religious and Cross Cultural Studies, 2011).
25 S. Tanuwidjaja, "Political Islam and Islamic Parties in Indonesia: Critically Assessing the Evidence of Islam's Political Decline", in *Contemporary Southeast Asia: A Journal of International and Strategic Affairs* 32, no. 1 (April 2010) pp. 29–49.
26 Ibid., p. 30.
27 Ibid., p. 37. Also see B. Platzdasch, op. cit.
28 There is a large body of literature that critically examines the use of the term "moderate" in post-9/11 western policy circles, and a backlash against the term in Muslim intellectual circles. See for example Asma Barlas, "The Excesses of Moderation", *The American Journal of Islamic Social Sciences* 22, no. 3 (2005): 158–65; Muqtedar Khan, "Islamic Democracy and Moderate Muslims: The Straight Path Runs Through the Middle", *The American Journal of Islamic Social Sciences* 22, no. 3 (2005): 39–50; and Yvonne Haddad and Tyler Golson, "Overhauling Islam: Representation, Construction, and Cooptation of 'Moderate Islam' in Western Europe", *A Journal of Church and State* 49, no. 3 (2007): 487–515.
29 NU defines itself as an organization following *Ahlus Sunnah Waljamaah* (which it refers to by the acronym Aswaja to differentiate itself from modernist Sunni groups) which is a theological methodology based on values of flexibility, *tawasuth, I'tidal, tawazun,* and *tasamuh.* See Fealy, "Ulama and Politics in Indonesia", pp. 64–68; Bush, *Nahdlatul Ulama and the Struggle for Power*, pp. 36–37; and K.H. Said Aqiel Siradj, *Ahlussunnah wal Jamaa'ah dalam Lintas Sejarah* (Yogyakarta: LKPSM, 1997).
30 See Asma Afsaruddin, "The Hermeneutics of Inter-faith Relations: Retrieving Moderation and Pluralism as Universal Principles in Qur'anic Exegeses", *Journal of Religious Ethics* 37, no. 2 (2009): 347–50, and indeed the entire article, for an excellent review of the range of interpretations of the term *wasat* in these Quranic verses. Afrasruddin argues there is prevailing consensus that the term "implies above all adherence to justice and temperateness". (p. 347). Also, for another interpretation of this verse, see Abdullah Yusuf Ali, *The Meaning of the Holy Qur'an*, 10th ed. (Beltsville, Maryland: Amana Publications, 1999), p. 58.

31. "Kang Said: Pesantren Mengemban Misi Sebagai Penengah", NU Online, 22 October 2005, available at <http://www.nu.or.id/page/id/dinamic_detil/1/3685/Warta/Kang_Said__Pesantren_Mengemban_Misi_Sebagai_Penengah.html> (accessed 15 March 2012).
32. Bagir, "Defamation of Religion", p. 2.
33. Bush, "Nahdlatul Ulama and the Struggle", pp. 65–110.
34. Ibid.; van Bruinessen, "What Happened to the Smiling Face of Indonesian Islam? Muslim Intellectualism and the Conservative Turn in Post-Suharto Indonesia", pp. 30–8.
35. Bush, "Nahdlatul Ulama and the Struggle", pp. 95–96; van Bruinessen, "Smiling Face of Indonesian Islam", pp. 31–34; and "Percakapan dengan Said Aqiel Siradj", in *Membela Kebebasan Beragama: Percakapan tentang Sekularisme, Liberalisme, dan Pluralisme*, edited by Budhy Munawar Rachman (Jakarta: Paramadina — LSAF, 2010), pp. 1405–06.
36. van Bruinessen, "Smiling Face of Indonesian Islam", pp. 25–35. Also, Djohan Effendi, *A Renewal Without Breaking Tradition: The Emergence of a New Discourse in Indonesia's Nahdlatul Ulama During the Abdurrahman Wahid Era* (Yogyakarta: Interfidei, 2008).
37. The author (Bush) observed these activities first-hand as part of her role as then-Program Officer at The Asia Foundation.
38. Indeed, Indonesian Islamic discourse at this time experienced a shift to the right across the board in the mid-2000s, as Islamist agendas dominated the public domain, and had a great deal of political momentum. On the growing conservatism within NU and Muhammadiyah, see Andree Feillard and Remy Madinier, *The End of Innocence? Indonesian Islam and the Temptations of Radicalism* (Singapore: National University of Singapore Press, 2011), pp. 240–47; and Ricklefs, "Religion, Politics, and Social Dynamics".
39. van Bruinessen, "Smiling Face of Indonesian Islam", p. 3.
40. van Bruinessen, "New Leadership, New Policies".
41. Piers Gillespie, "Current Issues in Indonesian Islam: Analysing the 2005 Council of Indonesian Ulama Fatwa No. 7 Opposing Pluralism, Liberalism, and Secularism", *Journal of Islamic Studies* 18, no. 2 (2007): 202–40; and van Bruinessen, "Smiling Face of Indonesian Islam", pp. 3–4. Also see Munawar Rachman, *Membela Kebebasan Beragama*, which contains interviews with 70 Indonesian intellectuals, 57 of them from NU and Muhammadiyah. This volume documents a range of views on the three core issues in the title.
42. See an insightful article on MUI history, composition, and these fatwa in particular — Syafiq Hasyim, "The Council of Indonesian Ulama (Majelis Ulama Indonesia, MUI) and Religious Freedom", *Irasec's Discussion Papers, No. 12* (December 2011), available at <http://www.irasec.com>. On the anti-Ahmadiyah fatwa, see Bernhard Platzdasch, "Religious Freedom in Indonesia: The Case of the Ahmadiyah", ISEAS Working Paper: Politics and Security

Series No. 2 (2011), available at <http://web1.iseas.edu.sg/wp-content/uploads/2010/11/Religious-Freedom-in-Indonesia1.pdf>.

43 Platzdasch, "Religious Freedom in Indonesia". Also the author (Rachman) in 2008–09 conducted research on the response of the Muslim community, especially within NU and Muhammadiyah, to the fatwa on secularism, liberalism and pluralism. This research was then published as a four-book series, *Islam Progresif dan Perkembangan Diskursusnya* (Jakarta: Gramedia Widiasarana Indonesia, 2010) — *Argumen Islam untuk Sekularisme; Argumen Islam untuk Liberalisme; Argumen Islam untuk Pluralisme;* dan *Sekularisme, Liberalisme dan Pluralisme.*

44 Both authors attended this public event, held in August 2005 at Lembaga Ilmu Pengetahuan Indonesia (LIPI). In addition, see Gillespie, "Current Issues in Indonesian Islam", pp. 223–28 for an excellent review of the range of opinions within NU on these fatwa, and in particular on the criticisms made by NU intellectuals of MUI's understanding and usage of concepts of "pluralism" and "liberalism".

45 Ibid., pp. 228–30.

46 Ibid., p. 228.

47 Feillard and Madinier, *End of Innocence*, pp. 245, 259.

48 Robin Bush, "Regional Sharia Regulations in Indonesia: Anomaly or Symptom?", in *Expressing Islam: Religious Life and Politics in Indonesia*, edited by Greg Fealy and Sally White (Singapore: Institute of Southeast Asian Studies Publishing, 2008), pp. 174–91.

49 Boy Pradana, "In Defense of Pure Islam: The Conservative — Progressive Debate within Muhammadiyah", unpublished thesis (Canberra: Australian National University, 2003).

50 Interview with Siti Ruhaini Dzuhayatin, 13 January 2012. Ruhaini is a well known feminist leader within Muhammadiyah that has served on the Majelis Tarjih (religious council) and is active within Aisyiyah, the women's branch of Muhammadiyah.

51 Interview with Syamsul Arifin, 27 January 2011 in Surabaya. Arifin is a professor of Islamic Studies at Universitas Muhammadiyah Malang (UMM). See also, "Tanfidz Keputusan Muktamar Satu Abad Muhammadiyah (Muktamar Muhammadiyah ke-46)", Yogyakarta, 3–8 July 2010, p. 148.

52 van Bruinessen, "New Leadership, New Policies"; other observers, however, drew different conclusions from the same Muktamar. Feillard and Madinier, noting that a decision was made at this Muktamar to sanction the practice of female circumcision, despite a strong effort of the women's branch Fatayat NU to have it forbidden, found that increasingly conservative elements were gaining ground within NU at the time. Feillard and Madinier, *The End of Innocence*, p. 253.

53 "Tanfidziyah", NU Online, available at <http://www.nu.or.id/page/id/static/22/Tanfidziyah.html> (accessed 15 March 2012).

54 van Bruinessen, "New Leadership, New Policies".
55 Hasyim, "Council of Indonesian Ulama", p. 20.
56 Bagir, "Defamation of Religion", p. 2; see also Michael Feener, "Official Religions, State Secularisms, and the Structure of Religious Pluralism", in *Proselytizing and the Limits of Religious Pluralism in Contemporary Asia* (forthcoming), edited by Juliana Finucane and R. Michael Feener. For an insightful analysis of this case in relation to proselytization and human rights.
57 "Percakapan dengan Abdul Moqsith Ghazali", in *Membela Kebebasan Beragama: Percakapan tentang Sekularisme, Liberalisme dan Pluralisme*, by Budhy Munawar-Rachman (Jakarta: Paramadina — LSAF, 2010), p. 86.
58 Ibid.
59 Rachman, "Percakapan dengan Bahtiar Effendy", p. 233.
60 For excellent coverage of the MUI Fatwa and of the Decree, see Plazdasch, "Religious Freedom in Indonesia"; and Ismatu Ropi, "Islamism, Government Regulation, and the Ahmadiyah Controversies in Indonesia", *Al-jami'ah Journal of Islamic Studies* 48, no. 2 (2010): 281–320.
61 Pernyataan Ketua Majelis Tarjih PP Muhammadiyah, Syamsul Anwar. See, "Muhammadiyah Telah Nyatakan Ahmadiyah Sesat Sejak 1930-an", *Format News*, 8 March 2011, available at <http://formatnews.com/beta/view.php?newsid=3287> (accessed 15 March 2012).
62 Jeremy Menchik, "The Origins of Intolerance toward Ahmadiyah", *The Jakarta Post*, 10 February 2012, available at <http://www.thejakartapost.com/news/2012/02/10/the-origins-intolerance-ward-ahmadiyah.html> (accessed 15 March 2012).
63 "PBNU Saat Dipimpin Gus Dur Pernah Keluarkan Fatwa Larangan Ahmadiyah", NU Online, 25 April 2008, available at <http://www.nu.or.id/page/id/dinamic_detil/1/12149/Warta/PBNU_Saat_Dipimpin_Gus_Dur_Pernah_Keluarkan_Fatwa_Larangan_Ahmadiyah.html> (accessed 15 March 2012). In another example of the internal variation even at the highest of levels within NU, this fatwa was issued during the period of Abdurrahman Wahid's leadership of the NU Board, and he immediately called a press conference refuting the fatwa and stating that it did not have legal basis.
64 Menchik, "The Origins of Intolerance toward Ahmadiyah".
65 "Sikap PBNU tentang Ahmadiyah", NU Online, 9 May 2008, available at <http://www.nu.or.id/page/id/dinamic_detil/6/12315/Taushiyah/Sikap_PBNU_tentang_Ahmadiyah.html> (accessed 15 March 2012). Pandangan tentang cara menghadapi masalah Ahmadiyah tanpa kekerasan ini memang menjadi pandangan NU. Interview with Imam Aziz, member of the PBNU, December 2011. For an analysis of the fatwa and violence, see Luthfi As-Syaukanie, "Fatwas and Violence in Indonesia", *Journal of Religion and Society* 11 (2009): 1–21.
66 Platzdasch, "Religious Freedom in Indonesia".

67. Interview with Imam Aziz, member of the PBNU, December 2011.
68. "Suryadharma Ali: Ahmadiyah Lebih Baik Dibubarkan, Daripada Dibiarkan", *Republika*, 19 March 2011.
69. "Ulama NU Berupaya Menyadarkan Ahmadiyah", *Suara Merdeka*, 9 February 2011, available at <http://suaramerdeka.com/v1/index.php/read/cetak/2011/02/09/136540/Ulama-NU-Berupaya-Menyadarkan-Ahmadiyah> (accessed 15 March 2012). Muzadi's point begs some scepticism, as only six religions are recognized by the Indonesian constitution; presumably an "Ahmadiyah" religion would not be one of them.
70. Ibid.
71. "Percakapan dengan Abdul Moqsith Ghazali", in Munawar-Rachman, *Membela Kebebasan Beragama*, p. 88
72. "Muhammadiyah Prakarsai Dialog dengan Ahmadiyah", Gerakan Pemuda Ansor, 11 June 2008, available at <http://gp-ansor.org/5094-11062008.html> (accessed 15 March 2012).
73. "Muhammadiyah Tak Ingin Terlibat Gerakan Bubarkan Ahmadiyah", *Antara*, 21 February 2011, available at <http://www.antaranews.com/news/247016/muhammadiyah-tak-ingin-terlibat-gerakan-bubarkan-ahmadiyah> (accessed 15 March 2012).
74. "NU-Muhammadiyah bahas Ahmadiyah", *Waspada*, 4 March 2011, available at <http://www.waspada.co.id/index.php?option=com_content&view=article&id=178818:nu-muhammadiyah-bahas-ahmadiyah&catid=17&Itemid=30> (accessed 15 March 2012).
75. Ibid.
76. The Wahid Institute, "Monthly Report on Religious Issues", Edition XXXV, August 2011.
77. "Ahmadiyah Brought Attacks on Themselves: Officials", *Jakarta Globe*, 10 February 2011, available at <http://www.thejakartaglobe.com/news/ahmadiyah-brought-attack-on-themselves-officials/421756> (accessed 15 March 2012).
78. "PBNU Kecam Perusakan Tempat Ibadah Ahmadiyah", NU Online, 26 December 2007, available at <http://www.nu.or.id/page/id/dinamic_detil/1/10900/Warta/PBNU_Kecam_Perusakan_Tempat_Ibadah_Ahmadiyah.html> (accessed 15 March 2012).
79. Interview with M. Imam Aziz, December 2011. See also, "Terkait Ahmadiyah, PBNU Imbau Perkuat Ukhuwah Nahdliyah", NU Online, 7 August 2010, available at <http://www.nu.or.id/page/id/dinamic_detil/1/24127/Warta/Terkait_Ahmadiyah__PBNU_Imbau_Perkuat_Ukhuwah_Nahdliyah.html> (accessed 15 March 2012).
80. "Pencopotan Ketua GP Ansor Wajar", Radar Cirebon, 2 August 2010, available at <http://radarcirebon.com/2010/08/02/pencopotan-ketua-gp-ansor-wajar> (accessed 15 March 2012). For the press release, see <http://www.mail-archive.com/forum-pembaca kompas@yahoogroups.com/msg105717.html>. Banser is

the "paramilitia" arm of GP Ansor, the NU young men's group. They have a history of being deployed to protect churches and religious minorities.

81 Camelia Pasandaran, "Government Supports Ahmadiyah Ban in East Java", *Jakarta Globe*, 1 March 2011, available at <http://www.thejakartaglobe.com/news/government-supports-ahmadiyah-ban-in-east-java/425918> (accessed 15 March 2012).

82 "Banser Jatim Siap Kawal SK Pelarangan Ahmadiyah", Detik Surabaya, 3 March 2011, available at <http://surabaya.detik.com/read/2011/03/03/135239/1583920/466/banser-jatim-siap-kawal-sk-pelarangan-ahmadiyah> (accessed 15 March 2012).

83 Ibid.

84 On the anti-Shi'I conflict in Indonesia, see Zulkifli, "The Struggle of Shi`is in Indonesia", Ph.D. dissertation (Leiden: Leiden University, 2009), pp. 276–97; on pro-Shi'a responses of NU and Muhammadiyah, see ibid., pp. 297–304.

85 Interview with Dwi Rubiyanti Khalifah, 26 January 2012. Khalifah is an NU activist, and also Country Representative of AMAN Indonesia. See also, "Dilema Kebebasan Beragama di Indonesia: Studi Kasus Pembakaran Rumah Ibadah di Sampang Madura" (Jakarta: The Asian Moslem Action Network [AMAN] Indonesia, 2012).

86 Interview with Dwi Rubiyanti Khalifah, 26 January 2012.

87 "Bela Syi'ah Tak Sesat, Said Aqil Siradj Khianati Khittah NU", Syiahali. wordpress.com, available at <http://syiahali.wordpress.com/2012/01/31/bcla-syiah-tak-sesat-said-aqil-siradj-khianati-khittah-nu-ustad-husain-ardilla-ketua-umum-pbnu-kh-said-aqil-siraj-merupakan-imam-syafii-nya-negara-indonesia/>.

88 Ibid.

89 "Astaghfirullah… Said Agil Siradj Mencatut Ulama, Berdusta demi Membela Syiah", Nahimunkar.com, 27 January 2012, available at <http://nahimunkar.com/10869/astaghfirullah-said-agil-siradj-mencatut-ulama-berdusta-demi-membela-syiah> (accessed 15 March 2012).

90 "Nah, Said Aqil Siradj tertangkap basah kerjasama dengan Syiah", Nahimunkar.com, 11 February 2012, available at <http://nahimunkar.com/11094/nah-said-aqil-siradj-tertangkap-basah-kerjasama-dengan-syiah> (accessed 15 March 2012).

91 "K.H Said Agil Siradj: Sunni-Syiah Memiliki Akar Budaya Yang Sama", Deleteisrael.pun.bz, 16 January 2012, available at <http://deleteisrael.pun.bz/k-h-said-agil-siradj-sunni-syiah-memilik.xhtml> (accessed 15 March 2012).

92 Zulhidayat Siregar, "PBNU: Pembakaran Pesantren Syiah di Sampang Bukan Konflik Agama", Rakyat Merdeka Online, 1 January 2012, available at <http://www.rakyatmerdekaonline.com/read/2012/01/01/50728/> (accessed 15 March 2012).

93 "Ketua Umum PP Muhammadiyah Prof. Din Syamsuddin: 'Syiah bukan ajaran sesat'", Syiahali.wordpress.com, available at <http://syiahali.wordpress.com/2012/01/14/ketua-umum-pp-muhammadiyah-prof-din-syamsuddin-syiah-bukan-ajaran-sesat> (accessed 15 March 2012).

94 Ibid.

95 See Zukifli, "The Struggle of the Shi`is in Indonesia".

96 Melissa Crouch, "Implementing the Regulation on Places of Worship in Indonesia: New Problems, Local Politics and Court Action" 34 (December 2010) Asian Studies Review 403–19.

97 "NU Chairman visits Solo Church Victims", *Jakarta Globe*, 27 September 2011; "Police see Link Between Solo, Cirebon Bombers", Antara News, 27 September 2011. .

98 Frequently one hears the phrase "beware of the dangers of radical salafiism" within both NU and Muhammadiyah. And both often hold seminars or workshops on the dangers of terrorism and radicalism. For example, in December 2011, Muslimat NU held a workshop in Park Hotel, Jakarta, titled "Religious Deradicalization Based on Pesantren and Pesantren Leaders". This was attended by senior Muslimat NU leaders from across the country, and included speakers such as Said Aqil Siradj and Yenny Wahid.

99 "Muhammadiyah Tawarkan Gedung untuk Ibadah Natal", *Suara Pembaruan Daily* as published on Muhammadiyah Studies, 22 December 2005, available at <http://muhammadiyahstudies.blogspot.com/2010/10/muhammadiyah-tawarkan-gedung-untuk.html> (accessed 15 March 2012).

100 Available at <http://www.gusdur.net/pemikiran/Detail/?id=105/hl=Harlah_Natal_Dan_Maulid>.

101 The Yasmin Church of Bogor has become one of the best-known and most controversial cases of church closure in Indonesia. In 2000, the church leaders applied for a licence to build a church near the Yasmin Garden, Bogor. They went through all of the legal processes at the time, and in 2006, the Mayor of Bogor granted them a licence, and the building of the church commenced. In 2008, the head of the Bogor city administration cancelled that licence, and local administrative officials sealed off the church, refusing to let construction or worship take place. The congregation took the case to the court, and it went all the way to the Supreme Court, which decided in December 2000 that the church did have legal status. Despite that, the local Bogor officials maintain that the authority to bestow that status lies with them, and they have to date refused to let the church conduct worship services. For more details, see Ihsan Ali-Fauzi et al., *Kontroversi Gereja di Jakarta* (Yogyakarta: CRCS, 2010).

102 "GP Anshor Kerahkan 1.200 Anggotanya Amankan Natal", Metrotvnews.com, 25 December 2011, available at <http://metrotvnews.com/read/newsvideo/2011/12/25/142064/GP-Anshor-Kerahkan-1,200-Anggotanya-Amankan-Natal> (accessed 16 March 2012).

103 El-Qum, Mukti Ali, "Pembangunan Gereja dan Batasan Toleransi menurut Kitab Kuning: Laporan Bahtsul Masail Rumah Kitab ke-II, 29 Agustu 2010", unpublished paper; further information on this event was obtained from interviews with participants in the Rumah Kitab Bahtsul Masail event including head of the Bekasi District branch of NU, KH. DR. Zamakhsyari Abd. Majid and Ustadz Sa'dullah Affandi, MA.

104 Available at <http://balitbangdiklat.kemenag.go.id/index.php?option=com_content&view=article&id=397:optimalisasi-peran-fkub-dki-jakarta-menuju-kehidupan-yang-harmoni&catid=38:jurnal-penelitian>.

105 See Melissa Crouch, "Implementing the Regulation on Places of Worship in Indonesia", op. cit; which explains in detail the challenges for obtaining a licence to build a church, which involves getting signatures from community members, and approval by the FKUB (Forum for Inter-faith Harmony), usually dominated by Muslim leaders. There are many cases in which a church congregation has gone through the entire process, been given the permit, and still faces opposition by the local community. Also see Ali-Fauzi, *Kontroversi Gereja di Jakarta*.

106 See the excellent report by the International Crisis Group (ICG), "Indonesia: 'Christianisation' and Intolerance" on the problem of church burnings and closures, and several sound theories as to the underlying dynamics and causes of this growing phenomenon, including a perception of aggressive proselytization on part of Christian communities. International Crisis Group, Asia Briefing No. 114, 24 November 2010, available at <http://www.crisisgroup.org/en/regions/asia/south-east-asia/indonesia/B114-indonesia-christianisation-and-intolerance.aspx>.

107 Indonesian Survey Circle (LSI) Survey, "Kajian Bulanan Edisi No. 23, Oktober 2010", available at <http://lsinetwork.co.id/wp-content/themes/kajian_bulanan/Kajian_Bulanan_Edisi_No_23_Oktober_2010.pdf>.

108 Survey results provided directly by The Asia Foundation, used with permission.

109 The authors, and other members of The Asia Foundation program leadership, engaged in frequent dialogue with these and other members of NU and Muhammadiyah at the time, to facilitate the productive exposure and dissemination of the survey results within the two organizations, prior to any public dissemination.

110 Maarif Institute for Culture and Humanity, available at <http://www.maarifinstitute.org> (accessed 16 March 2012); Yayasan LKIS, "Detil Publikasi: Membangun Pluralisme dari Bawah", available at <http://lkis.or.id/v2/publikasi-8-modul-belajar-bersama-membangun-pluralisme-dari-bawah.html> (accessed 16 March 2012).

111 See, for example, Mujamil Qamar's *NU "Liberal": Dari Tradisionalisme Ahlussunnah ke Universalisme Islam* (Bandung: Mizan, 2002), which describes the thought of nine NU intellectuals (Abdurrahman Wahid, Ali Yafie, Said Agiel

Siradj, Masdar Mas'udi, Sahal Mahfudh, Achmad Siddiq, Sjechul Hadi Permono, Abdul Muchith Muzadi, and Tholchah Hasan) and argues that they each have in different ways advanced "liberal" and "moderate" thought within NU.

[112] "Ketua NU: Ormas Islam Radikal Harus Bubar", Vivanews.com, 23 February 2012, available at <http://m.vivanews.com/news/read/290771-said-ormas-islam-radikal-harus-dibubarkan> (accessed 16 March 2012).

[113] "Ansor dan Banser Desak FPI Dibubarkan", TempoInteraktif.com, 18 February 2012, available at <http://www.tempo.co/read/news/2012/02/18/078384852/Ansor-dan-Banser-Desak-FPI-Dibubarkan> (accessed 16 March 2012).

[114] This was witnessed and participated in by author Budhy Munwar Rachman, who attended the Congress. Also, interview with M. Dawam Rahardjo, 20 January 2012.

[115] Interview with M. Dawam Rahardjo, ibid.

References

Afsaruddin, Asma. "The Hermeneutics of Inter-faith Relations: Retrieving Moderation and Pluralism as Universal Principles in Qur'anic Exegeses". *Journal of Religious Ethics* 37, no. 2 (2009): 347–50.

Ali, Abdullah Yusuf. *The Meaning of the Holy Qur'an*, 10th ed. Maryland, Beltsville: Amana publications, 1999.

Ali-Fauzi, Ihsan, Samsu Rizal Panggabean, Nathanael Gratias Sumaktoyo, Anick H.T., Husni Mubarak, Testriono, dan Siti Nurhayat, eds. *Kontroversi Gereja di Jakarta*. Yogyakarta: Gajah Mada University, Centre for Religious and Cross Cultural Studies, 2011.

Bagir, Zainal A. "Defamation of Religion in Post-Reformasi Indonesia: New Legal Issues in the Old Politics of Religion". Law and Religious Pluralism in Contemporary Asia conference. Singapore: Asia Research Institute, 17–18 December 2011.

Barlas, Asma. "The Excesses of Moderation". In *The American Journal of Islamic Social Sciences* 22, no. 3 (2005): 158–65.

Bayuni, Endy. "Indonesia Loses its Bragging Rights". *Foreign Policy*, 12 March 2012. Available at <http://transitions.foreignpolicy.com/posts/2012/01/11/indonesia_loses_bragging_rights/>.

Bush, Robin. *Nahdlatul Ulama and the Struggle for Power within Islam and Politics in Indonesia*. Singapore: Institute of Southeast Asian Studies, 2009.

———. "NU and Muhammadiyah: Changing Political Roles and Spheres of Influence". Muslim Religious Authority in Contemporary Asia conference, Singapore: Asia Research Institute, 24–25 November 2011.

Crouch, Melissa. "Implementing the Regulation on Places of Worship in Indonesia: New Problems, Local Politics and Court Action". *Asian Studies Review* 34 (2010): 403–19.

Damami, Mohammad. *Akar Gerakan Muhammadiyah*. Yogyakarta: Fajar Pustaka Baru, 2000.
Effendi, Djohan. *A Renewal Without Breaking Tradition: The Emergence of a New Discourse in Indonesia's Nahdlatul Ulama During the Abdurrahman Wahid Er*. Yogyakarta: Interfidei, 2008.
Fealy, Greg. "Ulama and Politics in Indonesia: A History of Nahdlatul Ulama, 1952–1967". Ph.D. dissertation, Monash University, 1996.
Feener, Michael. "Official Religions, State Secularisms, and the Structure of Religious Pluralism". In *Proselytizing and the Limits of Religious Pluralism in Contemporary Asia*, edited by Juliana Finucane and R. Michael Feener. (forthcoming).
Feillard, Andreé. *NU vis-à-vis Negara*. Yogyakarta: LKIS Press, 1999.
Feillard, Andrée and Madinier Rémy. *The End of Innocence? Indonesian Islam and the Temptations of Radicalism*. Singapore: National University of Singapore Press, 2011.
Gillespie, Piers. "Current Issues in Indonesian Islam: Analysing the 2005 Council of Indonesian Ulama Fatwa No. 7 Opposing Pluralism, Liberalism, and Secularism". *Journal of Islamic Studies* 18, no. 2 (2007): 202–40.
Haddad, Yvonne, and Tyler Golson. "Overhauling Islam: Representation, Construction, and Cooptation of 'Moderate Islam' in Western Europe". *A Journal of Church and State* 49, no. 3 (2007): 487–515.
Haidar, Ali M. *Ulama dan Islam di Indonesia*. Jakarta: Penerbit Gramedia, 1998.
Hasani, Ismail, ed. *Putusan Uji Materi Undang-undang No. 1/PNPS/1965 tentang Pencegahan Penyalahgunaan dan/atau Penodaan Agama terhadap Undang-undang Dasar 1945 di Mahkamah Konstitusi*. Jakarta: Publikasi Setara Institute, 2010.
Hasyim, Syafiq. "The Council of Indonesian Ulama (Majelis Ulama Indonesia, MUI) and Religious Freedom". *Irasec's Discussion Papers* 12 (2011). Available at <http://www.irasec.com/>.
Hefner, Robert W. "Where Have All the Abangan Gone? Religionization and the Decline of Non-Standard Islam in Contemporary Indonesia". In *The Politics of Religion in Indonesia: Syncretism, Orthodoxy, and Religious Contention in Java and Bali*, edited by Michel Picard and Rémy Madinier. London: Routledge, 2011.
Hilmy, Masdar. "The Politics of Negotiating the Authenticity: Problems and Challenges of Regulating Freedom of Religion in Indonesia". Law and Religious Pluralism in Contemporary Asia conference. Singapore: Asia Research Institute, 17–18 December 2003.
International Crisis Group (ICG). "Indonesia: 'Christianisation' and Intolerance". *Asia Briefing* 114 (2010).
Khan, Muqtedar. "Islamic Democracy and Moderate Muslims: The Straight Path Runs Through the Middle". *The American Journal of Islamic Social Sciences* 22, no. 3 (2005): 39–50.

Mujani, Saiful and R. William Liddle. "Muslim Indonesia's Secular Democracy". *Asian Survey* 49, no. 4 (2009): 588.

Nakamura, Mitsuo. *Crescent Arises over the Banyan Tree: A Study of the Muhammadiyah Movement in a Central Javanese Town*. Yogyakarta: Gajah Mada University Press, 1983.

Platzdasch, Bernhard. *Islamism in Indonesia: Politics in the Emerging Democracy*. Singapore: Institute of Southeast Asian Studies, 2009.

———. "Religious Freedom in Indonesia: The Case of the Ahmadiyah". *ISEAS Working Paper: Politics and Security Series* 2 (2011), available at <http://web1.iseas.edu.sg/wp-content/uploads/2010/11/Religious-Freedom-in-Indonesia1.pdf>.

Pradana, Boy. "In Defense of Pure Islam: the Conservative-Progressive Debate within Muhammadiyah". Unpublished thesis. Canberra: The Australian National University, 2003.

Qamar, Mujamil. *NU Liberal: Dari Tradisionalisme Ahlussunnah ke Universalisme Islam*. Bandung: Mizan, 2002.

Rachman, Budhy Munawar. *Membela Kebebasan Beragama*. Pasar Minggu, Jakarta: Lembaga Studi Agama dan Filsafat dan Paramadina, 2010.

———. "Percakapan dengan Abdul Moqsith Ghazali". In *Membela Kebebasan Beragama: Percakapan tentang Sekularisme, Liberalisme dan Pluralisme* 86. Jakarta: Paramadina — LSAF, 2010.

Ricklefs, Merle C. "Religion, Politics and Social Dynamics in Java: Historical and Contemporary Rhymes". In *Expressing Islam: Religious Life and Politics in Indonesia*, edited by Greg Fealy and Sally White. Singapore: Institute of Southeast Asian Studies, 2008.

Ropi, Ismatu. "Islamism, Government Regulation, and the Ahmadiyah Controversies in Indonesia". *Al-jami'ah Journal of Islamic Studies* 48, no. 2 (2010): 281–320.

Siradj, K.H. Said Aqiel. *Ahlussunnah wal Jamaa'ah dalam Lintas Sejarah*. Yogyakarta: LKPSM, 1997.

Syamsudin, Sirajuddin. "Religion and Politics in Islam: The Case of Muhammadiyah in Indonesia's New Order". Ph.D. dissertation. Los Angeles, CA: University of California, 1991.

Tanuwidjaja, Sunny. "Political Islam and Islamic Parties in Indonesia: Critically Assessing the Evidence of Islam's Political Decline". *Contemporary Southeast Asia: A Journal of International and Strategic Affairs* 32, no. 1 (2010): 29–49.

Ufen, Andreas. "Mobilising Political Islam: Indonesia and Malaysia Compared". *Commonwealth and Comparative Politics* 47, no. 3 (2009): 310.

van Bruinessen, Martin. "New Leadership, New Policies?" *Inside Indonesia*, 16 June 2010. Available at <http://www.insideindonesia.org/weekly-articles-100-apr-june-2010/new-leadership-new-policies/>.

———. "What Happened to the Smiling Face of Indonesian Islam?: Muslim Intellectualism and the Conservative Turn in Post-Suharto Indonesia". RSIS Working Paper no. 22 (6 January 2011): 30–38.

3

ISLAM, RELIGIOUS MINORITIES, AND THE CHALLENGE OF THE BLASPHEMY LAWS
A Close Look at the Current Liberal Muslim Discourse

Supriyanto Abdi

Debates on religious freedom and religious minorities have become more intense in post-New Order Indonesia. This is partly attributed to the increasing attention given to the international human rights discourse in the country's constitutional-legal framework of human rights. During the period of constitutional reforms (1999–2002), a new chapter on Human Rights, which includes provisions on freedom of religion or belief, was inserted into the 1945 Constitution. As noted by some scholars, this new chapter in the Constitution largely reflects the provisions contained in major international human rights documents.[1] Moreover, a number of key international human rights covenants, including the International Covenant on Civil and Political Rights (ICCPR), which contains international norms on freedom of religion or belief, were ratified by the Indonesian government, politically and legally signifying its commitment to international human rights law.[2] This led to significant questions and debates about how and to what extent the largely secular-liberal international human rights discourse should be interpreted and applied within the Indonesian constitutional, political, and cultural context.[3]

These questions featured prominently in the recent public and legal debate on Law No. 1/PNPS/1965 on the Prevention of Abuse of Religion and/or Blasphemy (the "Blasphemy Law"). The Law, which prohibits and criminalizes religious interpretations or practices considered "deviant" from the core tenets of six "official" religions in Indonesia (Islam, Catholicism, Protestantism, Hinduism, Buddhism, and Confucianism), was recently reviewed by the Indonesian Constitutional Court. The application for the judicial review of the Law was submitted to the Constitutional Court in late 2009 by the Religious Freedom Advocacy Team (Tim Advokasi Kebebasan Beragama), a coalition of human rights lawyers and activists. The Team requested the Court to repel the Law arguing that, among other things, it contradicted the provisions on freedom of religion or belief in the Indonesian Constitution and internationally recognized human rights law. In April 2010, after an intense public debate and a long series of court hearings, the Court decided that there were insufficient grounds to revoke the Law, declaring it valid. Contrary to the Religious Freedom Advocacy Team's arguments, the Court found no contradiction between the Law and the Indonesian constitutional provisions on religious freedom, suggesting that Indonesia has its own unique conception of religious freedom.

As has been the case in many other debates, Muslims with different persuasions became passionately involved in this debate, expressing opposite views. This chapter focuses on the voices of Muslim intellectuals and activists with liberal persuasions in the debate. Scholars have used different terms to refer to this sort of Muslim intellectual orientation such as "neo-modernist Islam", "cultural Islam", and "civil Islam", none of which has gained a general consensus.[4] More recently, the term "liberal" and "progressive" have been increasingly used interchangeably or in combination to characterize this stream of Muslim discourse, with both terms largely being associated with the same intellectual orientation developed by the so-called religious renewal movement (*gerakan pembaharuan keagamaan*).[5] The movement emerged in the early 1970s, with Nurcholish Madjid and Abdurrahman Wahid at the forefront.[6] Although the combination of "liberal and progressive" has been increasingly used in the recent literature, I will refer, however, to the Muslims' views discussed here as merely "liberal" Muslim voice to emphasize its close affinity with certain liberal philosophical and political discourses.[7]

The first part of this chapter will provide a brief overview of the normative framework for religious freedom in Indonesia and discuss some of its inherent ambiguities. This will be followed by a discussion on the extent to which the existence and enforcement of Law No. 1/PNPS/1965 on Blasphemy has posed challenges to the rights of religious minorities. The next part will discuss liberal Muslim discourses on religious freedom, including their critiques and challenges to the Blasphemy Law. Following this, their views on the judicial review of Law No. 1/PNPS/1965 will be elucidated. The chapter will be concluded by a brief analysis as to what extent the decision of the Constitutional Court to uphold the Law constitutes discursive limits for liberal Muslim voices on religious freedom and religious minorities in Indonesia.

OVERVIEW ON THE CONSTITUTIONAL-LEGAL FRAMEWORK OF RELIGIOUS FREEDOM IN INDONESIA

The normative framework for religious freedom in Indonesia is provided in the Indonesian Constitution of 1945 and has been strengthened during its amendments in the post-New Order period. In the initial Indonesian Constitution of 1945, religious freedom is guaranteed under Article 29 on Religion. Part of the Article reads that "The state guarantees every person the freedom of religion and worship, each according to his/her religion and belief."[8] In 2001, as part of the second amendment to the Constitution, Article 28E was inserted into a new chapter on Human Rights. This Article, as many other articles in this new chapter, largely reflect the provisions found in major international human rights treaties. Parts of the Article read that "Each person is free to profess his or her religion, and to worship in accordance with his/her religion; and "Each person has the freedom to possess convictions and beliefs, and to express his/her thoughts and attitudes. Article 28I(1) reaffirms that the right to freedom of religion or belief is part of a "human right that cannot be reduced under any circumstance".[9]

The legal framework for religious freedom has been also strengthened since the downfall of the New Order regime. In 1999, Law No. 39/1999 on Human Rights was introduced as the national legal framework for human rights, including freedom of religion or belief. Article 22 states that "Each person is free to profess his/her religion and to worship according to his/her religion and belief"; and "The state guarantees all persons the freedom of religion, each according to his/her religion and belief."[10] In 2005, the Indonesian government re-affirmed its commitment to international human rights law with the ratification of the ICCPR which contains an article on the freedom of religion and beliefs. Article 18 of the ICPPR reads: "Everyone shall have the right to freedom of thought, conscience and religion. This right shall include the freedom to have or to adopt a religion or belief of his choice, and freedom, either individually or in community with others, in public or private, to manifest his religion or belief in worship, observance, practice and teaching."[11] With the ratification of the ICCPR, Indonesia is legally bounded by its provisions, including those on freedom of religion or belief.

There are, however, certain qualifications made in some parts of the Constitution that render the normative guarantee for religious freedom in Indonesia highly ambiguous.[12] This is particularly true to the limitation clause set out in Article 28J(2) of the Constitution. The Article holds that:

> In carrying out his or her rights and freedoms, every citizen has responsibility to abide by restrictions set out by laws with the sole aim to guarantee the recognition and respect for the rights of others and to fulfil a just cause, taking into consideration morality, *religious values* (emphasis added), security, and public order in a democratic community.[13]

The limitation clause as set out in Article 28J(2) qualifies Indonesia's normative commitment to international human rights norms at least in two ways. First, it seems to blur the distinction carefully made in international human rights discourse between the so-called *forum internum* and *forum externum* of the right to freedom of religion or belief. The first refers to the internal realm of the right to freedom of thought, conscience, and religion which includes the freedom for all to have, adopt, maintain, or change their religion or belief. The second refers to the external expression of the right which includes the freedom, either alone or in community with others, in private or public, to manifest their religion or belief in teaching, practice, worship, and observance.[14] The prevailing understanding in the international human rights discourse suggests that limitations may only apply to the external expression (*forum externum*) of the right, but only to the extent that such limitations are prescribed by law and are necessary to protect public safety, order, health, morals, or the fundamental rights of others. As to the internal realm (*forum internum*) of the right, restrictions are not applicable even in times of public emergency.[15]

Second, the recognition of "religious values" as a permissible ground for the restriction on freedom of religion or belief in the Indonesian normative framework for freedom of religion or belief also forms a significant departure from the international human rights discourse. While allowing certain restrictions on the external expression (*forum externum*) of freedom of religion or belief, the international human rights discourse does not recognize "religious values" as a permissible ground for such restrictions.[16] Despite increasing push by some Islamic countries for the adoption of an international legal document on anti-defamation of religion, which would allow some restrictions on freedom of expression or freedom of religion or belief on the ground of protecting religion, the traditionally dominant understanding in the international human rights discourse has remained that respect or protection of religion *per se* is not a legitimate ground for such restrictions.[17] As will be demonstrated later, the recognition of "religious values" as the ground for restrictions on religious freedom is crucial to the debate and the Constitutional Court's verdict on the Blasphemy Law.

LAW No. 1/PNPS/1965 AND ITS CHALLENGES TO RELIGIOUS MINORITIES

In addition to the ambiguity arising from the limitation clause as mentioned above, the constitutional guarantee for freedom of religion or belief is also put into question by Law No. 1/PNPS/1965 on the Prevention of Abuse of Religion and/or Blasphemy. The Blasphemy Law, introduced as a law (*undang-undang*) by former President Soeharto in 1969, originated from the Presidential Decree No. 1/PNPS/1965 issued by his predecessor Soekarno in January 1965. Historically, the introduction of the decree — and later the law — was strongly influenced by political tensions and struggles for power between various groups, including the Communists, syncretist-mystical groups (*kebatinan*), and traditional and conservative Muslims.[18] Soekarno's decision for issuing the decree reflected the concerns of the government and conservative Islamic groups at that time over the growing influence and political mobilization of Communists and *kebatinan* groups.[19] The elevation of the decree to a law by Soeharto in 1969 was also strongly influenced by the political interests of the new regime. Soeharto found in the Decree a justification for his government's anti-communist campaign and its ambition to assert extensive political control over its peoples.

The Blasphemy Law consists of four key provisions. Article 1 of the Law contains a prohibition on publicly interpreting a religion or conducting religious activities which deviate from the core tenets of religions adhered by people in Indonesia. Three subsequent articles set out the administrative and criminal punishment for the breach of the provision of Article 1. This includes the initial "warning" by the relevant government bodies to those in breach of the provision (Article 2) and the banning of groups or organizations and imprisonment to maximum of five years for continuing the breach (Article 3). Article 4 then inserts a new provision, Article 156(a), into the Criminal Code which imposes a five-year prison sentence:

> for whoever in public intentionally expresses their views or engages in actions: a. that in principle incite hostilities and considered as abuse or defamation of a religion embraced in Indonesia; b. has the intention that a person should not practice any religion at all that is based on the Belief in The One Almighty God.[20]

The Elucidation (*Penjelasan*) of the Law specifically mentions six religions as the "recognized religions", namely Islam, Catholicism, Protestantism, Buddhism, Hinduism, and Confucianism. While it also states that other religions such as Judaism, Zoroastrianism, Shintoism, and Taoism are not prohibited, it implies that these religions, and particularly various local religion and beliefs (*agama dan kepercayaan lokal*), are not afforded the same level of protection and support from the state. Local religions or beliefs in particular seem to be considered "unhealthy" and having "second-class" status, with the stipulation in the Elucidation that "… with regard to the followers of streams of beliefs (*aliran kepercayaan*), the government shall direct them towards a healthy belief in One God".[21]

In practice, their mentioning in the Elucidation of Law established these six religions as "official religions" (*agama resmi*) or "recognized religions" (*agama yang diakui*), although what counts as "recognized religions" proved to be elusive and highly political. This is particularly true during the New Order years. In 1967, Soeharto's government, depicting the Communists as the country's main enemy, issued a Presidential Instruction (*Instruksi Presiden/Inpres*) No. 14/1967 that strictly limited Chinese religion, beliefs, and tradition for its allegedly close association with Communism.[22] While the Instruction did not explicitly negate Confucianism from the category of "recognized religion", it severely undermined the freedom of its followers to practise Confucianism. The relegation of Confucianism from the list of "recognized religion" was eventually formalized by the introduction of the Circular (*Surat Edaran*) by the Ministry of Home Affairs in 1978, which named only five religions, namely, Islam, Catholicism, Protestantism, Hinduism, and Buddhism as "recognized religions". It was not until 2000 that Confucianism regained its status as one of the recognized religions through the Presidential Decision (*Keputusan Presiden/Keppres*) No. 6/2000 issued by then President Abdurrahman Wahid.[23]

Since its introduction, the Law has posed challenges and obstacles for religious minorities to fully enjoy their right to freedom of religion or belief. These challenges and obstacles can be seen in several ways. First, the Law has severely discriminated against the followers of religions or beliefs outside these six (or five during most of the New Order era) "recognized religions". Followers of religions or beliefs, and especially indigenous religious communities, outside the six religions are often labelled as "people who do not yet have a religion" (*orang yang belum beragama*), as members of splinter religions (*agama sempalan*) who must return to the established religions, or as a potential threat to public and political order.[24] All these labels have made them highly vulnerable to enforced conversion to mainstream religions or become an easy target of the purification campaign launched by conservative religious groups. As Picard argues, the introduction of the Law had resulted in turning "state-sanctioned religions into mutually exclusive categories, putting increasing pressure on heterodox views to conform".[25]

The Law has also led to a systematic discrimination against religious minorities in relation to various civil and administrative rights. This happens in particular in the case of entitlement to the resident identity card, marriage and birth registration. In order to get an identity card, for example, many adherents of minority religions were forced to claim themselves as followers of a religion that is different from their actual religious conviction. Those who refused to choose one of those official religions were not given the card. The state's marriage policy also suggests that couples need to marry according to the official religions' requirements for their marriage to be legally recognized. Children of unregistered married couples would also face social and legal difficulties. As a result, many couples were forced to choose to marry according to one of the officially recognized religions although it might not be the religion they adhere to.[26] Some of these problems have been partially addressed in the Law of Administration of Population Affairs No. 23/2006. Under the new Law, followers of religions or traditional beliefs outside the six religions may have their identity cards granted or their marriage registered without being forced to choose one of the six "official" religions. But the category "people who do not yet have a religion" was formally inserted as a new option, implying that the existing exclusionary discourse of "recognized religions" persists and that it is being endorsed by the state.[27]

The enforcement of the Law, often on recommendation by the Coordinating Board for Controlling Mystical Beliefs in Society (Badan Koordinasi Pengawasan Aliran Kepercayaan Masyarakat/Bakorpakem), has also resulted in the banning of various religious minority groups. During the New Order, at least 29 religious minorities were reportedly banned at the national level on blasphemy charges. The noteworthy cases include the abolition of Javanese beliefs (*aliran kepercayaan*) such as Manunggal and Agama Jawa Sanyoto Ki Kere Klaten as well as Islamic *sufi* orders such as Tareqat Saufiah Samaniyah Syeik Ibrahim Medan, and Protestant sects such as Sidang Jemaat Kristus Raja Dame Joha Sihotang and the Children of God.[28]

Blasphemy charges under the Law, in most cases against Islam, have also led to the imprisonment of several people. One of the most high profile cases of blasphemy in the New Order was that of Arswendo Atmowiloto, the lead editor of the tabloid Monitor. Arswendo was sentenced to five years in prison on blasphemy charges for releasing the results of a survey in the magazine that placed the Prophet Muhammad at the eleventh as the most admired public figures, with several other names, including Soeharto and Arswendo himself were in higher rankings.[29]

Since 1998, there has been a new trend in blasphemy-related cases. As Crouch observes, under the New Order, blasphemy charges had more political undertones due to volatile political atmosphere at that time. In the post-New Order period, however, blasphemy allegations have increasingly being pursued by Muslim leaders and activists who seek to protect a particular interpretation of Islam.[30] Many of these blasphemy charges were preceded by *fatwas* issued by conservative or radical Islamic groups. The Indonesian Ulama Council (Majelis Ulama Indonesia [MUI]), in particular, has been more active in issuing *fatwas* against minority groups whose teachings are considered a challenge to the established or mainstream Islamic tenets.[31]

Those accused of blaspheming Islam have usually been small, local groups, or relatively unknown figures with no international networks or support, which make them easy target.[32] One example of this is the Lia Eden community, also known as Salamullah or God's Kingdom of Eden whose key leader, Lia Eden or Lia Aminuddin claimed to have had an encounter with Archangel Gabriel. Lia Eden and several other key members of this group have been convicted for blaspheming Islam under article 156a of the Criminal Code.[33] Another example was the highly publicized allegation of blasphemy against Yusman Roy, the leader of "Pondok I'tikaf Ngaji Lelaku", an Islamic boarding school in Malang, East Java in 2005. MUI's local branch in Malang, East Java, accused Roy of blaspheming Islam for conducting and preaching prayers in two languages (Arabic and Indonesian). He was brought to court, but ultimately convicted on the basis of Article 157 (not Article 156a) of the Criminal Code, which prohibits the dissemination of writings or drawings containing feelings of hostility, hatred, or contempt against or among groups with the intent to enhance their publicity. Roy was reportedly convicted on the basis of Article 157 to ease the anger of conservative groups as the breach of Article 156a could not be proven.[34]

However, it is the Ahmadis, followers of the Ahmadiyah movement founded by Mirza Ghulam Ahmad of India, who have suffered from constant and increasing violence in recent years for their allegedly blasphemous teachings. Departing from the majority understanding of Sunni Muslims on the finality of Muhammad prophecy, the Ahmadis believe in the prophecy status of their founder, Mirza Ghulam Ahmad.[35] As early as 1980, the MUI has issued a *fatwa* against the Ahmadiyah declaring that its teachings fell outside the bounds of Islam. During the New Order period, however, the *fatwa* went largely unnoticed and had little effect on government policies.[36] More recently, however, MUI has increasingly come under influence of conservative Islamists.[37] In 2005, it reissued its earlier *fatwa* on Ahmadiyah, declaring the group as deviant, and strongly urged the Indonesian government to issue a ban. There was no immediate response from the government. The *fatwa*, however, has been met by an unprecedented level of violence and attacks against Ahmadis. In response to the continuing hostility against Ahmadis and under the increasing pressure from conservative Islamic groups, a joint resolution (*Surat Keputusan Bersama* [SKB]) by the Ministry of Religion, the Ministry of Internal Affairs, and the Attorney General's Office was finally issued in 2008. While the Law No. 1/PNPS/1965 was not explicitly mentioned in the SKB, the wordings and spirit of SKB were clearly inspired by it.[38] The SKB implicitly put the Ahmadis in the wrong side of the law, forcing them to strictly limit their religious activities.

POST-NEW ORDER LIBERAL MUSLIM DISCOURSE ON RELIGIOUS FREEDOM

Partly in response to the increasing level of violence against religious minorities and "deviant" groups, the issue of religious freedom has increasingly become one of the main concerns for many liberal Muslim intellectuals and activists in the post-New Order era. At the level of social activism, this was reflected in the establishment by liberal Muslim activists of several non-governmental organizations (NGOs) working on religious freedom and religious minority issues such as Desantara, the International Centre for Islam and Pluralism (ICIP), the Wahid Institute, the Ma'arif Institute, and many others.[39] At the discursive level, the focus on religious freedom was reflected in a growing number of writings by liberal Muslim intellectuals on various topics of religious freedom.[40]

Several key ideas and arguments can be observed in the writings of liberal Muslim intellectuals on religious freedom issues. First, there is a strong support for the idea of religious freedom as an individual freedom. The firm belief in religious freedom as an individual freedom, for example, can be found in the works of Siti Musdah Mulia, a professor of Islamic law widely known for her liberal views on many religious and legal issues. In one of her writings, she argues that religious freedom is individual freedom that must be free from constraints and state-interference.[41] She grounded her firm belief in religious freedom as an individual freedom on two important concepts in the Islamic tradition: the principle that Islam recognizes no institutionalization of religious authority (*lā rahbāniyyah fi al-Islam*) and the principle of no coercion of compulsory in religion (*lā ikrāha fi al-din*). According to Mulia, these two principles cannot be reduced or restrained by any institutionalization of religious truths.[42] She goes even further suggesting that "religious freedom should provide room for the emergence of new religious sects or even new religions as long as they do not disturb public order and do not conduct activities that breach the law."[43] An important consequence of this, she contends, is that "no state or religious authority can issue a fatwa or legal decision that declares certain religious sects or beliefs as "deviant and misleading" (*sesat dan menyesatkan*)."[44]

Second, there is also a strong support among liberal Muslims for the idea of a religiously neutral state, this support can be found, for example, in the writings of Syafi'i Anwar, director of the ICIP. He argues that the state may not be a partisan to certain beliefs or religious understandings or use the logic of proportionality between majority and minority.[45] As he asserts,

> The state has to view all religions as having the same and equal position, and respect differing religious interpretations within society. The state also cannot enter the internal affairs or theological and doctrinal issues of each religion, let alone determine which [theological or doctrinal] view is right or wrong for each religion.[46]

Third, there are also great concerns among liberal Muslims over the rights of religious minorities in the face of discriminatory laws and discourse dictated by majoritarian logics. It is this concern for religious minorities and opposition regarding majoritarianism that brings the Law No. 1/PNPS/1965 on Blasphemy into critical scrutiny by liberal Muslim activists. The Law was severely criticized, for example, by Ahmad Baso, Ahmad Suaedy, and Rumadi, three prominent NGO activists within the circles of traditionalist Islam (NU). In their own ways, these Muslim activists argue that the Law is greatly in favour of religious establishments or mainstream religions and, as such, it can be easily used to persecute or criminalize minority religious practices or interpretations.[47]

LIBERAL MUSLIMS AND THE JUDICIAL REVIEW OF LAW No. 1/PNPS/1965

Liberal Muslims' critical discussions on religious freedom and their critiques of Law No. 1/PNPS/1965 have helped to push greater efforts among a wider section of civil society to legally and constitutionally challenge the Law. In October 2009, the petition for the judicial review of the Blasphemy Law was officially filed by the Religious Freedom Advocacy Team (Tim Advokasi Kebebasan Beragama) to the Constitutional Court. The Team was a coalition of human rights lawyers from seven human rights NGOs and four individuals as the formal applicants of the petition. These seven NGOs were Imparsial, the Indonesian Legal Aid Foundation (Yayasan Lembaga Bantuan Hukum Indonesia [YLBHI]), the Association of Indonesian Legal Aid (Perhimpunan Bantuan Hukum Indonesia [PBHI]), the Institute for Study and Community Advocacy (Lembaga Studi dan Advokasi Masyarakat [ELSAM]), the Centre for Study of Human Rights and Democracy (*DEMOS*), the Desantara Foundation and the Setara Institute. The four individual applicants were widely known liberal Muslim figures: former President Abdurrahman Wahid, Siti Musdah Mulia, Dawam Rahardjo, and Maman Imanul Haq. The first three have established themselves as widely respected figures and are well-known for their concerns on religious freedom and religious minorities. The last applicant, a young leader of a *pesantren* in Majalengka, West Java, is a relatively new, but increasingly influential figure in the Muslim grassroot movements devoted to religious freedom. Several other Muslim intellectuals and activists were also involved as expert witnesses in court. Some of them, including Luthfi Assyaukani, one of the founders of the Liberal Islam Network (Jaringan Islam Liberal/JIL) and M.M Billah, a senior human rights activist with a strong background in traditionalist Islam, were proposed by the Team to present their insights in court. Other well-known liberal Muslims such as Ulil Abshar-Abdalla, Azyumardi Azra, Komaruddin Hidayat, Moeslim Abdurrahman, and Jalaluddin Rakhmat, were independently invited by the Court.

The petition for the judicial review of the Law soon sparked a fierce public debate, hitting the newspaper headlines for several months by those who support the petition and those who oppose it. A large number of Islamic groups, however, expressed their anger over the proposal to revoke the Law. Conservative and radical Islamic groups were among the loudest critics of the proposal, with some accusing it as a pretext for hidden agendas of atheists and liberals who promote "unlimited freedom" (*kebebasan tanpa batas*).[48] Interestingly, the two largest mainstream Islamic organizations, the Nahdlatul Ulama (NU) and Muhammadiyah, were also among those who oppose the proposal, arguing that the Law is necessary for maintaining religious harmony and public order. Leaders of both organizations also claimed that the Law is primarily about the defamation of religion, which they saw as necessary to avoid horizontal conflicts, and not about religious freedom.[49] This position largely echoed and supported the similar position of the government as often represented by the comments by Minister of Religious Affairs, Suryadharma Ali (from the Islamist Unity and Development Party [PPP]) and Minister of Justice and Human Rights at that time, Patrialis Akbar (from the pluralist National Mandate Party [PAN]).[50]

Liberal Muslims, on the other hand, were largely supportive of the judicial review of the Law. In fact, some activists played a significant role in initiating the idea and Muslim NGOs such as the Wahid Institute facilitated various meetings and discussions leading up to this legal initiative.[51] It is important to note, however, that not all liberal Muslims shared the formal position of the Team which called for the revocation of the Law. Some, such as Azyumardy Azra, Komaruddin Hidayat, and Jalaluddin Rakhmat, suggested only significant revisions of the Law, not its revocation altogether.

Three main problems were associated with the Law by liberal Muslim intellectuals and activists. The first main problem was that the Law allowed too much room for state involvement and intervention in religious matters. This problem was identified, for example, by Luthfi Assyaukanie. In his address in court entitled *"Negara Harus Melindungi Semua Agama dan Keyakinan"* (the State has to protect all religions and beliefs), he argued that the Law is highly problematic because it allows the state to interfere into religious matters.[52] "Belief and faith are individual matters in which the state is not allowed to interfere."[53] The same view was also put forward by Ulil Abshar-Abdalla and Djohan Effendi. For Abdalla, the Law is problematic because it allows religious *fatwas* to be enforced by the state. This, for him, cannot be accepted since Indonesia is not a religious state, but a democratic state which must be neutral on religious matters.[54] Similarly, Effendy argued that the authority to adjudicate belief only belongs to God, and it cannot be taken over by the state.[55]

The second main problem of the Law identified by the liberal Muslim intellectuals is that it fails to provide an inclusive and equal guarantee for religious freedom by granting freedom only to certain religions and religious understandings whilst discriminating against others. This was again pointed out by Assyaukanie who argues that the Law is discriminatory and, as such, it is clearly in conflict with the inclusive and equal guarantee for religious freedom provided by the Constitution. For him, the Indonesian constitution "clearly protects all religions, without exception. There is no limitation on the number of religion or sects. Every religion and sect is protected to grow and develop".[56] Ulil Abshar-Abdalla and Jalaludin Rakhmat also found the Law problematic for its possibility of being manipulated by both the state and religious establishments to marginalize and suppress religious minorities.[57]

The third main problem of the Law highlighted by liberal Muslims is its tendency to blur the distinction between religious interpretations (*penafsiran agama*) and defamation of religion (*penodaan agama*). Most liberal Muslims argue for a clear distinction between the two, perceiving religion as being subject to multiple interpretations and pointing to the historical competition over interpretations, which included even fundamental religious issues. Assyaukanie, for example, stressed that historically, multiple interpretations, including those initially or for political reasons considered "heretical" or "deviant", have been central to the growth and development of religious traditions.[58] The conflation between interpretation and defamation is thus seen by liberal Muslims as potentially dangerous for unorthodox religious interpretations, including new interpretations critical to the established or mainstream interpretations.

LIMITS OF LIBERAL MUSLIM VOICES?

The Indonesian Constitutional Court ultimately rejected the call for the revocation of the Blasphemy Law. The Court's decision thus endorsed a broad interpretation of what it saw as legitimate limitations on religious freedom. Two particular grounds, "public order" and "religious values", appear to be the main justifications of the Law by the Court.[59] First, the Court agreed that in the interest of public order the state had the right to intervene in religious matters and restrict certain religious interpretations. Affirming the concerns expressed by many Islamic leaders and government officials, the Court argued that the revocation of the Law would lead to horizontal conflict and anarchy within the community.[60] Second, the Court also justified the Law on the ground of "religious values" as found in the Indonesian Constitution, but not in the international human rights law. Stressing what it considers as distinctive historical close relations between state and religion in Indonesia, the Court considered the Law "as a compromise between the state and religious leaders, allowing the state to restrict religious activities on the grounds of 'public order' or 'religious values' while also delegating some power to religious leaders to act as gatekeepers to define the 'correct' interpretation of their religion".[61] There was, however, one important dissenting opinion in this Court's decision, made by Maria Farida Indrati, the only female judge in the Court. She was of the view that the Law need a significant revision to accord with significant changes in the 1945 Constitution especially in relation to religious freedom. She argued that Law in practice has resulted in systematic discrimination against "non-official" religions and especially local or traditional beliefs in some areas such as civil and administrative entitlements to identity card as well as marriage, birth, and death registration.[62]

Dissenting opinion aside, the Court's decision and its underlying arguments are clearly at odds with the voices of liberal Muslims. Relying on some sort of cultural relativist arguments, the Court took a conservative position in this debate. While the Court maintained that its decision was purely based on constitutional grounds, politically it reflects growing conservatism in the political and public sphere of the post-New Order period. In general, this "conservative turn", as some scholars have identified it, has put liberal Muslims in a more defensive position and reduced some of its capacity to set terms of debate on major issues.[63] In this particular debate, liberal Muslims appeared to be even more "isolated", with traditionally moderate and politically more powerful organizations such as the NU and Muhammadiyah lending support to the government's and the conservatives' voices.[64]

For some liberal Muslim activists, the outcome of this legal challenge was not entirely unexpected. Assyaukanie, for example, who found some of the judges' questions during his testimony irrelevance and biased, and described the atmosphere of the court room as "terrifying" with the presence and intimidation of Islamist groups inside and outside the court building, was prepared with what he considers as not entirely impartial decision by the Court.[65] Yet, while unhappy with the end result of this legal initiative, some of them saw the whole process of deliberation inside and outside the Court was not entirely bad. For Abdalla, the positive side of this case was the fact that the highly sensitive issue of religion and blasphemy was publicly debated with small incidents of violence.[66]

The question remains, however, as to what extent the Court's decision poses discursive limits for liberal Muslim voices on religious freedom and religious minorities. With its legal status as the highest institution in the Indonesian legal system which offers the "official", if not the final, interpretation on the Indonesian Constitution, the Constitutional Court's decision on this case seems to effectively silence any other voices, including those of liberal Muslims and sealed off the debate. This, however, is not entirely true at least for two reasons. First, the fact that, as mentioned before, there was a dissenting opinion in the Court's decision suggests that the Indonesian Constitution remains open to multiple interpretations on the question of religious freedom and religious minorities. While, formally, certain interpretations have been adopted by the Court in this case, discursively, constitutional debates and new interpretations remain a possibility. This, at least in theory, offers some hope and room for new voices, including those of liberal Muslims. Second, while the legal debate in the Constitutional Court was important and will have significant impacts on constitutional-legal discourse in Indonesia, it is not the only site of contestations. Arenas of discursive contestations and struggles beyond formal structures and institutions remain open and have equal political and legal significance. This again offers some hope that debates and discursive struggles over religious freedom will continue. While their dominance in the public sphere has been increasingly challenged by conservative and radical Islamic discourses, liberal Muslims seem to remain an influential player in these discursive struggles. To what extent they will successfully negotiate their voices in these struggles, however, remains to be seen.

CONCLUSION

Liberal Muslims in post-New Order Indonesia have been one of the important players in the debates on religious freedom and religious minorities. The post-New Order era has particularly seen a renewed interest among younger generation of liberal Muslims on the question of religious freedom and religious minorities. This new interest and focus on religious freedom is demonstrated by the rise of several NGOs on religious freedom within the circles of liberal Muslim activists and the growing number of their writings on various topics of religious freedom.

A closer look at their writings reveals that there appears to be an increasingly critical engagement among liberal Muslim intellectuals and activists with the largely secular and liberal international human rights discourse on religious freedom and religious minorities. This can be seen primarily in their support, with some religious justifications, for some of the core principles in the international human rights discourse on the right of freedom of religion or belief such as the principle of equality or non-discrimination and the principle of state neutrality.[67] From a comparative perspective, Indonesian liberal Muslim discourse on religious freedom has been an important part of the growing critical discourse on religious freedom developed by contemporary liberal Muslim thinkers in other parts of the world, including those who reside in the West. While Indonesian liberal Muslim discourse on religious freedom remains largely influenced by the specific Indonesian context, broad similarities can be found between their views and those of liberal Muslim thinkers in the West such as Abdullahi Ahmed An-Na'im, Abdulaziz Sachedina, and Abdullah Saeed, to name a few. In their own ways, these Muslim thinkers have argued for religious freedom as an individual freedom and a religiously neutral state as the necessary institutional foundation for this freedom.[68]

The question remain, however, as to what extent the voices of liberal Muslims have been well-received and gained support in an increasingly competitive "market of ideas" in Indonesia. The Indonesian Constitutional Court's decision to uphold the Blasphemy Law, which was against the voices of liberal Muslims, seems to suggest that their liberal voice on religious freedom has a limited appeal. The Court's decision certainly poses considerable challenges for liberal Muslims. On the other hand, the decision seems to help conservative religious and political discourses to gain more resonance in political and legal discourse. It is too early, however, to conclude that the voices of liberal Muslims on religious freedom and religious minorities have been effectively silenced. Discursive struggles and contestations over state-religion relations and religious freedom will continue and liberal Muslims will remain an important part of these struggles.

Notes

1. See, for example, Nicola Colbran, "Realities and Challenges in Realizing Freedom of Religion or Belief in Indonesia", *The International Journal of Human Rights* 14, no. 5 (2010): 678; and Tim Lindsey, "Human Rights and Islam in South East Asia: The Case of Indonesia", in *Islam und Menschenrechte* (Islam and Human Rights), edited by Hatem Elliesie (Frankfurt: Peter Lang Verlag, 2010), p. 271.
2. The International Covenant on Civil and Political Rights (ICCPR) along with the International Covenant on Economic, Social and Cultural Rights (ICESCR) were ratified by the Indonesian government in 2005. Another key international human rights instrument, the International Convention on the Elimination of All Forms of Discrimination, had also been ratified.
3. Modern discourse on religious freedom in particular has religious, and for some particularly Christian, origins, but for very complex historical and political factors, it has left behind its religious origins and become more secular and liberal in character. For accounts on the intellectual history of modern discourse of religious freedom see, among others, Steven D. Smith, "Discourse in the Dust: The Twilight of Religious Freedom?", *Harvard Law Review* 122 (2009): 1878–79; and Richard Helmstadter, ed., *Freedom and Religion in Nineteenth Century* (Stanford, CA: Stanford University Press, 1997).
4. For analyses using these terms, see Greg Barton, "The Impact of Neo-Modernism on Indonesian Islamic Thought: The Emergence of a New Pluralism", in *Democracy in Indonesia: 1950s and 1990s*, edited by David Bourchier and John Legge (Clayton: Centre of Southeast Asian Studies, Monash University, 1997); Greg Fealy, "Islamisation and Politics in Southeast Asia Limits of Indonesian Political Islam", in *Islam and Political Legitimacy*, edited by Shahram Akbarzadeh and Abdullah Saeed (London, New York:

5. RoutledgeCurzon, 2003); and Robert W. Hefner, *Civil Islam: Muslims and Democratization in Indonesia* (Princeton and Oxford: Princeton University Press, 2000).
5. For recent usage of or reference to "liberal and progressive" Islam, see, for example, M. Syafi'i Anwar, "The Clash between 'Radical-Conservative Islam' and 'Progressive-Liberal Islam' in Post-New Order Indonesia", in *The Future of Secularism*, edited by T.N. Srinivasan (Oxford: Oxford University Press, 2007); Martin van Bruinessen, "Liberal and Progressive Voices in Indonesia", in *Indonesian Islam in Reformist Voices of Islam: Mediating Islam and Modernity*, edited by Shireen T. Hunter (Armonk, New York: M.E. Sharpe, 2009); Budhi Munawar-Rachman, *Sekulerisme, Liberalisme, dan Pluralisme: Islam Progresif dan Perkembangan Diskursusnya* [Secularism, Liberalism and Pluralism: Progressive Islam and Its Discursive Development] (Jakarta: Grasindo, 2010); and Suratno, "The Flowering of Islamic Thought: Liberal-Progressive Discourse and Activism in Contemporary Indonesia", *IRASEC Discussion Papers No. 8* (February 2011).
6. Other key actors of the "religious renewal movement" include Mukti Ali, Harun Nasution, Djohan Effendi and Ahmad Wahib. See, for example, Gregory James Barton, "The emergence of neo-modernism: a progressive, liberal movement of Islamic thought in Indonesia. A textual study examining the writings of Nurcholish Madjid, Djohan Effendi, Ahmad Wahib and Abdurrahman Wahid, 1968–1980", Ph.D. thesis, Monash University, Clayton, 1995; and Martin van Bruinessen, "Liberal and Progressive Voices in Indonesia", in *Indonesian Islam in Reformist Voices of Islam: Mediating Islam and Modernity*, edited by Shireen T. Hunter (Armonk, NY: M.E. Sharpe, 2009), pp. 187–207.
7. I am not suggesting, however, that all Muslims whose views are discussed here have the same degree of ideological affinity with liberalism and that all are happy with their identification as "liberal" Muslims.
8. Article 29 (2), the Indonesian Constitution of 1945.
9. Article 28I (1), the Indonesian Constitution of 1945.
10. Article 22, Law No. 39/1999 on Human Rights.
11. Article 18, the International Covenant on Civil and Political Rights (ICCPR).
12. Bernhard Platzdasch, "Freedom in Indonesia: The Case of the Ahmadiyah", *ISEAS Working Paper: Politics and Security Series*, no. 2 (Singapore: Institute of Southeast Asian Studies, 2011), p. 21.
13. Article 28J (2).
14. Nicola Colbran, "Realities and Challenges", p. 678.
15. Ibid., p. 678.
16. See Jeroen Temperman, "Blasphemy, Defamation of Religion and Human Rights Law", *Netherlands Quarterly of Human Rights* 26, no. 4 (2008): 525–56.

17. For a critical account on the "defamation of religion" debate, see Malcolm Evans, "Advancing Freedom of Religion or Belief: Agendas for Changes", *Oxford Journal of Law and Religion* 1, no. 1 (2012): 5–14.
18. Nicola Colbran, "Realities and Challenges", p. 681.
19. Melissa Crouch, "Law and Religion in Indonesia: The Constitutional Court and the Blasphemy Law", *Asian Journal of Comparative Law* 7, issue 1 (2012): 6.
20. Law No. 1/PNPS/1965. The full text of the law and its elucidation can be found in Weinata Sairin, ed., *Himpunan Peraturan di Bidang Keagamaan* (Jakarta: BPK Gunung Mulia, cetakan kedua, 1996), pp. 262–68 and *Kompilasi Kebijakan dan Peraturan Perundang-Undangan Kerukunan Umat Beragama*, edisi kesebelas (Departemen Agama RI Badan Litbang dan Diklat Puslitbang Kehidupan Keagamaan, 2009), pp. 182–89.
21. Elucidation of Law No. 1/PNPS/1965 as compiled in *Kompilasi Kebijakan dan Peraturan Perundang-Undangan Kerukunan Umat Beragama*, edisi kesebelas (Departemen Agama RI Badan Litbang dan Diklat Puslitbang Kehidupan Keagamaan 2009), p. 187.
22. Ismatu Ropi, "Defending Religious Freedom in Indonesia: Muslims, Non-Muslims and Legislation on Houses of Worship", in *Islam and the Question of Reform: Critical Voices from Muslim Communities*, edited by Benjamin MacQueen, Kylie Baxter and Rebecca Barlow (Melbourne: Melbourne University Press, 2008), p. 74.
23. Rumadi, *Delik Penodaan Agama dan Kehidupan Beragama dalam RUU KUHP* [*Religious Offences and Religious Life in the Legal Draft of the Indonesian Penal Code*] (Jakarta: Tifa Foundation and the Wahid Institute, 2007), p. 6.
24. Nicola Colbran, "Realities and Challenges", p. 680. See also Jane Monnig Atkinson, "Religion in Dialogue: The Construction of an Indonesian Minority Religion", in *Indonesian Religions in Transition*, edited by Rita Smith Kipp and Susan Rodgers (Tucson: The University of Arizona Press, 1987), pp. 171–86; and Michel Picard, "Introduction, 'Agama', 'adat', and Pancasila", in *The Politics of Religion in Indonesia*, edited by Michel Picard and Remy Madinier (London and New York: Routledge, 2011).
25. Michel Picard, "Introduction, 'Agama', 'adat', and Pancasila", p. 13.
26. Luthfi Assyaukanie, *Islam and the Secular State in Indonesia* (Singapore: Institute of Southeast Asian Studies, 2009), p. 156.
27. See Nicola Colbran, "Realities and Challenges", pp. 682–83.
28. Ismatu Ropi, "Defending Religious Freedom", p. 67.
29. Nicola Colbran, "Realities and Challenges", p. 685.
30. Melissa Crouch, "Opposition to Christian Proselytisation in Democratic Indonesia: Legal Disputes between Muslims and Christians in West Java (1998–2009)", Ph.D. thesis, University of Melbourne, Parkville, 2010, p. 203.

31 Ibid., p. 204.
32 Ibid., p. 203.
33 Ibid.
34 Nicola Colbran, "Realities and Challenges", p. 686.
35 See Bernhard Platzdasch, "Freedom in Indonesia", p. 2; Bush and Munawar-Rachman and Fuller, both in this volume.
36 Martin van Bruinessen, "What Happened to the Smiling Face of Indonesian Islam? Muslim Intellectualism and the Conservative Turn in Post-Suharto Indonesia", *RSS Working Paper*, no. 222 (January 2011): 4.
37 Ibid., p. 3. See also Syafiq Hasyim, "The Council of Indonesian Ulama (Majelis Ulama Indonesia, MUI) and Religious Freedom", *IRASEC's Discussion Papers*, no. 12 (December 2011): 12.
38 Bernhard Platzdasch, "Freedom in Indonesia", p. 15.
39 For further account on a number of NGOs run by liberal and progressive Muslim activists, see Budhi Munawar-Rachman, *Sekulerisme, Liberalisme, dan Pluralisme*; and Suratno, "The Flowering of Islamic Thought".
40 Collections of writings of liberal Muslim intellectuals on topics related to religious freedom can be found, for example, in *Bayang-Bayang Fanatisisme: Esai-esai untuk Mengenang Nurcholish Madjid* [The Shadow of Fanaticism: Essays on the Commemoration of Nurcholish Madjid], edited by Abd Hakim and Yudi Latif (Jakarta: Pusat Studi Islam dan Kenegaraan, Universitas Paramadina, 2007); and *Merayakan Kebebasan Beragama: Bunga Rampai 70 Tahun Djohan Effendi* [Celebrating Religious Freedom: An Anthology for the 70th Anniversary of Djohan Effendi], edited by Elza Peldi Tahir (Jakarta: Indonesian Conference on Religion and Peace and Kompas, 2009).
41 Siti Musdah Mulia, "Menuju Kebebasan Beragama di Indonesian" [Towards Religious Freedom in Indonesia], in *Bayang-Bayang Fanatisisme: Esai-esai untuk Mengenang Nurcholish Madjid* [The Shadow of Fanaticism: Essays on the Commemoration of Nurcholish Madjid], edited by Abd Hakim and Yudi Latif (Jakarta: Pusat Studi Islam dan Kenegaraan, Universitas Paramadina, 2007), p. 227.
42 Ibid., p. 227.
43 Ibid., p. 230.
44 Ibid.
45 M. Syafii Anwar, "Ketika Pluralisme Diharamkan dan Kebebasan Berkeyakinan Dicederai" [When Pluralism is Denied and Freedom of Belief Betrayed], in *Merayakan Kebebasan Beragama: Bunga Rampai 70 Tahun Djohan Effendi* [Celebrating Religious Freedom: An Anthology for the 70th Anniversary of Djohan Effendi], edited by Elza Peldi Tahir (Jakarta: Indonesian Conference on Religion and Peace and Kompas, 2009), p. 460.
46 Ibid.
47 See Ahmad Baso, *Islam Pasca Kolonial: Perselingkuhan Agama, Kolonialisme dan Liberalisme* [Postcolonial Islam: Unholy Alliance between Religion,

Colonialism and Liberalism] (Bandung: Mizan, 2005), p. 244; Ahmad Suaedy, "Islam, Negara-Bangsa, dan Kebebasan Beragama" [Islam, Nation-State and Religious Freedom], in *Merayakan Kebebasan Beragama* [Celebrating Religious Freedom], edited by Elza Peldi Taher (Jakarta: Indonesian Conference on Religion and Peace in Cooperation with Kompas, 2009), p. 417; and Rumadi, *Delik Penodaan Agama dan Kehidupan Beragama dalam RUU KUHP* [Religious Offences and Religious Life in the Legal Draft of the Indonesian Penal Code] (Jakarta: Tifa Foundation and the Wahid Institute, 2007).

48 Margiono et al., *"Bukan Jalan Tengah" Eksaminasi Publik atas Keputusan Mahkamah Konstitusi perihal Pengujian Undang-Undang Nomor 1 PNPS Tahun 1965 Tentang Penyalahgunaan dan/atau Penodaan Agama* ["Not the Middle Path" Public Examination on the Constitutional Court's Decision on the Judicial Review of the Law No.1/PNPS/1965 on Abuse of Religion and/or Blasphemy] (Jakarta: The Indonesian Legal Resource Centre, 2010), p. 25. See also "Ormas Islam Membela UU Penodaan Agama", Hukum Online, 10 February 2010, available at <http://www.hukumonline.com/berita/baca/lt4b68089ebf56a/lima-ormas-islam-membela-uu-penodaan-agama> (accessed 16 November 2010).

49 See "Kebebasan Beragama: Hasyim: Jangan Berlogika Terbalik", *Republika*, 10 February 2010 (accessed 15 December 2011).

50 See "Pemerintah Keberatan Pencabutan UU Penodaan Agama", available at <http://www.tempointeraktif.com/hg/hukum/2010/02/04/brk,20100204223522,id.html> (accessed 16 November 2011); see also Constitutional Court Decision No. 140/PUU-VII/2009, p. 139.

51 Interview with Rumadi, a senior researcher of the Wahid Institute, 27 December 2010

52 Luthfi Assyaukanie, "Negara Harus Melindungi Semua Agama dan Keyakinan", address to the Indonesian Constitutional Court, available at his personal website <http://www.assyauknie.com> (accessed 10 April 2011).

53 Ibid.

54 See Constitutional Court Decision No. 140/PUU-VII/2009, p. 217.

55 Ibid., p. 223; see also Margiono et al., *"Bukan Jalan Tengah"*, p. 20.

56 Luthfi Assyaukanie, "Negara".

57 Margiono et al., "Bukan Jalan Tengah", p. 19.

58 Luthfi Assyaukanie, "Negara".

59 See Melissa Crouch, "Law and Religion in Indonesia", pp. 42–43.

60 Ibid., p. 42.

61 Ibid., p. 46.

62 See Constitutional Court Decision No. 140/PUU-VII/2009, p. 321. See also her interview with Tempo, "Maria Farida Indrati: Sesat Bukan Ranah Negara", available at <http://www.elsam.or.id/new/index.php> (accessed 16 November 2010).

[63] Martin van Bruinessen, "What Happened to Smiling Face of Indonesian Islam", p. 3.
[64] For a further account on the NU's and Muhammadiyah's position on the judicial review of Law No. 1/PNPS/1965 and religious minority issues in general, see Bush and Munawar-Rachman in this volume.
[65] Interview with Luthfi Assyaukanie, 10 February 2011.
[66] Melissa Crouch, "Law and Religion", p. 45.
[67] For a further account on the centrality of state neutrality and non-discrimination principles in the international religious freedom discourse, see Heiner Bielefeldt, "Freedom of Religion or Belief — A Human Right under Pressure", *Oxford Journal of Law and Religion* 1, no. 1 (2012): 15–35.
[68] See Abdullahi Ahmed An-Na'im, *Islam and the Secular State: Negotiating the Future of Shari'a* (Cambridge, MA: Harvard University Press, 2008); Abdulaziz Sachedina, *Islam and the Challenge of Human Rights* (Oxford, New York: Oxford University Press, 2009); and Abdullah Saeed and Hassan Saeed, *Freedom of Religion, Apostasy and Islam* (Burlington: Ashgate, 2004).

References

An-Na'im, Abdullahi Ahmed. *Islam and the Secular State: Negotiating the Future of Shari'a*. Cambridge, MA: Harvard University Press, 2008.

Anwar, M. Syafi'i. "The Clash between 'Radical-Conservative Islam' and 'Progressive-Liberal Islam' in Post-New Order Indonesia". In *The Future of Secularism*, edited by T.N. Srinivasan. Oxford: Oxford University Press, 2007.

―――. "Ketika Pluralisme Diharamkan dan Kebebasan Berkeyakinan Dicederai". In *Merayakan Kebebasan Beragama: Bunga Rampai 70 Tahun Djohan Effendi*, edited by Elza Peldi Tahir. Jakarta: Indonesian Conference on Religion and Peace and Kompas, 2009.

Assyaukanie, Luthfi. *Islam and the Secular State in Indonesia*. Singapore: Institute of Southeast Asian Studies, 2009.

―――. "Negara Harus Melindungi Semua Agama dan Keyakinan". Available at his personal website <http://www.assyauknie.com>.

Atkinson, Jane Monnig. "Religion in Dialogue: The Construction of an Indonesian Minority Religion". In *Indonesian Religions in Transition*, edited by Rita Smith Kipp and Susan Rodgers. Tucson: The University of Arizona Press, 1987.

Barton, Greg. "The Impact of Neo-Modernism on Indonesian Islamic Thought: The Emergence of a New Pluralism". In *Democracy in Indonesia: 1950s and 1990s*, edited by David Bourchier and John Legge. Clayton: Centre of Southeast Asian Studies, Monash University, 1997.

Baso, Ahmad. *Islam Pasca Kolonial: Perselingkuhan Agama, Kolonialisme dan Liberalisme* [Postcolonial Islam: Unholy Alliance between Religion, Colonialism and Liberalism]. Bandung: Mizan, 2005.

Bielefeldt, Heiner. "Freedom of Religion or Belief — A Human Right under Pressure". *Oxford Journal of Law and Religion* 1, no. 1 (2012).

Colbran, Nicola. "Realities and Challenges in Realizing Freedom of Religion or Belief in Indonesia". *The International Journal of Human Rights* 14, issue 5 (2010).

Crouch, Melissa. "Opposition to Christian Proselytisation in Democratic Indonesia: Legal Disputes between Muslims and Christians in West Java (1998–2009)". Ph.D. thesis, University of Melbourne, Parkville, 2010.

———. "Law and Religion in Indonesia: The Constitutional Court and the Blasphemy Law". *Asian Journal of Comparative Law* 7, issue 1 (2012).

Evans, Malcolm. "Advancing Freedom of Religion or Belief: Agendas for Changes". *Oxford Journal of Law and Religion* 1, no. 1 (2012).

Fealy, Greg. "Islamisation and Politics in Southeast Asia: Limits of Indonesian Political Islam". In *Islam and Political Legitimacy*, edited by Shahram Akbarzadeh and Abdullah Saeed. London, New York: RoutledgeCurzon, 2003.

Hasyim, Syafiq. "The Council of Indonesian Ulama (Majelis Ulama Indonesia, MUI) and Religious Freedom". *IRASEC's Discussion Papers*, no. 12 (December 2011).

Hefner, Robert W. *Civil Islam: Muslims and Democratization in Indonesia*. Princeton, NJ: Princeton University Press, 2000.

Helmstadter, Richard, ed. *Freedom and Religion in Nineteenth Century*. Stanford, CA: Stanford University Press, 1997.

Kompilasi Kebijakan dan Peraturan Perundang-Undangan Kerukunan Umat Beragama, edisi kesebelas. Departemen Agama RI Badan Litbang dan Diklat Puslitbang Kehidupan Keagamaan, 2009.

Lindsey, Tim. "Human Rights and Islam in South East Asia: The Case of Indonesia". In *Islam und Menschenrechte* [Islam and Human Rights], edited by Hatem Elliesie. Frankfurt: Peter Lang Verlag, 2010.

Margiono et al. *"Bukan Jalan Tengah" Eksaminasi Publik atas Keputusan Mahkamah Konstitusi perihal Pengujian Undang-Undang Nomor 1 PNPS Tahun 1965 Tentang Penyalahgunaan dan/atau Penodaan Agama* ["Not the Middle Path" Public Examination on the Constitutional Court's Decision on the Judicial Review of the Law No. 1/PNPS/1965 on Abuse of Religion and/or Blasphemy]. Jakarta: The Indonesian Legal Resource Centre, 2010.

Mulia, Siti Musdah. "Menuju Kebebasan Beragama di Indonesia". In *Bayang-Bayang Fanatisisme: Esai-esai untuk Mengenang Nurcholish Madjid*, edited by Abd Hakim and Yudi Latif. Jakarta: Pusat Studi Islam dan Kenegaraan, Universitas Paramadina, 2007.

Picard, Michel. "Introduction, 'Agama', 'adat', and Pancasila". In *The Politics of Religion in Indonesia*, edited by Michel Picard and Remy Madinier. London and New York: Routledge, 2011.
Platzdasch, Bernhard. "Religious Freedom in Indonesia: The Case of the Ahmadiyah". *ISEAS Working Paper: Politics and Security Series*, no. 2. Singapore: Institute of Southeast Asian Studies, 2011.
Rachman, Budhi Munawar. *Sekulerisme, Liberalisme, dan Pluralisme: Islam Progresif dan Perkembangan Diskursusnya* [Secularism, Liberalism and Pluralism: Progressive Islam and Its Discursive Development]. Jakarta: Grasindo, 2010.
Ropi, Ismatu. "Defending Religious Freedom in Indonesia: Muslims, Non-Muslims and Legislation on Houses of Worship". In *Islam and the Question of Reform: Critical Voices from Muslim Communities*, edited by Benjamin MacQueen, Kylie Baxter and Rebecca Barlow. Melbourne: Melbourne University Press, 2008.
Rumadi. *Delik Penodaan Agama dan Kehidupan Beragama dalam RUU KUHP* [Religious Offences and Religious Life in the Legal Draft of the Indonesian Penal Code]. Jakarta: Tifa Foundation and the Wahid Institute, 2007.
Sachedina, Abdulaziz. *Islam and the Challenge of Human Rights*. New York, Oxford: Oxford University Press, 2009.
Saeed, Abdullah and Hassan Saeed. *Freedom of Religion, Apostasy and Islam*. Burlington: Ashgate, 2004.
Sairin, Weinata, ed. *Himpunan Peraturan di Bidang Keagamaan*. Jakarta: BPK Gunung Mulia, cetakan kedua, 1996.
Smith, Steven D. "Discourse in the Dust: The Twilight of Religious Freedom?" *Harvard Law Review* 122 (2009).
Suaedy, Ahmad. "Islam, Negara-Bangsa, dan Kebebasan Beragama" [Islam, Nation-State and Religious Freedom]. In *Merayakan Kebebasan Beragama* (Celebrating Religious Freedom), edited by Elza Peldi Taher. Jakarta: Indonesian Conference on Religion and Peace in cooperation with Kompas, 2009.
Suratno. "The Flowering of Islamic Thought: Liberal-Progressive Discourse and Activism in Contemporary Indonesia". *IRASEC Discussion Papers No. 8* (February 2011).
Temperman, Jeroen. "Blasphemy, Defamation of Religion and Human Rights Law". *Netherlands Quarterly of Human Rights* 26, no. 4 (2008).
van Bruinessen, Martin. "Liberal and Progressive Voices in Indonesia". In *Indonesian Islam in Reformist Voices of Islam: Mediating Islam and Modernity*, edited by Shireen T. Hunter. New York, Armonk: M.E. Sharpe, 2009.
———. "What Happened to the Smiling Face of Indonesian Islam? Muslim Intellectualism and the Conservative Turn in Post-Suharto Indonesia". RSS Working Paper no. 222 (January 2011).

4

READING AHMADIYAH AND DISCOURSES ON FREEDOM OF RELIGION IN INDONESIA

Andy Fuller

Islam in Indonesia is highly contested. Contesting Islam involves grappling with meanings of religious texts and of relating such texts to contemporary social and political conditions. Discourses on the meanings of the Qur'an intersect with readings of Indonesia's history and current trajectory. The fall of the Soeharto-led government in 1998 facilitated much openness in freedom of expression. The press, for years stifled under strict censorship and practices of self-censorship, became more vocal and critical: there was room for all sorts of voices to compete in debates of national, regional, and religious importance. Islam and expressions of being Muslim became increasingly debated. The manner in which Islam is invoked in the discourses on Ahmadiyah and freedom of religion is the subject of this chapter.

The process of democratization that emerged in 1998 was seen as a highly positive break from an authoritarian and highly centralized recent past. Decentralization, democratization, and a liberal press, however, also opened up space for intense conflicts to emerge. Some of the voices that have gained prominence in the post-New Order era have been highly anti-democratic and illiberal. This casts a question mark over Indonesia's reputation for fostering a supposedly "tolerant Islam". Muhammad Ali, for example, writes, "this era of political openness became a political opportunity for Muslim radicalism. Islamic hard-liners [...] came to the surface and became active" (Ali 2005, p. 3). Elsewhere, recent yearly reports on religious life in Indonesia have concluded rather negatively that acts of intolerance are increasing and that there are rising problems of religious harmony between members of different religious groups (Bagir et al. 2012; The Wahid Institute 2011).

A reading of the ongoing cases and controversies surrounding Ahmadi communities and Ahmadi faith is necessary in order to gain a deeper understanding of how public debates on Islam and religious freedom are changing and developing. This chapter draws on material from the mainstream liberal media as well as from texts that seek to condemn liberal thought. It explores some of the main ideas that are being circulated, critiqued, and debated concerning Ahmadiyah and the contestable legitimacy of the Ahmadi faith. I argue that such a reading will provide an insight into the range of views and perspectives on Ahmadiyah and freedom of religion. Does this multiplicity of voices indicate diversity and richness, or does it indicate a reluctance of some groups to understand and approach the religious other?

Divergent trends in interpretation and practice continue to develop in the contest over Islam. Matters of religion and Islam are points of significant importance and contestation: perhaps some debates are becoming more violent, more restrictive, and thus are indicative of a textualist approach to the Qur'an. For example, the books of writers such as Jaiz (2003) and Djamaluddin (1992) rely heavily on the repeating of Qur'anic quotations for their rhetorical legitimacy. There is a concomitant growth in liberal Islamic thought. This has been an ongoing and well-noticed trend in the study of Islam in Indonesia. Indeed, some scholars have criticized the emphasis on studying developments in "liberal" Islamic thought (Fealy 2008; Platzdasch 2009). They offer a set of discourses and values that are highly debated, contested, and challenged. The actors and agents in the debates are diverse with different backgrounds and interests. The values of "pluralism" and "liberalism" are varyingly viewed as signs of progressive tolerance, while others see pluralism as an indication of being "deviant" (*sesat*). Indeed, the condemnation of being "*sesat*" or belonging to an "*aliran sesat*" (a deviant sect) is a highly emotive accreditation.

The post-New Order era has seen a proliferation in the number of books published on Islam in Indonesian (Assyaukanie 2011). Religion and Islamic sentiment — feelings, memories — are invoked in political debates and in the campaigning of aspiring national and regional political leaders.

The fates of religious minorities in Indonesia are subject to a changing set of political, economic, and social circumstances and contexts. Some trends in the way Islam is being re-interpreted and re-practised show that "Indonesian Islam" is highly fragmented and fluid. Indonesia is home to a variety of Islamic identities, rather than a single all-encompassing Islamic identity. Organizations such as *Front Pembela Islam* (FPI; Islamic Defenders' Front) and *Lembaga Penelitian dan Pengkajian Islam* (LPPI; Institute for the Study and Teaching of Islam) seek to combat the fragmentation of Islamic identity through their campaigns against *Jaringan Islam Liberal* (JIL; Liberal Islam Network) and Ahmadiyah, for example.

Ahmadiyah doctrine is characterized by its acknowledgement of Mirza Ghulam Ahmad as a prophet; Ahmadi leaders themselves, however, sometimes like to "downgrade" Ghulam Ahmad's significance to that of a "mentor" or "teacher". In any case, the matter has a strong propensity to contradict Islam's fundamental belief in the Prophet Muhammad being the final prophet. This is the primary reason for Ahmadi belief being considered "deviant". Ahmadiyah is a religious community, distinct from Sunni Islam. Cantwell Smith writes that, "on 4 March 1889 [Mirza Ghulam Ahmad] announced that he had received from God a revelation authorizing him to accept *bay'at* [a pledge of allegiance]; and a small group was forthcoming of formal disciples (Smith 1960). Mirza Ghulam Ahmad is considered by his followers to be the *al-Masih* [Messiah] (Zulkarnain 2005, p. 90). That Ahmad is also believed to be the *al-Mahdi* is also a primary reason for many Muslims to consider Ahmadis as being 'outside of Islam'" (Platzdasch 2011, p. 2). In Ahmadi literature, Zahfrullah Khan points out that he was the "Promised Messiah and Mahd" (Ahmad 2009, p. vii). As with mainstream Islam, the Ahmadiyah sect believes in the *syahadat*, prayer, alms, fasting, pilgrimage, and other common beliefs across Muslims (Mulyono 2003, p. ii). The commonalities of Ahmadiyah doctrine with that of mainstream Islam is rarely invoked as being a reason for having empathy for the fate of Ahmadis.

Mirza Ghulam Ahmad's interpretation of "*jihad*" is also a significant cause of controversy for its divergence from that of the Muslim majority's perception (Burhanudin 2005). Jihad in Ahmadiyyah doctrine is articulated through a textual struggle (Sevea 2009, p. 135). The recognition of a prophet after the Prophet Muhammad is arguably the most offensive aspect of Ahmadi belief to other Muslims. Ahmadis believe that their practice and interpretation of Islam is the true Islam and that other Muslims are unbelievers. They believe that Ahmad revitalized Islam and was "divinely guided" by God (Smith 1960).

The Indonesian state's response and policy towards the Ahmadiyah community has been varied and has changed over time. Ahmadiyah was declared a lawful organization in 1953 (Platzdasch 2011, p. 3). The current stance, however, reflects a kind of ambivalence to their persecution. Crouch argues that protection of religious minorities in Indonesia is failing due to the "combination of state policies on religion and the practices of the criminal justice system" (Crouch 2012, p. 54). Indeed, in the wake of the murders of Ahmadis in Cikeusik in February 2011, none of the perpetrators was sentenced heavily (Crouch 2012).

In 1995, Nadlatual Ulama (NU) re-stated that Ahmadiyah teachings diverge from that of Islam. The Syuriah PBNU stated that Ahmadiyah teachings mix-up verses of the Qur'an and that they recognized the prophethood of Mirza Ghulam Ahmad. As such, they submitted a request to the Supreme Court for banning Ahmadiyah in Indonesia (Djamaluddin, p. 172).

Djamaluddin's book, Ahmadiyah dan Pembajakan Al-Qur'an (Ahmadiyah and the Plagiarising of the Qur'an, 1992) seeks to show how the *Tadzkirah* (*Tadhkirah*) is a corruption and plagiarism of the Qur'an. One chapter of the book provides a comparison of texts from the Qur'an with those from the *Tadzkirah* (Djamaluddin 1992, pp. 1–35). Djamaluddin's book, as well as containing a summary of Ahmadiyah beliefs (pp. 72–86), also contains re-printings of various rulings issued against the Ahmadiyah movement in Indonesia (Djamaluddin 1992, pp. 72–106). The author's arguments against the deviance of the Ahmadiyah movement are strengthened by these rulings issued by various national and regional authorities.

Expressions and practices of Islam in Indonesia has often been characterized to be "liberal", "plural", and "moderate". Moreover, Indonesia is often noted for an example of a successful Muslim-majority democracy. The process of democratization in the post-New Order era, however, is not something smooth and seamless; instead, it is a process that involves the negotiation of conflicts between societal groups that read Islam, the nation, and identity politics in highly divergent ways. Interpretations of the Qur'an have direct implications in fragile social and political situations, where religious authority is often directly linked to political power. Islam and Islamic thought, nonetheless, is undergoing a period of intense scholarship and critical inquiry in contemporary Indonesia (Hilmy 2010; Saeed 2005; Sukma and Joewono 2007); at the same time, Indonesia is undergoing similar contestations over the nation's identity and imagining.

Weintraub (2011) has argued that Indonesia is frequently overlooked in discussions and debates regarding the Muslim world. This does not appear to be the case anymore. Indonesia, however, can also be recognized for having fostered the development of much innovative and critical Islamic scholarship rather than just being important for the sheer weight of numbers of its Muslim population. Muslimness and the validity of Muslim expressions are two of the issues that are at the heart of this chapter. This is where orthodoxies of Muslimness and nonconformist interpretations of doctrine collide. In texts such as *Menangkal Bahaya JIL dan FLA* (Jaiz and Bashori 2003) the Muslimness (i.e., his orthodoxy) of Ulil Abshar Abadalla is often questioned.[1] And, similarly, Ahmadis are also called to recant and return to following the "true Islam". One such discourse on Ahmadis return from being "deviant" is recounted in *Mengapa Saya Keluar dari Ahmadiyah Qadian: Sebuah Kesaksian — Why I left the Qadian Ahmadiyah: A Testimony* (Hariadi 2008). Arguably, this text also speaks of diversity and fluidity: a multiplicity of voices represents a vibrant intellectual and an open political climate, rather than one which is homogenous and stifled.

Condemnations and categorizations of deviance, blasphemy, and apostasy have emerged at the same time as have limitations on the practices of religious minorities in Indonesia. As Assyaukanie has argued, *fatwas* — legal opinions — have had violent outcomes in contemporary Indonesia (Assyaukanie 2009).[2] This chapter intends to provide a reading of the debates on Ahmadiyah in order to provide a context in which these *fatwas* are issued. The competing discourses of the law, *fatwas*, and advocacy of religious pluralism rarely meet and complement. A kind of polyvocality seems to exist in contemporary discourses on Islam in Indonesia. On the one hand, this indicates richness; on the other, the discourses seem to be mutually exclusive.[3] There is, however, little room for laughter and play. Condemnations of deviancy are surrounded by rhetorical and real violence.

Three prominent discourses are those of the legal — the state authorities — the religious authorities (as argued by the Majelis Ulama Indonesia, Council of Indonesian Ulama, MUI), and those of Muslim activists and intellectuals — as represented by such diverse groups as FPI (Islamic Defenders' Front), and the Jakarta-based JIL (Liberal Islam Network). Culture and the national identity of Indonesia — exemplified primarily through the state doctrine Pancasila and a Muslim majority — are varyingly invoked as being sources of answers to solve recent violent religious conflict (for example, Dadang Kahmad 2012). Elsewhere, pluralist and open readings of Islam are given as reasons for why a religious minority should be protected, rather than condemned and banished from society. As Ali argues, the intellectuals affiliated with JIL, for example, play the role of a "counter-movement", critiquing and opposing the perceived advances of radical Islam (Ali 2005, p. 5). Munawar-Rachman's *Membela Kebebasan Beragama* (Munawar-Rachman 2010) is a two volume work consisting of interviews with liberal intellectuals, who seek to defend the ideas of secularism, liberalism, and pluralism against perceived threats to such values. Some writers, on the other hand, also produce texts to stem the influence of Ahmadiyah, liberal, plural, Islamic thought (Djamaluddin 2007, Husaini 2009; Rasyid 2009; Jaiz 2003; Putro 2004)[4].

MUI's *fatwa* against Ahmadiyah condemned the movement as being "*sesat*". This *fatwa* has served to strengthen the conviction of some groups that the Ahmadiyah movement should be disbanded. The *fatwa* was a reissuing of an earlier ruling against the sect (Crouch 2011; Platzdasch, 2011). That this *fatwa* gained such currency and controversy speaks of the changing circumstances in post-Soeharto era Indonesia. The *fatwa* states:

> The MUI re-affirms the fatwa of 1980 that Ahmadiyah is a sect that is outside of Islam is misguided and misguiding. The fatwa also declares that people who follow Ahmadiyah are *murtad* (that is, they have left Islam). As such, in the aforementioned fatwa, MUI implores those that have already started to follow Ahmadiyah, to return to Islamic teachings in accordance with the Qur'an and hadiths. MUI asserts that the government of Indonesia should forbid the dissemination of Ahmadiyah teachings, freeze the organisation and close down all its places of activity. (MUI 2005, p. 1)

A *fatwa*, argues liberal Islamic thinker Ulil Abshar Abdalla, is regarded as the internal business of a particular religion, while the law is something that is universal and cuts across different religious practices and interpretations (Abdalla 2008). Abdalla argues that there exists a kind of free-market for *fatwas*. That is, they are legal opinions that are not legally binding. Muslim organizations issue their own *fatwas*. Their members tend to look into the *fatwas* of their own organizations for guidance in determining proper conduct. Believers, that is, those who use *fatwas*, are able to choose *fatwas* that are most suitable for their belief. Such a condition is facilitated by the lack of a centre of authority within Islam. Instead, there are multiple centres of authority — which, as is seen in contemporary Indonesia — and are highly competitive and often seek to mutually deny one another. As Abdalla argues, religious elites intend to "freeze" an interpretation, an idea, something that is "fluid". That is, by asserting rules and laws and *fatwas* where there otherwise would be acknowledged as ethics and principles established by consensus of interpretations. Budiwanti describes the power invested in *fatwas* as follows:

For activist groups such as LPPI and FPI, a *fatwa* from MUI was considered as an expression of Islamic law and is therefore a basis for action, regardless of the arguments made by Muslim scholars that *fatwa* are only opinions and do not have the same status as *hukum* (law) (Budiwanti 2009, p. 19).

Abdalla's project, as an activist of JIL, indeed is to make fluid those interpretations and laws that have become frozen. His deconstructionist approach seeks to show how Islamic laws, principles, and interpretations are subject to social, cultural, and political conditions. He argues that "meaning" is not derived instantly and unproblematically from the Qur'an, but that the meaning is subject to a process. Ulil argues that Islam is something that is changing in process and open to varying interpretations and, moreover, that Muslims should not see themselves as an *"umat"* that are separate from other groups (Putro 2004, p. 192). A kind of unresponsive dialogue exists: laws and *fatwas* are issued only to be condemned and criticized by intellectual elites. While Ulil seeks to "refresh" Islamic thought, he is criticized by writers such as Putro for "limiting Islam" and "placing it in a stuffy corner" (Putro 2004, p. 46)[5]. Ironically, these two opposing views come to the same conclusion about the other. In turn, their critiques are unheard by the more conservative, yet, authoritative political and religious elite. Abdalla (2008) argues that:

> When the state is allowed to determine which interpretations are straight and those that are crooked, there is already a blurring between law and fatwa. The role of the state is to implement the law for all groups, sects; it is not a fatwa that is partisan [*partikular*]. The state that is the tool of a particular sect [*sekte*] to condemn another sect is a state of the middle-ages that has no right to be maintained. It appears that some groups within Islam are guiding the nation to this dangerous condition.

In 2008, MUI's *fatwa* was supported by a Joint Ministerial Decree (*Surat Keputusan Bersama* [SKB]). This Joint Decree was condemned by advocates of pluralism and the rights of religious minorities, for it seemingly gave into the demands of some of the more radical groups (Crouch 2009, p. 3). The former head of NU, KH Hasyim Muzadi, also strongly supported MUI's demand on prohibition (*mengharamkan*) of Ahmadiyah in Indonesia (Mahally 2006, p. xv). Like the *fatwa* of the MUI, this Joint Decree discourages practising beliefs that go against the accepted religions and not to promote deviant teachings. A final point of the decree is to warn people against taking the matter into their own hands (Crouch 2009, p. 6).

The Indonesian constitution, the *Undang-Undang Dasar* of 1945, provides guarantees regarding both the unitary character of the state and the rights of individuals. One of the fundamental rights for individuals is to practise their freedom or belief in accordance with their belief. As Ropi points out, however, the identity of what religion one can believe in (or legitimately state on one's ID card) is something that has developed with notions of Indonesianness. Ropi states that between 1967 and 1995, there were 51 rulings against religious sects. These were in the form of teachings, religious activities, books, and calendars, which according to the state were "false", had "diverged from the mainstream", or had blasphemed a particular tradition (Ropi 2008, p. 130). Ropi argues as follows:

> For the majority, no matter how much every regulation has the potential to intervene in their private lives, they still consider such regulations [of religion] as important to maintain a hegemony and competition with other groups (minorities), where such regulations which will be used as effective tools in maintaining their hegemony and their monopoly on the truth.[6]

The SKB (Joint Ministerial Decree) has mostly been used against the Ahmadis. At a presentation at the Asian Law Centre at The University of Melbourne, the prominent advocate Prof. Adnan Buyung Nasution told how he was one of the formulators of the SKB. He said that issuing the SKB in which Ahmadiyah is not banned but has its practices restricted was the compromise he could make with the minister for religion, the justice minister, and the interior minister. Throughout the course of the discussion, Nasution stated that representatives of Ahmadiyah had not been consulted prior to the release of the SKB. Nasution has recently been active in defending members of Ahmadiyah against their persecution. He has argued that the "intention" of the SKB was to prevent further acts of violence against Ahmadis. Platzdasch, however, points out the SKB left Ahmadis in a legal no-man's land (Platzdasch 2011, pp. 16–17).

The Joint Decree was supported by both hardline and mainstream groups such as FPI, *Forum Umat Islam, Hizb Ut-Tahrir Indonesia, Lembaga Penelitian dan Pengkajian Islam,* and *Forum Umat Ulama Indonesia.*[7] Nahdlatul Ulama, Muhammadiyah, Persis, and others supported the ban. Politicians of varying political parties have also taken action against Ahmadiyah. These groups all played a role in pressing the government and MUI to issue the SKB. Some members of the Indonesian parliament and legislature also supported the decree and called for its socialization (Khanif 2010, p. 261). The International Crisis Group (ICG) points out that although most Muslim leaders are very quick to condemn acts of violence, and there is a reluctance to challenge "radical positions" through mobilizing their masses. This reluctance may in part be due to the increasing pressure of radical groups and indeed also out of the belief that Ahmadiyah is in fact "deviant". The ICG report ends optimistically: "The decree on Ahmadiyah is a step backward for Indonesia, but if it galvanizes pro-democracy activists and constitutional defenders into action, there may yet be some positive outcome" (ICG 2008, p. 17).

MUI, however, seeks to maintain the orthodoxy of believers through issuing its *fatwas*. Banning the Ahmadiyah movement has also been argued as a means to "minimalize tension". Instead, however, the *fatwa* against Ahmadiyah and the SKB against Ahmadi practice have served to legitimize attacks (both discursive and violent) against Ahmadis. Azyumardi Azra, a prominent public intellectual and rector of Jakarta Islamic State University, argues that violence in the name of religion has been the result of an explosion in "freedom" that has not been accompanied by a similar increase in the capacity of the police forces to guarantee respect for the law, order, and civility (Azra 2012). Significantly, Azra also engages in a discussion of FPI's arguments for using violence. Azra seeks to engage in a dialogue with FPI and to treat their agendas with legitimacy, despite their broadly condemned actions. FPI's justification for using their violence is due to the police force's inability to combat sinful behaviour (*maksiat*) — such as gambling and prostitution — and that the government has not disbanded Ahmadiyah, which in their view, has diverged from Islam. Azra accepts a basic legitimacy of FPI's desire to use violence, but then condemns them, based on arguments from authoritative *ulama*. Azra (2012, p. 6) writes: "For authoritative *ulama*, in general, *dakwah* as a call for doing good and combating sin, must be based on wisdom, *maw'izah hasanah* (good learning) and *mujadalah* (discussion and civilized debates)."

Such a call for moderation doesn't necessarily hold in the face of a transgression of one of Islam's fundamental beliefs that the Prophet Muhammad is the final prophet. Azra compares violence in the name of religion (and in this case, Islam) to similar developments that have happened in the name of Christianity or Judaism. Drawing on Charles Kimball,[8] Azra sites five conditions that lead to violence being committed in the name of religion. They are (1) a group believes that only themselves have access to the truthful interpretation of a particular religious text; (2) a belief that the present is the right time for those who believe they are blessed by God to stop all kinds of injustice; (3) a blind faith in implementing religious practices; (4) justifying any means to reach their goal; and (5) waging a holy war against those who diverge from the particular religion. Azra's article is significant as it doesn't reject FPI out of hand. Azra, despite the distance between his role as an academic, engages in a dialogue (albeit brief) with the claims of FPI, a group that has little truck for academic formalities. Nonetheless, Azra does not look into how such radical values emerge. He argues that their needs to be a reorientation of an understanding of *dakwah*, an understanding that can be accepted by society in general. He argues that this needs to be complemented by a governmental stance against preventing anarchistic (i.e., outside the law) behaviour by *ormas* (*organisasi masyarakat*; society-based groups) (Azra 2012, p. 6).

CONCLUSIONS

This chapter has sought to show the varying forces at play in the negotiation and re-negotiation of Islamic thought and practice in contemporary Indonesia. This is a practice in which the law, state, and Islamic authority intersect. Importantly, Islamic authority is something that is highly contested and fluid. In some cases, state authority is highly limited. The post-New Order era has indeed been marked by a great contestation for what is acceptable and unacceptable within Islam. Some have argued for a greater fluidity of Islamic practice and thought, while others have actively sought to limit the flexibility and openness of Islam. It seems that this has been missing throughout the formulation of some recent laws and dialogues. Whatever the intentions of the SKB, it was flawed as it was conceived without the dialogue and negotiation with Ahmadi representatives. MUI's *fatwa* against Ahmadiyah has been supported by political and social conditions that have further marginalized the positions of Ahmadi communities in contemporary Indonesia. Despite the *fatwa* arguably being non-binding (Abdalla 2008), it has assumed a violent character (Assyaukanie 2009). The pluralism and diversity of Islamic practices in Indonesia is under contestation. Many intellectuals in Indonesia have contributed to a significant rethinking of Islamic thought. Nonetheless, these have been conducted in the relatively exclusive and elitist circles of highly educated urbanites in Jakarta, Yogyakarta, Surabaya, and elsewhere.

The discourses of religious pluralism and tolerance for religious minorities are highly contentious in many layers of Indonesian society. Tensions regarding the condemnation of Ahmadiyah as *sesat* (deviant) have emerged at a time of openness in Indonesia's political and cultural landscape. Writers and activists such as Putro, Djamaluddin, Hariadi, and groups such as FPI and organizations such as MUI have shown a clear reluctance to accept Islam as being subject to fragmentation, question, and variation. Islamic thought is being subject to an intense moment of renewal and critical inquiry. This is happening at different layers of Indonesian society. Groups that had been marginalized have become increasingly assertive. Liberal groups are struggling to maintain their position and practising "moderate" Islam.

Islam, however, at varying moments and throughout different regions, has been reduced and essentialized to something concrete evident in symbols and imagined as a set of limited beliefs. Religious minorities such as Ahmadiyah, regardless of their commonalities with mainstream Sunni Islam, have found themselves *othered* due to their apparent blasphemy. This has often been led by statements from official organizations such as MUI. The violence, however, has happened in a less structured manner. The condemnation of being deviant and blasphemous has been the main rhetorical tool in justifying violence against Ahmadis and their property.

Notes

1. Ulil also mentions this in "Anda Muslim Bukan?" [You're a Muslim, aren't you?], an essay on his website <http://www.ulil.net>.
2. For an outline of Ahmadiyah, see Platzdasch (2011). For an overview of the controversy surrounding Ahmadiyah, see Crouch (2011).
3. Richard Sennett writes of Bakhtin's idea of the "dialogic". This term names "a discussion which does not resolve itself by finding common ground. Though no shared agreements may be reached, through the process of exchange people may become more aware of their own views and expand their understandings of one another" (Sennett 2012, p. 19).
4. There is also a book, *Tikaman Ahmadiyah Terhadap Islam*, authored by Sayid Abul Hasan Ali Nadwi. The title is translated as "Ahmadiyah's Stabbing of Islam". The original title, however, was far more neutral: *Qadianism: A Critical Study*.
5. "[Ulil] *telah ... mempersempit Islam; dan menyudutkan Islam ke pojok yang pengap*" (Putro 2004, p. 46).
6. *Bagi kelompok mayoritas, betapapun setiap regulasi secara potensial mengintervensi kehidupan pribadi mereka, pada dasarnya regulasi itu tetap dianggap penting untuk*

mempertahankan hegemoni dan kompetisi dengan kelompok ang lain (minoritas) di mana dalam beberapa kasus regulasi itu digunakan sebagai senjata yang efektif untuk mempertahankan hegemoni dan memonopoli kebenaran.

7 Robin Bush's and Budhy Munawar Rachman's chapter in this volume provides details.

8 Author of *When Religion Becomes Lethal: The Explosive Mix of Politics and Religion in Judaism, Christianity and Islam* (Jossey Bass 2011).

References

Abdalla, U.A. "Hukum, Fatwa dan Ahmadiyah". *Tempo*, 21 April 2008.

Ahmad, M.G. *Tadhkirah*. Surrey: Islam International Publications, 2009.

Ali, M. "The Rise of the Liberal Islamic Network (JIL) in Contemporary Indonesia". *American Journal of Islamic Social Sciences*, 22 (Winter 1) (2005): 1–27.

Assyaukanie, L. "Fatwa and Violence in Indonesia". *Journal of Religion and Society* 11 (2009): 1–21.

———. "Recent Publications on Indonesian Islam". *Bijdragen tot de Taal-, Land-en Volkenkunde* 167, no. 1 (2011): 140–53.

Azra, A. "Atas Nama Agama". *Kompas*, 25 February 2012, p. 6.

Bagir Z.A. et al. *Laporan Tahun Kehidupan Beragama di Indonesia*. Yogyakarta: Program Studi Agama dan Lintas Budaya, 2012.

Budiwanti, E. *Pluralism Collapses: A Study of the Jama'ah Ahmadiyah Indonesia and Its Persecution*. Singapore: Asia Research Institute, 2009.

Burhanudin, A. *Ghulam Ahmad: Jihad Tanpa Kekerasan*. Yogyakarta: LKiS, 2005.

Crouch, M. *Indonesia, Militant Islam and Ahmadiyah: Origin and Implications*. Melbourne: Centre for Islamic Law and Society, 2009.

———. "Ahmadiyah in Indonesia: A History of Religious Tolerance Under Threat?". *Alternative Law Journal* 36, no. 1 (2011): 56–57.

———. "Criminal (In)Justice in Indonesia: The Cikeusik Trials". *Alternative Law Journal* 37, no. 1 (2012): 54–56.

Djamaluddin, A. *Ahmadiyah dan Pembajakan Al Qur'an*. Jakarta: Lembaga Pengkajian dan Penelitian Islam, 1992.

Fealy, G. "Indonesian Islamist Perspectives on Human Rights". In *Islam and Human Rights in Practice: Perspectives across the Ummah*, edited by S. Akbarzadeh and B. MacQueen. New York: Routledge, 2008.

Hilmy, M. *Islamism and Democracy in Indonesia: Piety and Pragmatism*. Singapore: Institute of Southeast Asian Studies, 2010.

Husaini, A. *Membendung arus liberalisme di Indonesia: Kumpulan catatan akhir pekan*. Jakarta: Pustaka Al-Kautsar, 2009.

Husein, F. "State and Religion in Indonesia: The Case of Inter-religious Dialogue". In *State, Law and Religion in Pluralistic Societies: Austrian and Indonesian*

Experiences, edited by R. Potz, S. Kroissenbrunner, and A. Hafner. Vienna: Vienna University Press, 2010.

International Crisis Group. *Indonesia: Implications of the Ahmadiyah Decree.* Jakarta/Brussels, 2008.

Jaiz, H.A. "Membedah Anatomi Aliran Sesat". *Sabili*, vol. 11, no. 9 (2003): 144–51.

Kahmad, D. "Religious Radicalism and Cultural Change". *Inside Indonesia* 107 (January–March 2012).

Khan, Z. "Foreword to the First English Edition". In *Tadkirah*, by M.G. Ahmad. Surrey: Islam International Publications, 2009.

Khanif, A. *Hukum dan kebebasan beragama di Indonesia.* Yogyakarta: Laksbang Mediatama, 2010.

Kimball, C. *When Religion Becomes Lethal: The Explosive Mix of Politics and Religion in Judaism, Christianity and Islam.* New Jersey: Jossey Bass, 2011.

Magnis-Suseno, F. "Interreligious Dialog: Indonesian Experiences". In *State, Law and Religion in Pluralistic Societies: Austrian and Indonesian Experiences*, edited by R. Potz, S. Kroissenbrunner, and A. Hafner. Vienna: Vienna University Press, 2010.

Majelis Ulama Indonesia. *Penjelasan Tentang Fatwa Aliran Ahmadiyah.* Jakarta: MUI, 2005.

Mulyono. *Bunga Rampai Paham Keagamaan Gerakan Ahmadiyah Indonesia* [Essays on Ahmadiyah Religious Interpretation in Indonesia]. Yogyakarta: Darul Kutubil Islamiyah, 2003.

Munawar-Rachman, B., ed. *Membela Kebebasan Beragama: Percakapan tentang sekularisme, liberalisme dan pluralisme* [Defending Religious Freedom: Conversations about secularism, liberalism and pluralism]. Jakarta: Lembaga Studi Agama dan Falsafat, 2010.

Platzdasch, B. *Islamism in Indonesia: Politics in the Emerging Democracy.* Singapore: Institute of Southeast Asian Studies, 2009.

———. "Religious Freedom in Indonesia: The Case of the Ahmadiyah". ISEAS Working Paper on Politics and Security Series no. 2 (2011). Available at <http://web1.iseas.edu.sg/wp-content/uploads/2010/11/Religious-Freedom-in-Indonesia1.pdf>.

Putro, P.W. *Membongkar Kesesatan Pemikiran Jaringan Islam Liberal.* Solo: Bina Insani Press, 2004.

Rahmat, M.I. *Arus Baru Islam Radikal: Transmisi Revivalisme Islam Timur Tengah Ke Indonesia.* Jakarta: Penerbit Erlangga, 2005.

Rasyid, D. *Melawan sekularisme.* Jakarta: Usamah Press, 2009.

Rofiqoh, L. "The Fatwas of the Majelis Ulama Indonesia on the Ahmadiyah Doctrines: The Problems of Religious Authority and Tolerance". Unpublished M.A. thesis, Leiden University, Leiden, 2008.

Ropi, I. "Hak-hak Minoritas, Negara dan Regulasi Agama". *Titik Temu* 1, no. 1 (2008): 117–30.

Saeed, A. *Interpreting the Qur'an: Towards a Contemporary Approach*. New York: Routledge, 2006.

———., ed. *Approaches to the Qur'an in Contemporary Indonesia*. Oxford: Oxford University Press, 2005.

Sennett, R. *Together: The Rituals, Pleasures and Politics of Cooperation*. New Haven: Yale University Press, 2012.

Sevea, I.S. "The Ahmadiyya Print Jihad in South and Southeast Asia". In *Islamic Connections: Muslim Societies in South and Southeast Asia*, edited by M. Feener and T. Sevea. Singapore: Institute of Southeast Asian Studies, 2009.

Siradj, S.A. "Mengurai Makna Kesesatan". *Suara Pembaruan*, 21 February 2012, p. 4.

Smith, W.C., Wilfred. "Aḥmadiyya". *Encyclopaedia of Islam*, 2nd ed., edited by P. Bearman, Th. Bianquis, C.E. Bosworth, E. van Donzel, and W.P. Heinrichs. Brill Online, 2012. University of Melbourne, 3 April 2012. Available at <http://www.brillonline.nl.ezp.lib.unimelb.edu.au/subscriber/entry?entry=islam_COM-0028>.

Sukma, R. and C. Joewono, eds. *Islamic Thought and Movements in Contemporary Indonesia*. Jakarta: Centre for Strategic and International Studies, 2007.

The Wahid Institute. *Laporan Kebebasan Beragama/Berkeyakinan dan Toleransi 2010*. Jakarta: The Wahid Institute, 2011.

Weintraub, A., ed. *Islam and Popular Culture in Indonesia and Malaysia*. London: Routledge, 2011.

Zulkarnain, Iskandar. *Gerakan Ahmadiyah di Indonesia*. Yogyakarta: LKiS, 2005.

5

SANCTIONS AGAINST POPSTARS ... AND POLITICIANS? INDONESIA'S 2008 PORNOGRAPHY LAW AND ITS AFTERMATH[1]

Helen Pausacker

INTRODUCTION

On 30 October 2008, Indonesia's Pornography Law (No. 44 of 2008) was passed after much controversy. The Bill was supported by a loose coalition of conservative Islamist groups and Islamic parties, including MUI (Majelis Ulama Indonesia, Indonesia's Council of Ulama, or religious teachers),[2] which issued an official statement, endorsing the immediate passage of the Bill[3] and more radical groups such as FPI (Front Pembela Islam, the Islamic Defenders Front). Despite the fact that the Criminal Code contains articles, which could be used to charge pornography, but which were not being properly enforced, the Islamic party PKS (Partai Keadilan Sejahtera, the Prosperity and Justice Party), supported by a number of other political parties, was keen to introduce a special Pornography Law, as a means of enforcing Islamic morality throughout Indonesian society. PKS's hopes for the Pornography Law were high. It stated that the Pornography Law would save current and future generations from moral depravity, that pornography is a deviation, and against Eastern culture (*budaya ketimuran*) (PKS 2006). In other words, Eastern culture was seen in oppositional terms to the "depraved West". Conservative Muslims called on the state to implement laws for the whole community, Muslim or otherwise, which fitted their own standards of morality. The reference to "Eastern culture" can be seen as a way to broaden their Islamic standards to other Indonesians of different religions. As such, it was part of an attempt to incorporate, at a national level, more conservative Islamic values into Indonesian society in general and its legal system in particular.

The Bill was rejected by a broad coalition of liberal Muslims, religious minorities, feminists, and artists. The groups most vocal in opposition to the Bill were religious minorities (particularly the predominantly Hindu Balinese and the predominantly Christian Papuans), who opposed domination of Islamic values (Kearney 2006; Sawitri 2006); feminists, who were concerned that the Bill would restrict women's daily lives and choices of clothing and behaviour (Arivia 2006; Allen 2009); and artists, who worried that the Bill could lead to a new moral censorship (Lindsay 2008). Liberal-thinking Muslims in this loose coalition of activists who opposed the Bill (who also overlapped with the above categories, of course), included the late Abdurrahman Wahid (Gus Dur), former Chair of Nahdlatul Ulama and former President of Indonesia (*Jakarta Post* 2006*b*). Liberals tend to view morality and religious belief as personal issues.[4]

Due to the strong feelings expressed in the debate, both for and against the Bill, it was withdrawn for further revision (Allen 2007), to focus on curbing the prevalence of obscene materials, rather than focusing on restricting individual behaviour (Sherlock 2008, pp. 164–65). By 2007, the DPR (Dewan Perwakilan Rakyat, the People's Representative Council, the legislature) Special Committee on the Pornography Bill had changed its name from the "Anti-Pornography and Porno-Action Bill" to the "Pornography Bill" and simplified the content of the Bill, cutting it from 93 articles to 30 articles (*Jakarta Post* 2007). Revised again, the final 2008 Law contained 45 articles.[5] However, the changes are not as widespread as this might suggest. In many cases, the idea of "porno-action" has simply been included, albeit more vaguely, in the definition of "pornography", as can be seen below.

Article 1(1) of the Law reads:

> [...] 1. Pornography is pictures, sketches, illustrations, photos, writing, voice, sound, moving pictures, animation, cartoons, conversations (*percakapan*), **movements of the body,** or other forms through a variety of communication media and/**or performances in public** which contain obscenity (*kecabulan*) or sexual exploitation which violates the moral norms (*kesusilaan*) in society [my translation, my bolding].

The pressure to introduce this law shows the increasing influence by conservative Muslim groups, following the decline of authoritarian social control in post-Soeharto Indonesia (the current period is known as *Reformasi* or reform era). The greater space for different groups in society to express their values and aspirations more openly has led to lobbying, demonstrations, and other means for influencing politicians. By this means, conservative Muslim groups exert an influence greater than their numbers.

This chapter outlines the challenges to the Pornography Law in the Constitutional Court (Mahkamah Konstitusi or MK) and the first cases prosecuted under the Law, which indicate that — as had occurred with the Criminal Code — cases pursued to date are focusing on individuals, rather than the widespread black market pornography business.

DECISIONS BY THE CONSTITUTIONAL COURT ON THE PORNOGRAPHY LAW[6]

The purpose of the Constitutional Court is to test whether specific laws conflict with the Constitution. Even after the Pornography Law was passed, many people remained dissatisfied with the Law, feeling that their original criticisms of the bill had not been resolved in the final law. They therefore took the Pornography Law to the MK to test whether various Articles in the Pornography Law conflicted with the Constitution. Three of the submissions wanted the Law to be less strict and one wanted the Law to be stricter. To date no challenges to the law have been successful.

SUBMISSIONS AGAINST THE PORNOGRAPHY LAW, HEARD ON 8 OCTOBER 2009

On 8 October 2009, the MK heard three submissions against the Pornography Law. The first submission (10/PUU-VII/2009) was brought by eleven organizations from Minahasa and Sulawesi, many of them Christian.[7] It criticized Article 1(1) (the definition of pornography, above), arguing that there was insufficient definition of "moral norms in society"; Article 4(1)d (prohibiting the making and distribution of items which contain "nudity or the impression of nudity"); and Article 10 (prohibiting nudity, sexual exploitation, explicit sexuality or intercourse in performances or in public).[8] In particular, this submission was concerned about the livelihood of artists and artisans in the Minahasa area, whose income depended on selling paintings, carvings, and statues, many of which depicted nudity. The petitioners emphasized that Indonesia was a "pluralistic country" and that different regions had different views on nudity. They argued that the definition of pornography should be altered so that it was suitable for all Indonesians (MK 2009a, pp. 3–4).

The second submission (17/PUU-VII/2009) was brought by six human rights, women's, Christian, and other organizations, as well as twenty individuals,[9] who also criticized the definition of pornography in both Articles 1(1) and 4(1) (the latter prohibiting the production and distribution of material containing nudity — or the appearance of nudity — or the exposure of sexual organs, sexual violence, masturbation, and child pornography). The petitioners argued that terms such as "indecency", "sexual exploitation", and "violating the norms of propriety in the community" lacked proper definition. In particular, they criticized the inclusion of lesbianism and homosexuality in a list of deviant sexual activities (such as sexual activity with a corpse or animal, oral sex, and anal sex),[10] commenting that lesbianism and homosexuality were natural orientations, not sexual acts, and that including homosexuality and lesbianism as sexual deviancies was a form of discrimination.[11] They also expressed concerns about the involvement of the community in socializing the Pornography Law (Articles 20 and 21), that is, they were concerned that the Law might encourage vigilante sweepings and raids. Finally, they argued against the obligation for citizens to destroy all pornography (Article 43 of the Pornography Law), stating that this would also make it illegal for people to keep homemade pornography, even as electronic files on their own computer (MK 2009b). "Homemade" pornography is made by the person/s for the person/s' own private viewing, as opposed to pornography made by other people (including pornography downloaded from the Internet).

The third submission (23/PUU-VII/2009) was also made by many human rights and women's organizations as well as individuals.[12] As with the previous submission, they criticized Articles 1(1), 4(1 and 2), 10, and 20 of the Pornography Law. In addition, they stated that Articles 23 (stipulating that violations of pornography should be tried in court, according to the rules of the Code of Criminal Procedures [*Hukum Acara Pidana* or KUHAP]) discriminates against women because the KUHAP does not recognize "psychological violence" (*kekerasan psikologis*, that is, threats, force, deceit) as a defence, if, for example, a woman was coerced into "consenting" to pose as a model for pornographic photos (MK 2009c).

The court called a number of expert and government witnesses to give evidence. While the petitioners queried specific articles in the Pornography Law, the expert witnesses, who supported the Law, spoke about the general evils of pornography and their support for the Pornography Law, but they did not address the content of this particular law in any detail. The expert witnesses included MUI's lawyer, Wirawan Adnan, who stated that MUI considered the Pornography Law was intended to "save the morals of our nation". He commented that although MUI had been disappointed that the Law had not included all of their suggestions, it was better than no law at all. He pointed out that the United States also had a type of Pornography Law to protect children from sexual exploitation (MK 2009*d*, pp. 8–14; MK 2009*e*). The conservative women's organization, Kowani (Kongres Wanita Indonesia or Indonesia's Women's Congress),[13] represented by Dr Charletty Choesyana, stated that the Pornography Law protected Indonesian citizens, particularly women and children. Kowani had supported the introduction of the Pornography Law, because it felt that the other laws which regulated pornography[14] had been insufficient. Dr Choesyana stated that pornography was spreading widely through the community and the easy access to pornography led to amoral actions, criminality, sexual violence, teenage pregnancies, sexually transmitted diseases, and abortion (MK 2009*d*, pp. 14–19; MK 2009*e*).

Government witnesses included psychologist, Elly Risman, who stated that many primary school children had already seen pornography and that this could negatively influence their psychological development. A neuroscientist, Dr Andre Mayza, then explained the neurological way in which pornography can become an addiction and cause damage to the brain (MK 2009*d*, pp. 47–50; MK 2009*e*), as shown in these short quotes from the long, detailed, and technical explanation:

> The problem with pornography is that if the need to satisfy [the arousal from looking at pornography] is not fulfilled in teenagers, in people who are not yet married and who are legally unable to marry, it can lead to sexual criminality. [...] (MK 2009*d*, p. 47, my translation)

> The damage [to the brain] results in a moral damage [...] (MK 2009*d*, p. 47, my translation)

> Comparison of the parts of the brain which are damaged as a result of pornography, [show that] almost all parts of the brain may be damaged as a result of exposure to pornography. We see that there are five parts of the brain which are damaged, in comparison to the use of cocaine which results in only three parts [of the brain] being damaged. (MK 2009*d*, p. 49, my translation)

The Constitutional Court handed down its decision relating to all three submissions on 25 March 2010. The Court found that no clauses in the Pornography Law were in contradiction to the Constitution. The Court stated that there were five areas not categorized as pornography: art, literature, customs (*adat istiadat*), knowledge (*ilmu pengetahuan*), and sport. These exceptions, they stated, would mean that artists and artisans who produced statues and other works would be able to continue production under the Law as it stood. Further, the Court commented that basic human rights, including freedom of expression, can be limited without violating the 1945 Constitution, providing these limits acknowledge and honour the rights and freedoms of other people and fulfil the just demands in a democratic society. The Court also refuted the claims that Articles 20 and 21 of the Pornography Law placed too much power in the hands of the community, stating that the Law was clear about the role of the community and prevented anarchistic actions by people who wished to take the law into their own hands (MK 2010*a*).[15]

Only one of the Constitutional Court judges, Maria Farida Indrati, dissented. She stated that the phrase "which violates the values of propriety within the community" in the first Article was vague and that this then tainted the rest of the legislation (MK 2010*a*, p. 6).

SUBMISSION AGAINST THE PORNOGRAPHY LAW, HEARD ON 7 OCTOBER 2010

The next submission against the Pornography Law (PUU-VIII/2010) was submitted by two individuals, Farhat Abbas and Agus Wahid. Farhat Abbas was the head of the organization which reported the high-profile pop star Nazril Irham (a.k.a. Ariel Peterpan) to police,[16] after a video showing Ariel having sex was released on the Internet (*Jakarta Post* 2010*b*. See further details of the case below). Where the previous submissions argued that the Pornography Law was too repressive, this submission argued that the Law was not strict enough, and argued against Article 4 and, particularly, the Elucidation of Article 6, which specifically states that "[t]he prohibition on 'owning or saving [pornography]' does not include for oneself and for one's own purposes",[17] Abbas and Wahid emphasized that rights and freedoms in the Constitution are restricted according to "moral considerations, religious values and public order" and asserted that Articles 4 and 6 of the Pornography Law contravened this restriction, by making it impossible to punish people who made pornographic videos for their own consumption (MK 2010*b*). In other words, they implied that the production of homemade videos for one's own consumption was "ungodly".

The case was heard on 7 October 2010, and the judges' decision, rejecting the submission, was handed down on 26 April 2011. The judges commented that the Law was intended to "respect [*menjunjung*] moral values which have their origins in religious teachings, to protect all citizens, and prevent the development of pornography and the commercialization of sex in the community" (MK 2011, p. 25, para 3.11.3, my translation). However, the judges added that if any particular religious rules prevented its believers from a [legal] pornographic action, which involved only themselves, strictly for personal use, then it was their personal responsibility to God to refrain from this (MK 2011, p. 26, para 3.11.5). The judges further commented that the Elucidations to Articles 4(1) and 6 clearly state that the prohibitions to "make", "possess", and "store" pornography did not include "for oneself and one's own purposes" and that this was not a contradiction, but a limit and exception to the prohibition (MK 2011, p. 27, para 3.11.7).

Judge Maria Farida Indrati had a different reasoning to the other judges. Her reasoning related to technical requirements in drafting laws. She commented that the Attachments [*Lampiran*] 149, 151, and 159 to Law No. 10 of 2004 concerning the Formation [*Pembentukan*] of Regulations and Laws clearly state that that the Elucidation must not include contents which might change the meaning of a law, and she felt that to avoid this, the material in the Elucidation should be included in the body of Articles 4(1) and 6. However, as the applicant had only queried the contents of the Elucidation, rather than the way the law was written, she generally concurred with the decision by the other judges on the panel (MK 2011, pp. 30–32).

ANTI-PORNOGRAPHY TASKFORCE

In March 2012, President Susilo Bambang Yudhoyono announced a new anti-pornography taskforce, which will be led by the Coordinating Welfare Minister, Agung Laksono, and managed by Religious Affairs Minister, Suryadharma Ali.[18] The taskforce will eventually consist of thirty members from ministries, government agencies, religious organizations, universities, and private institutions, and the taskforce will draw up regulations to enable similar taskforces at regional and local level. The funding for the taskforce will be drawn from the Religious Affairs Ministry's budget (Bachelard 2012; *Jakarta Post* 2012a), further highlighting that anti-pornography measures are now seen as a religious rather than a secular concern.

While this was reported in the press as a new initiative, it is mentioned in the 2008 Pornography Law, Article 42, which stated "an inter-departmental task force will be formed, from involved ministries and institutes, the provisions of which will be arranged through Presidential Regulation [Peraturan Presiden]". This, in turn, harked back to Articles 40–50 of the 2005–06 Bill, which set up the BAPPN (Badan Anti-Pornografi dan Pornoaksi Nasional, National Anti-Pornography And Porno-actions Agency), a venture that was dropped in the next two versions (presumably because it was unpopular).

At a press conference announcing the taskforce, Suryadharma Ali gave the wearing of mini-skirts (defined as "a skirt above the knee") as an example of a "pornographic act" which should be banned. The announcement followed reports that a woman wearing a knee-length dress at an anti-corruption dialogue with President Susilo Bambang Yudhoyono had been asked to move to the back row of seats. This was reportedly because the First Lady Kristiani Yudhoyono did not like women wearing Western-style dresses at presidential functions, preferring pants or ankle-length traditional dress (McBeth 2012). Marzuki Alie, the speaker of the DPR, also announced that he would ban female politicians and staff members from wearing mini-skirts, because "there have been a lot of rape cases and other immoral acts recently and this is because women aren't wearing appropriate clothes. You know what men are like. Provocative clothing will make them do things" (Bachelard 2012; Aritonang 2012*a*).

Later in the month, Suryadharma Ali elaborated further on the taskforce's plans. While conceding that areas, such as Bali and Papua, have "unique" cultures, and stating that stakeholders will have a chance to express their opinions, Suryadharma Ali has stressed that the taskforce will set "universal standards" throughout the archipelago, commenting that "[r]equiring women to wear skirts that fall below the knee will be one such criterion" (Aritonang 2012*c*).

The statements by the two ministers led to many counter-comments by women and women's groups. For example, spokesperson for the National Commission on Violence Against Women, Masruchah, stated the proposed regulation would be a "violation of women's rights" and stated that sexual harassment and assault had nothing to do with pornography or the length of women's skirts. She added, "Many women [who were] raped happened to wear very conservative clothing. They were raped anyway"

(Bachelard 2012). Or, as Prodita Sabarini, a journalist with the *Jakarta Post*, states:

> [I]n a world where men have a sense of entitlement over women, it is difficult to get across to them that women are individuals and not sexual objects nor reproductive machines. [...]
>
> The suffering of rape victims is horrendous enough without other people putting the blame on the victim for how they dress. No one has the right to violate another person. There are no excuses. The danger is in the eye of the beholder, not in the object of beauty. The culprit is the rapist, not the victim's torn clothes (Sabarini 2012).

Others, such as Rieke Dyah Pitaloka from Indonesian Democratic Party of Struggle (PDI-P), commented that the government had more important things to deal with, such as the impending rise in prices of fuel (Aritonang 2012*b*) and corruption cases within the Democratic Party (Bachelard 2012).

By mid-April, the taskforce commented that it had blocked websites with domain names that contain the words "porn" and "sex", but did not have a system to block websites which used other names. It stated that it had also worked with the Association of Internet Cafes to install pornography filters (*Jakarta Post* 2012*a*).[19]

While the taskforce targets skirts and obvious domain names on the Internet, trials for breaking the Pornography Law appear to be targeting individuals, rather than the hard-core pornography business.

CHARGES UNDER THE PORNOGRAPHY LAW

In addition to the challenges issued to the Pornography Law in the Constitutional Court, the scope of the application of the Law can be seen by the cases which have been brought to court so far. One factor that originally led critics to be sceptical about the Pornography Bill was that the Criminal Code was never properly enforced, so they saw little point in passing a stricter Pornography Law.[20] This scepticism appears to be founded.

Hard-core pornography was, and is, easily available on the Indonesian black market and sold quite openly. Police make occasional, widely-publicized raids on the petty sellers of pornographic magazines and VCDs, but shortly afterwards the items will be available again (Butt and Lindsey 2007, p. 401; Barker 2006). It is estimated that there is a daily turnover of billions of rupiah in the sale of illegal VCDs in Glodok and that vendors pay bribes to police and local officials, with police often re-selling confiscated videos (*Jakarta Post* 2008; Butt 2008, pp. 620, 629).[21] Disturbing the corrupt black-market activity where officials are involved could have repercussions on those who disrupted these activities. It is therefore not surprising that rather than targeting the black-market, commercial pornography industry, all cases charged under Law No. 44 of 2008 on Pornography (one of which appears to have been dropped) have to date involved individuals and either "pornographic acts" or homemade pornography.

EROTIC DANCERS

Nude Dancers in Serang District, Banten

The first case involved two young women, An and My, aged fifteen and sixteen years old, respectively. In October 2009, they were sentenced in the Serang District Court to four months imprisonment and fined Rp 300,000 (approximately US$31) each for naked table-top dancing at a private room in a karaoke club, New LM (Antara 2009). A forty-five-year-old woman who organized the dance was sentenced to ten months imprisonment and was imposed a similar fine (Osman and Adriyanto 2010).[22] Police became aware of the event, because a video of the performance circulated in the community (Antara 2009).

The three women were sentenced by a Council of Judges, headed by Judge Pinta Uli Boru Tarigan, a conservative Muslim judge, who later, in 2011, was criticized by Human Rights Watch, for her rude and biased treatment of an Ahmadi (Antara 2009; *Jakarta Post* 2011*b*). Whether her religious views coloured her sentencing is unclear, but the four month prison sentence for the two minors seems particularly harsh. Note that there were no charges against any of the people who were involved in commissioning the dance for the function[23] or those who circulated the video.

Bel Air Café, Bandung

The next case involved four female dancers, charged for erotic dancing in skimpy clothing at Bel Air Café, Bandung. The four women (three aged nineteen years and one twenty-seven years) were arrested in a dawn raid on 1 January 2010 after a New Year's celebration.

The police were accompanied on the raid by Bandung Mayor, Dada Rosada, who has introduced a programme of "religious Bandung" and previously attempted to shut down the red-light district, Saritem.[24] The raid was therefore, in part, publicity for the efficacy of his programme. The four women, their manager, and the café manager were tried in the Bandung District Court on 10 March 2010.

The Court, presided over by I Made Sukadana, found all those charged guilty under both the Anti-Pornography Law and Article 282 of the Criminal Code. They were each sentenced to two and a half months prison and fined Rp 1 million (approximately US$105) (*Jakarta Post* 2010*a*; Osman and Adriyanto 2010).

Fellaz Café, Padang

In September 2011, two women, Silfi and Nofera Aisyah, who performed a striptease dance in Fellaz Café in Padang were arrested. The women were each paid Rp 1 million (approximately US$105) for an hour's dance. Both women acknowledged that they had performed the acts out of economic motives — Silfi needed the money for medicine and Nofera Aisyah had outstanding debts for the payment of a motor bike. The three men who hired the two women (Edi, Andre, and an unidentified man) escaped in the police raid. On 9 March 2012, Silfi and Nofera Aisyah were sentenced in the Padang State Court to one year's imprisonment for violating Article 34 of the 2008 Pornography Law. Presiding Judge, Asmar, commented that their actions disquietened (*meresahkan*) the public and damaged the traditional values (*nilai adat*) of Minangkabau (Kistyarini 2012; Maruli 2012).

Karaoke, Malang

On 12 March 2012, the State Court of Malang tried two naked dancers, Yayuk (a.k.a Intan, aged 26) and Sarah Zuleha (also known as "Santi" and "Rhara", aged 19). The two women had been paid Rp 600,000 (approximately US$63) per hour by the karaoke club, The Loft Café, where they had danced. The Council of Judges, headed by Edward Harris Sinaga,[25] sentenced the two women to ten months prison and fined them Rp 3 million (approximately US$314), or an additional three months' imprisonment, for violating Article 36 of the 2008 Pornography Law. The manager (*pengelola*) of the karoke club, Ardi Zuliandi, was sentenced to two years imprisonment (Widianto 2012; Malang Raya 2012).

Similar court cases seem likely as newspapers have reported other raids. One raid occurred in February 2012 on the nightclub, Exclusive Club, in Pekanbaru, Riau and two women (known only as AM from Blitar, 22 years and IF from Jakarta, 22 years) were charged under Article 36 of the 2008 Pornography Law, for working naked as DJs. Five naked women dancers were also taken into custody, but only as witnesses, for appearing in front of an audience, which paid Rp 75,000 (approximately US$8) to observe the dancers (Ebo 2012). AM and IF were released from detention in July 2012 and neither they nor the manager of the nightclub have yet been tried in court (Haluan Riau 2012). In another raid occurred in February 2012, police arrested 16 striptease dancers and a number of hotel employees at the Golden Hands Hotel and Spa. It was reported that clients would pay Rp 1.5 million (approximately US$156) to watch the women dance (*Jakarta Globe* 2012). As in the cases above, none of the clients — who would also have been violating the Pornography Law — were arrested.

HOME-MADE VIDEOS

Ariel and Rejoy from Peterpan

The most highly publicized court case involved pop star Nazril Irham, a.k.a. Ariel, lead singer of the popular boy band, Peterpan. Home-made videos allegedly showing Ariel involved in sexual acts with two celebrities, Luna Maya and Cut Tari, were uploaded to the Internet (Suwarni 2010). Ariel initially stated that he was not the man in the videos, but Cut Tari testified that the videos did depict her and Ariel and were filmed around 2005–06, that is, before the Pornography Law was passed (Suwarni 2010).

Peterpan's musical editor, Reza Rizaldi, a.k.a. Rejoy, also faced charges for spreading pornography. Rejoy testified that it was part of his job as music editor of Peterpan to copy data from Ariel's computer and he then backed these up onto both the Peterpan office and his own home computer. In doing this, he unintentionally transferred the videos from Ariel's computer in 2006. Later, when Rejoy found the two files he rang Ariel, who asked him to delete them. However, it appears that copies on Rejoy's home computer were not deleted (Hardi 2010*b*; Suwarni 2010).

It was suspected that either Rejoy's cousin, Anggit Gagah Pratama, or Anggit's friends were involved in uploading the videos onto the Internet in 2010. The videos on the Internet are in smaller segments than on

Rejoy's computer, indicating that other people had been involved. In a press conference, Anggit admitted copying and watching the videos from Rejoy's personal computer in about 2009, and this was also reiterated in the summing up of the case by Judge Singgih Prakoso, although Anggit claimed that he did not upload the videos onto the Internet (Mustholih 2010; Hardi 2010*a*, 2010*c*). In the court case, a computer expert (*ahli telematika*) testified that after being installed on Anggit's computer, the files were distributed by about ten people through email, facebook and Bluetooth Blackberry and then put on the Internet (Hardi 2010*d*). Anggit has only been questioned as a witness, and neither he nor his friends have been charged (Mustholih 2010; Hardi 2010*c*), although it would seem that if anyone should be charged it would be the "distributor" of the pornography, the person/s who put the video clips on the Internet.

The trial of Ariel attracted demonstrations from Islamic groups, including FPI and the Gerakan Reformis Islam (Islamic Reformist Movement). They pelted the armoured police car, which brought Ariel to court, with rotten eggs and tomatoes and vandalized a number of cars, including those of human rights activists. Following this episode, Bandung Police Chief Senior Comrade Jaya Subriyanto said the police had not detained any of the attackers because the incident was "merely a misunderstanding", a rather meaningless phrase, given that the protestors throwing rotten eggs and tomatoes knew exactly whom they were throwing at. It may have indicated either that the police were in sympathy with the demonstrators or simply unable to control the crowd, and did not wish to admit to their inability (Suwarni and Dipa 2011; Krisna and Karana 2011).

The Council of Judges, headed by Judge Singgih B. Prakoso, in the Bandung District Court passed down the sentence against Ariel and Rejoy on 31 January 2011.[26] Ariel was sentenced to three and a half years in prison and ordered to pay Rp 250 million (approximately US$27,777) for violating Article 29 of the Pornography Law.[27] The Judge stated that the Pornography Law was not being applied retrospectively to when the sexual acts and the storing of the video files occurred in 2005 and 2006, but to when the video began to be circulated in June 2010, after the Pornography Law was in place. He stated that Ariel was careless (*ceroboh*) in how he stored the video on his computer. This had led Rejoy copying the video, and both Ariel and Rejoy were careless with not checking that all copies of the files were properly deleted (Hardi 2011*a*; Hardi and Erwin 2011).

Both Ariel and Rejoy (separately) appealed the decision in the Bandung High Court, but their appeals were rejected.[28] Rejoy's sentence was increased from two years to two and a half years, while Ariel's sentence remained the same (Hardi 2011c). Ariel was released on parole in July 2012, after serving two thirds of his sentence (*Jakarta Post* 2012b), at which point Rejoy had already been released (Felani 2012). High Court Decision Presiding Judge Sjam Amansjah commented that the court had taken "popular opinion" into consideration when it rejected the appeal. "We considered the people's opinion, especially [the reactions] of those who were present during the court proceedings", he said (Krisna 2011). Given that public opinion was divided, it seems that he had paid more attention to the opinion of the anti-Ariel demonstrators rather than his supporters — perhaps the rotten eggs and tomatoes were more persuasive! Violent demonstrations by groups against Ariel, and possibly a fear of further violence by these same demonstrators if the judges delivered a verdict they did not like, may have influenced the decision. Ariel's supporters were not violent and therefore less to be feared.

The charges against both Ariel and Rejoy are in a grey area of the law. As mentioned, the Pornography Law does not relate to the personal production and storage of pornography for one's own purposes. In addition, both the recording and original copying were done prior to the passing of the Pornography Law and laws generally cannot be applied retrospectively in Indonesia (Butt and Hansell 2004). Ariel's crime, therefore, hinges on his "carelessness" in the storage of the video files. Given Rejoy's copying of the videos was inadvertent, his violation of the Law is forgetting to delete all copies of the files, thereby violating Article 43 of the Pornography Law (anyone storing pornographic content should destroy it within thirty days after the law was endorsed).

Jhon and Erna, Pamekasan

"Jhon" (sic.), a thirty-seven-year-old motorbike mechanic and "Erna", a twenty-eight-year-old teacher in the village of Pakong (Pamekasan, East Java) were also charged under the Pornography Law in September 2010 for making a sex video of themselves, although it appears that they have not been convicted. The two produced the video to force Erna's parents (who had initially refused permission) to agree to their marriage. The tactic worked; the parents blessed the union and the two were married in November 2010. However, unfortunately for the couple, the video then began to circulate within the community, and in December the police identified the couple in the video. They were arrested on charges of violating Article 29 of Law No. 44 of 2008 on Pornography and were imprisoned, awaiting trial (Bisri 2010*a* and Bisri 2010*b*).

Hence, as in Ariel, Luna Maya, and Cut Tari's case, the participants of a home-made video (in itself a legal act) were charged, rather than the people who spread the video. The case does not appear to have been tried in court, indicating charges have been dropped.[29]

None of the cases described above targeted the more extreme end of pornography. The lucrative trade in black market hard-core VCDs has not been the target of prosecutions, any more than it was under the Criminal Code. The courts also seem to be acquiescing to the demands of conservative Islamic groups, as can be seen, for example, in the statement above by the Bandung High Court judge, Sjam Amansjah, who commented on "public" opinion having influenced the judges' decision.

ANOTHER LAW FOR RULERS

In 2006, the Islamic party PKS stated that the Pornography Law was necessary "to save the current and future generations from moral depravity" (PKS 2006). In an ironic twist, on 8 April 2011, a journalist, Irfan, from *Media Indonesia* photographed H. Arifinto, a PKS legislator, viewing a pornographic video on a tablet computer during a legislative session of the DPR. Initially Arifinto claimed that he had briefly opened the file inadvertently, but photos produced by Irfan indicated that the files were on Arifinto's computer and he had viewed the video for two minutes (Andriyanto, Rayda, and Rachman 2011; *Jakarta Post* 2011*a*).[30]

On 11 April, Arifinto resigned from the legislature, issuing a public apology (Andriyanto, Rayda, and Rachman 2011). However, Arifinto has not been charged, much less imprisoned (*Jakarta Post* 2011*a*). Despite PKS claiming strict discipline, a strong dedication to Islamic values and enthusiasm for the Pornography Law,[31] Fahri Hamzah, a PKS official, was quoted in the press, saying, "[Punish] the one who spreads pornography and not the one who keeps it" (Andriyanto, Rayda, and Rachman 2011).

Nor is Arifinto the only legislator in trouble. In March 2011, a sex video of Iwan Fajarudin and his second wife, a National Mandate Party (PAN, Partai Amanat Nasional) legislator in Purworejo's Legislative Council, has been circulated on the Internet. Fajarudin admitted the video might have been taken from his laptop which he had sold recently, and stated he may have been "reckless and foolish" in not deleting files, including those in the recycle bin of his computer (*Jakarta Globe* 2011*a*).[32]

Interestingly, despite this action being similar to Ariel's "carelessness", the legislator has not been charged, nor have hardline, radical Islamist groups demonstrated against him.

CONCLUSIONS

In the long-term, the response by PKS to Arifinto and other politicians may lead to the public becoming more disillusioned in the party, which had originally gained much of its public support through the image of its politicians being clean from corruption and through efforts by PKS to fight corruption, rather than necessarily through public support for its Islamic beliefs (Collins and Fauzi 2005). PKS and other conservative Muslim groups fought hard for the Pornography Law, but it would seem that the implementation of this law is no more effective than the articles relating to pornography in the Criminal Code in wiping out hard-core pornography. Nor does it seem to be lessening consumers' desire to access pornography (including even a conservative Muslim member of the very party which was keen to implement the law). The enforcement of the Pornography Law is similar to the enforcement of the articles in the Criminal Code; that is, the hard-core pornography industry is not being targeted, but (certain) individuals are rather randomly used as "soft targets", to demonstrate the Law is having an effect. These have included both the weak (in the case of the dancers) and high-profile teenage idols (in the case of Ariel) in highly publicized events.

The publicity and the desire to be seen to be producing results seems to be one of the main aims of the conservative Muslim groups. That is, they have a desire to show on a national level that Islamic values are being incorporated into Indonesian society and its laws.

Targeting these particular individuals may be aimed at dissuading young people to involve themselves in pornography, but this approach does not disturb the profits from the hard-core, illegal pornography industry, which are said to be an income stream for corrupt state officials. Attacking the industry would involve both systemic changes, a much more difficult process, and one which may have repercussions on the individuals which attack the system.

Notes

[1] This chapter is based on part of the author's Ph.D. thesis, submitted at the Melbourne Law School, the University of Melbourne in 2013. The author

thanks Tim Lindsey for comments on an earlier draft of this chapter and Bernhard Platzdasch for editorial suggestions.
2   For background information on the role of MUI, set up by former President Soeharto and its changing role in the *Reformasi* era, see Ichwan (2005).
3   For a copy of this statement, see <www.halalguide.info/index.php?option=com_content&task=view&id=242&itemid=29MUI2006ijtima>.
4   Assyaukanie (2009, p. 18) describes "liberal democrats" such as Nurcholis Madjid and Abdurrahman Wahid, as believing that religiosity is "entirely a private matter, in which the state has no right to intervene".
5   For more information on both the 2006 Bill and the final 2008 Pornography Law, see Allen (2007), Pausacker (2008), Pausacker (2009), Sherlock (2008), and Lindsey (2012, pp. 445–80).
6   Research for this section was also used in Lindsey (2012, pp. 445–80).
7   These included six Christian youth groups; three general university student groups; one Christian women's group and a group involved in *adat* (traditional customs) (MK 2009*a*, p. 1).
8   Constitution articles, in which the Pornography Law was said to have contradicted, included Article 28C(1) (the right to advance oneself through education, knowledge and technology, and art and culture); Article 28C(2) (the right to fight for rights in a collective fashion to develop the community, nation and state); Article 28I(3) (respect for cultural identity and traditional communal rights); and Article 32(1) (the state should advance the national Indonesian culture through protecting the freedom of the community and cultural values) (MK 2009*a*, pp. 2–3).
9   The six groups, most national, included two human rights organizations (one focused on women), one church peak body, a liberal Muslim research organization, an Ashram, a multi-ethnic, multi-religious movement, and twenty individuals including the actor Butet Kartaredjasa (MK 2009*b*, p. 1). Note that on the summary of the submission, the number is written as 17/PUU-VI/2009, but in the proceedings of the court, it is 17/PUU-VII/2009 (my underlining). I am assuming that the number on the summary is a typographical error as both of the other cases heard with this submission also have a VII.
10 Constitution articles said to be contradicted: Article 28D(1) (the right to protection of the law); Article 28E(2) (the right to freedom of belief, and to speak thoughts according to conscience); Article 28F (the right to communicate and obtain and convey information to develop oneself and the community); and Article 28I(2) (the right to protection from discrimination) (MK 2009*b*, pp. 3–7).
11 Homosexuality and lesbianism have never been illegal in Indonesia, but neither are the rights of homosexuals, lesbians, and *waria* (transgender people) specifically protected (Hapsari 2010).

12 Six women's rights organizations, one educational organization, and one individual, Acep Supriadi (MK 2009c, p. 1).
13 Kowani <http://kowani.or.id> was established in 1928. See Blackburn (2004, pp. 27, 227) for further information about Kowani's relationship with the state in the New Order and Reformasi era.
14 The Criminal Code (KUHP), Law No. 43 of 1999 on the Press; Law No. 32 of 2002 on Broadcasting; and Law No. 23 of 2002 on the Protection of Children.
15 This is, in fact, in the Elucidation to these Articles.
16 Farhat Abbas was also the lawyer for three of the Australian "Bali Nine" drug mules, Norman, Chen, and Nguyen (Fitzpatrick 2008).
17 My translation. The submission argued that this contradicted a number of Articles in the Constitution: Article 28D(1) (the right to protection and certainty of the law), Article 28J(1) (respect for other people's basic human rights in the order of life of the community) and Article 29(1) (Indonesia is a country based on belief in God).
18 Other members of the task force already named include other Cabinet Communications and Information Technology Minister Tifatul Sembiring, Law and Human Rights Minister Amir Syamsuddin, Women's Empowerment and Child Protection Minister Linda Gumelar, Education and Culture Minister Muhammad Nuh, and Home Minister Gamawan Fauzi (Aritonang 2012a).
19 There have been no further announcements in the press by the taskforce at the time of writing (early September 2012).
20 See for example, the comments by Leo Batubara of the Indonesian Press Council (Kearney 2006).
21 Barker (2006) also discusses the more recent phenomena of illegal amateur pornographic VCDs available on the Indonesian black market.
22 Antara (2009) gives the woman's age as forty years, whereas Osman and Andriyanto (2010) state she is forty-five.
23 Article 7 of the Pornography Law prohibits sponsoring (*mendanai*) or facilitating a pornographic act. Article 11 forbids involving a minor in a pornographic activity and/or as an object of pornography. A minor is defined as someone less than the age of eighteen (Article 1(4)).
24 The programme, first suggested by Dada Rosada in 2004, is not specifically Islamic. See Millie and Safei (2010) for further details of Dada Rosada's programmes.
25 Edward Sinaga is the Deputy Head of the State Court of Malang, available at <http://pn-malang.go.id/index.php?option=com_content&view=article&id=7&Itemid=43>. He was moved from the Surabaya State court in about May 2011, available at <www.jatimprov.go.id/index.php?option=com_content&task=view&id=10334&Itemid=2> (both websites accessed 28 June 2012).

26   Bandung State Court Decision No. 1401/Pid/B/2010/PN.Bdg for Ariel; No. 1402/Pid/B/2010/PN.Bg for Rejoy, dated 31 January 2011 (Source: Bandung High Court website, <http://www.pt-bandung.go.id/status-perkara-pengadilan-tinggi/perkara-pidana?field=&value=&v_f_date=01-07-2011&v_t_date=29-07-2011&show=100&fil=&start=1>).

27   Article 29 forbids someone from producing, making, duplicating, distributing, broadcasting, exporting, offering, selling, renting, or preparing pornography, in accordance with the terms in Article 4(1). The Elucidation to Article 4(1) states that home-made pornography by oneself for one's own use is not illegal. Both were also originally charged under the 2008 Law on Electronic Information and Transaction (Hardi and Erwin Z. 2011), but this is not mentioned in the final sentence.

28   Bandung High Court Decision No. 67/Pid/2011/PT-BDG for Ariel, No. 68/PID/2011/PT.Bdg for Rejoy, dated 19 April 2011 (Bandung High Court website, <http://www.pt-bandung.go.id/status-perkara-pengadilan-tinggi/perkara-pidana?field=&value=&v_f_date=01-07-2011&v_t_date=29-07-2011&show=100&fil=&start=1>).

29   It is not listed on the Pamekasan District Court website, and I could also find no further press reports about the case after December 2010.

30   This violated Article 6 of the Pornography Law: "It is illegal for anyone to allow pornographic products to be heard (*memperdengarkan*), to show (*mempertontonkan*), to use (*memanfaatkan*), to own (*memiliki*), or to save (*menyimpan*) pornographic products ..." (my translation, my underlining). It would seem that Arifinto both owned and saved pornographic products, and that these were not homemade pornography of himself, which would have been legal.

31   For further details about PKS, see Fealy (2010).

32   In the same week, Anis Matta, Deputy Speaker of the DPR and PKS politician, was also implicated in a feral sex video on the Internet, but investigation by police digital forensics unit indicated that the person in the video resembled him, but was not Anis Matta himself (Arnaz 2011).

References

Allen, Pam. "Challenging Diversity? Indonesia's Anti-Pornography Bill". *Asian Studies Review* 31, no. 2 (2007): 101–15.

——. "Women, Gendered Activism and Indonesia's Anti-Pornography Bill". *Intersections: Gender and Sexuality in Asia and the Pacific*, issue 19 (February 2009). Available at <http://intersections.anu.edu.au/issue19/allen.htm>.

Andriyanto, Heru, Nivell Rayda, and Anita Rachman. "Can Arifinto Be Charged Under the Porn Law?". *Jakarta Globe*, 12 April 2011. Available at <http://www.thejakartaglobe.com>.

Antara. "Dua ABG Penari Telanjang Dihukum Empat Bulan", 15 October 2009. Available at <http://www.antaranews.com>.

Aritonang, Margareth S. "'Miniskirts = Porn': Religious Affairs Minister". *Jakarta Post*, 28 March 2012a. Available at <http://www.thejakartapost.com>.

———. "Showing Thighs 'a Porn Crime'". *Jakarta Post*, 29 March 2012b. Available at <http://www.thejakartapost.com>.

———. "Discourse: Minister on Short Skirts, the Haj and Non-Islamic Radical Groups". *Jakarta Post*, 30 March 2012c. Available at <www.thejakartapost.com>.

Arivia, Gadis. "Aliansi Mawar Putih, Lahir dari Kebutuhan: Gerakan Sosial untuk Keadilan". *Jurnal Perempuan* 47 (May 2006): 91–95.

Arnaz, Farouk. "Police 'Digital Forensics' Clear Anis Matta in Sex Tape Scandal". *Jakarta Globe*, 19 March 2011. Available at <http://www.thejakartaglobe.com>.

Assyaukanie, Luthfi. *Islam and the Secular State in Indonesia*. Singapore: Institute of Southeast Asian Studies, 2009.

Bachelard, Michael. "'You Know What Men are Like': Indonesia to Ban Mini-Skirts over Links to Rape". *The Age*, 29 March 2012. Available at <www.theage.com.au>.

Barker, Thomas. "VCD Pornography of Indonesia". Conference paper presented at the 16th Biennial Conference of the Asian Studies Association of Australia in Wollongong, 26–29 June 2006. Available at <http://coombs.anu.edu.au/SpecialProj/ASAA/biennial-conference/2006/Barker-Thomas-ASAA2006.pdf> (accessed 20 October 2007).

Bisri, Musthofa. "Calon Menantu Buat Video Porno untuk Luluhkan Hati Mertua". *Tempointeraktif*, 5 December 2010a. Available at <http://www.tempointeraktif.com>.

———. "Disodori Rekaman Video Porno Anaknya, Calon Mertua Pasrah". *Tempointeraktif*, 5 December 2010b. Available at <http://www.tempointeraktif.com>.

Blackburn, Susan. *Women and the State in Modern Indonesia*. Cambridge: Cambridge University Press, 2004.

Butt, Simon. "Intellectual Property in Indonesia: A Problematic Legal Transplant". In *Indonesia: Law and Society*, 2nd ed., edited by Tim Lindsey. Annandale, NSW: The Federation Press, 2008.

Butt, Simon and David Hansell. "The Masykur Abdul Kadir Case: Indonesian Constitutional Court Decision No. 013/PUU-I/2003". *Australian Journal of Asian Law* 6, no. 2 (2004): 176–96.

Butt, Simon and Tim Lindsey. "Intellectual Property, Civil Law and the Failure of Law in Indonesia: Can Criminal Enforcement of Economic Law Work in Developing Countries?". In *Law Reform in Developing and Transitional States*, edited by Tim Lindsey. London: Routledge, 2007.

Collins, Elizabeth Fuller and Ihsan Ali Fauzi. "Islam and Democracy!". *Inside Indonesia*, no. 81 (January–March 2005). Available at <http://www.insideindonesia.org>.

Ebo, Aloysius Gonsaga Angi. "Lima Penari Striptis Tertangkap Saat Tanpa Busana". *Kompas*, 22 February 2012. Available at <http://regional.kompas.com>.

Fealy, Greg. "Front Stage with the PKS". *Inside Indonesia*, no. 101 (July–September 2010). Available at <http://www.insideindonesia.org>.

Felani, Jejen. "Pengedar Video Tak Senonoh Ariel Sudah Bebas dari Penjara", 5 June 2012. Available at <http://www.seputarinformasi.com>.

Fitzpatrick, Stephen. "Bali Nine Lawyer Farhat Abbas Asks to See Kevin Rudd". *The Australian*, 11 March 2008. Available at <http://www.theaustralian.com.au/news/bali-nine-lawyer-asks-to-see-rudd/story-e6frg6t6-1111115764514> (accessed 9 February 2012).

Haluan Riau. "2 Penari Striptis Bebas dari Jerat Hukum". *Sindikasi*, 17 July 2012. Available at <http://sindikasi.inilah.com>.

Hapsari, Arghea Desafti. "In Workplace, LGBTs Face Discrimination". *Jakarta Post*, 17 December 2010. Available at <http://www.thejakartapost.com>.

Hardi, Erick P. "Ariel Didakwa Memberi Kesempatan Video Porno Tersebar". *Tempointeraktif*, 6 December 2010*a*. Available at <http://www.tempointeraktif.com>.

———. "Ariel Minta File Video Porno Dihapus". *Tempointeraktif*, 20 December 2010*b*. Available at <http://www.tempointeraktif.com>.

———. "Rejoy Diperiksa Soal Pemindahan Video Ariel". *Tempointeraktif*, 20 December 2010*c*. Available at <http://www.tempointeraktif.com>.

———. "Saksi Ahli Sidang Ariel Dinilai Tak Memberatkan Rejoy". *Tempointeraktif*, 23 December 2010*d*. Available at <http://www.tempointeraktif.com>.

———. "Ini Pertimbangan Hakim Memvonis Ariel". *Tempointeraktif*, 31 January 2011*a*. Available at <http://www.tempointeraktif.com>.

———. "Pengganda Video Ariel Diganjar Dua Tahun Penjara". *Tempointeraktif*, 31 January 2011*b*. Available at <http://www.tempointeraktif.com>.

———. "Hukuman Rejoy Ditambah 6 Bulan". *Tempointeraktif*, 25 April 2011*c*. Available at <http://www.tempointeraktif.com>.

Hardi, Erick P. and Erwin Z. "Ariel Divonis 3,5 Tahun Penjara". *Tempointeraktif*, 31 January 2011. Available at <http://www.tempointeraktif.com>.

Ichwan, Moch. Nur. "Ulamā, State and Politics: Majelis Ulama Indonesia after Suharto". *Islamic Law and Society* 12, no. 1 (2005): 45–72.

Jakarta Globe. "Another Lawmaker in Hot Water after Sex Video Leaks", 4 March 2011*a*. Available at <http://www.thejakartaglobe.com>.

———. "16 Strippers Arrested at North Jakarta Hotel", 25 February 2012. Available at <http://www.thejakartaglobe.com>.

Jakarta Post. "Porn Bill Backers Come Out in Force", 22 May 2006*a*. Available at <http://www.thejakartapost.com>.

———. "Gus Dur, Gadis Honored with Press Award", 11 August 2006*b*. Available at <http://www.thejakartapost.com>.

———. "House Renames Pornography Bill", 25 January 2007. Available at <http://www.thejakartapost.com>.

———. "Pirated VCD Supplier Arrested", 26 January 2008. Available at <http://www.thejakartapost.com>.

———. "Six Arrested over Bandung New Year Striptease", 5 January 2010*a*. Available at <http://www.thejakartapost.com>.

———. "Farhat Abbas Proposes Polygamy to Ariel", 4 August 2010*b*. Available at <http://www.thejakartapost.com>.

———. "'Arifinto' Photo Journo Has Not Received Police Summons", 12 April 2011*a*. Available at <http://www.thejakartapost.com>.

———. "Rights Watchdog Wants More Oversight of Ahmadi Trials", 20 June 2011*b*. Available at <http://www.thejakartapost.com>.

———. "Task Force Touts 'Progress' on Internet Porn Crackdown", 24 April 2012*a*. Available at <http://www.thejakartapost.com>.

———. "Singer Ariel Free at Last", 23 July 2012*b*. Available at <http://www.thejakartapost.com>.

Kearney, Marianne. "Anti-Porn Measure Divides Indonesia". *Aljazeera*, 16 March 2006. Available at <http://english.aljazeera.net/news/archive/archive?ArchiveId=22173>.

Kistyarini. "2 Penari Striptis Divonis 1 Tahun Penjara". *Kompas*, 9 March 2012. Available at <http://regional.kompas.com>.

Krisna, Yuli. "Ariel's Sex Tape Appeal Gets Shot Down by High Court". *Jakarta Globe*, 25 April 2011. Available at <http://www.thejakartaglobe.com>.

Krisna, Yuli and Kinanti Pinta Karana. "Ariel Verdict Leaves Sour Taste". *Jakarta Globe*, 1 February 2011. Available at <http://www.thejakartaglobe.com>.

Lindsay, Jennifer. "A New Artistic Order? The Arts Scene has Changed Radically since 1998, but Some of the Old Uncertainties Remain". *Inside Indonesia*, no. 93 (August–October 2008). Available at <http://www.insideindonesia.org>.

Lindsey, Tim. *Islam and Law in Indonesia: Laws, Legal Institutions and the National Madhhab*. London: I.B. Tauris, 2012.

Malang Raya. "Purel Bugil 15 Menit, Polisi Baru Beraksi", 5 January 2012. Available at <http://malangraya.web.id>.

Maruli, Aditia. "Dua Penari Telanjang Divonis Satu Tahun Penjara". *Antara*, 8 March 2012. Available at <http://www.antaranews.com>.

McBeth, John. "All Hot over Indonesia's Latest Antipornography Drive". *Jakarta Globe*, 27 March 2012. Available at <http://www.thejakartaglobe.com>.

Millie, Julian and Agus Ahmad Safei. "Religious Bandung: Bandung's Government Opts for a Religious Program that Matches the City's Character".

Inside Indonesia, no. 100 (April–June 2010). Available at <http://www.insideindonesia.org>.

MK (Mahkamah Konstitusi). "Perbaikan Ringkasan Permohonan Perkara Nomor 10 /PUU-VII/2009 tentang Undang-undang Pornografi (Definisi Pornografi)", 2009*a*. Available at <http://www.mahkamahkonstitusi.go.id/Resume/resume_perkara%2010%20%20pornografi.pdf> (accessed 1 March 2011).

———. "Ringkasan Permohonan Perkara Nomor 17/PUU-VII/2009 tentang Undang-undang Pornografi (Kemajemukan Budaya yang Terlanggar)", 2009*b*. Available at <http://www.mahkamahkonstitusi.go.id/Resume/resume_sidang_perkara%2017%20%20pornografi.pdf> (accessed 1 March 2011). Front cover title is written as 17/PUU-VI/2009. See endnote 9 for further explanation.

———. "Ringkasan Permohonan Perkara Nomor 23/PUU-VII/2009 tentang Undang-undang Pornografi (Kemajemukan Budaya yang Terlanggar)". Jakarta: Mahkamah Konstitusi, 2009*c*. Available at <http://www.mahkamahkonstitusi.go.id/Resume/resume_sidang_perkara%2023%20%20pornografi.pdf> (accessed 1 March 2011).

———. "Risalah Sidang Perkara Nomor 10/PUU-VII/2009, Perkara Nomor 17/PUU-VII/2009, Perkara Nomor 23/PUU-VII/2009 Perihal Pengujian Undang-Undang Republik Indonesia Nomor 44 Tahun 2008 tentang Pornografi terhadap Undang-Undang Dasar Negara Republik Indonesia Tahun 1945". Jakarta: Mahkamah Konstitusi, 8 October 2009*d*. Available at <http://www.mahkamahkonstitusi.go.id/Risalah/risalah_sidang_Perkara%sidang_Perkara%2010,%2017,%2023%20%20PUU%20VII-2009,%208%20Oktober%20%2020 09%20final%20-%20Copy%20(2).pdf> (accessed 1 March 2011).

———. "UU Pornografi Untuk Selamatkan Moral Bangsa", 11 October 2009*e*. Available at <http://www.mahkamahkonstitusi.go.id/index.php?page=website.BeritaInternalLengkap&id=3400> (accessed 1 March 2011).

———. "Ringkasan Putusan". Jakarta: Mahkamah Konstitusi, 25 March 2010*a*. Available at <http://djpp.kemenkumham.go.id/files/litigasi/Putusan%20PUU%2010-17-23-2009%pornografi.pdf> (accessed 8 March 2011).

———. "Risalah Sidang Perkara Nomor 48/PUU-VIII/2010 Perihal Pengujian Undang-Undang Nomor 44 Tahun 2008 tentang Pornografi terhadap Undang-Undang Dasar Negara Republik Indonesia Tahun 1945. Acara Perbaikan Pemohonan (II)". Jakarta: Mahkamah Konstitusi, 16 September 2010*b*. Available at <http://www.mahkamahkonstitusi.go.id/Risalah/Perkara%20Nomor%2048.%20PUU-VIII.2010,%2016%20Sept%20201063.pdf> (accessed 1 March 2011).

———. "Putusan Nomor 48/PUU-VIII/2010". Jakarta: Mahkamah Konstitusi, 26 April 2011. Available at <http://www.mahkamahkonstitusi.go.id/putusan/putusan_sidang_Putusan%2048%20PUU%202010%20TELAH%20BACA.pdf> (accessed 9 December 2011).

Mustholih. "Anggit Bantah Jadi Penyebar Pertama Video Ariel". *Tempointeraktif*, 22 December 2010. Available at <http://www.tempointeraktif>.

Osman, Nurfika and Heru Andriyanto. "Sexy Dancers Jailed by Indonesia's Porn Law as Activists Fume". *Jakarta Globe*, 13 March 2010. Available at <http://www.thejakartaglobe.com>.

Pausacker, Helen. "Hot Debates: A Law on Pornography still Divides the Community". *Inside Indonesia*, no. 94 (October–December 2008). Available at <http://www.insideindonesia.org>.

———. "Indonesia's New Pornography Law: Reform Does Not Necessarily Lead to More Liberal Attitudes to Morality and Censorship". *Alternative Law Journal*, vol. 34, no. 2 (2009): 122–24.

PKS (Partai Keadilan Sejahtera). "Dewan Syariah Pusat PKS Dukung Pemberlakuan UU Anti Pornografi dan Porno Aksi", 22 February 2006. Available at <http://pks-jepang.org/archives/340> (accessed 28 July 2011).

Sabarini, Prodita. "By the Way ... Putting Men in a Tight Spot". *Jakarta Post*, 22 April 2012. Available at <http://www.thejakartapost.com>.

Sawitri, Cok. "Tolak Kebijakan I Belog yang Mengubur Dirinya". *Journal Perempuan* 47 (May 2006): 41–51.

Sherlock, Stephen. "Parties and Decision-Making in the Indonesian Parliament: A Case Study of RUU APP, the Anti-Pornography Bill". *Australian Journal of Asian Law*, vol. 10, no. 2 (2008): 159–83.

Suwarni, Yuli Tri. "Tari Admits that is Her in Sex Tape". *Jakarta Post*, 14 December 2010. Available at <http://www.thejakartapost.com>.

Suwarni, Yuli Tri and Arya Dipa. "Ariel Gets 3.5 Years; Unrest Outside Court". *Jakarta Post*, 1 February 2011. Available at <http://www.thejakartapost.com>.

Widianto, Eko. "Di Malang, Penari Telanjang Divonis 10 Bulan". *Tempo*, 13 March 2012. Available at <http://www.tempo.co>.

6

THE INTER-RELIGIOUS HARMONY FORUM, THE OMBUDSMAN, AND THE STATE
Resolving Church Permit Disputes in Indonesia?

Melissa Crouch

INTRODUCTION

Conflicts between religious communities over sacred sites and places of worship, particularly concerning religious minorities, frequently feature in the media and continue to be matters of global debate. At the heart of these issues are often legal attempts or proposals for reform to regulate where and how a religious community can build a place of worship. In Indonesia, the introduction of tighter legal regulations on permits for places of worship has done little to curb conflict over church permits, with difficulties experienced by some churches in the majority-Muslim province of West Java.

This chapter explores the role that the law plays in promoting religious harmony by regulating the permit process for a place of worship in Indonesia. It examines two institutions involved, the Inter-Religious Harmony Forum, which is the main committee at the regional level that approves permit applications, and the national Ombudsman, which can investigate complaints against government authorities. The Bogor Church

Permit Case will be discussed to demonstrate that in some areas, the Forum have exacerbated inter-religious tensions by recommending the cancellation of church permits and disputes have escalated beyond their control. This has led some Christian congregations to complain to independent bodies such as the Ombudsman, as well as taking action in the Administrative Courts (Pengadilan Tata Usaha Negara) to resolve the dispute. All cases in the Administrative Courts have been successful in favour of the church, but only some churches have been able to enforce the court decision and continue to build churches. Others, like the church in Bogor, continue to face opposition from the local government in defiance of the Administrative Court. This poses a threat to the integrity of the courts and raises questions about whether religious minorities can have faith in the law and legal processes in Indonesia.

PERMIT APPLICATION PROCESS

The Inter-religious Harmony Forum

The Inter-religious Harmony Forum was established by a Joint Regulation of the Minister of Religion and the Minister of Home Affairs[1] in 2006 following the escalation of violent attacks against religious minorities in 2004–05. It replaced a ministerial decree[2] that was widely considered to be in contradiction to the commitments the Indonesian government has made to human rights and religious freedom since the transition to democracy in 1998.

The Joint Regulation provides for the establishment of a forum that consists of representatives from each of the six recognized religions — Islam, Catholicism, Protestantism, Hinduism, Buddhism, and Confucianism[3] — in proportion to the percentage of adherents of these religions in each province and city/regency (Article 1(6)). There are twenty-one members of the provincial Forum and seventeen members of the city/regency Forum (Article 10(2)). The members of each Forum are chosen by the Inter-religious Harmony Advisory Council, which consists of representatives from relevant government departments (Article 11).

The role of the Forum is to conduct inter-religious dialogue among religious communities, formulate policy recommendations, and educate the community on laws related to religious harmony at the regional level (Articles 8(1); 9(1)). Importantly, the city or regency Forum has the additional responsibility of providing written recommendations for requests to build a place of worship (Article 9(2)), which I will focus on in this chapter.

The Forums are established by regulations of the governor and regent or mayor (Article 12). These regulations outline the tasks of the Forum and the reporting procedures, although these are generally along the same lines as the Joint Regulation. For example, they specify the criteria for representatives to the Forum and they determine the length of members' terms, which vary slightly from region to region.[4]

There have been complaints from both within and outside the Forum since its establishment. One of the main concerns of Forum members is that there is a lack of guidance from the Ministry of Religion on how to deal with disputes and conflict over proposals for places of worship that are not covered in the new regulation,[5] which I will discuss shortly. Some leaders of religious minorities have complained that the election of the chairperson and vice-chairperson has been unfairly decided because both positions are often held by the religious majority, whereas in their opinion one of those leadership positions should be held by a religious minority. There is also the more basic concern that decisions are made by the majority, whether that be Muslim representatives in Muslim-majority areas or Christian representatives in majority Christian areas.

Many non-government organizations (NGOs) have also criticized the Forum for being elitist and adding another unnecessary layer of bureaucracy to an already lengthy process (Wahid Institute 2007). Overall, reports remain mixed on whether the Forum can play a constructive role in facilitating the processing of applications,[6] although there are indications that it has been overshadowed and encumbered by religious bureaucracy and crippled by majoritarianism in its decision making. As I will demonstrate in this chapter, the Forum is ultimately only one of many authorities that applicants must satisfy. Therefore, there are multiple levels at which disputes over proposed places of worship of religious minorities can be opposed and stalled indeterminately.

Despite its promising name, the Forum has at times hindered, rather than facilitated applications for church permits and has yet to play a significant role in mediating church disputes.[7] There is a need to address the complicity of local governments and enforcement agencies, and support respected community leaders at the grassroots level who play a significant role in mediating these tensions. This clearly requires government attention if the concept of *kerukunan umat beragama* (inter-religious harmony) is to be more than empty rhetoric.

One final point to note is that although the Inter-religious Harmony Forum was created in 2006, it was not necessarily a new initiative, but was rather an effort by the government to capitalize on a successful grassroots model. In many areas of Indonesia where inter-religious violence broke out during 1996 to 2001, religious leaders established the Inter-religious Communication Forum (Forum Komunikasi Umat Beragama), a coalition of respected community religious leaders that could assist to facilitate and resolve any disputes that arose. Many of these organizations have since been conveniently converted into, or taken over by, the Inter-religious Harmony Forum, although given that it now has to fit the model set by the government, such as that representatives are only chosen from the six recognized religions, it receives government funding and it is closely linked to the Ministry of Religion; this raises questions about its independence.

The Forum must consider whether applications fulfil the requirements as set out in the Joint Regulation; and these new requirements have also been the cause of concern for some religious minorities, as I will discuss next.

NEW REQUIREMENTS

Aside from the Forum, the second change introduced by the Joint Regulation is the requirements that must be met in order for a religious community to obtain a building permit or renovate an existing place of worship. The general conditions stipulate that an applicant must demonstrate a "real need" for a place of worship regarding the total number of religious followers at the village level (Article 13(1)).[8] This is followed by the broad condition that construction must "respect inter-religious harmony and not disturb the community" (Article 13(2)). The applicants must also comply with the general administrative requirements for the construction of a building for "religious purposes" (Article 14(1)).[9]

One of the main issues is the requirement that a religious group must obtain the signatures and photocopies of the national identity cards of at least 90 members of the congregation and at least 60 "local residents" of another religion (Article 14(2)). This is known as the "90/60 Requirement". There was some dispute about these numbers at the time of drafting (Soefyanto 2009, p. 75). While no official reason was given for such a requirement, one possible explanation is that it may have been based on the position expressed in *Bulughul Maram*, a collection of Islamic *hadith* that is well known in Indonesia.[10] In *Bulughul Maram*, a *hadith* states that there must be a minimum of forty people in attendance at the mosque for Friday prayers.[11] According to Din Syamsuddin, Chairperson of Muhammadiyah,[12] many Muslim leaders felt that other religions should also be required to have at least forty members before they can build a church (Soefyanto 2009, p. 71).[13]

In practice, the requirement states that the 60 signatures must come from the "local community". Given that this document must be signed by the head of the village, it can be presumed that it must be the signatures of residents who live in the village (Article 14(2)(b)). The 90 signatures of religious followers must come from residents from the area,[14] which is actually a surprisingly low threshold. There are indications, however, that some misinterpretations about the application of this condition have emerged.

For example, the requirement of 90 signatures has been subject to various interpretations, with the Forum in some regions interpreting the requirement strictly so that it is difficult for religious minorities if they do not live in proximity to the land on which they intend to build the place of worship. According to the new regulation, however, as long as members of the congregation live in the same province as the church, this is not a ground for rejecting an application. There are also often strong suspicions in cases where there is opposition to a proposal that the signatures were obtained by deception, bribery, or coercion. In such cases, the Forum usually conducts a verification process.

The final requirement in the application process is that an applicant must obtain a written recommendation from the city or regency Ministry of Religion and from the city or regency Forum (Article 14(2)). The mayor must then use the recommendations of the Ministry of Religion and the Forum to support his decision to cancel the permit. The Ministry of Religion, along with the Forum, therefore still plays a significant role in determining applications for a permit. Some disputes, however, have quickly escalated beyond the control of the Forum and the Ministry of Religion, which highlights the importance of other avenues for redress, such as complaints to the Ombudsman.

DISPUTE RESOLUTION AND THE ROLE OF THE OMBUDSMAN

A report by Paramadina Institute on disputes over the construction of churches in Jakarta highlighted the need for checks on the role of the bureaucracy, including the local government and the police (Paramadina Institute 2011). It emphasized the way local governments bow to the pressure of hardline Islamic religious leaders or the campaigns of radical Islamic groups (Paramadina Institute 2011, pp. 79–80). It suggested that the position taken by local government leaders to church disputes directly affects the response of the police, who may charge a fee for their services (Paramadina Institute 2011, p. 18), often contributing to tension rather than assisting to resolve it. There is therefore a clear need for accountability mechanisms in terms of the actions of local authorities in these disputes.

There are several mechanisms available if religious minorities have a complaint against a local government authority regarding the processing, or cancellation of, a permit, and this may potentially contribute to resolving the conflict between religious communities. This chapter will focus on the Ombudsman given its prominence in these disputes more recently and in the Bogor Church Permit Case in particular. The National Indonesian Ombudsman was first established as part of the process of democratic reforms in 1999 (Crouch 2008, pp. 6–7) and later officially regulated by Law 37/2008 on the Ombudsman.[15] It has powers to receive complaints and conduct investigations into allegations of maladministration. It is a crime to obstruct the investigations of the Ombudsman, which carries a penalty of two years jail (Article 44). If the recommendations from its investigations are not followed, it can report government agencies to the legislature and the president (Article 38(4)). It is, however, a new concept in Indonesia and one that has struggled to gain national impact in the midst many other new and more prominent accountability mechanisms, such as the Corruption Eradication Commission.

Complaints have been made to the national Ombudsman,[16] to its regional branches, and to the local Ombudsman of Yogyakarta.[17] The national Ombudsman has received twelve cases up until 2011, six of these in West Java.[18] This may not seem like a large number, but this is partly because the Ombudsman can only receive complaints against government authorities, for example, not against other religious groups. The willingness and capacity of the Ombudsman to respond to such complaints often depends on whether the complaint is against a local government or against the Inter-religious Harmony Forum. The Ombudsman only has the power to investigate the actions of government institutions and therefore cannot pursue claims against the Inter-religious Harmony Forum, which is considered by the Ombudsman to be an independent body.[19] It is arguable, however, that the Forum should be classified as a government authority for the Ombudsman's investigations to ensure that it can be held accountable for its decisions, particularly given that it has a close association with the Ministry of Religion and its members may also work for the Ministry of Religion.

Nevertheless, the national Ombudsman has declined to respond to complaints in some cases. For example, in January 2007, a complaint was made to the National Ombudsman Representative Office for Central Java and the Special Province of Yogyakarta by the Indonesian Bethel Church about an application for a church permit in Purbalingga, Central Java.[20] In this case, the regent had rejected an application for a permit to build a church on the basis of the recommendation of the Forum.[21] After receiving the complaint, the Ombudsman responded to the complainant by determining that the case was outside its authority to investigate because it considered the Forum to be an independent body, not a government institution.[22]

Other churches have had more success in cities where a local Ombudsman office has been established. For example, in October 2008, the local Ombudsman of the province of Yogyakarta received a complaint about a church permit. The Ombudsman investigated the matter, facilitating consultations with the Inter-religious Harmony Forum, the Ministry of Religion, the church, and the local government. Several months later, on 24 March 2009, the local Ombudsman issued a recommendation concluding that the leader of the village had the power to reject permits, but must provide adequate reasons for his decision.[23] As no reasons had been provided in this case, the Ombudsman requested that reasons be given. There have been other cases, such as the Bogor Church Permit Case, where the recommendations of the Ombudsman have fallen on deaf ears.

BOGOR CHURCH PERMIT CASE

Before going into the details of this case, it needs to be clarified that this case is an exception. Out of only four cases of disputes over church permits that have gone to court, it is the only one that has not been resolved, that is, in which the court decision has not been enforced. It is also important to keep in mind that all four cases so far have occurred in West Java, a province with a majority-Muslim population and a history of radical Islam.

West Java is one of the most densely populated provinces in Indonesia, with only 4.6 per cent of the population, or about 2 million people, are Protestant, while just 1 per cent, less than 500,000 people, are Catholic (West Java Provincial Government 2012). The majority of the population, approximately 40 million people, identify as Muslim (West Java Provinical Government 2012). To cater for its Muslim population, West Java has the largest number of mosques of any province in Indonesia, with almost 38,000.[24] In contrast, there are only 1,075 Protestant churches and 117 Catholic churches.

West Java also has a history of hardline (*garis keras*) Muslims and is home to Darul Islam (Domain of Islam), a group that emerged in 1947 promoting the ideology of an Indonesian Islamic state (Dijk 1981). West Java has not only been a site for conflict between Muslims and Christians, but groups that are deemed to be "deviant" by some Islamic religious leaders have also been threatened and attacked. In terms of the city of Bogor in particular, the location of the church in the Bogor Church Permit Case is just a short drive down the road from the Jemaat Ahmadiyah Indonesia headquarters, which was attacked in 2005 because of concerns its teachings are "deviant" from Islam.[25] It is within this broader context that the Bogor Church Permit Case must be considered.

Origins of the Dispute

In 2008, the Indonesian Christian Church (Gereja Kristen Indonesia [GKI]) of Curug Mekar, Bogor, initiated a case in the Administrative Court for review of a decision by the local government to cancel its permit. In this case, which I will refer to as the Bogor Church Permit Case, the church challenged the power of the Head of the City of Bogor Administration and Planning Division to cancel its permit.[26] The church had initially applied for a permit from local authorities in 2002. The 1,700 member-church claims that it made numerous efforts to disseminate information about its plans, conducted community consultation, and even obtained video evidence of local residents agreeing to its proposal.[27] On 13 July 2006, four years later, the church was finally granted a permit to build.[28]

The permit was granted in 2006 during the transition phase from the old to the new permit regulation system, described earlier. Although the Joint Regulation was passed in March 2006, the new process had not yet been implemented in Bogor. According to the Chairperson of the Bogor Indonesian Ulama Council,[29] Mukri Adji, the Bogor Inter-religious Harmony Forum was only formed in 2007, so the dispute was already well underway by this time.[30]

The construction of the church initially appeared to have the full support of the local government, evident by the attendance of the mayor at the opening ceremony of the construction site to lay the first brick. Shortly after construction began, however, the church began to face increasing opposition from members of hardline Islamic groups such as the Islamic Defenders Front (FPI) and the Bogor Ulama Forum.[31] The lawyer for the church asserted that the church had amicable relationships with many long-standing Muslim residents in the area, but that it was Muslim residents who had moved into the area just two or three years ago who were encouraged by members of radical Islamic groups from outside the area to oppose the church.

On 14 February 2008, due to the staunch opposition, the City of Bogor Administration and Planning Department ("Bogor Administration") suspended the church's permit.[32] The church then took its case to court. In court, the Bogor Administration argued that one of the reasons that the church should not be built is because the road on which the church site is located was recently renamed after Islamic figure Kyai Haji Binu, the founder of Al Ghazali *pesantren* (Islamic boarding school) in Bogor.[33] The Bogor Administration also used evidence of high concentration of Muslim residents in the area to argue that a church should not be built in a "Muslim" area. This argument of course had no legal standing in court, and the church succeeded at the first instance. The Bogor Administration lodged a subsequent application to appeal the decision to the High Administrative Court in Jakarta, but it was dismissed. In January 2011, the Bogor Administration appealed to the Supreme Court, but the court refused to hear the case because, since 2004, it no longer has jurisdiction to hear appeals regarding complaints of regional government officials.[34] This means that the decision of the High Administrative Court stands and the church should now be able to continue construction.[35]

It is significant that this case was even taken to court, as a closer look at the situation demonstrates that religious minorities, in this case a Christian community, are often divided on the merits of taking legal action when such conflicts arise. According to the lawyer of the church in the Bogor Church Permit Case, it was difficult for the church to agree on instituting court proceedings because

> the image of the courts in Indonesia is very corrupt and they [the congregation members] were convinced we would lose ... one of the judges in the case was not embarrassed to say that he would accept the largest bribe.[36]

This suggests that the history of corruption within the judicial system is a significant deterrent for potential litigants in cases of religious intolerance. This case is not only remarkable because the church went to court, but also because it was successful. By law, this means the church can now recommence construction.

However, in a separate case, in June 2010 an Islamic coalition filed a complaint against the neighbourhood leader, alleging that he had forged signatures of local residents that were submitted by the church in support of its application for a permit. In January 2011, the District Court of Bogor found the neighbourhood leader guilty, although the church claimed that those signatures had not been included in the application for a permit.[37] It is unclear how this court decision affects the decision of the Administrative Court or whether it could be used as a basis to challenge the decision.

Law Enforcement beyond the Supreme Court

The dispute has continued to escalate since the Supreme Court declined to hear the case, which effectively affirmed the decision of the Administrative Court in favour of the church, with the mayor refusing to recognize the court decision in favour of the church. On 23 January 2011, several hardline Islamic groups, including Hizbut Tahrir and the Indonesian Muslim Communication Forum (known as Forkami) held a religious gathering in opposition to the church (Haryanto 2011). On 7 March 2011, a meeting was held between the church and the mayor in which the mayor offered to relocate the church to another building, although they refused. The mayor then issued a letter on 11 March 2011[38] in an attempt to cancel the permit for the second time. On the same day, the Chief of Police issued a letter[39] that stated that the church was not allowed to worship on the building site as it had been doing. Nevertheless, throughout 2011, the congregation continued to meet on Sundays on the side of the road outside the church property (Saudale 2011). They were occasionally met by Brimob[40] which at times broke up the gathering with water cannons. The church sent another letter to the Supreme Court requesting assistance. In June 2011, the Supreme Court issued a *fatwa*[41] stating that its 2010 decision not to hear the case was final and that it could not hear the church's concerns.

Having exhausted the legal system, the church leaders then complained to the national Ombudsman. The case was handled by one of the eight members of the Office of the Ombudsman, Budi Santoso.[42] In the course of their investigations, which included summoning the mayor to their office, they found that the mayor had lied about his alleged attempts to mediate with the church congregation, as such efforts had never been made (Rachman and Saudale 2011). In the course of the investigation, the Office of the Ombudsman received many letters from individuals and members of organizations such as Amnesty International and Human Rights Watch, including from countries such as Canada, Switzerland, the United States, Germany, the Netherlands, France, Japan, and Australia. These letters supported the church and called for the Ombudsman to ensure that the court decision is respected and enforced by the regional government.

On 8 July 2011, the Ombudsman issued a recommendation[43] instructing the mayor to cancel the letter he had issued on 11 March, advising the Minister of Home Affairs to monitor the situation to ensure the church could begin building, and warning the mayor to comply with a sixty-day deadline.[44] The Ombudsman therefore reinforced the need for the local government to respect the decision and authority of the Supreme Court.

This has not brought an end to the dispute, however. On 24 August, the mayor responded to the Ombudsman in a letter[45] in which he claimed that it was local residents who were protesting and that the church had falsified documents to obtain the permit. The local government decided that the best option for the church was to relocate and it would form a "relocation team" to facilitate the process, although the church rejected this proposal.

The sixty-day ultimatum lapsed and, given the failure of the mayor to respond adequately to the recommendations, the Ombudsman submitted its report to the legislature (Dewan Perwakilan Rakyat [DPR]) and the president.[46] They reported the mayor's continued defiance of the Administrative Court decision, and they did this in the hope that it may lead to the impeachment of the mayor.

The dispute then openly entered the political arena. It is reported that the then mayor of Bogor, Diani Budiarto, (who was serving his second term as mayor after being re-elected in 2009) was initially supported by several political parties, including the Indonesian Democratic Party of Struggle (PDI-P), Golkar, and the Islam-based Prosperous Justice Party (PKS). As a consequence of the recommendations of the Ombudsman, PDI-P has since withdrawn its support for the mayor, although Golkar and PKS still appear to be maintaining their support (Sihaloho 2011*b*). The mayor also made headlines in his own right, being dubbed "Indonesia's most controversial mayor" not only for his stance against the church, but also because he practises polygamy and took a fourth wife, who was just nineteen years old (*Jakarta Globe* 2011).[47] His controversial lifestyle aside, there appeared to be no political movement at the local level to place pressure on the mayor to comply with the court decision.

Several attempts at the national level had been made by the legislature to mediate between the local government and the church. In September 2011, the mayor was called to Commission III of the legislature to answer questions about his failure to enforce the Supreme Court decision (Rachman 2011). In November 2011, another meeting was held between representatives from the Bogor church and the legislature. This meeting proved controversial, however, with the Speaker of the legislature, Marzuki Alie, suggesting that negotiations facilitated by the legislature could substitute for the decision of the Supreme Court, and that it was not realistic for the court's decision to be enforced (Sihaloho 2011*a*). This stirred debate about authority of the courts and the right of the legislature to intervene in such disputes.

This dispute remains ongoing at the time this chapter was written and demonstrates the limited reach of the law without the political will to ensure law enforcement of court decisions that are in favour of religious minorities. Despite the limitations of a legal approach, there have been calls for reform to the Joint Regulation, which could affect the way disputes over permits are handled in the future.

DRAFT LAW ON INTER-RELIGIOUS HARMONY

Despite the fact that there continue to be issues with the Joint Regulation, there remain calls for a law to further regulate inter-religious relations. As early as 1982, in response to inter-religious conflicts and calls for government intervention, the Ministry of Religion proposed a Draft Law on Religious Harmony. This failed to receive support, although a similar draft was proposed again in 1989 and 1997 (Aqsha et al. 1995, pp. 93–97). Then in 2002, the Ministry of Religion recommended discussions about the possibility of a Law on Religious Harmony.

In 2003, a Draft Law on Inter-religious Harmony was circulated and the Department of Research of the Ministry of Religion held a press conference explaining the Draft Law (*Tempo Interactive* 2003). The Draft Law addressed a wide range of issues, including religious education, marriage, blasphemy, places of worship, and burial practices. The key provisions of the 2003 Draft Law favoured the position of the Indonesian Ulama Council (MUI), endorsed by officials from the Ministry of Religion, as expressed through various *fatawa* over the years on key issues such as proselytization, religious celebrations, places of worship, family issues, and blasphemy.

In 2006, however, the issue of places of worship was dealt with by the Ministry of Religion through a Joint Regulation. Part of the reason for this regulation was to contain vigilante acts of violence against churches, although these have continued since 2006. As a result, there have been some calls from hardline Islamic religious leaders for the Ministry of Religion to upgrade this regulation to the status of a law, and one of the ideas that has been suggested is to include the provisions of the 2006 Joint Regulation in a Draft Law on Inter-Religious Harmony.

This proposal was put forward as recently as August 2011 with the overall idea being that the Draft Law would be a "legal umbrella", incorporating existing ministerial regulations on religious activities into one law to regulate inter-religious relations. Somewhat surprisingly, the 2011 version of the Draft Law on Inter-religious Harmony takes a different approach to the requirements for an application for a permit and would potentially make significant changes if it replaced the Joint Regulation, although it is unclear whether these changes would improve the permit application process.

The Draft Law 2011 would retain the Inter-religious Harmony Forum as a "consultative body" (Article 35(2)) to facilitate permits and promote good relations between religious communities, which it defines by the principles of tolerance, togetherness, non-discrimination and orderliness (Article 2). The composition and responsibilities of the Forum and its role in approving permit applications would remain largely the same.

The main difference, however is that there is no 90/60 requirement. The main provisions on permits for places of worship are set out in Chapter 3. Article 24 contains provisions that the application must be based on a real need for a place of worship similar to Article 13 of the Joint Regulation. Article 25 then sets out a more specific list of authorities that an applicant would have to obtain permission from, including the Ministry of Religion and the local village head, who must consult with religious organizations and leaders in the area. Although this list is not included in the Joint Regulation, in practice it is usually necessary for applications to go through these authorities in order to obtain permission. Article 26 has a more specific set of requirements an application must satisfy. These include a list of all the members of the religious group that live in the area and will use the building, and a list of the committee members who oversee the construction of the place of worship. This is different from the current requirement, which only requires an application to include at least 90 members of a religious group. The elimination of the 90/60 requirement could potentially be an improvement if it means that groups with lower than 90 members may still have the opportunity to obtain a permit if they satisfy the other requirements. On the other hand, it is not often this requirement that is the real obstacle, with religious minorities often being able to satisfy the threshold number of 90 members, but still facing opposition and therefore not being granted a permit. In addition, the Draft Law does not provide any further guidance over how disputes are to be resolved if and when they arise (Article 27).

Although the Draft Law 2011 failed to be passed as law, it remained on the legislative agenda for 2011–14. It is unlikely to be approved by 2014, however, as the Draft Law 2011 provoked conflicting reactions from members of the legislature and criticism from NGOs. At this stage, it appears that the legislature is unable to come to an agreement on what the provisions of the Draft Law should contain. Further, the real concern here is that the government appears to be focused on the need for more laws, rather than addressing the more pressing need of improving law enforcement.

CONCLUSIONS

This leads us to the question of whether religious minorities in democratic Indonesia can have faith in the legal system. Despite court success in challenging the decision of regional governments to cancel their permits, only some Christian congregations have been able to continue to build churches. Others, like the Bogor Church Permit Case, continue to face opposition from local government, in defiance of the court order. This poses a threat to the integrity of the courts and raises questions about the practical effect of court decisions, which is a problem in many areas of law, including for cases concerning religious minorities. There are real concerns among NGOs that if a local mayor remains allowed to defy a decision of the Supreme Court, this will have negative consequences on the rule of law and respect for the authority of the courts in Indonesia. This demonstrates that government policy on religious tolerance may be undermined by the uncertainty of law enforcement and the failure to uphold court decisions.

On the positive side, the Bogor Church Permit Case was a boost to the Office of the Ombudsman, which has struggled to gain influence in

Indonesia amidst the range of new commissions and agencies created to improve government accountability and transparency in the transition to democracy (*Jakarta Globe* 2011). The complaint made to the Ombudsman by the church leaders not only generated significant publicity and media for the Bogor Church Permit Case, but also for the Office of the Ombudsman itself. This has helped to raise the profile of the Office of the Ombudsman as an avenue of complaints against government agencies and has potentially educated other minority groups about the possibility of complaining to the Ombudsman regarding maladministration issues.

It needs to be kept in mind, however, that this case is something of an exception. For example, a report by Paramadina Institute also found that there are encouraging efforts being made by some local leaders to resolve church permits at the grassroots level, consistent with Indonesia's long history of religious diversity and tolerance (Paramadina Institute 2011). The report suggested that it is local community leaders, often the head of the local neighbourhood unit (RW/RT), who are the most powerful determinants in the outcome of a dispute over a church. It also highlighted the importance of personal relationships between the church and the wider local community and demonstrated the many ways some church leaders actively try to connect with local community leaders, while also encouraging churches to continue to make these bridge-building efforts.

Finally, disputes over permits for places of worship of religious minorities are complex and affected by a wide range of issues, which may not adequately be captured by the labels of "religious minority" and "religious majority". The dispute may be between a religious minority and local government authorities who, to some extent, may be supported by hardline Islamic groups that only represent a minority of the Muslim community. In other areas of Indonesia where the population is majority Buddhist or majority Christian, similar difficulties are encountered by minority Muslim communities seeking permits. The debate in Indonesia over the extent to which the law can and should be used to regulate inter-religious relations is complex and will continue for some time to come. In the Bogor Church Permit Case, if efforts to impeach the mayor are not successful, it may be up to voters at the next local election to express their voice at the ballot box. More broadly, in seeking resolutions to these disputes, we can only hope that Indonesia's strong tradition of tolerance at the grassroots level will prevail.

Notes

1. Joint Ministerial Regulation Nos. 8 and 9 of 2006 on the Implementation of the Task of the District Head/Representative of the District Head to Maintain Religious Harmony, Equip the Religious Harmony Forum and Regulate the Building of Places of Worship.
2. Joint Decree of the Minister of Religious and Internal Affairs No. 1/1969 on the Implementation of Government Mandates for Ensuring Law and Order and the Effective Administration of Religious Development and Worship by Religious Followers.
3. The six recognized religions are Islam, Protestantism, Catholicism, Hinduism, Buddhism, and Confucianism, as set out in the Elucidation to Presidential Decision 1/1965 on the Prevention of Misuse and/or Disrespect of Religion. This does not mean that other religions or beliefs, such as Judaism, Zoroastrianism, Shintoism, and Taoism are banned. As long as they do not disturb the community, adherents of other religions are also free to practise their religion in principle. It does mean that other religions or beliefs do not get a seat on the Forum. For a detailed explanation of this law, see Crouch (2012a).
4. For example, members are elected for three years to the provincial Forum of Central Kalimantan, while members to the provincial Forum of Yogyakarta are elected for five-year terms. See Regulation of the Governor of Central Kalimantan 6/2007 on the Inter-religious Harmony Forum, Article 2; Regulation of the Governor of Yogyakarta 10/2007 on the Inter-religious Harmony Forum, revised by Regulation 31/2008, Article 3, respectively. Other regulations establish the Forum in broad terms and do not provide details about the criteria for members or the terms of membership. For example, see the Regulation of the Governor of Riau 21a/2006 on the Inter-religious Harmony Forum.
5. This concern was expressed at the first Bi-Annual Forum Congress held on 6–10 December 2007 in Jakarta; see Forum Kerukunan Umat Beragama, *Rumusan Keputusan Komisi A Kongres FKUB*, Ministry of Religion, North Jakarta, 7–9 December 2007.
6. For example, Wijsen and Singgih (2009) conducted a survey of the views of thirty Protestant ministers and students from Duta Wacana Christian University, Yogyakarta, on the Joint Regulation and the Forum. The survey revealed a very wide range of attitudes about the influence of the new regulation on churches. See also Wahid Institute (2007, 2008).
7. See generally Paramadina Institute (2011).
8. If there are fewer than sixty members of a congregation in the village, then the total number of religious followers in the sub-regency, city/regency, or province can be relied on Article 13(3). Law 28/2002 on the Construction

of Buildings, Article 5(3); Government Regulation 36/2005 on the Construction of Buildings, Article 4(2).
9   A building has a "religious function" if its primary use is as a place of worship, such as a mosque or *musholla* (small room set aside for prayer), a church or chapel, a Hindu temple (*pura*), Buddhist monastry (*vihara*), or Confucian temple (*kelenteng*).
10 According to Federspiel (1995, p. 39), "*Bulughul Maram* is a well-known text on tradition criticism and usage by Ibnu Hajarul Asqalani (d. 1448) which has had long usage in Indonesia." See also Feener (2007, p. 36).
11 For an Indonesian translation of *Bulughul Maram*, see Hassan (1964).
12 Muhammadiyah is the largest modernist Islamic organization in Indonesia.
13 For further discussion of the opinions of the different schools of law on the numbers prescribed for Friday prayers, see Bakhtiar (1996, p. 103); Abd al-Rahman al-Jaziri (2009, pp. 509–11).
14 As defined by Article 13(3), that is, at least in the same province as the proposed location of the church: Article 14(2)(a).
15 See also Law 25/2009 on the Public Service which refers to the role of the Ombudsman in investigating complaints concerning the public service.
16 Although the national Ombudsman began in 2000 by Presidential Decree 44/2000, it was not established by law until 2008: Law 37/2008 on the national Ombudsman. Local Ombudsmen also exist in Indonesia, but these remain the initiatives of particular provinces and do not come under the authority of the national Ombudsman: Crouch (2007), pp. 17–18; Crouch (2008).
17 The offices of the regional Ombudsman are not under the umbrella of the national Ombudsman, but are rather separate initiatives of particular local governments.
18 Indonesian National Ombudsman, *Laporan Kepada Ombudsman 2001–2010* (Jakarta: Ombudsman Nasional, 2010). This figure does not include any cases that may have been received by the branches of the Ombudsman based outside of Jakarta. In November 2011, the office had just received a case concerning a dispute over the construction of a mosque in North Sumatra.
19 Law 37/2008 on the National Ombudsman, Article 6. Interview with Ahmad Baso, 2 December 2010.
20 Letter of the Purbalingga Inter-religious Harmony Forum No. 03/FKUB/IX/2007 concerning the Request for a Permit for a Place of Worship, dated 21 September 2007.
21 Recommendation of the Purbalingga Inter-religious Harmony Forum No. 450/01/2007 rejecting the application for a permit for a place of worship on No. 20B Kapten Street, Sarengat.
22 Letter of the Ombudsman No. 0157/SRT/00821.2009/yg-11/VIII/2009 from the Head of the Office of the Ombudsman Regional Office, Yogyakarta and Central Java, dated 14 August 2009.

23 Rekomendasi Lembaga Ombudsman Daerah Provinsi Daerah Istimewa Yogyakarta berkaitan Laporan Pemanfaatan Bangunan Untuk Rumah Ibadah, dated 24 March 2009.
24 This number excludes *musholla*, prayer rooms, see Ministry of Religion, "Table 2: Places of Worship 2008", 2010, available at <http://www.depag.go.id>.
25 See also Fuller and Bush and Munawar-Rahman in this volume. For an analysis of the bans issued by local governments, including Bogor, against Ahmadiyah see generally Crouch (September 2012*b*).
26 Administrative Court Decision No. 41/G/2008/PTUN-BDG in the Bogor Church Permit Case, dated 2 September 2008.
27 Interview with Fatmawati Djugo, lawyer, Jakarta, 14 December 2009.
28 Letter of the Mayor of Bogor, No. 645.8-372/2006 concerning a building permit, dated 13 July 2006.
29 The Indonesian Ulama Council (Majelis Ulama Indonesia) is a national organization of Islamic religious leaders that is recognized by the Department of Religion and claims to speak on behalf of the Islamic community.
30 Interview with Mukri Ali, Jakarta, 10 November 2009.
31 Administrative Court Decision No. 41/G/2008/PTUN-BDG in the Bogor Church Permit Case, dated 2 September 2008, pp. 24–25.
32 Letter of the Head of the City of Bogor Administration and Planning No. 503/208-DTKP concerning the suspension of a permit, dated 14 February 2008.
33 Administrative Court Decision No. 41/G/2008/PTUN-BDG in the Bogor Church Permit Case, dated 2 September 2008, p. 27.
34 This is according to Article 45A(2)(c) that was introduced by Law 5/2004 concerning Amendments to Law 5/1986 on the Administrative Courts. A challenge to the constitutionality of this provision failed in the Constitutional Court: Decision No. 23/PUU-V/2007 issued on 14 January 2008.
35 Decision of Supreme Court, Letter No. 127 PK/TUN/2009 that it cannot hear the case and that the decision of the High Administrative Court of Bandung is final, dated 2 December 2010.
36 Interview with Fatmawati Djugo, lawyer, 14 December 2009, Jakarta.
37 District Court of Bogor, Decision No. 265/PidB/2010/PN, Bogor, in the case of Munir Karta.
38 Letter of the Mayor of Bogor, No. 645.45-137/2011.
39 Letter of the Chief Police of Bogor, No. B/1226/3/2011.
40 Mobile Brigade, or Brigade Mobil, is a special operations unit of the Indonesian police force.
41 *Fatwa* of the Supreme Court, No. 45/Td.TUN/VI/2011. *Fatwa* here refers to a guideline issued by the court, rather than an Islamic legal decision.
42 Interview with Budi Santoso, one of eight members of the National Office of the Ombudsman, Jakarta, 8 November 2011.

43 Recommendation of the National Ombudsman No. 0011/REK/0259.2010/BS-15/VII/2011.
44 The sixty-day deadline for compliance with the recommendations of the Ombudsman is set out in Article 38(2) of Law 37/2008 of the National Ombudsman.
45 Letter of the Mayor of Bogor No. 452.2/2085-huk to the National Ombudsman.
46 If the recommendations of the Ombudsman are not followed, the Ombudsman may then submit the report to the legislature and the President, according to Article 38(4) of Law 37/2008 of the National Ombudsman.
47 Law No. 10/1983 on Permission to Marry and Divorce for Civil Servants states that civil servants may only have more than one wife if they have obtained permission from their superiors.

References

Abd al-Rahman al-Jaziri. *Islamic Jurisprudence According to the Four Sunni Schools*, vol. 1, translated by Nancy Roberts. Canada: Fons Vitae, 2009.

Aqsha, Darul, Dick van der Meij, and Johan Dendrik Meuleman. *Islam in Indonesia: A Survey of Events and Developments from 1988 to March 1993*. Jakarta: INIS, 1995.

Bakhtiar, Laleh. *Encyclopedia of Islamic Law: A Compendium of the Major Schools*. Chicago: ACB International Group, 1996.

Crouch, Melissa. "Regulation on Places of Worship in Indonesia: Upholding the Right to Freedom of Religion for Religious Minorities?" *Singapore Journal of Legal Studies* (July 2007): 1–21.

———. "Indonesia's National and Local Ombudsman Reforms: Salvaging a Failed Experiment?" In *Indonesia: Law and Society*, 2nd ed., edited by Tim Lindsey. Sydney: Federation Press, 2008.

———. "Implementing the Regulation on Places of Worship in Indonesia: New Problems, Local Politics and Court Action". *Asian Studies Review* 34 (December 2010): 403–19.

———. "Law and Religion in Indonesia: The Blasphemy Law and the Constitutional Court". *Asian Journal of Comparative Law* 7, no. 1 (May 2012*a*).

———. "Judicial Review and Religious Freedom: The Case of Indonesian Ahmadis". *Sydney Law Review* 34, no. 3 (September 2012*b*): 545–72.

Dijk, C. van. *Rebellion Under the Banner of Islam: The Darul Islam in Indonesia*. The Hague: Nijhoff, 1981.

Federspiel, Howard. *A Dictionary of Indonesian Islam*. Athens: Centre for International Studies, Ohio University, 1995.

Feener, Michael. *Muslim Legal Thought in Modern Indonesia*. Cambridge: Cambridge University Press, 2007.

Haryanto, Ulma. "Indonesian Hardliners Rally against Bogor Churches Arrogance". *Jakarta Globe*, 30 November 2011. Available at <http://www.thejakartaglobe.com>.

Hassan, A. *Tardjamah Bulùghul-Maràm: Beserta Keterangannja, Dengan Muqaddimah Ilmu Hadits dan Ushul-Fiqih*. Bandung: Diponegoro, 1964.

Jakarta Globe. "Bogor Mayor Takes Teenager as His Fourth Wife", 24 June 2011. Available at <http://www.thejakartaglobe.com>.

———. "Ombudsman's Office Struggles to Stay Afloat", 26 September 2011. Available at <http://www.thejakartaglobe.com>.

Paramadina Institute. *Kontroversi Gereja Indonesia* [Disputed Churches in Jakarta]. Jakarta: Centre for the Study of Religion and Society (CRCS) and Paramadina, 2011. Available at <crcs.ugm.ac.id/get/PCjk>.

Rachman, Anita. "Bogor Mayor Lashed by Lawmakers for 'Sick' Logic in Yasmin Church Row". *Jakarta Globe*, 15 September 2011. Available at <http://www.thejakartaglobe.com>.

Rachman, Anita and Vento Saudale. "Ombudsman to Refer Bogor Mayor to SBY over Church". *Jakarta Globe*, 19 September 2011. Available at <http://www.thejakartaglobe.com>.

Saudale, Vento. "Satpol PP in Bogor Clash with GKI Yasmin Faithful". *Jakarta Globe*, 10 October 2011. Available at <http://www.thejakartaglobe.com>.

Sihaloho, Markus Junianto. "Indonesian Church Fight Is Job for DPR, Not Courts: Marzuki Claims". *Jakarta Globe*, 30 November 2011*a*. Available at <http://www.thejakartaglobe.com>.

———. "Golkar Stands by Bogor Mayor, for Now". *Jakarta Globe*, 9 November 2011*b*. Available at <http://www.thejakartaglobe.com>.

Soefyanto. *Pendirian Rumah Ibadat dan Catatan Perkembangan Pembahasannya*. Jakarta: Universitas Islam, 2009.

Tan, Chrestella. "Ombudsman Comes Through for Embattled Bogor Church". *Jakarta Globe*, 19 July 2011. Available at <http://www.thejakartaglobe.com>.

Tempo Interactive. "UU Kerukunan Umat Beragama tidak Diperlukan", 2 December 2003. Available at <http://www.pdat.co.id>.

Wahid Institute. "Forum atau Birokratisasi Kerukunan Umat Beragama?" *Nawala* no. 3 (July–October 2007). Available at <http://www.wahid-institute.org>.

———. "Menapaki Bangsa yang Kian Retak". Annual Report on Belief and Religious Pluralism in Indonesia, 2008. Available at <http://www.wahid-institute.org>.

West Java Provincial Government. "Total Number of Religious Adherents in West Java According to City or Regency". Available at <http://www.jabarprov.go.id> (accessed 10 January 2012).

Wijsen, Franz and Gerrit Singgih. "Regulation on Houses of Worship: A Threat to Social Cohesion?" In *Religion, Civil Society and Conflict in Indonesia*, edited by Carl Sterkens, Muhammad Machasin and Frans Wijsen. Wien: Lit, 2009.

7

IN EACH OTHER'S SHADOW
Building Pentecostal Churches in Muslim Java

En-Chieh Chao[1]

"For the pillars of the temple stand apart And the oak tree and the cypress grow not in each other's shadow."

— Kahlil Gibran

INTRODUCTION

Home to the world's largest Muslim population, Indonesia would seem an unlikely destination for a Christian revival. The rapid growth of Pentecostal congregations across the archipelago in recent years, however, reveals just such a development. Today, Indonesia not only nourishes numerous vibrant Pentecostal communities, it also accommodates dozens of auditorium-size mega-churches filled with thousands of worshippers in several Muslim-majority cities. The historians Aritonang and Steenbrink suggest that among the 17 million Indonesian Protestants, at least 6 million are Pentecostals, including those who are still registered in mainline churches (2008, pp. 882–83). In its celebration of the Holy Spirit's gifts — speaking in tongues, healing, and prophesying — Pentecostalism is particularly successful in converting mainline Protestants[2] and Catholics (Chao 2011; Nagata 2005; Robinson 2005). Over the last twenty years, almost in parallel to the children of Javanist Muslims[3] turning into consciously orthodox

Muslims, the offspring of Indonesian mainline ethnic church members have embraced the identity of born-again Christians in great numbers.

Charismatic churches are growing apace in Indonesia amidst rising tensions between religious communities. In West Java during the last decade, animosities between certain hardline Islamizers and aggressive evangelicals have triggered attacks against churches (Jones 2010, p. 1). On the other end of the archipelago, Pentecostalism has been a major rallying point among the Dani of Irian Jaya in opposition to the rising number of Muslim migrants (Farhadian 2007, p. 117). In 2011, a suicide bomber struck the Bethel Full Gospel Church in Surakarta in Central Java — a Pentecostal church affiliated with the best-selling author Rick Warren's megachurch in the United States — and injured 28 people (Kumar 2011). In the same region earlier that year, extremists[4] had vandalized three churches in retaliation for the allegation that local Pentecostal churches were converting Muslims.

Despite these attacks, evangelical Christian and Pentecostal communities continue to find ways to erect churches throughout the country. As the renowned Indonesian evangelical preacher Stephen Tong commented defiantly when his new mega-church opened in Jakarta in 2008, "I've built a bigger one than all the destroyed churches combined" (Ng 2008). But it is difficult to predict whether the erection of mega-churches would incite more anti-Christian sentiments. As Christian and Islamic movements continue to assert their public influence, it is urgent to understand how people across religious borders live together, negotiate their various worldviews, and achieve a kind of religious tolerance and civility that is feasible and meaningful to them.

In taking up this line of inquiry, the following discussion focuses on the pattern of religious pluralism in the Central Javanese city of Salatiga. The research is based on twelve months of fieldwork between 2009 and 2010 with two middle-class Pentecostal congregations, Fendi and Ester (pseudonyms), with 400 and 150 members, respectively, leaders of the mainstream Muslim organizations Nahdlatual Ulama and Muhammadiyah, college students of the State Islamic Institute (STAIN), and general occurrences in the city proper. The contrast between Muslims' and Christians' views on Christian worship facilities will help us to problematize the idea of religious pluralism.

Two points are crucial in understanding the alternating perspectives of religious pluralism. First, throughout human history pluralism in practice always works in favour of privileged groups and is never simply a matter of equal expression for all. The current situation of Salatiga is no exception. On the one hand, Christians have to be extra cautious in

Muslim-majority areas and make efforts to downplay any acts or words of theirs that might imply they are part of a plot to Christianize the society, which is locally known as "Christianization" (*Kristenisasi*) — a term that carries an unequivocally negative connotation. Even if Christians have qualms about what they perceive as their vulnerability, they confine these within the walls of churches. On the other hand, despite their numerical predominance and the flowering of Islamic resurgence over the last two decades, Muslims continue to feel threatened by Christianity. Muslims' critiques of Christianization are widely circulated in public, and we will discuss the rationales behind the critiques.

The second lesson of the story of Salatiga is the importance of seeing inter-religious relations as constitutive of religious identities, rather than merely their by-product. Christian and Muslim communities are ever mindful of one another, and they take each other into consideration when formulating their opinions and actions. In others words, religious communities develop dialectically, not independently. A focus exclusively on one single community would lose sight of this entangled aspect of pluralism and overlook the fact that even the activities of religious minorities can critically reshape the identities of religious majorities. The periodical Muslim protests against the alleged plot to Christianize Indonesia in the national context are good examples, which I turn to in the following section.

ONE COMMUNITY'S ANXIETIES — ANOTHER'S SACRED RESPONSIBILITY

Christian missionary activities in Muslim-majority areas in Indonesia have never ceased to be controversial. During the colonial period, Christianity was typically viewed as the "white men's religion" and one of the forms of colonial domination, cultural invasion, and communal destruction. After independence in 1945, the perception of Christianity as being intrinsically connected to colonialism has partially faded away due to the state policy that has granted Christianity legitimacy in the country, yet its culturally imperial image lingers. Christian missionary societies have advanced and triumphed in education and medicine given their connections to and resources from the West. Moreover, the international discourse of "religious freedom" also privileges — often insensitively — the right to proselytize over the right against cultural invasion. A cautious sensibility against Christian expansion thus has long troubled Indonesian Muslim intellectuals, as much as their Middle Eastern counterparts (Laffan 2007). One must modernize with self-dignity, many great Muslim thinkers argue, in ways not unlike the nineteenth-century Japanese thinkers in their encounters with Western powers (Wakabayashi 1986). The goal was to modernize, but not under the shadow of the West and Christianity. Thus, despite the fact that Protestantism and Catholicism are among the state-approved religions that a citizen can legally choose to fulfil the universal requirement of religious affiliation, which was instituted following the 1965–66 anti-communist campaign, there is always a social implication of disloyalty if one converts to Christianity.

The state-endorsed pluralism has its limitations, and it certainly has promised different things to different constituencies. For Christian activists, it promises the right to choose religion and to change one's religion (Sidjabat 1960, p. 288), given their individualistic presumption about what religion is and should be. For many Muslim leaders, however, it grants the right for diverse religious communities to coexist, not a license for freely undermining other religious communities (Mujibrahman 2005). Seeing the steady growth of Christianity in the country, Muslim activists ever since lobbied the Department of Religious Affairs to restrict the activity of Christian missionaries in Muslim-majority areas; some Christian activists argued that this was a violation of human rights, but others decided to defer to the larger community. Eventually, the Ministry of Religion concluded in favour of the Islamic viewpoint by issuing two decrees in 1978 stating that it is forbidden to direct a new religion to a person or persons who already adhere to a particular faith (No. 70), and that official permission is required to build a new worship facility, or to receive foreign missionaries and funds (No. 77). In 2006, the laws were revised to require a larger number of signatures of approval from people living in the neighbourhood where a new worship place was to be built before construction could begin.

The controversy surrounding religious freedom appeared on paper with the two decrees, but in reality it never was. Like the difficult question posed by the contradiction between freedom and equality that has long troubled Western philosophers, the contradiction between individual freedom and communal solidarity has let to no easy answer. Christians were still active among non-Christians, although often in more cautious manners. Whenever churches received new converts who "already had another religion", evangelizers had to emphasize that it was a thoroughly voluntary act on the part of converts, that is, the result of mission without missionaries. Competing definitions of religious pluralism remain fundamentally incompatible and Muslims' fears of Christianization have remained acute, as will be shown in the Salatiga case.

CONTESTING THE IDENTITY OF SALATIGA

Salatiga is a picturesque hilly town situated forty kilometers south of Semarang, the provincial capital, and surrounded by volcanic ridges. It numbers about one hundred seventy thousand residents, with 21 per cent of whom consisting of Protestants or Catholics. This is a high percentage in a province where 96 per cent of the population is Muslim, even higher than the nationwide proportion of Muslims which is 88 per cent. Due to such a sizable Christian community, mutually influenced by the presence of the renowned Christian University of Satya Wacana, Salatiga is known in Central Java as "a Christian city".

But Salatiga has been changing. On 2 March 2008, 5,000 Muslims gathered in the mosque *Al-Atiq Kauman* and walked to the residence of Salatiga's incumbent Christian mayor John Manuel Manoppo to demand the right to the state-owned land called White Cross (Salib Putih). In the late nineteenth century, White Cross was used by the Salvation Army and a huge part of the land is currently used by the Javanese Christian Church (GKJ). In the 2000s, the lease for Salib Putih was up for renewal after thirty years of use. In 2007, the Muslim mayor who had won re-election in 2006 passed away, and his Christian vice-mayor Manoppo succeeded him with a new Muslim vice-mayor. Still, not all Muslims were happy with "a Christian mayor". No sooner than Manoppo had taken up the post, Muslim groups demanded access to Salib Putih. The protesters came from various Islamic organizations such as the Indonesian Network of Mosque Youth (JRMI), the Muslim Students Association (HMI), the Union of Indonesian Muslim Students Action (KAMMI), the Student Movement of Indonesian Islam (PMII), Ansor (the youth branch of Nahdlatul Ulama [NU], the largest Muslim organization in Indonesia), and Pemuda Muhammadiyah (the youth wing of the largest modernist organization in the country). They were coordinated by the Salatiga branch of the Indonesian Council of Ulamas (MUI). The dispute remained unsettled; it only led to more resistance against "*Kristenisasi*" (Christianization).

In tandem with the protests on the ground, Muslim discontent over Salib Putih also spread on the internet. An article was circulated among college students online titled "Salatiga, Under the Shadow of Christianity" (*Salatiga, Di Bawah Bayang-bayang Kristen*) (Sukur 2002). In this article, the author criticizes Indonesians' impression of Salatiga as a Christian city despite its Muslim majority. He asserts that there are many signs of Christianization in the Salatiga region and calls for more *da'wah* (Islamic proselytization) among fellow Muslims in the city. The gist of the article is this: Christians are the minority, but they dominate the city. Why does the

Muslim majority accept this? With its provocative tone, the article framed the need for an Islamic revival in Salatiga as inextricably linked to defend Muslims against Christianization. The article even appeared on a short-lived hardline Muslim blog called "Pious Salatiga Muslims On the Net" (*Santri Salatiga On the Net*). The editors of the blog, whose identities were not revealed, promoted a project called "Salatiga, the City of Pious Muslims" (*Salatiga Kota Santri*) to raise awareness among Muslim citizens in order to diminish the influence of Christianity in Salatiga.

All these contestations surrounding the religious identity of the city, however, are but the new manifestations of an ongoing project of religious transformation. In fact, for at least two decades, and thus well before the protest in 2008, Salatiga had been less and less of a "Christian city". If anything, Salatiga has never been more Islamic. The most visible changes are the mushrooming of shops displaying vast collections of headscarves, veiled women heading towards Islamic sermon meetings, traffic jams around the main mosques prior to Friday prayers, and, above all, the much greater number of mosques. While the relative proportions of religious adherents have been in equilibrium since the 1970s (see Figure 7.1),[5] the number of worship facilities

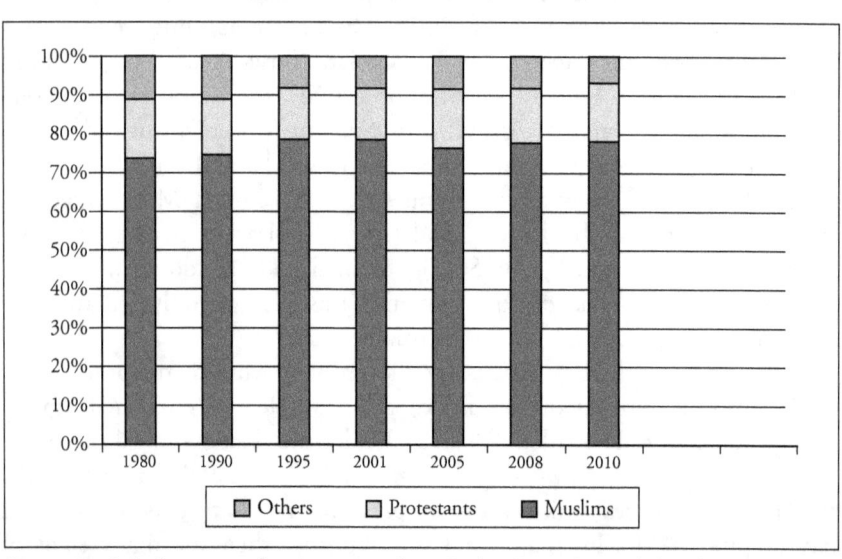

Figure 7.1
Religious Populations in Salatiga

Source: Statistical reports of various years from Badan Pusat Statistik (BPS) Kota Salatiga and Badan Perencanaan Pembangunan Daerah (BAPPDA) (Religional Development Planning Board).

has grown at a great pace. More than any other worship places, mosques have had the highest growth rate, 642 per cent since 1980 (from 26 to 193 buildings, see Figure 7.2, compared to 22 and 72 Protestant churches).

The growth of mosques may be more impressive than these numbers might suggest. This is because, unlike a church, a mosque relies on a different type of social ecology to grow. While a large mosque may serve a wider congregation beyond the residents of its location, most mosques in the city are still embedded in local neighbourhoods, the most important social community besides the family in Javanese society. By contrast, a church congregation is a group of volunteers whose members are most often not neighbours and whose social relations are not defined by location. Because of this, there is an incentive for the smallest neighbourhood unit to refrain from building more mosques once it has obtained sufficient facilities. It would therefore be incorrect to directly relate the proportion of the number of worship facilities to the religious population per capita and conclude that Protestant Christians have a slight advantage. Given the different social ecology mosques and churches rely on, the overall advantage for Muslims should not be overlooked.

**Figure 7.2
Number and Types of Worship Facilities in Salatiga**

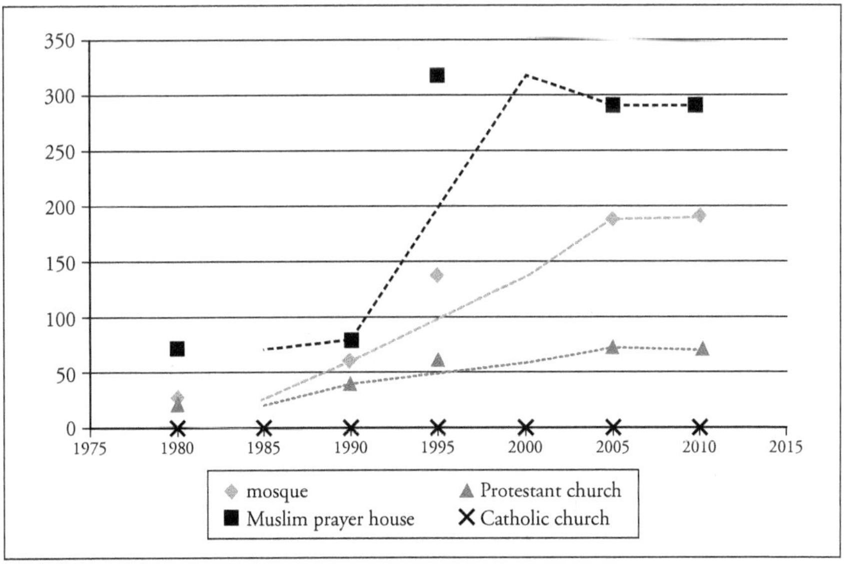

Source: Statistical reports of various years from Badan Pusat Statistik (BPS) Kota Salatiga and Badan Perencanaan Pembangunan Daerah (BAPPDA) (Religional Development Planning Board).

One might rightfully ask, first: since Islamic facilities have so successfully permeated almost every corner of the city, what do 5,000 Muslim protesters see in White Cross, besides a piece of land, without which Muslim facilities still thrive? Second, how are Christians to deal with the accusation that their presence casts a "shadow" over the city?

In early January, 2010, I was invited to speak on a panel in the national intermediate training of HMI held in Edi-Mancoro, a *pesantren* (Islamic boarding school) located on the outskirts of Salaitga that has a reputation for promoting civic pluralism and holding regular inter-religious prayer events. The HMI training invited scholars from various backgrounds to give talks on democracy, pluralism, gender justice, and other topics. Once I talked to the members of HMI in private and I asked about their perceptions of inter-religious relations in Salatiga. Mbak Sri,[6] a second-year student of STAIN and the head of the women's wing in HMI at Salatiga, told me in agitation:

> The issue of Christianization (*Kristenisasi*) is a serious one. Many people have the impression that this is a Christian city, while the truth is that it is *not*. [Yet] even though Christians are the minority, they are strong. We [Muslims] are the majority, but we are not united. Recently we again see a new church being built, just around the Pancasila Plaza. This is but one sign of Christianization in this city. That's why we Muslims have to work together. That's why we allied with all other Muslim organizations to protest at the continuing domination over the land of White Cross by Christians (field notes, 8 January 2010).

With regard to viewing things from Mbak Sri's standpoint, I came to realize that the configuration of her resistance to *Kristenisasi* has a genealogy that predates the publishing of the article "Salatiga, Under the Shadow of Christianity". Her concerns share a great deal with the thoughts of the revered Indonesian thinker Hamka in his firm critique of the Western colonization of mentality. The fear of *Kristenisasi* and the erosion of Muslim community, while seemingly hyperbolic in Java, definitely can strike mass sentiments forcefully in Salatiga. In this manner, Islamic resurgence in Salatiga has been partially, but critically, tied to the fear of Christianization. One has to look into the part of the religious self that is shaped by its outlook on the religious other, in order to make sense of the persistent insecurity of both the minority and the majority.

It is in the mode of learning to detect these insecure feelings that we will proceed to explore two kinds of insecurities under the same shadow.

In the case of Pentecostal churches, it is the miracle narratives that help the believers justify their existence. In the case of the Muslim mainstream leaders of NU and Muhammadiyah, it is a call for an alliance across different Muslim factions to face a common enemy.

MIRACLE DISCOURSES SURROUNDING THE BUILDING OF CHARISMATIC CHURCHES

A forty-seven-year-old son of a Catholic family, Toni Yusuf, converted to Pentecostalism after his wife's miraculous pregnancy in 1988 despite numerous medical confirmations of her infertility. One day in 1990, he reports having had a dream. In this dream, a beam of light brought him to a familiar space in the dormitory run by his mother-in-law. The rooms were nice and empty, but he could hear the imminent noise of cheerful crowds moving towards him. Another light led him to see a banner on top of the building, and there, the word "Ester" was glaringly inscribed on it, foreign to him. The dormitory became a church, and the Pentecostal convert awoke (interview with Toni Yusuf, 10 December 2010).

Toni Yusuf told his wife about his dream and learned from friends about the existence of a church named Ester, but he soon forgot about the dream. Several years later he was encouraged by a spiritual mentor (*bapak rohani*) from an Ester congregation based in Semarang to organize a bible study group (*Family Altar* [FA]). His FA was successful enough that he was often asked by different people if he wanted to build a church, but he always denied having any such plans. But the mentor kept telling him "This will become a church. It definitely will" (interview with Toni Yusuf, 25 January 2010).

Toni did not believe it. He had no place and no money. Most importantly, he did not wish to become a pastor. Years later, when Toni wrote an article addressing the history of his congregation for the church website,[7] he cited Psalm 127:1 "Unless the Lord builds the house, its builders labor in vain" (interview with Toni Yusuf, 10 December 2009). Toni's church opened in 1998, built upon the renovated dormitory that belongs to his mother-in-law. The prophetic dream became reality.

Toni Yusuf's story is not only popular among the local congregation, but also received some attention from local and national Christian media. His experience was understood as a miracle. It was published in a Christian magazine based in Salatiga and in the official Ester magazine in Surabya, arguably the "capital" of Pentecostalism in Indonesia. The latter is circulated nation-wide.

A similar story is said to have taken place at almost exactly the same time in the city. This time, it was with a sixteen-year-old boy named Dimas.[8] Dimas observed that thousands of freshmen arrived at the Christian University of Satya Wacana each year. He did not notice that, despite the religious affiliation of the university, the majority of the students were Muslim. What Dimas highlighted was that some of the Christian students, once detached from their families, stopped going to church. Dimas was disappointed to see that the newcomers were eroding the reputation of Salatiga as "a Christian city". As a result, he started a worship group with a few other enthusiastic friends. As the worship group grew bigger, Dimas was encouraged by a pastor from Semarang to initiate a church. The young leader rejected the idea, protesting that he had no intention to build a church. In fact, in order to show just how much he disagreed with the idea, he disbanded the fellowship and ordered his followers to go to other churches.

That move did not work out well. All of a sudden, Dimas' followers stopped going to church. He felt guilty because he was the one who brought them to Jesus, but also the one who abandoned them. As a result, in order to bring these "lost sheep" back again to Jesus Christ, Dimas finally agreed to start a congregation in 1998, which became Fendi church. The inception of both Fendi and Ester is thus narrated not as deriving from human intention, but presented in public as the result of divine intervention through *mujizat*, or miracles. In the case of Dimas, the miracle is the mysterious working of God that first confused the young leader and his followers, but eventually brought them to submit to the idea of starting a new congregation. In the case of Pak Toni, the miracle is the prophetic dream and the fulfilled prophecy.

In telling these origin stories of the congregations, Ester and Fendi are sending a similar message: It was never their intention to build a church. Rather, the initiators were chosen by destiny or divine will. Although not explicitly stated, the undertone regarding the Christian minority's status behind these narratives is clear: Just like one can rarely admit the intention to convert Muslims into Christians, one can rarely "have the intention" to build a church. Christianization is such a taboo that the denial of an intent to build a church has logically become the part of churches' own origin stories.

Although human initiatives weigh significantly in the process of building a new Pentecostal church, they are downplayed within the miracle narratives. Before remembering his dream, Toni Yusuf in fact had looked at several different places as candidates for the location of his church-to-be, only to meet objections from neighbourhoods and other established churches in the city. His plans were at such an impasse in late 1996, when he failed to gain permission several times, that his wife reminded him of the prophetic dream in which his mother-in-law's boarding house was turned into a church. Similarly, before Dimas could start a new church, he had led his followers through the "vagrant" phase where they moved from unused classrooms, a rented place in a GKJ church, and other temporary places. These difficulties and endeavours to secure a worship place are not mentioned in the officially documented origin story.

The discourse of fantastic wonder and divine intervention, of course, is not unique to Pentecostalism in Indonesia.[9] But for Indonesian Pentecostals, the stories about *mujizat* serve a particular function to situate their churches in the larger society. Not only are there prophetic dreams and allegedly miraculous occurrences, there are also stories about mysterious donors who would appear unexpectedly to rescue a church-building project. The origin stories that feature a mysterious donor tend to emphasize not the capacity and aspiration of a particular Christian evangelizer, but the humble origin of the church, the financial difficulty of the building project, and the mysterious source of finance. Mysterious donors are often depicted as indigenous, whose money is thus not an illegitimate donation from a foreign missionary society that could be construed as part of an international conspiracy of Christians to undermine Indonesia's Muslim community. Both the re-establishment of the Indonesian Bethel Church (GBI)'s Johar Salatiga branch and the Pentecostal Church of Isa-Almasih at Salatiga (GPIAI) fit this category of miracle stories, and so do those of many other churches in Indonesia.[10]

Miraculous Pentecostal origin stories in Java thus show a slight deviation from the theology of a strong individual voluntarism that characterizes Pentecostalism worldwide (Marshall 2009, p. 45; Martin 2002, p. 145; Maxwell 2000, p. 249; Schram 2010, p. 465). What distinguishes the deviation of the founding stories is their emphasis on passivity in narrating the inception of their churches in an environment where their presence is not always welcome. Miracle stories are significant because they serve as the justification mechanism in the local struggle for church-planting in an environment that imposes strict surveillance on worship facilities and where admitting the intention to build churches would guarantee controversy.

As such, a church-building story can be highly sensitive for Muslim–Christian relations and serve as a diplomatic strategy to situate the church in the wider society. Such sensitivity is perhaps best epitomized by the legend of the founding father Abraham Alex Tanuseputra, commonly referred to as Pak Alex, of the Bethany Church, one of the fastest-growing Pentecostal denominations in the country today. Pak Alex decided to launch his ministry after he caused a terrible car accident and the badly injured victim was — so goes the story — miraculously cured in the late 1960s. He later managed to build fourteen churches in the suburbs of Surabaya, East Java, but failed to secure a place to build a church in the city proper. One day in 1985, he had a dream. He saw a building and a number: 38. He did not know the meaning of the dream, and upon waking, kept searching for a possible location to build his church in Surabaya. One day, he learned about a wealthy Muslim landlord who was in a coma. He went to the hospital, prayed for this Muslim and God awakened him.[11] This Muslim man in turn generously donated, a piece of land for the new church. The land is precisely at 38 Manyar Rejo II Road in Surabaya (interview with Faradhy Henky, 20 March 2010).

In this narrative, the role of miracles and that of Muslim–Christian relations are all the more accentuated. The identity of the grateful and compliant donor, a Muslim, serves to legitimize the acquisition of land for the church. Moreover, healing a Muslim and peacefully winning the Muslim land through the belief in a miraculous deed by God cleverly dissociates the evangelizer from the agentive position and helps him avoid the accountability for building a new church.

This certainly begs the question: Who believes in the truthfulness of these stories? Do they effectively help Pentecostals justify their churches in a society whose majority objects to churches being built in their neighbourhoods? The answer is yes and no. Pious Pentecostals believe these miracle stories wholeheartedly.[12] In fact, miracle stories are constantly told in sermons and printed in best-selling books, many of which are not merely local, but also translated from English-speaking countries. Miracle narratives are an integral part of the basic repertoire for a Pentecostal sermon, just as common at a service as Christian rock music. More importantly, they are powerful stories that express the Pentecostals' identity in the context of a wider Christian-phobic society.

However, there is more to the miraculous origin stories than a cagey gesture to disavow responsibility for creating potential discord with the mainstream society. A bold statement is behind the miracle narratives: the foundation of the church is authorized by God. In other words, God's mighty power stays on the side of the "chosen few", which is testified by the accomplishment of the church. Revelatory dreams and miracles, then, serve as a meaningful instrument through which something which is normally taboo can be bravely embraced, and proudly presented.

Most Muslims are not aware of these miraculous stories. After all, what many Muslim leaders have been trying to do is to warn their congregations to stay away from missionaries and evangelizers. The bulletins printed by Pentecostal churches often carry a "for internal members only" caption, so that they will not be interpreted as tools of proselytization. But just like all other origin stories that tell much about a people's self-identity and about who they are in this world, the miraculous building of charismatic churches empowers the Pentecostals to deal with Christian-phobia in Indonesian society.

THE PERENNIAL WORRIES OF MUSLIM LEADERS

In grasping the fear of Christianization among Muslims in Salatiga, one has to take into account the influence of the perceived national and even global status of Islam *vis-à-vis* Christianity. The basis for Muslims feeling threatened by Christianity is never merely a matter of a domestic counting of religious populations. It is always related to the ways Islam and Christianity have become linked to the dynamic of both local and transnational identity politics.

In many Muslim-majority lands, the discourse of self-empowerment of Islam has been invoked again and again since the advent of European colonization. More recently, in the wake of the global Islamic resurgence since the 1970s, the competition between Islam and Christianity in some parts of the world has been particularly intense. In Nigeria, for example, demonization of Islam has become commonplace among Pentecostal congregations. The famous priest Adeboye even went so far as to suggest that Islam was *the* obstacle to God's plan to make Nigeria a Christian nation that would initiate the eschatological revival out of Africa to the rest of the world (Ojo 2001 cited in F.-K. Ukah 2009; F.-K. Ukah 2009).

Pentecostalism and Islam are politicized to a much greater degree in Nigeria than in Indonesia, but their competition in both countries is comparable: their horizons are the globe, not merely the nation. Indonesian Muslims are afraid that the presence of vibrant Christian activities in Indonesia would advance the encroachment of Christianity at the expense of the global Muslim community, while Indonesian Christians are careful to confine speeches that might be considered provocative to insiders' circles only. Yet, Christians never fully stop proselytizing or "undermining" other religious communities.

Despite their strong nationalistic devotion to the Republic of Indonesia, both Muslims and Christians often stretch their networks beyond the borders of the nation. With such widened horizons in mind, a local Pentecostal sermon can be just as global in its nature. At a city-wide pre-Christmas celebration in the Ester congregation in mid-December of 2009, a famous charismatic pastor invited from Jakarta gave the following speech to the Salatiga Christians:

> They do not understand. (They ask): "Huh, how come God can be *born?*" Then they are like this: "Jin–gle–be–ll ... Jin–gle–bell" (imitating the style of Arabic chanting, with the congregation bursting into laughter). I say God comes to be with us, God will save us! They do not understand that when the End of Time comes, eventually Christians will win (the audience clapping, the pastor paused for a while). ... Foolish. Truly foolish those who do not believe. ... The Gospel and Jesus Christ is not a religion for westerners. The Gospel and Jesus Christ is for everyone. Even not all the Arabs are Muslims! Thank God, there are still Christian Arabs in the Middle East! (The congregation applauds enthusiastically) (field notes, 15 December 2009)

The sermon unequivocally presents the ridiculed position of Christianity in the Muslim-majority society and boldly retaliates by mocking Islamic chanting and praising Arab Christians. With the globe in sight, the preacher envisions the Middle East, the most "Muslim" place, as a battleground. He implies: Even in the most Islamized place, God does not fail Christians, and one day Christians will win even in the most Islamized place. In a way, the preacher pictures and celebrates Muslims' worst nightmare: the Christianization of the world.

The scope of the Muslim awareness in Salatiga is equally global. On the day of *Idul Adha* in 2009, thousands of people gathered in the city's Pancasila Plaza to pray together. The preacher who gave the sermon on behalf of other Muslim leaders was Dr Zulfa, a lecturer in STAIN and a member of Muhammadiyah. Part of his sermon dealt with the suffering of Muslims in the world:

> Today we gather again in celebration of *Idul Adha* as a symbol of the unity of the Muslim community. More than a billion Muslims at this moment are knitting togetherness into a sturdy bond of faith. Far out there, different races, nations and languages now unite in a great ritual, namely the holiday of *Idul Adha* ... The teaching of Islam is very loaded with guidance of social justice and the same rights between human beings ... thousands or even millions of people in other places perhaps do not have things to eat, [and] they cry over

their fate. They are hungry and thirsty, [and] they lost their property and residence. They lost their children, wives, husbands, parents or relatives ... they may even have to flee from their homeland due to disaster or conflict ... Isn't it an act of brutality if we just let them suffer there, while we do not bother to help them? Because of this I ask you who are capable of donating some parts of your property to help diminish the suffering of our fellows ... (the city-wide *Idul Adha* sermon, 27 November 2009)

According to Pak Zulfa Machasin, "those who suffer" include all the poor, the Palestinians and victims in the Iraq War and Afghanistan War. Pak Zulfa's speech echoes the group solidarity and sympathy towards Muslim fellows whose nations are ravaged by foreign powers, a sentiment that is widespread in Indonesia. This sentiment is often manifested in anti-Israel protests that periodically take place in Jakarta and other cities including Salatiga and in the charitable donations to Palestine. One recent accomplishment is the "Rp 20,000 (about US$2) per person movement" since 2008 that granted the Indonesian NGO Medical Emergency Rescue Committee a total of Rp 21 billion (about US$2.18 million) to complete the Indonesian Hospital in Gaza. From this perspective, Muslims in Indonesia cannot be called a majority in an absolute sense. When the boundaries of the imagined community extend beyond national borders and confounded by a sense of resistance to Western hegemony, the status of majority and minority can be easily reversed.

Linked to the contemporary position of fellow Muslims in the world, the self-consciousness of being Muslim is repeatedly pronounced lest the people of Islam forget their struggle in a still troubled world. The theme of the unity and the togetherness of the Muslim community in the sermon is more than a commonsense cliché. Without taking into consideration the ways Muslims position themselves in global politics, the theme of *Idul Adha* cannot be logically linked to the theme of the unity of the *umat*.

As Muslims in Salatiga perceive themselves as a community in need of empowerment, it is not surprising that the discourse of Christianization of the nation can be so frightening for some, especially when from a statistical perspective, the discourse is not entirely unfounded. The Christian population of the total Indonesian population was 2.8 per cent in 1933, 7.5 per cent in 1971, and 8.9 per cent in 2000. In Central Java, it was merely 0.2 per cent in 1971, and 2 per cent today, and above 10 per cent in bigger cities (Ricklefs 2001, p. 379). With the constantly growing percentage of Christians in the total population since the late 1970s, not to mention the mass conversion due to state policies since the late 1960s,[13] there is a good reason to ponder whether the slow but steady Christian expansion will continue in the long run.

Under such fear of Christianization, the character of an Indonesian city that has a large Christian population often becomes a site of contestation. The Northern Sulawesi city of Manado, for example, has almost exactly the same problem as Salatiga. More than Salatiga, Manado is viewed as "a Christian city" because 60 per cent of the population is Christian. Yet, Manado Muslims still account for about 30 per cent of the residents. There, churches broadcast their hymns and rock gospels more vehemently than mosques. In recent years, Muslims have also started to be more observant. As a result, Christians accuse Muslims of "acting as if they were living in a Muslim city", whereas Muslims jibe that the Christians "act as if they were living in a Christian country".[14] The logic of identifying as the majority or the minority is always situated for one's present argument.

This "as if" logic over the appropriate character of Manado can only be partially translated into the situation in Salatiga. Unlike Christians in Manado, Christians in Salatiga could not complain that Muslims are acting *as if* they were living in an Islamic city, because Muslims are numerically the majority. Nevertheless, Muslims could well complain that Christians were acting as if they were living in a Christian city. And they indeed have. They pointed out that it was time for the "invisible" Muslims to come out of the shadows.

Ironically, despite the steadily rising number and further improvement of mosques and Islamic schools in the city, the shadow of Salatiga as a "Christian city" still looms large even in the minds of mainstream Muslim leaders. Regardless of the remarkable Islamic revival in Salatiga, the growth of Christian facilities has concerned the local leaders of Muhammadiyah and NU. The chairwoman of Aisyiyah, the women's wing of Muhammadiyah, Ibu Zulfa, for example, harbours strong feelings on this matter.

Born in Yogyakarta in 1955, Ibu Zulfa or Haja Untari moved to Salatiga in 1981 after marriage. She has assumed the position of the head of Aisyiyah in Salatiga since 2004 with a goal to revive the women's Islamic organization in the city. She often recounts her life in Yogyakarta, where Muhammadiyah was founded in 1912 and where its headquarters has remained ever since. Compared to her birthplace, the scale and strength of Aisyiyah in Salatiga is rather small. The reason behind this, according to Ibu Zulfa, is because of the "Christian character" of Salatiga (interview with Ibu Zulfa, 16 November 2009). She considers the Christian influence partially responsible for the relative weakness of Muslim NGOs in the city, where Muslims of various factions and sects have redirected more of their efforts into their immediate communities, the neighbourhoods.

From this perspective, the Islamization of Salatiga for Ibu Zulfa is an ongoing project. She and her husband, therefore, devoted themselves to building a Great Mosque (*masjid raya*) at STAIN where Pak Zulfa taught. Up until 2010, Salatiga did not have a Grand Mosque (*masjid agung*) that could be compared to those in Semarang, Solo, Demak, and other major cities in Central Java. Rather, there were only two Big Mosques (*masjid besar*), namely Masijd Pandawa and Masijd Kauman. For the Zulfas, a Great Mosque would enhance the Islamic character of a city, even though an even bigger Grand Mosque is still awaited (field notes, 27 November 2009).

The same doubt about the Christian influence in the city is also cast by Mbak Nur Hidayati, a twenty-nine-year-old *madrasah* teacher and a member of NU. With regard to the controversy over "Christian domination" in Salatiga, she argues:

> To "dominate" ... well ... this sounds very disturbing in its connotation ... But it is true that now in all [Indonesian] cities, or in the city [here], there are many Christian worship places (*peribadatan Nasrani*) ... almost in every corner, and at every moment there are perhaps some [who] observe that Christian [facilities] are much bigger or that there is a much greater number [than Muslim facilities], whereas if we look at the data we realize they are but a minority ... it is not just [that there are] many worship places, but also many schools ... even Muslim children — many of them also go to Christian schools. Then, those who ... how should I put this ... who have a strong faith in Islam would of course hold a more critical attitude about these matters ... so if a person wants to say that "Christians dominate Salatiga", it is up to her/him (interview with Nur Hidayati, 19 November 2009).

Latent fears about *Kristenisasi* are thus not just part of an extremist agenda but shared sentiments among leaders of the mainstream, pro-pluralist, Muslim organizations such as NU and Muhammadiyah. Like Ibu Zulfa, Mbak Nur rejects Islamic political agendas such as the implementation of the codified modern *sharia* as national law and holds that there should be no discrimination against people of different religions. Despite such pro-pluralist views, when it comes to worship facilities, Mbak Nur shares fears that Christianity was spreading in the country, and that their facilities were built in numbers disproportionate to the status as a minority regardless of the feelings of the majority in society.

The perception about a thriving Christian minority has been addressed through initiatives to amplify Islamic facilities and strengthen the community, so that the Islamic character of Salatiga would not be overshadowed. This line of thought was unequivocally conveyed in the sermon of the citywide worship of *Idul-Fitri*, the last day of the fasting month Ramadan, held again at the Pancasila Plaza in 2010. This event was the largest ceremony for Muslims in the city proper. Following the morning worship, the head of the Religious Ministry of the city government gave the following sermon:

> *Idul Fitri* reminds us of one aspect of co-religious life (*hidup berjamaah*) based on awe towards God The Most Glorified … The Islamic *umat* has to unify steps in one goal of the magnificence of Islam by putting aside the differences between streams (*aliran*), factions, colors and social class. Togetherness and unity represents great strength so that *umat Islam* will not be defeated. The Islamic community does not want to become like foam in the middle of the sea. We don't want to become a Muslim community whose existence cannot set an example. We must not become the Muslim community once pointed out by the Apostle of God (Muhammad) in his dialogue with [his] companions: "An era will come, in which other religious communities will arrive and seize you, almost like a gang of people who are gluttonous, clustering and fighting with one another around the dish of their food". … Hearing the utterance of the Apostle of God about the fate of a generation of the Muslim community like that, companions asked: "Can it be that because at the time our Muslim community numbers little as a minority, Apostle of God?" The Apostle replied: "No, your number at the time is a lot! However your quality is like foam adrift on the waves". (the city-wide *Idul-Fitri* sermon, 23 August 2010)

The scene depicted in the dialogue between the Prophet and his companions is a cautionary tale insinuating the fear of failure of *umat Islam*. The advantage of a domestic majority disappears if the quality of the majority is low, the preacher warns, and he imagines that the diverging streams within the Muslim community weaken it in the face of a common enemy. Although such a concern misrepresents the heavily fragmented Christian community as a united force, it enables the discourse of Christianization to justify the cause of the Islamization as the vaccine against the loss of self-esteem of *umat Islam*.

If the struggle of Christians in this land is to gain legitimacy, the struggle of Muslims is to match the legitimacy that the latter believe has been accorded to them. The performance of Christians is to hide controversy and seek conversion; the expectation of Muslims is to be a dignified people in the face of the religious other. Such dialectical relations will continue to show their relevance, and peaceful coexistence between these religious communities will demand constant renegotiations.

Notes

1. The materials presented in this chapter are part of a dissertation project on how women's religious activities and Muslim–Christian relationships reshape religious identities in Salatiga, Central Java. Support for the research was provided by a National Science Foundation Dissertation Improvement Grant and a Mellon/ACLS Dissertation Completion Fellowship. I would like to thank Robert Hefner, Nancy Smith-Hefner, Robert Weller, Kimberly Arkin, Dan Slater, Rachel Rinaldo, Daniel Birchok, and Anna Tsing for providing insights for revisions on the earlier versions of this chapter. Finally, thanks go to Nat Tuohy, as always.
2. They are members of mainline churches, including the Javanese Christian Church (GKJ), the Indonesian Christian Church (GKI), the Batak Protestant Church (HKBP), Sumbanese Christian Church (GKS), and so forth.
3. On the rise and fall of Javanist Muslim (*abangan*), see Ricklefs (2007) and Hefner (2011).
4. I decline to use the term "Islamist extremist" since I do not wish to imply that extreme devotion to Islam ("Islamism") necessarily leads to violence. Such a usage is unfair to the vast majority of peace-loving Muslims.
5. All data is from various statistics published by BPS Kota Salatiga from 1980s to 2010 and BAPPDA.
6. All of the names used in this chapter are pseudonyms, except in instances where a person's identity would already be apparent from their professional titles and activities.
7. To protect the privacy of the informants, the website is purposefully concealed.
8. Many Indonesians only have a single name. Although "Dimas" is a pseudonym, this is how the person is referred to in the officially documented story of the Fendi church.
9. Prophetic revelation is a Qur'anic tradition in Islam. Yet, the exercise of *muzijat* is strictly limited to prophets, such as Moses, Abraham, and Muhammad as opposed to saints' *karamat*. Here, the democratization of *muzijat* takes place in Indonesian Pentecostalism, which deserves greater attention and more analyses and cannot be addressed in this chapter.

10   A famous example is the origin story of the Pentecostal Church in Surabaya, Indonesia in which the mysterious donor appears while the pastor was napping. The identity of the donor is concealed in the story.
11   The story is recounted by Rev. Faradhy Henkky in the headquarters office of Bethany Indonesia in Surabaya.
12   This was expressed to me in numerous informal conversations.
13   See Hefner (1993) for a socio-political account of mass conversions to Christianity after 1965.
14   This observation was shared by Professor Dan Slater in Ann Arbor on 9 December 2011.

References

Aritonang, Jan and Karel Steenbrink. *A History of Christianity in Indonesia*. Leiden, Boston: Brill, 2008.

Chao, En-Chieh. "Blessed Fetishism: Language Ideology and Embodied Worship Among Pentecostals in Java". *Culture and Religion* 12, no. 4 (2011): 373–99.

Farhadian, Charles E. *Christianity, Islam and Nationalism in Indonesia*. New York: Routlege, 2007.

Hefner, Robert W. "Of Faith and Commitment: Christian Conversion in Muslim Java". In *Conversion to Christianity: Historical and Anthropological Perspectives on a Great Transformation*. Berkeley: University of California Press, 1993.

———. "Where Have All the *Abangan* Gone? Religionization and the Decline of Non-Standard Islam in Indonesia". In *The Politics of Religion in Indonesia: Syncretism, Orthodoxy, and Religious Contention in Java and Bali*, edited by Rémy Madinier and Michel Picard. London and New York: Routledge, 2011.

Jones, Sidney. "Indonesia: 'Christianisation' and Intolerance". International Crisis Group, 2010.

Kumar, Anugrah. "Another Bomb Found at Church in Indonesia". *The Christian Post*, 25 October 2011. Available at <http://www.christianpost.com/news/another-bomb-found-at-church-in-indonesia-56481/>.

Laffan, Michael. *Islamic Nationhood and Colonial Indonesia: The Umma Below the Winds*. New York: Routledge, 2007.

Marshall, Ruth. *Political Spiritualities: The Pentecostal Revolution in Nigeria*. Chicago: University of Chicago Press, 2009.

Martin, David. *Pentecostalism: The World Their Parish*. Oxford: Blackwell, 2001.

Maxwell, David. "'Catch the Cockerel Before Dawn': Pentecostalism and Politics in Post-Colonial Zimbabwe". *Africa: Journal of the International African Institute* 70, no. 2 (1 January 2000): 249–77.

Nagata, Judith. "Christianity among Transnational Chinese: Religious Versus (Sub)ethnic Affiliation". *International Migration* 43, no. 3 (2005): 99–130.

Ng, Nathaniel. "Indonesia's Mega-Churches: Resisting Christiano-Phobia in Numbers". *The Christian Post Singapore*, 9 September 2008. Available at <http://sg.christianpost.com/dbase/asia/676//1.htm>.

Ojo, Tony. *Let Somebody Shout Hallelujah! The Life and Ministry of Pastor Enoch Adejare Adeboye*. Lagas: Honeycombs Cards and Prints, 2001.

Ricklefs, M.C. *A History of Modern Indonesia Since C. 1200*. Stanford, CA: Stanford University Press, 2001.

———. *Polarizing Javanese Society: Islamic and Other Visions, 1830–1930*. Singapore: National University of Singapore Press, 2007.

Robbins, Joel. "The Globalization of Pentecostal and Charismatic Christianity". *Annual Review of Anthropology* 33 (2004): 117–43.

Robinson, Mark. "The Growth of Indonesian Pentecostalism". In *Asian and Pentecostal: The Charismatic Face of Christianity in Asia*, edited by Allan Anderson and Edmond Tang. Oxford: Regnum Books International, 2005.

Schram, Ryan. "Finding Money: Business and Charity in Auhelawa, Papua New Guinea". *Ethnos* 75, no. 4 (December 2010): 447–70.

Sidjabat, Walter Bonar. "Religious Tolerance and the Christian Faith: A Study Concerning the Concept of Divine Omnipotence in the Indonesian Constitution in the Light of Islam and Christianity". Unpublished Th.D. thesis, Princeton Theological Seminary, 1960.

Sukur, Bahrul. "Salatiga, Di Bawah Bayang-bayang Kristen", 2007. Suara Hidayatullah: Agustus 2002. Available at <http://www.hidayatullah.com>.

Ukah, Asonzeh F.-K. "Contesting God: Nigerian Pentecostals and Their Relations with Islam and Muslims". In *Global Pentecostalism: Encounters with Other Religious Traditions*, edited by David Westerlund. London: I.B. Tauris, 2009.

Wakabayashi, Bob Tadashi. *Anti-foreignism and Western Learning in Early-modern Japan: The New Theses of 1825*. Cambridge, MA: Harvard University Asia Center, 1986.

8

CHRISTIAN–MUSLIM RELATIONS IN POST-CONFLICT AMBON, MOLUCCAS
Adat, Religion, and Beyond

Birgit Bräuchler

INTRODUCTION[1]

Indonesia is a religiously plural state. Freedom of faith is constitutionally granted — at least concerning the six officially acknowledged religions. Pluralism in Indonesia thus not only implies diversity, but also the "right of every religious ... community to be itself and maintain its own traditions, practices and attitudes" (Sharpe 2005, p. 43). However, as recent acts of religious intolerance show — be it the forced closure of Christian churches, attacks on Ahmadiyah Muslims or, earlier, the "religious war" in the Moluccas — religious pluralism is often at stake and constantly needs to be renegotiated and put into action again. During the authoritarian Soeharto regime, any tensions, conflicts or media reporting having to do with issues of ethnicity, religion, race or class (SARA) were kept in check or suppressed. After his stepping down in May 1998, SARA tensions all over the country exploded or were taken as a welcome excuse to instigate conflicts and mobilize local people for violence. This chapter aims to outline two ways of how Indonesians in the Moluccas try to cope with inter-religious clashes: one being focused on *adat*, that is tradition and customary law, as a seemingly neutral means to reintegrate people, the other being focused on religious dialogue. The contribution intends to deconstruct the simplified image of a harmonious traditional past versus religious strife that neglects the diverse and complex processes of negotiation in which the two domains — religion and *adat* — have always been involved in.[2]

The Moluccas are part of Eastern Indonesia, a region that stands out against the rest of the country due to its (colonial) history, its former importance as spice granary, and its religious composition (Bräuchler and Erb 2011). In Muslim-majority Indonesia, the Christian share of the population in Eastern Indonesia is substantial; in some of its provinces Christians even constitute the majority. According to recent government statistics, the Moluccan population is almost 50 per cent Muslim and 50 per cent Christian (comprising Protestants and Catholics) (Badan Pusat Statistik Propinsi Maluku dan Badan Perencanaan Pembangunan Daerah 2010).[3] Spending some time in the Moluccas, it is obvious that religion very much determines daily life. The majority of people is, one way or the other, on a regular basis busy with social or praying activities organized by churches or mosques. This has a strong impact on social networks in the Moluccas. However, as this chapter also aims to argue, whilst pre-war Moluccan society was renowned for inter-religious harmony throughout the country, inter-religious relationships were based on passive tolerance and inter-religious dialogue was missing. This made it relatively easy for religion to become the mobilizing force for violence. The conflict was fought out mainly between Christians and Muslims and lasted from 1999 until 2003. When violence seemed to take no end though and the majority of the population had suffered for too long in all areas of life, people became disillusioned by what their religion has made out of Moluccan brother and sisterhood. What had happened to those cultural mechanisms that preceded the arrival of both Christianity and Islam in the area and once united its inhabitants? Was the conflict, as many Moluccans like to believe, a punishment for having abandoned their common *adat* and ancestry?

A short overview of the history of Islam and Christianity in the region, in particular the Central Moluccas, reveals that relations between the two denominations have in fact never been easy and that the relationship between the world religions and local *adat* greatly depended on the changing sociopolitical context. To explore those complex relationships, I then take the Moluccan conflict as a peg and introduce two different ways how people try to come to terms with the aftermath of the violence: one based on expectations towards the integrative character of *adat*, in this case embodied by a traditional village union, the other one based on religious dialogue.[4] A closing section aims to draw some conclusions about the reconciliatory potential of *adat* and religion.

CHANGING RELATIONS OF ISLAM, CHRISTIANITY, AND *ADAT*

Whereas Islam came as a peaceful concomitant to trade and had already established itself in various parts of the Central Moluccas by the late fifteenth century, Christianity was forcefully imposed on the Moluccan peoples. As the first European colonial powers, the Portuguese arrived in the Moluccas in 1512 and brought Catholicism to the islands. The Dutch established themselves in the region in the early seventeenth century in the form of the Dutch East India Company (Vereenigde Oost-Indische Compagnie [VOC]) and forced those who had been baptized by the Portuguese to convert to Protestantism (Becker 1996, p. 57; Enklaar 1963, pp. 38–39). In the early nineteenth century, the VOC was replaced by the Dutch colonial government, and the Dutch Missionary Society (active from 1815 to 1865) initiated a more systematic proselytization. In 1935, the Moluccan church achieved independence, making the Protestant Church of the Moluccas (Gereja Protestan Maluku [GPM]) the oldest evangelical church in Asia (Cooley 1966, 1968, pp. 52–53). The lack of professional Protestant missionaries was compensated for by the high number of laymen and indigenous preachers who were stricter than those from abroad in promoting a purified Christianity and in taking action against *adat* that was not in line with it, thus adding to anti-Christian feelings among Muslims (Bartels 2003, pp. 136–37, Müller-Krüger 1968, pp. 105–06, 146–47, Wawer 1974, pp. 212, 214).

Christian (i.e., Protestant) missionary activities met with political village structures that had already been largely established by the Dutch based on their successful efforts to control the population and local *adat*. This was a crucial additional factor for the antagonism between Christianity and *adat*. *Adat* and the church thus constitute two different institutional hierarchies that are opposed to each other, with the village head and the priest commonly competing for the peoples' favour (F.A.K. v. Benda-Beckmann 1988, pp. 204, 206–09). To the contrary, Islam had encountered a still fairly flexible social and political setting. The long-term isolation of Moluccan Muslims during the Dutch spice monopoly from the seventeenth to nineteenth centuries thus led to a harmonious fusion of Islam with local *adat* and a strong overlap, if not congruity, between *adat* and religious functionaries (Franz and Keebet v. Benda-Beckmann 1988, 1993, Chauvel 1980, p. 44, Cooley 1961, p. 290, Fraassen 1972). This substantially changed in the nineteenth and twentieth centuries, when the improving transport system and the rising number of pilgrims from

Indonesia to Mecca caused a rapidly increasing influx of reformatory ideas from the Middle East and led to a split in the Muslim community in Indonesia into the modernist and traditionalist streams or *aliran* (see Becker 1996, pp. 203–04; Benda 1958; Mulder 1966, p. 73; Wawer 1974, p. 10; Wertheim 1956, p. 208). This new reformist movement spilled over into the Moluccas, enabled by the lifting of the spice monopoly in 1863. Whereas in some parts of the Moluccas, it proved unable to penetrate society, leaving the particular Islam-*adat* linkage untouched (sometimes by forcefully expelling the unwanted intruders) (Chauvel 1980, pp. 56–57; 1990, pp. 162–68), in others the reformist thought was able to get a foot in the door, which led to a split in the Muslim community there (see below).

Ever since the Portuguese introduced Christianity to the region, religion had become increasingly politicized. In their deadly effort to push through the spice monopoly, the colonial powers made massive use of existing local power struggles and traditional rivalries, thus sharpening existing group boundaries. Under Dutch colonial rule, Christians were given preferential treatment in education and the bureaucracy, while Muslims — being the "natural" enemies of the Europeans and moreover competitors in the spice trade — were either neglected or treated with hostility (Andaya 1993; Schumann 1995, p. 287; Tjandrasasmita 1971, p. 6; Wertheim 1956). Under the Japanese occupation, and even more so after independence, Muslims increasingly gained equal access to education and better jobs, which led to the emancipation of their community. Between 1945 and 1949, when the Dutch persistently refused to grant the Indonesian people independence, hundreds of Christians in the colonial army fought side by side with the Dutch against their brothers and sisters who favoured an independent Republic of Indonesia. Still today, Ambonese Christians are reproached for their closeness to the former colonial government and their (previous) claim for superiority (Cooley 1966, pp. 125–26; Kraemer 1958, pp. 13–14, 17). However, discrimination against Muslims was not only a strategic move by the colonial government, it was also based on a prevailing attitude among Muslims that, for example, sending their children to Dutch schools would be tantamount to making them convert to Christianity.

After independence, the situation remained at least as complicated as before since Christians were now living in a predominantly Muslim country. Indonesia's first president Sukarno immediately turned the federal state of Indonesia, as the Dutch had left it, into a unitary state, thus robbing the Eastern Indonesian State of its special status. Many Christian

Moluccans feared being abandoned by the Dutch and to be overpowered by a Muslim majority, which on 25 April 1950 led a minority of Western-educated and politically active Moluccan figures to proclaim the independence of a South Moluccan Republic (Republik Maluku Selatan [RMS]). However, Moluccan independence — a stigma that still affects Moluccan Christians today — was short-lived and crushed by the Indonesian military only a couple of months later. Soeharto became Indonesia's second president after the suppression of an alleged communist coup in 1965 and the murder of hundreds of thousands of alleged communists throughout the country. From then on Indonesian citizens had to profess one of the official religions by law, thus making religion an inherent identity marker. Due to Soeharto's unification efforts and the weakening of the *adat* system, the increasing infiltration of church organizations into daily life, the rising influx of non-Moluccan Muslims through spontaneous and government-sponsored transmigration, and the government's pro-Islamic turn from the early-1990s onwards, the role of Islam and Christianity as identity markers was amplified further (see also Bartels 2010).

In a nutshell, religion has often been used as a political weapon, be it by the colonial power in its endeavours to convert the local population to Christianity in order to create bonds of loyalty whilst fighting the "common" enemy, the Muslims, or in current power struggles over political control. At the same time, *adat* itself underwent massive changes and declining authority over the centuries (see case studies below), especially over the last decades. However, inter-religious violence in the Moluccas has never been so explicit, so all-embracing, so bloody, and so persistent as in the conflict at the turn of this century. This notwithstanding, Moluccan Christians and Muslims retain a great deal in common, such as family ties, the common struggle against (neo)colonial forces, a common history, ancestry, myths, and *adat* (see also Chauvel 1980), which has, despite all outside influences, frequently been able to come to the fore and proving able to maintain inter-religious harmony. This legacy makes use of both *adat* and religion as means for peace ambivalent, challenging, and with erratic results.

THE MOLUCCAN CONFLICT AND THE HOPE IN *ADAT*

The Moluccan conflict broke out in Ambon town on 19 January 1999, when Muslims were celebrating the end of the fasting month. Estimates of casualties from both sides range from 5.000 to 15.000. Almost a third of the Moluccan population was displaced for various periods of time and Moluccan society became completely divided along religious lines.[5] A minor and not unusual quarrel between a Christian bus driver and a (migrant) Muslim at the border of the neighbourhoods of Kudamati and Batumerah is commonly said to have triggered the mass violence. Other catalysts were Christian–Muslim clashes in Dobo (Aru, Southeast Moluccas) in mid-January 1999 (also caused by a spat over a trivial issue), in Kupang in late November 1998 following a protest march against church-burnings in Indonesia, and in Ketapang, Jakarta in November 1998. The latter incident was triggered by a dispute between local gangs (involving Moluccan Christians and Muslims) over a gambling establishment, resulting in the destruction of a mosque and several churches plus the government-initiated return of a mob of Ambonese youngsters who have been involved in the clashes on both sides. Taking their enmity with them back to Ambon, these gangs were a likely additional factor in fueling the mass violence. Whereas initially it looked as if Christian Ambonese mainly targeted migrant Muslims in Ambon town, religion soon became the principal marker defining conflict lines. Rumours that central mosques and churches had been set alight and the fact that Ambon town is home to people from all over the Moluccas put the conflict on a higher (transcendental) scale and made it spread rapidly throughout the whole Moluccan archipelago. Although it is not clear in how far the military was involved in setting up or provoking the conflict, it was obvious that both military and police did not act neutrally and often took sides, the former with Muslims; the latter with Christians, thus further escalating the conflict. The conflict had already undergone several hot and cool phases, when the arrival of the Laskar Jihad, a militant Muslim group that had set off from Java to save their Muslim brothers in the Moluccas from extermination (so they argued), led to new scales of destruction and violence.

For years, the Indonesian government seemed willing to leave it up to the Moluccan people to solve "their own" problems; law enforcement did not take place. Countless peace initiatives had been undertaken by local, national, and international actors from the very beginning of the conflict by the time the government organized peace talks in Malino, Sulawesi (February 2002), which put at least an official end to the violence. Single ninja-style attacks occurred until 2004 and tension continues to run high in Moluccan society until today.

Among Muslims, this polarization brought memories of past repression to the fore, as well as the trauma of the RMS period and pride in the anti-colonial resistance. Among Christians, it triggered fear of extinction.

Notwithstanding or maybe precisely due to this fear, students, religious and *adat* leaders appealed to the Moluccan people from the very beginning of the conflict to honour their common roots and shared *adat* to stop the conflict. Whereas those pleas were not very successful first, after several years of violent conflict, people from all levels of society put their hopes in *adat* as a foundation for overarching alliances that can bridge the religious divide or, more concrete, in the revival, strengthening, and re-adaptation of certain elements of *adat*. In the centre of attention are traditional concepts of Moluccan culture such as *siwalima*, which implies a cultural dichotomization of Moluccan society (*siwa* and *lima*) that, however, can only exist in its unity, traditional alliances that bind villages together irrespective of their religious affiliation (*pela*), and other village alliances based on common ancestry. *Pela* has always been held responsible for religious harmony in the Moluccas (before the outbreak of mass violence). It has become the symbol for Moluccan brotherhood and for the resilience of *adat* in the face of possible conflict (see, for example, Bartels 2003; Bräuchler 2009*a*). In the following section, I focus on a village union that has received little attention by outside observers but has played a prominent role in the post-conflict years and whose members claim it to be the key to peace in the Moluccas. The union is highly interlinked with other villages through *pela* and other family or *adat* ties. Its foundation is common ancestry, a factor figuring most prominently in the establishment of harmonious inter-religious relations (see also Kraemer 1958).

Uli Hatuhaha or Hatuhaha Union lies on the northern half of Haruku, a neighbouring island of Ambon.[6] Although unique in its particular composition, the village federation is worth a closer look since it also embodies the complexity of relations between *adat* and religion, Christianity and Islam, as well as of internal religious disputes and violence, and thus opens up a window to look at more general problems and challenges in post-conflict Ambon. Hatuhaha is also a good example of how borders between *adat* and religion or between different religions shift or blur depending on the changing socio-cultural context and what is known as "the segmentary principle" in anthropology.[7] The union goes back to a mythical event in the past in which five brothers came from the mother island of Seram to Haruku, climbed Alaka Mountain and founded *Hatuhaha Amarima Lounusa* (literally "five villages gather on the island on a rock"), where they jointly converted to Islam: Rohomoni, Kabauw, Kailolo, Pelauw, and Hulaliu villages. *Uli* are traditional Moluccan village federations. Most of them were destroyed by the Dutch for fear that such overarching societal structures could challenge their supremacy. Due to its remoteness and, generally, the past isolation of the Muslim community in the Moluccas from developments in the Muslim communities in the rest of the country, and the rest of the world as described above, the adaptation of Islam to local circumstances and *adat* was quite radical. Hatuhaha Islam thus developed peculiarities such as its weekly prayer on Friday instead of the obligatory five daily prayers, a particular architecture of the mosque integrating pre-Islamic elements, the reduction of the yearly fasting period to three days, the calculation of Muslim festivals such as Idul Fitri or Idul Adha according to *adat* elders, and the pilgrimage (*haj*) to a local shrine (*keramat*) instead of to Mecca.

The Hatuhaha union — a stronghold of anti-colonial resistance and strong opposition to the RMS — was constantly being harassed by the Portuguese and the Dutch who finally succeeded in converting Hulaliu to Christianity (Rumphius 1910, p. 275; Titaley 2007). Given the claimed forced nature of this conversion, Hatuhaha Muslims today still see Hulaliu village as part of their *adat* union, or even celebrate it as making a heroic sacrifice for the sake of the others, who were then able to save their Muslimness. After Hulaliu had turned away from Islam, its Muslim relics were distributed among the four other villages. Up until now Hulaliu has to participate in Hatuhaha ceremonies such as the renovation of the Hatuhaha Mosque. Hatuhaha people in turn also help out when a church or a mosque needs to be built. In other words, these five villages have preserved at least parts of their common *adat* and present a harmonious unity to the outside world to this day, thus making them an example of *adat*'s supposedly unifying potential. The union still shares a traditional meeting place to deliberate over common matters (the *asari* in Pelauw) and a mosque (*Mesjid Hatuhaha* in Rohomoni), and they still come together for important ceremonies and the renovation of mosques and traditional community houses. However, at the same time, Hulaliu's conversion to Christianity was one of several factors contributing to the weakening of the Hatuhaha union (see also Sahusilawane and Sopacua 1996/1997). Another was the relocation of the union's former settlements (*aman*) from Alaka Mountain to the coast and its division into autonomous village units, called *negeri*, by the Dutch in the mid-seventeenth century. A more recent factor was the village law passed by the Indonesian government in 1979 in an effort to unify governmental structures down to the village level, which had an immense impact on local *adat* throughout Indonesia. Hatuhaha's unity was severely undermined, and its functions were reduced to *adat* ceremonies (Sopacua, Pattinama and Noya 1996, pp. 56–59, 68–72). These factors did, of course, not only affect Hatuhaha but also many villages in the Moluccas and many other parts of Indonesia.

But the union has not only been weakened by external factors, but also by internal quarrels. These quarrels have been an integral part of the union since its foundation (thus contradicting a rather Western notion of the mutually exclusive character of conflict and peace), and they have been severely aggravated due to power struggles related to higher level politics and the recent Moluccan conflict. This case study gives expression to the fact that *adat* does not only stand for harmony and integration but also for conflict and exclusion. In seeming contradiction to the depiction of an ideal Hatuhaha union, Hatuhaha is internally torn by conflicts, power struggles, and religious clashes — not between Christians and Muslims, but between Muslims. The encroachment of reformist Islamic ideas in the nineteenth and twentieth centuries led to a split in the Muslim community in Hatuhaha into traditionalists (*kaum/golongan adat*), who continue to stand for the Hatuhaha-specific version of Islam (*Islam Hatuhaha*), and modernists (*kaum/golongan syariat*), who support a purified version of Islam (*Islam syariat*) and thus aim to move closer to the broader non-Moluccan Muslim community, both within and beyond Indonesia. As Bartels (2010, p. 229, n. 12) argues, this split led to "fanaticism and religious polarization" in parts of Hatuhaha, which in turn led to the reduced involvement of Hulaliu in *adat* matters after 1910. However, as the only Christian village in the union, Hulaliu is seen less as a religious opponent and occasionally even acts as a mediator in these internal fights.

The arrival of modernist/reformist Islam led to violent confrontations and the division of Pelauw village in the 1930s. The followers of *Islam Hatuhaha* stayed in Pelauw, while the followers of *Islam syariat* were moved to a place called Ori that is located east of Pelauw's neighbouring Christian village Kariu, thus making Kariu a buffer between the two opposing Islamic streams. To elucidate the expellees' position, a former head of the high school in Ori compared their situation with that of Hulaliu, which, although converted to Christianity, still follows most of the Hatuhaha *adat* ceremonies. This is meant to express a good relationship but has nothing to do with religious beliefs. As a retired teacher in Ori expressed it, *adat* must not be "religionized" (*mengagamakan adat*).[8] Today, the population of Pelauw has become divided again over the reformist-traditionalist divide, a potential additional factor to cultivate violence, which has become increasingly accepted as a means to solve conflicts during the communal unrests. To this day, the divide is an extremely sensitive topic. Involved in all this are struggles between village clans over who has the power to define what *adat* is, what needs to be continued, and what can be replaced or adapted to the wider cultural and religious context. But increasingly involved also get power struggles related to high-level politics: that is, the competition among (Muslim) Hatuhaha clans whose turn it is to get an influential position in the district or provincial government.

The Moluccan conflict, at least momentarily, had reunited Hatuhaha Muslims. It brought up common experiences of past repression and made them fight on the front lines against Christians. Kariu, the neighbouring Christian village of Pelauw that is not part of the Hatuhaha union, was completely destroyed in February 1999 and its population forced to flee.[9] At the end of 1999, Hulaliu was attacked by its Muslim Hatuhaha "brothers" as a result of the overpowering religious polarization and the exceptional violence in the whole of the Moluccas.[10] However, the attackers only destroyed some of the houses at the village periphery. They did not enter the village's centre and they did not demolish the church. Instead they soon withdrew. Several of my interlocutors emphasized that this was due to what the attackers felt was their ancestors' spiritual power or voice, strongly opposing to the clashes among "brothers". This was followed by a Hatuhaha internal reconciliation ceremony, a peace march to Ambon town in 2002, and a two-week long ceremony to celebrate the restoration of the Hatuhaha Mosque in Rohomoni in 2006 to promote Hatuhaha as a symbol of internal unity and peace between Christians and Muslims.

Internal problems among Muslims were hushed up (although they did not end); the focus was now on the relationship with Hulaliu as a Christian member of the *adat* family and on their relationship with other (former) Christian enemies. Illustrative is here also one of Hulaliu's *pela* partners, the Muslim village Tulehu on the eastern coast of Ambon Island that soon joined the Hatuhaha Muslims in their efforts to bridge the religious divide.

REINTEGRATING SOCIETY THROUGH RELIGIOUS DIALOGUE

Although the revival of *adat* for peace seems to be quite successful and Moluccans are very enthusiastic about it,[11] a complementary approach is needed given the popularity of religion and the overall weakened *adat* system, an approach that initiates and fosters religious dialogue. One such initiative is the Moluccan Interfaith Council (Lembaga Antar Iman Maluku [LAIM]). The Council was founded in December 2003 and consists of representatives of the main religious bodies in the Moluccas: the

Moluccan Protestant Church (GPM), The Catholic Diocese of Amboina, and the Indonesian Council of Muslim Clerics (Majelis Ulama Indonesia [MUI]). The Council is described as "an attempt to raise awareness about the commonalities between the religions and to teach the positive values inherent in each faith that guarantee peaceful co-existence". The Council thus provides a forum for religious leaders to meet and discuss pressing socio-economic and political issues and respond to any arising communal tensions, but it also wants to extend its activities to the general population to strengthen inter-community relationships and promote interfaith education (Maluku Reconciliation and Reconstruction Meeting 2004). This is quite a challenging task, not only in the face of the Moluccan conflict, which left deep scars in the peoples' psyche and the social, and the resulting territorial segregation between Muslims and Christians. One of the biggest problems in the fabric of Moluccan society, I would argue, is that the relationship between Christians and Muslims is merely based on passive tolerance, not on mutual respect and understanding of the others' religion. This is very much rooted in history as sketched above. The way Kraemer (1958, p. 22) described the relationship between Muslims and Christians based on the perceptions of church members almost a century ago is illustrative of this: "They leave each other completely alone." Although interactions took place as daily routines and *pela* pacts were celebrated regularly, no dialogue took place with regard to religion. Although Christians and Muslims used to visit each other for festivities such as Christmas or Idul Fitri, religion was generally a topic not to delve into. There was no significant mutual inspiration based on religious debate or exchange.

Due to this absent tradition of inter-religious dialogue on the grassroots level, there was nothing to fall back on during and after the conflict — nothing except shared *adat* traditions and local belief systems that go beyond the world religions. One of the first workshops organized by the Interfaith Council, which took place in July 2006 on Ambon, was entitled "Building peace: Learning from the failure of religions" and was very much focused on such shared *adat* traditions. More generally, the Council wants to advance a more open attitude towards *adat* and a more in-depth understanding of others' religions in religious institutions. More concrete actions include an arrangement in 2007 for imams and priests, with a Muslim family hosting a priest for a night at their home and a Christian family hosting an imam another night at theirs. The intention of this arrangement was to foster dialogue by enabling people to talk on a personal level and to reduce stereotypes about the other's religion. In 2009, the Council set up a teleconference between hundreds of Christian and Muslim youths in

Ambon and Solo (Java). To stimulate discussion, guest speakers were invited on both sides, among them (former) hardliners such as Jafar Umar Thalib, an Islamist leader who had sent his *jihad* troopers to the Moluccan conflict. In 2010, LAIM organized a youth exchange, where Muslim youths stayed in Christian neighbourhoods for four nights and vice versa, concluded by a session to reflect on how the perception of "the other" has changed, in almost all cases leading to positive results. The exchange was followed by a youth camp where all participants came together again in Ambon town in early 2011 to build up an inter-religious youth network.[12]

Another initiative undertaken by LAIM is the exchange of lecturers between Christian and Islamic universities such as the Indonesian Christian University of Maluku (UKIM) and the State Institute of Islamic Studies (IAIN) in Ambon. Muslim lecturers were to teach about the history, the social, political, and cultural perspectives of Islam at UKIM and vice versa. However, the programme has thus far been restricted to students of religious studies (both Islam and Christianity). One important additional initiative would be to introduce joint religious classes into primary and high schools. Another strategic move in the peace process has been to open a Reconciliation and Mediation Centre at IAIN in 2010. IAIN has been known as a radical hotspot during the conflict but more recently has aspired setting an example by transforming itself into a centre for dialogue and encounter.[13] MUI Maluku had earlier (2002) established a special Sector for Interreligious Harmony (Bidang Kerukunan Antar Agama). According to the sector's head, the organization uses the Interfaith Council, in which he is also involved, to put their ideas into action. All these initiatives are important steps in getting a more far-reaching and inclusive inter-religious dialogue going.

GOING BEYOND *ADAT* AND RELIGION?

A simple conclusion would be that conflict lines in the Moluccas are complex, dynamic, and thus difficult to grasp. The relations between followers of various (local and world) religions remain potentially belligerent; Christianity and *Islam syariat* remain in an ongoing competition with *adat* and vice versa; and there remain conflicts internal to both *adat* and religion. So is the solution to go beyond (a potentially exclusivist and weakened) *adat* and the world religions and look for something else that can actually reunite Moluccans?

Countless peace initiatives were undertaken in the Moluccas by national and international NGOs and the government, but common people were often not even aware of them. For them, peace and reconciliation came about rather naturally, without interference from the outside, due to the resumption of daily economic, educational, and social ties. The relationship between Muslim and Christian office mates in Ambon town, between Christian teachers and Muslim pupils, or between Christians in Kariu and Muslims in Pelauw could be described in such terms. Kariu is located right in the middle of the Hatuhaha village federation, but does not belong to it. It is not connected to any of the villages through kinship or *adat* ties. Its relationship with neighbours such as Pelauw is mainly determined through daily economic interaction, such as the exchange of fish and vegetables, or teachers from Kariu being employed in Pelauw's schools. The resumption of those activities that John Braithwaite et al. (2010, p. 43) would call "rituals of everyday life" facilitated the return to normalcy and (at least superficial) peace. Conducting research in India, Ashutosh Varshney (2002) argues that those communities that have a higher level of daily interaction between their Hindu and Muslim populations compared to others are much less prone to communal violence. As Carolyn Nordstrom's (1997) ethnographic research in Mozambique vividly shows, it is local agency and creativity that is most essential for rebuilding peace. In post-war Mozambique, it was first and foremost daily routines and processes on the local level that helped to reduce violence such as fishmongers travelling the country to sell their fish, thus crossing linguistic and ethnic borders, forging trade and social networks and contributing to social reintegration. All these studies suggest that daily interactions of various kinds can help to reduce violent encounters. However, as the Kariu–Pelauw and many other cases in Maluku prove, such relationships were ultimately not strong enough to resist religious mobilization. Drawing on case studies in the Balkans and South Asia, Robert Hayden similarly warns of the "simplistic assumptions that coexistence is evidence of a positive valorization of pluralism. Instead, coexistence may be a matter of competition between members of different groups manifesting the negative definition of tolerance as passive noninterference and premised on a lack of ability of either group to overcome the other" (Hayden 2002, p. 206). Tolerance needs to be defined and realized in a positive sense instead, as Hayden suggests, namely by recognizing and respecting the others, which does not imply the agreement with the others' beliefs or practices (p. 205).

The integrative potential of *adat* helped the Moluccan people to reconcile rather naturally (*secara alami*) by recalling and restrengthening (an imagined) common ancestry or shared *adat*. Crucial in such a setting is the extent to which local traditional structures, mechanisms, and norms are still intact. As the Hatuhaha case illustrates, the integrative force of *adat* almost failed not only due to the explosion of exceptional violence during the years of conflict but also due to the weakened state of the union, but in the end it was able to resist the religious "challenge" and might even emerge out of the conflict stronger than before. As this case study shows, *adat* has the potential to be an important integrative factor, yet it has exclusivist traits as well. Kariu was in the deplorable situation that it belonged not only to the religious "other side" but also that it wasn't part of the Hatuhaha *adat* union. A tradition of daily interaction could not prevent religion and *adat* to take their toll.

No single option thus seems to be sufficient on its own for building sustainable peace: daily interaction based on daily needs, *adat* or religion. They are all components of a dynamic Moluccan culture coexisting and competing with each other. It would rather be more productive for Moluccans to acknowledge their roots and history, but not by unreflectively instrumentalizing or politicizing them, but by their creative adaptation to precarious circumstances. The Moluccan conflict restored peoples' awareness of old conflict lines and new scales of violence; it has severely influenced notions of future coexistence. People have painfully experienced the exclusivist side of religion, which made them celebrate the inclusive character of *adat*. However, exclusivism is also part of *adat* as my case study shows; a fact that is not sufficiently taken into account yet in the current revival hype. It is thus necessary to explore and to (re)create the integrative potential inherent in both religion and *adat*. *Adat* has always been adapted to changing circumstances. Based on an inclusive approach, it now needs to be adopted to the post-conflict situation and serve as means to actively integrate "others" and "outsiders" that often have been living in the Moluccas for generations (but have so far not been considered to be part of local *adat*), and assign them an active role in a shared social world. *Adat* unions such as Hatuhaha need to provide more space for religious variation and interpretation of its *adat* rituals that allows for the integration of all Hatuhaha people, be they Christian or followers of *Islam Hatuhaha* or of a more orthodox version of Islam. Otherwise, the conduct of, for example, shared rituals that include religious practices that are not integrative might rather make people more aware of their differences and thus widen the gap between them. At the same time, in order to establish a broader basis for peace, an informed and integrative inter-religious dialogue needs to be fostered at all social strata that promotes active tolerance, the exchange of religious ideas and the accommodating nature of religion and that prevents Christianity and Islam to be used again as mobilizer for violence. This is an option that is only slowly gaining ground, probably due to the traumatic experience of years of brutal conflict and after so many Moluccans lost their lives in a purportedly "religious war".

Notes

1. An earlier, more comprehensive version of this chapter will appear in a book, *Dynamics of Religion in Southeast Asia: Magic and Modernity*, edited by Volker Gottowik, to be published by Amsterdam University Press in 2014. Research for this project was supported by the Asia Research Institute, National University of Singapore, and the Fritz Thyssen Stiftung (Germany).
2. By contrasting religion with *adat*, I refer to the world religions Christianity and Islam in contrast to local *adat* systems, which at the same time involve local belief systems or religions.
3. The Moluccan archipelago was divided into two provinces in 1999: the Moluccas (Maluku) and the Northern Moluccas (Maluku Utara). Here, I am referring to the former. Those statistics are not necessarily reliable. Especially in the Moluccas, there was a lot of changes in the composition of the population due to an enormous immigration of Muslims from other parts of the country to the area and due to movements connected to the conflict.
4. This is based on ethnographic fieldwork I have conducted in the Moluccas over the last couple of years. In case no source is provided in this chapter, data and interpretations are based on my fieldwork and participant observation and interviews I conducted there.
5. On various aspects and interpretations of the Moluccan conflict (with a focus on the Central Moluccas), such as its local roots, instrumentalization theories, the role of the media, and the role of the Laskar Jihad, a militant Islamist group from Java, see, among others, Aditjondro (2001); Benda-Beckmann (2004); Bertrand (2002); Braithwaite et al. (2010); Bräuchler (2003, 2005); Human Rights Watch (1999); International Crisis Group (2000, 2002); Klinken (2001, 2007); Pannell (2003); Schulze (2002); Spyer (2002).
6. For a more detailed discussion of the Hatuhaha case, see Bräuchler (2010*a*). I will use part of the material here.
7. This principle denotes the belief that humans tend to be at variance or unite depending on what is at stake and who is the (common) enemy. For example, A is fighting B, but concerning a certain issue they together oppose a common enemy C; and they might unite with C, when under attack by another enemy D, and so forth.
8. Interviews conducted by the author in 2008.
9. For a detailed account of the conflict in Kariu and Hatuhaha, their search for peace and the culturally informed repatriation ceremony of Kariu, see Bräuchler (2009*b*).

¹⁰ The use of "brothers" echoes the essence of the Hatuhaha union: the highlighting of a common ancestry regardless of a possible different religion (i.e., Islam versus Christianity).
¹¹ Taking up local voices emphasizing the importance of the empowerment of *adat* for reconciliation and peace, I have been doing research on that movement and its problems for the last couple of years. Interestingly, peace actors on all levels (local, national, international) and from all strands of society (villagers, NGOs, academics, *adat* leaders and even some religious leaders, government, etc.) jumped on that bandwagon and started to support the revival or reconstruction of specific *adat* elements (see, for example, Bräuchler 2007, 2009*a*,*b*, 2010*b*, 2012).
¹² This is not an exhaustive list of the Interfaith Council's programmes, but examples of its major activities.
¹³ This has been a continuous and ongoing process that involved, among others, the co-option of one of the former radicals who was then appointed head of the IAIN and thus made to change his mind and foster dialogue.

References

Aditjondro, George Junus. "Guns, Pamphlets and Handie-Talkies: How the Military Exploited Local Ethno-religious Tensions in Maluku to Preserve Their Political and Economic Privileges". In *Violence in Indonesia*, edited by I. Wessel and G. Wimhöfer. Hamburg: Abera-Verlag, 2001.

Andaya, Leonard Y. *The World of Maluku: Eastern Indonesia in the Early Modern Period*. Honolulu: University of Hawaii Press, 1993.

Badan Pusat Statistik Propinsi Maluku dan Badan Perencanaan Pembangunan Daerah. *Maluku Dalam Angka 2010* [Maluku in Figures 2010]. Ambon, 2010.

Bartels, Dieter. "Your God is no longer mine: Moslem-Christian Fratricide in the Central Moluccas (Indonesia) After a Half-Millennium of Tolerant Co-Existence and Ethnic Unity". In *A State of Emergency: Violence, Society and the State in Eastern Indonesia*, edited by S. Pannell. Darwin: Northern Territory University Press, 2003.

———. "The Evolution of God in the Spice Islands: Converging and Diverging of Protestant Christianity and Islam in the Moluccas During the Colonial and Post-Colonial Periods". In *Christianity in Indonesia*, edited by S. Schröter. Reihe Southeast Asian Modernities. Berlin: LIT, 2010.

Becker, Dieter. *Die Kirchen und der Pancasila-Staat. Indonesische Christen zwischen Konsens und Konflikt* [The Churches and the Pancasila State: Indonesian Christians between Consensus and Conflict]. Erlangen: Verlag der Ev.-Luth. Mission Erlangen, 1996.

Benda, Harry J. *The Crescent and the Rising Sun: Indonesian Islam under the Japanese Occupation 1942–1945*. The Hague: W. van Hoeve, 1958.

Benda-Beckmann, F. von and K. von. "Adat and Religion in Minangkabau and Ambon". In *Time Past, Time Present, Time Future: Perspectives on Indonesian Culture*, edited by H.J.M. Claessen and D.S. Moyer. Verhandelingen van het Koninklijk Instituut voor Taal-, Land- en Volkenkunde 131. Leiden: KITLV Press, 1988.

———. "Eine turbulente Geschichte im Verhältnis zwischen Religion und Volksrecht: die Molukker in Indonesien und den Niederlanden". In *Sprache, Symbole und Symbolverwendungen in Ethnologie, Kulturanthropologie, Religion und Recht*, edited by W. Krawietz, L. Pospisil, and S. Steinbrich. Festschrift für Rüdiger Schott zum 65. Geburtstag, Berlin: Duncker and Humblot, 1993.

———. "Law, Violence and Peace Making on the Island of Ambon". In *Healing the Wounds: Essays on the Reconstruction of Societies after War*, edited by M.-C. Foblets and T. v. Trotha. Oxford and Portland Oregon: HART Publishing, 2004.

Bertrand, Jacques. "Legacies of the Authoritarian Past: Religious Violence in Indonesia's Moluccan Islands". *Pacific Affairs* (Spring 2002).

Braithwaite, John et al. *Anomie and Violence: Non-truth and Reconciliation in Indonesian Peacebuilding*. Canberra: ANU E. Press, 2010.

Bräuchler, Birgit. "Cyberidentities at War: Religion, Identity, and the Internet in the Moluccan Conflict". *Indonesia* 75 (April 2003): 123–51.

———. *Cyberidentities at War: Der Molukkenkonflikt im Internet*. Bielefeld: Transcript, 2005.

———. "Ein Comeback der Tradition? Die Revitalisierung von Adat in Ostindonesien" [*A Comeback of Tradition? The Revitalisation of Adat in Eastern Indonesia*]. *Zeitschrift für Ethnologie* 132. Special issue "Die Revitalisierung von Tradition/The Revitalisation of Tradition", edited by Birgit Bräuchler and Thomas Widlok, 2007.

———. "Cultural Solutions to Religious Conflicts? The Revival of Tradition in the Moluccas, Eastern Indonesia". *Asian Journal of Social Sciences* 37, no. 6 (2009*a*): 872–91.

———. "Mobilising Culture and Tradition for Peace: Reconciliation in the Moluccas". In *Reconciling Indonesia: Grassroots Agency for Peace*, edited by B. Bräuchler. London/New York: Routledge, 2009*b*.

———. "Integration and Exclusion: *Islam Adat* in Central Moluccas". *Indonesia and the Malay World* 38, no. 110 (March 2010*a*): 65–93.

———. "The Revival Dilemma: Reflections on Human Rights, Self-Determination and Legal Pluralism in Eastern Indonesia". *Journal of Legal Pluralism and Unofficial Law* 62 (2010*b*): 1–42.

———. "Intangible Cultural Heritage and Peace Building in Indonesia and East Timor". In *Routledge Handbook of Heritage in Asia*, edited by P. Daly and T. Winter. London/New York: Routledge, 2012.

Bräuchler, Birgit and Erb Maribeth. "Introduction — Eastern Indonesia under Reform: The Global, the National and the Local". *Asian Journal of Social Sciences* 39 (2: Special issue "Eastern Indonesia under Reform: The Global, the National and the Local", edited by Birgit Bräuchler and Maribeth Erb, 2011), pp. 113–30.

Chauvel, Richard. "Ambon's Other Half: Some Preliminary Observations on Ambonese Moslem Society and History". *Review of Indonesian and Malaysian Affairs* 14, no. 1 (1980): 40–80.

―――. *Nationalists, Soldiers and Separatists: The Ambonese Islands from Colonialism to Revolt, 1880–1950*. Verhandelingen van het Koninklijk Instituut voor Taal-, Land- en Volkenkunde 143. Leiden: KITLV Press, 1990.

Cooley, Frank L. "Altar and Throne in Central Moluccan Societies: A Study of the Relationship between the Institutions of Religion and the Institutions of Local Society Undergoing Rapid Social Change". A Dissertation presented to the Faculty of the Department of Religion Yale University. New Haven: Yale University, 1961.

―――. "Das Gesicht der ältesten evangelischen Kirche in Asien". In *Indonesia Raja: Antlitz einer großen Inselwelt*, edited by T. Müller-Krüger. Bad Sulzfelden: Verlag für Missions- und Bibelkunde, 1966.

―――. *Indonesia: Church and Society*. New York: Friendship Press, 1968.

Enklaar, I.H. *Joseph Kam "Apostel der Molukken"*. Den Haag: Boekencentrum, 1963.

Fraassen, Chris Frans van. *Ambon-Rapport: Doktoraalskriptie*. Leiden: Stichting Werkgroep Studiereizen Ontwikkelingslanden, 1972.

Hayden, Robert M. "Antagonistic Tolerance: Competitive Sharing of Religious Sites in South Asia and the Balkans". *Current Anthropology* 43, no. 2 (2002): 205–31.

Human Rights Watch. "Report on Violence in Ambon". A Human Rights Watch Report 11, no. 1 (C) (March 1999). Available at <http://www.hrw.org/sites/default/files/reports/indon994.pdf>.

International Crisis Group. "Indonesia: Overcoming Murder and Chaos in Maluku". *Asia Report* no. 10 (19 December 2000). Jakarta/Brussels: International Crisis Group, 2000.

―――. "Indonesia: The Search for Peace in Maluku". *Asia Report* no. 31 (8 February 2002). Jakarta/Brussels: International Crisis Group, 2002.

Klinken, Gerry van. "The Maluku Wars: Bringing Society Back In". *Indonesia* 71 (April 2001): 1–26.

―――. *Communal Violence and Democratization in Indonesia: Small Town Wars*. Routledge Contemporary Southeast Asia Series 15. London/New York: Routledge, 2007.

Kraemer, Hendrik. "Report on Amboina and the Minahassa". In *From Missionfield to Independent Church: Report on a Decisive Decade in the Growth of Indigenous Churches in Indonesia*, edited by H. Kraemer. The Hague: Boekencentrum, 1958.

Maluku Reconciliation and Reconstruction Meeting. Recommendations for Reconciliation and Reconstruction in Maluku, January 2004. London: Islamic Christian Organisation for Reconciliation and Reconstruction (IICORR Ltd.) and British Foreign Office, 2004.

Mulder, D.C. "Unter dem Halbmond". In *Indonesia Raja: Antlitz einer großen Inselwelt*, edited by T. Müller-Krüger. Bad Sulzfelden: Verlag für Missions- und Bibelkunde, 1966.

Müller-Krüger, Theodor. *Der Protestantismus in Indonesien: Geschichte und Gestalt.* Stuttgart: Evangelische Verlagswerk GmbH, 1968.

Nordstrom, Carolyn. "The Eye of the Storm: From War to Peace — Examples from Sri Lanka and Mozambique". In *Cultural Variation in Conflict Resolution: Alternatives to Violence*, edited by D.P. Fry and K. Björkqvist. Mahwah, NJ: Lawrence Erlbaum Associates, 1997.

Pannell, Sandra, ed. *A State of Emergency: Violence, Society and the State in Eastern Indonesia.* Darwin: Northern Territory University Press, 2003.

Rumphius, Georgius Everhardus. "De Ambonsche Historie". *Bijdragen tot de Taal-, Land- en Volkenkunde van Nederlandsch-Indië* 64 (Deel I), 1910.

Sahusilawane, Florence and L. Sopacua. *Dari Aman Hurariu ke Desa Hulaliu: Sejarah Pembentukan Negeri Hulaliu — Suatu Tinjauan Sosial Budaya di Kecamatan Pulau Haruku, Kabupaten Maluku Tengah, Propinsi Maluku* [From Aman Hurariu to Desa Hulaliu: Formation History of Hulaliu Village — A Sociocultural Review in the Subdistrict of Haruku Island, Central Moluccan District, Maluku Province]. Ambon: Balai Kajian Sejarah dan Nilai Tradisional, 1996/1997.

Schulze, Kirsten E. "Laskar Jihad and the Conflict in Ambon". *The Brown Journal of World Affairs* IX, no. 1 (2002): 57–69.

Schumann, Olaf. "Christian-Muslim Encounter in Indonesia". In *Christian–Muslim Encounters*, edited by Y.Y. Haddad and W.Z. Haddad. Gainesville, FL: University Press of Florida, 1995.

Sharpe, Eric J. "The Study of Religion in Historical Perspective". In *The Routledge Companion to the Study of Religion*, edited by J.R. Hinnells. London/New York: Routledge, 2005.

Sopacua, L., W. Pattinama and T. Noya. *Laporan Penelitian Perlawanan Rakyat Amarima Hatuhaha Terhadap Imperialisme dan Kolonialisme Portugis dan Belanda Pada Abad 16 (Perang Alaka) di Pulau Haruku* [Research Report about the Resistance of the Hatuhaha People against Portuguese and Dutch Imperialism and Colonialism in the 16th Century (Alaka War) on Haruku Island]. Ambon: Balai Kajian Sejarah dan Nilai Tradisional, 1996.

Spyer, Patricia. "Fire without Smoke and other Phantoms of Ambon's Violence: Media Effects, Agency, and the Work of Imagination". *Indonesia* 74 (October 2002): 21–36.

Titaley, M.M. "Injil Masuk Negeri Hulaliu". Paper presented to the Seminar Sehari HUT ke 100 Gedung Gereja Bethlehem, Hulaliu, 20 June 2007.

Tjandrasasmita, Uka. "Peranan dan sumbangan Islam dalam sedjarah Maluku". Paper presented to the Seminar Sedjarah Maluku ke-1, Ambon, 5 s/d, 10 October 1971.

Varshney, Ashutosh. *Ethnic Conflict and Civic Life: Hindus and Muslims in India.* New Haven, CT: Yale University Press, 2002.

Wawer, Wendelin. *Muslime und Christen in der Republik Indonesia.* Beiträge zur Südostasienforschung 7. Heidelberg: Südasien-Institut, Universität Heidelberg, 1974.

Wertheim, Willem Frederik. *Indonesian Society in Transition: A Study of Social Change.* Den Haag/Bandung: W. van Hoeve, 1956.

9

CHINESE MUSLIM CULTURAL IDENTITIES
Possibilities and Limitations of Cosmopolitan Islam in Indonesia

Hew Wai Weng

INTRODUCTION

[The] Prophet Muhammad urges Muslims to seek knowledge even as far as China. Since many ethnic Chinese reside in Indonesia, Indonesian Muslims are lucky enough that we can learn from them without traveling to mainland China (field notes, 16 October 2008).

Tan Mei Hwa, a popular female Chinese Muslim preacher, delivered this message to her audience of mostly Javanese Muslims during a *halal-bihalal* (a meeting for mutual forgiveness) in Surabaya in 2008. Dressed in stylish Islamic dress, she also claimed that some of the Walisongo (Muslim saints popularly credited with for bringing Islam to Java) were of Chinese descent.[1]

Also in 2008, at a breaking of the fast function during Ramadan, another Chinese preacher, Syaukanie Ong, wearing red traditional Chinese dress, spoke in front of Muslims crowded into the compound of the Muhammad Cheng Hoo Mosque, a Chinese-style mosque in Surabaya.[2] These two events combine Chinese cultural symbols and Islamic messages, as well as bring together Chinese preachers and Muslim audiences, to challenge the widely held perception by both non-Muslim Chinese and non-Chinese Muslim Indonesians that "Chineseness" and Islam are incompatible.

During the New Order (1966–98), Chinese Indonesians who converted to Islam had always been assumed to have lost their "Chineseness", and assimilated themselves into various local ethnic majorities. Today, there are increasing numbers of Chinese Muslims who are publicly performing their Chinese ethnicity along with Islamic religiosity, exemplified by the popularity of Chinese preachers, the establishment of Chinese-style mosques, the celebrations of Chinese New Year in mosques, and the engagement of Chinese converts in various Islamic movements. Who and why promotes Chinese Muslim cultural identities? What does the emergence of Chinese Muslim culture tell us about Islamic pluralism in Indonesia? This chapter sketches answers to these questions.

CONTEXTUALIZING CHINESE MUSLIMS IN CONTEMPORARY INDONESIA

The emergence of Chinese Muslim cultures is an outcome of several interrelated processes that occurred in Indonesia and abroad from the 1990s onward. Such events include China's growing economic and diplomatic power; improving relations between China and Indonesia after the Cold war; the establishment of Indonesian democracy, the recognition of Chinese cultures after the fall of the New Order regime; the rise and diversification of Islamic consumer markets; the divergent pluralist and conservative tendencies of Indonesian Islam.

Chinese Muslims can be seen as a double minority in Indonesia: a minority within Chinese Indonesians and a minority within Muslim Indonesians. Some studies put the number of Chinese Muslims at about 5 per cent (Ananta, Arifin, and Bakhtiar 2008), whereas another study claims that there are about 30,000–50,000 Chinese Muslims across Indonesia (Jahja 2005), which is roughly 1–2 per cent of the Chinese population and a very tiny proportion of Muslim Indonesians. However, the attempt to figure out the number of Chinese Muslim itself is very problematic. During my fieldwork, I met some Chinese Muslims who married non-Chinese Muslims and do not regard themselves as Chinese anymore. I also encountered a few Javanese Muslims who refer to themselves as "Chinese Muslims" because parts of their ancestors have Chinese blood. I met many Chinese Muslims who are very pious and practise every details of Islam, but I also encountered a few non-practising (i.e., nominal) Chinese Muslims.

Indeed, the public manifestation of Chinese Muslim cultural identities does not reflect an existing ethno-religious reality but rather brings a new reality into being. It does not reflect the heterogeneity of cultural interactions and religious practices of many ordinary Chinese Muslims. While many popular Chinese preachers parade their "Chineseness", there are ordinary Chinese Muslim individuals who reject being labelled "Chinese Muslim" and claim to be "biologically Chinese, culturally Javanese" (field notes during 2008). While some Chinese Muslim leaders celebrate Chinese New Year in mosques, there are also a few Chinese Muslims who insist that Chinese New Year celebrations are *haram* (prohibited according to Islamic law). Also, most Chinese Muslims today are converts. There are various reasons for conversion, including political strategy, business consideration, religious interest, and intermarriage. Conversion factors together with religious experiences, economic statuses, social networks, and localities influence the identity negotiation of different Chinese converts.[3]

Despite these diversities, we witness a shift from the dominant discourse of "assimilation of Chinese Indonesians through Islam" (*asimilasi lewat Islam*) during the New Order period to "preaching Islam through cultural approaches" (*dakwah dengan pendekatan budaya*) in the past decade. During the New Order, the public expression of Chinese was prohibited. Even the Mandarin translation of Qur'anic text was banned. Some Chinese Muslim leaders, such as Junus Jahja, suggested conversion to Islam as a solution to the prejudice and discrimination against Chinese Indonesians since the majority of Indonesians were Muslims. In his view, Chinese Muslims should ultimately assimilate into the larger Indonesian Muslim population (Jahja 1981, 1990). However, after the fall of Soeharto, Chinese Indonesians regained the freedom to publicly express their cultural identities (Hoon 2008). Some Chinese Muslim preachers deliberately perform Chineseness in public talk to attract audiences, as well as to preach the universality of Islam.

Theoretically speaking, this chapter engages with academic debates on vernacular and religious cosmopolitanism (Kahn 2006; Robinson 2008; Werbner 2008). The notion of cosmopolitanism, despite being highly contested, has been deployed by many scholars to examine, theorize, and sometimes promote the ideal of people from different ethnicities and religions living together. In this research, I use religious cosmopolitanism to indicate its openness to difference, inclusiveness to diversity, and willingness to transform itself. Therefore, Islamic cosmopolitanism is not only about its tolerance of inter-religious diversity, but also its acceptance of diverse religious opinions, expressions, and practices among Muslims. In the following parts of this chapter, by examining the establishment of Chinese-style mosques, the popularity of Chinese Muslim preachers, and the celebrations of Chinese New Year in mosques, I look into the possibilities and limitations of Islamic cosmopolitanism in contemporary Indonesia.

CHINESE-STYLE MOSQUES

Since the collapse of the Soeharto regime, at least five Chinese-style mosques have been built across Indonesia. The first one is the Cheng Hoo Mosque in Surabaya, which was established by East Java PITI (Persatuan Islam Tionghoa Indonesia, Indonesian Chinese Muslim Association) in 2002. The Cheng Hoo Mosque has been inspired by the design of the Niu Jie Mosque in Beijing. According to the mosque handbook (YHMCHI 2008), its outlook resembles the architecture of *klenteng* (Chinese temple) and is intended to display the "Chineseness" of Chinese Muslims. The main hall of the mosque is as large as 11×9 meters with an eight-sided roof (*pat-kwa*). The length of 11 meters symbolizes the initial measurement of the *ka'bah*, demonstrating the commitment to Islamic faith. The length of 9 meters represents the number of Walisongo (the nine saints who are said to have brought Islam to Java), showing an appreciation towards local Javanese tradition. Meanwhile, the usage of Chinese *pat-kwa* suggests that the acceptance of Islamic and Javanese tradition does not necessarily mean the fading of Chinese cultural identity. This mixture of traditions reflects the desire of Chinese Muslim leaders to show that Islamic, Javanese, and Chinese elements are not conflicting.

Through the interior design of the mosque, PITI would like to send a message that the mosque belongs to all Muslim groups in Indonesia, including both Nahdlatul Ulama (NU) and Muhammadiyah (YHMCHI 2008). A *bedug* (a drum for calling to prayer) was placed on the side of the mosque, which is common for NU followers. Meanwhile, the pulpit used by an *imam* to deliver a sermon is designed to suit Muhammadiyah practices, as its front is closed rather than open. On the right side of the mosque, there is a relief of Admiral Cheng Ho and his fleet, illustrating his journey from China to Indonesia in the fifteenth and sixteenth centuries, to promote his contribution to the spread of Islam in Indonesia.

The mosque is an attempt of PITI to manifest a symbolic unity of Chinese Muslim identity. As the founder of the mosque, Bambang Sujanto said:

> The population of Chinese Muslims is small, diverse and scattered. As happened in the past, our identity will easily disappear or be assimilated into the Muslim majority. Thus, we need a physical space — a mosque that can project and uphold our identity. The structure of the mosque could stand for long time, and sustain our uniqueness over a few generations. Converting to Islam does not mean giving up our Chinese cultural identity. There can be a Chinese way of being Muslim (interview, Bambang Sujanto, 27 Novermber 2008).

Chinese Muslim leaders also believe that the Surabaya Cheng Hoo Mosque could highlight that Islam is a universal religion and not a religion for "indigenous" Indonesians only. In fact, most of Indonesian Muslim organizations, including NU and Muhammadiyah, endorse the establishment of Chinese-style mosques as a form to *dakwah* (preaching) to Chinese Indonesians. As stated by former chairperson of NU East Java, Ali Maschan:

> Chinese-style mosques will help the development of the *dakwah* movement in Indonesia, especially among ethnic Chinese, who will potentially convert to Islam. Even though they do not convert to Islam, at least, the mosque will reduce their prejudice toward Islam (interview, Ali Maschan, 27 November 2008).

PITI believes that the establishment of the Cheng Hoo Mosque will not be a success without additional support from non-Muslim Chinese. Given that the mosque is situated in a majority non-Muslim neighbourhood, PITI consulted local residents in order to gain their support for the mosque. To ensure non-Muslim Chinese residents are not disturbed, the mosque does not use loud speakers when calling for the morning praying session (*azan subuh*). Besides, most of the donors to the mosque are non-Muslim Chinese, who have contributed about 70 per cent of the total construction cost.[4] As some Chinese Muslim leaders told me, the non-Muslim Chinese have supported the construction of the Cheng Hoo Mosque, because they acknowledged the role of PITI in protecting them from possible "anti-Chinese" riots, as well as in bridging the divide between Chinese and Muslims in Surabaya.

CHINESE-STYLE MOSQUES AS TRANSLOCAL ETHNO-RELIGIOUS IMAGINATION

Following the success of Surabaya Cheng Hoo Mosque, many Chinese Muslims in other localities have expressed their intentions to build

Chinese-style mosques. The Al-Islam Muhammad Cheng Hoo Mosque in Palembang, which was inaugurated in 2008, is the second Chinese-style mosque in Indonesia named after Admiral Cheng Ho. This mosque was initiated by PITI South Sumatra, after its branch leaders visited their counterparts in Surabaya.

Painted in green and red, this mosque combines Chinese, Palembang, and pan-Islamic architectural features. It has a dome with a crescent and star and two minarets which resemble the design of a Chinese pagoda. Both minarets have ornaments with the shape of a goat's horn — a Palembang feature. According to the mosque handout (PITI Palembang 2009), its design reflects the similarity between Chinese and Palembang–Malay culture. The handout also states that the mosque is a reflection of the cultural accumulation of Islamic practices among Chinese Muslims, resembling the traditions of Javanese and Minangkabau Muslims. It is an important argument, as it is suggesting the imagination of "Chinese Islam" as another form of ethno-religious tradition in Indonesia. Given that Chinese Muslims from Medan to Makassar are extremely diverse, mosque architecture that adopts Chinese features can be seen as a symbolic unifying form for them.

Besides PITI, individual Chinese Muslims have also engaged in the construction of Chinese-style mosques. For an example, Anton Medan, a Chinese preacher had built a mosque that resembles the architectural design of an ancient Chinese palace in his Islamic boarding school in Bogor. In Pandaan, Pasuruan, East Java, even non-Chinese Muslims have built a mosque, resembling the outlook of the Surabaya Cheng Hoo Mosque, to support social blending (*pembauran*) and promote religious tourism.

THE SURABAYA CHENG HOO MOSQUE AS A COSMOPOLITAN SPACE

The establishment of the Cheng Hoo Mosque and its significance have to be examined in a larger Indonesian context in 1998 and onwards. It was marked by events such as "anti-Chinese" riots in 1998, the Bali Bombing, Majelis Ulama Indonesia (MUI; Indonesian Ulama Council) *fatwas* against pluralism, attacks against churches. Responding to such events, mainstream Muslim organizations, despite internal frictions, have continued to promote Islamic moderation and religious pluralism (Hefner 2005; Robinson 2008). Within such contexts, Cheng Hoo Mosque can be seen as a symbolic marker of the acceptance of Chinese culture in

Indonesia society, as well as a clear statement of the tolerant face of Indonesian Islam.

Both NU and Muhammadiyah leaders have lend their support towards Chinese-style mosques. Syafiq Mughni, a Muhammadiyah leader, welcomed the Surabaya Cheng Hoo Mosque because it reflected the universality of Islam and helped preaching Islam to non-Muslims. He urged Indonesian Muslims to learn from the spirit of Cheng Ho which emphasized togetherness and tolerance (interview, Syafiq Mughni, 18 September 2008). Meanwhile Rubaidi, a NU activist, suggests that the mosque shows that Indonesian Islam is open towards the inclusion of ethnic cultural symbols and practices. As a proponent of the indigenization of Islam, he sees it as a form of resistance against the "Arabization" of mosque architecture in Indonesia (interview, Rubaidi, 15 November 2008).

Now, let us explore the social reality of inclusive practices in Surabaya Cheng Hoo Mosque — a place where Chinese and non-Chinese Muslims and non-Muslims converge as well as a space where religious and social activities coexist. The busiest day of the week is Friday, when hundreds of men of various ethnic backgrounds come to the mosque for afternoon prayers. The mosque can only accommodate about 200–300 people, so every Friday a temporary shelter is set up to cater for another 1,000 people. With the exception of a few Chinese Muslim leaders, almost all Muslims who perform Friday prayers at the mosque are non-Chinese who are either working or residing nearby.

During a Ramadan night in 2008, while Muslims (both Chinese and non-Chinese) were performing their evening *taraweh* prayer in the mosque, non-Muslims (mostly Chinese) were practising *Qi Gong* (Chinese breathing exercise) at the corridor of the PITI's office in the mosque compound. For the *taraweh* prayer, the mosque organized two versions, one with 11 *rakaat* (prostration during prayer) and another one with 23 *rakaat* to accommodate the need of Muslims from different groups. The mosque also exercises its inclusivity through collaborations with other socio-religious groups. PITI, for instance, organized a mass circumcision at the mosque for poor Muslims in cooperation with Al-Irsyad, an Arab Muslim organization. Together with a Buddhist organization, Tzu Chi, PITI have donated goods for flood victims. Also parts of the mosque compound are PITI's offices, a few multipurpose rooms, a kindergarten, a canteen, an acupuncture clinic, and badminton courts.

This inclusivity shows that Islamic cosmopolitanisms are not only found in Islamic texts also in its historical encounters and cultural syncretism, but also in the everyday life strategies of a minority group. To a certain extent, the Surabaya Cheng Hoo Mosque promotes "cosmopolitan Islam" as not only a prayer house for all Muslims regardless of their affiliations, but also a gathering place for non-Muslims to conduct various social activities.

CHINESE MUSLIM PREACHERS

Chinese Muslim preachers such as Tan Mei Hwa and Anton Medan are popular religious figures among not only Chinese converts but also non-Chinese Muslim Indonesians. They appear regularly in religious programmes on TV and give public talks. Tapping into the rising consumer culture, many successful preachers in contemporary Indonesia have become media celebrities, who are skilled at tailoring their messages and fashioning their appearances to a media audience (Fealy 2008). Chinese preachers appear to have a special marketing pull, because of their ethnicity and their status as converts. Their Chinese appearance stands out as exotic trademarks in the crowded preaching market. In addition, some Muslims are concerned with what they see as a process of "Christianization" in Indonesia, and so they view the conversion of Chinese Indonesians to Islam — a community that is almost 40 per cent Christian — as a welcome phenomenon.[5]

At the same time, many Muslims think that having experienced the spiritual journey towards piety, these "converts-turned-preachers" can provide a persuasive role model for non-practising Muslims. Many Chinese Muslim preachers are aware of their distinctive qualities and thus, they strategically use their differences to augment their popularity. Yet, Chinese preachers are not a singular entity. Their preaching takes varying forms and each of them has different messages, reflecting their varying socio-economic backgrounds, cultural outlooks, conversion experiences, and religious education. The following section presents a few case studies.

Tan Mei Hwa: Singing, Dancing, Preaching

Tan Mei Hwa is both a preacher and an entertainer. Her Chinese identity and engaging style of preaching make her one of the most popular preachers in East Java. Always dressed in fashionable and colorful Muslim attire with a *jilbab* (headscarf), her easily digested religious messages and down-to-earth preaching style are welcomed by many ordinary Muslims, especially women and girls. She intersperses her message with singing, plenty of jokes, and sometimes even dancing. She also makes extensive use of "social talk" (*bahasa gaul*) — the slang used by the Indonesian youth — to interact with her audience.

What makes her most striking, however, is her expression of Chineseness. First, although she is not a fluent Mandarin speaker, she often sprinkles a little Mandarin in her talk. Second, she always highlights the role of Chinese Muslims in promoting early Islamization in Java. Third, she tries to present a positive image of Chinese Indonesians to the Muslim crowd by saying that not all Chinese are rich or exclusive. Fourth, she uses her Chinese name, Tan Mei Hwa, in order to differentiate herself from other preachers who have Arabic or Indonesian names.

Tan Mei Hwa also creatively makes references to religious texts in her preaching. In a public talk in Surabaya in 2008, she urged the crowd, who were mostly non-Chinese Muslims, to acknowledge and respect difference. She began her talk by stating that she converted to Islam because she was interested in the (popular) concept of "*rahmatan lil 'alamin*" (a blessing for all) in Islamic teachings. Later, she recounted a short conversation between two Muslim girls one of whom had refused to go to a *pengajian* (Islamic study session) because it was being led by a Chinese preacher. She then cited Qur'anic texts and told her audience the following:

> I was born as Tan Mei Hwa. Is it a sin to be Chinese? There is no Qur'anic text that obliges someone to be ethnic Chinese or not. God creates us in different shapes and colors. Some have slanted eyes, and some have broader eyes. Some have darker skin, and some have fairer skin. We are all brothers and sisters. We should respect each other. (field notes, 16 October 2008)[6]

She further likes to claim that Cheng Ho, the Chinese admiral, played an important role in the early Islamization in Java, and that some of the Walisongo were of Chinese descent. Such messages help promote a better image of Chinese Indonesians and bolster her credentials as a Chinese preacher.

Koko Liem: Chinese Package, Islamic Message

Born Liem Hai Thai, Koko Liem adopted a Muslim name, Muhammad Utsman Anshori after converting to Islam. However, he prefers to be called Koko Liem in his preaching, because it is more down to earth. Koko is a word derived from the *Hokkien* dialect and means "brother", and Liem is his Chinese surname. Besides his name, Koko Liem's other preaching hallmark is his traditional Chinese clothing with a Chinese skullcap.[7]

He wears this outfit because it looks interesting and is different from what other preachers wear. As he likes to say, "Preachers don't have to wear a *jubah* with turban, or a *baju koko* with *peci*. I am a Chinese preacher. That is why I dress in Chinese clothing" (interview, Koko Liem, 26 April 2008).[8] He also explained that it was a preaching strategy to show that Islam is a universal religion and compatible with Chinese cultural traditions.

Koko Liem can be seen as one of the most creative Chinese Muslim preachers, since his Islamic business career goes beyond public preaching, but also includes religious travel and SMS services. In his latest SMS religious-themed service, *Lampion Hati* (A Lantern for the Heart), which offers Islamic-based advice, teaching, and ring tones to subscribers, Koko Liem combined Chinese cultural symbols with Islamic messages to attract customers. Against a red background decorated with pictures of Chinese lanterns and the silhouette of a mosque, Koko Liem features in a posture of prayer, wearing green (the color of Islam) traditional Chinese clothing. The advertisement for his SMS service declares his goal to "illuminate your heart and faith with Islamic advice" (*Terangi Hati dan Imanmu dengan tausiyah-tausiyah Islami*).

Irena Handono: From Church Activist to Islamic Preacher

Irena Handono was a Catholic activist and nun before converting to Islam. Different from Tan Mei Hua and Koko Liem, Irena Handoko does not position herself as a "Chinese" preacher. She also eschews much of the entertainment-focused approach, concentrating instead on smaller-scale preaching tours and Islamic activism. She is active in numerous Islamic organizations, most of which are conservatively inclined, including Forum for the Anti Pornography and Porno-action Movement (FORGAPP, Forum Gerakan Anti Pornografi dan Pornoaksi). She also established Irena Centre to educate Muslims and prevent apostasy.

Whenever she preaches, Irena emphasizes her experience of conversion to Islam. She makes detailed theological comparisons between Christianity and Islam, which always end by asserting Islam's superiority: that Islam is the only true religion recognized by God, and that the Christian concept of the "trinity" is deceptive. Not only criticizing those non-practising, she also routinely blames the well-known religious scholar Syafi'i Ma'arif for suggesting that both Muslims, Christians and Jews are offered a place in heaven. Her messages draw criticism from Christians and moderate Muslim leaders. They worry that her effort to rid Christianity of "weaknesses" after having found the "Islamic truth" will worsen inter-religious relationships in

Indonesia. On the contrary, hardline Muslim groups, especially those who worried about the threat of "Christianization" welcome her talks.

Anton Medan: From *Preman* (Gangster) to *Dai* (Preacher)

Anton Medan, or Tan Kok Liong, is another controversial character in the Chinese Muslim community. He was a *preman* (gangster) before he became a popular *dakwah* figure. His involvement in murder, robbery, and illegal gambling led him to spend 18 years of his life in prison. After converting to Islam, he started his preaching career amongst prisoners and prostitutes, before becoming popular in public.

Anton Medan sees himself as a bridge between ethnic Chinese and Muslim Indonesians. He is occasionally involved in inter-faith activities and helps some non-Muslim Chinese solve their conflicts with Muslim leaders. For instance, during my visit to his boarding school, a couple of Chinese women from Medan were asking for his help in dealing with some Muslim leaders who opposed the building of a Chinese temple in Medan, Sumatra (field note, 9 January 2009).

However, far from being a liberal Muslim, Anton Medan claims to be an advisor to the Islamic Defenders' Front (FPI, Front Pembela Islam). He expressed regret that the FPI chairman Rizieq Shihab had been sentenced for two years for his involvement in the MONAS incident in May 2008, involving a clash between hardline Muslims and an alliance of organizations that support religious freedom.[9] In 2008, at an Islamic study session in Cirebon to celebrate the Islamic New Year, he openly criticized the well-known liberal-minded NU leader, Maman Imanulhaq, a speaker at the same event. He blamed Maman Imanulhaq for supporting religious freedom and urged him to repent (*"tobat"*). He even suggested the audience to disperse and not listen to Maman Imanulhaq's speech (Wahid Institute 2009, p. 1).

From Converts to Preachers — Pluralizing the Islamic "Market"?

Always dominated by "indigenous" and Arabic-descent Muslims, the *dakwah* activities of Chinese Muslims have pluralized the Indonesian religious market. Muslim preachers use not only Arabic and Indonesian names but also Chinese names. Muslim preachers wear not only *peci* with *baju koko*, or long robes and turbans but also Chinese clothing with skullcaps. To a certain extent, this hybrid form of Islamic expression is an antidote to increasing puritanism that is hostile to local cultural traditions. However, this diversity does not necessarily contribute to a more critical understanding of Islam. Like other celebrity preachers, many Chinese preachers tend to embrace "a socially conservative Islam, albeit with a light touch" and do not "provide the tools for critical thinking and nuanced religious interpretation" (Howell 2008, p. 59). In other words, Chinese preachers may diversify the appearance of preaching — simply because they look Chinese — but they do not necessarily add greater pluralism to the substance of religious belief and practice.

Indeed, many Chinese Muslim preachers are rather conservative regarding religious and social matters, especially when preaching in public.[10] Irena Handono is one extreme case. Her constant criticism of Christianity not only alarms non-Muslims but also alienates her from moderate Muslim audiences. Other Chinese Muslim preachers are moderate and tolerant in their preaching, yet sometimes restrict themselves to certain orthodox interpretations of Islamic teaching. For example, Anton Medan, Tan Mei Hwa, and Koko Liem respectively held that "Muslims should avoid wishing 'Merry Christmas' to their Christian friends" (interview, 7 November 2008), that "women are not suited to become leaders" (field notes, 23 November 2008); and that "Muslims cannot celebrate Valentine's Day" (Koko Liem 2009). For converts, subscribing to a rather conservative understanding of Islam is not surprising, as this is a way of proving the sincerity of one's conversion and demonstrating one's credentials as a preacher.

CHINESE NEW YEAR CELEBRATIONS IN MOSQUES

Along with Chinese-style mosques and Chinese preachers, Chinese New Year (also known as "Imlek" in Indonesia) celebrations in mosques is another form of identity performance, bringing together Islamic messages and Chinese cultural symbols, thus forging a hybrid Chinese Muslim identity.[11] Imlek celebrations in mosques have various meanings. First, they suggest another possibility of a hybrid Islam along with other local Muslim streams such as "Javanese Islam". Second, it shows there is another way of expressing Chineseness: the celebration of Imlek is not limited to Confucian and Buddhist temples but also churches and even mosques. Third, it is a way of spreading Islamic messages using Chinese culture.

Imlek ceremony of Chinese Muslims in Yogyakarta was first held in 2003 and the celebrations became livelier in the following years. In

2003, despite protests from some conservative Muslim individuals and groups, about 200 Muslims from Chinese and non-Chinese backgrounds participated in the inaugural Imlek ceremony in Syuhada Mosque in Yogyakarta. This celebration was organized by the Indonesian Chinese Muslim Association (PITI), Yogyakarta, and attended by local figures from MUI, NU, Muhammadiyah, and the provincial administration. As the main organizer of the event Budi Setyagraha pointed out, the Imlek celebration in the mosque was modest and its rituals had been modified to suit Islamic teachings, which includes a *pengajian* (Islamic studies session), *sholat hajat* (a blessing prayer for a prosperous and healthy year), and *sujud syukur* (a prayer to express gratitude to God) (interview, Budi Setyagraha, 12 February 2009).

Encouraged by the success of the 2003 Chinese New Year celebrations, PITI continued to hold them in the following years. In 2004, PITI organized the Imlek ceremony in the Syuhada Mosque in a more obvious way, decorating with red lanterns (Susanto and Sudiarno 2004). There were also activities such as the distribution of traditional Chinese New Year Cake (*kue keranjang*) and the giving of *ang pao* (money in red envelopes). The 2005 PITI Imlek celebration of PITI was a very lively affair with lion dance performances outside the Syuhada Mosque. In 2006, the Imlek ceremony moved to the An Nadzar Mosque and a special *pengajian* was conducted to celebrate both Chinese New Year and Islamic New Year (*hijrah*), which fell on very close dates that year. In 2007 after the earthquake in Yogyakarta, PITI and other local Chinese organizations arranged "Festival Imlek Bantul 2007" (2007 Bantul Imlek festival) with the theme "Imlek for the recovery of Bantul".

DAKWAH THROUGH CULTURAL APPROACHES: DISTINGUISHING RELIGION FROM CULTURE

Imlek celebrations in mosques are not without controversy, as some conservative Muslims see it as "improper innovation" and "un-Islamic". However, by differentiating Chinese "religious" rituals from "cultural" traditions, PITI Yogyakarta successfully convinced many local Muslim leaders that the celebration of Chinese New Year is not violating Islamic principles. They promote Chinese New Year celebrations as a form of "*budaya*" (culture), and sometimes, "*adat*" (custom) or "*tradisi*" (tradition), not as a religious festival. Statements such as "Imlek is not a religious practice. It is a Chinese custom" (interview, Rudiansyah, 16 February 2009); and "Imlek does not belong to any religion. It is a cultural event shared by all Chinese" (interview, Merry Effendi, 8 February 2009); and so on are commonly used by Chinese Muslims to justify their celebrations of Chinese New Year.

Through the enactment of rituals and abandonment of "un-Islamic" practices, Chinese Muslim leaders show that Imlek celebrations are not only compatible but also complementary to Islamic values. During Imlek ceremonies in mosques, Chinese Muslims do not worship deities or burn incense and perform any other rituals related to Chinese folk beliefs. Instead, they perform Islamic prayers. Chinese Muslim leaders also endorse activities such as paying visits to relatives and friends as a form of "*silaturahim*" (maintaining good relationships). At the same time, they retain Chinese cultural symbols such as red decorations and ornaments, whilst scrapping "un-Islamic" practices, such as the consumption of *haram* food and gambling.[12]

Arguing that there was no contradiction between Chinese culture and Islamic religiosity, some Chinese Muslims active in accommodating Chinese cultural elements in their Islamic preaching call it "*dakwah pendekatan budaya*" (*dakwah* through cultural approaches). During Idul Fitri 2008, a Chinese Muslim leader in Surabaya, Abdul Chalim Lee, organized an open house called "*Lebaran bernuansa budaya Tionghoa*" (Celebration of Idul Fitri with Chinese cultural features). He decorated his home with red Chinese lanterns, ornaments, and calligraphy. As well as serving Indonesian cuisine, he also provided both *halal* Chinese food, such as *mee sua* (long noodles, symbolizes long life) and Arabic dates. Beyond the festivities, Chinese-style mosques, Chinese *nasyid* (Islamic music) group, and Chinese *halal* restaurants, that combine both Chinese cultures with Islamic messages, are other creative forms of "*dakwah* through cultural approaches".

To some extent, their efforts are reminiscent of the early efforts of Muslim saints who appropriated the Javanese traditions to disseminate Islamic messages (Dijk 1998; Woodward 1989). Indeed, appreciation of ethnic cultural practices is not new to Indonesian Islam. Today, not only the traditionalist NU but also the modernist Muhammadiyah have a more relaxed attitude towards local cultural traditions (Daniels 2009; Syamsul 2005). Over the last few years, under the notion of "cultural *dakwah*" (*dakwah kultural*), some Muhammadiyah activists have been striving to accommodate local traditions, while attempting to reform religious practices.[13] Yet, the different cultural manifestations of Islam are not without critics, as many conservative Muslims see such practices as "improper innovations" and thus "un-Islamic".

IMLEK AS RELIGIOUS DEBATE: *HALAL* OR *HARAM*

How do Muslim leaders perceive Chinese New Year celebrations among Chinese Muslims? Is it considered *halal* or *haram* (permitted or prohibited according to Islamic principles)? According to a feature report by *Nurani* magazine in 2008, entitled *"Fatwa MUI: Boleh Rayakan* Imlek *di Masjid"* [MUI *Fatwa*: It is permissible to celebrate Imlek in mosques], the national board of MUI issued a *fatwa* (religious opinion) that the Imlek celebration is permissible (*diperbolehkan*) as long as it does not contain customary rituals.[14] According to Mahruf Amin, head of the MUI *fatwa* commission, the *fatwa* decision was based on Qur'anic texts. To support his argument that Islam acknowledges cultural and ethnic differences, Mahruf Amin first quoted a Qur'anic verse from Chapter Al-Hujurat, which holds: "People, We created you all from a single man and a single woman, and made you into races and tribes so that you should recognize one another. In God's eyes, the most honored of you are ones most mindful of Him: God is all knowing, all aware."[15]

He then describes Qur'anic verses 26–30 from Chapter Al-Zukhruf, which state that Islam strongly prohibits idolatry and polytheism (*syirik*), associating God with other human inventions. According to Mahruf Amin, the Chinese New Year tradition is not part of a religious ideology, but a social and cultural tradition. Chinese Muslims are thus allowed to celebrate Imlek in mosques to show their gratitude towards God by welcoming a new year. He says the Imlek ceremony is only *haram* if it involves non-Islamic praying rituals, such as deity worship and consumption of forbidden food, such as pork. He stresses that Islam is not hostile to cultural traditions and perceives cultural expressions of Islam as variations of *syiar* (Islamic preaching).

While most mainstream Muslim leaders share MUI's viewpoint on Imlek, some Muslims disagree and even argue that Chinese New Year celebration is *haram*. Such opinion is well represented in an article entitled, *"Imlek adalah hari raya agama kafir bukan sekedar tradisi Tionghoa: Haram atas Muslim turut merayakannya"* [Imlek is a religious holiday for heathens, not merely a Chinese tradition: Muslims are forbidden to join the celebrations], which was written by Shiddiq al-Jawi, a HTI (Hizbut Tahrir Indonesia) activist in 2007. Referring to a book, entitled *"Mengenal Hari Raya Konfusiani"* [Understanding Confucian Holidays] (Winarso 2003), Al-Jawi concludes that Chinese New Year is an integral part of Confucian (i.e., religious) teachings and therefore not merely a cultural event. He follows Winarso's book argument that Imlek signifies the birth of Confucius and is an important day to pray *Tian* (God), to back up his view that the Chinese New Year festival has a religious connotation.

Highlighting that the Qur'an and the *Hadith* are the only references for Muslims, he further contends that the question over whether Muslims are allowed to carry out a certain practice or attend a particular event is not related to whether the practice or event is part of a cultural tradition or a religious ritual, but on whether it is stated in the religious scriptures or not (Al-Jawi 2007). Like most other conservative Muslims, the author views those practices not specifically mentioned in the scriptures as improper innovations. The Chinese New Year celebration is thus violating Islamic principles, even though it does not involve "un-Islamic" rituals. On a separate note, some Chinese Muslims, too, discourage Imlek celebrations, as they might lead a convert to observe "un-Islamic" activities, such as drinking beer, eating pork, and gambling (Laison 2008).

CONTEXTUALIZING *FATWA*: THE POSSIBILITIES AND LIMITATIONS OF ISLAMIC COSMOPOLITANISM

In the previous section, I discussed Muslim opinions on Chinese New Year celebrations; now I will locate the discussion within the larger debate on Islamic cosmopolitanism in Indonesia. The MUI *fatwa* that allowed the celebration of Imlek was a surprise for some people, as the conservative-inclined council had previously issued *fatwas* against religious pluralism. For example, in 1981, MUI issued a *fatwa* proposing it was *haram* for Muslims to attend Christmas celebrations, and some Muslim leaders even argued that Muslims should avoid wishing Christians "Merry Christmas". In 2005, MUI issued a *fatwa* describing pluralism, secularism, and liberalism are "un-Islamic" (Gillespie 2007). In 2009, the West Javanese branch of MUI issued another *fatwa* that prohibited Muslims from celebrating Valentine's Day,[16] a view shared by Mahruf Amin.[17] As I discussed, the "culture-religion" distinction is one of the main reasons why MUI have different attitudes towards Imlek and Christmas. MUI views Imlek as a cultural tradition but treats Christmas as a religious celebration that is incompatible with Islamic teachings.

I would like to further argue that, to a certain extent, MUI *fatwas* allowing Imlek yet prohibiting Christmas celebrations among Muslims reflect the possibilities and limitations of religious pluralism in contemporary Indonesia. Paradoxically, while there is an increasing acceptance of cultural diversity among Muslim leaders, there is also a rising intolerance towards religious intermingling and intra-religious differences within some sections of the Indonesian Muslim society. To support this argument, I compared the responses of Indonesian Muslims towards a variety of issues. As I noted, while most Indonesian Muslim leaders are agreeable and, at times, even openly support the establishment of Chinese-style mosques, some hesitate to endorse Chinese New Year ceremonies in mosques. Many Muslims, including the conservatively inclined MUI, allow the celebration of Chinese New Year if it does not involve non-Islamic rituals, yet keep themselves alway from Christmas celebrations. When it comes to Ahmadiyah, fewer Muslim scholars lend their support to the minority Muslim sect which was deemed "deviant" according to MUI's *fatwa*.

CONCLUSIONS

Despite their relatively small number, studying the religious beliefs of Chinese Muslims against the backdrop of their socio-cultural heritage provides relevant insights into the possibilities and limitations, and the patterns and paradoxes, of cosmopolitan Islam in contemporary Indonesia. First, the rise of Chinese Muslim cultures reflects an overall acceptance of Chinese culture in Indonesian society and the tolerance of Islam towards different cultural expressions. Second, although tending towards religious conservatism, Chinese Muslim cultures do embrace a limited kind of cosmopolitan Islam, in which the assertion of Islamic religiosity does not mean racial segregation and religious exclusion, but can act against them. The Surabaya Cheng Hoo Mosque is a prime example of religious inclusivity — it is a socio-religious place where both Chinese and non-Chinese, Muslims, and non-Muslims can converge and interact with each other. Third, Chinese Muslim culture is able to reconcile prevailing stereotypes of an alleged incompatibility between Islam and Chineseness. But the amalgamation of Islam and Chinese culture does not necessarily pluralize Islamic discourses. For instance, many Chinese Muslim preachers creatively mix Islamic teachings and Chinese cultural symbols to promote the universality of Islam, yet they do not contribute to a more critical understanding of Islam. Instead of challenging some widely held conservative viewpoints, many preachers choose to conform to them to avoid controversy.

Notes

1. The term "Walisongo" refers to the nine saints who are mythologized as the individuals who spread Islam in Java. On several occasions, the late NU leader and former Indonesian President Abdurrahman Wahid stated that he had Chinese heritage and that some of the Walisongo were of Chinese descent. He claimed that he is a descendant of Tan Kim Han or Sheik Abdul al-Shini Qodir, a Chinese Muslim who has helped Raden Patah seize power from the Majapahit kingdom and founded the Islamic kingdom of Demak (Al-Qurtuby 2003, p. 125).
2. Cheng Ho is a Hokkien pronunciation for Zheng He (as pronounced in Mandarin). Given that most Chinese in Java are Hokkien, Cheng Ho is more commonly used to refer to the prominent Chinese Muslim admiral. Cheng Ho is often spelt with one "o". However, the mosque in Surabaya is called "Masjid Muhammad Cheng Hoo" (Muhammad Cheng Hoo Mosque), spelt with two "o". In this chapter, I use "Cheng Ho" to refer to the Chinese Muslim figure, whereas "Cheng Hoo Mosque" refers to the Chinese-style mosque in Surabaya. Recently, despite being highly contested, there is a growth of historical re-articulation to support the role of Cheng Ho in the early Islamization in Indonesia.
3. For a detailed discussion of diverse religiosity and flexible piety of Chinese converts in contemporary Indonesia, see Hew (2011).
4. According to the mosque handbook (YHMCHI 2008), the first phase of its construction cost Rp 500 million, collected through selling the trilingual "*Saudara Baru/Juz Amma*" ("New Convert/Selected Verses from Qur'anic texts"). Meanwhile, the total construction cost amounted to Rp 3,300 million. Most of it came from public donations.
5. "Christianization" is a term that generally refers to both Christian efforts to convert Muslims and the alleged growing influence of Christianity in Muslim-majority Indonesia. Some Muslim groups use it as a justification for mass mobilization and vigilante attacks. For more discussion of "Christianization" in Indonesia, see International Crisis Group, "Indonesia: 'Christianization' and Intolerance", available at <http://www.crisisgroup.org/en/regions/asia/south-east-asia/indonesia/B114-indonesia-christianisation-and-intolerance.aspx> (accessed 27 December 2010).
6. The Qur'anic verse she quoted is from Chapter Al-Hujurat (49, p. 13). The verse can be translated as "People, We created you all from a single man and a single woman, and made you into races and tribes so that you should recognize one another. In God's eyes, the most honored of you are ones most mindful of Him: God is all knowing, all aware" (Abdel Haleem 2004).
7. The trademark Chinese clothing of Koko Liem is *Tangzhuang*, or Tang suit. *Tangzhuang* refers to a Chinese jacket the origins of which can be traced to the end of the Qing Dynasty (1644–1911). It evolved from *Magua*, a Manchurian

clothing, which was in turn adopted by the Han Chinese during the Qing Dynasty. Today, *Tangzhuang* is one of the main formal clothing for Chinese men on various occasions. At the Asia-Pacific Economic Cooperation Summit in Shanghai, China, in November 2001, the host presented its silk *Tangzhuang* jacket as the Chinese traditional national costume. Since then, some Chinese overseas have also worn the *Tangzhuang*, either as a fashion statement or for cultural expression.

8   *Jubah* is a long flowing robe, similar to Arabic garments. Meanwhile, *peci* is a rimless cap and *baju koko* is a collarless shirt, which is one of the most common clothing styles of male Indonesian Muslims. Some Indonesians have suggested that the *koko* shirt has Chinese roots. According to historian J.J. Rizal, such collarless long or short-sleeve shirts were modified from a *tuikhim* shirt, which was commonly worn by male Chinese in Indonesia until the early twentieth century (Isnaeni 2010).

9   The MONAS incident refers to an attack by FPI on members of the National Alliance for Freedom of Religion and Faith (AKKBB, Aliansi Kebangsaan Untuk Kebebasan Beragama dan Berkeyakinan) who rallied around the National Monument, MONAS in June 2008. AKKBB is a coalition that promotes religious freedom and which also sympathizes with Ahmadiyah, a controversial Islamic sect. FPI urges the Indonesian government to ban Ahmadiyah activities as it was deviant.

10 By stating that a preacher holds certain "conservative" viewpoint, it does not necessarily mean I see him or her as a "conservative" preacher. Indeed, a preacher can have "conservative" view on one issue, but hold a "progressive" stand on another matter.

11 Imlek is a Hokkien term (*Yinli*, in Mandarin), which means Chinese lunar calendar. In Indonesia, it is also used to refer to Chinese New Year. I will use Imlek and Chinese New Year interchangeably in this chapter.

12 Pork is one of the main dishes during Chinese New Year dinner and gambling is one of the leisure activities for some Chinese during the festival. Yet, for Muslims, both pork consumption and gambling are *haram*.

13 Discussions of "cultural *dakwah*" began during Muhammadiyah's national congress in 1995 and it gained greater momentum during 2002 and 2003. The concept, however, remains contested in the organization. For more discussion, see Daniels (2009, pp. 107–13), Hadi (2007), and Syamsul (2005).

14 See "Rayakan Imlek di masjid, why not?" [Celebrating Imlek in mosques, why not?], *Nurani*, February 2008.

15 The Indonesian translation, quoted in *Nurani*'s report is "*Allah menciptakan Manusia dari seorang laki-laki dan perempuan, dan menjadikan manusia berbangsa-bangsa dan bersuku-suku supaya kamu saling mengenal. Sesungguhnya yang paling mulia di sisi Allah adalah manusia yang bertakwa*". The English translation I used here is quoted from Abdel Haleem (2005).

16 See "MUI Jabar Haramkan Peringatan Valentine Day" [MUI West Java Disapprove Valentine's Celebration], *Kompas*, 14 February 2009.
17 See "Ketua Komisi Fatwa MUI: Perayaan Valentine Haram" [Head of *Fatwa* Commission of MUI: Valentine's Celebration *Haram*], *Kompas*, 13 February 2008.

References

Abdel Haleem, M.A.S. *The Qu'ran: A New Translation*. Oxford: Oxford University Press, 2004.
Al-Jawi, Muhammad Shiddiq. *"Imlek Adalah Hari Raya Agama Kafir Bukan Sekedar Tradisi Tionghoa: Haram Atas Muslim Turut Merayakannya"* [Imlek is a religious holiday for heathens, not merely a Chinese tradition: Muslims are forbidden to join the celebrations], 2007. Available at <http://hizbut-tahrir.or.id/2010/02/10/imlek-adalah-hari-raya-agama-kafir-bukan-sekedar-tradisi-haram-atas-muslim-turut-merayakannya/> (accessed 16 February 2007).
Al-Qurtuby, Sumanto. *Arus Cina-Islam-Jawa, Bongkar Sejarah atas Peranan Tionghoa dalam Penyebaran Agama di Nusantara Abad XV and XVI* [Chinese-Islam-Javanese Flow]. Yogyakarta: Inspeal Ahimsakarya Press, 2003.
Alfitri. "Religious Liberty in Indonesia and the Right of 'Deviant' Sects". *Journal of Comparative Laws* 3, no. 1 (2008): 1–27.
Ananta, Aris, Evi Nurvidya Arifin, and Bakhtiar. "Chinese Indonesians in Indonesia and the Province of Riau Archipelago: A Demographic Analysis". In *Ethnic Chinese in Contemporary Indonesia*, edited by L. Suryadinata. Singapore: Institute of Southeast Asian Studies, 2008.
Appiah, Kwame Anthony. "Cosmopolitan Patriots". In *Cosmopolitics: Thinking and Feeling Beyond the Nation*, edited by P. Cheah and B. Robbins. Minneapolis, MN: University of Minnesota Press, 1998.
Bayat, Asef. "Everyday Cosmopolitanism". *ISIM (International Institute for the Study of Islam in the Modern World) Review* 22 (2008): 5.
Bhabha, Homi. "Unsatisfied: Notes on Vernacular Cosmopolitanism". In *Text and Nation*, edited by L. Garcia-Morena and P.C. Pfeifer. London: Camden House, 1996.
Budianta, Melani. "Discourse of Cultural Identity in Indonesia during 1997–98 Monetary Crisis". *Inter-Asia Cultural Studies* 1, no. 1 (1999): 109–28.
Budiwanti, Erni. *Pluralism Collapses: A Study of the Jama'ah Ahmadiyah Indonesia and Its Persecution*. ARI Working Paper Series. Singapore: Asia Research Institute, NUS, 2009.
Chiou Syuan-Yuan. "Building Traditions to Bridging Differences: Islamic Imaginary Homelands of Chinese-Indonesian Muslims in East Java". In *East–West Identities: Globalization, Localization, and Hybridization*, edited by C. Kwok-bun, J.W. Walls and D. Hayward. Leiden: Brill, 2007.

Daniels, Timothy. *Islamic Spectrum in Java*. Farnham: Ashgate, 2009.
Dickson, Anne. "A Chinese Indonesian Mosque's Outreach in the Reformasi Era". 17th Biennial Conference of the Asian Studies Association of Australia, Melbourne, 1–3 July 2008.
Dijk, Kees Van. "Dakwah and Indigenous Culture: The Dissemination of Islam". *Bijdragen tot de Taal-, Land- en Volkenkunde* [Journal of the Humanities and Social Sciences of Southeast Asia and Oceania] 154, no. 2 (1998): 218–35.
―――. "National Pride and Foreign Influences: The Shape of Mosques in Southeast Asia". *Off the Edge* (August 2009): 24–27.
Fealy, Greg. "Consuming Islam: Commodified Religion and Aspirational Pietism in Contemporary Indonesia". In *Expressing Islam: Religious Life and Politics in Indonesia*, edited by G. Fealy and S. White. Singapore: Institute of Southeast Asian Studies, 2008.
Gillespie, Piers. "Current Issues in Indonesian Islam: Analysing the 2005 Council of Indonesian Ulama Fatwa No. 7 Opposing Pluralism, Liberalism and Secularism". *Journal of Islamic Studies* 18, no. 2 (2007): 202–40.
Hadi, H. Abd. "Gerakan Pemikiran Muhammadiyah dari Puritanisme ke Dinamisme". *Paramedia* 8, no. 4 (2007). Available at <http://ejournal.sunan-ampel.ac.id/index.php/Paramedia/article/view/197/182>.
Hefner, Robert W. "Muslim Democrats and Islamist Violence in Post-Soeharto Indonesia". In *Remaking Muslim Politics: Pluralism, Contestation, Democratization*, edited by R.W. Hefner. Princeton, NJ: Princeton University Press, 2005.
Hew Wai Weng. "Identiti Cina Muslim di Malaysia: Persempadanan, Perundingan and Kacukan Budaya" [Chinese Muslim Identities in Malaysia: Boundary-making, Negotiation and Hybridity]. MPhil thesis, Institute of Malaysian and International Studies (IKMAS), National University of Malaysia (UKM), Bangi, 2005.
―――. "Marketing the Chinese Face of Islam". *Inside Indonesia* 99 (2010). Available at <http://www.insideindonesia.org/edition-99/marketing-the-chinese-face-of-islam>.
―――. "Negotiating Ethnicity and Religiosity: Chinese Muslim Identities in Post-New Order Indonesia". Ph.D. thesis, The Australian National University, Canberra, 2011.
Hoon Chang Yao. *Chinese Identity in Post-Suharto Indonesia: Culture, Politics and Media*. Brighton: Sussex Academic Press, 2008.
―――. "More Than a Cultural Celebration: The Politics of Chinese New Year in Post Suharto Indonesia". *Chinese Southern Diaspora Studies* 3 (2009): 90–105.
Howell, Julia Day. "Modulations of Active Piety: Professors and Televangelists as Promoters of Indonesian 'Sufisme'". In *Expressing Islam: Religious Life and Politics in Indonesia*, edited by G. Fealy and S. White. Singapore: Institute of Southeast Asian Studies, 2008.

Isnaeni, Hendri F. "Koko Masuk Islam". Available at <http://www.majalah-historia.com/majalah/historia/berita-302-koko-masuk-islam.html> (accessed 23 August 2010).

Jahja, Junus. *Asimilasi dan Islam*. Jakarta: BAKOM-PKB, 1981.

——— . "Sang Pemula Karim Oei 'Nasionalis Indonesia, Muslim Taat dan Pengusaha Sukses'". Jakarta: Yayasan H. Karim Oei, 2005.

Kahn, Joel S. *Other Malays: Nationalism and Cosmopolitanism in the Modern Malay World*. Singapore: Singapore University Press, 2006.

——— . "Other Cosmopolitanisms in the Making of the Modern Malay World". In *Anthropology and the New Cosmopolitanism: Rooted, Feminist and Vernacular Perspectives*, edited by P. Werbner. Oxford: Berg, 2008.

Koko Liem. "Valentine's Day". *Koko Liem website*, 2009. Available at <http://www.kokoliem.com/Artikel_Islami/_01_Artikel_Umum/04_ValentineDay/index_AI.html> (accessed 26 October 2010).

Laison, Nugroho. "Imlek: antara Budaya dan Aqidah" [Imlek: Between Culture and Faith], 2008. Available at <http://nugon19.multiply.com/journal/item/71/TANYA-FOR_MUSLIM_AND_MUALLAF_Imlek_Antara_Budaya_dan_Aqidah_> (accessed 26 February 2008).

Lombard, Denys and Claudine Salmon. "Islam and Chineseness". In *The Propagation of Islam in the Indonesian-Malay Archipelago*, edited by A. Gordon. Kuala Lumpur: Malaysian Sociological Research Institute, 2001.

Muzakki, Akh. "Negotiating Identity: The Cheng Hoo Mosque and Ethnic Chinese Muslims in Post-Soeharto Indonesia". *Chinese Southern Diaspora Studies* 3 (2009): 193–203.

PITI Palembang. *Masjid Al-Islam Muhammad Cheng Ho* [Al-Islam Cheng Ho Mosque]. Palembang, 2009.

Robinson, Kathryn. "Islamic Cosmopolitics, Human Rights and Anti-Violence Strategies in Indonesia". In *Anthropology and the New Cosmopolitanism: Rooted, Feminist and Vernacular Perspectives*, edited by P. Werbner. Oxford: Berg, 2008.

The Siauw Giap. "Religious Adaption: The Moslem Chinese in Indonesia, A Preliminary View". In *Cina Muslim di Indonesia*, edited by R. Saidi. Jakarta: Yayasan Ukhuwah Islamiyah, 1990.

Susanto, Slamet and Tarko Sudiarno. "Chinese Muslims Celebrate 'Imlek' in Mosque". *Jakarta Post*, 24 January 2004.

Syamsul, Hidayat. "Dakwah Kultural dalam Dinamika Purifikasi Gerakan Muhammadiyah". *Jurnal Studi dan Dakwah Islam* 19, no. 2 (2005): 6–18.

The Wahid Institute. "Ketegangan Berbasis Agama Terus Terjadi". *Monthly Reports on Religious Issues* 17 (2009). Available at <http://www.wahidinstitute.org/files/_docs/17.MonthlyReport-XVII-Bhs.pdf> (accessed 16 October 2010).

Werbner, Pnina. "Vernacular Cosmopolitanism, Special Issue 'Problematising Global Knowledge'". *Theory, Culture and Society* 2, no. 3 (2006): 496–98.

———, ed. *Anthropology and the New Cosmopolitanism: Rooted, Feminist and Vernacular Perspectives*. Oxford: Berg, 2008.

Werbner, Pnina and Tariq Madood, eds. *Debating Cultural Hybridity: Multi-Cultural Identities and the Politics of Anti-Racism*. London: Zed Books, 1997.

Winarso, Hendrik Agus. *Mengenal Hari Raya Konfusiani* [Understanding Confucian Festival]. Semarang: Effhar and Dahara Prize, 2005.

Woodward, Mark R. *Islam in Java: Normative Piety and Mysticism in the Sultanate of Yogyakarta*. Tucson: University of Arizona Press, 1989.

YHMCHI (Yayasan Haji Muhammad Cheng Hoo Indonesia). *Sekilas Tentang Masjid Muhammad Cheng Hoo Indonesia* [About Cheng Hoo Mosque]. Surabaya, 2008.

10

MAJORITY AND MINORITY
Preserving Animist and Mystical Practices in Far East Java

Nicholas Herriman

Banyuwangi is the easternmost of more than eighty administrative districts in contemporary Java.[1] In this district, there are several small but identifiable minorities, including Hindus, Catholics, Protestants, and modernist Muslims. However, the minorities this chapter is concerned with are adherents to mystical and animist practices and beliefs residing in several unique villages. The question I seek to address is how to account for the animist and mystical adherence in these villages in relation to widespread conformity to traditionalist Islam. To answer this, I point to cultural revitalization, state's multicultural, and tourism policies in the face of an Islamic revival. I first provide a brief overview of the religious history of Banyuwangi (I will use the term "Banyuwangi" to refer to the whole district; when referring specifically to the large urban area which is the capital, I will use the phrase "Banyuwangi City"). I then describe the religious culture of the traditionalist majority in Banyuwangi. Following this, I consider the small minority of mystics and animists who are, for the most part, limited to a cluster of four villages. Finally, I consider the historical forces, which account for the uniqueness of the animists and mystics against the widespread conformity in the rest of Banyuwangi.

Map 10.1
The Districts (*kabupaten*) of East Java.

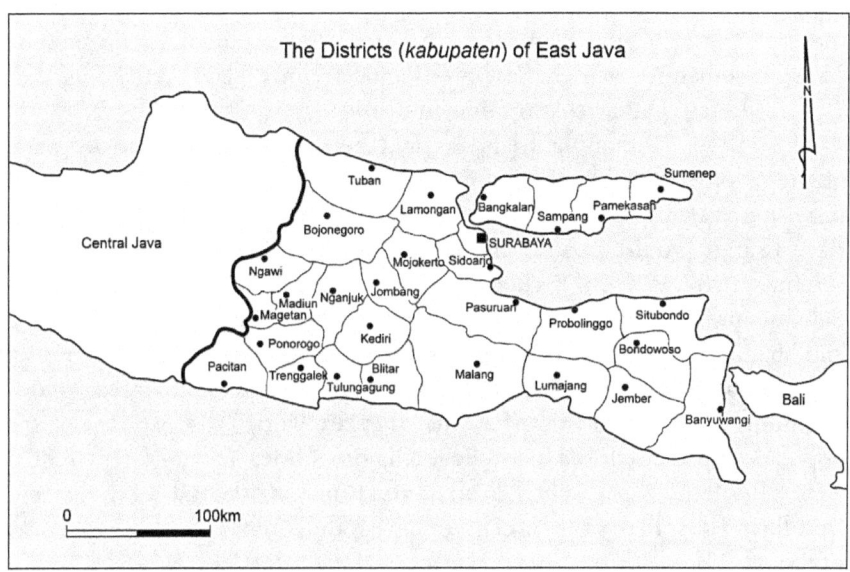

Banyuwangi District can be seen in the far east.
Source: Reproduced with kind permission from Joanne Byrne.

RELIGIOUS HISTORY OF BANYUWANGI

The earliest evidence of human inhabitation in this area is provided by megalithic remains excavated in Bondowoso, to the west of the Banyuwangi district. Dated around 670–1360, these comprise a stone enclosure and a number of dolmen (stone grave sites) (Prasetyo 2006, p. 167). They are consistent with the pre-Indic, local ancestral, and animistic beliefs and practices of the Southeast Asian region in the pre-historic period (Reid 1993, pp. 136–40; Warren 1993*a*, pp. 44–45). By 1316, a Hindu–Buddhist dominion called "Blambangan" existed within the borders of contemporary Banyuwangi. Blambangan (c. 1316–1767) was at the eastern reaches of the Majapahit kingdom (1294–1478) and seems to have swung between autonomy and subjugation to Majapahit.

The decline of Majapahit coincided with the rise of the first Islamic kingdoms in Java. Accompanying this, according to Javanese legend, was an exodus of Hindu–Buddhists from these newly Islamic areas towards Blambangan and Bali, which still adhered to Hindu–Buddhist beliefs

(Cortesao 1944, p. 198; Hakluyt 1904, pp. 338–39). For the next three hundred years, Blambangan's history can be understood with reference to these Islamic kingdoms and the emerging Hindu Balinese kingdoms to the east. Nevertheless, Blambangan resisted the spread of Islam and, by 1579, Blambangan was the last pre-Islamic realm in Java, remaining that way until after Dutch colonization in 1767.

Instead of containing Islam, as had been the policy in many parts of the colony, local Dutch colonists promoted the religion. By encouraging their vassal rulers to embrace Islam, the Dutch reckoned that Banyuwangi would be less influenced by the Balinese Hindu enemy (Hefner 1987, p. 87; Ricklefs 2001, p. 132; Wolbers 1992, p. 45). Subsequent Islamization was apparently gradual; for example, animistic and shamanistic beliefs were apparently noted in a 1920s colonial report (Stoppelaar 1926, pp. 413–19). Eventually, Islam made great gains. According to 1999 statistics (for what they are worth), 95 per cent of the population professed Islam as their religion. Other religions represented were Hindu (2.5 per cent), Protestant (1 per cent), and Catholic and Buddhist (less than 1 per cent each) (Kabupaten Banyuwangi 1999, pp. xxxv, 86).

To start with the listed minorities, Protestants and Catholics are most commonly ethnic Chinese and tend to reside in Banyuwangi City and small towns. Hindus can be found in several majority Hindu villages. Against the 95 per cent, these minorities are tiny. So how can we understand the apparently overwhelming adherence to Islam?

In Banyuwangi, as in the rest of Indonesia, Islam is overwhelmingly Sunni as opposed to Shia. Under a Soeharto regime policy, one of the five officially recognized religions had to be selected for one's identity card (KTP). This means that animist and mystical religious outlooks could not be accounted for. People with such beliefs might have selected Islam for their official affiliation. Certainly, in some parts of Java, it has been reported that animist and mystical beliefs were associated with the Communist party. Therefore, in the wake of the 1965–66 massacres, people had chosen "Islam" to protect themselves from being seen as associated with the party. In other parts of Java, either Hinduism or Christianity was selected (Hefner 1987, p. 540). For these reasons, people might profess to be Islamic, although they might not be Muslim in their own or others' eyes, thus inflating the 95 per cent figure. However, I suggest below that this may not be the case in Banyuwangi: the statistical information might reasonably reflect the way people viewed their own adherence, such that those who chose "Islam" as their religion on the identity card regard themselves and are identified by others as Islamic. The majority of this 95 per cent, I will argue, would identify with traditionalist Islam.

To make this argument, I will draw on a year's fieldwork based on Tegalgaring village (a pseudonym) in Banyuwangi, 2001–02, where I studied state and society in relation to the problem of sorcery. As such, a major focus of this research was religious and magical beliefs. I participated and observed daily life in Tegalgaring village, but also, accompanied more often than not by my host-father, conducted more than 150 interviews, mostly taking place in other villages around Banyuwangi. In these villages, I met people of Osing ethnicity (who are believed to be indigenous to Banyuwangi) as well as Javanese and Madurese (who are believed to have migrated to the Banyuwangi in the past two centuries). As I will maintain, the religious adherence of these three groups is characterized by beliefs and practices associated with *kiai*, rituals, *ngaji*, and magic.

Generally, Islam in Java has been indigenized or domesticated such that it reflects both local and foreign influences. Like some other "world religions" (Christianity, and, perhaps, Judaism), Islam provides generalized or universal as opposed to piecemeal approaches to existential problems; transportable beliefs and rituals which are suited to a larger social macrocosm rather than local circumstances; a transcendent as opposed to immanent divine; a promise of salvation to an entire religious community (Geertz 1973; Hefner 1987; Reid 1993; Weber 1991). Nevertheless, when transported to new areas, these religions are generally accommodated or blended with local practices and customs — a process known as syncretism.

Clifford Geertz's *Religion of Java* (1960) provides an influential study of syncretism. The town Geertz studied, "Modjokuto", being a pseudonym for the town of Pare in East Java. Pare was populated by people of Javanese ethnicity. (The Javanese primarily inhabit Central and Eastern Java.) Geertz (1960, p. 6) characterized their religious culture as an "overall Javanese syncretism". Within this overall syncretism, he posited three variants, or cultural types, defined in terms of their "religious beliefs, ethical preferences, and political ideologies" (1960, p. 4). The *abangan* "variant" emphasized animistic elements; the *santri*, Islamic; and the *priyayi*, Hindu elements within this syncretism. If one were to apply this schema to contemporary Banyuwangi, *santri* Islam would be seen to be predominant; however, in Bayu and nearby villages, a small minority of animists and mystics could be roughly associated with *abangan* and *priyayi*, respectively.

To clarify, almost all the people I met in rural Banyuwangi identified themselves as *santri*. I will define *santri* Islam as a form of Islam which insists on the Islamic dogmas (fasting, pilgrimage, tithing, prayers, and monotheism). When local residents identified themselves as "*santri*", it could mean one of the following three things. First, "*santri*" means the "pupils" (past and present) of a particular "*ulama*" or "*kiai*", who is a religious teacher, scholar, and leader. The second meaning, infrequently used, of "*santri*" is "followers" as opposed to "pupils". A *santri* is one of these followers who, though never having been a *kiai*'s pupil, lives in the *kiai*'s village and respects him.

Third, and most importantly, "*santri*" refers to the members of a general "Muslim community". In this sense, *santri* is roughly synonymous with "*ummat*" (religious community) in Indonesia at least. This sense of a religious community is central to Islam (Esposito 1991, p. 10). Geertz (1960, p. 127) wrote that when the residents of "Modjukuto" used the word "*santri*", this referred to an insistence "on the necessity of unreserved belief and faith in the absolute truth of Islam". However, when local residents of contemporary Banyuwangi identify themselves as "*santri*", it does not connote the intense commitment that Geertz associated with the term. Even people who are in practice lax about praying five times a day, or strictly adhering to fasting, consider themselves to be *santri*, because to be otherwise seems to be equated with not really being Muslim. And thus, I imagine that most of the 95 per cent who identified their religion, for official purposes, as Islam, would think of themselves as *santri*.

Santri Islam in Banyuwangi had two main forms: traditionalist and modernist. Traditionalist Muslims incorporate many aspects of Javanese "tradition" (including animism and Hindu–Buddhism), and centuries of learned commentaries on Islam (*fiqh*). As Beatty (1999, p. 120) puts it, they "stress the complementarity of religion and custom". Modernist Muslims seek to rid Islam of these traditions in order to modernize it. In other words, they tend to advocate embracing "progress" and stripping off non-Islamic traditional accretions. Aside from these two forms, puritanical Islam seeks to emulate a Middle Eastern form of Islam and is hostile to both traditionalism and modernism in Islam. Rather than being a characteristic of a social group or an area, puritanism seems limited to a small number of individuals in many locations. The larger groups are traditionalists and modernists.

Amongst the *santri* of rural Banyuwangi, conformity to traditionalist Islam is most widespread. Local residents usually refer to their traditionalist Islam as "NU Islam". By contrast, they refer to the Islam of the modernist as "Muhammadiyah Islam" ("Islam Muhammadiyah"). This can be attributed to the organizational dimension of the religious cleavage, dating back to 1912 with the formation, elsewhere in Java, of the modernist organization Muhammadiyah. Nahdlatul Ulama (NU) is the name of the traditionalist organization formed in 1926, partly in response to Muhammadiyah. Informal competition for legitimacy, power, and status has characterized relations between the two organizations, even spanning to contemporary times. For example, traditionalist Muslims harbour a sense of acrimony towards Muhammadiyah Islam. In contemporary Banyuwangi, NU is the predominant "civil society" institution in the villages of Banyuwangi. Beatty notes that that aside from Bayu, "in other … villages in the region … Nahdlatul Ulama (NU), is well represented" (1999, p. 131). Indeed, as far as I can recall, all the villages (with the exception of Hindu villages) I visited in Banyuwangi had NU representation. Nevertheless, the NU in the villages is an ineffective organization, its representatives rarely possessing status or influence due to their organizational position. The NU leader in my village had been, for instance, a man of little status, and he obtained very little status when he became leader. Notwithstanding, at the sub-district and district levels, NU leaders can be quite influential. However, NU-Muhammadiyah distinction in contemporary Banyuwangi is not merely organizational.

The traditionalist-modernist divide also has other ramifications. The traditionalist outlook tends to be tolerant and even protective of other religious persuasions; a popular reference for NU people is the Qur'anic verse that declares, "your religion is for you, and my religion is for me". Socially, modernists tend to be urban and wealthier, whereas traditionalists are rural and poorer. Demographically, traditionalist and modernist Muslims often live in separate villages, or separate neighbourhoods. Thus, the term "NU Islam" (Islam NU) symbolizes, in Durkheim's sense, the traditionalist community itself, the "*nahdliyin*" as it is known. This means that beliefs and practices aside, to not identify as NU Islam, is to not really be part of the large rural community. Thus, "NU Islam" partly denotes organization and partly an idea of community. Finally, the term also partly denotes a lived reality, a religious culture which incorporates *kiai*, ritual meals, *ngaji*, and magic.

CONFORMITY TO TRADITIONALIST ISLAM

What defines traditionalist Islam more than anything else is its culture of *kiai* (religious scholars). This is not surprising given that NU means "revival of the religious scholars" — it was created with the interests of *kiai* at the forefront. As Geertz (1960*a*, p. 240) noted, Islam of the traditionalist is a "*kiai* Islam". For traditionalist Muslims, according to the adage, "if there's no *kiai*, there's no community." In the absence of a centralized formal organization (as distinct from Shia Islam or Roman Catholicism), the *kiai* is the central figure around whom religion is socially organized. This absence of a centralized formal organization also means that it is up to the community to determine who is or is not a *kiai*, largely, it seems, on the basis of the following criteria. Ideally, as the following paragraphs describe, a *kiai* is a scholar, is a teacher, has magical abilities, and is the son of a *kiai*.

First, a *kiai* is a scholar of Islam. Typically, he — for *kiai* are always male — has been a pupil of an Islamic school. He can read the Koran and *Hadith* written in Arabic, as well as other Islamic texts. And he can explain and provide his insights into their contents. He provides his often witty and entertaining orations at *ngaji, ceramah* (informal presentations), after evening prayers, and sometimes during a sermon (*chotbah*) at Friday prayers.

Second, a *kiai* teaches boys or girls. The word "*kiai*" is roughly synonymous to "*ulama*", although the latter is used in more formal contexts, and often refers to a *kiai* of higher status, who, as one informant explained, "has a boarding school" (*pondok pesantren)* attended by hundreds of pupils. He wields significant political, social, and economic power, and inspire sincere devotion among their pupils, past and present. At the other end of the "teacher" spectrum, the word "*kiai*" is used to describe a man who has only a dozen pupils. He does not have a boarding school to speak of, but will probably have a small prayer house (*langgar, musholla*) attached to his house. His pupils are locals who come to his prayer house for education in the afternoon and evening. In Tegalgaring, there were three such minor *kiai*. Without sufficient reputation, not to mention accommodation, these *kiai* were hard pressed to attract any pupils to board. If a man has only a few pupils, he might instead be called a *guru ngaji*, that is, a man who provides religious instruction to neighbouring children, typically for a couple of hours every day. The scale for which the term "*kiai*" is used in relation to teaching seems to slide.

Third, consulted daily by visitors seeking assistance, the *kiai* uses what are believed to be supernatural powers to heal, to solve personal problems, and so on. For example, a local *kiai*, who blessed water and used it to cure people, explained to me in an interview that this was part of "the Muslim tradition *a la* NU". While some local residents deny the importance of the attribute, in practice, a *kiai*'s stature grows with his ability to advise successfully in supernatural matters. The *kiai* himself is typically wary of the idolatrous implications of saying he is a healer and will prefer to say that he simply prays for the patient's well-being. But most "lay" people believe that the *kiai* intercedes, magically, on behalf of the patient.

Last, the son of *kiai* might inherit the title "*kiai*" from his father, but this is not the case always, and a man whose father was not a *kiai* might also become a *kiai*. Thus, it is still necessary for a man to establish himself independently as a religious scholar, curer, and teacher. These attributes seem to be sufficient but not necessary, as someone not in possession of all may yet be called "*kiai*".

Aside from the role of *kiai*, another important aspect of traditionalist religion is the ritual meal. Geertz called them "*slametan*", and different words might also be used in different circumstances. In a ritual meal, the host invites neighbours and friends for a child's birthday, for the successful sale of land, or to bid farewell to a relative visiting from the city. With the help of the guests' wives, the host's wife prepare the meal, usually consisting of a small plate of rice with some meat, at the side of the host's house. Usually, the husbands gather in the front room (*ruang tamu*) of the host's house after evening prayers, and led by someone knowledgeable, recite passages from the Koran. Then, they eat the rice dish, share jokes, smoke cigarettes, and after that the guests leave with a takeaway pack of food. Leftovers are shared with the guests/wives and kids who happen to be around.

Ngaji is another important social institution for traditionalist Muslims in Banyuwangi. People in Banyuwangi use the Javanese term *ngaji* with a nominal use similar to the use of *pengajian* in Indonesian, which means something like "religious instruction" or "preaching". This can refer to a religious scholar (*kiai*) teaching his students at a religious school (*pondok pesantren*) (Julian Millie, personal communication). In the villages of Banyuwangi, it has also assumed a wider significance to refer to meetings in which there is a formal address pertaining to "Islamic" matters and chanting. Almost any night of the week, in any village in Banyuwangi, various *ngaji* are occurring. The best translation I could come up with to cover all the uses is "any meeting of people in which the participants recognize the purpose to be religious but which is not among the rituals prescribed in traditionalist Islam". Thus, performing one of the five obligatory daily prayers or a funeral ritual is not considered "*ngaji*", but the following real examples are:

- Five to six children learning Arabic script at house of a "*guru ngaji*" (*ngaji* teacher) who is a neighbour or lives down the lane.
- Up to thirty children learning religious lessons under the tutelage of a *kiai*.
- A group of women who regularly gather at a different member's house to study the Koran or *Hadith*. A microphone and loudspeakers broadcast these events, which are referred to as a *pengajian*.
- Occasional large communal prayer sessions for adults that are devoted to chanting, and sermons from *kiai* and other guests, at a mosque.
- A soccer field full of paying people listening to a celebrity preacher.
- Infrequently, ritual meals are also referred to as *ngaji* (probably because a religious expert leads chanting).

Apparently, a good *ngaji* entertains and educates, but it also reaffirms a sense of religious community within the culture of traditionalist Islam.

Belief in magic is another aspect of NU Islam. Some traditionalist Muslims I met were embarrassed about the possible idolatrous implications of magic beliefs and openly denied their beliefs. Others were more candid, including one who emphasized that "the Muslim community must believe ... they must believe that magic exists. [Magic] is a supernatural entity that must be believed in". By contrast, I found a more pronounced tendency among modernist Muslims in Banyuwangi to openly question the existence of magic, although, privately, some were also convinced of its reality. In summary, in addition to the role of the *kiai*, ritual meals, *ngaji*, and a belief in magic characterize traditionalist Islam in rural Banyuwangi.

Although NU Islam boils down to these four elements, a cursory reading of the Qur'an and *Hadith* would not necessarily lead one to these. So, while many local accretions accommodated within Javanese syncretism have been stripped away to reveal this traditionalist religious culture, NU Islam is still steeped in local culture. Conformity to the culture of NU Islam, rather than variety, is the more marked and enduring phenomenon in Banyuwangi. It is against this background of conformity to NU Islam that one can appreciate the animism and mystical beliefs and practices which characterize the Banyuwangi's most famous religious minority in Bayu and nearby villages.

MINORITY OF ANIMISTS AND MYSTICS

The religious minority I discuss here is the animists and mystics identified in scholarship regarding Bayu, Olehsari, Cungking, and Bakungan. Although only a quarter of an hour's drive up the slopes of the Ijen mountain from Banyuwangi City, these villages have preserved traditional dance, music,

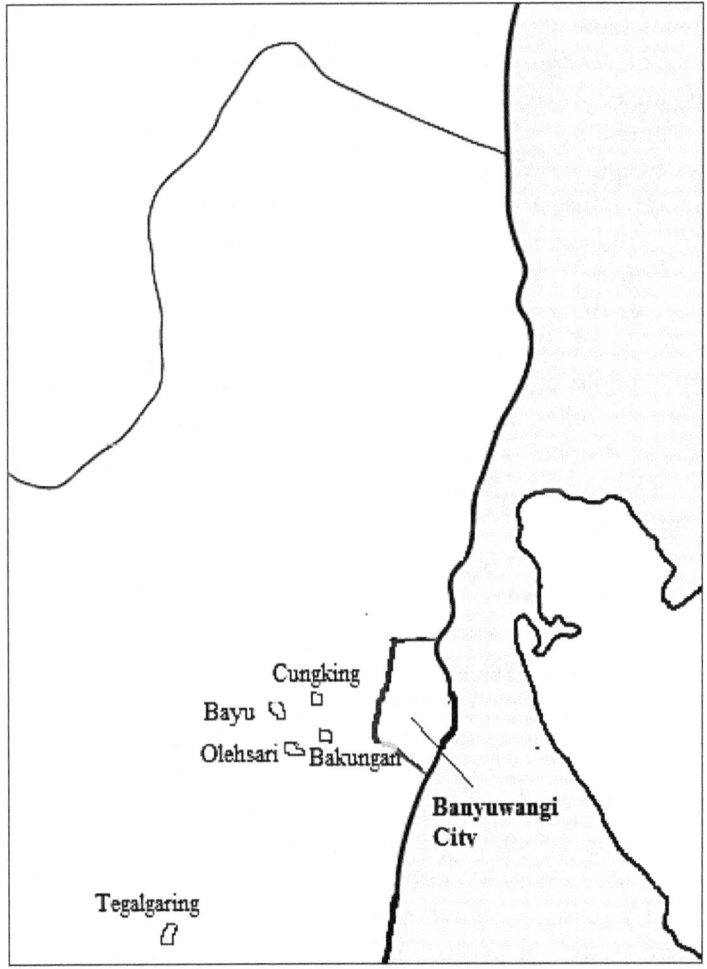

Map 10.2
Banyuwangi District

Banyuwangi City, the large area, is portrayed in relation to the cluster of villages; Bayu, Bakungan, Olehsari, and Cungking. My fieldwork location Tegalgaring is also depicted. All the locations are approximate in order to preserve the pseudonyms.

and beliefs which have been recorded in some outstanding scholarship. Arps (1992) studied the recital of Javanese poems. Wessing (1999, pp. 644–45) studied *seblang*, a ritual that is performed only in Bakungan and Olehsari and in which a young or old woman contacts village spirits, goes into trance, and begins to dance, in the belief that it will ensure the fertility of the village. Beatty (1999, pp. 59–78; 2009, pp. 55–67) studied the *barong* ritual; the *barong* belongs to the Bayu's guardian spirit. Wolbers (1992) studied *gandrung*, the dance for which Banyuwangi is famous. Gandrung is often performed on official occasions, especially for weddings and circumcisions all around Banyuwangi. However, Bayu is considered the home of *gandrung*. Thus, the recital of poems, *seblang*, *barong*, and *gandrung* are either centred on or unique to, these villages. And, as a result, almost all published scholarships on religion in Banyuwangi have focused on these exceptional villages.

The religious culture of "Bayu" village, in particular, has been intricately studied by Andrew Beatty in two publications: *Varieties of Javanese Religion* (1999) and *A Shadow Falls* (2009). Beatty depicts a continuum of the religious culture. At one end are animists (whose rituals and beliefs are focused on local spirits) and mystics (who emphasize worldly symbols of divinity, such as the human body, forests, and foods). At the other end is puritan Islam. This pious form of Islam is "a puritan grass roots Islam hostile to tradition and political compromise" led by a "hectoring" (Beatty 1999, p. 183) "vanguard" of "reformers and zealots" (Beatty 2009, p. 217). With such frankness, it is no surprise that the negative portrayal of puritanical Islam in this book was debated (Semedi, Peletz, Wieringa and Beatty 2010). In between these two poles, Beatty searches, in *Varieties of Javanese Religion*, to find the common- or middle ground of religious practices in this village. For Beatty (1999, pp. 115–17), this religious common ground is what he calls "practical Islam". This "practical Islam", as described by Beatty, is very similar to what my informants called NU Islam.

The specific problem Beatty addresses is "the effect of diversity upon Javanese religion" (1999, p. 1). This was in the context of what he saw as the advance of puritanism and the predicaments this advance presented to mystics and animists. A central question is thus, "how to get on with people of a different religious persuasion?" (1999, pp. 1–2). The answer, Beatty suggests, lies in "multivocality". Privately, people interpret the symbolic meaning of different rituals in their own way and are not aggrieved by different interpretations; publicly these differences are brushed over (1999, pp. 49–50, 125–26). For a pious Muslim, the red and white porridge of a ritual simply represent Adam and Eve. For the mystic, Adam and Eve are "mere intermediaries". The majority of people have an opinion "falling somewhere in between … the two extremes" (1999, p. 38). Thus, each symbol in the ritual "represents nobody's views in particular" (1999, p. 25). The result is a profound, subtle, and insightful study of how adherents to different religious cultures — animist, mystical, and traditionalist and puritanical — get along with each other.

The division between puritans and the animists-mystics Beatty describes seems limited to these villages. I have not encountered such divisions elsewhere in Banyuwangi, so the question of why puritans have targeted or singled out these villages, if this is, in fact, what they have done, remains open. Nevertheless, some authors have assumed this deep division to be typical of Banyuwangi district as a whole. From his reading of Beatty, Sidel (2006, pp. 142–53), for example, portrays Banyuwangi district as riven between mystical, animist religious culture, and NU Islam. Based on my experience, this portrayal is without foundation. In other words, Beatty's books are studies of a unique area of Banyuwangi. As Beatty astutely observes, his research concerns "religion in a particular corner of Java but it is not conceived as a regional study". So how are the beliefs and practices centred on, or unique to, these villages, distinct from the majority NU Islam?

The contrast between NU Islam and the animist-mystical adherence of these villages is, in some ways, obvious. In Bayu and surrounding villages, ritual meals often incorporate offerings explicitly made to spirits through, for example, red and white rice porridge. By contrast, elsewhere in Banyuwangi, this is uncommon — indeed none of the ritual meals I attended had such offerings and thus no different coloured porridges. In no cases was reference made to spirits, only to "Allah". Furthermore, the ritualized spirit possession of the *seblang* and *barong* can, to my knowledge, only be found in Bayu and surrounding villages. Finally, for the majority of residents in rural Banyuwangi, belief in house, ancestral village, and other spirits is idolatrous, while animists in Bayu apparently take it for granted. In these ways, the contrast can be clearly articulated.

In other ways, the differences are less obvious. Outside the villages, one might find what appear to be remnants of beliefs in spirit possession. In the village of Watukebo, for instance, I saw a *jaranan* ritual, in which men dancing as horses enter trances — this seems to be popular entertainment at weddings. However, this slips under the moral radar by being dressed up as *seni* (art). In Muncar, a Madurese area, there is an annual sea offering. But here again spirit propitiation, as found in Bayu and surrounding villages, is apparently absent. Instead, rituals are stripped off the spirits and are merely festivities. The religious adherence is thus also subtly distinct.

The existence of these differences raises the issue of tolerance. As noted by Beatty, for the minority of Middle Eastern style puritans, the practices in these villages were tantamount to idolatry. On the other hand, the animists and mystics seemed to have put up with the puritans. Beatty (1999, p. 138), nevertheless, describes an instance where rocks were thrown on the roof of one puritan's prayer house. Leaving aside the puritans, what could be said about the adherents to NU Islam; the religious majority in Banyuwangi? Rather than adopting a fanatical attitude, traditionalists tend to be fascinated by animist and mystics. In a district dominated by NU Islam, the "go to" place for what appear to be strange and exotic rituals is Bayu and nearby villages. A *Seblang* ritual "attracted" as Beatty (2009, p. 117) notes, "crowds ... schoolchildren taking notes ... [and] an Indonesian film crew"; similarly, a marriage ritual fascinated "reporters and school students, jostling for pictures, noting down 'Osing custom'" (Beatty 2009, p. 243). Moreover, in a fortnight of idly watching Indonesian television (9 January 2011– 22 January 2011), I saw two programmes concerning dance and ritual in Bayu, but none concerning other villages in East Java, let alone Banyuwangi. The religious practices and beliefs of Bayu seem rather quaint and exotic, even to people from other parts of Banyuwangi. Thus, no press reported Friday prayers, a *pengajian*, or a ritual meal in my Osing fieldwork village or any of the 200+ other villages in Banyuwangi, and nor would we expect them to; given the conformity to NU Islam. Having outlined the differences between the mystical and animist minority and the traditionalist majority, the question I now seek to address is how to account for the uniqueness of Bayu and surrounding villages and the conformity of religious adherence to NU Islam elsewhere in the district.

UNIQUENESS AND CONFORMITY

As to the uniqueness of Bayu and surrounding villages, topography and communication might be important factors. Typically, the religious cultures of mid- and up-slope areas of Java emphasize animism, local cults, and other apparently indigenous elements. Perhaps being somewhat "cut off", these villages were once less affected by newer trends in religious culture. Nevertheless, other more isolated, upland villages in Banyuwangi conform to NU Islam. So topography and communication are of limited application.

Rather, two phenomena might help explain the maintenance of a religious minority. First is cultural revivalism. When I visited Bayu, I was surprised to observe that local residents had identified a local form of crafts, architecture, and performance, which they actively sought to preserve. Indeed, they identified themselves, and were identified by others, as being responsible for maintaining what they hold to be the true, indigenous, or Osing, identity of Banyuwangi (Wolbers 1992).

Second is state cultural policy. The Indonesian state has openly maintained a policy of multiculturalism including "recognition" of minority cultures. Indeed, this policy stretches down to the district level. As Wolbers (1992, p. 70) notes, the Banyuwangi district offices for culture and education sought to list and preserve, as well as maintain control over a variety of genres of cultural performance in Banyuwangi. Moreover, Bayu village was singled out by the district government to be established as a tourist destination, with the intention of promoting and preserving its distinct cultural attributes. As Jones (2005, 2012, 2013) has shown, Indonesian state cultural policy is closely tied up with governance. At the same time, these policies have modified, tamed, and limited the observance of local beliefs and customs (*adat*) of certain groups in Indonesia (Acciaioli 1985, 2002; Foulcher 1990; Hefner 1987; Yampolsky 1995). It is entirely appropriate for these scholars to question how and to what end the state has gone about "preserving" local "cultural" forms. The effect is nevertheless the "preserving" of "tradition", albeit in a state-sanctioned form. In summary, the animism and mysticism in Bayu and nearby villages have been developed and maintained by forces from below (cultural revivalism within the villages) and from above (tourism and state multicultural forces).

On the other hand, contradictory historical forces could be seen to erode the unique religious culture of the villages. Internationally, since the 1960s, the Muslim revitalization (*dakwah*) has been a call to a more scriptural form of Islam, and it is a call to which millions in Asia have responded (Keyes, Hardacre, and Kendall 1994). Nationally, tensions between the PKI (whose rural supporters included many animists) and the NU (who were strongly anti-communists) culminated in a massacre of PKI members throughout

Java. In the wake of these massacres, the NU emerged in a stronger position. Furthermore, in the following decades of the Soeharto era, there was a "*santri*-fication" (Barton 2002, pp. 63–64; Desker 2002, 385) (c. 1966–98). For example, in Java, societal and state forces, including state education, commercialization, increased communications, and the relative strength of orthodox Islamic organizations, both modernist (Muhammadiyah) and traditionalist (NU), brought about the "relative decline" of Javanist Islam characterized by the syncretic forms in Bayu and neighbouring villages (Hefner 2000, p. 18). In Central and East Java, Islamic boarding schools (*pesantren*) may have had a more important role in the spread of Islam accounting for an adherence to Islam that was more orthodox than if, for example, royal courts or wandering mystics had been largely responsible for proselytization (Greg Barton, personal communication, 2010).

Generally, local religions integrate fundamentally into a local society, culture, and economy. By contrast, world religions tend to be generalized, universal, and abstract, and thus adhere more easily to societies in which outside connections are as influential as internal integrity (Hefner 1987, pp. 73–74). As East Java has become increasingly incorporated into a national imagined "community" and international economy, world religions are possibly more appropriate to this modern experience. Perhaps these historically specific and general reasons help explain why NU Islam predominates in rural Banyuwangi.

I have argued that conformity to "NU Islam" characterizes the religious culture in Banyuwangi. This conformity can be attributed to several historically specific factors as well as the general spread of world religions. There are several exceptions to conformity to NU Islam. Thanks to Beatty, Wolbers, and Arps, we have a deep understanding of the isolated phenomena of a cluster of several villages in the mountains of Banyuwangi. We are also fortunate that Beatty has studied one of a number of Hindu villages in Banyuwangi (Beatty 1999, pp. 211–38). And to further understand the exceptions, we still lack studies of Buddhists, Protestants, and Catholics, who if we are to believe the statistics together constitute less than 5 per cent of the population. Nevertheless, at this stage, scholarship on religious adherence in Banyuwangi is mostly limited to a few exceptional villages neighbouring Bayu. To revive the general picture of religious culture in Banyuwangi, more research is also needed on the religious majority, what local people call "NU Islam".

CONCLUSION

In conclusion, the religion of rural Banyuwangi is characterized by adherence to a traditional form of Islam called "NU Islam". Small minorities of Hindus Protestants and Catholics, and modernist Muslims can also be found within the district's borders. Recently, too, there has been a rise in puritanical, Middle Eastern style Islam. However, the religious minority I have been concerned with in this chapter is an animist and mystical religious culture as studied by Arps, Wolbers, Beatty, and Wessing, which one can find in a cluster of villages. I have suggested that historical factors, both general and specific, might account for the widespread adherence to NU Islam and for the uniqueness of the cluster of villages described above.

Note

[1] Thanks to Achmad Habib, Haji Hotip, Greg Acciaioli, David Bourchier, Robert Hefner, Andrew Beatty, Carole Herriman, and Joanne Byrne.

References

Acciaioli, G. "Culture as Art: From Practice to Spectacle". *Canberra Anthropology* 8, issues 1 and 2 (1985): 148–71.

———. "Re-Empowering the 'Art of the Elders': The Revitalisation of Adat among the To Lindu People of Central Sulawesi and throughout Contemporary Indonesia". In *Beyond Jakarta: Regional Autonomy and Local Societies in Indonesia*, edited by M. Sakai. Belair: Crawford House Publishing, 2002.

Arps, B. *Tembang in Two Traditions: Performance and Interpretation of Javanese Literature*. London: School of Oriental and African Studies, University of London, 1992.

Barton, G. *Gus Dur: The Authorised Biography of Abdurrahman Wahid*. Jakarta: Equinox, 2002.

Beatty, A. *Varieties of Javanese Religion: An Anthropological Account*. Cambridge: Cambridge University Press, 1999.

———. *A Shadow Falls in the Heart of Java*. London: Faber and Faber, 2009.

Cortesao, A. *The Suma Oriental of Tomé Pires and the Book of Francisco Rodrigues*. n.p.: Hakluyt Society, 1944.

Desker, B. "Islam and Society in South-East Asia after 11 September". *Australian Journal of International Affairs* 56, no. 3 (2002): 383–94.

Esposito, J.L. *Islam: The Straight Path*. New York: Oxford University Press, 1991.

Foulcher, K. "The Construction of an Indonesian National Culture: Patterns of Hegemony and Resistance". In *State and Civil Society in Indonesia*, edited by A. Budiman. Clayton: Monash University Centre of Southeast Asian Studies, 1990.

Geertz, C. "The Javanese Kijaji: The Changing Role of a Cultural Broker". *Comparative Studies in Society and History* 2, no. 2 (January 1960): 228–49.

———. *The Religion of Java*. Chicago and London: The University of Chicago Press, 1960.

———. "Thick Description: Toward an Interpretive Theory of Culture". In *The Interpretation of Cultures: Selected Essays by Clifford Geertz*, edited by C. Geertz. London: Hutchinson, 1973.

Hakluyt, R. *The Principal Navigations Voyages Traffiques and Discoveries of the English Nation Made by Sea of Over-land to the Remote and Farthest Distant Quarters of the Earth at Any Time within the Compasse of the 1600 Yeeres*. Glasgow: James MacLehose and Sons, 1904.

Hefner, R.W. "Islamizing Java? Religion and Politics in Rural East Java". *Journal of Asian Studies* 46, no. 3 (1987): 533–54.

———. "The Political Economy of Islamic Conversion in Modern East Java". In *Islam and the Political Economy of Meaning: Comparative Studies in Muslim Discourse*, edited by W.R. Roff. London: Croon Helm, 1987.

———. "The Politics of Popular Art: Tayuban Dance and Culture Change in East Java". *Indonesia* 43 (1987): 75–94.

Jones, T. "Indonesian Cultural Policy, 1950–2003: Culture, Institutions, Government". Ph.D. dissertation, Curtin University of Technology, 2005.

———. "Indonesian Cultural Policy Post-Suharto". *Indonesia* 93 (2012): 147–76.

———. *Culture, Power, and Authoritarianism in the Indonesian State: Cultural Policy across the Twentieth Century to the Reform Era*. KITLV: Leiden, 2013.

Kabupaten Banyuwangi. *Kabupaten Banyuwangi Dalam Angka 1998*. BAPPEDA Kabupaten DATI II Banyuwangi, Kantor BPS Kabupaten Banyuwangi, 1999.

Keyes, C.F., H. Hardacre, and L. Kendall. "Introduction: Contested Visions of Community in East and Southeast Asia". In *Asian Visions of Authority*, edited by C.F. Keyes, H. Hardacre, and L. Kendall. Honolulu: University of Hawaii Press, 1994.

Prasetyo, B. "Austronesian Prehistory from the Perspective of Comparative Megalithic". In *Austronesian Diaspora and the Ethnogeneses of People in Indonesian Archipelago: Proceedings of the International Symposium*, edited by T. Simanjuntak, I.H.E. Pojoh, and M. Hisyam. Jakarta: LIPI Press, 2006.

Reid, A. *Southeast Asia in the Age of Commerce 1450–1680*. New Haven and London: Yale University Press, 1993.

Ricklefs, M.C. *A History of Modern Indonesia since c.1200*. Houndmills: Palgrave, 2001.

Semedi, P., et al. "Debate: Andrew Beatty, a Shadow Falls; In the Heart of Java". *Bijdragen, tot de Taal-, Land- en Volkenkunde* 166, nos. 2/3 (2010): 315–30.
Sidel, John T. *Riots, Pogroms, Jihad: Religious Violence in Indonesia*. Ithaca, NY: Cornell University Press, 2006.
Stoppelaar, D.J.W.d. "Een Paar Aanteekeningen Over Banjoewangi". *Koloniaal Tijdschrift* 15 (1926): 413–19.
Warren, C. "Disrupted Death Ceremonies: Popular Culture and the Ethnography of Bali". *Oceania* 64 (1993): 36–56.
Weber, M. "The Social Psychology of the World Religions". In *From Max Weber: Essays in Sociology*, edited by H.H. Gerth and C. Wright Mills. Great Britain: Routledge, 1991.
Wessing, R. "A Dance of Life: The *Seblang* of Banyuwangi, Indonesia". *Bijdragen, tot de Taal-, Land- en Volkenkunde* 155, no. 4 (1999): 644–82.
Wolbers, P.A. "Maintaining Using Identity through Musical Performance: Seblang and Gandrung of Banyuwangi, East Java, Indonesia". Ph.D. dissertation, University of Illinois at Urbana-Champaign, 1992.
Yampolsky, P. "Forces for Change in the Regional Performing Arts of Indonesia". *Bijdragen, tot de Taal-, Land- en Volkenkunde* 151, no. 4 (1995): 700–25.

11

AN *ABANGAN*-LIKE GROUP IN A *SANTRI* ISLAND
The Religious Identity of the *Blater*[1]

Yanwar Pribadi

INTRODUCTION

There are, besides *kiai* (religious leaders),[2] other variants of local leadership in Madura. These include *klebun* (village heads) and the *blater*. The *blater* are feared local strongmen who have a high position in society and who are held in awe (*disegani*) by the local population. Despite their special status and public recognition of the *blater* as a non-religious group, they follow certain religious traditions and beliefs which, I argue, place them at the peripheries of what is commonly perceived as a religious minority. This chapter thus deals with the religious identity of the *blater* and their position as a religious minority in the larger Madurese society. Among the questions addressed are: What is the origin and nature of the *blater* in society? How does *remo*, the *blater*'s special feast, contribute to the way of life of the *blater* and distinguish them from *santri* (orthodox Muslims)? What is the nature of local mystical belief in Madura? How have the religious beliefs of the *blater* adapted to *santri* Islam in daily life?

In Madura, many of the local traditions and customs, such as *tellasan topa'* (an extra celebration of Eid Al-Fitr on the eighth day of Shawwal month after observing six days of voluntary fasting) and *padusan* (a communal bathing performed one day before the fasting month of Ramadan to purify one's heart and soul), have become linked with the common *santri* culture. However, there are also several local traditions that are closely related to non-*santri* culture, such as *kerapan sapi* (bull racing) and *sabung ayam* (cock fighting). These two traditions are deeply embedded in the lives of many non-*santri* that I identify as *abangan*-like people. Therefore, I argue that Madura is not only a home for *santri* groups but also for non-*santri* groups, like the *blater*.

According to Clifford Geertz' renowned trichotomy — the *santri*, the *abangan*, and the *priyayi* — in his book *The Religion of Java* (1960), *santri* are orthodox Muslims in Java. The *santri* religious tradition consists not only of a set of basic Islamic rituals but also includes a whole complex of social, charitable, and political Islamic organizations. Meanwhile, *abangan* is a variant within the general Javanese religious system whose religious tradition is made up primarily of the ritual feast called the *slametan*, as well as an extensive and intricate complex of spiritual beliefs and a whole set of theories and practices of curing, sorcery, and magic (Geertz 1960, pp. 5–6). Unlike Geertz, however, I do not describe *blater* practices as un-Islamic. There are several similarities between Javanese *abangan* and *blater* as far as cults, spirit beliefs, and ritual practices are concerned, which lead me to identify them as *abangan*-like. In the *pesantren* (Islamic boarding school) tradition, *santri*[3] are pupils of *kiai*. In this chapter, *santri* refer primarily to the majority of Madurese Muslims as the proponents of a more orthodox Islam that is based on global influences of Sunni Islam, whereas the *abangan blater* belong to a minority of Madurese Muslims who practise a non-orthodox Islam grounded in local beliefs and customs.

Several authors seem to neglect the existence of other variants of Islam in Madura, besides the *santri*. They suggest that "[t]he conceptual distinction between *abangan* and *santri* does not exist; the Central Javanese *abangan* religion, with its many magico-mystical influences from Hinduism and Buddhism, never developed to a large extent on Madura" (Koentjaraningrat 1972, p. 54); "With the exception of occasional eccentrics, religious uniformity among the Madurese makes it difficult for us to observe overt representatives of a strange tradition comparable to Javanese *abanganism*" (Mansurnoor 1990, p. 4), and *"Dalam masyarakat Madura tidak dikenal adanya pembagian golongan abangan dan putihan, sebagaimana di masyarakat Jawa* (In the Madurese society, the division of *abangan* and *putihan* [a term also denoting *santri*] like in Java is not recognized)" (Moesa 1999, p. 53). Unlike the three authors, I would argue that the whole island is not completely characterized only by *santri*-style orthodoxy.

Madurese Islam is in fact plural, and at least two forms of Islam can be identified. The first is based on global viewpoints of Sunni Islam and the other is based on local perspectives. The former adheres more to the largest denomination of Islam, *Ahl as-Sunnah* or Sunni Islam and the latter, while also adhering to Sunni Islam, is influenced more by local mystical belief systems. According to Mark Woodward (1989) and Martin van Bruinessen (1999), similar traditions of the supposedly non-Islamic Indonesia's local culture can in fact be found in other Muslim civilizations as well. Furthermore, like in Java, it is important to note that each form of Islam in Madura itself shows heterogeneous characters. Therefore, the categorization of *blater* as an *abangan*-like group does not mean that they are the same group as the one identified by Geertz in Java. What I intend to do is to make a distinction between the two divergent groups: the *santri* and the *blater*.

ORIGIN AND NATURE

Blater are local strongmen who often gain their reputation by the fear they spread amongst the local population. One has to perceive those local strongmen different from strongmen in politics. The latter exercises authority through money and social control, whereas the former can be seen as a sub-type of local gangsters who benefit from their fearsome reputation in order to reap economic benefits and political influence. Many *blater* become private security forces of entrepreneurs in Madura as well as in neighbouring cities in the East Java province. Local entrepreneurs often regard them as more reliable than the police. Many *blater* who are unable to find a "job" in the private security world instead offer pseudo-protection at a lower level, such as in bus terminals or traditional markets. Drivers in bus terminals or retailers in traditional markets in turn hand out *jatah preman* (illegal rents) to the *blater* in charge of their locale. In doing so, the clients at the same time avoid being harassed by the *blater*. The distinction between the *blater* and the *bajingan* (a common term for scoundrel and a more derogatory term sometimes used for *blater*, see below) is quite hazy — a common perception among locals in Madura and East Java. Even if they no longer offer their protection services and are no longer active in *remo* (a feast characteristic to the *blater* community) *blater* — not unlike the *jawara*, local strongmen in Banten — they continue to be recognized as a *blater*.

Blater are strongmen who are known to possess martial arts skills, and some are even believed by locals to have magical powers and have attained invulnerability. The *blater's* physical appearance is not different from any other person, yet their presence is made apparent through *remo*, the celebration in which several tens of *blater* with their own group gather on a regular basis. On this occasion, they usually but not exclusively wear *pesa'an* (traditional Madurese black-coloured shirts) with typical red-white stripes t-shirt (*sakera*) inside, *gombor* (traditional Madurese black-coloured trousers), and *odheng* (traditional Madurese head accessories).

Blater are not attached to a distinctive institution, such as the *pesantren* in the case of the *kiai*. Moreover, *blatership* cannot be considered a "proper" occupation; it does not appear in official statistics. Consequently, counting the number of the *blater* is impracticable. Moreover, there is no "official" organization of *blater* under a central leadership. Tens of *blater* may form a small group on grounds of sharing the same working area or place of origin. Such a group is usually headed by an influential *blater*. He collects a regular contribution (*iuran*) for various purposes, such as making a donation if a fellow *blater* holds rite of passage-style ceremonies, such as *slametan*, for his family members, and makes sure that his group is invited to every *remo*. It is indeed in *remo* that the presence of *blater* in groups is obvious. By and large, they do not appear in a group on a daily basis.

While the *blater* is predominantly a Madurese phenomenon, they belong to the long tradition of strongmen in the archipelago. That includes the vanished *jago* in the nineteenth-century Java and the aforementioned *jawara* — both who offer protection to those who need it and those who are thought to need it. This includes petty traders in traditional markets as well as big entrepreneurs. Nevertheless, one should note that every strongmen group has its specific features, and different groups differ considerably from one another. Unlike the *jago* who were portrayed as masters of the underworld or the *jawara* who were mostly known as political brokers during the New Order as well as the post-Soeharto era, the *blater* are distinctive perpetrators of cultural violence in Madura. Johan Galtung defines cultural violence as "any aspect of a culture that can be used to legitimize violence in its direct or structural form. Examples of cultural violence are indicated, using a division of culture into religion and ideology, art and language, and empirical and formal science" (1990, p. 291). In the *blater* traditions such as *remo* (further described in the next section), a *blater* can commit acts of violence (for example, fighting using sharp weapons) if he is interrupted by another *blater* when he is dancing with a *tandhak* (dancer) as part of *remo*. This act of violence is legitimized by a set of rules in *remo* which all *blater* are expected to follow. Moreover, aside from *remo*, they are also engaged in *kerapan sapi* and *sabung ayam*, other *blater*-style symbols of machismo, which are frequently used in order to emphasize their influence.

The word *blater* cannot be found in Madurese-Dutch dictionaries. In H.N. Kiliaan (1905) and P. Penninga and H. Hendriks (1936), one can find the word *"badjingan"* (a word that is used to refer to *blater* by many Madurese today) that means *landloper* ("tramp" in English). In an older dictionary of Dutch-Madurese (1898), Kiliaan translates *schurk* to *bangsat* or *bhangsat* (a word that is sometimes used to refer to *blater* today). In two Madurese-Indonesian dictionaries written by Asis Safioedin (1975 and 1977), I did not find the word *blater* or *bajingan*. Only in the recent dictionary of Madurese-Indonesian, one can find the word *blater* (Pawitra, 2009). According to that dictionary, *blater* means a figure who is regarded as a charismatic *jagoan* (*jago*) due to his strong influence in his village, and the term has a negative connotation.

Moreover, I have not been able to trace the emergence of *blater* in colonial records. No newspaper of the colonial period appears to provide accounts on *blater*. Today's East Javanese papers also hardly make references to *blater*. Even local Madurese newspapers that came into existence mainly after the New Order have hardly talked about *blater*. Sometimes, the media fear to be critical of the *blater*. If a *blater* commits a crime, the media will refer to the perpetrator only by his name without explaining that he is a *blater*. At the same time, some journalists seem to believe that the word *blater* is less popular than other similar terms in Madura and East Java, such as *bajingan* or *preman* (hoodlum, the term has become more popular since 1980s).

It may seem that *blater* is a relatively new word, at least when compared to the older words *jago* or *jawara*, terms that already existed in the nineteenth century. Nonetheless, the *blater* or the *blatership* are not new phenomena. In Kiliaan (1904), one can find the words of *remo(h)* and *tjarok* (*carok*). This obviously indicates that these cultural forms already existed, at least in the first decade of the twentieth century. These traditions are in fact older and were already recorded in Dutch sources.[4] In a general sense, it is possible to suggest that the concept of *blater* came into being some time before the twentieth century. More importantly, since *remo* and *carok*,[5] which play an important part in *blater* life, were already prevalent in the nineteenth century, it is possible that *blater* first appeared around the same time. A possible argument is that *blater* might have another name that was not recognized by the Dutch[6] or that the distinction between *bajingan* and *blater* did not exist yet (see the following paragraph for the distinction between *bajingan* and *blater*).

Today's *blater* frequently assert to know when the term first appeared. In confidential interviews with several *blater*, many of them claim that the word already existed when they were young. Some of them spent their childhood in the 1930s and 1940s and are convinced that the word *blater* was used at that time to identify strongmen in villages. Although such a claim is unverifiable, it is still useful to indicate that *blater* wish to highlight their presence by stressing their historical significance. Many Madurese identify *blater* as *bajingan* or *preman*: the first is a common but not an exclusive term for scoundrel in Madura and East Java, whereas the latter commonly being used in Jakarta; *blater* themselves, however, will most surely object being categorized as *bajingan* since that term has a negative connotation, while *blater* has an honorific meaning to them.

According to Abdur Rozaki (2004, pp. xx, 9), *blater* are a social community who possess habits or customs that are different to those of *kiai* or *santri*. They engage in *remo*, *sandur* (Madurese dancing), *sabung ayam*, and gambling. Other characteristics of *blater* include their predilections for magic, invulnerability skills, and martial arts. Rozaki and Latief Wiyata perceive the *blater's* consumption of alcohol, gambling, and womanizing as forms of crime (2006, p. xix). The view of these Madurese authors that the standing of the *blater* in their own society is unequivocally negative seems, however, exaggerated.

Blater, however, are not as simply local gangsters as Rozaki, Wiyata, or Pawitra suggest. *Blater* are a group who are able to sustain their distinctive norms in society using their charisma and means of intimidation against their potential enemies or whomever they consider as opponents. They are strongmen who can act as power brokers and have a mutually beneficial relationship with authorities and religious leaders and thus they hold a high standing in society.

In studying the Sicilian mafia, Anton Blok (1974) and Diego Gambetta (1993) make a clear distinction between the mafia and common criminals. The *blater* can similarly be described as entrepreneurs of protection, as individuals who offer protection to various groups that range from commoners to political parties in order to get political and economical benefits.[7] For instance, in interviews with three *kiai* (one of whom was a former functionary of the United Development Party, Partai Persatuan Pembangunan [PPP]) and a former functionary of the PPP in Bangkalan, they claimed that during the New Order many *blater* were employed by Golkar to persuade — or to intimidate if the persuasion did not succeed — villagers to vote for it. Yet, they admit that they also used the *blater* to protect themselves from their political adversaries during campaign times.[8] These *blater* who protected the PPP functionaries were said to be those whose religious orientations were still relatively influenced by the *santri* culture and who still maintained a relationship with their former religious teachers who also acted as the PPP functionaries. According to one of the three *kiai* (who was a former PPP functionary) and a former PPP functionary above, there was a prominent *blater* in Galis sub-district of Bangkalan in the 1970s and 1980s who supported the PPP. In the first three elections during the New Order, he (a prominent *blater* in Galis sub-district of Bangkalan) was a PPP supporter. In 1987 he was promised by Golkar functionaries of Bangkalan a position as a *klebun* in his village should he became a Golkar supporter. He accepted the offer and joined and afterwards he was "given" the *klebun* position through an alleged fraudulent village head election. Following the downfall of the New Order and the subsequent unpopularity of Golkar, he returned to the PPP and remained with the party until his death. Meanwhile, in Tanah Merah sub-district of Bangkalan, another *blater* who was also a PPP supporter was promised a *klebun* position if he could contribute to the victory of Golkar. Although he was not able to persuade the villagers to vote for Golkar, it was said by PPP functionaries that he was able to interfere with the final results of the general election in 1992. Following the victory of Golkar, he was "awarded" the *klebun* position.[9]

REMO AS THE ULTIMATE *BLATER* CHARACTERISTIC

What distinguishes *blater* from other strongmen in Indonesia is *remo*. *Remo* is an exclusive all-*blater* meeting that signifies the importance and existence of *blater* in Madurese society. *Remo* is a feast for *blater* and also serves as a rotating savings and credit association. A guest has to give money (*bhubuwan*) to the host, and in return, when he becomes a host, he will receive money from the former host and other guests, who will eventually become hosts as well. In this sense, *remo* may have a significant aspect of economic benefits for the host. Nevertheless, it does not mean that the host will directly become affluent from the gathering. In principle, when he becomes a guest for a *remo* which is held by a fellow *blater*, he has to provide the host (who was himself a guest at an earlier occasion) with more cash than he received from him earlier (*ngompang*). If he gives the same amount of money or even less, the host may consider this as an insult. Consequently, he may be removed from the membership of *remo*. However, exceptions do frequently occur, as many hosts show no real objection if they receive the same amount of money considering the possibility that they may not have sufficient amount of money to attend a *remo* held by a fellow *blater*, and that money is not the main reason when a *blater* holds a *remo*. *Remo* is a means of establishing new fraternities or fortifying old brotherhoods (*nyareh taretan* or *nyareh kancah*).

Remo also entails art performances such as a *tayub* performance.[10] Unlike *tayub* in Java, *remo* is not performed by female dancers. The dancers are men dressing as women. The purpose of replacing female dancers with male performers is said by the *blater* to reduce unwanted trouble that may arise if the dancers are women. Nonetheless, like in Javanese *tayub*, the act of *napel* (giving money to the dancer(s) by putting it on the dancer's chest) is prevalent and in fact it symbolizes the level of affluence of the cash-giver.

Another significant characteristic of *remo* is the consumption of alcohol, mostly but not exclusively, beer. Younger *blater* tend to show their ability to drink significant quantity of alcohol to prove their machismo, whereas older *blater* are less determined to do so. In general, *remo* is very much essential for *blater* to showcase their authority. Although many Madurese will deny the accusation that they like to show off, in fact, Madurese are stereotyped by many outsiders as individuals who like to do so. The involvement of *blater* in *remo* by showing their money to the host and other *blater*; the ability to dance with the *tandhak* and to *napel*; and the ability to drink large quantity of beer actually confirm the stereotyping. While many *kiai* and people may condemn the gathering, *blater* will ignore the complaints and continue to preserve their main cultural identity in order to assert their standing in society.

LOCAL BELIEF IN MADURA

The belief system of the common Madurese villagers centres on supernatural powers. While *kiai* as the core of the *santri* culture sustain close connections with Islam, local villagers believe in supernatural powers of spirits that mediate between them and God. From this point of view, common Madurese believe that events occur because of God's will, while others take place because of unknown powers or according to the laws of nature. Therefore, in order to put everything in order, supernatural powers of spirits have to be gratified regularly. In Java, collective ritualistic festivities, such as *bersih desa* (spirit shrine ritual), are held to keep people safe and free from trouble. It also holds true for the Madurese who hold *rokat* festivities, such as *rokat bandaran* or *rokat tase* (fishermen's celebration) and *rokat desa* (annual ritual to bless a village) to ask protection from the spirits of their ancestors, to avoid calamities as well as to get blessings so that they will benefit from their farm if they are farmers or the sea if they are fishermen. Mansurnoor who conducted an ethnographic research in Pamekasan points out that *se areksa*, the immanent supernatural powers, are a key element in the everyday relations between villagers and the supernatural world (1990, pp. 3–4). This holds true for many Madurese in daily life. Yet, they also tend to pray five times a day, adhere to other pillars of Islam (*Rukun Islam*), and believe in the six articles outlined in *Rukun Iman*.[11] At the same time, *dukun* (shamans, healers, or fortune-tellers) function as the prime mediators between the real world and the unseen world. *Kiai*, too, are also regarded as the key mediators between the two worlds; yet, several *kiai* reject this because of its association with *shirk* (the sin of polytheism) practices. They are afraid that the deification of anyone or anything other than God will lead to *shirk* practices which are a serious sin. Therefore, for instance, several *kiai* will refuse requests for *jimat* (amulet) or to bless one's business. Other *kiai*, however, believe that they are the intermediaries between the two worlds, and in fact, they attempt to maintain this status by consciously keeping away from villagers, so that villagers are convinced that they are different from common people. They, for instance, uphold their sacred position by preserving a prevalent belief in society that people will have their *barakah* (blessing) and *karomah* (dignity) if they visit and ask guidance in any matter from *kiai*. They are usually called *kiai dukun*. Meanwhile, other *kiai* — and they are actually the majority — are a mixture of two kinds of *kiai*. *Dukun*, meanwhile, frequently incorporate Islamic elements, such as recitation of Qur'anic verses (often blended with Madurese and Javanese words, considered un-Islamic) and declaring that their practices are approved by Allah and the Prophet. This is somewhat a compulsory practice among Madurese *dukun* where even though many Madurese still visit *dukun* up to the present day, they do not wish to be labelled un-Islamic individuals and hence they always believe that who they visit are *dukun Islami* (Islamic *dukun*) and this is not regarded as an un-Islamic practice.

In principle, the perceived power of mystical beliefs and practices are embedded in supernatural practitioners. Be that *dukun* or *kiai*, they have great power associated with them. This great power is said to have bridged worlds and to heal spiritual diseases, such as spirit possession (*kesurupan*) and to predict the future by applying divination practices or interpretation of dreams. Islam in Madura has been incorporated into indigenous practices as a matter of fashion, and all the parties involved — *kiai*, *dukun*, and common people — are all supporters of the long tradition.

RELIGIOUS ASPECTS OF THE *BLATER*

Blater like to claim that they are Muslims, yet unlike most Madurese, they are not *santri* who practise the common *santri* culture. They possess a mystical syncretist belief of Islam that, to a large degree, is different from that practised by *kiai* and *santri*; in fact, they tend to promote their own culture, especially *remo*, *vis-à-vis* that of *santri* individuals. Nevertheless, many *blater* reportedly have studied in a *pesantren* or at least informally in a village *langgar* (small mosque) during their childhood.[12] They thus may be categorized *santri* in the sense of having been pupils of *pesantren* during their childhood. For several reasons, mainly to seek wealth, influence, and fame, some time in their life the young *santri* leave the *pesantren* and transform into *blater*. Therefore, it is not uncommon that *blater* have the ability to read the Qur'an, although like many other Madurese, they do not understand the meaning of the words. When asked what their religion is, like most Madurese, they will definitely answer that Islam is their religion.

Similar to that of the Javanese *abangan*, the *blater's* religious tradition is composed primarily of syncretist religious activities, such as *slametan*, *khaul* (annual celebrations on the death anniversaries of religious leaders), and *ziarah* (pilgrimage to graves), as well as predilections for magic, invulnerability skills, and martial arts. Despite their claim that they are Muslims, many *blater* may not practise Islamic values as suggested by *kiai* since they may not perform *salat* (prayer) nor may they fast during Ramadan (in addition to a liking for drink and gamble). *Kiai* are certainly aware of these matters, like to keep hands-off attitude. Typically, they harbour ambiguous feelings towards the *blater*, a mix of aversion and respect.[13]

Aside from religious and mystical-supernatural purposes, *blater* also attend religious activities and if only for social, political, and economical reasons. Prominent *blater* do not wish to stand in the shadow of a *kiai*. For political purposes, for example during the New Order, they could cooperate with *kiai* of Golkar because they both were co-opted by the ruling party. In the post-New Order era, they can cooperate with *kiai* of any party for political power reasons.

Khaul of prominent *kiai*, such as that of *Kiai* Kholil, the *kiai* of Batuampar and the *kiai* of Guluk-Guluk are believed to bring blessings to attendees of religious events. These *khaul* even tempt prominent *blater* who dislike certain *kiai* who have somewhat ambiguous feelings towards the *blater* to appear at the celebration to seek blessings and to acquire the charisma of the deceased *kiai*. In a way, the coming of the *blater* functions as a free "advertisement", and it is good for their standing to show face. Besides *khaul*, another means to obtain blessings and charisma is via *ziarah* to the holy graves of *kiai* or royal families or other holy places, such as *gunung keramat* (sacred mountain), huge old trees, or big stones. The charisma of the leaders ensures the loyalty and obedience of their followers (Pribadi 2011, p. 178). Although some *blater* pay less attention to the general population in their village, prominent *blater* certainly need to maintain good relations with their neighbours in order to keep their influence in society. These *blater* are consciously aware of the fact that *kiai* preserve their position in society by following the same approach. In this sense, they mirror the tactics of *kiai* in how they form relations with villagers. By appearing at *slametan* held by their neighbours, *blater* are better able to assert their position than if they did not attend these occasions.

These visits have thus social, political, and economic motives. The following story illustrates the pragmatic purpose of these visits.[14] In 2009, the village of Sontang (a fictitious name) held its *klebun* election. Two candidates competed in a lively contest. Rustam (pseudonym) was a forty-four-year-old *blater* whose reputation extended beyond his village, but no further than the sub-district where he resided. He had three *taksi* (local public transport, in Java it is usually called *angkot*) and a *lapak* (stall) in the main market in Bangkalan. Mat Hosen (pseudonym) was a fifty-nine-year-old retired civil servant. Rustam actively involved in religious events during the campaign, not only in his village but also in neighbouring villages. He knew that many of his fellow villagers regularly attended religious congregations in a *pesantren* of a neighbouring village. Besides attending the ritual events, the villagers also frequently visited the *kiai* of the *pesantren* to ask for guidance in daily matters. By attending religious events in the *pesantren*, Rustam hoped that fellow villagers would help creating an image of him as a pious *blater* who had transformed from a less-orthodox (i.e., nominal) Muslim public figure to a religious person. More importantly, attending religious events in the *pesantren*, he hoped to be noticed by the *kiai* of the *pesantren*, as he knew that the *kiai* would advise his fellow villagers regarding the upcoming *klebun*. Moreover, Rustam frequently participated in fellow villagers' religious rituals. When his neighbour held a *slametan* as a result of his *nazar* (*nadhr* — a religious vow), Rustam provided a goat for the meal. He knew that fellow neighbours would also enjoy the feast, and by letting them know that he had contributed to the gathering, he was subtly campaigning for the election. Rustam won the election in Sontang by a slim margin. Nevertheless, he had already won over the voters during his sympathetic campaign. Rustam was known as a generous person, and so people did not really see his acts as part of his campaign. The three months campaign period provided Rustam with numerous opportunities to promote a first-rate image of himself among the villagers. In many villages, whose inhabitants expect to be able to see the elected *klebun* in his office at any time, and as he (the *klebun*) attends communal events and discusses public concerns on a regular basis, the villagers very much prefer a reliable candidate.

On a higher level, the local or regional (in this case East Java province) state apparatus are usually invited to attend grand *khaul* (*khaul akbar*) of renowned *kiai*. Their coming also indicates how such *khaul* are politically, economically commoditized. The presence of local or regional officials helps enhance the prestige level of such *khaul*. For instance, although for a long time the *khaul* of *Kiai* Kholil (died sometime between 1923 and 1925)[15] had already attracted a great number of visitors, the appointment of Fuad Amin Imron, a great-grandson of *Kiai* Kholil, as the regent of Bangkalan from 2003 to 2008 and 2008 to 2013, has increased the significance of the occasion more than even. Since *blater* form patron–client relationships with the state apparatus, in which the former are the client and the latter are the patron, their being there constitutes a good sign of "obedience" to the officials. For *blater*, besides maintaining their good relationship with the bureaucrats, it is not uncommon that they obtain governmental or partisan "projects", such as controlling the security of a sacred burial ground (*pasarean*),[16] on such occasions.[17] Such practices mirror those in other parts of Indonesia, especially in Jakarta.[18]

Ziarah to holy graves provide *blater* with opportunities similar to those obtained from attending *khaul*. During Muslim holidays, such as Eid Al-Fitr and Eid Al-Adha, famous *pasarean* attract many pilgrims from all over Madura and Java. Like the event of *khaul*, *ziarah* also attract both state officials and *blater*. Royal Pasarean Ratu Ebu in Bangkalan or royal Pasarean Asta Tinggi in Sumenep, like the graves of renowned *kiai*, are known to attract tens of thousands of pilgrims every month. Officials and *blater* seemingly coincidentally meet on these occasions. However, since *blater* have a network of informants, they first find out when the officials will come to the cemeteries. Not surprisingly, the officials — whether or not they are aware that *blater* will come — actually expect that they will meet their clients there at a certain time and location. In other words, *blater* are expected to know when state officials will visit. Meetings in *pasarean* are not necessarily intended to discuss significant matters between the two sides. It acts mostly as a form of *silaturahmi* (good relationship). However, *silaturahmi* between patron and client certainly also indicates a high degree of obedience of the latter to the former.

Other occasions that attract many important pilgrims are elections, be they *pemilu* (general elections), *pilkada* (elections to vote for provincial or municipal head), or *klebun* elections. Prior to the elections, many candidates who run for various positions typically visit holy graves of *kiai* or royal families. This is believed to bring luck and confidence for the candidates running in the elections. The *juru kunci* (the custodians of graveyards) of Pasarean Ratu Ebu, Makam Agung, and Makam Tengah (all located in Bangkalan) claim that famous national figures generally visit their *pesarean* prior to general elections. Although such claims are unreliable — these kinds of stories are also found in many graveyards and although some famous national figures may indeed come, the numbers are in fact never revealed — many Madurese pass this story on to other visitors. For them, this justifies visiting such graves: if important people can have their wishes granted, then there is also an opportunity for other visitors to get blessings. However, when asked whether *blater* come to these last resting places, *juru kunci* strongly deny it. They claim that bad people (*orang jahat*) never come to holy places because their wishes will not come true and more importantly, instead of getting blessings, they will have bad luck if they dare enter the cemeteries with unholy wishes.

> *Blater* never come here. They do not dare to ask [for anything] because their bad intentions are already known when they enter the grave. Their bad intentions are unveiled by the holy people who are buried here, not by me. Those who come here are important people (*orang besar*). If they come here, they usually become someone important (*jadi orang*-here means they occupy important positions). If not governor, at least regent or member of parliament. But bad people will not have their wishes granted (*dikabulkan*) (interview with the *juru kunci* of Makam Agung, 24 February 2011).

It is important to note, however, that it is a well-known secret that *blater* regularly visit holy graves of *kiai* or royal families, the reasons explained earlier. The denial of the *juru kunci* is part of an unobserved contestation between the *blater* and the *santri*. In fact, I would argue that the *blater* have been promoting a counterculture, which is apparent in the objections by supporters of the *santri* culture, very much including the *juru kunci* of these holy graves. *Juru kunci*[19] is an inherited position in Madura. The holders of this position are the auxiliary hands of religious leaders. In order to keep their places sacred, religious leaders need to keep them clean of unwanted people. *Blater* who do not practise the *santri* culture are regarded by some *kiai* as their latent enemies. Although on other occasions, the two sides can cooperate in a loose relationship, it is exactly in the religious domain that the two sides have conflicting opinions.

All the above examples may seem to indicate that *blater* are pragmatic individuals. However, their supposed pragmatic attitudes would not last if they were not sustained by a strong sense of their own identity. As I have mentioned earlier, *blater* have been pushing their counterculture *vis-à-vis* the *santri* culture, which is very influential in Madurese society, even at the lowest level. Nevertheless, the *blater* do not publicly attack the *santri* culture since its main supporters, the *kiai*, are highly regarded by many elements of society, including the *blater* themselves. Even though they leave the *pesantren* after they graduate, many *blater* still consider the *kiai* as their teachers. In Banten, to oppose *kiai* was a serious breach of etiquette, with both social and spiritual consequences. On a spiritual level, a rebellious pupil runs the risk of *kawalat* (accursed and struck down by calamity) (Tihami 1992, pp. 99–100 and Wilson 2003, p. 246). This situation also holds true in Madura.

CONCLUSIONS

Blater have displayed various roles they play: from their roles as entrepreneurs of protection, perpetrators of cultural violence to their leading roles as power brokers. As with many other strongmen groups in the Indonesian archipelago, the origin of *blater* is not clearly known. It seems that it is not a new phenomenon (at least it must be older than a hundred years) and the emergence of *blater* in Madura may show parallel patterns with other distinctive groups such as the *jago* and *jawara*. Like other strongmen in Java, they are strongmen who have acted as cultural and political brokers and intermediaries.

Meanwhile, *remo* is the distinctive *blater* characteristic that counteracts the dynamics of piety that *kiai* and *santri* promote. In fact, seen together with *kerapan sapi* and *sabung ayam*, which play an important part in *blater* life, these cultural forms are so distinctive that it seems that no other strongmen in Java are counteracting the *santri* culture as much as *blater* do, at least when we look at the special feast of *remo*, which other strongmen such as *jawara* do not have. *Blater* have their own sets of religious beliefs that, to a large degree, differ from those of *kiai* and *santri* individuals. It shows us that Madura is also actually home to less orthodox Muslims and a place where *abangan*-like spiritual beliefs as a variant of Islam are appreciated by some segments of society.

Blater, together with much of the general Madurese population acknowledge supernatural powers of spirits that mediate between them and God, the highest power. What I want to emphasize is that the power of mystical beliefs and practices are perceived to be embedded in supernatural practitioners, such as *dukun* or *kiai* who act as *kiai dukun*, considered to have great power and be able to interact with the unseen world.

Even though that in terms of religious ideas and practices *blater* are a minority, in daily life they have well adapted to the mainstream Islam of the Madurese. They have never really experienced pressure as a minority among the majority *santri* adherents. There are in fact many Madurese, who, apart from their adherence to *santri* culture (the prayers, the fast, the almsgiving), visit *dukun* or *kiai dukun* on a regular basis and perform collective ritualistic festivities, such as the *rokat* traditions. While *kiai* and other main supporters of the *santri* culture, such as the pupils in *pesantren* and other people in the religious network of *pesantren* openly promote their religious orientations, *blater* and other non-orthodox Muslims do not explicitly demonstrate their religious views. In fact, they do not seem to directly oppose the *kiais*' religious authority. What they promote are their distinctive institutionalized characteristics, *remo*, and violent traditions, such as *kerapan sapi* and *sabung ayam*. With these cultural forms, the *blater* and the supporters of the *abangan*-like culture clearly signify the difference between the common *santri* culture and their own counterculture.

Notes

[1] I am grateful to Kees van Dijk for commenting on earlier versions of this chapter, Amrih Widodo, Greg Fealy, and Phillip Winn for their valuable suggestions, and Bernhard Platzdasch for his guidance during the revision process of this chapter. Financial support of this research was provided by Training Indonesia's Young Leaders, Leiden University; the Australia-Netherlands Research Collaboration (ANRC); and Leiden University Fund (LUF).

[2] I use the terms *ulama* and *kiai* interchangeably.

[3] In Indonesian languages such as Javanese, Madurese, and Bahasa Indonesia (the official language of Indonesia), the term *kiai* and *ulama* can be used in both singular and plural forms. Other non-English terms in this chapter can be used in both singular and plural forms as well.

4   About *carok*, Dutch sources state: "When a Madurese was made to be ashamed (*malo*), he pulled his knife and immediately avenged the insult or waited until an opportunity arose to avenge himself. Fights, murder, and homicide (*carok*) were the order of the day, if one can believe it. One assumed the adage 'an eye for an eye, a tooth for a tooth'" (*De Java-Post* 1911, pp. 9–22, 345), and "Even 'small insults' were 'answered with a knife'" (Wop 1866, p. 284). Both are quoted in de Jonge (1995), p. 13. Further: "Before the prohibition of carrying weapons in 1863, *carok* was also committed with spears, lances, swords, broadswords, and *kris*." See de Jonge (2002), p. 147. About *remo*: "The Madurese are also crazy about festivities. That is when they kick over the traces, followed again by a long period of saving. It is often said about the inhabitants of the western part of the island that they drink *tuak* or palm wine ('the population of West Madura is addicted to alcohol') and that festivities there often got out of hand. For a long time parties were only permitted there under police supervision" (Surink 1933, p. 196; Van Gennep 1895, p. 270) (quoted in de Jonge 1995, pp. 15–16).

5   *Carok* is a distinctive Madurese fight using sharp weapons, mostly but not exclusively sickles, and is considered a last resort in defending one's honour.

6   It is possible for one particular phenomenon to have many different terms. For instance, the word *gali* in Indonesia (*gabungan anak-anak liar* — "groups of wild boys" literally) was not popular before the 1980s although individuals who acted like *gali* already existed in the 1960s and 1970s. The term became popular only during the *petrus* (*penembak(an) misterius* [literally "mysterious shootings" of suspected criminals and hoodlums] and shortly afterwards (personal communication with Prof. Robert Cribb).

7   According to Blok, the central characteristic of the mafia is "the private use of unlicensed violence as a means of control in the public arena" (Blok 1974, p. xiv). Meanwhile, Gambetta defines mafia as an industry, an enterprise which offers private protection as its main product (see Gambetta 1993, p. 1).

8   Confidential interviews with *Kiai* MF, a former PPP functionary on 1 December 2009, *Kiai* AS on 16 December 2009, *Kiai* MS on 23 December 2009, and FR, a former board member of the PPP chapter of Bangkalan on 19 November 2009.

9   Confidential interviews with *Kiai* MF, a former PPP functionary on 1 December 2009 and FR, a former board member of the PPP chapter of Bangkalan on 19 November 2009.

10 *Blater* call the art performance *sandur* or *sandhor* instead of *tayub*.

11 *Rukun Islam* or the Five Pillars of Islam are the acts in Islam considered obligatory for Sunni Muslims. They are: (1) The *shahada* (creed); (2) *Salat* (daily prayers); (3) *Sawm* (fasting); (4) *Zakat* (almsgiving); and (5) *Hajj*

(pilgrimage to Mecca) if it can be afforded. *Rukun Iman* or the Six Articles of Faith is a set of articles of faith in the Islamic creed that consist of (1) Belief in God; (2) Belief in the Prophets (acknowledged in the Sunni tradition); (3) Belief in the Angels; (4) Belief in Divine Books; (5) Belief in the Day of Judgment; and (6) Belief in *Qadr* (fate).

12 Confidential interviews with *Kiai* MF, a former PPP functionary on 1 December 2009, R, a *blater* on 13 January 2011, K, a *blater* on 21 February 2011, and MG, a *blater* on 24 February 2011.

13 In interviews with two *kiai*, one (*Kiai* NR) states that "we never touch on (*mengusik*) them [the *blater*] as long as they do not touch on us either. Even though they are *blater*, they still *mengaji* (learning to read the Quran, sometimes with Arabic lessons) and respect *kiai* and *santri*. It does not matter if they don't pray, as long as they behave appropriately in [the] presence of a *kiai*. It is important that we respect their braveness. We have to remember that there are two kinds of [public] figures, the *ulama* and the *blater*. The two must not clash (*bentrok*) in Madura. Negative is that the *blater* sometimes gives inappropriately obtained money to *kiai*, despite being seen as a sin" (interview with *Kiai* NR on 1 December 2009). Meanwhile, *Kiai* MF reveals that "in my opinion, *blater* are a group whose professions are unpleasant for the people (*tidak menyamankan masyarakat*), but on the other hand [they] bring many benefits … in my opinion, from one side the *blater* can be utilized as security forces. If one who is facing a threat of being robbed (*ditodong*-by a *preman*, for instance) mentions a certain *kiai* or *blater* name, he will be safe [from the robbery]" (interview with *Kiai* MF on 1 December 2009).

14 This is based on my fieldwork in 2009.

15 The most famed *kiai* in the history of Madura is *Kiai* Muhammad Kholil of Bangkalan. Nowadays a considerable number of Madurese and Javanese *kiai* consider him their indirect guru, because many leading *kiai* in Java, such as two of the founders of the NU *Kiai* Wahab Hasbullah of Tambakberas, Jombang, and *Kiai* Hasyim Asyari of Tebuireng, Jombang, studied in his *pesantren*.

16 In the 2003 regency head election of Bangkalan, two pairs competed (Sulaiman–Sunarto and Fuad–Muhammadong). Wars of support and support gatherings arranged by local leaders appeared prior to the election. In a confidential interview, a *blater* informed that initially he was not concerned about who would become the regent of Bangkalan, as long as the successful candidate would help the *blater*'s business. He said that Fuad's camp had promised him to take over the security of a *pasarean* because of his support, and also positively mention that Fuad's people had seen him in the *Kiai* Kholil *pasarean* (interview with MK, a *blater* on 23 April 2011).

17 William R. Liddle shows how political parties in Sumatra in order to be successful on the local level have had to adapt to local socio-economic and cultural circumstances (see Liddle 1972, pp. 126–78). In Banten, through the local chairman of PPPSBBI (a *jawara* organization), *jawara* could act as bridge between the military, the bureaucracy, and Golkar, through which many governmental projects came under their control, as they maintained closed patron–client relationships with the officials (see Pribadi 2008, p. 59).

18 In Jakarta and provincial capitals, many governmental or partisan projects are obtained during informal occasions, as during golf games. According to Anton Lucas, many senior members of Indonesia's bureaucratic elite are devoted golfers, or aspire to be. See Lucas (1997), p. 237.

19 Based on colonial records, *juru kunci* had a distinctive position among those who had to provide service to royal families. They were awarded tax-exempted land (*pakuncen*) as rewards for their service (see de Jonge 1989, p. 71).

References

Blok, Anton. *The Mafia of a Sicilian Village, 1860–1960: A Study of Violent Peasant Entrepreneurs*. Oxford: Blackwell, 1974.

de Jonge, Huub. *Madura dalam Empat Zaman, Pedagang, Perkembangan Ekonomi, dan Islam: Suatu Studi Antropologi Ekonomi* [Madura in Four Periods, Merchants, Economic Development, and Islam: An Economic Anthropology Study]. Jakarta: Gramedia, 1989.

———. "Stereotypes of the Madurese". In *Across Madura Strait: The Dynamics of an Insular Society*, edited by Kees van Dijk, Huub de Jonge and Elly Touwen-Bouwsma. Leiden: KITLV Press, 1995.

———. "Rather White Bones than White Eyes: Violent Self-Help among the Madurese". In *Violence and Vengeance: Discontent and Conflict in New Order Indonesia*, edited by Frans Hüsken and Huub de Jonge. Saarbrücken: Verlag fürEntwicklungspolitik Saarbrücken, 2002.

Galtung, Johan. "Cultural Violence". *Journal of Peace Research* 27, no. 3 (1990): 291–305.

Gambetta, Diego. *The Sicilian Mafia: The Business of Private Protection*. Cambridge: Harvard University Press, 1993.

Geertz, Clifford. *The Religion of Java*. Glencoe: The Free Press, 1960.

Kiliaan, H.N. *Nederlandsch-Madoereesch Woordenboek* [Dutch-Madurese Dictionary]. Batavia: Landsdrukkerij, 1898.

———. *Madoereesch-Nederlandsch Woordenboek, Eerste Deel* [Madurese-Dutch Dictionary, First Part]. Leiden: Brill, 1904.

———. *Madoereesch-Nederlandsch Woordenboek, Tweede Deel* [Madurese-Dutch Dictionary, Second Part]. Leiden: Brill, 1905.

Koentjaraningrat. "Madurese". In *Ethnic Groups of Insular Southeast Asia Vol. 1: Indonesia, Andaman Islands and Madagascar*, edited by Frank M. LeBar. New Haven, CT: Human Relations Area Files Press, 1972.

Liddle, R. William. "Ethnicity and Political Organization: Three East Sumatran Cases". In *Culture and Politics in Indonesia*, edited by Claire Holt, Benedict Anderson and James Siegel. Ithaca, NY: Cornell University Press, 1972.

Lucas, Anton. "Land Disputes, the Bureaucracy, and Local Resistance in Indonesia". In *Imagining Indonesia: Cultural Politics and Political Culture*, edited by Jim Schiller and Barbara Martin-Schiller. Athens, OA: The Center for International Studies, Ohio University, 1997.

Mansurnoor, Iik. *Islam in an Indonesian World: Ulama of Madura*. Yogyakarta: Gadjah Mada University Press, 1990.

Moesa, Ali Maschan. *Kiai and Politik dalam Wacana Civil Society*. Surabaya: Lepkiss, 1999.

Pawitra, Adrian. *Kamus Lengkap Bahasa Madura Indonesia: Dengan Ejaan Bahasa Madura Tepat Ucap*. Jakarta: Dian Rakyat, 2009.

Penninga, P. and H. Hendriks. *Practisch Madurees-Nederlands Woordenboek, 2^e Vermeerderde Druk*. s-Gravenhage: G.C.T. van Dorp, 1936.

Pribadi, Yanwar. "Jawara in Banten: Their Socio-Political Roles in the New Order Era 1966–1998". M.A. thesis, Faculty of Humanities, Leiden University, 2008.

———. "Strongmen and Religious Leaders in Java: Their Dynamic Relationship in Search of Power". *Al-Jamiah Journal of Islamic Studies* 49, no. 1 (2011): 159–90.

Rozaki, Abdur. *Menabur Kharisma Menuai Kuasa: Kiprah Kiai dan Blater sebagai Rezim Kembar di Madura* [Strewing Charisma Reaping Power: The Roles of *Kiai* and *Blater* as Twin Regimes in Madura]. Yogyakarta: Pustaka Marwa, 2004.

Safioedin, Asis. *Kamus Sederhana bahasa Madura–bahasa Indonesia*. Surabaya: [s.n.], 1975.

———. *Kamus bahasa Madura–Indonesia*. Jakarta: Pusat Pembinaan dan Pengembangan Bahasa, Departemen Pendidikan dan Kebudayaan, 1977.

Tihami, M.A. "Kyai dan Jawara di Banten: Studi tentang Agama, Magi, dan Kepemimpinan di Desa Pasanggrahan Serang, Banten" [*Kyai* and *Jawara* in Banten: A Study of Religion, Magic, and Leadership in Pasanggrahan Village, Serang, Banten]. M.A. thesis, Department of Anthropology, University of Indonesia, 1992.

van Bruinessen, Martin. "Global and Local in Indonesian Islam". *Southeast Asian Studies* 37, no. 2 (1999): 158–74.

Wilson, Ian Douglas. "The Politics of Inner Power: The Practice of *Pencak Silat* in West Java". Ph.D. dissertation, School of Asian Studies, Murdoch University, 2003.

Wiyata, Latief. *Carok: Konflik Kekerasan dan Harga Diri Orang Madura* [*Carok*: Violent and Self-Esteem Conflicts of the Madurese]. Yogyakarta: LKiS, 2006.

Woodward, Mark. *Islam in Java: Normative Piety and Mysticism in the Sultanate of Yogyakarta*. Tucson, AZ: The University of Arizona Press, 1989.

MALAYSIA

12

INTRODUCTION

Johan Saravanamuttu

FROM PLURALISM TO CENTRALIZED ISLAM

Malaysian society was from the outset depicted as a "plural society" (Furnivall 1948) with the connotation that such a society, with its diverse ethnicities, was held together by dint of colonial power. The corollary was that such a social formation was neither socially cohesive nor politically integrated. Since achieving its independence from the British, the Malaysian political class has fashioned a degree of power-sharing and political accommodation to keep peace among Malaysia's different ethnic communities in most areas of political and social life. Ethnic peace has endured except for an episode that saw the eruption of race riots on 13 May 1969 and almost two hundred people killed. No major riots of this sort has occurred for over some four decades, except the Kampung Medan incident of 2001, when Malays clashed with Indians and some six persons of the latter community died. While no serious upheavals have occurred since then, ethnic and religious conflicts continue to afflict Malaysian society, and in more recent years, religious divisions have become particularly prominent. Such conflicts have occurred even as a more universal notion of citizenship has found expression among Malaysia's multicultural populace through the agency of a vibrant civil society.

Paradoxically, the emergence of social activism and an expressive civil society has also given rise to a backlash of religious atavism and religious intolerance in society, evidenced by incidents of Hindu temple desecration and demolitions and church burnings, hitherto absent in the country. By and large, such incidents have been the work of fringe groups, but the worry is that state authorities or the ruling group have condoned these acts. It is clearly evident that mitigating these developments of religious extremism is now integral to the rise of a more tolerant Malaysian middle-class society. Related to the rise of an educated middle class is the emergence of a new participatory politics, which now challenges an old authoritarian politics, based on a model of power-sharing dominated by ethnic elites, which over-privileged the Malay-Muslim community. New politics in Malaysia has given sustenance to a path of social relations and political engagement of citizens cutting across, and to some extent, transcending ethnic boundaries. This by no means suggests that the old path of politics has been eliminated, but rather that the contestation has arguably entered a more progressive phase.

The study of non-Muslim minorities in Malaysia is still relatively sparse. Among the pioneers of such work are Raymond Lee and Susan Ackerman (1997). One of the few book-length studies dealing directly with a religious minority is Andrew Wilford's (2006) path-breaking ethnographic work on Malaysian Tamils. Wilford shows how a politicized Hinduism has engaged and coped with a state-driven ethno-religious nationalism. Most recent work on Islam focuses on the Malays. The important anthropological work of Michael Peletz (2002) sheds considerable light on how middle-class Muslims are increasingly drawn within the rubric of a Malaysian civil society through modern institutions such as the courts. Similarly, Gerhard Hoffstaedter (2011), using a sociological approach, provides important hints as to how modern Muslim identities intersect with those of their non-Muslim counterparts.

The writers in this book examine, through their different disciplines and lenses, how religious minorities have invariably been drawn into the whirlwind of Malaysia's new politics. As shown by the chapter writers, Malaysia's religious minorities which comprise of Buddhists, Christians, and Hindus in the Peninsula have become increasingly engaged with issues pertaining to politics, primarily because of the increasingly intrusion of Muslim-driven state agendas. Indigenous Christian communities in Sarawak have also similarly felt the weight of Islamic policies. Malaysian ethnic minorities and their engagement with the state have become part of the landscape of Malaysia's new politics. Of paramount importance today in Malaysia is how a predominantly Muslim society comprising about 60 per cent of the population accommodates religious minorities. More pointedly, we need to ascertain the extent of tolerance and the new terrains of inter-religious conflict and friction and the manner by which they are to be overcome in a Muslim-dominant state such as Malaysia. Furthermore, how have religious minorities managed their relations with the Muslim majority and *vis-à-vis* Muslim state authorities?

Religious minority groups mentioned above have largely remained on the periphery of politics in the past but have increasingly been brought into contention with a rising religiosity of the Muslim majority and inevitably impacting directly on social relations and politics. Since the 1970s, the resurgence of Islam has impelled a state-led Islamization project, with its complex ramifications on everyday Islamic practices and inter-religious relations. Islamic resurgence and the Islamization process have been well-documented and analysed by scholars (Nagata 1984; Martinez 2001; Liow 2004, 2009; Noor 2004; Mohamad 2004, 2010, 2011; Lee 2010) but its impact on religious minorities has been less studied.[1] The writers in this volume show that the political engagement of religious minorities with the Malaysian state has taken various forms, but outcomes have not altogether been positive for these communities. What is evident, however, is that a continuous engagement has been possible through the mediation and agency of civil society organizations.

The rise of a centralizing Islamic bureaucracy has seemingly narrowed the terrain of toleration in inter-religious relations and even in intra-religious relations, giving rise to both deliberate and unintended acts of religious intolerance. What is particularly worrisome is that religion-related conflicts have increasingly become part of the leitmotif of mainstream politics and contestations in the public sphere and even in everyday social interactions. This said, Malaysia's underlying multiculturalism (Saravanamuttu 2004) and cosmopolitanism (Kahn 2006) and its overall cultural open-endedness, coupled with a more engaged civil society, has spawned new modes of political accommodation and management of religious conflicts. In particular, a newly shaped reformist politics has also helped to ameliorate religious conflicts and kept them to tolerable levels. To be sure, by the early 2000s, many issues and conflicts pertaining to religious minorities have surfaced prominently onto the Malaysian social and political landscape. At the same time, non-governmental organizations (NGOs) have provided much-needed agency in reducing such conflicts and altercations. The chapters that are in this section of the book deal specifically with how such issues and conflicts have impacted Christians, Buddhists, Hindus, and the Syiah Muslims. The responses of these religious minorities, as our contributors show, have been for each specific community to engage with the state but also for these communities to collectively respond to common issues through a multi-religious platform. Before we delve further into the specifics of the areas of conflict and the level of tolerance for religious minorities as well as their responses, it would be germane to first provide a brief overview of the process of Malaysia's Islamization and its relevance to this discussion.

ISLAMIZATION

Under the Malaysian Constitution, Islam is "the religion of the Federation" but other religions may be followed in peace (Article 3) and furthermore religious minorities are free to profess their respective religions subject to the caveat of not propagating them to Muslims (Article 11). However, through a complex web of laws and regulations at the state and federal levels, the policy of Islamization was given much sway by the 1980s. The government had introduced this policy partly because of the political rivalry between the two contending Malay political parties in the face of an Islamic revivalism throughout the country. Thus, the United Malays National Organization (UMNO)-led government was obliged to progressively introduce Islamic legislation at the two major levels of governance, via state governments and federal authorities. Given the centralized character of Malaysian federalism, this invariably led to the setting up of a federal Islamic authority known as JAKIM (*Jabatan Kemajuan Islam Malaysia*), or "Department for the Advancement of Islam in Malaysia". JAKIM as an entity was the product of the bureaucratic upgrading of the Islamic Affairs Division (BAHEIS)[2] of the Prime Minister's Department in 1997. JAKIM has been given oversight in all matters related to the administration of Islam outside the courts.

We now turn to Article 121 which refers to the power vested in the Malaysian High Court. In 1988, the controversial amendment of "1A" effectively prevented the High Court from intervening in *Syariah* Court rulings, that is, in matters affecting Muslims.[3] Farid S. Shuaib (2003, pp. 2–6) argues that the new legislation was necessitated by the fact that the Court of Judicature Act of 1964 allowed civil courts to supersede *Syariah* courts and caused jurisdictional conflicts. Thus, with the promulgation of Article 121(1A), this effectively insulated the *Syariah* courts from the civil court system. In the meantime, the *Syariah* Court system, which had previously mainly dealt with Muslim family law and inheritance, has expanded to three tiers of courts — Subordinate Court, High Court, and Appeals Court — and by 1991 all thirteen states and federal territories in Malaysia had instituted all three levels of *Syariah* courts. Moreover, a plethora of laws have been passed going well beyond the matters of inheritance, marriage, divorce, custody, and maintenance.

Examples include the *Syariah* Criminal Offences Law of 1983 (Kelantan), and laws in 1987 sanctioning various types of whipping for transgressions in Islam — *Kaedah-Kadeah Hukum Sebat* (Mohamad, 2011, p. 176).

Contestation over Islamization reached a crescendo with the promulgation, by Kelantan in 1993 and Terengganu in 1999, of *Hudud* and *Qisas* laws, which deal with mandatory punishment for criminal offenses as derived from the Qu'ran and Sunnah. *Kanun Jenayah Syariah* (II) was enacted in 1993 and officially known as *Enakmen Undang-undang Kanun Jenayah Syariah (II) 1993 (Hukum Hudud)*. Under *Hudud,* theft, robbery, illicit sex, alcohol consumption, and apostasy were to be considered chargeable as Islamic offenses. Punishments for these are corporeal in nature involving whipping, stoning to death, and amputation of the limbs. *Qisas* law refers to offenses that involve bodily injury or loss of life. The punishment is death or imprisonment but compensation in the form of money or property is acceptable if the guardian of the victim forgives the offender.[4] However, the Kelantan and Terengganu state enactments saw no actual progress so long as the Barisan Nasional (BN)-controlled federal government chose not to endorse such legislation.

Not to be outdone, in late 2001, ironically after the 11 September event, the then Prime Minister Mahathir Mohamad attempted to "out-Islamize" the Islamic party, PAS (Parti Islam Se-Malaysia), by declaring that Malaysia was already a practising Islamic State ("*Negara Islam*").[5] There was some justification to Mahathir's statement as the Islamization project was initiated under his tenure as Prime Minister and had gone a considerable distance by the time he made this announcement. However, the move was poorly orchestrated and a booklet purporting to explain the contours of Malaysia's version of the Islamic state was hastily withdrawn after objections from civil activists and intellectuals. PAS then called for the matter of the "Islamic state" to be openly debated as did the Democratic Action Party (DAP) from a different standpoint. The DAP had by then left the defunct Barisan Alternatif (BA) in August 2001 because of a fundamental disagreement with PAS over the Islamic state issue. However, today both parties are part of the People's Alliance (Pakatan Rakyat) even though the issue of Islamic state has not been satisfactorily resolved. A *modus vivendi* between the UMNO and PAS appeared to be in the horizon when the so-called unity talks started in 2008 after the general election of that year. These talks have seen no real progress as PAS has remained firmly committed to its alignment with the opposition alliance.

A shift in the nuance of UMNO's Islamic politics had apparently occurred more or less coinciding with the landslide electoral victory of the BN in 2004 under the leadership of Abdullah Badawi. After assuming the helm in October 2003, Abdullah had introduced a softer version of a modernist and moderate Islam known as "*Islam Hadhari*" or "civilizational Islam" defined as follows:

> An approach to human development, society and the Malaysian state that is comprehensive based on the parameters of growing Islamic civilization with the view of producing individuals and an Islamic society which is spiritual, intellectual, with material strength, self-reliance, competitiveness, is forward-looking, innovative as well as capable of handling current challenges in a manner is wise, rational and peaceful (Saravanamuttu 2010, p. 286).

The ten principles of *Islam Hadhari* were outlined by Abdullah Ahmad Badawi in his keynote address to the UMNO General Assembly in September 2004, and the former premier has himself penned a book about the concept (Abdullah Ahmad Badawi 2006). Interestingly, principle number seven concerns the rights of minority groups and women's rights.[6] This shift in policy has not prevented what has been the continual and increased centralization and bureaucratization of Islam at various levels of governance (Mohamad 2010, pp. 513–14). Increasingly, Islam came under the charge of both the Federal level authority JAKIM and other state-level institutions. The prevailing practice of Islam that is officially sanctioned by JAKIM is the *Ahlus Sunnah Wal Jamaah* (ASWJ) practice of Sunni Islam.

Constitutional provisions since the time of independence in 1957 allowed for what could be called a Muslim exceptionalism, which has become the basis for the legal penetration of Islamic practices. This has been brought about by the enhancement of the *Syariah* Court system and a growing plethora of federal institutions and agencies, premised on Islam's designation as the religion of the federation. With the amendment of "1A" to Article 121 in 1988, as noted earlier, the status of the *Syariah* Court system was put on a par with the civil court system. Moreover, *Syariah* courts were *ipso facto* not subjected to judicial oversight by the Malaysian High Court or the Federal Court.[7] Appellate *Syariah* courts were also convened at the state level, as religion is a state matter. This created a conundrum particularly for non-Muslims as to where they could seek legal redress on matters of Islam. Muslims who have sought redress on issues of Islam in civil courts have invariably failed and non-Muslims who have sought redress in civil courts have had only limited success. These developments in effect have elevated the *Syariah* Court to the status of the

High Court and even the Federal Court. There are now some prominent cases regarding conversion to Islam that have been brought appellate courts that have become the cause célèbre of non-Muslims as will be shown in some chapters of this volume. Further below, I discuss the troubling case of Lina Joy, a Muslim woman who converted to Christianity and turned to the civil courts for a ruling but failed in her attempt to remove the word "Islam" from her identity card. The former Chief Justice of Malaysia Abdul Hamid Mohamad delivered a judgement in July 2007 in which he raised the problem of the Article 121(1A) legislation, where he argued that "Clause (1A) of Article 121 was not introduced for the purpose of ousting the jurisdiction of the civil courts." He added, "The question to be asked is: are such laws constitutional in the first place? And the constitutionality of such laws is a matter for the Federal Court to decide — Article 128" (Maznah Mohamad, Zarina Aziz, and Chin Oy Sim, 2008, p. 93).[8]

Both UMNO-led and PAS-led Islamization led to the further expansion of Islamic bodies and bureaucracies at the state and federal levels. Malaysia could well be considered a "hybrid state" when it comes down to constitutional practices with respect to religious freedom (Saleem Faruqi 2005; Saravanamuttu 2010). Constitutional experts differ at two extreme poles of the debate as to whether Malaysia has become an "Islamic state". For example, Fernando (2006) maintains that Malaysia is a secular state in conception and intention, while Bari (2005) is equally resolute that Islamic moral precepts are embedded in Malaysia's constitutional provisions. Social scientists such as Martinez (2001), Liow (2004), and Weiss (2004) are closer to the spectrum of scholarship that argues that a deepening Islamization has yet to produce a full-fledged Islamic state. Going further, some contend that an Islamic state may already be the order embedded in the nature of Islamic governance or cultural practice (Noor 2003, 2004; Shamsul 2005). Finally, some scholars have shown in no uncertain terms that the Islamic legal structure has grown through the institutionalization of *Syariah* courts, while the promulgation of a series of *Syariah* enactments has spawned a veritable Islamic bureaucracy (Hamayotsu 2003). An interesting view holds that the centralization of Islamic practice under a set of rationally embedded laws administered by a "divine" bureaucracy has given rise to the "secularization" of Islam (Mohamad 2010).

AREAS OF TOLERATION AND CONFLICT

For everyday social relations and politics, a thoroughgoing Islamization has impacted palpably Malaysian society both with respect to Muslims and non-

Muslims. For the Muslim majority, they have had to follow more closely the norms and practices of the Sunni-Shafi'i school of behaviour known as the ASWJ. This has meant that Malaysian Muslims are subject to a particular form of Islam and would suffer the opprobrium of punishment if they transgress the newly set rules and would pay dearly if they deviate from the ASWJ, or worse, if they became "apostates" (Mohamad 2010, pp. 72–78). Two examples would suffice to substantiate the point about this "ring-fencing" (ibid.) of Muslims. The first case relates to a man known as "Ayah Pin" who started a cult known as "Sky Kingdom" in Terengganu in July 2005. The kingdom in question was a commune with structures and quaint buildings looking like teapots. The "Sky Kingdom" commune was attacked by unidentified assailants and later raided by a religious authority. Ayah Pin went into hiding, but his wife, Kamariah Ali, who boldly declared herself an apostate was thus subjected to charges in a *Syariah* Court and imprisoned for two years after a three-year trial. In this volume, Norsharil Saat reveals the same sort of intolerance shown towards the Syiah Muslim community because it falls outside the purview of the ASWJ.

The second example has become the *cause célèbre* of civil society.[9] Lina Joy (Azlina Jailani), a Muslim woman of 43 years who embraced Christianity in 1988, applied to the National Registration Department (NRD) for a change of name and religious status in 1997. In 1998, the NRD allowed the name change, but not the change of religion. Lina Joy appealed against this decision in the High Court in 2001. The High Court ruled against the change of religion stating that the jurisdiction in conversion matters lay solely in the hands of the *Syariah* Court. In 2004, Lina Joy's case to the Court of Appeal was dismissed on the grounds that the *Syariah* Court or any other Islamic authority did not confirm her renunciation of Islam. In her appeal, Lina Joy's application to have her conversion to Christianity validated was struck off by the highest court of the land, the Federal Court, on 30 May 2007, ending a ten-year legal battle. The Court ruled in a 2–1 split decision that the NRD was correct to ask Lina Joy to seek a declaration from the *Syariah* Court to confirm her conversion. The Chief Justice, who sat on the three-man bench, argued that Muslims could not change their religion at their own whims and fancy. The dissenting judge, a Christian, argued that the NRD's demand on Lina Joy was unreasonable, discriminatory, and unconstitutional.

As indicated clearly in the chapter on Christians in this volume, the Lina Joy case has led to grave concern that Islamization could also encroach on their rights. It was in response to the Lina Joy ruling that the human rights subcommittee of the Malaysian Bar Council tried to lobby for the formation of an Inter-Faith Commission in 2005. It was felt that the Malaysian Consultative Council for Buddhism, Christianity, Hinduism, Sikhism, and Taoism (MCCBCHST) was inadequate to deal with inter-faith matters not least of all because Muslims were not members of the MCCBCHST. The long and short of it was that eventually after many meetings a broad consensus was arrived at to hold a national conference to discuss the setting up of the IFC. The holding of the conference, involving some 200 multi-faith participants, representing various faiths, was itself an achievement. It was also interesting that a minister, Rais Yatim, a lawyer by profession, officiated at the event. But the inevitable happened. A coalition of thirteen Muslim groups calling itself the Allied Coordinating Committee of Islamic NGOs (ACCIN) demanded that the government scuttle the idea of the IFC.

It became a supreme irony that the very idea of an inter-faith commission proposed by civil society groups turned out to be an issue requiring the eventual intervention of politicians and the prime minister no less. Prime Minister Abdullah Badawi stepped in at the height of the controversy to pronounce that the IFC idea should be shelved and that the government was only prepared to consider it at a later time. Many constitutional experts have argued that the Malaysian state remains one not based on any particular religion but one that guarantees freedoms of all faiths as stipulated in Article 11 of the Constitution. However, in 1988 when Amendment 121 (1A) was passed, the *Syariah* courts were seemingly given absolute discretion over matters of Islam. This introduced yet another perhaps intended consequence on matters pertaining to religious freedom as we shall see below.

Amendment 121 (1A) has been invoked specifically in many controversies regarding conversions to Islam. Among the more contentious cases was that Moorthy Maniam (@Mohammad Abdullah)[10] whose body was seized in December of 2005 by the Kuala Lumpur religious authority, JAWI,[11] on the ground that he had converted to Islam some time prior to his death. Just prior to his conversion to Islam, Moorthy had been celebrated as a national hero who had scaled Mount Everest. JAWI approached the KL *Syariah* Court on 22 December and got the ruling that Moorthy's conversion to Islam was valid. This was however disputed by his wife S. Kaliammal, who took the matter to the High Court which heard the case on 28 December. The three-panelled court of appeal ruled that there was no "relief" for Kaliammal on the grounds that Article 121(1A) of the Malaysian Constitution proscribed a civil court from ruling on matters of Islam. The above examples show that the level of tolerance for deviation from the norm is greatly restricted for Muslims, given a high degree of *Syariah* compliance in the state, and, one might say, the unwillingness of the civil court system to challenge the competency of *Syariah* courts in matters pertaining to Muslims. The Moorthy and Lina Joy cases also indicate the level of toleration to any non-Muslim challenge of Islamic primacy or predominance on matters of religion.

Legal tussles over religious matters have also led to some dire and direct consequences for inter-religious relations. A case in point is the tussle over the ban on the use of the word "Allah" by the Catholic weekly magazine "*Herald*" in its Malay edition. In 2009, the Catholic Church took the matter to court for a ruling that the banning of the word was unconstitutional. The High Court ruled in the Church's favour in January 2010 but the decision was met with a storm of protest from Muslim NGOs as well as from UMNO. On 8 January 2010, a church was fired bombed, and by the middle of the month, nine churches, one Sikh temple, one girls' convent school, and three mosques were damaged, with two mosques finding wild boar heads tossed into their compounds (Mohamad 2011, p. 187). The work of agent provocateurs cannot be ruled out, and it is a measure of the broad tolerance of Malaysian society that these incidents did not spark any actual or direct confrontations between religious communities. However, hardly a day passes without some religious or inter-faith issue surfacing in Malaysia. By August 2013, a plethora of issues have surfaced ranging from bloggers and dog trainers being hauled up and arrested for insulting Islam to calls for non-Muslim conversions to Islam to be unchallengeable through further constitutional amendments and to the Kedah and Pahang state governments gazetting laws proscribing the teachings of the *Syiah* sect.[12] The National Fatwa Council had made this ruling as early as 1996.

The chapters in this volume show that a dominant form of Islam in Malaysia has indeed impacted the social and political life of non-Muslim minorities as well as that of the small *Sy'iah* group. They deal with religious pluralism in Malaysia's most populous and cosmopolitan cities; Christian and Buddhist responses to perceived Muslim encroachment in their affairs and their perception of religious intolerance on the part of state authorities; localized Christian minorities resisting and also accommodating hegemonic Muslim or Islamic presence and the intolerance of a dominant Sunni Islamic practice *vis-à-vis Sy'iah* Muslims.

Following this introduction, the Malaysian section begins with a chapter by Gerhard Hoffstaedter suggesting that Malaysia's strong syncretic tradition of the interplay of *adat* (custom) and non-Islamic religious traditions have been overtaken by a new Islamic praxis, based on strict orthodoxy. However, the contestation over the Islamic space in Malaysia continues, and Hoffstaedter's ethnographic vignettes show the persistent syncretic praxis of *bomohs*, Sufi *tariqas*, and cultural art forms and demonstrate how they circumvent, evade and oppose the instrumentalization of religion by reactionary, orthodox, and bureaucratic institutions. In Chapter 14, Yeoh Seng Guan writes with some persuasion that Kuala Lumpur has not crossed the threshold of becoming a "fundamentalist city" where minority groups are not just forced to conform to dominant religious strictures but could also be denied access to specific public spaces, and worse, when this becomes normalized and self-policed in the everyday behaviour of minority groups. Yeoh demonstrates nonetheless that Kuala Lumpur's "cosmopolitanisms" are constantly at variance with the embedding of Muslim exceptionalism. Examining everyday encounters of non-Muslims with Muslims, Yeoh finds that "public spaces, lifestyles, an array of consumer goods and worldviews are being re-assessed and re-configured along these Islamic coordinates" with palpable ramifications on the affective domains of Kuala Lumpur's cosmopolitan citizens. However, the political moment that came with the spectacular outcome of the 2008 general election has perhaps given voice to newer generations of urbane and cosmopolitan Malaysians who "will play a greater role in deciding how they want their city and country to be governed and shaped".

Chapters 15 and 16 by Chong and by Tan, respectively, give us perspectives from the largest non-Muslim minorities, namely Christians and Buddhists. Both authors tell a tale of the perceptible and palpable intrusion of Muslim authorities into the religious terrain and space of these minority communities. Both authors allude to the state's programme of Islamization and how the two groups have responded to issues such as restrictions to the building of churches and temples. Chong writes about the "Allah" proscription issue, the lock-down on the importation of Bahasa Indonesia bibles, and the generally high level of intolerance for a variety of Christian activities. The net effect of such intolerance has been to push Christians to respond more effectively by engaging the public sphere via their umbrella Christian Federation of Malaysia (CFC). Christians as a whole have also become increasingly politicized, particularly during and after the 2008 general election.

Tan writes about the emergence of a "political Buddhism" in the Malaysian context. According to him, Buddhist organizations have voiced their discontent publicly through the civil engagement of the

Young Buddhist Association of Malaysia (YBAM) with the state. Political engagement which was non-confrontational had hitherto been effected through the mainstream Buddhist association the Malaysian Buddhist Association (MBA). However, in more recent years, a more radical or direct approach has been carried out by the lay-dominated YBAM. The YBAM has publicly protested against the idea of an Islamic state and has championed the secular state as the means to safeguard the rights of Buddhists.

In Chapter 17, Arunajeet Kaur writes about the emergence of the Hindu Rights Action Force (Hindraf) as a response to Islamization. The Moorthy "body snatching" case, already mentioned above, proved to be a catalyst for the founding of Hindraf on 29 December 2005. Arunajeet suggests that the series of occurrences that included the demolition of Hindu temples reinforced the commonly perceived notion of Indians as a backward class of people with limited access to opportunities within a social political system that favoured the majority Malay-Muslim population. The culmination of Hindraf's championing of the Indian cause came with a 30,000-strong rally in Kuala Lumpur on 25 November 2007, where the group highlighted its petition to the British Crown for a sum of US$4 trillion (RM14 trillion) — or US$2 million for every Indian currently residing in Malaysia — in compensation for the community's discrimination and marginalization in present-day Malaysia. Arunajeet argues that the articulation of Malay-Muslim hegemony in the Malaysia state has cast a pall of pessimism on Hindraf's demands and the recognition Hindu rights.

In Chapter 18, Norshahril notes that the Syiah minority is considered to be "deviant" because of the practice in Malaysia of an exclusivist Islam, namely the officially sanctioned form of Islam, the AWSJ. A *fatwa*, or religious edict, in May 1996 virtually outlawed any practice of Sy'ism in Malaysia. The state has gone to the extent of using the draconian Internal Security Act (ISA) to detain adherents of Sy'ism on the grounds that these individuals were a security threat. Norsharil delves into the historical schism that led to the Sunni–Syiah split in Islam but maintains that tolerance for religious diversity has always been the norm in Islam. He concludes that the treatment of the Syiah minority is not just an affront to human rights but "contradicts the very foundation of the Quran" and that "Islam is inherently diverse and inclusive, not only towards different faiths, but also towards different views."

Two chapters on Christian minorities in Sarawak bring to a close the chapters of the Malaysia section. Poline Bala, in Chapter 19, writes of

Introduction

the experiences of the Kelabit and Lun Bawang of northeastern part of Sarawak, highlighting the ways in which these "small" communities and cultures grapple with the growing saliency of Malay culture and Islamic identity in national politics. Although the Kelabit and Lun Bawang have been "mute spectators" of Islamic resurgence and Malay politics, there has been an increasing sense of anxiety about powerful, assertive, and intolerant Muslims. There is a growing unease that these tendencies might be a threat to the Kelabit's and Lun Bawang's religious identity. Yet at the same time there are ongoing debates among the Lun Bawang and Kelabit as to how as Christian communities they ought to respond with kindheartedness and tolerance in their everyday encounters and engagements with people of other faiths including their Muslim friends, visitors, and relatives.

In Chapter 20, Liana Chua writes about how a religious-cum-indigenous community, the Bidayuh, has responded to a dam construction, which has necessitated a resettlement of some of their families. Chua's ethnographic study shows the complex manner development (*pembanguan*) is viewed by Bidayuhs. She suggests that rather than entering into open conflict with the government and Islam, many Bidayuhs find alternative means of dealing with the upheavals around them by recourse to the religious and cultural influences in their lives: Christianity and old rituals (*adat gawai*). She observes that "religious toleration and conflict look less like dichotomous states than like intertwined strands in a tangled and ever-shifting relational bundle" for her Bidayuh acquaintances.

As shown by the chapters in this volume, the changing character of Malaysian politics and its capacity to deal with religious diversity would be put fully to the test in the coming years. It is evident from the writers in the volume that Malaysia's religious minorities and leaders have shown exemplary tolerance and a high level of acumen in engaging with a Muslim-dominant state. Although it may be true that some communities remained conflicted and ambivalent about how they should deal with many new issues, the civil engagement of their leaders and their NGOs with the state ensures that problems are usually resolved through peaceful processes. The state authorities on their part exhibit some level of flexibility in engaging with religious minorities, but this has often been stymied by the state's role as guardians of the majority Muslim faith.

Notes

[1] One such study is by Maznah Mohamad (2011) dealing directly with the impact of Islamization on women and religious minorities.

2   In Malay, "*Bahagian Hal Ehwal Islam*".
3   In point of fact, in 1988, two crucial amendments were made to the Federal Constitution. After 1988, Article 121(1) states that the High Court "shall have such jurisdiction and powers as may be conferred by or under federal law". The Judiciary was thus made subservient to Parliament. The second significant amendment in 1988 was the inclusion of a new clause (1A) into Article 121 that stated: "The courts referred to in Clause (1) shall have no jurisdiction in respect of any matter within the jurisdiction of the syariah courts." Available at <http://www.malaysianbar.org.my/members_opinions_and_comments/article_1211a_what_does_it_really_mean_.html> (accessed 1 August 2013).
4   See "Q & A on the Hudud and Qisas Enactment", *Aliran Monthly* 22, no. 6 (2000): 25–29.
5   It should be noted, however, the competition of "out-Islamization" by PAS and UMNO is only part of the explanation, the other part being the rise of a large and powerful Islamic bureaucracy and as argued by Maznah Mohamad (2010), pp. 507–8.
6   The ten principles are: faith and piety in Allah; a just and trustworthy government; a free and independent people; a vigorous pursuit and mastery of knowledge; a balanced and comprehensive economic development; a good quality of life for the people; the protection of the rights of minority groups and women; cultural and moral integrity; the safeguarding of natural resources and the environment; and strong defence capabilities (Abdullah Ahmad Badawi 2006, p. 4).
7   It has been suggested that JAKIM should resolve this conundrum by appointing eminent jurists to discuss and adjudicate on issues of "Hukum Shara" or Islamic jurisprudence (Farid Sufian Shuaib 2003, p. 5). This has been done for commercial matters through a *Syariah* Advisory Council of eminent persons set up by the Central Bank.
8   Article 128 refers to the overriding powers of the Malaysian Supreme Court, now called the Federal Court.
9   See the book edited by Tan and Lee (2008), which is devoted entirely to the Lina Joy controversy.
10 Corporal Moorthy, who died at the age of thirty-six from serious head injuries, was one of the ten individuals in the Malaysia team, two of whom reached the peak of Mount Everest on 23 May 1997, the first Malaysians to achieve the feat. Moorthy was posthumously promoted to the rank of sergeant in the midst of the controversy.
11 *Jabatan Agama Wilayah Persekutuan* (Federal Territory Religious Department).
12 Syias are said to number about 250,000. See <http://www.theedgemalaysia.com/political-news/249131-home-ministry-shia-followers-now-at-250000.html> (accessed 12 August 2013).

References

Abdul Aziz Bari. "The Enforcement of Morality through the Law". Paper presented at the National Law Symposium 2005, organized by the Law Students Society, International Islamic University Malaysia, Nikko Hotel, Kuala Lumpur, 2005.

Abdullah Ahmad Badawi. *Islam Hadhari: A Model Approach for Development and Progress*. Petaling Jaya: MPH Publishing, 2006.

Farid Sufian Shuiab. *Powers and Jurisdiction of Syariah Courts in Malaysia*. Kuala Lumpur: IIUM and LexisNexis, 2003.

Farish A. Noor. "The Localization of Islamist Discourse in the Tafsir of Tuan Guru Nik Aziz Nik Mat, Murshid'ul Am of PAS". In *Malaysia: Islam. Society and Politics*, edited by Virginia Hooker and Norani Othman. Singapore: Institute of Southeast Asian Studies, 2003.

———. *Islam Embedded: The Historical Development of the Pan-Malaysia Islamic Party PAS (1951–2003)* 1 and 2. Kuala Lumpur: Malaysian Sociological Research Institute, 2004.

Faruqi, Shad Saleem. "The Malaysian Constitution, the Islamic State and Hudud Laws". In *Islam in Southeast Asia: Political, Social and Strategic Challenges for the 21st Century*, edited by K.S. Nathan and Mohammad Hashim Kamali. Singapore: Institute of Southeast Asian Studies, 2005.

Fernando, Joseph M. "The Position of Islam in the Constitution of Malaysia". *Journal of Southeast Asian Studies* 37, no. 2 (2006): 249–66.

Furnivall, J.S. *Colonial Policy and Practice: A Comparative Study of Burma and Netherlands India*. Cambridge: Cambridge University Press, 1948.

Hamayotsu, Kikue. "Politics of Shariah Reform: The Making of the State Religio-Legal Apparatus". In *Malaysia: Islam, Society and Politics*, edited by Virginia Hooker and Norani Othman. Singapore: Institute of Southeast Asian Studies, 2003.

Hoffstaedter, Gerhard. *Modern Muslim Identities: Negotiating Religion and Ethnicity in Malaysia*. Copenhagen: Nias Press, 2011.

Kahn, Joel S. *Other Malays: Nationalism and Cosmopolitanism in the Modern Malay World*. Singapore: NUS Press, 2006.

Kahn, Joel S. and Francis K.W. Loh, eds. *Fragmented Vision: Culture and Politics in Contemporary Malaysia*. Sydney: Allen & Unwin, 1992.

Lee, Julian C.H. *Islamization and Activism in Malaysia*. Kuala Lumpur and Singapore: SIRD and Institute of Southeast Asian Studies, 2010.

Lee, Raymond and Susan Ackerman. *Sacred Transitions: Modernity and Religious Transformation in Malaysia*. Columbia, SC.: University of South Carolina, 1997.

Liow, Joseph Chinyong. "Political Islam in Malaysia: Problematising Discourse and Practice in the UMNO-PAS 'Islamisation Race'". *Commonwealth and Comparative Politics* 42, no. 2 (July 2004): 184–205.

Martinez, Patricia. "The Islamic State or the State of Islam in Malaysia". *Contemporary Southeast Asia* 23, no. 3 (December 2001): 474–503.

Mohamad, Maznah. "The Ascendance of Bureaucratic Islam and the Secularization of the Shariah in Malaysia". *Pacific Affairs* 83, no. 3 (September 2010): 505–24.

———. "Creating a Muslim Majority in Plural Malaysia: Undermining Minority and Women's Rights". In *The Politics of Religion in South and Southeast Asia*, edited by Ishtiaq Ahmed. London and New York: Routledge Press, 2011.

Mohamad, Maznah, Zarizana Aziz, and Chin Oy Sim. "Private Lives, Public Contention: Muslim-non-Muslim Family Disputes in Malaysia". In *Muslim-non-Muslim Marriage: Political and Cultural Contestations in Southeast Asia*, edited by Gavin W. Jones, Chee Heng Leng, and Maznah Mohamad. Singapore: Institute of Southeast Asian Studies, 2009.

Nagata, Judith. *The Reflowering of Malaysian Islam: Modern Religious Radicals and Their Roots*. Vancouver, BC: University of British Columbia Press, 1984.

Peletz, Michael G. *Islamic Modern: Religious Courts and Cultural Politics in Malaysia*. Princeton, NJ: Princeton University Press, 2002.

Saravanamuttu, Johan. "Malaysian Multicultural Policy and Practices: Between Communalism and Consociationalism". In *The Challenge of Ethnicity: Building a Nation in Malaysia*, edited by Cheah Boon Kheng. Singapore: Marshall Cavendish, 2004.

———. "Malaysia: Multicultural Society, Islamic State or What?" In *State and Secularism: Perspectives from Asia*, edited by Ten Chin Liew and Michael Heng Siam-Heng. Singapore: World Scientific, 2010.

Shamsul, A.B. "Islam Embedded: 'Moderate' Political Islam and Governance in the Malay World". In *Islam in Southeast Asia: Political, Social and Strategic Challenges for the 21st Century*, edited by K.S. Nathan and Mohammad Hashim Kamali. Singapore: Institute of Southeast Asian Studies, 2005.

Tan, Nathanial and John Lee. *Religion under Siege: Lina Joy, the Islamic State and Freedom of Faith*. Kuala Lumpur: Kinibooks, 2008.

Weiss, Meredith L. "The Changing Shape of Islamic Politics in Malaysia". *Journal of Southeast Asian Studies* 4, no. 1 (2004): 139–73.

Wilford, Andrew. *Cage of Freedom: Tamil Identity and the Ethnic Fetish in Malaysia*. Ann Arbor, MI: University of Michigan Press, 2006.

13

ISLAMIC PRAXIS AND THEORY
Negotiating Orthodoxy in Contemporary Malaysia

Gerhard Hoffstaedter

INTRODUCTION

Malaysia, and the greater Malay world, has a rich history of syncretic religious and cultural traditions that have seen disparate theological norms and theories wedded with culturally inflected actions and practices. Islam in the Malay world, accordingly, has a rich syncretic and pluralistic history (Ellen 1983). Traders and Sufi missionaries (Islamic scholars of the Muslim mystical and spiritual tradition) are credited with bringing Islam to the Malay world from India, China, Persia, and the Arab peninsula and as such introducing a range of interpretations as well as practices in a diffuse manner that only slowly and regionally displaced earlier practices of animism, Hinduism, and Buddhism (Federspiel 2007). Sufism is attuned to otherness and a communion with the divine that goes beyond prayer or orthodox Islamic praxis and thus is seen as instrumental in the process of conversion from other spiritual traditions to Islam. The mode of transmission is debated with some arguing that Islam penetrated the region often through elites who acted as advisors to royal households (Milner 1982), whereas others focus on the emancipatory power of Islam for ordinary Malays (Wertheim 1956). Another debate focuses on whether it was traders or Sufi missionaries who were the first and most important for Islam's successful entrée into the region (van Leur 1955; Johns 1961). One moment many agree upon as pivotal is the conversion of the ruler of Malacca in the fifteenth century (even if debates still surround whether the first or second ruler converted and precisely when). Upon the ruler's conversion, his subjects would also convert; however, religious praxis and cosmological thinking were often syncretic, merged, and connected by adherents, religious leaders, and rulers. Thus, a long history of religious pluralism and hybridity continued in the Malay world with the advent of Islam.

Over time, Islam in the Malay world became interwoven with local *adat* (custom) into regionally distinct traditions that often accommodated pre-existing beliefs, rituals, and customs. These processes have produced an abundance of locally distinct customary practices that complement Islam (Sharifah Zaleha Syed Hassan 2000). There continues a long and sometimes fierce debate about the impact of Islam on the Malay world, its rulers, and people. For the prominent Islamic scholar Syed Muhammad Naquib Al-Attas, Islam made possible the "liberation of man first from magical, mythological, animistic, national-cultural tradition opposed to Islam, and then from secular control over his reason and his language" (Al-Attas 1993, p. 44). In time, Al-Attas argues, Islam activated the mind of the Malays and enabled an exchange of science, philosophy, and other intellectual pursuits based on the Arabic script and language, thus making the advent of Islam a monumental occasion for the Malay world, both historically and civilizationally (Al-Attas 1969, 1972). Al-Attas has since driven an agenda to Islamize knowledge and Malay(sian) history and culture that, in effect, seeks to expunge pre-Islamic cultural, religious, and even linguistic attributes. This project of Islamization, I have argued elsewhere, has been very successful and has become totalizing in its aims. Islamization of a state, a nation's history, and its culture leads to the Islamization of the public sphere and an ingrained social habitus (Hoffstaedter 2011, 2013).

This process also partly coincided with the religious revival or *dakwah* movement that swept the world in the 1970s, which had a major impact on Malaysian Islam (Hussin Mutalib 1990; Zainah Anwar 1987; Muzaffar 1987; Nagata 1984). The revival spawned a range of civil society organizations and religious movements that were courted by politics leading to the inclusion in government of the outspoken student leader Anwar Ibrahim, who had been a student of Al-Attas and a vocal proponent of an Islamization of the state and its institutions. Subsequently, Anwar Ibrahim implemented a series of policies that embedded Islam and the Islamic educational system into the mainstream Malaysian education system (Ahmad Fauzi Abdul Hamid 2010, pp. 34–36). All these processes facilitated the overall Islamization that was taking hold within the burgeoning Malay middle class and managed to create powerful orthodox Islamic discourses that have become dominant and have silenced minor Islamic praxis and theology across the nation.

Today the plural and hybrid history of Islam in Malaysia has been displaced by a statist and orthodox version that places great emphasis on outward appearances and adherence based on observable practices, such as the consumption of *halal* products (Fischer 2008). Such practices can be policed by the state and federal Islamic departments that are in charge of enforcing *Syriah* law. As such, Muslims in Malaysia have become, as Maznah Mohamad's has argued, ring-fenced by bureaucratic Islamists (Maznah Mohamad 2012). In addition, Islam in Malaysia has become a *de facto* state religion. It is termed the "official religion of the federation" in the constitution and has been given a range of government funding in terms of propagation and support of the *hajj* or pilgrimage to Mecca. In spite of the state sponsorship and regulation, plural and syncretic Islamic practices persist in Malaysia. Through the exploration of syncretic practices of Sufis, traditional healers, and popular Muslim musicians, this chapter shows how Muslims in Malaysia negotiate Islamic traditionalism and orthodoxy.

THE SELF AND THE INSTITUTIONAL POWER OF ISLAM

Islam encapsulates within its long and diverse history the entire gamut of self-actualization and emancipatory movements to some of the most autocratic and totalitarian regimes. In terms of Islamic praxis and theory, there is an important moment in Islamic history when individual powers were subjugated to elite discourses. This moment is called the closing of the gates or doors of *ijtihad* (individual reasoning) beginning around five hundred years after the time of the Prophet Muhammad. Individual reasoning had been a powerful process for people to contribute to theological debates; however, as a professionalized class of people invested in Islamic law and its precedents (as found in the *Sunnah* and *Hadith* or sayings and actions of the prophet) grew, so did its power to act as final arbiters in debates. As the practice of *ijtihad* diminished in the Muslim world, the state and religious authorities took its place and cemented their role by formulating *syariah* (Islamic law) (Schacht 1964). Thus, the potentially uncontrollable use of individual reasoning (*ijtihad*) was replaced by reason within *taqlid* (unquestioned imitation) (Roff 1983).

Roff describes a confrontation between modernists (*kaum muda*) and traditionalists (*kaum tua*) in Kelantan in the 1930s over whether the crown prince of Kelantan could keep a dog as a pet. The debate between *kaum tua* (literally, the old generation) conservatives and *kaum muda* (the young generation) modernists continued to vex and excite, especially, academic debate (Rahim 2006). Yet, the debate between what kind of Islam should be practised and within what kind of legislative framework was just beginning in Malaysia.

During one of my early fieldwork experiences, I stayed with a Malay family that uncharacteristically owned a dog. Lassie, as he was named, belonged to the eldest son of the family, who would occasionally take him for a walk around the neighbourhood. If the son was out, I was deputized to walk the family pet. Often, neighbourhood children would run up to the dog and then quickly retreat when the young collie tried to approach them. The family's youngest daughter Zariah sometimes accompanied me on afternoon walks with Lassie. She was afraid to touch the dog though because she feared "Allah's punishment when she dies". She told me her *ustaz* at her afternoon Islamic classes had told her that it was "*haram*" (forbidden) to touch a dog and that Allah would punish all those who did so. She was, however, willing to take the leash once I had attached it to Lassie's collar. Her friends were similarly cautious about disobeying the words of the *ustaz*, but also took pleasure in taking the leash for a while, on occasion dropping it if Lassie came too close to them.

The *ustaz*'s orthodox views on dogs clearly had a profound impact on the interaction Zariah and her friends had with the pet. There is evidently a strong influence of orthodox views upon practice, but practice also asserts itself and allows for tactics to circumvent the rules and regulations in novel ways. Not only do some Muslims keep dogs as pets, they do so in spite of social and peer pressure. For Zariah and her family, keeping the dog was an act of mercy that was not couched in Islamic terms as either good or bad, *haram* or *halal* — the dog had appeared in front of the eldest son one night and looked close to death so he adopted it there and then, bringing it back to the house and nursing it back to health. Everyday interactions were regulated by the theological orthodoxy of the local *ustaz*, but family members engaged in imaginative circumventions to be close to their pet nonetheless.

While the practice of Muslim identity and Islam as a whole remains heterodox, it is under constant threat by religious authorities, normative discourses, and state interventions. Islamic theory or its theology with a particular orthodox interpretation is overlayering the multitude of praxis and attempting to level it out in order to minimize the difference and maximize the sameness in theological, legal, and political structures as well as everyday praxis. In the northern state of Perlis, Wahhabism, the Arabian fundamentalist revival movement that began in the eighteenth century and has had a lasting effect on global Islam, has been embraced by the state religious authorities to guide the theological framework and diminish pre-Islamic or heterodox practices.

RELIGIOUS MANIFESTATIONS

Perlis was also the site of some of my encounters with traditional healers known as *bomoh* in Malaysia. Their practices demonstrate the continued significance of mysticism in Malaysia today as well as reveal now the important role of Islam in the traditional healing practices. The ongoing importance of *bomoh* highlights that even in a state that has ostensibly adopted a fundamentalist interpretation of Islam, divergent practices persist. In 2006, I spent time with an influential *bomoh*, recording my visits in field notes which I will recount, in part, here.

It is mid-afternoon and I am sitting in the living room of a well-appointed house in a middle-class neighbourhood of a small town in the northern state of Perlis with my host mother, who has come to seek relationship and financial advice. I am about to meet a *bomoh* who will tell us about our futures. This occasion is special only insofar as this *bomoh* is said to possess special powers and commands the respect of not only just the many ordinary people who seek out his advice but also of members of a Malay royal family. I had visited *bomohs* earlier for health-related issues and they offered herbal, homeopathic, and also religiously infused cures. The latter was usually in the form of incantations such as the *shahadah* (Islamic declaration of faith) or Islamic sayings. On this occasion, however, religion and the divine was going to play a much greater part in our encounter. Waiting in the living room, we were brought tea and biscuits by the *bomoh*'s wife. She quickly withdrew after exchanging some pleasantries. Minutes later, the *bomoh* arrived and everyone stood up to greet him. He was a wiry man of distinguished features with a greying moustache and wearing a white baju Melayu with a chequered sarong and a white skull cap. We sat down and discussed how he had come to be a powerful, respected, and influential *bomoh*. His transformation was radical and had taken considerable time and effort as he explained that he had had a tough life working as a farmer and later supervisor on a sugar cane plantation. One day, fifteen years ago, he felt he needed to change his life's trajectory and decided to meditate in a nearby cave for three months. It is here that he found Allah and his special powers to channel Muslim spirits from times gone by (spanning the time of the Prophet Muhammad to the late colonial period in the Malay world). During several sessions with this *bomoh*, I witnessed his transformation before me, sitting cross-legged on a rug in his study, singing and chanting incantations, and luring the other mystical side to him or losing himself within it. He would become quiet and sometimes rocked gently back and forth before speaking in an altered voice about distant issues. Then one was able to ask the medium for advice, and the medium would respond with the wisdom of the ages as well as Islamic wisdom from distant shores. Even mundane questions about love affairs and investments would become couched in an Islamic framework from which the medium would put things into perspective, relating the issue at hand to the time of the medium's life, for example, the time of the prophet, and provide advice. The advice was often clear and straightforward, but the accompanying story and setting provided more gravitas.

The *bomoh* described above is not a prophet or even sect leader, of which there are numerous across the Malay peninsula. Nor does he claim legitimacy from his "family and intellectual genealogies (*silsilah; isnad*) and the personal bond with [his] students and disciples" (Nagata 2012, p. 23) that usually mark out forms of Muslim spiritual authority. His humble beginnings and transformation into a spiritual healer and medium was based on his personal spiritual journey and the trust locals placed in his abilities to apply his spiritual currency to their ailments and problems. On a theological level, he sees himself as a vessel for transmitting the timeless truth of Islam and its practice across time and space. As such, he is a connection to vague memories of a syncretic and cosmopolitan past in the Malay world (Kahn 2006), as well as a reminder of alternative modalities of being Muslim that transcend the national/ethnic straitjacket so dominant in contemporary Malaysia.

Bomohs continue to excite the masses as well as retain their authority with the many middle-class Malaysians who visit them. Their power remains bathed in folklore and the supernatural, nowadays more often than not with an added ingredient — Islam. The magic is often imbued with Muslim incantations and the power of Allah who is invoked to bless as well as demand justice for clients.

BEING MUSLIM AND DOING ISLAM

Being Muslim is often simply an ontological factum Muslims interpret, perform, or inhabit in a multiplicity of ways. As anthropologists we are most attuned to the performative identity experiences. In what follows, I will recount some fieldwork experiences to bring to the fore the often conflicted and conflicting Islamic praxis and theory in Malaysia.

One young Malay Muslim exemplified this phenomenon of internal tension and identity crisis of, especially the urban middle-class, Islamic praxis in Malaysia. She told me that she did not eat pork, but had tried it before. She drank alcohol and had taken drugs in the past. This was common in her circle of friends. She felt at odds with, what she termed, the secular West and Malaysia's religious authorities and theologians. She was Muslim and this meant a great deal to her, but her Islam was personal, flexible, and situational. At the same time, and this was the apparent contradiction, her life, actions, and worldview were deeply anchored in an Islamic framework. This framework was derived from early lessons about Islam in primary and secondary school as well as a perfunctory reading of the Qur'an at home. She was deeply disturbed by her late father having two wives and her mother marrying a man who already had a wife. She told me that she would never tolerate this behaviour, but acknowledged that it was the right of Muslim men to do so. She weighed her hands back and forth and said that it was a personal decision in the end. I asked what she would do if her husband took a second wife, without consulting her. She thought about it for a while and then said that she would not marry someone capable of such disrespect towards her. I pressed her: "What if you misjudged him, and he married again." "Then I would divorce him, lah!", she exclaimed. She did not sound convinced herself and added: "It's difficult, men have the right to do it, but I have the right to leave him, right?" The question raises an important aspect of the power of orthodox views in mainstream Malaysia. Muslims are subject to *Syariah* law in their respective state, but they are usually neither well versed in the law nor in its theological roots. Thus, they abrogate responsibility of negotiating the licit, permissible, or encouraged forms of Islam to the religious authorities. Moreover, many of the young people I interviewed for my Ph.D. research in Malaysia in 2006 reported that they did not hold the Islamic authorities in high esteem, nor did they think much of the *Syariah* legal system. They did not, in fact, consider *Syariah* as a law in the same way as criminal laws, but more of a tantalizing chance to be a rule breaker by drinking alcohol, for instance. They were all aware of the fines and potential incarceration, but also reiterated to me that they knew enough people who had been caught and let off by paying either a bribe or the fine. No one they knew had been jailed for drinking, allowing them to believe in the very possible circumvention of Islamic law. Some even acknowledged that the existence of the prohibitions within *Syariah* made them more aware of their (sometimes daily) transgressions and acted as a limiting influence. One respondent remarked: "Here, I know I am doing something wrong, drinking alcohol. When I am abroad there are no limitations for me. It's better for me to have laws that tell me I am doing something wrong, to remind me how to be a good Muslim."

This sentiment was not uncommon amongst those who had studied in Western countries and had found themselves to take, in their own view, too much advantage of their new-found freedom. This sometimes engendered a reaction upon their return to Malaysia that was channelled into an invigoration of their Islamic identity. As Kahn has observed, Malays can get "obsessed with their own uniqueness with respect to a godless, cultureless, but nonetheless imperialist 'West'" (Kahn 2003, p. 148). This "imperialist West" also beckons in the cities, and one friend of mine living in the Klang Valley often reminisced about his time at a religious school in Kelantan where he could be "a true Muslim", whereas in the city "looms temptation and an inauthentic Muslim life".

Tawada claims that Muslims strive to be "better Muslims" or "more Islamic" and seek an ideal and utopia, that is, ultimately, unachievable (Tawada 1998, p. 57). In order to make sense of some of the tensions of being Muslim and transgressing, Tawada employs Swift's concept of *malu*, or embarrassment/shame, (Swift 1965). He argues that *malu* functions as a normalizing force, as no-one wants to feel *malu*, thus one's fear of it sanctions one's behaviour (Tawada 1998, p. 58).

But *malu*, too, can cause contradictions. Tawada recounts a story about a Kelantanese village where a father-in-law brings *malu* upon himself because he does not scold his son-in-law for not carrying out the morning prayer because scolding a grown man would also bring *malu*. In another anecdote politics is mediated through religion. The imam officiating at a wedding shames (brings *malu* upon) the bridegroom by asking him difficult theological questions about marriage. The imam, it turns out is a PAS (Partai Islam se-Malaysia) supporter who seeks to purify folk traditional Islam and at the same time presents himself and his party as the pure representatives of Islam. These conversations attest to the ongoing interplay between the multiple forms of Islam practised in Malaysia and "the range of difference in individual behaviour and opinions shows the dynamic of Malay Islam as it is continually renewed in social reality, by each Malay, at each moment" (Tawada 1998, p. 67).

Although in my fieldwork I have not encountered people interpreting their actions within the framework of *malu*, there were many instances where Malay Muslims were aware of their actions being opposed to social norms and *Syariah* law. They often did not feel guilty per se, but felt that they should atone at some point. Often these parts of conversations were framed in terms of "when I am an adult" or "when I have a family". On one occasion, I witnessed remorse rather than embarrassment, when I asked about what a good Muslim is like.

> If you want to be a Muslim, you must find a true Muslim and learn from him. You can only learn from a true Muslim, I too am not a true Muslim. I have met and found a true Muslim and I have felt what it feels like. I want to return to that feeling. Now I am nothing, *kosong* (zero/empty).

GOOD MUSLIMS, PURE HEARTS

Some people take the wish to be "good Muslims" further through ongoing educational activities, which stretch from afternoon community-led reading sessions, Quranic reading groups, and seminars to the Islamic education sector offering primary to secondary education. In peninsular Malaysia the Islamic school system of pondoks (Islamic religious, often boarding, schools)[1] sits beside the national school system, with an increasing number integrated into the national education system through funding arrangements and recognition. Many pondoks have a bad educational reputation due to their (sometimes) exclusive focus on Islamic studies and the neglect of mathematics, foreign languages (apart from Arabic), and other skill sets.

In one of the pondoks in the northeast of Peninsular Malaysia in the state of Kelantan, I was told about the importance of purity and the search for the true Islam within all of us. The *ustaz* (religious teacher) reflected: "purity [*ikhlas*] helps me to reach Allah faster, to gain spiritual advancement" and every good deed was a demonstration of the purity of one's heart that brings one closer to Allah. He went on: "Pondok students are considered closer to Allah" and so they are "asked to pray at all people's houses to reach Allah better". This often attracts donations, but also allows for pondok students to take up an elated position of access to the divine and prepares them for a study of Islam that goes beyond the theology. In this particular pondok, students were instructed to use Quranic incantations and holy water (usually Zamzam water from Mecca)[2] to heal and treat a variety of ailments. Students were often dispatched to surrounding villages where they could practise and earn some money for the school. These unorthodox practices were pared with very conservative Islamic teachings at the school. Students did not see a paradox between the two as for them one was a natural extension of the other. The medium of their traditional healing was so fully Islamic, either because it was transformed by the Qur'anic incantations or the power of association with Islam that it had lost its pre-Islamic history of local practice.

The multiplicity in Islamic praxis extends throughout society. A bifurcated view would suggest a governmental and bureaucratic endeavour to streamline, standardize, and regiment Islamic praxis, but this is too a simplistic view as Malaysian government departments, at the federal or state level and enforcement agents, do not conform to one singular view or interpretation of the religious orthodoxy.

At the higher levels of government, there are many high-profile admirers of Sufi masters whose Sufi practices and syncretic forms of religious practice could otherwise be termed deviant (by religious authorities). I had the pleasure of meeting with Al Sheikh Afeefuddin Al Gaylani who is the leader of the Qadiriyya *tariqa* and currently resides in Malaysia. His authority is clearly based upon a genealogical link to the Prophet Muhammad and the spiritual authority he has inherited from his father within the *tariqa*. I met the *sheik* at a function at the Kuala Lumpur Convention Centre during Ramadan. I was invited to break fast with him and his entourage and to meet him at his house on the outskirts of Kuala Lumpur some time later. At his beautiful and splendid compound, we sat in his living room discussing his life, Sufi teachings, and his presence in Malaysia. He had fled Iraq when the security situation became untenable and was offered residence and anything else he needed in Malaysia by rich backers. He arranged weekly meetings with a small group of his followers in Malaysia, which occurred behind closed doors. He mentioned that this was unusual for him, as he had many followers in Iraq and around the world. He recounted that when he flies to Indonesia to give talks, thousands of people attend, but in Malaysia this was unthinkable. His position here was in a safe and secure environment that nonetheless did not afford him the opportunity to preach as he did elsewhere. Indeed he mentioned that Malaysians would follow him to Indonesia to see him there.[3] Thus, in Malaysia he was most influential amongst the elite and some middle-class followers.

His religious views were couched in cosmopolitan and spiritual terms in which we fight our greater *jihad* with ourselves for self-improvement. "Striving for peace of mind and peace in one's heart, [those] are our biggest struggles", he said, adding: "as we keep struggling, sincerity is the key". He kept returning to the heart and its importance for Muslims, focusing on the need to purify one's heart. Sufism, according to him, "touches the heart and enters the mind through the heart", highlighting the importance of experience and feeling that can influence and change one's thoughts and ideas. He also warned that because "Sufism is Islam, they distributed Islam in the world" it requires a teacher to lead the interpretative quest and act as a good example for the community. But Sufism also "breaks the ego in ourselves" forever reminding Muslims of the ummah around us and Allah within us. Indeed, he stated: "Allah does not focus on your body, but your heart."

The focus on the heart and experiential level of being Muslim and what that means is a common theme amongst urban middle-class and upper-class Malays. One told me that Islam for him was "like music". He quickly added that for him there was no categorization in music such as Rock, Blues, or Jazz: "people who adhere to that don't understand music". For him, Allah is spirituality, something everyone can tap into and experience, following the example of the Prophet Muhammad. He went on: "everyone has ears to listen to music, to hear it — those who propagate orthodox and restrictive Islam don't hear the music, they only know the categories." Listening and being receptive to the sounds of Islam, be they the muezzin's call to prayer, the imam's sermon, or one's own recitation of prayer, are potent experiential manifestations of belief in the everyday.

Many scholars and observers have focused their attention on the potency of music in religion in Malaysia, most prominently the impact of *nasyid* music, a form of Islamic devotional pop poetry (Sarkissian 2005; Tan 2007; Kahn 2003; Barendregt 2012). Its origins date all the way back to the time of the prophet in terms of its devotional aspects, but its modern form is imbued with pop beats and percussion instruments. Thus, it is often seen as a modern Islamic art form that bridges traditional messages with modern delivery methods. By deploying the boy/girl band model of Western music pop *nasyid* groups spread an Islamic message of love and traditional values to the young and new audience.

Kahn juxtaposes the modern *nasyid* phenomenon with P. Ramlee films that marked the 1950s to 1970s and accompanied Malaysia's path to independence and its early years of crafting a national consciousness. Modern Malayness, Kahn argues, was not so much the product of Muslim theologians and nationalist intellectuals during the colonial period (see Milner 1995; Roff 1967), but the modern popular entertainment industry. Thus, for Kahn it was not the printing press (cf. Anderson 1991), but popular entertainment, especially the cinema, that shaped Malay self-perception. Thus, *nasyid* groups are reorienting popular conceptions of

Malayness through the prism of a global Islam as evidenced in generic (often Arab) Muslim dress codes. Whereas Ramlee often used the *kampung* or village as a set, Middle Eastern imagery aids *nasyid* groups in its transnational Islamic setting. Ramlee's Malay subjects were often based on the subaltern peasantry, whereas the *nasyid* groups are based on Malay urban middle class. *Nasyid* thus "implies a subtle but nonetheless significant shift in the patterns of racialization in popular Malaysian discourse" (Kahn 2003, p. 161)

At a local primary school concert a *nasyid* band successfully engaged the children (and parents) in dancing and singing along to their songs which espoused the values of being a good student and being grateful towards their parents. The songs were interspersed with a Qur'an reading competition, in which students read and sang a surah from the Qur'an, sometimes backed up by the *nasyid* group, who, on occasion, would be moved to sing along or expand the recitation with chants and praises to Allah. The mood was jubilant, spiritual, and electric. There are hints in the *nasyid* genre at a transnational Islam that is at home in modernity, yet deeply Islamic. It is capturing the imagination of many young people and perhaps like the Sufi missionaries of times gone by is connecting to their specific desires and paradoxes and offering a soothing spiritual answer to existential questions.

CONCLUSION

Islam in Malaysia has never been and will never be a monolithic static "thing" or identity. Instead, it continues to be a multifaceted identity and experienced in a range of ways. The state, religious authorities, and the media continue to standardize, polarize, and curtail diversity of Islamic praxis and theory in Malaysia, but people's ingenuity, tactics, and also laziness all contribute to the ongoing negotiation between structures, norms, and orthodoxy and the divergent practices of "other" Muslims. Thus, the syncretic practices of Sufi *tariqa*, traditional healers or *bomohs*, and *nasyid* bands will continue to move some people and infuriate others. Muslim praxis remains a multiverse of experience and practice, whereas Islamic theory becomes ever more firmly curtailed and straitjacketed. The state and its agents are only as powerful as society allows them to be and the agents of the state are often themselves conflicted, which all points to the Malay world in general and Malaysia in particular continuing its heritage of plurality and multiplicity in Muslim religiosity.

Notes

1. For more on the pondok schools and Islamic education, see Ahmad Fauzi Abdul Hamid (2010).
2. The Zamzam well is considered to be a gift from Allah to Hagar, Abraham's second wife, whose son Ismael was crying for water. The well is located in Mecca.
3. For more on the importance of the transnational in Sufi *tariqa*, see Ahmad Fauzi Abdul Hamid (2012).

References

Ahmad Fauzi Abdul Hamid. "Islamic Education in Malaysia". Nanyang University 2010. Available at <http://www.rsis.edu.sg/publications/monographs/Monograph18.pdf>.

———. "The Aurad Muhammadiah Congregation: Modern Transnational Sufism in Southeast Asia". In *Encountering Islam: The Politics of Religious Identities in Southeast Asia*, edited by Yew-Foong Hui. Singapore: Institute of Southeast Asian Studies, 2012.

Al-Attas, Muhammad Naguib. *Preliminary Statement on a General Theory of the Islamization of the Malay-Indonesian Archipelago*. Kuala Lumpur: Dewan Bahasa dan Pustaka, 1969.

——— *Islam dalam sejarah dan kebudayaan Melayu* [Chet. 1.], ed. Kuala Lumpur: Penerbit Universiti Kebangsaan Malaysia, 1972.

———. *Islam and Secularism*. Kuala Lumpur: International Institute of Islamic Thought and Civilization, 1993.

Anderson, Benedict R. O'G. *Imagined Communities: Reflections on the Origin and Spread of Nationalism*. Rev. and extended ed. London: Verso, 1991.

Barendregt, Bart. "Sonic Discourses on Muslim Malay Modernity: The Arqam Sound". *Contemporary Islam* 6, no. 3 (2012): 315–40. doi: 10.1007/s11562-012-0221-z.

Ellen, Roy. "Social Theory, Ethnography and the Understanding of Practical Islam in South-East Asia". In *Islam in South-East Asia*, edited by M.B. Hooker. Leiden: Brill, 1983.

Federspiel, Howard M. *Sultans, Shamans, and Saints: Islam and Muslims in Southeast Asia*. Honolulu: University of Hawai'i Press, 2007.

Fischer, Johan. *Proper Islamic Consumption: Shopping among the Malays in Modern Malaysia*. Copenhagen: NIAS Press, 2008.

Hoffstaedter, Gerhard. *Modern Muslim Identities: Negotiating Religion and Ethnicity in Malaysia*. Copenhagen: NIAS Press, 2011.

———. "Secular State, Religious Lives: Islam and the State in Malaysia". *Asian Ethnicity* (2013): 1–15. doi: 10.1080/14631369.2013.759763.

Hussin Mutalib. *Islam and Ethnicity in Malay Politics*. South-East Asian Social Science Monographs. Oxford: Oxford University Press, 1990.

Johns, Anthony H. "The Role of Sufism in the Spread of Islam to Malaya and Indonesia". *Journal of the Pakistan Historical Society* 9, no. 3 (1961): 143–60.

Kahn, Joel S. "Islam, Modernity and the Popular in Malaysia". In *Malaysia: Islam, Society and Politics*, edited by Virginia Hooker and Norani Othman. Singapore: Institute of Southeast Asian Studies, 2003.

———. *Other Malays: Nationalism and Cosmopolitanism in the Modern Malay World*. Singapore: NUS Press, 2006.

Maznah Mohamad. "Legal-bureaucratic Islam in Malaysia: Homogenizing and Ring-fencing the Muslim Subject". In *Encountering Islam: The Politics of Religious Identities in Southeast Asia*, edited by Yew-Foong Hui. Singapore: Institute of Southeast Asian Studies, 2012.

Milner, A.C. *Kerajaan: Malay Political Culture on the Eve of Colonial Rule*. Tucson, AZ: University of Arizona Press, 1982.

———. *The Invention of Politics in Colonial Malaya: Contesting Nationalism and the Expansion of the Public Sphere*. Cambridge: Cambridge University Press, 1995.

Muzaffar, Chandra. *Islamic Resurgence in Malaysia*. Cet. 2. ed. Petaling Jaya: Fajar Bakti, 1987.

Nagata, Judith. *The Reflowering of Malaysian Islam: Modern Religious Radicals and Their Roots*. Vancouver, BC: University of British Columbia Press, 1984.

———. "Authority and Democracy in Malaysian and Indonesian Islamic Movements". In *Encountering Islam: The Politics of Religious Identities in Southeast Asia*, edited by Yew-Foong Hui. Singapore: Institute of Southeast Asian Studies, 2012.

Rahim, Rahimin Affandi Abd. "Traditionalism and Reformism Polemic in Malay-Muslim Religious Literature". *Islam and Christian-Muslim Relations* 17, no. 1 (2006): 93–104. doi: 10.1080/09596410500400090.

Roff, William R. *The Origins of Malay Nationalism*. Yale Southeast Asia Studies. New Haven, CT: Yale University Press, 1967.

———. "Whence Cometh the Law? Dog Saliva in Kelantan, 1937". *Comparative Studies in Society and History* 25, no. 2 (1983): 323–38.

Sarkissian, Margaret. "'Religion Never Had It So Good': Contemporary Nasyid and the Growth of Islamic Popular Music in Malaysia". *Yearbook for Traditional Music* 37 (2005): 124–52.

Schacht, Joseph. *An Introduction to Islamic Law*. Oxford: Clarendon Press, 1964.

Sharifah Zaleha Syed Hassan. "A Fresh Look at Islam and Adat in Malay Society". *Sari* 18 (2000): 23–32.

Swift, M.G. *Malay Peasant Society in Jelebu, Monographs on Social Anthropology* 29. London: Athlone Press, 1965.

Tan Sooi Beng. "Singing Islamic Modernity: Recreating Nasyid in Malaysia". *Kyoto Review of Southeast Asia* 8 (2007).
Tawada, H. "Reconsidering Malay Islam as a System of Meaning in Social Reality". In *Japanese Anthropologists and Malaysian Society: Contributions to Malaysian Ethnography*, edited by A.B. Shamsul and T. Uesugi. Osaka: National Museum of Ethnography, 1998.
van Leur, Jacob C. *Indonesian Trade and Society: Essays in Asian Social and Economic History*. Translated by James S. Holmes and A. van Marle. The Hague: W. van Hoeve, 1955.
Wertheim, Willem Frederik. *Indonesian Society in Transition: A Study of Social Change*. The Hague: W. van Hoeve, 1956.
Zainah Anwar. *Islamic Revivalism in Malaysia: Dakwah Among the Students*. Petaling Jaya, Selangor: Pelanduk Publications, 1987.

14

RELIGIOUS PLURALISM AND COSMOPOLITANISM AT THE CITY CROSSROADS

Yeoh Seng Guan

INTRODUCTION

In recent years, various scholars have drawn attention to the way traditional definitions of citizenship based exclusively on the framework of the nation-state are being recalibrated under the forces of global capitalism with its pervasive space–time compression and speeding up of transnational flows. James Holston and Arjun Appadurai (1999, p. i), for instance, have suggested that "cities are both a strategic arena for the reformulations of citizenship and a stage on which these processes find expression in collective violence". To be sure, for the last two or three centuries, the historic primacy of urban citizenship has been incrementally dismantled and replaced by the imaginary and ideological frame of the nation-state (cf. Anderson 2006 [1983]). Nevertheless, in more recent times, it is more often the case that:

> [T]he cities' streets conflate identities of territory and contract with those of race, religion, class, culture and gender to produce the reactive ingredients of both progressive and reactionary political movements. Like nothing else, the modern urban public signifies both the de-familiarizing enormity of national citizenship and the exhilaration of its liberties (Ibid., p. 2).

Said differently, the public spaces of a country's major cities have become microcosms of the nation-state where citizenship issues of belonging are re-imagined, mis-recognized, played out, and contested. On a similar note, AbdouMaliq Simone understands a central feature of a city — what he calls its "city-ness" — in terms of its cosmopolitan "crossroad" attributes. As he puts it, cities are places "where people take the opportunity to change each other around by virtue of being in that space, getting rid of the familiar ways of and plans of doing things and finding new possibilities by virtue of whatever is gathered there" (2010, p. 192). In comparison to small rural agricultural settlements, cities are seen as dynamic places where the potentialities for cosmopolitan encounters are multiplied manifold.

Be that as it may, under certain historical conditions, cities can become un-cosmopolitan or de-cosmopolitanized. For instance, critical scholars have tended to view contemporary urban citizenships in globalizing modern cities to be increasingly fragmented and splintered. Among others, exclusionary urban enclave cultures in the shape of gated communities, neo-liberal urban renewal policies criminalizing informal housing and the homeless, and having differential policies for different classes of trans-migrant workers have lend themselves to the further weakening of historical cosmopolitan conditions and encounters (eg., AlSayyad and Roy 2005; Caldeira 2000; Yeoh 2004).

In this respect, a related phenomenon has been the post-secular transformation of the urban milieu through the assertion of radical religiosities into the making of "fundamentalist cities". As a working hypothesis, Nezar AlSayyad (2010) has delineated four attributes of these kinds of cities. *First*, the city "categorically excludes by law, tradition, declared policy or latent practice individuals who are adherents of another religion or who belong to a different ethnicity than those of the ruling power or majority population" (p. 15). Minority residents, whether in the shape of ethnic or religious groups, are denied access to public spaces and basic urban services. *Second*, minority groups are expected to "conform to all the rituals of public behaviour prescribed in the religious code of the majority" (p. 16). *Third*, the city is strongly gender segregated such that women have little access to public space. *Finally*, the city "normalizes most of the above-mentioned forms of control or oppression in everyday life to the extent that the minority ceases to question them" (p. 16).

Malaysia is often mistaken to have an Islamic theocratic polity given the prominence of an array of markers of Islamic religiosity. Although Islam is accorded a special status ("Islam is the official religion of the Federation"), the country is constitutionally a secular state with safeguard provisions for other religions. Another closely related exigency of (post)colonial realpolitik has been the crafting and institutionalization of a racialized political landscape centred around the notion of Malay-Muslim exceptionalism. While this has arguably not adversely undermined inter-religious and inter-ethnic relations in the past, many observers and scholars have nevertheless noted that the global phenomenon of Islamic fundamentalism and the nature of ethnicized politics in Malaysia has recalibrated this state of affairs in the past two or three decades.

Is Kuala Lumpur stealthily becoming a "fundamentalist city" in the manner characterized by Nezar AlSayyad? If so, in what ways has Kuala Lumpur's cityscape been reconfigured by the politics of the majority? What kinds of urban citizens are being hailed? I begin by narrating two events in 2012 to give a flavour of how recent encounters with non-Muslim faiths have been largely construed by certain Muslim social actors. In the following section, I describe how Kuala Lumpur has been enveloped by two countervailing forces in recent times. On the one hand, it is being re-imagined to be a cosmopolitan world class city as part of larger project of the modernist trajectory of *Wawasan 2020* (Vision 2020). On the other, the emergent cosmopolitan citizens created in its wake continue to be subjected to the disciplinary parochialism of Malay-Muslim exceptionalism. Finally, I provide brief ethnographic snippets from my fieldwork data to illustrate how majority–minority religious relations manifest on the ground in two different sites in the city.

A TALE OF TWO RELIGIOUS DILEMMAS

On 10 February 2012, the controversial Perak Mufti, Tan Sri Harussani Zakaria, was reported as saying that Najib Abdul Razak, the Prime Minister of Malaysia, had "performed an idolatrous act" and "sacrificed his [Muslim] faith" by attending an annual Hindu Thaipusam festival at the Batu Caves pilgrimage shrine, situated just on the outskirts of Kuala Lumpur city.[1] Instead of attending the event, as the Prime Minister has been doing since 2010, Harussani opined that Najib should have delegated this task to a Hindu cabinet minister.

The Perak Mufti was not alone in his judgement. Many Muslim groups similarly voiced their alarm at the actions of the Prime Minister. To evince wider support, Harussani reiterated the public stance of the *Islamic Advancement Department of Malaysia* (JAKIM) which forbade Muslims from being present at non-Muslim religious rituals as they could encourage polytheism and idolatry among the Muslim community. However, Harussani later retracted his statement after Najib had personally clarified to him that he had merely given a speech at an adjoining building complex and had not entered into the cave temple proper. The Perak Mufti, moreover, conceded that as a national leader, it is not wrong for Najib to join in these festive celebrations so long as he does not endorse or participate in the rituals of other religions.[2] Indeed, Muslims are permitted to attend functions celebrating the customs and cultures of "other races" as a mark of mutual respect for those of other faiths. Ibrahim Ali, the leader of the right wing Malay rights group, *Perkasa*, well known for expressing parochial views on defending "Malay supremacy" surprisingly came out in support of Najib's action. He said that perhaps the Prime Minister did not have time to consult with religious leaders beforehand in wanting to bring the "torch of unity" to Batu Caves.

But the matter was not laid quickly to rest given the opportunities for enhancing political capital in the light of imminent 13th general elections and the religio-political significance of the Batu Caves shrine during the historic Hindraf rally of November 2007.[3] The rising young opposition woman politician Nurul Izzah Anwar, the Member of Parliament of the Kuala Lumpur constituency of Lembah Pantai and Vice-President of Parti Keadilan Rakyat (People's Justice Party), criticized the Perak Mufti for being a "hypocrite" and "flip-flopping" over the issue.[4] Nurul had also consented to attending the Thaipusam celebrations. But she had consulted with former Perlis Mufti Dr Asri Zainul Abidin beforehand, and was assured that it was okay for Muslims to attend religious festivals as long as they stayed un-involved in the practices.[5]

Dr Asri added another layer to the inter-religious conundrum when he shared his own experiences on the matter with the media. He had posted up a photo image of Najib's visit to the Batu Caves shrine on his Facebook page, which quickly attracted close to a thousand negative comments and some "politically motivated *fatwas*" on the matter. By contrast, his photo of the opposition leader, Anwar Ibrahim, attending Thaipusam in the northern town of Ipoh was regarded as a forgery by many of his readers. Dr Asri surmised that critics of Najib were using religion to further their own agenda and cautioned this "minority group of Muslims" that it was a "big sin" to exploit Islam to support their political biases.[6] To arrest this growing trend, he suggested that guidelines for Muslim–non-Muslim interaction be drawn up as both the government and the opposition groups have abused Islam by accusing each other of being "un-Islamic", and causing confusion as to what can be sanctioned. Dr Asri opined that

Muslims must return to a scripture-based "original Islam" to address the dilemma — "If not, there will be UMNO *fatwas*, PAS *fatwas*, PKR *fatwas*, DAP *fatwas*, non-aligned *fatwas*. Everyone will create so many things and say this is allowed, this is not. This is politics."[7]

During the same period, a similar dilemma over the hazy or porous boundaries between religion and culture came to the foreground, but in this instance implicating Christianity. As in the previous year (2011), the incident elicited a wave of lively and amusing commentary in the comparatively freer space of social media. The *Ulama Association of Malaysia* (Persatuan Ulama Malaysia [PUM] had reiterated its stance of wanting the Malaysian government to intervene in the print and electronic media so that "there will not be any campaigns, advertisements, TV series, films and articles that will encourage Muslims to participate in the Valentine's Day celebration".

The youth wing of the opposition party, Part Islam Se Malaysia (PAS, Islamic Party of Malaysia) espoused a similar line. While not pushing for a ban on the observance of Valentine's Day among non-Muslims, it nevertheless urged the government to spearhead a campaign aimed at discouraging all Malaysians from celebrating the event, which it believes promotes premarital sex and promiscuity. The PAS Youth Chief, Nasrudin Hassan Tantawi, was reported as saying, "We are not trying to assume the role of moral police here but we want to help save youngsters from falling into the Valentine's Day trap that promotes immoral activities."[8] As in the previous year, a similar campaign code-named "Awas jerat Valentine" ("Beware Valentine's trap") was launched by JAKIM together with the Kuala Lumpur Federal Territory of Islamic Affairs Department (JAWI) and Raudhah, a Muslim non-governmental organization, to forewarn young Muslims of the inherent grave dangers embedded in observing Valentine's Day.

In February 2011, the onslaught was more tightly orchestrated. A scripted sermon read at all mosques in Kuala Lumpur and Selangor at Friday prayers had been reported in the online media, and subsequently elicited robust accusations and counter-accusations from both sides of the Muslim–non-Muslim divide. The sermon had underscored that the declining morals of Malay Muslims in big cities like Kuala Lumpur are due to sensuous activities like Valentine's Day which encouraged the free mixing of unmarried couples and illicit sex. To buttress this claim, statistical evidence was provided. It noted that 257,411 unwanted pregnancies were reported between the years 2000 and 2008 as a consequence of the passions ignited on Valentine's Day.[9] It also repeated a 2005 ruling by the National Fatwa Council which had stated that Valentine's Day "had elements of Christianity that contradict Islam". A Muslim celebrating Valentine's Day was thus additionally opening him/herself to the charge of treachery as several centuries earlier the event was declared by Queen Isabella to be in commemoration of the victory of Christianity over Islam in Spain. The sermon text concluded by reminding Muslims that Jews and Christians would continue to deceive them and would do everything possible to undermine their *aqidah* (faith) and weaken their resolve to be practising Muslims. High-profile "immorality" raids were subsequently conducted at various public spaces and budget hotels. Whereas in 2011, close to 100 unmarried Muslim individuals were reported detained for compromising *khalwat* (in close proximity with the opposite sex) positions in Kuala Lumpur and Selangor alone, much lesser numbers were churned up in 2012.

Both the Christian Federation of Malaysia and the Council of Churches of Malaysia issued press statements (in 2011) to refute the tenuous connections made between modern day Valentine's Day and Christianity. Briefly, they stated that this inference was a factual error as Valentine's Day is no longer observed as a religious event by churches in Malaysia nor by any other Christian denomination in the world. It is currently a secular celebration taken over by the business world. They urged the National Fatwa Council to retract the ruling as it was "hurtful" to Christians.[10] They had also identified a particular instalment of a Muslim programme, *Halaqah*, aired two years earlier (February 2009) on a Malaysian public television (TV9) as "offensive" to Christians. It featured a well-known motivational speaker on the television circuit Ustazah Siti Nor Bahyah Mahamood and he stated that the immoral activities unleashed on Valentine's Day were firmly within the "traditions of the Christian community". Soon after the press statement was publicized, the producers of the programme had issued a public apology for the slip-up. However, the video clip continues to be available virally in cyberspace.

KUALA LUMPUR, *WAWASAN 2020* AND MALAY-MUSLIM EXCEPTIONALISM

Kuala Lumpur city, as experienced on the cusp of the new millennium, is a qualitatively different space from what it was two or three decades ago. Familiar localities, buildings, and road traffic systems that were relatively unchanged since the post-war period have been destroyed or transformed. Large swathes of forests, plantations, and squatter settlements that used to make up much of Kuala Lumpur cityscape have been possessed for the construction of iconic high-rise buildings, integrated shopping complexes, gated condominiums, sprawling residential estates, and an elaborate system of city highways. This construction boom has not only altered landscapes and skylines but also fomented a kaleidoscopic array of urban aesthetics and temposcapes in motion, morphing further its already fragmented spaces (cf. King 2008). Especially for old-timer residents, it is a truism that many parts of Kuala Lumpur have become unfamiliar and unrecognizable primarily because of the *speed* and *scope* of the change, and they feel like "strangers" in a city they consider their home.

Kuala Lumpur has also become materially and socially complex for other reasons as well. Since its beginnings as a multi-ethnic trading post in the mid-nineteenth century and subsequent incarnations as the capital of Selangor, British Malaya, and independent Malaysia, the city has continued to be a powerful magnet for a diverse and sizeable mix of migrants for the array of commercial, educational, employment, and personal freedom opportunities that it offers.[11] Today, they range from Malaysian citizens originating from all the component states of the country as well as non-Malaysian expatriates, migrant workers, and refugees. Different parts of Kuala Lumpur replicate or index partially these variegated ethnoscapes, and for the cosmopolitan, this pluralism validates the city's — and by implication the country's — celebrated multicultural vitality.

Nevertheless, as the two anecdotes recounted suggest, there have been recent countervailing trends that belie competing notions of urban citizenship. Thus, running alongside and against these cosmopolitanizing trajectories have been a perceived trend in the systematic Islamizing of Kuala Lumpur primarily through the religious idiom of *halal/haram* (religiously permissible/forbidden) dialectic, a feature which was comparatively weak in the past. Public spaces, lifestyles, an array of consumer goods and worldviews are being re-assessed and re-configured along these Islamic coordinates. Their ramifications extend beyond the affective domains of Muslims to non-Muslim residents of Kuala Lumpur.

Several scholars have suggested that the seeds for this current state of affairs can be genealogically traced to the racializing, segregational and bureaucratizing strategies of British colonial rule (e.g., Ackerman and Lee 1990; Kahn 2006; Roff 1998; Shamsul 2005). But apart from making the salient point that these instrumentalities of rule can be read as emergent regimes of rule primarily aimed at producing visible, regulated, and docile bodies, and which have since been appropriated by post-colonial elites, I will not rehearse them here. Instead, my point of departure for appreciating the radical morphing of Kuala Lumpur city (and beyond) and its accompanying disjunctions begins from the long reign of Mahathir Mohamad as Prime Minister (1981–2003) and to subsequent Prime Ministers onwards.

In 1991, claiming overall success for the economic growth generated by the "Look East", "privatization", and "Malaysia Incorporated" neo-liberal policy initiatives launched in the 1980s, Mahathir promulgated a bolder and more coherent plan. With the protean catchphrase of *Wawasan 2020* (Vision 2020) to designate a teleological point of arrival in the year 2020, the goal is to transform Malaysia into a modernist "developed" nation-state by then through an average growth rate of 7 per cent per annum for the intervening 30 years. In this scheme of things, the master plans prepared for the growth and development of Kuala Lumpur (in 1984 and 2004, respectively) exhibit a re-imagining of the city in ambitious and globalist terms. Kuala Lumpur was viewed beyond its administrative limits as an expansive and interconnected metropolitan region, and expected to become a second tier "world class city" in the near future through the provision of high-end services and infrastructure while increasingly better positioned to become a premier "global city" in the as-yet indeterminate future.

Also integral to Mahathir's plan was the role of the Malaysian citizenry in bringing about and embodying this transformed nation. In the 1960s, Mahathir's radical stance had seen him proposing the notion of "constructive protection" to address the economic under-achievement of Malays *vis-à-vis* their "special privileges" as embedded in the Federal Constitution (Maznah 2011, p. 43f; Ariffin 2003, p. 17). This eventually became the prototype for the New Economic Policy (NEP) which ran officially from 1971 to 1990. Among other wide ranging economic and political reforms, the NEP enabled preferential policies through a quota system in business, employment, education, and housing in order to economically and socially uplift Malays to be on par with entrepreneurial and middle-class Chinese. While the NEP envisaged improving inter-ethnic relations by redressing this economic disparity, its implementation arguably also fomented agonistic inter-ethnic relations as many deserving non-Malay Malaysians saw themselves as being marginalized by the NEP despite their merits.

By the time *Wawasan 2020* was promulgated two decades on, a sizeable Malay-Muslim middle class had been created. Moreover, Malay Muslims also dominated demographically all levels of the much expanded civil service bureaucracy through the auspices of the NEP. The NEP had prompted Malays to "modernize" by moving to urban centres, and in the process dissolve the colonial legacy of a spatial duality between non-Malay urban residents and Malay rural *kampung* (village) dwellers. In particular, Kuala Lumpur has been the favourite destination, and its stereotyped image of being predominantly a "Chinese town" has begun to ring less true in demographic terms.[12]

Under these changed material conditions, Mahathir proposed a revised racial imagery that seemed, at first glance, to be more accommodative of difference. He said that there was need for a unitary *Bangsa Malaysia* ("Malaysian race") in contributing to:

> a united Malaysian nation with a sense of a common and shared destiny ... at peace with itself, territorially and ethnically integrated, living in full harmony and full and fair partnership ... with political loyalty and dedication towards the nation.[13]

However, in other contexts, Mahathir also spoke of the necessity of weaning away the dependency of Malays from continued state assistance. Instead, the "New Malay" is one who imbibes modern entrepreneurial qualities, has shed the attitudinal deficiencies of old, and is able to compete with others on equal terms. Nevertheless, despite the aura of liberality, Maznah Mohamad (2011, p. 46) has observed that:

> In fact, it was not racial equality that he was seeking after all, but the creation of multiple but equally hegemonic racial blocs. It would not be enough that Malays already constituted the 60 per cent majority in the country. In Mahathir's rhetoric, they must all think alike and unite under the banner of a singular Malay politics.

Governmentally producing a "singular Malay politics", as crystallized in the pithy slogan *Ketuanan Melayu* ("Malay lordship/supremacy"), has been powerfully buttressed by the rallying and centripetal powers of religion. While the Federal Constitution has principally delineated the privileged position of Malays and Islam in the national imaginary (inter alia, Article 3, Article 153), and the NEP has created the space for diverse nascent Islamic groups to grow and consolidate, it was not until Mahathir Mohamad's premiership that these potent Islamic spiritual energies were seized as opportunities for the further strengthening of UMNO (United Malay National Organization), the key partner in the ruling Barisan Nasional (BN) coalition. The administration adopted the twin strategy of coercion and accommodation by "fighting Islam with more Islam ... and absorbing

Islam in government institutions and centralizing power over it" (Maznah 2010, p. 71). Through a series of government fiats, the "Islamization" of Malaysian society unfolded relentlessly through education, cultural policy, financial institutions, and, most significantly, *Syariah* law supported by a burgeoning religious bureaucracy. The cumulative effect, as Maznah Mohamad insightfully observes, has been to create:

> ... a sacred Muslim majority immune from the adjudication of secular laws or given exceptions whenever Islamic supremacy is invoked. The jurisdiction of the syariah is then ring-fenced around this majority, making it a legal majority and legitimizing *Ketuanan Islam* as the ideological construct of the authoritarian state (Ibid., p. 70).[14]

Electorally, that state also needed to craft a statist Islam that would ensure UMNO's relevance for both Muslims and non-Muslims alike. Thus, in comparison to the "Islamic radicalism" of PAS, UMNO is consistently portrayed as the guardian and arbitrator of the "right" moderate Islam for the former and as guardian of Malaysia's ethnic peace for the latter (Ibid., p. 72).

Hegemonic ideological constructs further require celebratory or fantastical manifestations in order to be persuasive to its subjects. The state has thus invested much in the cultivation of Islamic cultural capital in fashioning the politics of the majority. Although they are usually generated through the dissemination of Islamic high arts, literature, and heritage artifacts, the interpellative function of modern architecture has also been conscripted. Several iconic and monumentalist buildings imbued with Middle Eastern (rather than Southeast Asian) Islamic architecture have been built since the 1990s. Of these, the 88-storey Petronas Twin Towers is the most significantly impressive. Standing in the centre of the most expensive commercial real estate in Kuala Lumpur, it is commonly known that Mahathir Mohamad was closely involved in the design, construction, and contracting details of the Petronas Twin Towers. At its launch, Mahathir had propositioned:

> As an internationally recognised landmark, the Petronas Twin Towers are a national pride to the people of Malaysia. Indeed, they stand out prominently against the skyline of Kuala Lumpur to symbolize courage, ingenuity, initiative, and determination, energy, confidence, optimism, advancement and zest of a nation that will bring worldwide recognition and respect to all Malaysians.

I would also suggest that at a more demotic level, substantial shifts in the consumption landscape in Kuala Lumpur through the enforcement and practice of *halal* requirements and standards have contributed to building up Islamic cultural capital as well. Beyond hitherto parochial production, marketing and consumption chains among homogeneous ethno-religious groups, *halal*-certified products and processes have become more visibly commonplace and include a wide array of consumer items (and not just cuisine) in view of the substantial urban Malay-Muslim market now found in cities throughout the country. Conversely, many small entrepreneurial Malay-Muslim food businesses have taken to learning about and modifying the cuisine of non-Muslims and in the process broaden their usual food fare to a more cosmopolitan menu than before. Large established non-Muslim businesses — including international food chains like Kentucky Fried Chicken, Pizza Hut, and McDonalds — have similarly modified their production processes, entered into business partnerships with Muslims, and updated their marketing strategies in view of the "halalization of consumption" in Malaysia (Fischer 2008).

Cultivating this invincible aura of Malay-Muslim exceptionalism in the pursuit of modernity, however, have not been always convincing nor spiritually fulfilling for many of the Muslim faithful, and other alternatives have been sought. However, these competing "deviationist" alternatives have not been tolerated and have instead been criminalized and extinguished by the state. In recent years, the most resilient has been Darul Arqam. For several years, Darul Arqam was successful in setting up a thriving commune on the outskirts of Kuala Lumpur and had attracted a sizeable following among middle-class Malays. Its leader Ashaari Muhammad was also able to set up self-sufficient satellite communes in Southern Thailand, Southern Philippines, and Singapore. Darul Arqam was a hybrid experiment that tried to combine elements of modernity with that of the anti-modern as well as the pre-modern (Maznah 2011, p. 49). Eventually seen as a serious threat against the modernization project of the state, its leaders were detained under the Internal Security Act (ISA), and the group disbanded.

Likewise, smaller scale attempts by individual Muslims (or converts to Islam) in seeking judicial recognition from the civil courts in renouncing Islam or re-converting back to their original faith have met with unjust outcomes for the aggrieved parties. Instead, the civil courts have consistently ruled they have no jurisdiction in protecting the faith choices of individuals like Ayah Pin (and his followers) and Lina Joy @ Azlina Jailani, and that their legal fate lies in the hands of the *Syariah* courts.

Under *Syariah* law, the renunciation of Islam amounts to the offence of apostasy and their defence lawyers have posited, to no avail, that *Syariah* law can only apply to persons who continue to profess Islam. An individual who no longer professes Islam as his/her personal faith should thus be free from the jurisdiction of Islamic law. This jurisdictional conundrum stems from a key controversial amendment made to Article 121 of the Federal Constitution in 1988 during the Mahathir Administration, and which has, in effect, created two spheres of competing jurisdiction between the civil and the *Syariah* courts.

Indeed, the codification of Islamic "norms", "values", and "morals" into state legislation have created another layer of legal surveillance over the activities of Malay Muslims in the first instance, and indirectly on non-Muslims given the porosity of everyday interactions. Under *Syariah* criminal laws, Muslims are subject to restrictions on various "immoral" behaviour ranging from prohibition of alcohol, gambling, and *khalwat*; the enforcement of fasting during the month of Ramadan; observance of prayers; and "decency" requirements in dressing and leisure. JAWI conducts frequent "moral" raids throughout Kuala Lumpur city in search of Muslims infringing these stipulations based on their own surveillance as well as tip-offs from the public. These raids are often widely reported in the mass media as a strategy in not only shaming the offenders but also disciplining would-be offenders. In these raids, Malay-Muslim women, in particular, have frequently become targets of humiliation and intimidation by JAWI officers.[15] In a number of documented cases, civil society groups have argued that over-zealousness in conducting these "morality raids" into the private lives of Malaysian citizens and the improper behaviour of the JAWI enforcement officers have violated human rights standards.[16] In response, Muslim groups have tended to characterize these criticisms as "anti-Islam" or "insulting Islam".[17]

The moral policing of ordinary Malay Muslims has extended to the virtual and sensorial world of images and fantasies produced by the mass media for entertainment, which, by its commercial calculus, are aimed at an ecumenically broad audience. Over the years, various Muslim-based organizations have criticized local TV stations for producing and airing entertainment programmes that purportedly undermine moral values and contradict Islamic teachings. For example, in July 2004, a minister in the Prime Minister's Department reportedly said that the trend of broadcasting "talent search" entertainment programmes simulating *American Idol* — like *Malaysian Idol, Akademi Fantasia*, and *Audition* — are not in accordance with the government's efforts in promoting Islamic values. Similarly, rock concerts organized by entertainment companies have been a regular target for PAS Youth, *muftis*, and other Islamic groups.[18] These events are said to be *haram* because they have negative consequences such as free mixing between boys and girls, drug abuse, adultery, and rape. The spectre of moral danger due to concerts featuring foreign artistes and bands like Beyonce, Elton John, and Scorpions is heightened given their alleged Western "hedonist" sensuality and sexuality, and deemed "unsuitable" for Malaysians, Muslim or non-Muslim.

EVERYDAY RELIGIOUS SPACES IN KUALA LUMPUR

In this section, I turn to briefly looking at the conundrums of everyday spaces as experienced by informants drawn from my fieldwork experience conducted in two different kinds of localities in the city. The first is a high-rise flat situated on the outskirts of Kuala Lumpur and occupied by mainly working-class Tamil-Hindus and Malay Muslims who have been displaced from neighbouring squatter settlements and gathered together into one structure. The other is a historic commercial enclave known as "Little India/Masjid India" situated in central Kuala Lumpur. Though certainly not representative of the ethos of the whole city, I would suggest they illustrate some of the everyday pragmatics of subaltern inter-religious relations in Kuala Lumpur removed from the decorum of high-level inter-faith consultations and conferences.

As noted earlier, the rapid material and symbolic transformation of Kuala Lumpur saw the sites of numerous "illegal" squatter settlements — many of which predate Independence — being re-developed from the 1990s onwards in order to create a "squatter-free city". Although not legally compelled to do so, some residents of these settlements have been provided with subsidized high-rise housing flats either on humanitarian grounds or as a consequence of the intervention of local-level politicians and civil society groups. Typically ensconced in these settlements is an array of places of worship of differing faith traditions, and even within them of different theological persuasions. The provision of alternative housing by the government authorities or private developers, however, rarely extended to places of worship. When alternative sites were offered, they came with the imposition of certain limiting conditions. For instance, small Hindu temples and roadside shrines were required to merge with each other even though they might have different patron gods/goddesses and founding genealogies. Moreover, in comparison to Muslim *suraus* which are easier to re-constitute, the alternative sites offered to Hindu (and Chinese) temples did not always fully comply with the requirements of respective religious geomancy. Moreover, over the years, human rights groups have further documented the brusque and arbitrary manner in which these demolitions and relocations of places of worship were executed.[19] Cumulatively, these narratives of victimhood by ethno-religious minorities, especially salient in metropolitan Kuala Lumpur, have become widely disseminated through the amoebic sharing of testimonies and the deployment of social media.

Accompanying the significant demographic increase of Malay Muslims in Kuala Lumpur has been a corresponding mushrooming of new mosques in residential areas and public spaces to accommodate their spiritual needs. Older mosques have also been expanded and renovated. Most of these new mosques have adopted Middle-Eastern architectural motifs and are strikingly larger in size. By comparison, a long-standing lament of non-Muslim religious groups has been that land to build places of worship in new residential suburbs has not been readily made available by local authorities. An array of church denominations has thus resorted to renting conference halls in hotels, buying over shop houses and factory lots in order to conduct their worship services. Moreover, in many documented instances, applications to local authorities to build churches and temples have been objected to by Malay-Muslim residents of the same locality.

Besides the mutating politics of public religious spaces noted above, the texture of lived domestic spaces also has a bearing in enlivening the folds of everyday religious pluralism. Unlike elite and middle-class housing which have the luxury of bigger spaces acting as buffer zones, my fieldwork with working-class Tamil-Hindus residing in a high-rise flat suggests the fomenting of sentiments that do not enhance inter-religious relations at close quarters. While the authorities may have formally addressed the security of tenure, the architectural design of these structures leaves much to be desired.[20]

In comparison to their former landed modest squatter homes which have allowed for organic modifications when circumstances permit, living in these high-rise structures is considered an alienating daily experience. First, for three-generational households extending to grandparents, the cramped conditions of these two-bedroom flats have been physically and emotionally challenging for these families. Second, the current architectural design of the common areas does not allow the effective dispersal of an array of sounds and smells emanating from the units. Instead, they reverberate and circulate along the narrow passageways of the building.

Third, the high density of residents coupled with the poor maintenance of these buildings have quickly disfigured these structures into vertical "slums" and places of unhealthy ferment. Ironically, the stated goal of "social upliftment" through modern housing appears to be incredulous and self-defeating when these material conditions are taken into account.

Compared to their current abode, their former squatter *kampung* ("village") had allowed for the gradual cultivation of various mutually recognizable buffer zones because of the horizontal spread of squatter settlements predominantly segregated along ethno-religious lines. By contrast, these vertical structures have compressed these zones to a compact and dense space, heightening frictions caused by intrusive soundscapes and smellscapes. For instance, many of my Hindu-Indian informants usually use a hand bell during their daily domestic *pujas* (prayers). Although they are clearly audible to neighbouring units, the "religious noises" that are produced are momentary and localized. By comparison, most of my informants feel that the amplified and reverberated sound of the Muslim *azan subuh* (call to prayer at dawn) issuing out of a *surau* located within the building is of a different scale. These enforced wake-up calls are not religiously relevant to them and are seen as pragmatically intrusive especially when much needed sleep is needed after long hours of work. But because they fear causing ill-feelings to their Muslim neighbours and inviting possible retaliatory action from both local Muslim residents and entrepreneurial local politicians who want to be seen as defending Islam against its detractors, they have not publicly sought any redress with the local *surau* leaders.[21] In short, despite the creative array of everyday risk-avoidance strategies adopted by my informants, they are required to labour much in keeping inter-religious relations on a convivial plane.

Even in commercial precincts which have been ethno-religiously pluralist for decades, the interplay between changing government policies, demographic changes, and local-level entrepreneurial politics has sometimes led to reduced economic opportunities being interpreted along racialized lines. This was a point of contention in one of the oldest and lucrative commercial enclaves in Kuala Lumpur — "Little India/Masjid India" — where I conducted fieldwork between 2004 and 2006 (Yeoh 2009*a*). In the past, "Little India/Masjid India" has had a far more varied, fluid, and unregulated ethnoscapes — Chinese, Punjabis, Malays, and Tamils — eking out a living. But in part prompted by the overarching policies discussed earlier and by more recent urban planning innovations, "Little India/Masjid India" has been re-branded as a destination for a host of *halal* cuisine and goods, and for tourists to visit and gaze at the "old Malay quarter" of Kuala Lumpur. Subsequently, long established non-Muslim businesses have also found it financially necessary to voluntarily re-locate or change their usual wares and services to cater to the Muslim clientele.

At the time of my fieldwork, the religious festivals like Hindu Deepavali and Muslim Hari Raya Puasa were in very close temporal proximity. Street vendors who had been setting up temporary stalls along the spine of the enclave during their respective festivities for several years without any problems suddenly found themselves caught in a novel crossroad. The Kuala Lumpur City Hall had decided to allot Malay-Muslim traders with 78 per cent of the 556 bazaar lots. Disgruntled Indian-Hindu traders contended that they were more accustomed to at least 350 lots instead. To suggestions by City Hall that they shift to the Indian-Hindu enclave of Brickfields during this special period, the traders reiterated their desire of doing business in familiar places. When City Hall officials did not relent on their decision, the affected traders read this episode as yet another instance of their continued neglect and marginalization as working-class Hindu-Indians.[22]

CONCLUSION

In concluding, it would be pertinent to view contemporary inter-religious relations in Malaysia in relation to the spatial politics of right-wing Hindutva nationalism in India. For this, I draw from Mrinalini Rajagopalan's (2010) insightful study on Hindutva politics as played out in Delhi to make spectral comparisons of attempts at the ideological re-making of Kuala Lumpur into a post-secular urban cityscape.

Hindutva nationalism is a movement that essentially aims to reclaim the nation-state of India as a Hindu homeland. This notion of Hindu-ness rests on three pillars — geographical unity, similarity in "racial" features, and a common culture. Since India is considered the motherland of the Hindu nation, the loyalty of India's Christians and Muslims is considered suspect as they do not look upon India as their holy land. A Hindutva nation-state, if realized, would thus have diminished rights for citizens who belong to minority religious groups. Instead of anchoring their vision of a sovereign India emancipated from British colonial rule, the founders of Hindutva promote a contrasting view that Hindus are a vulnerable group who have been oppressed and humiliated by an imagined pre-colonial Other (Muslims) (Rajagoplan 2010, p. 263).

A cornerstone of Indian secularism embedded in the Indian Constitution is the role of the state as the protector of minorities (ethnic, religious, and caste-based) and their rights. From the 1980s onwards, the Hindutva movement has seized on disillusionments with the socialist ideals and the ravages of globalization to argue that major political parties like the Indian National Congress (INC), which has a modern secular liberal platform, have largely given in to minority rights to the detriment of the majority Hindus. By contrast, Hindutva politicians have contended that the politics of the majority should prevail and that religious minorities should accept their status as second-tier citizens in a Hindu nation-state. Thus, rather than seen as being anti-secular, Mrinalini Rajagopalan counter-intuitively argues that Hindutva has in fact appropriated secularist rhetoric to promote a "rational model of republicanism that simply represents the rights of the majority demographic over others" (p. 265).[23]

Notwithstanding the different historical particularities and complexities of India and Malaysia — in terms of ethno-religious demographics, ideological spectrum of competing party politics, and economic policies *vis-à-vis* globalization — what is strikingly similar is the stock of spatial strategies deployed in undergirding the politics of the majority. Attentive energies are devoted to re-configuring pluralist urban spaces into the idealized image of a "homeland", past and prospective, that is parochially rather than ecumenically framed. Religious interactions and mixing with the homogenized Other is eschewed, if not abhorred. To underscore and buttress radical difference, selective past histories of religious afflictions and humiliation are recuperated. The "glorious past" is, moreover, re-materialized in the built form of the present, whether through modernist architecture utilizing religious motifs or through the textual re-appropriations of ancient cities and civilizations in history books and museums. Cosmopolitan and pluralist city spaces are typically assessed as places infused with grave moral and sexual danger, afflicting especially nubile and vulnerable female bodies. This logically necessitates the intervention of masculine valour to guard the integrity and honour of both female bodies and the re-imagined homogenous ethno-religious social body as both are conflated with each other. Finally, the force of law is a key recruitment in producing the legitimation for regulating permissible religious/moral behaviour.

In light of my discussion above, does Kuala Lumpur qualify to be a "fundamentalist city" (AlSayyad) despite the overt "world class city" aspirations of its planners? Is the religious majority unilaterally morphing the capital city of Malaysia into a kind of post-secular urban citizenry that confirms primarily to stringent Islamic coordinates? Or would it be more sanguine to see these contesting configurations merely as another passing feature of the "crossroads" dialectic of "city-ness"? Prior to the unanticipated spectacular results of the 12th general elections (March 2008) and a continuation of this electoral trend in the subsequent 13th general elections (May 2013), many would have been more inclined to see Kuala Lumpur's slide towards the "fundamentalist city" mode as inevitable. However, the significant change in political mood and political will since March 2008 has recalibrated these doomsday and self-fulfilling predictions. Despite the highly vocal pronouncements of individuals and groups professing to represent the sentiments of the majority or re-affirming the politics of the majority, this trajectory is less assured than before. The electoral voice of newer generations of urbane and cosmopolitan urban citizens — across ethnic and religious differences — residing in Kuala Lumpur has played a more vocal role in deciding how they want their city (and country) to be governed and shaped. A significant majority of this constituency has opted for more moderation and integration despite the narrow racialist and religious overtures of some political parties and non-governmental organizations.

Nevertheless, if these sea changes are to be truly cosmopolitan and socially just, to their growing voices must be added those of Kuala Lumpur's working class and other marginalized groups who have to bear heavier burdens or suffer greater costs in the current ideological and ethical warfare between religious parochialism and religious cosmopolitanism.

Notes

[1] See <http://www.themalaysianinsider.com/malaysia/article/najib-sacrificed-his-faith-to-attend-thaipusam-do-says-perak-mufti/> (accessed 19 February 2012). Thaipusam is dedicated to the male ascetic deity, Lord Murugan. Originally more popular among Tamil Hindus, the festival has since become arguably the most participated in the Hindu religious calendar in Malaysia with the Batu Caves shrine as the key gravitational centre for pilgrims from all over the country. The Malaysian Tourism Board has also cashed in on Thaipusam as one of many events showcasing Malaysian multiculturalism branded as the "Colours of Malaysia".

[2] Unlike the mainstream newspapers, the stance of the Perak Mufti was severely criticized and ridiculed by readers in the comments section of independent online newspapers, *Malaysian Insider* and *Malaysiakini*. See, for example, <http://www.malaysiakini.com.ezproxy.lib.monash.edu.au/news/189273>.

3   The visits by political leaders from both sides of the political divide are significant because of the results of the March 2008 general elections which saw the BN losing its two-thirds parliamentary majority for the first time in four decades. Billed by the media as a "political tsunami", the candidates of the Malaysian Indian Congress (MIC), a component member of the multi-ethnic–based BN, which hitherto had strong support of Indians in the country, was decimated as large droves of Indian voters turned their backs on the party. Among others, a key reason for their defection is MIC's political impotence in addressing the deepening marginalization of Indians in the country as dramatized in MIC's complicity in not condemning how Indian demonstrators were treated during the historic Hindraf (Hindu Rights Action Force) rally of November 2007. For an account see Yeoh (2009*b*). See also Arunajeet Kaur, this volume.

4   Nurul Izzah Anwar is also the daughter of Anwar Ibrahim, the current *de facto* leader of the opposition coalition, Pakatan Rakyat (People's Pact/Coalition), comprising three key parties, Democratic Action Party (DAP), Parti Islam Se Malaysia (Islamic Party of Malaysia, PAS), and Parti Keadilan Rakyat (People's Justice Party, PKR). Anwar Ibrahim was the former deputy Prime Minister of Malaysia before he was deposed by Mahathir Mohamad at the beginning of the Asian financial crisis on allegations of sodomy and corruption. He has denied these allegations saying that the real reason is because of his deep personal disagreement with Mahathir on how the financial crisis was to be managed.

5   See <http://www.themalaysianinsider.com/malaysia/article/nurul-izzah-harussani-hypocrite-for-retracting-thaipusam-comment/> (accessed 19 February 2012).

6   See <http://www.themalaysianinsider.com/malaysia/article/be-fair-asri-tells-thaipusam-visit-naysayers/> (accessed 19 February 2012).

7   See <http://www.themalaysianinsider.com/malaysia/article/asri-politicians-causing-need-for-inter-religious-guidelines/> (accessed 19 February 2012).

8   See <http://www.malaysiakini.com.ezproxy.lib.monash.edu.au/news/188707> (accessed 21 February 2012). See also "PAS: Sinful to Promote Valentine's Day", *The Star*, 9 February 2012.

9   No detailed explanation was provided on how this statistical correlation was gathered and verified. In social media, this putative link was especially lambasted and ridiculed.

10 See "V-Day: CCM 'hurt' by Assumptions Made in Fatwa", *Malaysiakini*, 11 February 2011, available at <http://www.malaysiakini.com.ezproxy.lib.monash.edu.au/news/155775> (accessed 21 February 2012).

11 For a historical account of the genesis and evolution of early Kuala Lumpur, see Gullick (2000).

12 For instance, the 2000 census figures indicate that although ethnic Chinese still constitute the majority at 43 per cent of the Kuala Lumpur population of 1.4 million, the "Bumiputra" (literally, "prince of the soil" to denote Malays

and indigenous peoples) component has increased substantially by 77 per cent over the past two decades to make up 38 per cent of the city (*Kuala Lumpur Structure Plan 2020: A World Class City*, p. 4–4).

13 Available at <http://www.wawasan2020.com/vision/index.html>.
14 Drawing parallels from the Palestinian situation, Gerhard Hoffstaedter (2011, p. 215f) has argued that the paternalistic treatment of Malays by the Malaysian state over the years amounts to "politicide", with the goal of "ultimately silencing of the Malay majority by the political elite. ... The spectre of Malay supremacy is used to seemingly provide the Malay majority with economic privileges whilst their rights to sovereignty and political will are diminished".
15 For example, see *Suaram Human Rights Report* (2004), p. 105f.
16 Ibid., p. 105. In the early days of the NEP, the spectre of waves of young and single Muslim women migrating to Kuala Lumpur for education and employment purposes was a cause of anxiety and concern for Muslim male leaders. Among other practices, these women were told to wear the *tudung* (head covering) and dress conservatively as a sign of their moral and religious difference. For a feminist anthropological critique of these disciplinary practices, see Ong (1987).
17 For more details, see Lee (2010), Liow (2007), Riddell (2005), and Yeoh (2011, 2005*a*).
18 Thus, while both UMNO and PAS are overt political nemesis, the parties arguably share similar outlooks in the primacy of Islam in managing multi-religious and multicultural Malaysia.
19 See the annual human rights reports produced by the NGO, Suaram, <http://www.suaram.net>.
20 For a discussion of inter-ethnic relations in their settlement before they were evicted and relocated into high-rise housing, see Yeoh (2001, 2005*b*).
21 Unaccustomed to a Muslim soundscape, the issue of "religious noise" extends as well to ethno-religiously mixed middle-class residential areas where new mosques with powerful loudspeakers allow for greater aural reach than before.
22 From anecdotal evidence, similar feelings of discontent are multiplied elsewhere throughout the country. This groundswell was well harnessed by the Hindraf leaders and contributed to the spectacular Hindraf rally of November 2007.
23 Said differently, the Hindutva project is essentially an attempt to re-calibrate constitutional secularism in India. In this project, Hindutva represents India as a Hindu territory in need of protection by valiant Hindu male subjects, defined as by militant prowess and physical valour (p. 261). Moreover, Dehli's archaeological past is particularly viewed with great interest as an avenue to fortify claims of an ancient imperial ur-city of the Hindu epic Mahabharatha pre-dating all Islamic cities (p. 269).

References

Ackerman, Susan and Raymond Lee. *Heaven in Transition: Non-Muslim Religious Innovation and Ethnic Identity in Malaysia.* Kuala Lumpur: Forum, 1990.
AlSayyad, Nezar and Ananya Roy. "Medieval Modernity: On Citizenship and Urbanism in a Global Era". *Space and Polity* 10.1 (2006): 1–20.
AlSayyad, Nezar and Mejgan Massoumi, eds. *The Fundamentalist City? Religiosity and the Remaking of Urban Space.* London and New York: Routledge, 2010.
Anderson, Benedict. *Imagined Communities: Reflections on the Origins and Spread of Nationalism.* Rev. edn. [1983]. London: Verso, 2006.
Ariffin, S.M. Omar. "Origins and Development of the Affirmative Policy in Malaya and Malaysia: A Historical Overview". In *The "Bumiputera Policy": Dynamics and Dilemmas*, edited by Richard Mason and Ariffin S.M. Omar. Special Issue of *Kajian Malaysia* 21, nos. 1–2 (2003).
Caldeira, Teresa P.R. *City of Walls: Crime, Segregation and Citizenship in Sao Paulo.* Berkeley, CA: University of California Press, 2000.
Fischer, Johan. *Proper Islamic Consumption: Shopping among the Malays in Modern Malaysia.* Copenhagen: Nordic Institute of Asian Studies, 2008.
Gullick, John. *A History of Kuala Lumpur, 1856–1939.* Kuala Lumpur: Malaysian Branch of the Royal Asiatic Society, 2000.
Hoffstaedter, Gerhard. *Modern Muslim Identities: Negotiating Religion and Ethnicity in Malaysia.* Copenhagen: Nordic Institute of Asian Studies, 2011.
Holston, James and Arjun Appadurai, eds. *Cities and Citizenship.* Durham: Duke University Press, 1999.
Kahn, Joel. *Other Malays: Nationalism and Cosmopolitanism in the Modern Malay World.* Singapore: National University of Singapore Press, 2006.
King, Ross. *Kuala Lumpur and Putrajaya: Negotiating Urban Space in Malaysia.* Singapore: National University of Singapore Press, 2008.
Kuala Lumpur Structure Plan 2020: A World Class City. Kuala Lumpur: City Hall, 2004.
Lee, Julian C.H. *Islamization and Activism in Malaysia.* Singapore: Institute of Southeast Asian Studies, 2010.
Lefebvre, Henri. *The Production of Space*, translated by Donald Nicholson-Smith. Oxford: Wiley-Blackwell, 1991.
Liow, Joseph Chin-Yong. "Political Islam in Malaysia: Legitimacy, Hegemony and Resistance". In *Islamic Legitimacy in a Plural Asia*, edited by Antony Reid and Michael Gilsenan. London and New York: Routledge, 2007.
MaznahMohamad. "The Authoritarian State and Political Islam in Muslim-majority Malaysia". In *Islam and Politics in Southeast Asia*, edited by Johan Saravanamuttu. London and New York: Routledge, 2010.
———. "Like a Shady Tree Swept by the Windstorm: Malays in Dissent". In *Melayu: The Politics, Poetics and Paradoxes of Malayness*, edited by Maznah

Mohamad and Syed Khairudin Aljunied. Singapore: National University of Singapore Press, 2011.
Ong Aihwa. *Spirits of Resistance and Capitalist Discipline: Factory Women in Malaysia*. Albany, NY: State University of New York, 1987.
Rajagopalan, Mrinalini. "Post-secular Urbanisms: Situating Delhi within the Rhetorical Landscape of Hindutva". In *The Fundamentalist City? Religiosity and the Re-making of Urban Space*, edited by Nezar AlSayyad and Mejgan Massoumi. London and New York: Routledge, 2010.
Riddell, Peter G. "Islamization, Civil Society and Religious Minorities in Malaysia". In *Islam in Southeast Asia: Political, Social and Strategic Challenges for the 21st Century*, edited by K.S. Nathan and Mohammad Hashim Kamali. Singapore: Institute of Southeast Asian Studies, 2005.
Roff, William. "Patterns of Islamization in Malaysia, 1890s–1990s: Exemplars, Institutions and Vectors". *Journal of Islamic Studies* 9, no. 2 (1998): 210–28.
Shamsul, Amri Baharudin. "Making Sense of the Plural-religious Past and the Modern-secular Present of the Islamic Malay World and Malaysia". *Asian Journal of Social Sciences* 33 (2005): 449–72.
Simone, AbdouMaliq. *City Life from Jakarta to Dakar: Movements at the Crossroads*. New York and London: Routledge, 2010.
Suaram Human Rights Report. Petaling Jaya: Suaram Komunikasi, 2004.
Willford, Andrew. *Cage of Freedom: Tamil Identity and the Ethnic Fetish in Malaysia*. Ann Arbor, MI: University of Michigan Press, 2006.
Yeoh, Brenda. "Cosmopolitanism and Its Exclusions in Singapore". *Urban Studies* 41, no. 12 (2004): 2431–45.
Yeoh Seng-Guan. "Producing Locality: Space, Houses and Public Culture in a Hindu Festival in Malaysia". *Contributions to Indian* (n.s.) 35, no. 1 (2001): 33–64.
———. "Managing Sensitivities: Religious Pluralism, Civil Society and Interfaith Relations in Malaysia". *The Round Table: The Commonwealth Journal of International Affairs* 94, no. 382 (2005*a*): 629–40.
———. "House, Kampung and Taman: Spatial Hegemony and the Politics (and Poetics) of Space in Urban Malaysia". *Crossroads: An Interdisciplinary Journal of Southeast Asian Studies* 17, no. 2 (2005*b*): 128–58.
———. "Limiting Cosmopolitanism: Streetlife Little India, Kuala Lumpur". In *The Other Global City*, edited by Shail Mayaram. London and New York: Routledge, 2009*a*.
———. "The Streets of Kuala Lumpur: City-space, 'Race' and Civil Disobedience". In *Dissent and Cultural Resistance in Asia's Cities*, edited by Melissa Butcher and Selvaraj Velayutham. London and New York: Routledge, 2009*b*.
———. "In Defence of the Secular? Islamization, Christians and (New) Politics in Urbane Malaysia". *Asian Studies Review* 35, no. 1 (2011): 83–103.

15

THE CHRISTIAN RESPONSE TO STATE-LED ISLAMIZATION IN MALAYSIA

Chong Eu Choong

The state-religion relationship in Malaysia is a complex matter wherein all non-Islamic religious relations are mediated by the state's preferential relationship with Islam, as befitting Islam's constitutional status as the religion of the country.[1] Islam's status has meant that the Malaysian government is obliged and empowered to regulate and administer the Islamic religious sphere while staying out of any direct involvement in the non-Islamic religious sphere.[2] As a result, administrative decisions involving Islam have been made largely without considering the interests of other religions. It should be borne in mind that such decisions are not necessarily intentional or by design. Quite often, it is simply that the concerns of other religions do not fall within the ambit of the government, legally speaking. However, the practical effect of the government's involvement in the Islamic religious sphere has been the increasing intrusion by the government into the non-Islamic religious sphere. The intrusion of the government in the religious and social spheres of the non-Muslims has provoked a response by the latter to circumvent such intrusion. In this chapter, I will be discussing the response by the minority Christian community in Malaysia.[3]

ETHNICITY AND RELIGION IN MALAYSIA

One of the major projects of all post-colonial states is the quest for a national identity that seeks to transform its diverse population into a modern nation. However, as Geertz (1973) had noted almost fifty years ago, the state's attempt at nation-building will inevitably run into the resistance of primordial sentiments (traditional identities and loyalties) that have a more concrete reality than that of the abstract notion of nation-state. What results from this encounter is a complex interplay between the state's nation-building project, and these traditional identities and loyalties that would deeply affect the political, social, and economic structures of a given post-colonial society. Malaysia has not escaped this fate.

Therefore, the Malaysian state's project that aimed at wholeness is mired with the contingencies of a plural society that reflects a basic division between the indigenous Malays and non-Malays.[4] One needs to look no further on this issue than at the Federal Constitution of Malaysia. As with other modern constitutions, it explicitly carries the modern notions of citizenship. Interestingly, the same document also defines who is a Malay, a definition that carries with it certain social and political privileges.[5] The founding document of Malaysia has officially created two basic categories of citizens, Malays and non-Malays. Consequently, ethnicity has played an important part in forming social identities in Malaysia where social relationships are largely determined by "*kaum*" or "*bangsa*" (race, ethnicity). Apart from serving as an identity marker that helps one to identify oneself *vis-à-vis* others, ethnicity also serves a political purpose, that is, as a tool of the state for political control and resource allocation (Ackerman and Lee 1990, p. 4).

Since its independence in 1957, Malaysia has experienced rapid economic growth and social transformation even as religion has remained deeply embedded in Malaysian society (Nagata 1984; Lee and Ackerman 1997). Like ethnicity, religion is deeply intertwined with the individual's sense of self, and what complicates the picture is increasing potential for political mobilization (Ackerman and Lee 1990, p. 4). The enjoining of ethnicity and religion in the country has dichotomized the religious sphere into two separate fields, that is, Muslim and non-Muslim. The Muslim field is principally a Malay domain since all Malays are by definition Muslims. Those who voluntarily leave this field lose the social and political privileges as well as face state sanctions, implying that Malay-Muslim identity is materially and politically reinforced (Ackerman and Lee 1990, p. 4).

The non-Muslim field, on the other hand, is basically a non-Malay domain where identity and ethnicity are more loosely defined, and more importantly, it is not under-girded by any political and material privileges. Non-Malays are free to associate themselves with any religion of their choice although typically a Chinese is a Buddhist-Taoist whereas an Indian a Hindu. However, religions such as Christianity have attracted followers from non-Malays. Religious affiliation among non-Malays does not carry any socio-economic privileges. Although the connection between religion and ethnicity is loose in the non-Muslim field, "there is an undefined sense of solidarity among non-Malays that they are not Muslims" (Ackerman and Lee 1990, p. 5).

The relationship between the Malays and non-Malays in the present period assume a greater significance as the latter are confronting the Malays on the question of the rights of non-Islamic religions. The root of this conflict can be traced back to the mid-1970s when Islamic fundamentalism began to spread among urban Malay youths.[6] Generally speaking, this phenomenon can be partially attributed to the rising Islamic consciousness among Muslim societies worldwide as well as to the alienating effects of modernization on the Malays (Chandra 1987; Shamsul 1997). More importantly, given heightened ethnic consciousness in the country after the 13 May racial riots, the spread of Islamic fundamentalism among Malay youths can be interpreted as an attempt by the Malays to use Islam as an ethnic boundary to distinguish themselves from the non-Malays.[7] As Ackerman and Lee (1990, p. 6) pointed out: "Relatively speaking, the Malays — despite their factions and conflict — are more united politically under the banner of Islam ... The emergence of Islamic fundamentalism in the 1970s has revitalized Malay ethnicity."

The growing influence of Islamic fundamentalism among the Malays egged on the government to respond by initiating its own Islamization agenda that aimed at moralizing economic and social policies through a modernist interpretation of Islam:

> One consequence of this moralizing Islamic discourse has been an increasing reification of ethnic and religious boundaries through their bureaucratic codification and materialization of political representation (Willford 2005, p. 45).

This, in turn, has brought about the government's increasing encroachment on the lives of not only the Malays but also the non-Malays.

ENCROACHING ON THE CHRISTIAN RELIGIOUS FIELD

In line with the Islamization policy that was implemented in the 1980s, the government had steadily sought to impose its authority over the lives of the Muslim (and largely Malay) community.[8] However, in so doing, the non-Muslim (and non-Malay) community, particularly the Christians, has also been affected. This has stirred up a few controversies in the past few years. The government's encroachment in the Christians' religious field is most keenly felt in the administrative interference in areas such as the construction of new churches and the use of the national language in the Bible.

Administrative Interference in Constructing New Churches

Generally speaking, the government respects the non-Muslims' right to worship. However, for non-Muslims getting permission to build new places of worship tend to be a slow and arbitrary process (Suara Rakyat Malaysia 2005, p. 102). Take for example, the experience of the Latter Rain Church. "We bought a piece of land in Selangor twenty years ago with the goal of constructing a church building on it", said Reverend Dexter Low.[9] "Following the building by-laws, we applied for a permit with the local authorities to build the church at that time but it was only recently that we were given the green light to start construction", he continued.[10]

Apart from administrative difficulties in constructing new churches, such construction projects also face the obstacles of protest by local Muslim communities, which can delay if not stop such construction projects. Perhaps the most well-known case concerning the administrative difficulties and the political sensitivities of getting permission to build a church is the case of the proposed Catholic Church in Shah Alam. In 1977, the Catholic Church applied to the Selangor state government for land to build a church. The state government eventually approved and sold a piece of land in Selangor for this purpose in 1985. Formal approval for building the church was given by the Shah Alam Municipal Council in May 1993 and construction started in June of the year. On 16 August 1993, the *Menteri Besar* (Chief Minister) of Selangor received a memorandum sent by a group of Muslims in the district protesting the building of a church in Shah Alam. Within three days, the *Menteri Besar* instructed the municipal council to withdraw its approval of the proposed church building (Chew 2000, p. 272). This resulted in the stop of the church building project that was already underway. What followed were a few rounds of appeals and negotiations by the Catholic Church with the state government that dragged on until 2001 when a compromise was reached, and the church was built on an alternate place in the city.[11]

Bahasa Malaysia and the Christian Community

Although the national language of Malaysia is *Bahasa Malaysia* (the Malay language) nonetheless since the 1980s, nine states in the peninsula have legislated enactments that restrict the use of various terms and expressions in the national language by non-Muslims. These words are said to be reserved solely for the use of Muslims and cannot be associated with a non-Islamic religion.[12] Perhaps the most sensitive word in the *Bahasa Malaysia* vocabulary is the word "Allah" (God) which appears to be the property of Muslims according to the government's interpretation. Datuk Abdullah Mohd Zin, the Minister in charge of Islamic affairs, stated on 31 December 2007 that only Muslims could use the word 'Allah' because "the use of the word "Allah" by non-Muslims may arouse sensitivity and create confusion among Muslims in the country".[13] The use of any banned words by non-Muslims can bring about action not only by the state government but also by the federal government.

This issue gained national attention when *The Catholic Herald* (the major newspaper of the Malaysian Catholic Church) faced problems in getting its annual publishing permit renewed in December 2007.[14] This problem was caused by the use of the word "Allah" in the newspaper's *Bahasa Malaysia* section. The use of this word, according to the Deputy Minister of Internal Security Johari Baharum, is forbidden outside the context of Islam and would only confuse people (Suara Rakyat Malaysia 2009, p. 119). It was reported that the Internal Security Ministry had asked the newspaper to remove its entire *Bahasa Malaysia* section or there would be a risk getting its permit not renewed. However, the Ministry later reversed its earlier decision and renewed the newspaper permit without any condition. Nonetheless, on 4 January 2008, the Federal Cabinet decided that *The Catholic Herald* could not use "Allah" it is publications.

The banning of the use of certain words in *Bahasa Malaysia* inevitably meant that the sacred scripture of the Christians which had been translated in different languages faces difficulties in getting the *Bahasa Malaysia* version printed in the country. There is no *Bahasa Malaysia* version of the Bible. Hence Christians use the *Bahasa Indonesia* (Indonesian language) version, that is, *Alkitab* which is imported from the neighbouring country. In December 1981, the Home Affairs Ministry banned the importation of *Alkitab* under the Internal Security Act (ISA) but after much protest from Christians the ban was partially lifted. Under the concession, the book was allowed to be imported by certain bookshops. (Chew 2000, p. 280).

Nonetheless, the importation of such books still faces administrative difficulties at the implementation level as "Customs and enforcement officials from the Internal Security Ministry continued to confiscate not only *Alkitab* but also other *Bahasa* Christian publications at entry points at ports and airports as well as bookshops" (Teoh 2010, p. 6). For example, it was reported that the government confiscated 30,000 copies of *Alkitab* destined for Christians in Sabah and Sarawak in December 2011.[15]

Generally speaking, the issue of the *Alkitab* (and related *Bahasa* Christian publications) does not really affect Christians in the peninsula who rely on English, Chinese, and Tamil versions. However, Christians from Sabah and Sarawak use *Bahasa Malaysia* for worship and communication. The government also maintained a policy of banning certain religious books on grounds that such books were either twisting the facts and true Islamic teachings or containing elements that would mislead the faithful and humiliate the prophets. The problem with this policy is that it affects non-Muslims as well, as some of the books banned were Christian publications (National Evangelical Christian Fellowship 2008, p. 171).

For example, a consignment of Sunday school educational materials of the Sabah *Sidang Injil Borneo* (SIB) Church was confiscated by the Customs Department and subsequently handed over to the Ministry of Internal Security in August 2007. The reason for the confiscation according to the Ministry was that the materials contained prohibited Malay words such as "Allah" and "*Solat*" (prayer) among others which it deemed as being exclusive to the Islamic faith. In fact, the materials were destined for Sabahan Christians who have used *Bahasa Malaysia* as their medium in their liturgy, prayer, and sermons for generations (National Evangelical Christian Fellowship 2008, p. 171).

REPRESENTING CHRISTIANS: THE CHRISTIAN FEDERATION OF MALAYSIA

The government's encroachment on their religious sphere is perceived by Christians (and non-Muslims in general) to be a consequence of the government's Islamization policy that began from the 1980s onwards crowned by an announcement of Dr Mahathir Mohamad (the Fourth Premier) on 29 September 2001 that Malaysia was already an Islamic state (Martinez 2003).[16] At the heart of the Christians' (and other non-Muslims') concern was the government's infringement on the fundamental right of freedom of religion as guaranteed under the Federal Constitution. The steps taken by the government to strengthen the position of Islam in the country and the specific instances of government intrusion into the religious and private spheres of non-Muslims were viewed as measures taken to marginalize non-Islamic religions in the country.[17] The lack of official interest in Christian opinions reinforced such a view.

Robert Hunt (quoted in Riddell 2005, p. 173) speaks for Christians in the country when he noted that:

> Christians have felt systematically excluded from discussion and debate on Islamization and its implications. Non-Muslim criticism, or even comment, on government policies promoting Islamisation has been regarded as highly offensive by Muslims, despite the fact that such policies impact the entire Malaysian society.

Christians were also concerned with the growing polarization between Muslims and non-Muslims in the country. Islamic revivalism among the Malay Muslims has made the community more self-contained where religion became a key consideration for social interaction. As a reaction, non-Muslims began to place emphasis on their own religious identity as witnessed by a parallel revivalism of non-Islamic religions among non-Malays during the 1980s.[18] Unsurprisingly, social interactions between the different ethnic groups in the country became more and more infrequent (Riddell 2005, p. 174).[19] It was inevitable that non-Muslims would begin to mobilize their co-religionists in an attempt to respond to, what they perceived as, the government's infringement on the right of religious freedom in the country. What follows is a discussion of the steps taken by Christians in responding to the government's encroachment on their religious sphere.

FORMATION OF THE CHRISTIAN FEDERATION OF MALAYSIA

As reflection of global Christianity, Christians in Malaysia can be divided into two main groups, that is, Catholics and Protestants. The Protestants in turn can be sub-divided between the mainstream Protestant churches (such as Methodist, Lutherans that have a governing national council) and Evangelical churches (that is made up of autonomous local churches). The drift towards Islamization has provoked concerns among church leaders across the denominational divide. Church leaders, recognizing the progressive marginalization of Christianity since independence, came to the conclusion of the need for unity among the different denominations in order to be able to effectively respond to the increasing encroachment of the government on the non-Islamic religious sphere (Ackerman and Lee 1990, p. 64).

In 1982, the Council of Churches Malaysia (CCM), which represents the mainstream Protestant churches, organized a national conference which saw the participation of delegates from the entire range of the community. The end result of the conference was a resolution to form a national Christian body. In 1985, leaders from CCM, the National Evangelical Christian Fellowship (NECF), and the Catholic Church met together to fulfil the resolution. It was decided that the three Christian bodies, which represented the majority of Christians in the country, form the CFM (Kana 2004, p. 85).

> The stated objectives of the CFM were (i) to bring together all Christians who accept the authority of the Holy Bible and who subscribe to the cardinal doctrines of Christianity as set forth in the Apostles' Creed; (ii) to reinforce and extend, where possible, through dialogue and consultation, the common areas of agreement among the various Christian groups in the country; (iii) to look after the interests of the Christian community as a whole with particular reference to religious freedom and rights as enshrined in the Federal Constitution; (iv) to represent the Christian community in Malaysia on all matters that affect or are of interest to it; and (iv) to consult and work with Government and non-Government bodies (religious and secular) at all administrative levels, on matters of common interest and concern (Christian Federation of Malaysia n.d., p. 2).

CFM was envisioned as the national body that would represent the voice of the community to the government. "We are committed to engaging the government through private and official channels to present our position and recommendations on issues that affect the religious liberties of non-Muslims as provided by the Federal Constitution", said Bishop Ng Moon Hing, the current president of CFM.[20] As the national body representing Malaysian Christians, CFM actively sought to attract the government's attention by releasing media statements at appropriate times and contexts, in order to present the community's position on national issues, especially with regard to religious liberties.[21] One of the major occasions where CFM releases its press statements is on National Day. For example, on Malaysia's 45th National Day in 2002, CFM called upon the government:

> To continue to act against attempts by some to misuse religion for domination and to assert apartness which has profoundly affected the delicate fabric of harmony in a multi-ethnic and multi-religious society. (Quoted in Riddell 2005, p. 175).

General elections are an important channel for CFM to get their message across to the government. In the run up to the 1999 general election, for example, CFM released a press statement urging Christians to vote on the basis of "how far views expressed and political programmes espoused meet with God's standards and Christian values" (quoted in Riddell 2005, p. 177). The statement was a thinly veiled criticism against candidates who were campaigning on a specifically Islamist platform. CFM's statement expressed the hope that:

> The coming election campaign will be fair and that there will be no attempt by politicians to publicly misrepresent or miscast any particular religion, or, subject any particular religious community to unfair and adverse publicity for the purpose of political gain (quoted in Riddell 2005, p. 177).

In the run up to the 2008 general election, CFM released a press statement urging Christians "to vote wisely". In the statement, CFM urged Christians "to pray for an election campaign that is clean, fair and that does not heighten ethnic and religious tensions [and] to encourage all eligible Christian voters to exercise their right to vote".[22] They also produced a brochure entitled "Vote Wisely in the 2008 General Election" which advised Christians to consider the track record and political manifestos of the respective political parties to judge whether they "reflect God's standards and Christ-like values".[23]

Press statements aside, CFM also attempt to engage the government by presenting their list of grievances concerning administrative decisions that affect the Christian community. For example, in response to the government prohibition on the usage of certain terms in the national language which it deemed Islamic, the CFM drew up a memo to the then Premier, Mahathir Mohamad, in 1989 stating:

> It is inconceivable to us that the Bible in any translation can be regarded as a threat to national security in any country ... Nowhere else in the world, as we know, have people been forbidden to use words which are part of their National Language (quoted in Walters 2007, p. 254)

In 2005, the CFM voiced their dismay to the cabinet concerning the statement made in Parliament by Mohd. Nazri Abdul Aziz, a cabinet minister, that Christians were not allowed the free use of the *Bahasa Malaysia* and *Bahasa Indonesia* versions of the Bible. The CFM argued that *Bahasa Malaysia* was the national language of the country regardless of race or religion. Therefore, the right of Christians to use the Bible in the national language should not be an issue (Walters 2007, p. 255). As the national body that represents Christians in the country, the CFM is responsible for organizing the biennial national Christian conference which is aimed at providing a platform for church leaders from all sectors of the community to come together to discuss issues that confront the community and to plan for joint action on these issues.[24]

> CFM also participates in dialogue with conservative and liberal Muslim non-governmental organizations such as the Allied Coordinating Committee of Islamic NGOs (ACCIN) and Sisters in Islam (SIS) in order to facilitate dialogue and understanding with Muslims so as to improve Christian-Muslim relations

said Mr Tan Kong Beng, the Executive Secretary of CFM.[25]

The Malaysian Consultative Council of Buddhism, Christianity, Hinduism, Sikhism and Taoism

Running parallel to the attempt to achieve ecumenism among the various constituents in the Christian community is the effort by Christians and other non-Islamic religious communities, for example, Buddhists, Hindus, and Sikhs, to come together under a national umbrella body in order to work together for the common goal of limiting the intrusion of the government into non-Islamic religious affairs.

An inter-religious body called the Malaysian Consultative Council of Buddhism, Christianity, Hinduism and Sikhism (MCCBCHS) was formed in 1983 for this purpose.²⁶ In 2006, the body was enlarged with the inclusion of the Taoists resulting in its new MCCBCHST acronym. The aim of the council is to provide a platform for inter-religious dialogue and understanding, as well as for the non-Islamic religious communities to convey their views to the government on issues that affect non-Islamic religions (Walters 2007, p. 203). The official stand of the MCCBCHST can be found in the document entitled "Declaration on Freedom of Religion or Belief and on the Elimination of Intolerance and of Discrimination based on Religion and Belief" published in 1988. In the document, the MCCBCHS stated:

> Everyone shall have the right to freedom of thought, conscience and religion. This right shall include freedom to have or to adopt or to change one's religion or belief of one's choice, and freedom, either individually or in community with others and in public or private, to manifest one's religion or belief in worship, observance, practice and teaching (quoted in Riddell 2005, p. 176).²⁷

Since its inception, the MCCBCHST has attempted to present a unified stance to the government through organizing seminars and press statements as well as presenting their grievances to the government. The aim of the Council is to raise awareness among non-Muslims on the increasing encroachment of the government on their daily lives and the need to defend the right to freedom of religion in the country (Kana 2004, pp. 86–87).²⁸

THE CHANGING RESPONSE OF CHRISTIANS, 2001–2008

In general, the Christian response to the government's infringement on their religious affairs between the 1980s and 1990s was conducted mainly through the CFM or their national representative bodies. However, the announcement by Dr Mahathir that Malaysia was an Islamic state in 2001 added a new sense of urgency among Christians — and non-Muslims — to actively engage with the government on its policy of Islamization and its implications on the rights of non-Islamic religions in the public sphere. The year 2001 also witnessed more active participation of the Christian community in the public sphere.

The active participation of Christians into the public sphere was triggered by two events that took place between 2001 and 2002. First, the

Parti Islam Se-Malaysia (PAS) controlled state governments of Kelantan and Terengganu announced their intentions to set up Islamic governments in their states. Second, and as a response to PAS, Dr Mahathir announced that the country was already an Islamic state (Riddell 2005, p. 182).

These events projected Christians into the public sphere where they registered their anxiety. The NECF articulated this anxiety through its periodical *Berita* NECF:

> PAS' public declaration of its intent to set up an Islamic government should it come into power has once again sent jitters through the non-Muslim community ... The resurgence, consolidation and expansion of Islam is expected to continue irrespective of whichever party is in control, an alarming trend to communities of other religious faiths. Generally, the Government is of the view that religious freedom — as enshrined in our federal constitution — is a pre-requisite for national harmony and integration. In reality, however, the practice is not consistent with this view (Berita NECF September–October 2001).

The CFM also issued a statement in response to the Prime Minister's announcement. It stated that:

> the assurances by the Prime Minister and *Barisan Nasional* leaders that the constitution will not be tampered [with] do not offer sufficient guarantee that Malaysia will not degencrate into something of the Islamic model which PAS is promoting. Rhetoric may lead to reality (*Catholic Asian News*, March 2002).

Apart from issuing press statements, other Christian responses included holding meetings and seminars to discuss their concerns and anxieties. All three-component members of the CFM held forums between 2001 and 2002 on this issue (Riddell 2005, p. 184). For example, the NECF organized a forum of fifty leading evangelicals who issued a call for the Malaysian Constitution to be upheld and defended to ensure that the right to freedom of religion in the country would not be threatened by calls for an Islamic government (Berita NECF, September–October 2001).

This anxiety reached its climax in 2005 when the controversial "Moorthy case" occurred. Briefly, the Hindu family of the deceased Moorthy contested the claim of the Federal Territory Islamic authorities that the deceased had converted to Islam and as such should be given Islamic burial rites as opposed to the wishes of the family that Moorthy be given Hindu burial rites.

Although this issue involved a Hindu family nonetheless it gained the attention of the Christian community because it demonstrated the government's willingness to use its machinery on behalf of Islam whenever the religious rights of non-Muslims come into conflict with the government's Islamization agenda. This controversy was followed by other cases such as the conversion of Lina Joy (a Malay Muslim) to Christianity, as well as several divorce cases that involved a Muslim convert and his/her non-Muslim spouse and custody rights on the children, which have implications for the religious upbringing of the children.[29]

Accordingly, there occurred a marked shift in the non-Muslims' response to the government's Islamization policy beginning from 2005. That year, the Hindu community formed the Hindu Rights Action Force (Hindraf) that comprises a coalition of thirty Hindu non-governmental organizations. Hindraf called for an end to the destruction of Hindu temples and the encroachment of Islamic laws on the lives of non-Muslims. Since its formation, Hindraf had taken a confrontational stand against the government by organizing rallies on the issue of the religious rights of Hindus climaxing in a massive demonstration in Kuala Lumpur in November 2007 although the demonstration was banned.[30] The subsequent arrest of its leaders under the ISA resulted in a loss of its initial momentum.[31]

As I have argued at the beginning of this chapter, the enjoining of ethnicity and religion has transformed Malaysian political dynamics. Up until 2001, the nation's political discourse was dominated by the question of ethnicity. However, in recent years, with the dichotomization of Malay-Muslim and non-Malay and non-Muslim fields, the question of the religious rights of minority communities has come to the forefront.[32] The post-2005 period also witnessed a growing public engagement by non-Muslims over the political implications of the government's policy on Islam in public forums such as in the Article XI movement and the initiative for setting up the Interfaith Commission.[33] The response from the Christian community towards the state's encroachment of its religious sphere is a reflection of the changing trend in attitudes among the non-Muslim population.

Seeking Legal Recourse: *The Catholic Herald*

Among the many decisions made by the government that affect the Christian community, perhaps the most contentious issue is the prohibition of the use of certain words in the national language, that is, *Bahasa Malaysia*, by non-Muslims. This had resulted in the arbitrary confiscation of religious literature in *Bahasa Indonesia*, which is essentially similar to the national language. Although the dominant language of the Christian community in the peninsula is English, Christians in Sabah and Sarawak predominantly use the national language in their church services. And since more and more Sabahans and Sarawakians have migrated to the peninsula in search of jobs and other opportunities, church services in the peninsula have also begun to be conducted in the national language too, to cater to these migrants.

The problem came to a head when the Ministry of Home Affairs in 2008 banned the *Bahasa Malaysia* version of the Catholic weekly "The Herald" for using the word "Allah" which belongs to the list of words proscribed for use by non-Islamic religions.[34] The newspaper responded by seeking a judicial review on the constitutionality of the government's decision. "We are asking the court to say the decision was wrong and quash it and declare that The Herald can use the word '*Allah*' in its publication", said Porres Royan, the newspaper's counsel.[35] "The Constitution says Malay is the national language so why can't we use the national language in Malaysia?", said Father Lawrence, the newspaper editor, clarifying why the Catholic Church was seeking judicial review of the government's decision.[36] "More than 50 per cent of our congregation are *Bumiputera* and two of our bishops are *Bumiputera*", he added.[37] In short, the newspaper's contention is that that Malay language is the national language as enshrined in the Constitution, and Christians (particularly those from Sabah and Sarawak) have the right to use the national language for religious purposes.

As a result, the church came before the judiciary in early 2008 seeking the right to challenge the decision of the Home Affairs Ministry. In April 2009, the High Court granted the church the right to challenge the government on this issue. Throughout this period, the newspaper continued publishing its Malay section using the word "Allah" when necessary. On 31 December 2009, the High Court ruled in favour of the church. The government immediately filed a notice to appeal the court's decision.[38]

Engaging in the Political Process: The 2008 General Election

Unlike the campaigning period of the nation's previous general election where the Christian community avoided making a visible presence in the run up to the elections, the 12th general election witnessed a markedly visible Christian presence and participation in the electoral process.

The first visible public presence of the community was a letter issued by the CFM to the community at large encouraging them to exercise their right to vote. The letter stressed that considerations should be given to questions such as the "future for you and the generations to come" and "the citizens' rights on freedom of religion, conscience and speech" among others when deciding which party to support.[39] The same message was reinforced by a pastoral letter issued by the Catholic Bishop of Penang, Antony Selvanayagam, through the official website of the Penang Diocese highlighting the same points raised in the CFM letter.[40]

In addition to sending out letters to the community at large, churches across the denomination divide also organized dialogue sessions between the candidates and church members as well as talks on electoral issues by noted Christian public figures in the run up to the 12th general elections. All these activities were well attended.[41] It should be emphasized that such sessions were scrupulously neutral with regard to campaigning for any particular political party. Instead, the sessions were meant to be educational, so as to help the Christian voters decide how to vote, and a chance for them to get to know the political parties and their candidates. In addition, certain pastors and priests began to discuss the significance of the upcoming election in their sermons and prayers (collectively and individually), exhorted their members to come out to vote, and to consider the issues that affected the body politic (which include the issue of freedom of religion).

For example, the evangelical Latter Rain Church of Malaysia, had as early as 2000, used the pulpit to teach members to consider political principles (from a Christian perspective), congregational prayer on political issues that affect the nation and approaching the Member of Parliament of their constituency (who happened to be a Christian) to give pastoral support and research input to issues which would be brought up to the Parliament for debate. During the run up to the 2008 election, "the church encouraged its members to exercise their right as voters on Election Day and also encouraged members who had not registered as voters to register with the Election Commission as soon as possible", said Mr Elijah Low, the Head of Operations of the Latter Rain Church of Malaysia.[42] The church also encouraged its members to consider issues like the candidate's integrity, party positions when considering whom to vote for.[43] "Some pastors were definitely more involved this time round through their messages in the pulpit by giving the congregations points to ponder on when they consider which party to support on election day", said Reverend Sivin Kit, pastor of the Bangsar Lutheran Church and social activist.[44]

Apart from churches mobilizing their members to participate in the upcoming elections, there were a few instances where individual members took the initiative to get their church involved. In one instance, Ms A, an Indian evangelical Christian in her early fifties, attempted to persuade the church leadership and members to exercise their rights as voters.[45] Ms A, in her capacity as a citizen, organized a "Get to know your MP" campaign in the Subang Jaya constituency. She also disseminated political news and information from the alternative media to her network of contacts apart from attending the political talks and forums that took place in the run up to the election. She also volunteered herself as a campaign staff for one of the political candidates contesting in the Kelana Jaya constituency.[46]

There have also been cases where the more partisan individual church members became volunteers for the candidate of the chosen political party in a given constituency.[47] "I know of cases of Christians, particularly those ages 25 to 35, who actively campaigned for political parties of their choice. Some became party members as well", said Reverend Sivin Kit.[48] "Some of us were more involved, in the sense, we volunteered ourselves ... my church members, at least one-fourth of us, as counting and polling agents for political parties even though we have no political affiliation. We did it because we felt the need to be involved in the electoral process", he continued. "Compared with the 2004 General Elections, Christians have definitely become more politically conscious and involved in the last elections. I was in a [Lutheran] pastors' prayer meeting where they talked about the elections and invited two politicians from the opposing sides to give their views on the elections. It was unheard of", said Reverend Sivin Kit. "I also helped to organize some forums on the elections in my personal capacity and not as a pastor", he added.

Engaging Civil Society

Christian engagement is not limited to the electoral process. It overflowed into civil society activities too. A significant involvement of the community was when individual Christians including members of the clergy participated in peaceful demonstrations on political issues such as electoral reform and the abolishment of the ISA.[49]

Another significant involvement of the community was the participation of Christians in candle light vigils in major urban centres of the country throughout 2008 demanding the repeal of the notorious ISA and the immediate release of ISA detainees.[50] An indication of the new involvement of the community in this protest were the special services and vigils held in certain churches for this purpose. Perhaps the most dramatic of these vigils was that conducted in the Cathedral of the Holy Spirit (Catholic) in Penang which was celebrated by half a dozen priests and attended by 800 people on 15 September 2008.[51] The Saint Francis Xavier church (Catholic) also held a vigil on the same day not only to protest the ISA but also demanding a release of one of their parishioners, Ms Teresa Kok a Member of Parliament, who was detained on 12 September 2008.[52]

As well, Christian participation also extended to the use of new media and the setting up of the new so-called research organizations outside the traditional institutional setting of the church. Among the earliest new research organizations was Kairos Research Centre which was formed in 1993 by a group of evangelical Christians. The objectives of Kairos are (i) to encourage and facilitate Christian research and scholarship on issues relevant to Malaysian Christianity and (ii) to contribute towards the intellectual development of Christian leaders and thinkers.[53]

Since its founding, Kairos has been involved in organizing forums on topics ranging from culture to politics and its implications for Malaysian Christians, the publication of its magazine "*Understanding the Modern World through Christian Eyes*" which covers social, political, and other issues of concern to the Christian community and other publications on topical issues that affect the community.[54] The other significant Christian research organization is the Oriental Hearts and Mind Institute (OHMSI). "OHMSI was founded in 2004 with the aim of engaging in the public sphere from a Christian perspective", said Dr K.J. John, the founder and director of OHMSI.[55] "OHMSI is independent of the institutional church support because we don't want to be tied down with the politics that comes with such support. Our funding comes from donations from individual Christians and pastors", he added.

Its stated aims are: (i) standing up for issues of public interest and articulating views on behalf of affected Malaysian communities; (ii) engaging communities to support or initiate action on specific issues relevant to them; and (iii) promoting scholarship and mentorship by developing and transforming worldviews.[56] Between 2005 and 2007, OHMSI organized the "National Congress on Integrity" which sought to engage Malaysian Christians on the issue of good governance.[57] Themes of past congresses included "Corruption", "Christian citizenship and Local Government", "The Concept of Integrity from the Islamic and Christian perspectives", and "Federal Accountability and Local Government". OHMSI have also organized public forums on the 2008 elections and political duties of a Christian.[58] "OHMSI also offer the Maxwell's Million Leaders Mandate program to young people in order to develop the next generation of leaders which the country will need. The program is not limited to Christians. It is open to anyone who wishes to become a leader in his own right", said Dr K.J. John. "OHMSI is a young setup and we are still in the midst of developing our organization and exploring ways in which we can fulfil our aims. Ultimately, the vision of OHMSI is to become a critical think-tank for Malaysian Christians with a global recognition", he added.

The spread of the Internet usage in Malaysia, particularly in the past five years, have enabled individual Christians to participate in the public sphere using this medium. In the past couple of years, there have been many websites and blogs created to comment on the nation's political and social situation. The contents in most of these websites and blogs are personal in nature and do not offer much in terms of critical analysis of the contemporary political and social issues compared with the website created by *Aliran* (a human rights non-governmental organization).[59] Most of the electronic sites do not last long in cyberspace as they usually fall quickly into disuse because of the neglect of its owners to update their websites and blogs.

However, one noteworthy exception is the website "The Micah Mandate" (TMM) created by a group of like-minded pastors and Christian activists.[60] The goal of TMM is to develop a "Christian-based public interest advocacy that seeks a transformation of our nation through justice, mercy and humility".[61] Since its founding in 2007, the website has offered commentaries on the political and social issues of the country from a Christian perspective.[62] One of the interesting ways in which the community seeks to engage civil society is through the "Malaysia National Prayer Network" (MNPN) project. The project was launched on 19 March 2008 by a group of Protestant church leaders aimed at mobilizing all believers, whether as individuals or as groups, to engage in prayer that "call upon God for revival of the Church and transformation of our nation".[63] One of its aims is "to mobilize prayer channels to communicate specific and urgent national issues that may arise from [sic] time to time". This project is noteworthy because for the first time church leaders are attempting to get Christians to use prayer on specific national issues as a corporate body.[64] Traditionally, corporate prayer activity, that is, prayer meetings, in the local churches is centred upon the needs of the church and its members while skirting around social and political issues of the day.

The MNPN, on the other hand, organizes corporate prayer, which calls attention to specific political and social issues of the day that Christians should pray over. The MNPN disseminates such prayer items through email to its list of contacts, on its website, and through its weekly prayer meetings in Kuala Lumpur and Petaling Jaya. The project is a step forward by the community in engaging civil society. It is a reminder to Christians that they are part of the larger society and should be concerned with national issues that affect society.

Certain local churches have also begun to initiate projects that seek to contribute to a mutual understanding between Christians and Muslims on each other's concerns and perspectives. In mid-June 2009, I attended a forum on interfaith dialogue hosted by a local church in Kuala Lumpur. This event was a rarity in itself because half of the audience was Muslims and the other half non-Muslims (and mostly Christians) in a church with two Muslims and a Christian engaging in a dialogue on how to live together in a society with diverse faith chaired by the church's pastor. The pastor later told me that the event was jointly organized by a Christian and Muslim organization which had approached him on the feasibility of his church hosting the event which he readily agreed. "I think this is one of those rare moments when you can find Muslims and non-Muslims sitting together and talking to each other in a church setting", he said.[65]

SHIFTING RESPONSES IN A DIVIDED COMMUNITY

The post-2008 general election situation has seen the community becoming more aware of the need for Christians to publicly engage civil society on pressing political and social issues. This is best reflected in the changing political perception among individual Christians across the denominational divide.

Consider the case of Mr B, a Chinese Catholic in his late twenties, who said that he was concerned with the impact of the government's Islamization policy on non-Muslims.[66] "Christians from all denominations should come together to discuss this issue and work out a plan on how the community should respond on this issue", he added. Ms P, a Chinese Catholic in her early thirties agreed. "The church is part of the larger community and cannot isolate itself. The church cannot take a backseat when there are cases of infringement of the right to freedom of religion in our society. The church cannot disassociate itself with what is happening in society. The church must take a stand on such cases", she said.[67]

Ms A, an Indian evangelical Christian in her mid-fifties, added "I am distressed with what is happening in our politics in the last few years. Issues such as the infringement on the non-Muslim religious right, corruption and public scandals have made me more politically aware that Christians must involve themselves in the political process. I don't mean joining political party or anything like that but becoming citizens who are willing to participate as voters and engaging civil society to bring about a more just society."⁶⁸

Mr Z, an Indian mainline Protestant in his mid-forties, added that:

> cases such as the right of Moorthy's widow to bury her husband according to the Hindu rites should have been respected. We are seeing an increasing infringement by the government on non-Muslims' religious rights. Christians need to politically engage the government to ensure our religious rights are not circumscribed.⁶⁹

Mr M, a Chinese evangelical church leader in his mid-fifties, summed up this changing political awareness among Christians when he said that "Christians cannot ignore politics because our political process allows it. More importantly, I think the church must play a role in developing political consciousness in order to make Christians better citizens."⁷⁰

Such awareness is not limited to the laity but also the clergy. "Many of the Lutheran pastors are from Perak. The recent Perak constitutional crisis really pushed a few of them off the edge … and they shared with me their concern with what is happening there even though they are based here now. Even our Bishop, who is from Perak, is concerned with the political situation in Perak", said Reverend Sivin Kit.⁷¹ "I became politically aware during the Moorthy case particularly with its implications for the right to freedom of religion in this country", he added.

Reverend Anthony Loke said:

> I do know of a couple of colleagues in my denomination who are concerned with the recent events [i.e., the government's infringement on the non-Muslim religious sphere]. As for myself, I became more politically aware in 2000 when I started to do some research on *Operasi Lalang* and the community's response towards that incident. Since then, I have taken an interest in the political events of the country, particularly those which have an impact on the community.⁷²

"The priest in the church, which I attend, is known for his strong views on the political situation in the country. He worked into his sermons and prayers political issues of the day", said Ms P.⁷³

Although there is a growing awareness among individual members of the community on the need to engage civil society and the political process, such awareness has not always been translated into action. "What I usually do is to email my circle of like-minded friends on news and issues that affect our community. I also attended some related public talks and seminars on issues of religious freedom", said Mr B. "As for me, I just follow the news of what is happening but I don't get involved in protests or related activities", said Mr Z.

Nonetheless, even among those who are committed to engagement, their responses vary. There are some who choose to participate in civil society or joining a political party. "I am upset with what is happening in the country. That is why I have participated in public rallies such as the anti-ISA vigils, BERSIH, Article XI. I am also a member of the *Saya Anak Bangsa Malaysia* movement. I believe that convictions alone are not enough. We must put them into action", said Ms A.[74] In a similar vein, Mr R, a Chinese evangelical in his mid-forties said, "I have joined the *Saya Anak Bangsa Malaysia* movement because I am concerned with the racial polarization that is happening today."[75]

"I choose to join a political party in the opposition because I am fed up not only with the government infringing upon the rights non-Islamic religions but also the general political situation where political scandals are abound", said Ms P.

Others choose to work within the community. "I'm against ISA. What I do is I talk about this issue not only in my classes but also in some churches. I also blog about why ISA should be abolished. Anyway, I also attended some anti-ISA candlelight vigils as a show of support on this issue", said Reverend Anthony Loke. "I see my task as that of an educator. Someone who helps Christians to think about issues that affect them. The greatest threat to the community is the *tidak apa* (apathy) attitude", he added. Of course, there are those who choose to engage both with civil society and within their own community such as Reverend Sivin Kit and Dr K.J. John as I have discussed earlier.

Everyone has not greeted the engagements of individual members of the community with unanimous support. Some consider such actions as contrary to the spirit of the church. The focus of the church, for these Christians, should be the realm of the sacred, and politics has no right to intrude into the sacred realm. "I don't think the church should involve itself in politics. If not, the church would find itself in a situation where it would not focus on spiritual concerns but worldly concerns", said Ms J, a Chinese evangelical Christian in her early thirties.[76] "I think the only way to resolve our social and political problems is when we learn to love one another", she added.

Ms C, a Chinese Catholic in her mid-fifties, agrees. "I don't think it is proper for any priest to bring up political issues during Sunday mass. Some people will think that this is wasting time. What people want is something spiritual. I don't like to go to a church where politics is discussed. This is not the venue for it", she said, "there are other avenues to talk about it [politics]. Sunday mass should only focus on our spiritual needs."[77]

"Not everyone in my church is comfortable with the sermons and prayer of our priest", said Ms P, "some have left for a church further down the road where the sermons and prayers leave out politics and social concerns."[78] Ms A added: "I work with a Christian organization but every time I talk about the political situation that is affecting our country, my colleagues will politely turn to other topics. They are not interested in politics."[79] Reverend Sivin Kit, who pastors the Bangsar Lutheran Church, admits that "not all members of my congregation are happy when I touch on the subject of politics in my sermons. A few of them have left the church."[80] "I would say that most pastors won't preach politics in their sermons. Generally in Malaysia, most pastors will stay away from politics. It is very rare for them to speak about it. Speaking for my denomination, we have not really taken on politics as an area of concern", said Reverend Anthony Loke.[81] "I think that this is partly because Christians have been taught that politics deals with the temporal while the church deals with the spiritual", he added.

CONCLUSION

The Christian community's changing response to the government's intrusion into their religious field is a reflection of the growing anxiety felt by the non-Muslim (and non-Malay) community over the government's policy of neutrality in the field non-Islamic religions. Ever since the implementation of the government's Islamization policy in the early 1980s, non-Muslims began to experience a growing restriction not only in their religious field but also increasingly in their everyday life.

The anxiety of non-Muslims reached its climax in late 2005 with cases such the Moorthy case and the forbidding of the use of certain religious words in the national language outside the Islamic context among others. Such cases have sparked a growing awareness among non-Muslims on the need to engage the government using the courts and public demonstration as a way of responding to the increasing infringement of the government in their religious field.

Although the Christian community's response to the government may have been initially motivated by the intrusion of the government into its religious field, nonetheless, there are some for whom engaging the government meant more than just ensuring that their religious field is not intruded upon. They are also motivated by the pressing political issues of the day, for example, strengthening democratic institutions and the increasing divide in society along racial lines. Nonetheless, at the institutional level, for example, the CFM, the Christian response has been limited to issues pertaining religious freedom. Unsurprisingly, much of CFM's energy have been devoted to building alliances with like-minded bodies in civil society, for example, the MCCBCHST, while not giving much attention to organizations that does not dovetail with its interest.

It should be noted that there is as yet no consensus within the community on how best to respond to the government's intrusion into the Christians' religious sphere. The community is still divided as to whether Christians should actively engage with the government. That said, it is also evident that parts of the Christian community have signalled that active engagement with the government must become a permanent part of their response to the government's intrusion into the non-Islamic religious sphere.

Notes

[1] Article 3(1) of the Federal Constitution stated "Islam is the Religion of the Federation".

[2] Article 11 of the Federal Constitution guarantees freedom of religion in the country. There is no provision in the Federal Constitution that obliges and empowers the government to involve itself in the non-Islamic religious sphere with the exception of 11(4) which states that "[s]tate law and in respect of the Federal Territories of Kuala Lumpur and Labuan, federal law may control or restrict the propagation of any religious doctrine or belief among persons professing the religion of Islam."

[3] Christians form 10 per cent of the Malaysian population. See Poline Bala in this volume for a discussion of the Christian community response in Sarawak.

[4] See Cheah (2002).

[5] Article 160(2) states that "Malay" means a person who professes the religion of Islam, habitually speaks the Malay language, and conforms to Malay customs.

[6] I am aware that the term "Islamic fundamentalism" is a contentious term which some have interpreted in a pejorative sense. However, in this chapter, fundamentalism simply means revisiting its "cumulative body of ritual,

behavior, and thought that reaches back to the time of origins" (Ruthven 2004, p. 15) as a response towards modernity.

7   See Nagata (1984), Chapter 3.
8   See Chong (2010). In Chapter 3, I gave a detailed account of the government's attempt at imposing surveillance and discipline among Muslims and the spillover to non-Muslims.
9   Reverend Dexter Low is the founder and CEO of the Latter Rain Church. The interview was conducted on 13 May 2009.
10 Although state governments have jurisdiction over land matters, the federal government may, for the purpose of uniformity of law and policy in all states, enact laws with respect to land matters as provided by the Federal Constitution, that is, Article 76(1)(b), with the exception of Sabah and Sarawak. The relevant law here is Town and Country Planning Act 1976. Basically, this law requires the relevant local authority to create a development plan that determines the use of land of a given area. If an area does not have land allocated for non-Muslim religious usage, then strictly speaking Christians cannot erect a church or use any building for religious purpose. Once a draft has been completed, it must be publicized to the public to garner feedback. It is during this stage that the Christian community can appeal to the local authority over its omission of allowing land to be used for non-Muslim religious purpose. Once the plan is finalized, no alteration is allowed. This law together with the arbitrariness of local authorities on matters relating to non-Islamic religions made it difficult for Christians to erect church buildings. For a more detailed discussion on this issue, see Kairos (2004), Chapter 3.
11 <http://www.divinemercyshahalam.com/history.htm> (accessed 10 October 2008).
12 The Malay words which non-Muslims are prohibited from using vary from state to state. Nonetheless, the words listed in the different enactments are: *Akhirat; Allah; Al-Quran/Quran; Al-Sunnah; Azan; Baitullah; Dakwah; Fatwa; Firman Allah; Fitrah; Hadith/Hadis; Haji/Haj; Hajjah; Hauliak; Ibadah/Ibadat; Imam; Injil; Kaabah; Kadi; Karamah/Qaramah; Khalifah; Khutbah; Masjid; Mubaligh; Mufti; Mussabaqah; Mussala; Nabi; Qiblat; Rasul; Salat/Solat; Sahadah/Syadah; Sheikh; Surau; Syariah; Tabligh; Ulama; Wahyu; Wali; Zakat.* Some Malay words are used by Christians, particularly the native Christians of Sabah and Sarawak, in their Malay language worship service. These words are Allah, *firman, iman, nabi, rasul, wahyu* (Kairos 2004, pp. 52–53).
13 Hong (2008).
14 Under the Printing Presses and Publications Act 1984, all forms of printed media must apply for an annual printing licence from the Ministry of Internal Affairs (now known as the Home Affairs Ministry).

15 "Christian Protest: Government Block 30 thousand Bibles in Malay", *Asia News*, 3 December 2011, available at <http://www.asianews.it/news-en/Christians-protest:-government-blocks-30-thousand-Bibles-in-Malay-21010.html> (accessed 20 January 2012).
16 See Chong (2010), Chapter 2 for an account of the Islamization policies during the Mahathir era.
17 See also Tan (2004); Riddell (2005); and Ng (2008).
18 See Ackerman and Lee (1990). Cf. Lee and Ackerman (1997). For a discussion on Hindu revivalism, see Ramanathan (1996) and Willford (2007).
19 See also Lim (2007).
20 He is also the Anglican Bishop of West Malaysia. The interview was conducted on 27 May 2009.
21 Interview with Bishop Ng Moon Hing on 27 May 2009. "CFM does not make much noise but we do make known our position to the government through press statements particularly our Merdeka Day message", said Mr Tan Kong Beng, the Executive Secretary of CFM, in an interview conducted on 10 November 2008.
22 Christian Federation of Malaysia, "Vote Wisely", 11 February 2008, available at <http://www.ccmalaysia.org/reports/20080211vote_wisely.htm> (accessed 5 October 2008).
23 Christian Federation of Malaysia, "Vote Wisely in 2008 General Election", 11 February 2008, available at <http://www.ccmalaysia.org/reports/CFM-vote_wisely_English_final.jpg> (accessed 5 October 2008).
24 The last two conferences that were held in 2005 and 2009 centred on the theme of Islamization and the Church's response. The objective of both conferences was to find a joint response by the community to the increasing infringement of the government in their religious affairs.
25 Interview with Mr Tan Kong Beng conducted on 10 November 2008.
26 Naturally, the CFM is the Christian representative in the council.
27 See also MCCBCHST (n.d.), *Unity Threatened by Continuing Infringements of Religious Freedom* for a list of non-Muslim grievances on the government's intrusion on their religious and private spheres. This document reiterates the MCCBCHST position on freedom of religion as proclaimed by the 1988 document produced above.
28 See <http://harmonymalaysia.wordpress.com/> on the organizational structure, aims and objectives, and press statements of the MCCBCHST.
29 In the aftermath of the Moorthy controversy as well as other non-Muslim grievances over their religious rights being overlooked by the government, nine non-Muslim cabinet ministers submitted a memorandum to the then Prime Minister Abdullah Badawi on January 2006. The memorandum called for the Prime Minister to protect the rights of religious minorities (see "Memo to PM", *The New Straits Times*, 20 April 2006). It was withdrawn a couple

of days later with the Prime Minister announcing that the matter have been resolved (see "Memo Withdrawn", *The Star*, 22 January 2006).

30   Apart from the Government of Malaysia, Hindraf also focused its grievances against the British government alleging that the former colonial master neglected the interest of the Hindu community when it granted independence to Malaya which resulted in the socio-economic deprivation which they suffered. Hindraf planned a mass rally to submit a memorandum to the British High Commissioner in Kuala Lumpur on 25 November 2007 to urge Queen Elizabeth II to appoint a Queen's counsel to argue for their case in a British court. In the days leading to the rally, the Malaysian police obtained a court order to stop the rally, set up roadblocks, and even arrested three leaders of Hindraf to prevent the rally from happening ("Facing Malaysia's Racial Issues", *Time Word*, 26 November 2007, available at <http://www.time.com/time/world/article/0,8599,1687973,00.html> (accessed on 15 June 2012).

31   For a more detailed discussion of Hindraf as a response to Islamization in Malaysia, see Arunajeet Kaur in this volume. For a discussion on the Buddhist response, see Tan Lee Ooi in this volume.

32   See Chong (2010) for a more detailed argument of the changing political dynamics in Malaysia.

33   See Chong (2010), Chapter 3.

34   "Malaysian Catholic Weekly in Allah Controversy Still Waiting on License Renewal", *Catholic News Agency*, 30 November 2008, available at <http://www.catholicnewsagency.com/new.php?n=14654> (accessed 6 March 2009).

35   "Malaysia's Catholic 'Herald' fights to Use 'Allah' in paper", *The China Post*, 26 April 2008, available at <http://www.chinapost.com.tw/asia/malaysia/2008/04/26/153686/Malaysia%27s-Catholic.htm> (accessed 12 July 2008).

36   "BM Edition of Catholic Paper Banned: Editor", *My sinchew*, 1 January 2009, available at <http://www.mysinchew.com/node/19712?tid=14> (accessed 1 June 2009).

37   "BM Edition of Catholic Paper Banned: Editor", *My sinchew*, 1 January 2009, available at <http://www.mysinchew.com/node/19712?tid=14> (accessed 1 June 2009).

38   See Debra Chong, "Four Reasons for Controversial Allah Ruling", *Religious Liberty Watch*, 31 December 2009, available at <http://libertysentinel.wordpress.com/2010/01/17/high-court-judgment-on-allah-controversy-home-minister-wrong-in-four-major-areas> (accessed 20 February 2012).

39   Christian Federation of Malaysia, "Vote Wisely in 2008 General Election", 11 February 2008, available at <http://www.ccmalaysia.org/reports/CFM-vote_wisely_English_final.jpg> (accessed 5 October 2008).

40   Anthony Selvanayagam, "Pastoral Letter: 2008 General Election", 17 February 2008, available at <http://www.penangdiocese.org/pages/the-bishop/messagesletters/pastoral-letter-on-the-election.php> (accessed 16 June 2009).

41 For example, the Oriental Heart and Mind Study Institute (a Christian organization) organized a talk on the upcoming election on 26 January 2008 at St. Paul's Church (Anglican). It was so well attended that they had to shift from a small seminar room slated for the talk to a larger hall to accommodate the size of the audience — the anecdote was related to me by a member of the church on 28 April 2009.
42 Interview with Mr Elijah Low conducted on 5 May 2009.
43 Interview with Mr Elijah Low conducted on 5 May 2009.
44 Interview with Reverend Sivin Kit conducted on 14 May 2009.
45 Interview with Ms A conducted on 19 March 2009.
46 Interview with Ms A conducted on 19 March 2009.
47 Interview with Mr L, a Christian who is a member of the Democratic Action Party, conducted on 8 November 2008.
48 Interview with Reverend Sivin Kit conducted on 14 May 2009.
49 "I think one reason which pushed Christians to be more involved in the political process prior to the March 8 elections was the *Bersih* rally where pastors and lay Christians participated in the public demonstration. I would have participated myself if not for some pressing business to attend to", said Reverend Sivin Kit in an interview conducted on 14 May 2009.
50 Interview with Mr Tan Kong Beng conducted on 10 November 2008.
51 For a reporting of the event see Anil Netto, "Catholic Cathedral in Penang Denounces ISA", 15 September 2008, available at <http://anilnetto.com/christianity/catholic-cathedral-in-penang-denounces-isa/> (accessed 10 March 2009).
52 "Catholics in Vigil for Detained Malaysian MP", *Catholic News*, 15 September 2008, available at <http://www.cathnews.com.au/article.aspx?aeid=9008> (accessed 10 August 2009).
53 Available at <http://www.cornerstone-msc.net/kairos/index.cfm> (accessed 10 August 2009). Kairos is funded by the same group of evangelical leaders — interview with Dr Ng Kam Weng, the Director of Kairos, 2 December 2008.
54 Available at <http://kairos-malaysia.org/index.cfm?menuid=62&parentid=9999> (accessed 10 August 2009).
55 Interview with Dr K.J. John conducted on 6 November 2008.
56 <http://www.ohmsi.net/index.cfm?menuid=3> (accessed 10 August 2009).
57 Interview with Dr K.J. John conducted on 6 November 2008.
58 <http://www.ohmsi.net/> (accessed 10 August 2009).
59 See <http://www.aliran.com> for a sample of their content. *Aliran* also publishes a monthly magazine entitled "*Aliran*".
60 See <http://www.themicahmandate.org/>.
61 <http://www.themicahmandate.org/about-us/> (accessed 12 August 2009).
62 In the "Allah" controversy, the website posted commentaries by leaders of the Christian community on why Christians have the right to use the word "Allah" in their religious services. For example, Pastor Eu Hong Seng's

"Why I Use Allah: A Layman's Perspective", *The Micah Mandate*, 21 January 2010, available at <http://www.themicahmandate.org/2010/01/why-i-use-allah-a-laymans-perspective/comment-page-1/#comment-495> (accessed 8 March 2010). Pastor Eu is the Senior Pastor of Full Gospel Tabernacle, Subang Jaya and the Chairman of the NECF.

63 Available at <http://www.prayer.net.my/index.cfm?menuid=9> (accessed 14 August 2009).
64 See <http://www.prayer.net.my/index.cfm?menuid=6> for a survey of the prayer items. It should be noted that the items are presented in a scrupulously neutral manner of presenting them as facts that required attention of Christians for prayer.
65 The conversation took place after the forum on 16 August 2009.
66 Interview with Mr B conducted on 6 August 2008.
67 Interview with Ms P conducted on 8 August 2008.
68 Interview with Ms A conducted on 19 March 2009.
69 Interview with Mr Z conducted on 15 December 2008.
70 Interview with Mr M conducted on 14 August 2008.
71 Interview with Reverend Sivin Kit conducted on 14 May 2009.
72 Reverend Anthony Loke pastors a church in Seremban, Negeri Sembilan, and is a lecturer in a seminary. The interview was conducted on 11 December 2008.
73 Interview with Ms P conducted on 8 August 2008.
74 Interview with Ms A conducted on 19 March 2009.
75 In a conversation which took place on 12 June 2009. *Saya Anak Bangsa Malaysia* movement advocates the concept of a *Bangsa Malaysia* (Malaysian nation) and the need to respect diversity in the country through its projects, available at <http://apps.facebook.com/causes/80669?recruiter_id=9041670> (accessed 13 August 2009).
76 Interview with Ms J conducted on 30 July 2008.
77 Interview with Ms C conducted on 8 August 2008.
78 Interview with Ms P conducted on 8 August 2008.
79 Interview with Ms A conducted on 19 March 2009.
80 Interview with Reverend Sivin Kit conducted on 14 May 2009.
81 Interview with Reverend Anthony Loke conducted on 12 November 2008.

References

Ackerman, Susan E. and Raymond L.M. Lee. *Heaven in Transition: Non-Muslim Religious Innovation and Ethnic Identity in Malaysia*. Kuala Lumpur: Forum, 1990.

Chandra Muzaffar. *Islamic Resurgence in Malaysia*. Petaling Jaya: Penerbit Fajar Bakti, 1987.

Cheah, Boon Kheng. *Malaysia: The Making of a Nation*. Singapore: Institute of Southeast Asian Studies, 2002.

Chew, Maureen K.C. IJ. *The Journey of the Catholic Church in Malaysia 1511–1996*. Kuala Lumpur: Catholic Research Centre, 2000.

Chong Eu Choong. "Modernity, State-led Islamisation and the non-Muslim Response: A Case Study of Christians in Peninsular Malaysia". Ph.D. thesis, School of Social Sciences, University Sains Malaysia, 2010.

Christian Federation of Malaysia. *Constitution of Persekutuan Kristian Malaysia (The Christian Federation of Malaysia)*, s.n.

Geertz, Clifford. "The Integrative Revolution: Primordial Sentiments and Civil Politics in the New States". In *The Interpretation of Cultures*, edited by C. Geertz. New York: Basic Books, 1973.

Hong, Carolyn. "Malaysia: Catholic Paper Can't Use 'Allah' After All", January 2008. Available at <http://www.asiamedia.ucla.edu/article.asp?parentid=84871> (accessed 8 February 2009).

Kairos. *Doing the Right Thing: A Practical Guide on Legal Matters for Churches in Malaysia*. Petaling Jaya: Kairos Research Centre Sdn. Bhd., 2004.

Kana, Maria P. "Christian Missions in Malaysia: Past Emphasis, Present Engagement and Future Possibilities". Master dissertation, School of Theology, Australian Catholic University, 2004.

Lee, Raymond M.L. and S.E. Ackerman. *Sacred Tensions: Modernity and Religious Transformation in Malaysia*. Columbia, SC: University of South Carolina Press, 1997.

Lim Heng Seng. "Religious Freedom after 50 Years of Merdeka". *Kairos Magazine*, September 2007, pp. 16–19.

Martinez, Patricia. "Mahathir, Islam, and the New Malay Dilemma". In *Mahathir Administration: Performance and Crisis in Governance*, edited by Khai Leong Ho and James Chin. Singapore: Times Media Private Ltd., 2003.

———. "Islam, Constitutional Democracy, and the Islamic State". In *Civil Society in Southeast Asia*, edited by Lee, H.G. Singapore: Institute of Southeast Asian Studies, 2004.

MCCBCHST. *Unity Threatened by Continuing Infringements of Religious Freedom*. Kuala Lumpur: MCCBCHST, n.d.

Nagata, Judith. *The Reflowering of Malaysian Islam: Modern Religious Radicals and Their Roots*. Vancouver, BC: University of British Columbia Press, 1984.

National Evangelical Christian Fellowship Malaysia (NECF). "Report on the State of Religious Liberty in Malaysia for the Year 2007". In *Religious Liberty after 50 Years of Independence*, edited by Samuel Ang, Lee Min Choon, and Lim Siew Fong. Petaling Jaya: NECF, 2008.

Ng Kam Weng. "Human Dignity and Religious Liberty". In *Religious Liberty after 50 Years of Independence*, edited by Samuel Ang, Lee Min Choon, and Lim Siew Foong. Petaling Jaya: NECF, 2008.

Ramanathan, K. "Hinduism in a Muslim State: The Case of Malaysia". *Asian Journal of Political Science* 4, no. 2 (1996): 42–60.

Riddell, Peter G. "Islamization, Civil Society, and Religious Minorities in Malaysia". In *Islam in Southeast Asia: Political, Social and Strategic Challenges for the 21st Century*, edited by K.S. Nathan and Mohammad Hashim Kamali. Singapore: Institute of Southeast Asian Studies, 2005.

Ruthven, Malise. *Fundamentalism: The Search for Meaning*. Oxford: Oxford University Press, 2004.

Shamsul, Amri Baharuddin. *From British to Bumiputera Rule: Local Politics and Rural Development in Peninsular Malaysia*. Singapore: Institute of Southeast Asian Studies, 1986.

———. "Identity Construction, Nation Formation, and Islamic Revivalism in Malaysia". In *Islam in An Era of Nation-States: Politics and Religious Renewal in Muslim Southeast Asia*, edited by R.W. Hefner and P. Horvatich. Honolulu: University of Hawai'i Press, 1997.

Suara Rakyat Malaysia. *Malaysia: Human Rights Report 2004*. Petaling Jaya: SUARAM Kommunikasi, 2005.

———. *Malaysia: Human Rights Report 2008*. Petaling Jaya: SUARAM Kommunikasi, 2009.

Tan, Paul S.J. *Alkitab and Related Subjects*. s.n., n.d.

———. *Islamization of Malaysian Laws*. No publisher, 2004.

Teoh, Bob. *Allah: More Than Just A Word*. Malaysia: Zomiky Media, 2010.

Walters, Albert S. *Knowing Our Neighbour: A Study of Islam for Christians in Malaysia*. Petaling Jaya: Council of Christian Churches Malaysia, 2007.

Willford, Andrew C. "The Modernist Vision from Below: Malaysian Hinduism and the 'Way of Prayers'". In *Spirited Politics: Religion and Public Life in Contemporary Southeast Asia*, edited by A.C. Willford and K.M. George. Ithaca: Cornell Southeast Asia Program, 2005.

———. "Cage of Freedom: Tamil Identity and the Ethnic Fetish in Malaysia". Singapore: National University of Singapore Press, 2007.

Online News Portals

Anil Netto. "Catholic Cathedral in Penang Denounces ISA", 15 September 2008. Available at <http://anilnetto.com/christianity/catholic-cathedral-in-penang-denounces-isa/> (accessed 10 March 2009).

Baradan Kuppusamy. "Facing Malaysia Racial Issues". *Time World*, 26 November 2007. Available at <http://www.time.com/time/world/article/0,8599,1687973,00.html> (accessed 15 June 2012).

"BM Edition of Catholic Paper Banned: Editor". *My Sinchew*, 1 January 2009. Available at <http://www.mysinchew.com/node/19712?tid=14> (accessed 1 June 2009).

"Catholics in Vigil for Detained Malaysian MP". *Catholic News*, 15 September 2008. Available at <http://www.cathnews.com.au/article.aspx?aeid=9008> (accessed 10 August 2009).

Chong, Debra. "Four Reasons for Controversial Allah Ruling". *Religious Liberty Watch*, 31 December 2009. Available at <http://libertysentinel.wordpress.com/2010/01/17/high-court-judgment-on-allah-controversy-home-minister-wrong-in-four-major-areas> (accessed 20 February 2012).

"Christian Protest: Government Block 30 Thousand Bibles in Malay". *Asia News*, 3 December 2011. Available at <http://www.asianews.it/news-en/Christians-protest:-government-blocks-30-thousand-Bibles-in-Malay-21010.html> (accessed 20 January 2012).

Eu Hong Seng. "Why I Use Allah: A Layman's Perspective". *The Micah Mandate*, 21 January 2010. Available at <http://www.themicahmandate.org/2010/01/why-i-use-allah-a-laymans-perspective/comment-page-1/#comment-495> (accessed 8 March 2010).

Hong, Carolyn. "Malaysia: Catholic Paper Can't Use 'Allah' After All". *Asia Media News Archive*, January 2008. Available at <http://www.asiamedia.ucla.edu/article.asp?parentid=84871> (accessed 8 February 2009).

"Malaysian Catholic Weekly in Allah Controversy still Waiting on License Renewal".*Catholic News Agency*, 30 November 2008. Available at <http://www.catholicnewsagency.com/new.php?n=14654> (accessed 6 March 2009).

"Malaysia's Catholic 'Herald' Fights to Use 'Allah' in Paper". *The China Post*, 26 April 2008. Available at <http://www.chinapost.com.tw/asia/malaysia/2008/04/26/153686/Malaysia%27s-Catholic.htm> (accessed 12 July 2008).

16

THE POLITICS OF BUDDHIST ORGANIZATIONS IN MALAYSIA

Tan Lee Ooi

INTRODUCTION

Attention to the link between Buddhism and politics has re-emerged with the shocking images of the persecution of the monks who led the *Saffron Revolution* in Myanmar. At the same time, terrorism, which has been associated with religion since the attacks of 9 November, has attracted intense academic research into the political roles played by various world religions. The study of political Buddhism is already a major focus in South and Southeast Asian studies. However, the study of political Buddhism has mostly centred on Buddhist majority states, such as Myanmar, Sri Lanka, Thailand, and Indochina. Undoubtedly, this broader context has created intense political activism and hence sparked vigorous theoretical conversations about Buddhism and politics. In Malaysia, the Buddhist minority faces the domination of another religious community — the Muslim majority. This chapter explores the Buddhist minority context in Malaysia to help fill the gap in political Buddhism studies of Buddhist minority states.

Islam is the most widely practised religion in Malaysia, and Malay Muslims are the dominant ethno-religious group in the country. In 2010, Muslims comprised 61.3 per cent of the total population. Buddhists, Christians, and Hindus comprised 19.8 per cent, 9.2 per cent, and 6.3 per cent of the total population, respectively. As of August 2007, there were 41,528 organizations registered with the Registry of Societies Malaysia.

Amongst the thirteen categories of organizations, the category of religion has the highest number of organizations: 7,228. According to the Registry of Societies' categorization system, the organizations in the religion category include Islam, Christianity, Buddhism, Hinduism, Sikhism, and Chinese Temple, among others. The registrar does not provide further breakdowns for these numbers by religion; however, according to estimations by the Malaysian Buddhist Association (MBA), the Buddhist group consists of 878 organizations, with 496 temples and 382 organizations.[1]

In 2010, nearly 83.6 per cent of Malaysian Chinese were listed as Buddhists, who are the largest minority religious group in the country. Malaysian Buddhists reflect the diversity present at the beginning of community formation. Various immigrant communities of Chinese, Thais, Burmese, and Sinhalese brought different Buddhist traditions, doctrines, and practices to Malaysia, and the current organizations that have evolved since the early years reflect this diversity of the Buddhist community. Buddhist groups are less centralized than Christian groups but more organized than Hindu groups. Christianity in Malaysia is divided into different denominations and independent churches, with a training system for professional religious administrators and clerics, and Christians have a more established national organization compared to Buddhists. The fragmentation of authority has shadowed the Buddhist community. Nevertheless, the effort to unite Buddhist groups has increasingly been strengthened through two major centralized organizations, the MBA and the Young Buddhist Association of Malaysia (YBAM). The former is for all Buddhist groups, and the latter is for Buddhist youth groups. Neither group is directly associated with any political party, as both groups assert themselves to be politically neutral.

The politics of Malaysian Buddhism are subtly articulated at the associational level without direct linkages to the existing political parties. Muslim political parties, such as Parti Islam Se-Malaysia (Islamic Party of Malaysia [PAS]), is an Islamist political party with the aim of establishing Malaysia as an Islamic state, and even the dominant ruling secular party, United Malays National Organization (UMNO) has an agenda of uplifting Islam. However, non-Muslim political parties have no religious agenda in their political struggle. None of the political parties has any direct aim of elevating and emphasizing the interests of Buddhism. Hence, Buddhist organizations have been playing their roles often in obscurity, resulting in a Malaysian political landscape with insufficient representation from the Buddhist community.

POLITICAL BUDDHISM IN THE MALAYSIAN CONTEXT

The political participation of Buddhists manifests itself in many forms globally. These include the enduring ethnic conflict of "Buddhism betrayed" in Sri Lanka (Grant 2009; Tambiah 1992; Wickremeratne 1995), the *Saffron Revolution* of "angry monks" in Burma (Smith 1965; U Maung Maung 1980), nationalist Buddhism in Tibet (Burman 1979; Schwartz 1994), "engaged Buddhism" in Vietnam (Topmiller 2002), and "political Buddhism" or "Dhammic socialism" in Thailand (Buddhadasa 1986; Jackson 1989; Smith 1978; Suksamran 1977, 1982). What can Malaysia's case offer to the understanding of the political participation of Buddhists?

Unlike in Buddhist-dominated societies, the contestation of the Buddhist community in the public sphere in a multi-religious society has its own complexities. There are contestations not only among Buddhists, but also between Buddhists and Muslims, as well as Taoists, Christians, Hindus, and Sikhs to a lesser extent. The minority context limits and cultivates the political behaviour of Malaysian Buddhists. The political setting of Islam as a state religion has a major impact on the political activism of Buddhists. These settings have provided an experience of political Buddhism, especially at the organizational level, that can be seen through the worldly actions of groups such as the YBAM and the MBA in the public sphere.

Under the setting of the minority context in a Muslim majority state, political Buddhism in Malaysia is a form of civil activism. The rules of the game have been framed by the setting of a modern nation-state. There is political space for the Buddhist community to engage with the state and other religious groups. The case of the Malaysian Buddhists provides a type of political Buddhism that may be termed "civil Buddhism". Both of the organizations studied here preach politics of peace in a Muslim majority state. Although the YBAM is more vocal and active in responding to state policies, it always accepts the final decision of the state. As a minority, the Buddhist organizations have voiced their discontent without a strong and confrontational political activism.

MALAYSIAN BUDDHIST ASSOCIATION (MBA)

The MBA's constitution clearly states, "MBA shall not take part in political activities, and its premises shall not be used for political purposes."[2] It also states that any member of the MBA, "shall be disqualified from membership if he/she participates in politics using the name of the MBA".[3]

However, in reality and practice, the MBA and its members are directly or indirectly connected with politics. The MBA's activities relate to politics in a variety of ways and forms, mostly involving collaboration and cooperation with the ruling coalition at different levels and dimensions. This organization generally rejects a "confrontational approach" in dealing with issues.

The MBA has played the politics of unity since its inception. It has 37 branches, 767 affiliate organizations, and 26,818 individual members throughout the country.[4] It aims to act as a Buddhist supreme body serving "mainly in uniting traditional Chinese temples and associations" (Sik 1992, p. 15). This orientation is paralleled with the political inclinations and trends in the Chinese community during the 1970s. At the beginning of its formation, the MBA took the discourse of unity as its major argument. In the early 1950s, before the MBA was established, Guang Yu, one of the founding members of the MBA, argued that Malaysian Buddhists were divided like "a heap of loose sand"[5] and that this had undermined the development of Malaysian Buddhism; thus, he urged the Buddhist organization to unite under the MBA (Shi 1985a, p. 34). On the 25th anniversary of the MBA, President Kim Beng claimed that Buddhism in Malaysia needed a main body to unite the Buddhist communities and that the MBA was the organization to fill the shortcoming (Shi 1985b, pp. 31–32).

MBA AND POLITICS

In the eyes of Buddhist communities, the MBA seems to have been withdrawn from politics. However, the MBA has been tainted by collaboration with ruling coalitions, especially the non-Muslim political parties Malaysian Chinese Association (MCA) and Gerakan. It has always maintained a good relationship with the ruling coalition. The making of friendly relations with local or national ruling parties is a political strategy adopted by the MBA and has allowed the organization to tackle issues affecting the Buddhist community. Over the years, the MBA has relied on three ways of offering gestures of friendship to the ruling party. First, political leaders were invited to official social events of the MBA to handle opening ceremonies or to deliver speeches. These events included anniversary celebrations, Buddhist festivals, opening of new buildings and commemorations. The establishment of the MBA in 1959, for example, was officiated by the first Prime Minister of Malaysia, Tunku Abdul Rahman. Second, political leaders in the ruling parties have served as advisers or committee members in the organization's National Council and sub-committees. Third, the

MBA's leader has shown willingness to receive honorary awards from the state ruler. The King conferred its second President, Kim Beng, with the award of A.M.N.[6] This action showed the close relationship of the MBA with the state and ruling power because the award candidate had to be recommended by an in-power ruling political leader.

There are at least three issues raised by the MBA. These comprised of three types of relations of the Buddhist community with the state, which are Buddhist-society relations, Buddhist-state relations, and Buddhist-society-state relations. The first includes protection of the image of Buddhism in various situations that involve relationships with other actors in society. The second includes an interpretation of the history and contemporary concerns of Buddhist rights that involve the state as the main actor. The third covers issues that involve Buddhist-society relations affected by the intervention of state machinery to resolve issues.

An issue involving Buddhist-society relations that has been taken seriously by the MBA is the "activities of bogus monks who are out to deceive the public".[7] The number of "bogus monks" who ask for donations at shopping complexes, hawker centres, and other crowded public spaces has been noticeable even at midnight. The Sangha identity has been used to collect money. In certain cases, after collecting money, the so-called bogus monks were discovered changing clothes, smoking, and drinking alcohol. Some have even been found to be married. The general public, especially the Chinese religious believers, cannot distinguish ordinary monks under the proper Buddhist order from the "bogus monks". This issue has consistently been raised by the MBA in order "to maintain and defend the dignity and credibility of Buddhism and the Buddhist Order", and it is a key mission that has been stated in its constitution since the formation of the MBA, with its cleric-oriented nature. To defend the image of Sangha, the MBA has decided to introduce an identification card system for Sangha members in the country to prove their respective identities. The MBA announced that under this policy, all registrations "will be forwarded to the Home Ministry and Police Department for reference", and that, further, those Sangha identity card holders "must strictly observe the precepts of the Sangha; failure to do so will result in the withdrawal of their IC after due consideration by the panel of senior Sangha members" and their "name will be revealed to the mass media".[8]

The MBA adopts a non-confrontational approach in Buddhist-state relations as well as on issues related to Buddhist rights. Usually, the MBA depends on community leaders who wish to seek public attention as a way of wielding political legitimacy. The MBA usually will initiate its own proposals by sending letters to relevant ministries. Efforts by the MBA in the interest of Buddhists included campaigns to declare Wesak Day as a national public holiday and efforts to correct the history of Buddhism in school textbooks.

The successful story of the MBA in demanding Wesak Day as a national public holiday has been highlighted as one of MBA's milestone contributions to Buddhism in Malaysia. The recognition of Wesak Day as a public holiday served as a symbol of acquiring an official status for Buddhism. This was accomplished through political connections with ruling leaders. A memorandum was drafted by the MBA in 1959. In 1960, Senator Cheah Seng Khim, who was also the Chairperson of the Penang Wesak Celebrations Committee, brought the appeal to a meeting of the Senate in Kuala Lumpur. In 1961, a Buddhist delegation met the Finance Minister, Tan Siew Sin, to seek support. The Minister "suggested that as many signatures as possible should be obtained from all Buddhist temples and/or organizations, prominent Buddhists and supporters for presentation to the Minister of Interior" (Lim 1985, pp. 54–57). One year later, the federal government declared Wesak Day as a public holiday. Evidently, the MBA had taken the approach of using personal and internal relationships to obtain official approval of Wesak Day as an official holiday.

Improving the history curriculum taught in national schools in the aspect of the history of religions is one of the MBA's political concerns. Before the arrival of Islam, Hinduism and Buddhism were part of the early history of small kingdoms in Peninsular Malaya. Official discourses arguing that Islam is the only religion inherited from the past in Malaysia have caused the sidelining of the early histories of other religions (Lim 2003). In 1979, the MBA urged that the Ministry of Education to review the history textbooks to incorporate an early century kingdom Langkasuka in the northern part of Malaya. The MBA also suggested that the history of the visit of a prominent monk, I-Ching from China, be included in the coverage of syllabus in school textbooks.[9]

In the Malaysian Buddhism Development Master Plan of 2002, the MBA proposed the formation of a Non-Muslim Affairs Commission.[10] Non-Muslim Ministers and NGOs have taken this suggestion seriously. In 2007, the Minister in Cabinet and the ex-President of the MCA, Ong Ka Ting, said that the cabinet had discussed the possibility of establishing a Non-Muslim Affairs Commission.[11] The Prime Minister had also reacted by saying that the government would sincerely consider the suggestion.[12] However, due to the pressure from Muslim groups, this commission has not materialized.

The MBA has an active role in protecting the image of Buddhism. In certain cases, it seeks the state intervention in solving problems. Sometimes, this way of inviting the state power to address issues related to the "image of Buddhism" has caused criticism from public intellectuals. During the group's early years in the 1960s, the MBA had "assisted the National Film Censorship Board to prevent the broadcast of films which taint the sanctity of Buddhism".[13] For example, in 1966, the MBA protested the screening of a film with the content of fake monks involved in criminal and sexual deviancy. The MBA even sent a memorandum to the Malaysian monarch, along with complaint letters to the Prime Minister, the Minister of Home Affairs, and the National Film Censorship Board. As a result, the National Film Censorship Board banned the film. This case clearly showed that the MBA has used state power to deal with its relations with society. Furthermore, the MBA has secured a representative position in the National Film Censorship Board.

In 2000, a sacred Buddhist mantra — The Great Compassion Mantra — was remixed with rock music and used by nightclubs as music for the purpose of consuming *ecstasy* in the southern part of the Malaysian Peninsula, Johor Bahru. The President of the MBA, Chek Huang, told the press that the protest would be taken to nightclub owners and legal action would follow if there was no immediate response. The MBA also wrote a complaint letter to the Ministry of Home Affairs. Consequently, the Ministry issued a formal ban of the public broadcasting of mantras in rock music.[14] The local authority also took action against the nightclubs.

For issues that will affect other religions and directly confront the ruling regime, the MBA prefers to settle concerns with the involvement of a "symbolic representation" of a non-Muslim organization, known as the Malaysian Consultative Council of Buddhism, Christianity, Hinduism, Sikhism and Taoism (MCCBCHST). This inter-religious council officially was formed in 1983. It was the outcome of "non-Muslim efforts to face the perceived threat of Islamic expansionism" (Lee and Ackerman 1997, p. 23). The president's post in the MCCBCHST is rotated every two years among representatives of the five largest religions. In MCCBCHST, the MBA can take a stronger political stand in voicing religious matters and grievances. Issues such as religious education for Buddhists, the amendment of Islamic laws that affect Buddhists, restrictions on places of worship, the lack of burial grounds, and the control of the free practice and propagation of Buddhism have been continuously channelled to the state authority through MCCBCHST. "Non-Muslims perceive [Islamic laws] as instruments of government policy to limit their resources and block their growth" (Lee 1988, pp. 400–18).

In recent years, court cases have politicized the religious communities, and this was especially evident in the general election of 2008. MCCBCHST took the opportunity of the national polling to call voters to "cast their vote wisely without fear and favour according to their conscience".[15] One of the critical issues was that "the constitutional guarantees of religious freedom have been badly infringed upon over the years and in recent times". It emphasized that the "assurances by the authorities must be demonstrated by actual implementation" because "no religious community should be subjected or forced to conform to the religious rules of another religion".[16] In contrast to the past elections, in which the MCCBCHST normally stood apart from political campaigning, the election in 2008 marked the history of open political engagement of the non-Muslim organization, with involvement of the MBA.

YOUNG BUDDHIST ASSOCIATION OF MALAYSIA (YBAM)

There have been several attempts by Buddhist youths to form a platform since the 1950s, but these efforts have failed. Nevertheless, the YBAM has succeeded to institutionalize a Buddhist youth movement and continued the mission. The YBAM was formed by a group of Buddhist graduates in 1970. With its stated first objective, "to be the national organization of all Buddhist youths in Malaysia",[17] this national body was able to represent Buddhist youths and spread across different educational backgrounds, languages, ethnic groups, and traditions of Buddhism. Although during a few terms the YBAM National Council was led by monks, it is a lay-oriented and lay-dominated organization in terms of its executive committee members, affiliate organization members, and group-targeted activities. Most of the former presidents were laymen.

The Puzhao Buddhist Vihara Controversy

The origins of the episode involving the controversial construction of the Puzhao Buddhist Vihara began with a one-storey old wooden temple owned by an eighty-seven-year-old lady named Lim Hong in Kluang, Johor. Lim donated the old temple in 1986 and the landowner agreed to release a seven-acre tract of land to the YBAM. A Puzhao Buddhist Vihara Planning Committee was formed to take charge of planning the construction to develop a multi-purpose Buddhist training, education, research, and cultivation centre. The YBAM appointed the Venerable Sik Chi Chern as the temple abbot. The construction was to cost RM10 million. The first phase, which was estimated to cost RM2 million, was expected to have been completed in March 1992.[18] The endowment from the Buddhist community exceeded the target, and RM2.6 million was collected, but trouble came before the construction could be completed.

Although most of the time the YBAM had insisted on a neutral stance in political participation, the visible hand of politics directly halted the Puzhao Buddhist Vihara project. The construction of the Puzhao Vihara was suspended without direct clarification from the committee because, as the committee noted, "YBAM is keeping a low profile in handling the suspension ... in view of sensitivity of a multi-religions society and to take care of the feelings of all parties. At the same time, it was because some of the decisions were listed as official secrets, which could not be announced to the public."[19]

The project was approved by North Kluang District Council on 26 November 1990 and gazetted on 25 April 1991. The construction of the project officially started on 28 May 1991, which was also Wesak Day. The Puzhao Vihara proposed site was near to a *Surau*, which was built by the Agricultural Department. The old wooden temple was built earlier than *Surau*, but it was nonetheless brought up as an issue by UMNO youth because the Johor Security Council's regulation does not allow "any other religious premises to be built within 1.5 km of the *Surau*".[20] Midway through the construction, the UMNO youth, together with villagers, protested the building of Puzhao Vihara, resulting predictably in raising racial tensions (Goh 1993, p. 39).

Several arrangements were made to save the project. These included a dialogue with local residents organized by members of Parliament from the ruling party. In a dialogue with the Chief Minister, a member of the Johor Security Council warned that "burning the Puzhao Vihara would solve the problem easily" (Goh 1993, p. 41). The ex-deputy president of the YBAM, Ang Choo Hong, "received a bullet as a threat to his life"[21] on the same day. Before 13 May 1992, rumours of a demonstration were spreading in the area, and leaflets protesting the building of a Buddhist temple in the Muslim area were distributed. On 13 May 1992, "more than 100 policemen surrounded Puzhao Vihara in case there was any demonstration".[22] At the end of 1992, the District Council ordered a stop to the construction work. The YBAM initially refused to halt before finally succumbing "under the request from District Officer for the sake of overall public interest".[23] The construction was only completed up to the third level.

The attempts to recommence the construction did not stop there. Several meetings with the ruling party's members and another dialogue with the Chief Minister were organized. The YBAM was "negotiating with all means", but "the difficulties and miseries that YBAM encountered could not be explained" easily.[24] In 1993, the State Security Council imposed eleven conditions for the resumption of construction, and the YBAM was "working hard days and nights to strive for better and less restrictive conditions for resumption".[25] In a press statement in 1994, the YBAM stated that "for the sake of overall public interest and to resume construction as soon as possible, we [YBAM] decided to accept MCA's advice to act according to the solution procedures".[26] In fact, the YBAM had strong political associations at that moment such as with the ex-Chief Minister of Penang, Koh Tsu Koon, who was its advisor. The latter's low-profile way of handling the issue did not achieve the desired end.

Before the tenth general election in 2004, the Kluang District Council brought good news of the possible approval, only for the project to be delayed again in a series of events creating much anguish and despair for the Buddhist youth. Given their experience of unfulfilled promises, the Buddhist community placed little hope on the likelihood of the project ever making a recovery. Surprisingly, before the twelfth general election, in January 2008, the construction of the temple was suddenly approved with a caveat that it had to comply with nine conditions. The Buddhist community considered two of the conditions to be "unfair" and "illogical". First, no religious activities were to be allowed in the temple. Second, Buddhist statues were prohibited as part of the design around the compound area of the Puzhao Buddhist Vihara.

In YBAM online discussion forums, the outbursts and angst of Buddhist youths were palpable. A posting by an anonymous participant using the nickname "Yahui" held that "the 16 years struggle of Puzhao Buddhist Vihara is the most important history in Malaysian Buddhism, and Buddhists should know this history".[27] Another posting on the eve of election day advised the Buddhist voters to "vote wisely".[28] A monk quoted a section on religious freedom in the Federal Constitution to argue that Puzhao Buddhist Vihara's restoration conditions were violating constitutional assurances.

During the national general election campaigning period, seminars on religious freedom were organized by the YBAM in accordance with this "illogical" regulation to restrict the restoration of the project. Criticism of the ruling party via mobile phone messaging over this issue spread among the Buddhist community a few days before the election.[29] The signs of anger among Buddhists were also shown in the political materials created and distributed through the social media. For example, a video on YouTube on a Buddhist temple demolition was circulated multiple times through email during the general election.[30] A poster titled "Buddhist Vote for Change" used the *Saffron Revolution* of the Burmese monks as a background and urged Buddhists to reject the hegemony of the National Coalition. This poster was spread via email.

Puzhao Vihara has served as a "grand vision" for the Buddhist youth movement. It is not only a usual temple for religious functions but also "a training centre for Buddhist teachers, professionals and researchers, which includes the Sangha and the laymen". It offers a means "to promote the Buddhist academic research and to further enhance the connections with other local and foreign Buddhist research centres or colleges".[31] The materialization of this grand vision will be a crucial milestone for the YBAM in promoting Buddhism in Malaysia. Unfortunately, politicians racialized the issue through the power of Islamic influence in the district administration. As a result, Malaysian Buddhist youth have experienced the frustration and defeat of their "grand vision". In the YBAM 11th Biennial National Convention in December 1992, two resolutions related to the issue expressed this frustration:

> to urge all the political parties to act with responsibility and uphold the interest of the people, especially by refraining from politicizing religious issues that bring about misunderstanding and fear among the followers of various religions; and to oppose any attempt by any one religion to impose its religion ideals on the followers of other religions.[32]

The Puzhao Vihara issue was not merely a disappointment for the YBAM in terms of the contestation for physical space, but it also symbolized the subordination of a Buddhist religious cosmological order in a Muslim majority state. It created a remarkable Buddhist resurgence yet a painful memory which aroused and politicized youths as well as nation-wide sentiments in the Buddhist community.

YBAM'S RESPONSE TO ISLAMIZATION

First Period: 1970s to the Late 1980s

In the early establishment period of the 1970s and 1980s, the YBAM had been silent on most Islamization policies implemented by the UMNO. It had not actively engaged in debates on the policies, such as the Islamization of the judiciary system and public policy. However, the YBAM did concern itself with some issues related to religious freedom.

One major issue during the 1980s involved the religious influence on non-Muslim students in school. Non-Muslim parents were particularly sensitive to the introduction of Islamic rituals in national schools. The "religious trivialities in demarcating the new boundaries of Islam" (Lee 1988, p. 403) have been seen in public education institutions in programmes involving dress, diet, and course syllabus school prayers and the like. Compared to other civil groups, the YBAM was not vocal in expressing the unease of non-Muslim parents regarding these programmes. However, in 1983, the YBAM opposed the introduction of Islamic common prayers as compulsory for all students in secondary school. After a meeting with the Deputy Minister of Education, "the common prayers were not instituted" (Yeap 1987, p. 29).

Second Period: The Late 1980s to the Late 1990s

The YBAM was passive regarding the Islamization of government machinery until the intensification of the Islamic State debate occurred when the opposition Islamic political party recaptured the state of Kelantan in 1990. After regaining the Kelantan state government, the PAS tried to implement Islamic penal code, *Hudud* laws. The PAS set up a committee led by the party's Deputy President, Abdul Hadi Awang, to introduce *Hudud* laws. The proposal of *Hudud* laws was submitted to the Kelantan State Legislature but ultimately failed because the motion was contradicted the Federal Constitution. Article 75 of the Federal Constitution states that any state law that is inconsistent with a federal law should be voided.[33] This Islamic State motion of PAS in the early 1990s alarmed the non-Muslim communities.

During the 11th YBAM Biennial National Convention in 1992, a special resolution on the objection to an Islamic law was endorsed by the Convention. It raised the concern that the YBAM should play a greater role "to actively resist proposals to amend the Federal Constitution with the intention of introducing the Islamic Criminal Law in the country".[34] When the debate between PAS and UMNO on Islamic Law escalated during the 1990s, the President of the YBAM, Sik Chi Chern, expressed the anxiety of non-Muslims in a commentary (Sik 1994, p. 2). Since then, the issue of the implementation of Islamic law by PAS in Kelantan has become a continuing political concern of the YBAM.

Third Period: Politicization since the Late 1990s

The political reform movement *Reformasi* influenced, activated, and politicized the civil society groups in the country when the national political crisis started with the sacking of Anwar Ibrahim as Deputy Prime Minister and Finance Minister in 1998. However, the YBAM appeared to be passive. In the YBAM's Fourth Six-Year Plan (1998–2003), the element of political affairs was downplayed again because the YBAM was more focused on issues related to religion, especially the Islamization policies that might directly affect the rights of the Buddhist community. Islamic politics were manipulated by both the opposition and ruling parties with the escalation of the contestation that started during the late 1990s.

The Islamic state debate took centre stage when ex-Prime Minister Mahathir proclaimed Malaysia an Islamic state on 29 September 2001. PAS had criticized the administration of the ruling coalition, especially UMNO, as being "an un-Islamic party plagued with rampant corruption and progenitors of unjust authoritarian security laws" (Liow 2004, p. 194). The debate was prolonged even after the new Premier, Abdullah Badawi, took power. Badawi, emphasizing his own Islamic credentials, responded to this political contestation with the introduction of the concept of *Islam Hadhari*. By the beginning of the 2004 general election, to counter UMNO's challenge, PAS published a "monumental document" on how to establish an Islamic state, which itself generated more controversy and criticism.[35] The contestation on the status of Malaysia as an Islamic state between UMNO and PAS served to reawaken the YBAM.

In the Fifth Six-Year Plan (2004–10) of the YBAM, two specific roles were outlined. First, the YBAM intended "to strive for Buddhist rights" in terms of securing government funding and other rights.[36] Second, it planned "to express Buddhists' views on current affairs and contemporary issues" through forums or seminars and to establish a Current Affairs Buddhist Commentary Group and Response Team to take immediate action against negative incidents.[37]

Previously, the YBAM had been actively responding to the attempt by PAS to establish an Islamic state. After the announcement that Malaysia was already an Islamic state, the YBAM became more aware of the unseen yet influential hand of the Islamization process, which it had ignored for so long. In fact, UMNO achieved far-reaching power because of its institutional and bureaucratization of Islam, "where tensions between forces of moderation and fundamentalism have in fact become internalized in the ruling regime" and "Islam moved from the fringe to the political mainstream" (Liow 2004, p. 199). In response to the Islamic state declaration by the ruling party, the YBAM issued a press statement as a form of protest.

In addition, the new tension between Civil Law and *Syariah* Law in the judiciary system served to further sharpen the degree of alertness. This policy involves legal jurisdictions for contesting interpretations of law between Muslims and non-Muslims. Tension resulted from a series of ongoing controversial court cases. The cases were highlighted by the media and served to reinforce Muslim and non-Muslim boundaries at the communal level. The issue has become one of the inescapable concerns that the YBAM has had to confront. Interestingly, the 17th YBAM Biennial National Convention's theme was *Becoming a Learning and Socially Engaged Organisation for Fulfilling Our Contemporary Commitments*. This departed from previous themes, which revolved around the duty of Buddhism propagation. The convention's presidential speech highlighted the issue of religious freedom:

> YBAM is against all forms of an Islamic state. The ground for objection to the declaration of Malaysia as an Islamic state is the social contract made by our forefathers, which has clearly been enshrined in the Federal Constitution: Malaysia is a secular state. (Goh 2004, p. 29)

YBAM's attention towards politics has been largely triggered by the political developments, and the President of the YBAM in the 2004 Convention opined that: "politics affect every aspect of living including the development of Buddhism in the society. Buddhists and Buddhist organizations should be concerned regarding political developments and vote for a government that upholds freedom of religion. Cherishing the vow of the Buddhisatta, 'not tolerating the decline of the Buddha Dharma and not tolerating the suffering of sentient beings'"[38] (Goh 2004, p. 29). However, he insisted that they "should be neutral in [their] political stand" (ibid.).

COMPARISON OF THE YBAM AND THE MBA

Table 16.1 shows the different political behaviours of the YBAM and the MBA in terms of actors, tactics, issues, and levels of involvement. The nature of the YBAM as a lay-dominated civil organization has contributed to its more active initiative in responding to state policies. In contrast, the cleric-dominated MBA has intentionally conveyed a passive and cooperative approach in responding to discontent over public policy.

Both organizations have articulated the concerns of Buddhists with the same aim, but through different means and modes of communication with the ruling power. They have adjusted their ways of interaction according to the expectation of the public and with an eye towards the ruling coalition. Indeed, both have provided the basis for mutually facilitated lobbying in the greater interest of Buddhist communities in Malaysia. With the constraints and limitations of their minority context, they have played their various roles and acted as important players in the religious sector of civil society of Malaysia.

Table 16.1
Comparison of Political Behaviour between YBAM and MBA

	YBAM	MBA
Political actors	Lay-dominated	Cleric-dominated
Political tactics	Lobbying and protests	More inclined towards cooperation
Political issues	Responds to state policies	Responds to issues on Buddhism (but through MCCBCHST when opposing state policies)
Level of political involvement	More active	More passive

CONCLUSION

Prior to the YBAM's 18th Biennial National Convention, a seminar with the theme "Non-Muslims' Rights in Malaysia" was held. The President of the YBAM reiterated that the movement should be proactive and continue to improve to build a mature and liberal society because the shortcomings of democracy coupled with racial and religious political rivalry have created obstacles to the development of Malaysian Buddhism. He stressed that all possible checks and balance mechanisms should be brought into play to stop developments detrimental to Malaysian Buddhism.[39] Of the five resolutions accepted in the convention, two were related to this new politics. In Resolution 2, the YBAM urged "the government, the judiciary and the parliament to uphold the supremacy of the Federal Constitution to ensure the basic human rights of all religious followers are safeguarded".[40] Also, Resolution 3 was "concerned with the predicament faced by converts to Islam and their non-Muslim family members". The YBAM called for "Buddhists to be fully aware of the implications of conversion to Islam and their legal rights and their non-Muslim family members".[41]

Majority-dominated groups occasionally impose their religious privilege on other religious groups. The contestation of different religious groups has triggered tension that has been directly intensified by public policy-makers who do not appear to be neutral because of conflicts of interest. The YBAM constantly defends and insists on the secular nature of the state because a secular state is the only way to safeguard the Buddhists' fundamental civil rights as citizens. Liow (2009) has argued that the game of "piety-trumping" would be very difficult to reverse with dire consequences not only for the ethnic minorities of Malaysia but also for their democratic system as a whole. Political Buddhism in Malaysia will continue responding through its different actors engaging with the Muslim majority.

The Buddhist minority context provides a form of civil Buddhist expression in a Muslim majority state. Political context, circumstances and religious demography have affected the kinds of orientations that political Buddhism has taken, Malaysia being a rather interesting and unique case in point. The multi-religious and diverse nature of political Buddhism has brought about the complexity of civil Buddhist expressions. In the Malaysian context, given the complexity of dealing with the religio-political public sphere, civil Buddhism is involved in interactions not only between religious and secular citizens but also among citizens with different religions. Political Buddhism is an important analytical concept, which has to be further theorized for the better understanding of the tensions and conflicts that occur in Buddhist majority and minority regions. This study of the Buddhist minority in a Muslim majority state can hopefully contribute to the ongoing debate of political Buddhism.

Notes

1. MBA, "Affiliate Organisations", available at <http://www.mba.net.my/public_html/Chi/MainFrame-SubOrganisation.htm> (accessed 8 May 2009).
2. "The Malaysian Buddhist Constitution (Revised in 2001)", available at <http://www.mba.net.my/public_html/Chi/MainFrame-Constitution.htm> (accessed 8 May 2009).
3. Ibid.
4. "Introduction to MBA", available at <http://www.mba.net.my/public_html/Chi/MainFrame-%20BriefIntro.htm> and "Member Organizations", available at <http://www.mba.net.my/public_html/Chi/MainFrame-SubOrganisation.htm> (accessed 6 June 2009).
5. Yipan Sansha. This is a popular idiom in Chinese language to describe the lack of unity and cooperation.
6. *Ahli Mangku Negara* (Member of the Order of the Defender of the Realm) is a fifth rank award.
7. "Issue[s] Raised", available at <http://www.mba.net.my/public_html/Chi/MainFrame-MBAArchives.htm> (accessed 11 June 2009).
8. "Sangha's IC", available at <http://www.malaysianbuddhistassociation.org.my> (accessed 12 June 2009).
9. "Xiuding Gaozhong Lishi Kecheng Gangyao" [Review of the Content of Higher Secondary School Textbooks], available at <http://www.mba.net.my/public_html/Chi/MainFrame-%20BriefIntro.htm> (accessed 16 June 2009).
10. "Dierzhang: Duizhengfu De Qiwang" [Second Chapter: Expectations toward Government], available at <http://www.mba.net.my/MyBuddhism/MasterPlan/MPMain02.htm> (accessed 16 June 2009).
11. "Huangjiading: Bizaiwai Hanhua Fangshi Youxiaoshe Feihuijiaotu Shiwulihui Shishihou" [Ong Ka Ting: Better than Discuss Outside, Forming of the Non-Muslim Affairs Commission More Effective], *Sin Chew Daily*, 19 December 2007.
12. "Yadoula: Kaolv Feizhengfu Zhuzhi Jianyi Nishe Feihuijiaotu Shiwu Lihui" [Abdullah: Consider NGO's Suggestion on Non-Muslim Affairs Commission], *Sin Chew Daily*, 19 December 2007.
13. "Issue[s] Raised", op. cit.

14 "Fojiao Jingwen Dabeizhou Beigaibian Chengwei Yaotou Yinyue" [Buddhism Mantra *Nīlakaṇṭha Dhāraṇī* Became Music for *Ecstasy*], available at <http://www.mba.net.my/public_html/Chi/MainFrame-%20BriefIntro.htm> (accessed 23 June 2009).
15 "MCCBCHST Calls for Prayers as the Nation Goes to the Polls", available at <http://www.bangkit.net/2008/02/21/mccbchst-calls-for-prayers-as-the-nation-goes-to-the-polls> (accessed 1 July 2009).
16 Ibid.
17 YBAM, "Introduction", available at <http://www.ybam.org.my/cms/zuzhijiagou/mafoqing/526.html> (accessed 9 May 2009).
18 Yeoh Kia Gee, "Puzhao Buddhist Vihara: The Buddhist Research and Retreat Centre of YBAM", *Berita YBAM* 67 (August 1991): 2.
19 YBAM, "To Dear Devotees", *Berita YBAM* 74 (June 1994): 12.
20 Ibid., p. 13.
21 Before the meeting to settle the problem, State Exco Lau Boon Hong, Member of Parliament Kang Chow Oh, senator Syed Hamid and the District Officer Haji Johari also received bullets as death threats (Goh Tuan Huee 1993, p. 42).
22 YBAM, *Berita YBAM* 74 (June 1994): 13.
23 Ibid.
24 Ibid.
25 Ibid.
26 Ibid., p. 14.
27 YBAM Forum, available at <http://www.ybam.org.my/forum/viewtopic.php?t=502&postdays=0&postorder=asc&start=0> (accessed 10 September 2009).
28 YBAM Forum, available at <http://www.ybam.org.my/forum/viewtopic.php?t=502&postdays=0&postorder=asc&start=45> (accessed 10 September 2009).
29 "Hoo Seong Chang: Duanxun Bushi, Puzhasi Chetu Meiwenti" [Hoo Seong Chang: Wrong SMS, Puzhao Vihara's Building Plan No Problem], *Sin Chew Daily*, 7 March 2008.
30 "Destroy temple", available at <http://www.youtube.com/watch?v=j8o12E7ejlY> (accessed 9 October 2009).
31 *The Third YBAM Six-Year Plan (1993–1998)*, pp. 129–30.
32 "Resolution Committee Report", *Berita YBAM* 70 (December 1992): 14.
33 Constitution of Malaysia, "Part VI — Relations Between the Federation and the States, Chapter 1 — Distribution of Legislative Powers", available at <http://www.helplinelaw.com/law/constitution/malaysia/malaysia06.php> (accessed 27 May 2009).
34 "Resolution Committee Report", *Berita YBAM* 70 (December 1992): 14.
35 PAS, *Islamic State Document*, available at <http://www.parti-pas.org/IslamicStateDocument.php> (accessed 28 May 2009).
36 *The YBAM 5th Six-year Plan (2004–2010)*, p. 2.
37 Ibid., p. 4.

38 Buren Shengjiao Shuai, Buren Zhongsheng Ku.
39 "The 18th YBAM Biennial National Convention", *Berita YBAM* 116 (December 2007): 32 and 35.
40 "Resolutions", *Berita YBAM* 116 (December 2007): 37.
41 Ibid., pp. 37–38.

References

Buddhadasa, Bhikkhu. *Dhammic Socialism*, translated and edited by Donald K. Swearer. Bangkok: Thai Inter-religious Commision for Development, 1986.
Burman, Bina R. *Religion and Politics in Tibet*. New Delhi: Vikas, 1979.
Goh Tay Hock. "President Speech". *Berita YBAM* 111 (2004): 29.
Goh Tuan Huee. *Puzhaosi Fengbo Ji* [*The Conflict of Puzhao Vihara*]. Batu Pahat: Perusahaan Emas Jaya, 1993.
Grant, Patrick. *Buddhism and Ethnic Conflict in Sri Lanka*. Albany, NY: SUNY Press, 2009.
Jackson, Peter A. *Buddhism, Legitimation, and Conflict: The Political Functions of Urban Thai Buddhism*. Singapore: Institute of Southeast Asian Studies, 1989.
Lee, Raymond L.M. "Patterns of Religious Tension in Malaysia". *Asian Survey* 28, no. 4 (1988): 400–18.
Lee, Raymond L.M. and Susan A. Ackerman. *Sacred Tensions: Modernity and Religious Transformation in Malaysia*. Columbia: University of South Carolina, 1997.
Lim Kit Siang. "Half of Form IV history subject is now on Islamic history as compared to one-sixth in the textbook used for over a decade — a consequence of the '929 Declaration' that Malaysia is an Islamic State and indication of more Islamisation to come", 2003. Available at <http://dapmalaysia.org/allarchive/English/2003/aug03/lks/lks2558.htm> (accessed 1 June 2013).
Lim Teong Aik. "Weisaijie Gonggong Jiaqi" [Wesak Public Holiday]. In *25th Anniversary: Malaysian Buddhist Association, 1959–1984*, by Malaysian Buddhist Association. Penang: MBA, 1985.
Liow, Joseph Chinyong. "Political Islam in Malaysia: Problematising Discourse and Practice in the UMNO–PAS 'Islamisation Race'". *Commonwealth and Comparative Politics* 42, no. 2 (2004): 184–205.
———. *Piety and Politics: Islamism in Contemporary Malaysia*. New York: Oxford University Press, 2009.
Malaysian Buddhist Association. *25th Anniversary: Malaysian Buddhist Association, 1959–1984*. Penang: MBA, 1985.
Schwartz, Ronald D. *Circle of Protest: Political Ritual in the Tibetan Uprising*. London: Hurst and Co., 1994.

Shi Guang Yu. "Malaiya Fojiaohui Chengli Qianhou" [The Establishment of Malayan Buddhist Association]. In *25th Anniversary: Malaysian Buddhist Association, 1959–1984*, by Malaysian Buddhist Association. Penang: MBA, 1985*a*.

Shi Kim Beng. "Fozongde Dangshengyu Jinzhang" [The Birth and Development of MBA]. In *25th Anniversary: Malaysian Buddhist Association, 1959–1984*, by Malaysian Buddhist Association. Penang: MBA, 1985*b*.

Sik Chi Chern. "Striving Towards the Establishment of Malaysian Buddhist Supreme Bodies". *Berita YBAM* 70 (December 1992): 15.

———. "Shehui Xinli De Pingheng Shi Hexie Jichu" [The Balance of Psychological Needs Is the Foundation of Harmony]. *Berita YBAM* 74 (June 1994): 2.

Smith, Bardwell L., ed. *Religion and Legitimation of Power in Thailand, Laos, and Burma*. Chambersburg, PA: ANIMA Books, 1978.

Smith, Donald E. *Religion and Politics in Burma*. Princeton, NJ: Princeton University Press, 1965.

Suksamran, Somboon. *Political Buddhism in Southeast Asia: The Role of the Sangha in the Modernization of Thailand*. London: C. Hurst and Co., 1977.

———. *Buddhism and Politics in Thailand: A Study of Socio-political Change and Political Activism of the Thai Sangha*. Singapore: Institute of Southeast Asian Studies, 1982.

Tambiah, Stanley J. *Buddhism Betrayed? Religion, Politics, and Violence in Sri Lanka*. Chicago, IL: University of Chicago Press, 1992.

Topmiller, Robert J. *The Lotus Unleashed: The Buddhist Peace Movement in South Vietnam, 1964–1966*. Lexington, KY: University Press of Kentucky, 2002.

U Maung Maung. *Sangha and Laity: Nationalist Movements of Burma, 1920–1940*. ANU Monographs on South Asia. Canberra: Australian National University, 1980.

Wickremeratne, Ananda. *Buddhism and Ethnicity in Sri Lanka: A Historical Analysis*. New Delhi: International Centre for Ethnic Studies, Kandy, Vikas Pub. House, 1995.

YBAM. *15th Souvenir Magazine*. Penang: YBAM, 1987.

Yeap Tor Hor. "History of YBAM, 1980–1986". *YBAM 15th Souvenir Magazine*. Penang: YBAM, 1987.

Websites
MBA, <http://www.mybuddhist.net/cms>.
YBAM, <http://www.ybam.org.my/cms>.

Organization Publications
Anniversaries reports of MBA and YBAM.
Berita YBAM [YBAM News]
YBAM Six-Year Plan (various years)

17

HINDRAF AS A RESPONSE TO ISLAMIZATION IN MALAYSIA

Arunajeet Kaur

The Hindu Rights Action Force (Hindraf) of Malaysia was formed on 29 December 2005 when 29 Indian NGOs met in Kuala Lumpur in response to the "body snatching" case of the Everest climber Moorthy (Uthayakumar 2010, p. 53). The Moorthy case was one of the several incidences involved in the controversy of religious conversions in Malaysia. It was believed that M.Moorthy, an army corporal in the Malaysian armed forces, who had gained recognition as one of the Mount Everest climbers for Malaysia, had converted to Islam without the knowledge of his family before dying. The Selangor Islamic Religious Department authorities "snatched" his dead body for burial according to Muslim rites from his wife Kaliammal and family who were unaware of his conversion to Islam and claimed that he was a practising Hindu. The family sought legal redress, but the *Syariah* Court ruled that he was a Muslim whereas the High Court said it had no jurisdiction over the matter (Malaysiakini, 13 January 2006). The founders of the Hindraf found the court rulings of both the *Syariah* and the High Court to be a violation of non-Muslim minority rights. The Moorthy case was simply a catalyst to the founding of Hindraf in a series of occurrences that include the demolition of Hindu temples and the fact that Indians in Malaysia are commonly perceived as a backward class of people due to limited access to opportunities within a social political system that favours privileges for the majority Malay-Muslim population.

The Hindraf was to gain national and international attention when it organized a rally on 25 November 2007 in the heart of Kuala Lumpur, at the Ampang area, in a bid to submit a petition to the Queen of England. In August 2007, Waythamoorthy, one of the leaders of Hindraf, filed a suit against the British government at the Royal Court of Justice, London, for bringing Indians to Malaysia as indentured labourers and exploiting them for 150 years (Malaysiakini, 24 November 2007). Furthermore, the suit sought a declaration that the Reid Commission Report 1957 failed to incorporate the rights of the Indian community, resulting in discrimination and marginalization to the present day. The quantum sought was US$4 trillion (RM14 trillion) — or US$2 million for every Indian currently residing in Malaysia. Following the filing of the suit, the Hindraf held nationwide roadshows explaining to the community's grassroots about the case. The petition to be presented on the November 25th rally sought to lobby the British Queen to appoint a Queen's Counsel to represent Waythamoorthy's suit. The rally drew an unprecedented crowd of 30,000 Malaysian Indians in protest and caused alarm to the local authorities who then proceeded to deal with the gathering with armed police attempting to disperse the crowd with tear gas and chemical laced water cannon (Malaysiakini, 25 November 2007). The nature of the rally revealed that although the Hindraf was protesting the local marginalization of Indians within the Malaysian state, the catalyst of its formation, the Moorthy conversion case, was a response to the increasing Islamization of the Malaysian state. The situation that accompanied the body-snatching conversion cases was that of Hindu temple demolitions by the Malaysian authorities. The latter especially was to further affect the low morale of the Malaysian Hindu community as described by Nagarajan in quoting a devotee, "Why do they have to tear down our temples? We are poor and our only comfort is our temples and now we are losing that also" (Nagarajan 2009, p. 378). The Hindraf is an activist group in Malaysia for Malaysian Indian rights, but this chapter will show that its key motivations and objectives were spurred by the increasing Islamization of the Malaysian state. This served to intimidate non-Muslim minorities, and Hindraf stands out as a key example of one such non-Muslim Hindu minority in protest.

ISLAM IN MALAYSIA AND THE REACTION OF NON-MUSLIM MINORITIES

In October 2001, Dr Mahathir Mohamed, the then Prime Minister of Malaysia, declared that Malaysia was already an Islamic State (Riddell

2005, p. 164). In July 2007, the Deputy Premier, Datuk Seri Najib Razak, affirmed this when he announced at the opening of the "International Conference on the role of Islamic States in a Globalised World 'that we have never, never been secular ... we are an Islamic state'" (Dzulkifli 2008, p. 127). The reaction to these announcements was obviously the expected resistance by non-Muslims, but some Muslims were perturbed as well. It was clear to the political spectators in Malaysia that these announcements were another manoeuvre by the United Malays National Organisation (UMNO) party to beat the opposition Parti Islam Se-Malaysia (PAS) party in the Islamization race and secure the support of the majority votes of the Malay electorate in Malaysia. Another dimension to this strategy is linked to the fact that Islam forms an integral aspect of Malay identity as defined in the Constitution. Since UMNO has always been known as the champion of Malay rights and identity, declaring Malaysia an Islamic state would portray UMNO as having remained steadfast in its original commitment to being the most effective protector of Malay dominance and rights (*Ketuanan Melayu*).

Non-Muslim advocates argue against the Islamic discourse by frequently quoting the intentions of the departing British government at Independence (the creed of the Reid Commission), the attitudes of the founding fathers such as Tunku Abdul Rahman and the "social contract" that bound the Malays with the non-Malay communities. Lim Kit Siang, Opposition Party Leader, DAP, retaliated in 2007 to Datuk Najib's comments, citing the first three prime ministers and their commitment to keeping Malaysia a secular state as agreed in the "Merdeka social contract" (Lim 2008, p. 9). Lim Kit Siang quotes the first Prime Minister, Tunku Abdul Rahman, on his 80th birthday celebrations in 1983 stating that Malaysia was set up as a secular state with Islam as the official religion and the constitution must be respected and adhered to, viz., "There have been attempts by some people who tried to introduce religious laws and morality laws. This cannot be allowed. The country has a multi-cultural population with various beliefs" (Lim 2008, p. 9). This is reiterated in K.J. Ratnam's (1965) work, which quotes the Tunku as having said, "Our country has many races and unless we are prepared to drown every non-Malay, we can never think of an Islamic administration." Basing his findings and arguments through examination of the report of the Reid Constitutional Commission, the White Paper on the Constitutional Bill, Parliamentary proceedings and newspaper reports and judgements handed down by the courts in the immediate post-independence period, Fernando (2006) takes a historical approach when stipulating that Islam as a religion of the Malay federation was very reluctantly added to the Malayan Constitution taking into account the concerns of non-Muslims and the Sultans, who feared that their own power as asserted through overseeing the practice of Islam would be usurped by the Federal government. Instead Fernando quotes two former Chief Justices, Lord President Tun Mohamed Suffian Hashim and Tan Sri Mohamed Salleh Abbas, as having declared that "Islam was made the official religion primarily for ceremonial purposes, to enable prayers to be offered in the Islamic way on official public occasions, such as the installation or birthday of the Yang Pertuan Agong, Independence Day and similar occasions" (Fernando 2006, p. 266). Opponents of the UMNO position that Malaysia is an Islamic State are premising their arguments on Malaysia still being a secular, democratic state whereby there is space for political lobbying of equal rights for non-Muslims. But observers of Malaysian politics have noticed that, especially since the era of Islamic resurgence in Malaysia, noticeably from the 1970s onwards, the expanded influence of the *dakwah* movement, coupled with state policies of Islamization. Since the era of Dr Mahathir as Prime Minister, the boundaries between Malaysia being a secular state or theocracy have become somewhat blurred. Critics of the UMNO government argue that the UMNO — Barisan Nasional (BN) regime welcomes this secular — religious ambivalence in Malaysia as a strategy "to keep the nation divided and subdued" (Dzulkifli 2008, p. 127).

Although there have been advocates for an Islamic state since the nationalist struggle for independence in the form of the Islamic party PAS and its predecessors, most scholars of the *dakwah* movement point to the emergence and success of Islamist organizations such as the Tabligh groups, Darul Arqam, and especially the ABIM (Angkatan Belia Islam Malaysia) organization as being responsible for the trend of Islamic resurgence among particularly the newly emergent, fast urbanizing Malay middle class since the enforcement of the NEP (New Economic Policy), post-1969. But this is not to dismiss that the local kampong (village) religious leaders and teachers also played a crucial role in propagating Islam to the rural, Malay underclass. The impact of the *dakwah* movement was visible in the increased popularity of Islamic attire, decline in social communication between the sexes, greater display of piety among Malaysian Muslims through the practice of *haj* (pilgrimage), *zakat* (donation), and prayers. However, the quest for greater piety was most visible in the heightened insistence on *halal* foods and products.

Muzaffar (1987) observed that the *dakwah* movement was to inevitably lead the Malay Muslims asserting a more "separate and distinct identity" to the point of exclusivity. This was further heightened when the Islamic resurgence received state patronage particularly under Mahathir as Prime Minister. Mauzy and Milne (1983–84), write in the 1980s that "ten years ago Islam was just one of the emotional issues used by PAS, the major Malay opposition party, to win the political allegiance of the rural Malays away from the dominant government party, UMNO. Now Islamist politics is centre stage. Since the mid-1970s the country has experienced radical Islamization, a process which has picked up momentum under the Mahathir administration." Previously, under the first three Prime Ministers, the Malaysian government tried to keep Islam out of mainstream politics; at best certain concessions were made such as the establishment of PERKIM (Pertubuhan Kebajikan Islam se Malaysia) by Tunku Abdul Rahman in 1960. However, Mahathir attempted to co-opt the Islamic resurgence in Malaysia as a state-led trend, especially, after Anwar Ibrahim, Leader of ABIM, joined UMNO. It has been explained already how Mahathir launched government projects that marked the UMNO patronage of Islamization in Malaysia.

Non-Muslim minorities in Malaysia were caught in a dilemma when reacting to the Islamic resurgence in Malaysia. Post-1969, they were caught by the constitutional amendments that forbade the discussion of Malay rights and identity in Malaysia, which would include Islam. Zainah Anwar (2005) reveals that the initial "shroud of silence" from non-Muslim quarters was due to the fact that non-Muslim opposition party leaders, especially from the Democratic Action party (DAP), were silenced whenever they tried to raise objections or questions about Islamic practices. She writes, "They were usually drowned by the jeering and thumping by the UMNO Muslim backbenchers who claim that Chinese MPs as non-Muslims do not have a right to talk about Islam. Thus they are prevented from playing their law making role when it comes to Islamic matters" (Anwar 2005, p. 125). Mauzy and Milne posit the suggestion that the portrayed apathy and even acceptance of non-Muslim communities to the initial processes of *dakwah* was actually a reaction in fear of speaking up. They write that Chinese political leaders "fear a Malay backlash if they publicly express their concern" (Mauzy and Milne 1983–1984, p. 638) and that it was better to support the UMNO moderates versus the PAS fundamentalists. However, over time even this non-Muslim strategy was to give way as it became obvious to them that in reacting to the fundamentalists, UMNO might be conceding too much in the name of Islam and "the onslaught is to become greater and most oppressive".

Non-Muslims have felt the pressures of rising Islamization primarily through the ambivalence and lack of clearly defined boundaries between the jurisdiction of Islamic laws (*syariah*) and civil law. This takes us back to the argument if Malaysia has now moved towards being a theocracy, or at least behaving like one, foregrounding Islamic law. This dilemma about jurisdiction of the law was most obviously felt by non-Muslims in issues of conversion and apostasy. It was contemplated in the late 1970s to extend Muslim law over all Malaysians regardless of religion especially in the matter of sexual offenses, such as *khalwat* (compromising proximity) and *zina* (adultery). Barraclough (1983) writes that the government was pressured to establish a committee to investigate the possibility of punishing non-Muslims involved with Muslims who transgress Islamic law on matters of sexual morality. *The Straits Times* on 27 July 1979 registered a protest by Lim Kit Siang who stated, "that the committee … infringes a fundamental constitutional provision that non-Muslims would not be brought under the purview of Muslim laws and customs …" (Barraclough 1983, p. 958). The Constitutional provision being referred to is Article 11 that states, "Every person has the right to profess and practise his religion." This is further supported by Article 8 of the Constitution that proclaims all persons to be equal before the law and prohibits discrimination on the grounds of religion, race, and descent.

However, there have been numerous cases to show that the above-mentioned constitutional provisions have often been transgressed. The most controversial and publicized of these cases have been the Lina Joy case in 2007, Maniam Moorthy's case in 2006, and Subashini's case in 2006. Lina Joy alias Azlina Jailani, born a Muslim but a convert to Christianity, attempted to get the classification of Islam removed from her National Registration Identity Card (NRIC). When the National Registration Department (NRD) instructed her to obtain the relevant papers (a certificate of apostasy) from the *Syariah* Court, she by-passed the procedure by filing a suit in the High Court. On 30 May 2007, the Federal Court issued a 2–1 judgement holding that Joy was not entitled to an NRIC without the word Islam. This episode drew international attention, with the press decrying its claim to a multi-religious and multicultural society when freedom of religion was not allowed. The Lina Joy case also became a focal point for tensions between Muslims and religious minorities. Some Muslim organizations such as the PEMBELA (Muslim Organisations in Defence of Islam) and ABIM expressed relief with the judgement that justice had been served, but the response from the Muslims was not homogeneous. The World Muslim Congress declared that it was un-Islamic to keep someone a Muslim against their wishes. Most non-Muslim organizations such as the Hindu Sangam and the Council of Churches criticized the judgement, citing the violation of Article 11 of the Constitution. The point of contention was the process through which Lina Joy would have had to undergo if she was to apply for certificate of apostasy from the *Syariah* Court, which entailed detention at a rehabilitation centre for at least a year whereby she would be indoctrinated against leaving the Islamic faith. This would have caused her separation from loved ones, leave from job and career obligations and inevitably would have incurred psychological trauma.

Some have argued that the Lina Joy case was an internal matter amongst Muslims and keeping their believers within the fold. This cannot be claimed in the cases of Maniam Moorthy alias Mohammad Abdullah, a former soldier and member of the Malaysian team which scaled Mount Everest in 1997. Described by his wife as a Hindu at the time of his death in 2005, she was prevented from burying him as one after *Syariah* courts ruled that he had converted to Islam in 2004, even though there was no documentary evidence of this conversion in his military identity card. When Moorthy's wife filed an application with the civil courts to allow her to claim Moorthy's body, the High Court rejected her application, claiming it had no jurisdiction over the matter and that she (as a non-Muslim) should revert to the *Syariah* Court. This same confusion over the role and jurisdiction of *Syariah* and civil courts was displayed in T. Saravanan and Subashini's case. In 2006, T. Saravanan, a Hindu, converted to Islam after which he proceeded to file for divorce in the *Syariah* courts and claimed custody over his two children with R. Subashini. Subashini being a non-Muslim applied for an injunction from the High Court to prevent Saravanan from dissolving their civil marriage in the *Syariah* Court. Once again the legal system conceded in the direction of Muslim rights with the Court of Appeal rejecting her appeal (Tan and Lee 2008, p. 137). A more severe case in reflecting the curbed constitutional rights is Revathi Mossosai's case. A practising Hindu but born to Muslim parents and registered as a Muslim with a Muslim name was raised by a Hindu grandmother. She is married to a Hindu husband and later gave birth to a daughter who is also Hindu. In January 2007 when she applied to be officially recognized as a Hindu, she was sent to a Muslim rehabilitation centre where she was forced to wear a Muslim headscarf, recite Muslim prayers, and eat beef, which is anathema to Hindus.

Critics observe that these measures in dealing with issues of conversion are more a concern for Malay identity than Islamic orthodoxy in Malaysia.

Many non-Malays regard the Islamic resurgence as an expression of Malay insecurities rather than an indication of greater religious piety (Barraclough 1983, p. 966), while critics of the government claim that it is more about politics and the politicization of religion. It is about maintaining Malay-Muslim hegemony and the power of the ruling coalition party. It is about preserving the special privileges accorded to Malays in the name of national unity and ethnic "tolerance". More importantly, it is about having the Malay majority rule the country without contest ever. Therefore, since Islam is inextricably linked with Malay ethnicity, maintaining Muslim rights in Malaysia is more of a matter of policing ethnic boundaries.

Besides curbing individual constitutional rights, certain policies and legislation have also had a negative impact on non-Muslims such as policies that include different allocation ratios for mosques and non-Muslim places of worship, with preference given to the building of mosques. Federal legislation passed in 1989 forbade the use by non-Muslims of forty-two Islamic terms. In 1991, this list was reduced to four terms including *Allah*, *Kaabah*, *Baitullah*, and *Solat* (Riddell 2005, p. 167). On 2 November 2001, the issue was raised in Parliament over the shortage of burial ground for non-Muslims. Another piece of legislation forbids Muslims to possess a copy of the Bible, while non-Muslims are not allowed to possess the Quran. Restrictions have been placed on non-Islamic religious literature and/or media, while public television and radio airtime have increasingly given coverage to Islamic symbols, prayers, and programmes. The practice of Yoga amongst Muslims has also been censured as the yoga postures are practised together with specific Hindu mantras and are meant to induce a meditative state (which is considered un-Islamic). Islamic practices and symbols are also pervasive in the public sphere with the broadcasting of the call to prayer (*azan*) from mosques which have been known to extend to lengthy recitations of the Quran and sermon over loudspeakers.

Farish Noor (2005) describes the situation of non-Muslims in Malaysia along the Muslim-*kafir* (unbeliever) divide. He employs concepts which are familiar to those who engage in post-colonial thought, such as "the Other", differentiation, and alterity. Borrowing from Spivak and Said, Noor employs the term "Other", usually used in context to describe how colonialist scholars/orientalists viewed the colonized so as to naturalize differences and justify colonial rule, to the Malay-Muslim hegemony in Malaysia. He points out that the Malaysian propensity to think in terms of binaries such as non-Malay/*bumiputera* with the Islamic resurgence has only hardened into Muslim-*kafir* or Muslim-Other. Although he problematizes this binary, stating that ethnic categories are never simple homogeneous entities to be reduced to such binaries, nonetheless he reflects on the realities of majoritarian Malay communal impulses to view the "towkay Cina" as the "evil *kafir*".

Non-Muslims in Malaysia have been under no illusions about their position *vis-à-vis* the Muslims in Malaysia. Abu Bakar notes that initial non-Muslim silence in response to *dakwah* gave way to the formation and resurrection of numerous non-Muslim organizations, of which the most consolidated non-Muslim response was the formation of the Malaysian Consultative Council of Buddhism, Christianity, Hindus, and Sikhism in 1984. For the Hindus, the most recent incarnation of resistance against Malay-Muslim hegemony has been the formation of the Hindu Rights Action Force (Hindraf).

HINDRAF LOBBIES FOR MALAYSIAN INDIAN-HINDU RIGHTS

The M. Moorthy case instigated the formation of Hindraf, partly because Moorthy was a high-profile member of the Indian community, being part of the Malaysian Everest Team. In turn, the Hindraf presented, from a Malaysian Indian standpoint, the grievances of the non-Muslim minorities over the blurred boundaries between civil and *Syariah* proceedings in two documents: (1) The proposals of the Hindraf to combat the unjust decision of Kuala Lumpur High Court dated 28 December 2005 which ruled Moorthy's case as a matter for *Syariah* law;[1] (2) Moorthy's struggle in terms of procedures for conversion to Islam, procedures on renunciation, the issue of court jurisdiction over these conversion cases, and the constitutional crisis caused as a result of blurred court jurisdiction.[2]

The first document, which was presented on 28 December 2005 to the Kuala Lumpur High Court, ruled that the High Court had no jurisdiction in the matter of Kaliammal, the wife of late M. Moorthy, who brought legal action against the Majlis Agama Wilayah Perseketuan and the Director of Kuala Lumpur General Hospital. A team of lawyers comprising A. Sivanesan, M. Manoharan, K. Gengadaran, P. Waythamoorthy, Kulasegaran, and Mohan Gandhi represented Kaliammal at the Kuala Lumpur High Court hearing on the 27 and 28 December 2005. They argued that the late Moorthy had never embraced Islam and that his pay slips and identity card reflected his Hindu name. Until the time of his death, he had never performed circumcision, and at all times he had practised Hinduism by participating in Hindu festivals and prayers. Therefore, based on these arguments the Majlis Agama Wilayah Persekutuan did not have the right to claim the body of the late Moorthy and the *Syariah* Court order dated 22 December 2005, according to Kaliammal's lawyers, was null and void. With the High Court ruling that it had no jurisdiction over Moorthy's case, Hindraf argued that this had grave consequences for non-Muslim citizens of Malaysia since they did not have the right to challenge decisions made about them by *Syariah* courts. Hindraf put forward that this was fundamentally wrong as *Syariah* courts are inferior to civil courts, which were a creation of the Federal Constitution, because *Syariah* courts do not listen to both parties. In the proposals of Hindraf to counter the High Court decision, Hindraf pledged a local and international campaign. The local campaign was to create a petition to be submitted to the Yang Di Pertuan Agong to sack Judge Md Rauf and launch an email and sms campaign as well as hold nationwide roadshows to create awareness of cases such as Moorthy's. In terms of the international campaign, Hindraf wanted to help Kaliammal lodge an official compliant with the United Nations Human Rights Commission.

In the second document, Hindraf discussed the legal implications of Moorthy's case in greater detail. There was a struggle between Kaliammal and the Federal Territory Religious Department (JAWI) over Moorthy's body. Since the High Court ruled it had no jurisdiction over the matter, which was a High Court case, Moorthy's body was buried according to Islamic rites. His widow managed to get all the financial benefits posthumously. The significance of the Moorthy case is that non-Muslims in Malaysia do not get their say if they are embroiled in family situations when one member of the family has converted and there are ramifications in financial matters, burial rites, and custody rights. The High Court refused to give a hearing to Moorthy's family, claiming that the case was under the jurisdiction of the *Syariah* Court. Since Kaliammal was a non-Muslim she could not bring her case to the *Syariah* Court and was therefore denied a hearing. In the issue of estate and inheritance a Muslim convert may dispose of one third of his estate by will provided two conditions are satisfied: (1) the disposition is to a Quranic heir; (2) the disposition must not benefit a person opposed to Islam. The remaining two-thirds of the estate is disposed according to Islamic law. The Islamic Office (*Jabatan Agama Islam*) would issue a certificate, *sijil faraid*. The distribution would be according to *sijil faraid*.[3] This means that Moorthy could only make a will on one-third of his property. The rest of his property had to be administered according to Islamic law. This also covered his provident fund and insurance claims. If Moorthy's infant children were deemed to be Muslim then their custody would be determined by Islamic law, with the likelihood that since Kaliamal is not a Muslim, she might lose the custody of her children.

The loopholes amidst the blurred boundaries between civil and *Syariah* courts are many. If a non-Muslim is identified as a Muslim and it is disputed, a suit cannot be brought to the civil courts to challenge the case. It is also very easy to allege that someone has converted to Islam. For example, there were no documents to prove Moorthy's conversion, only two words of his army colleagues. There could be a variety of situations where a non-Muslim could be wrongly classified as a Muslim, such as being caught in a sexually compromising position (*khalwat*) with a Muslim and then being forced to convert, and mistakes in entering data over religion into birth certificates and the Identification Card (*Mykad*) is also commonplace.[4] If a person's personal documents erroneously say that he or she is a Muslim, then that person falls under the *Syariah* Court.[5] There are also great difficulties in renouncing Islam. Islam prohibits converting out of Islam, which is punishable by death according to the Quran, but according to Malaysian *syariah* law, "Any Muslim who willfully either by his action or words or in any manner claims to denounce the religion of Islam or declares himself to be non-Muslim is guilty of an offence of deriding the religion of Islam and shall on conviction be liable to a fine not exceeding three thousand ringgit or to imprisonment for a term not exceeding two years or to both."[6] This is very harsh if someone is caught in Islam due to administrative glitches or social circumstances.

The Hindraf legal team lobbied for a re-examination of Article 121(A) of the Federal Constitution. In 1988 the Malaysian Constitution was amended to include Article 121(A) that says civil courts have no jurisdiction over any matter that falls within the jurisdiction of the *Syariah* courts.[7] This has caused a dual legal system whereby people of especially non-Muslim religious identification could become embroiled in such cases as (1) non-Muslims mistaken for Muslims; (2) Muslims wanting to get out of Islam; (3) non-Muslim spouses of Muslims; (4) children who have one parent who is a Muslim and the other a non-Muslim, and (5) non-Muslim parents or siblings of Muslims. Hence, considering the jurisdiction of the *Syariah* court the abovementioned do not get a right to a hearing, which imposes a sense of inequality and social hierarchies within the Malaysian social fabric.

The second pressing issue for the Hindraf was the demolition of Hindu temples. On 24 March 2006, Hindraf sent Prime Minister Abdullah Ahmad Badawi an open letter, "Hindu temples/shrines continuously haunted by unscrupulous demolishment."[8] In this letter

Hindraf invoked Article 11 of the Malaysian Federal Constitution which guarantees the freedom of worship and religion in Malaysia. Hindraf also pointed out that the Federal Constitution "unreservedly declares this state to be secular".[9] However, there were impediments to Article 11 with the demolition of the Sri Ayanar Satishwary Alayam Hindu Temple that was erected some 60 years ago. The Hindraf stated that the temple had some 3,000 devotees and was a place of service and welfare for the public that organized charitable and spiritual events and even public forums from time to time. According to the Hindraf, the act to demolish the temple by state authorities was considered "a most deplorable repulsive and regrettable act" and "barbaric and satanic" considering that the Malaysian government is "aggressively and vehemently advocating racial co-existence, national unity, mutual respect and appreciation between multiple races in the country". There was great emotional outpouring in this letter as in the other letters sent out to the Prime Minister and other officials. One wonders if these emotional outbursts are a strategy to incite sympathy from the relevant authorities or simply a demonstration of shock and outrage at the mentioned occurrences.

On 10 May 2006, the Hindraf sent another letter to the Prime Minister and the Minister of Law, Mohamed Nazri Bin Abdul Aziz, "Another Unlawful Act of 'Cleansing' about the demolition of the 110-year-old ancient Hindu shrine located at Midlands Estate Seksyen 7 Shah Alam by Shah Alam City Hall on 9 May 2006."[10] In this letter Hindraf pointed out that in their perspective the government was not demolishing temples to make way for development but that the "Mayor of Shah Alam is unlawfully engaged in a silent agenda to 'cleanse' ancient Hindu shrines".[11] This put the demolition of Hindu temples into direct co-relation with Hindu ethnic marginalization due to rising Islamization in Malaysia. Hindraf accused the government authorities of using obsolete laws to justify the demolition of these Hindu temples. For instance, the notice of demolition for the Hindu shrine issued in April 2006 states that the demolition was intended to be of an "illegal squatter building".[12] Hindraf questioned the moral/legal authority of City Hall to interpret a shrine that was built 110 years ago (before the existence of City Hall) as an illegal squatter building. Once again there was a clear expression of a high intensity of emotional outpouring of the Hindraf on behalf of the Indian community as the letter reveals that the shrine management had appealed to the Chief Minister of Selangor seeking his assistance and an NGO, the Consumer Association of Klang, had made appeals to City Hall. The letter states that despite these the City Hall had **arrogantly** and **deliberately** proceeded to demolish the ancient Shrine. It appears the Shah Alam City Hall Mayor acted **mala fide** and on **frolic of his own** with ill intentions to cause racial hatred, anger and humiliation among the non-Muslim population in Malaysia.[13]

Here we witness the ethnic binaries being confirmed between Muslims and non-Muslims in the Malaysian context and the pressure sustained by non-Muslims regarding the demolition of their temples since Muslims mainly form the authorities in Malaysia.

The Hindraf petitioned the Prime Minister for social justice. It called on him to (1) arrest and charge the Mayor of Shah Alam; (2) to issue a stern written directive to all state governments/chief ministers/city and local councils to immediately halt any form of cleansing/demolition of places of worship; (3) to instruct the Culture Arts and Heritage Ministry to immediately take positive steps to protect ancients shrines belonging to non-Muslims; (4) appoint a minister to oversee matters pertaining to religious rights and freedom of non-Muslims; (5) provide and allocate sufficient funds for building, maintenance, and upkeep of places of worship belonging to non-Muslims; (6) provide and allocate sufficient funds for the building, maintenance, and upkeep of places of worship belonging to non-Muslims; and (7) seriously implement existing legal provisions for the erection and building of places of worship for non-Muslims in new townships.[14] While these demands for reconciliation over Indian communal hurt due to the demolition of Hindu temples, especially heritage site Hindu temples, seem reasonable in the context of good governance and an egalitarian social and political scenario, it seems unrealistic in Malaysia. Given Malaysia's trajectory towards hardening ethnic boundaries with affirmative action policies for the Malays and the declaration of Malaysia as an Islamic state by prime ministers and important members of the cabinet, the UMNO government would find these demands unreasonable and as they have done in the past, ignore several if not all of the memorandums and letters of appeal sent to important dignitaries and the government.

Several of the letters such as the ones to the Sultan of Selangor and Attorney General of Malaysia were telling of the emotions and causes of grievances of the Indian community over the temple demolition issues.[15] The Indians were alarmed at the rate at which Hindu temples were scheduled for demolition. For example, within two-and-a-half months, twelve temples were demolished, deities stolen and smashed, and the roads to the temple closed. The letter to the Sultan of Selangor dated 3 August 2006 also pleaded that the further eleven Hindu temples in Selangor scheduled to be demolished in the next four and half months be stopped.[16] The letter dated 28 June 2006 to the Attorney General explains how Hindu deities were smashed before the devotees in the demolition of the Hindu temple Om Sri Balakrishna Muniswarer on 8 June 2006. It also described the Royal Police Force colluding with gangsters and a Malay-Muslim mob during the demolition as an intimidation tactic against the Hindus present.[17] Hindraf highlighted in this letter that the caretakers of these temples were mainly "downtrodden, poor, uneducated, ignorant and a defenseless class of the Indian ethnic community that could not defend themselves against the sledgehammers that were used to destroy the Hindu deities before their eyes".[18] The letter to the Attorney General also explains that the offers for the relocation of Hindu temples were unreasonable. For example, the sixty-year-old Om Sri Balakrishna Muniswarer Temple was located on a piece of land approximately 20,000 square feet and was scheduled to be demolished to make way for a highway development project. The temple serves 800 devotees of mainly the laboring class. The relocation land assigned to the temple was a piece of land measuring 10' × 10' which the Hindraf felt was "nothing but a calculated attempt to humiliate and belittle the Hindu faith and customs and its labouring class devotees".[19] The Hindraf also questioned why pre-independence Hindu temples had not been made into temple reserves, gazetted, and had the temple land alienated by the government before allowing the developer to acquire the said land, as is being done for Muslim places of worship.[20]

Since the letters and memoranda sent out by the Hindraf did not elicit a response from local authorities, Hindraf approached international organizations such as the United Nations. In a letter dated 16 August 2006 to the United Nations Secretary General, Kofi Annan, the Hindraf explained the crisis of demolition of Hindu temples in Malaysia.[21] It was explained that it was an imbedded belief amongst the Hindu-Tamil community that they should not live in a village that does not have a temple. The Hindraf described the Hindu-Tamils as a temple-building community. As the Hindu migrants settled in different parts of Malaya, various temples were built in those areas, therefore it was not surprising that a community in a rubber estate of 100 acres would have twenty temples in that area. This was because the migrant Hindu population originated from various clans and villages and each clan and village had its own deity with its own unique style of worship. The consecration of these temples was allowed and encouraged by the colonial masters as not only the spiritual lives but also the social lives of the Hindu-Tamil estate workers were centred around the temple. Problems ensued after Malayan/Malaysian Independence when estates belonging to British land owners were bought over by private businessmen and companies and later acquired by the government using the Land Acquisition Act for development purposes. When the land was acquired by the government or sold to private developers, these temples were not given recognition as sacred places of worship of the minority Hindu-Tamil community. Instead, they were declared buildings of illegal squatters and demolished. Hindu temples remained without a status, unlike mosques and *madrasahs*. Hence one witnesses the unequal treatment as meted out by the government towards the different races and religions that reinforced social hierarchies and Malay-Muslim supremacy.

The retort of the Malaysian authorities to these allegations was that there were too many Hindu temples in the country, which hampered development. The Indian community, too, acknowledged this and issued planning guidelines for "Places of Worship for Non-Muslims: Primarily Hindu Temples".[22] These guidelines explain the significance of the Hindu places of worship, their priests, and Hindu pooja (prayer). The main point made was that of *Agamas* (specific categories) of religious texts which gave detailed guidance regarding temple building and temple worship. Hindu *Agamas* (scriptural instructions) specify that Hindu temples should be built in a fertile place with a clean environment, central location, and accessible to the devotees. While these guidelines informed the government, these were also a polite protest against the numerous times Hindu temples had been relocated next to an oxidation tank, mining land, transmission line, or river reserve.[23] Despite this amount of protest, temple demolitions continue on state land that is under the charge of the UMNO or the Opposition.

CONCLUSION

With the Malaysian government ignoring memoranda and letters of protest by the Hindraf, it demonstrated that the dialogue between the state and the Hindraf group was non-existent. Instead, there was a sense of inflamed emotional finger-pointing at the UMNO. In referring to the Reid Commission, it is as though the Hindraf was looking to a point of genesis to correct the imbalances in the distribution of national resources and to hold the Malaysian government accountable. The Hindraf had failed to realize that, as in all institutions, state and communal identities, the Malaysian national identity, as determined by the UMNO-led government, has evolved. BN has had to alter the state image to cope with mounting pressures from the Islamic opposition party, PAS as well as the Malay-Muslim middle class that has increasingly started to participate in more rigid Islamic practices. Based on the discourse of the 18-point demand, Hindraf at best can be seen as a pressure group that through its refutation of the social contract, Malay special privileges, is testing the boundaries of the state to concede more to the Indian minority community. And while the November 2007 rally displayed that Hindraf was able to draw unprecedented support from the Indian community, despite state countermeasures and repression of the Hindraf spokesmen, a sense of pessimism prevails that the task in attaining equal rights or recognizing Hindu rights against a backdrop of a Malaysian Islamic state is an insurmountable one.

Notes

1. Hindraf memorandum titled, "Hindu Rights Action Force: A Joint Committee of Malaysian Hindu NGO's to combat the unjust decision of Kuala Lumpur High Court dated 28th December 2005".
2. Hindraf memorandum titled, "Moorthy's Struggle, Islam, Procedures for Conversion, Procedures on Renunciation, Jurisdiction, Constitutional Crisis, Prepared by Hindraf".
3. Ibid.
4. Ibid.
5. Ibid.
6. Ibid.
7. Ibid.
8. Open letter, dated 24 March 2006, addressed to Prime Minister of Malaysia, Dato Seri Abdullah Ahmad Badawi, "Hindu Temples/Shrines Continuously Haunted by Unscrupulous Demolishment", by P. Waythamoorthy, Chairman of Hindraf.
9. Ibid.
10. Letter addressed to both Prime Minister Abdullah Ahmad Badawi and the Minister of Law, Mohamed Nazri Bin Abdul Aziz, dated 10 May 2006, "Another Unlawful Act of 'Cleansing' demolishment of 110 years old ancient Hindu shrine located at Midlands Estate Seksyen 7 Shah Alam by Shah Alam City Hall on 9 May 2006", by P. Waythamoorthy, Chairman of Hindraf.
11. Ibid.

12 Ibid.
13 Ibid.
14 Ibid.
15 Letter addressed to Sultan Sharafuddin Idris Shah, ibni Almarhum Sultan Salahuddin Abdul Aziz Shah Al-Haj, dated 3 August 2006, by P. Waythamoorthy, Chairman of Hindraf. Letter addressed to Tan Sri Abdul Gani Patail, dated 28 June 2006, by P. Waythamoorthy, Chairman of Hindraf.
16 Ibid.
17 Ibid.
18 Ibid.
19 Ibid.
20 Ibid.
21 Letter addressed to Kofi A. Annan, dated 16 August 2006, by P. Waythamoorthy, Chairman of Hindraf.
22 Planning guidelines for "Places of Worship for Non-Muslims: Primarily Hindu Temples" submitted by a coalition of Hindu organizations, submitted to the Malaysian government in 2006.
23 Ibid.

References

Ahmad, Dzulkifli. "The Great Malaysian Paradox". In *Religion under Siege*, edited by Nathaniel Tan. Malaysia: Kinibooks, 2008.

Anwar, Zainah. "Law-making in the Name of Islam: Implications for Democratic Governance". In *Islam in Southeast Asia: Political, Social and Strategic Challenges for the 21st Century*, edited by K.S. Nathan and Mohammed Hashim Kamali. Singapore: Institute of Southeast Asian Studies, 2005.

Barraclough, Simon. "Managing the Challenges of Islamic Revival in Malaysia: A Regime Perspective". *Asian Survey* 23, no. 8 (1983): 958–75.

Fernando, Joseph M. "The Position of Islam in the Constitution of Malaysia". *Journal of Southeast Asian Studies* 37, no. 2 (2006): 249–66.

Lim Kit Siang. "Lina Joy Case Biggest P.R. Disaster for Malaysia". In *Religion under Siege*, edited by Nathaniel Tan and John Lee. Malaysia: Kinibooks, 2008.

Mauzy, Diane K. and R.S. Milner. "The Mahathir Administration in Malaysia: Discipline through Islam". *Pacific Affairs* 56, no. 4 (1983–84): 617–48.

Muzaffar, Chandra. *Islamic Resurgence in Malaysia*. Petaling Jaya: Fajar Bakti Sdn. Bhd., 1987.

Nagarajan, S. "Marginalization and Ethnic Relations: The Indian Malaysian Experience". In *Multiethnic Malaysia: Past, Present and Future*, edited by Lim Teck Ghee, Alberto Gomes, and Azly Rahman. Petaling Jaya: Strategic Information and Research Development Centre; Kuala Lumpur: MIDAS, UCSI University, 2009.

Noor, Farish A. *From Majapahit to Putrajaya: Searching for Another Malaysia*. Kuala Lumpur: Silverfish Books, 2005.
Ratnam, K.J. *Communalism and the Political Process in Malaysia*. Kuala Lumpur: University of Malaya Press, 1965.
Riddell, Peter G. "Islamization, Civil Society and Religious Minorities in Malaysia in Islam". In *Islam in Southeast Asia: Political, Social and Strategic Challenges for the 21st Century*, edited by K.S. Nathan and Mohammed Hashim Kamali. Singapore: Institute of Southeast Asian Studies, 2005.
Tan, Nathaniel and John Lee. *Religion under Siege; Lina Joy, the Islamic State and Freedom of Faith*. Kuala Lumpur: Kinibooks, 2008.
Uthayakumar, P. "25 November 2007: Hindraf Rally". Kuala Lumpur, 2010.

18

"DEVIANT" MUSLIMS
The Plight of Shias in Contemporary Malaysia

Norshahril Saat

INTRODUCTION

In December 2010, Islamic officials in Selangor detained 200 Muslims, said to be members of *The Lovers of the Prophet's Household*, a Shia-leaning group. The arrests were made following a raid on a shop in Sri Gombak (Selangor) by the Selangor Islamic Department (JAIS). This is not only a clear denial of the people's right to practise their faith freely as enshrined in the constitution, but also a manifestation of intolerance of the religious authorities on Islamic beliefs that do not conform to their interpretations. Is Malaysia swerving to an era of the centralization of religion that allows for only one school of thought to prevail? Many would not disagree. Nonetheless, arrests made against Shias are not unprecedented in Malaysia. Alleged followers of Shiism have been placed under the draconian Internal Security Act (ISA), which before its proposed abolition in 2011, warranted detention without trial. In 1997, seven Shia followers were detained for spreading deviationist teachings (Liow 2009, p. 163). Between October 2000 and January 2001, six Shia followers were also arrested under the ISA (Saeed and Saeed 2004, p. 128).

In contemporary Malaysia, the Shias are deemed as "deviant" from mainstream Islam by the dominant religious authorities, and this is reflected in the religious enactments, *fatwa* (legal opinion), publications, and sermons. The main purpose of this chapter is to examine what constitutes the label "deviant Shias". It also seeks to analyze critically the style of thought of the prominent religious elite that triggers such labelling. I argue that the treatment of the religious authorities towards the Shias manifest an "exclusivist" orientation of Islam that emerged out of the greater centralization of the religious bureaucracy. This exclusivist orientation upholds that the official variant of Islam, *Ahlus Sunnah Wal Jamaah* (ASWJ), must be stringently followed. Exclusivism is also manifested in the attitude that is totally dismissive towards alternative interpretations of what constitute ASWJ. The centralization "exclusivist" Islam, coupled with the emergence of a powerful religious bureaucracy, ensures that the practice of Malaysia's official Islam — in what they define as ASWJ — is safeguarded and adhered to by all Muslim groups through legal and even draconian means such as the use of ISA. By and large, Shiism is regarded as deviant mainly on three grounds: it is theologically different from the ASWJ; it is mainly a political minority not only in Malaysia, but also in the Islamic world; and it represents a security threat to the religious harmony in Malaysia.

EMERGENCE OF AN EXCLUSIVIST ISLAM

Exclusivist Islam emerged out of the greater centralization of the Islamic bureaucracies particularly during the Mahathir government (1981–2003). The government increased the power and authority of the federal bureaucracies in accommodating the demands made by the Islamic resurgence (or revivalism) movement of the 1970s. Although the Islamic resurgence movement was heterogeneous, with different *dakwah* organizations having diverse ideologies and goals, all groups fundamentally agreed on the need for a greater Islamization of governance and Malaysian society.[1] In their attempt to appease the movement, Islam was incorporated and appropriated into the "national" vision of the state during the Mahathir government (Hamayotsu 2002). Mahathir operationalized this national Islamic vision by setting up of the Islamic Bank and Islamic Economic foundation; upgrading of *Pusat Islam*; airing the *azan* (prayer call) on national television (RTM); building massive mosques; setting up of Islamic Universities (International Islamic University of Malaysia); and co-opting Muslim activists and leaders, such as the charismatic Malaysian Youth Islamic Movement (ABIM) leader Anwar Ibrahim into UMNO, Dean of Faculty of Islamic Studies from the National University of Malaysia (UKM) Yusuf Noor, and the Director of Pusat Islam (Islamic

Centre) Zainal Abidin Kadir into the government. Amendments were also made to the legal aspect. From 1988, Article 121(1A) of the Federal Constitution was amended to allow for an expansion and systemization of the Islamic judicial and legal systems.

However, the centralization of the religious bureaucracy had its roots a decade before Mahathir's rule, during the final years of the Tunku Abdul Rahman government (1957–70). Before 1968, the federal government had very minimal involvement on Islamic affairs, as Islam is a state's matter. Various state Islamic departments (*Jabatan Agama Islam*) were mainly responsible for Islamic affairs. Basically, the respective Sultans function as the head of Islamic affairs in various states and the Yang-Dipertuan Agong (King) oversees the territories such as Kuala Lumpur, Labuan, Penang, Malacca, Sarawak, and Sabah. Much of the power in various religious departments lies with the respective Mufti(s), who sit as the ex-officio members of the religious councils (Funston 2006). However, this clear federal separation of powers were altered significantly with the formation of a more centralized, federal-level *Majlis Kebangsaan Bagi Hal Ehwal Ugama Islam* (Malaysian National Council of Islamic Affairs) in 1968. Even though the constitutional provision, which indicated "Islam as a state matter" is still upheld today, the authority and significance of the federal-level *Majlis Kebangsaan* increased significantly. The fact that this council has a secretariat in the Prime Minister's Office serves as a strong indicator of its authority. The expansion and upgrading of this council later culminated in 1997 in the formation of what is known today as the Malaysian Department of Islamic Advancement (JAKIM) (Funston 2006, p. 55). Moreover, in ensuring that all Islamic laws are consistent across the states, the National Fatwa Council Committee was established in 1970 at the federal level, which at present is a part of JAKIM.

The greater role and authority accorded to the federal institutions such as JAKIM — in coordinating programmes and funding; in training, educating, and managing research projects; and in providing policy consultation on *shari'a* and Islamic information — allowed for the expansion of the *shari'a* (Maznah 2010, p. 513), even though the foundations of the Malaysian state is largely secular. The expansion of *shari'a* is evident when the Attorney General's Chambers was tasked to oversee the *shari'a* law-making processes. Besides, more laws, including criminal and family laws, were placed under *shari'a* statutes. Controversially, certain crimes are deemed exclusively Islamic even though there is a common penal code for Malaysians (Maznah 2010, pp. 515–16). "Islamic" crimes include lesbianism, fornication, sodomy, prostitution, eating during the day of Ramadhan, and alcohol consumption.

To be sure, the centralization of the religious bureaucracies is hugely responsible for the creation of "exclusivist Islam" in the hands of the official *ulama* (religious scholars). By 1982, the Federal government had over 100 *ulama* in the Department for Islamic Development in the prime minister's office and some 715 religious elites in the Ministry of Education (Norani, Zainah, and Zaitun 2005, p. 90). The numbers are likely to be higher today. Centralization handed these *ulama* in the religious bureaucracies the authority to be directly involved in the formulation of "Islamic" policies and *fatwa*. Furthermore, the *ulama* appointed as members of the National Fatwa Council are given direct access to provide recommendations to the Council of the Rulers on matters pertaining to Islam. More importantly, they are given the authority to define, delineate, and promote what constitutes "true" Islam.

A clear expression of this exclusivity was reflected during the banning of Darul Arqam movement in 1994 on the grounds that it bred a "deviant" theology. The movement was founded by a religious teacher Ustaz Ashaari Muhammad in 1968. Ashaari was well known for his oratorical skills, and his charisma captivates many young and old Muslims, particularly amongst the Malay middle class. Many questions were raised about the banning of this organization that at one time was estimated to have as only about 10,000 members including prominent personalities, politicians, and top academics. While the official reasons given for its banning were theological grounds, such as the theological validity of Aurad Muhammadiyah which form the basis of Darul Arqam's teachings (Ahmad Fauzi 2005, p. 96), some believed the challenge posed to the "exclusivity" of the religious officials in JAKIM by Ashaari as having played a momentous part. Ashaari's followers criticized the religious officials and politicians of "immoral" practice and "corruption" (Kamarulnizam 1999, pp. 273–74). Ashaari was later arrested and placed under ISA. Clearly, "exclusivist" Islam maintains that the official *ulama* have the sole and unquestionable right, close to infallibility, to ascertain the rightness and wrongness of theological positions. In the same vein, the religious authorities clearly set out the agenda of returning the society to the Islamic orthodoxy, adhering to the doctrines of ASWJ.

However, political challenges posed to the ruling elites, whom the official *ulama* obtain legitimacy and patronage, may also explain why disunity amongst the "exclusivist" camp could not be afforded. In the 1980s, UMNO faced the strongest electoral rivalry from the Islamic

Party of Malaysia (PAS). PAS leadership was taken over by a group of young charismatic clerics such as Nik Aziz Nik Mat, Abdul Hadi Awang, and Fadhil Noor, whose popularity at the grassroots level in some ways undermined the status of the state muftis who were widely seen as "lackeys" of the government. Also, PAS's organizational restructuring in the 1980s, said to be inspired by the Iranian model of "leadership by the ulama", presented an alternative system of Islamic governance rivaling UMNO's Malay supremacy. The essence of UMNO's model includes loyalty to the Malay Royalty. Associating political opponents with Shiism mainly served as a strategy to undermine them, a strategy deployed till this day. For instance, during the 2013 Malaysian General Elections, UMNO's Mukhriz Mahathir tried to link PAS's top leaders, such as Mat Sabu, as Shia followers (*New Straits Times*, 18 May 2013). Ironically, his father the former Prime Minister Mahathir Mohammed is a strong advocate for Sunni-Shia dialogue. On 22 May 2013, Mahathir, together with the former Iranian President Mohammad Khatami, urged the Organization Islamic Countries (OIC) to review the divisions between Sunnis and Shias in the name of unity.[2]

SUNNI-SHIA DIVIDE IN ISLAMIC HISTORY

When challenged by alternative viewpoints or interpretation of facts, emotions overwhelm rationality and objectivity in the way Islamic history is narrated, represented and written. Majority Sunni and Shia scholars today are guilty of this. Both maintain that their own set of traditions as absolute "truths", denying the possibility that narrations of traditions passed from generation to generation may have undergone numerous interpretations, (mis)-representations, and are subject to biases. In essence, such exclusivist orientation is not peculiar to the Malaysian case, but also other Muslim countries. At present, the Sunni-Shia divide has not moved beyond the contest of whose history and traditions are more "authentic". Though relatively peaceful today, this division has triggered many bloody wars and conflicts in the past.

The emergence of the Sunni-Shia divide after the demise of Prophet Muhammad (632 AD) is both ideological and political. The fundamental disagreement centres on who should take charge of the young Islamic polity after the Prophet's demise. Put succinctly, the Sunnis believed that the Prophet's ideal replacement was Abu Bakr. Abu Bakr deserved to be the Caliph because he was the most senior and closest companion of the Prophet. Abu Bakr is well known for his distinguished qualities, charisma, faith in Allah and knowledge. It was popularly narrated that Abu Bakr during his lifetime had sacrificed much his wealth in the name of religion. Abu Bakr was famously known to be the companion who accompanied the Prophet during his life-threatening migration from Mecca to Medina (*hijrah*). During the final days of his life, when the Prophet was very ill and too frail to lead the prayers (*solah*) at the mosque, Sunnis believed that Abu Bakr was appointed to lead the prayers on behalf of the Prophet. Many Sunnis interpreted this as a sign that Abu Bakr was the ideal replacement to lead the community of faith after the Prophet. It was also understood that after the Prophet's death, the Islamic community conducted the *Bay'ah of Saqifah* (pledge of allegiance and loyalty), which in modern manifestations, is to democratically elect Abu Bakr as the first Caliph of Islam. According to the Sunni belief, Abu Bakr's right to become the Caliph was strengthened by several evidences: indirect verses from the Quran, narrations of the *hadith* (sayings from the Prophet), universal consensus, and democratic elections (As-Sallaabee 2007, pp. 221–47). Upon Abu Bakr's death, Sunnis agreed that the leadership succession to be in the order of Umar Al-Khatab, Uthman Ibn Affan, and lastly Ali Abi Thalib.

The Shias, on the other hand, believed that leadership of the Islamic community was only reserved for the members of the "House of Prophet". Hence, the rightful Caliph immediately after the Prophet's demise should be his cousin, Ali Abi Thalib, who is also his son-in-law (married to the Prophet's daughter Fatimah). Several arguments were forwarded by the Shias to strengthen their claim. First, Ali was the first person in the Prophet's household to accept Islam. Second, the Shias believed that Ali was preserved from error and sin in his actions and sayings, making him a perfect and a knowledgeable individual (Allāmah Sayyid Muhammad Husayn Tabātabā'ī 1975, pp. 40–41). Third, during his lifetime, Ali had performed valuable services and remarkable sacrifices for Islam, a position which the Sunnis would not object. For example, Ali slept on the Prophet's bed in place of the Prophet on the night the latter migrated to Medina. Ali risked his life, because the Quraysh Meccans were trying to kill the Prophet that night. Fourth, Ali also led many battles such as the Badr, Uhud, Khaybar, Khandaq, and Hunayn. However, the central justification for Ali's right to be the Caliph was the event of Ghadir Khumm. The Shias believed that it was during this event that the Prophet assigned Ali for the "general guardianship", or the *wali*, to the Muslims (Muhammad Husayn Tabataba-I: 4.).

What began as theological schisms between the Sunnis and the Shias turned out to be bloody episodes and power struggles that coloured Islamic history. This was manifested in the uprising of Muawiyah against Ali (when Ali became the Caliph after Uthman), and later during the beginning of the Umayyad Caliphate (AD 680). During Muawiyah's leadership, the Prophet's grandson Hassan (son of Ali and Shias second imam) was believed to have been poisoned to death. Likewise, Imam Husayn, the third Shia imam and the second grandson of the Prophet, was massacred when he tried to rebel against the leadership of Yazid, Muawiyah's son, who became the Caliph upon his father's death. This failed rebellion is what Shias remember today as the Karbala tragedy.

Nevertheless, it was much later in Islamic history that both groups gain self-reflection of their existence. The ideological movements ASWJ and the Imami Shiism were later developments in Islamic history. In Sunnism, they had undergone a radical change, indeed a metamorphosis, in relation to the original state and the teaching of the Quran (Fazlur 2000, p. 30). The same can be said about the Imami Shiism, which arguably took a definite shape only between 874 and 920 (Watt 1983, p. 21). In Malaysia today, ASWJ is declared as the only true theology. There is a lack of objectivity in the presentation of history. To some extent, the skewed presentation of history may not be based on the motivation to deceive or conceal certain historical facts, but may arise out of the unconscious selection of religious facts and traditions, and not grappling with alternative viewpoints, perspectives, and sources of tradition objectively. This is evident in various ways to discredit Shias.

FATWA ON SHIAS: THE THEOLOGICAL PERSPECTIVE

Theological arguments have often been proffered by the religious elite to treat Shiism as a deviant sect. Several reasons are commonly underlined to justify this stance by the religious authorities in Malaysia, which include the members of the religious councils, state Muftis, politicians, and popular preachers. For instance, a *fatwa* has been passed by many states in Malaysia. Although in many parts of the Islamic world a *fatwa* is deemed a non-binding legal opinion, a *fatwa* in Malaysia is legally binding once they are gazetted. A *fatwa* in Malaysia not only operates as guides for judges in both *shari'a* courts and civil courts, it has a force of law once gazetted. Contravening a gazetted *fatwa* in Malaysia is a punishable offence. As stated earlier, due to the federal-state system, a *fatwa* can be issued at the federal level by the National Fatwa Council administered by JAKIM. However, for a *fatwa* to be enforced and obtain legal status, it has to be gazetted at the various state levels. Each state in Malaysia has its own religious council, headed by a Mufti, who reports directly to the Sultans (King). For states that do not have Sultans — such as Penang, Malacca, Sabah, and Sarawak — they answer directly to the Yang di-Pertuan Agong (Malaysian King).

A total ban on Shiism is a relatively recent phenomenon. In the past, the religious authorities were more relaxed on some sects within Shiism. Some discussions at the federal level on the status of Shias were held in 1984, but it was only in 1996 a decision about their condition attained a legal status. A *fatwa* committee was convened on 5 May 1996 to discuss the status of Shias in Malaysia. The 40th Special *Muzakarah* (Conference) of the Fatwa Committee of the National Council for Islamic Religious Affairs Malaysia agreed with the decision of the Fatwa Committee Muzakarah (Conference) held on 24–25 September 1984 (paper no. 2/8/84, Article 4.2(2)) concerning Shiism. The decision made in 1996 nullified the 1984 statement that "the Committee has decided that only the Zaidiyyah and Jafariyyah Shia sects are accepted to be practiced in Malaysia".[3] It was decided that Muslims in Malaysia must only follow the teachings of Islam based on ASWJ on creed, religious laws, and ethics. The *fatwa* clearly stipulates that the publication, broadcasting, and distribution of any books, leaflets, films, videos, and others relating to the teachings of Islam that contradicted the doctrine of ASWJ were to be prohibited and unlawful. Most states have accepted this *fatwa* issued by the federal *muzakarah* committee, although not all of the states have gazetted it. Among the states that have accepted and gazetted this *fatwa* are Wilayah Persekutuan or Federal Territories (1997), Negeri Sembilan (1998), Melaka (1997), and Pulau Pinang (1997). The states Kelantan and Perlis have agreed with the federal committee, though the *fatwa* is not gazetted. Kedah and Pahang, in August 2013, indicated that they would gazette the 1996 *fatwa*.

The review of the earlier *fatwa* that accepts the Zaidiyyah and Jafariyyah schools are within the fold of Islam is worthy of note. Before 1984, both schools were accepted as one of the many branches of Islam. What amounted to this review remains puzzling as not much explanation for the shift was given. Two factors may have contributed to this. First, this could have resulted from political considerations, particularly the growing influence of the Iranian revolution of 1979. There is a growing fear that the impact of the revolution may spill over to the Malay world, which may result in political instability and threaten the ruling elites in Malaysia then. Evidently, many of the *dakwah* movements were inspired by this revolution back then. Second, one should not downplay the significance of the *Wahabbi* influence from the Middle East, namely Saudi Arabia. One can only speculate that the strong ties established between the Malaysian government and organizations with their counterparts in Middle East during this period, as a result of the oil boom, led to the penetration of more puritanical religious ideas into the Malay world. Traditionally, the Wahabbi–Sunni orientated regimes have strong views against Shiism. Many Sunni-dominant Middle Eastern countries do not have good diplomatic ties with the Shia-orientated Iranian regime. As a result of wanting to align itself to the Middle Eastern regimes during the oil boom period, particularly Saudi Arabia, such *fatwas* on Shiism were passed.

The *fatwa* issued by the religious council of Kelantan is particularly interesting for it mainly explains its rationale for accepting the federal *muzakarah* position on Shias. The council's arguments centre on three reasons: mainly differences in faith, *shari'a* (laws), and attitudes. Their main contention in relation to faith is how the Shias understand the concept of "imam". In deliberating this point, the *fatwa* cited the views of Muhamad bin Ya'akob Al- kalini to represent the Shia's theological viewpoint. On Islamic laws, the *fatwa* charged that Shias did not place enough emphasis on prayers (*solat*), tithe (*zakat*), and *haj*, which was deemed to have derived from the views of Jaafar as-Saddiq, a Shia imam. In addition, the *fatwa* accused the Shias of encouraging the short-term, contract marriages (*mutah*), which the *fatwa* claimed is based on fabricated *hadith* (traditions of the Prophet).[4]

It is not within the interest of this chapter to determine the correctness or wrongness of theological positions. But the style of thought that underlies the *fatwa* issued — which mainly sees groups as homogenous, static categories, and refers to selective theological positions — manifests this Islamic "exclusivity" at its core. Referring to only a handful of Shia scholars as representative of the whole group ignores the diversity of opinions within Shiism. For instance, there are many other works that may disagree with the views of Muhamad Bin Ya'cob Ak Kulini. A work by progressive Indonesian *ulama*, Quraish Shihab (2007), underscored the multiple voices and viewpoints within Shiism. Moreover, to charge Shias as not placing enough emphasis on the five pillars of Islam is disputed by many progressive scholars — both from the Sunni and the Shia camps. According to eminent Islamic scholar Khaled Abou El-Fadl (2007), both Sunnis and Shias concur with the five basic pillars of Islam-confession of faith, prayers, fast, tithe, and *haj* (pp. 117–18). Shia Muslims perform the same five prayers, but instead of doing five separate prayers, the prayers are performed on three separate times. Collapsing such prayer timings are also practised by some Sunni schools. Shia Muslims are also required to perform a congregational prayer in the mosque once a week, which is the *Jumuah* prayer (Friday).

The inaccuracies about theological positions adopted by the Shias are also seen in terms of the rituals that are practised. This is clearly seen in a *Penjelasan Ajaran-Ajaran Sesat Di Negeri Pulau Pinang* (An Explanation of Deviant Teachings in Pulau Pinang) published by the office of Mufti of the State of Pulau Pinang. Among the rituals deemed deviant include (1) visiting the shrine of Saidina Hussein that promises heaven, (2) to inflict pain on 10 Muharram to commemorate the death of Saidina Hussein or the Karbala incident, (3) to insult the wives of the Holy Prophet, and (4) to collapse prayers (Jabatan Mufti Pulau Pinang 2008, pp. 4–5).

There is a failure to engage in the diversity of opinions found in the group they categorized as Shias. In fact, not all Shias agree with the claims mentioned in the *fatwa*, that all the Shia imams are infallible, that they receive revelation from God, and that they disputed the Qur'an. There is a diversity of opinions amongst the Shias themselves, which is manifested within the different Shia sects: Twelve-Imam Shiism, Ismailism, and Zaydism (Muhammad Husayn Tabataba-I, p. 82). For example, the issue of the infallible position of the imam, which is upheld by Shias according to the Kelantan *fatwa*, is mainly common among the Twelve-Imam Shia group. However, this position is not shared by the Zaydis, who do not consider the imamate to belong to the Household of the Prophet. Ismailism, on the other hand, believes that the imamate revolves the number seven, not twelve, and the Prophecy does not end with the Prophet Muhammad. Even then, some contemporary Muslim scholars, including Sunni *ulama*, opine that the extreme understanding of imamism that equates imams to the divine no longer exists today (Quraish 2007, p. 70).

SHIAS AS THE "MINORITY"

Apart from differences in terms of theological viewpoints, Shias are deemed to be minority in the Islamic world. By clinging on to selective interpretation of religious traditions, their "minority status" is also deemed to mean their theology is skewed. For instance, in attempting to prove the deviance of other sects apart from ASWJ, the President of PAS (Islamic Party of Malaysia), Abdul Hadi Awang, cited a Prophetic *Hadith* as narrated by Abu Daud and Ibnu Majah:

The Jews will break into 71 sects. One will go to Heaven, the others to Hell. The Christians will break up into 72 sects. 71 will go to Hell, the remaining one to Heaven. Muslim will break up into 73 sects. One will achieve Heaven the others Hell. When asked who is this one group (to achieve paradise), the Prophet responded by saying the one in Jamaah. (Abdul Hadi Awang 2008, p. 2)

By referring to this tradition, the ASWJ is positioned by the religious elite as the "Jamaah" or the mainstream. Essentially, the ASWJ is treated as synonymous to being Sunnis, even though the Prophet may have used the term to refer to something else. Membership to this group is held as the only way one can assure salvation and heaven, as opposed to Muslims who fall outside the fold.

Such reading of this *hadith* ignores the controversies surrounding it. Some Shias also call themselves followers of the Sunnah (Quraish 2007, p. 60). For instance, a Shia academic based at Sorbonne University wrote a book *Asy-Syiah Hum Ahlussunnah*, translated as "*The Followers of the Imamah as the followers of Sunnah*". At the same time, Sunni scholars of the past cannot agree who fall within these 73 sects as pointed out by the Hadith. For instance, one notable scholar, As'Syary counted there were more than 100 sects that are not within the fold of Islam, referring to the "*Muktazilah*" as one category. On the other hand, another notable scholar, Asy-Syahrastani, divided the "*Muktazilah*" into 17 further sub-categories, which could add to As-Syary's denominations. Another scholar, Fakhruddin ar-Razy, during his time, observed there were more than 73 sects than being defined by the *Hadith*. He concluded that the Prophet may have referred to large denominations only (pp. 44–45). These interpretations show that scholars, even in the Sunni world, cannot agree on which denominations make up these 73 deviant sects.

On the other hand, there are many alternative traditions that are not analyzed by the religious elite. In one tradition, the Prophet stated that, "Muslims will break up into 70 sects. All will achieve paradise except for one" (p. 45). Another prophetic tradition, narrated by Anas (the Prophet's companion deemed authoritative by Sunnis), stated that, "The Muslims will break into 70 sects. All will go to paradise except *az-Zanadiqah*" (p. 46). Clearly, such alternative traditions did not feature in the religious elite's discourse. Had these traditions been considered, the Shias may not be seen as a minority.

The religious elite's use of traditions accords the ASWJ as the only God-sanctioned sect in Islam that assures them as the true followers of the authentic traditions of the Prophet. Other sects are either seen as derailed from the "truth", or believed to have been manipulated by the leaders for their own benefits. Unfortunately, no consideration is given to the fact that the ASWJ, as a movement or ideology, did not exist during the time of the Prophet and the Caliphs. It was only later in Muslim history that the movement grew self-conscious of its position in response to opposing factions. Even then it had also undergone a tremendous change from the "original" state and the teachings from the Quran (Fazlur 2000, pp. 30–60). The theological debate occurred and developed in the context of political conflict into which religion was woven.

In emphasizing their minority status, the dominant view in Malaysia is that Shia Muslims only constitute 10 per cent of the Muslim world.[5] It is observed that three Shia groups exist in contemporary Malaysia — Taiyibi Bohra (Dawoodi Bohra), Ismailiyah Agha Khan, and Ja'fariyah @ Imamiyah Itsna Asyariyah (Twelver Imam). The Taiyibi Bohra group is believed to have originated from India. In Malaysia, they are believed to be the owners of the "Bombay" shop and are believed to be centred in Kelang, where the cemeteries and mosques are also situated. There are about 200–400 followers. (A recent report has put the total figure of Shias in Malaysia at 250,000.)[6] The Ismailiyah Agha group, on the other hand, is well known by the name Peerbhai shop. They are also believed to be located in Lembah Kelang, but the number of followers are less than that of the Bohra group. Lastly, the Ja'fariyah group was believed to have originated from Iran, and their influence grew after the Iranian Revolution in 1979. Their influence grew as a result of the importation of reading materials and individuals coming to Malaysia. It is argued that the problem became more accentuated when some local lecturers in local universities in Malaysia tried to spread their teachings to the students in the higher learning institutions (JAKIM 1996, Jabatan Mufti Negeri Pulau Pinang 2008).

Based on the descriptions of Shiism in Malaysia by the religious authorities, details of their existence remains sketchy, and their numbers are too meager to be seen as a security threat. Ironically, while there is an attempt to point out that Shias have minimal following (in the world and in Malaysia), hence treating them as theologically "deviant" and not mainstream, much attention is given to their "significant" and "increasing" presence in Malaysia. The figures cited show that very little data is obtained about the Shias in Malaysia by the religious authorities. For example, JAKIM in 1996 published some rough estimates about the number of Shias in Malaysia. However, the exact same figures and description were cited by the Jabatan Pulau Pinang in 2008. This gives the impression that the numbers have either not grown, which is unlikely, or that they are mainly based on rough estimates (Jabatan Mufti Negeri Pulau Pinang, pp. 2–3). This again brings the question whether the Shias do pose any security threat to the legitimacy of the state.

SHIA AS A SECURITY THREAT

Shiism in Malaysia has, to some extent, been framed as a national security issue. In 1997, seven Shia followers were detained for spreading deviationist teachings (Liow 2009, p. 163). They were arrested for allegedly threatening religious harmony and the nation's political and economic development. As a precondition for their release, they were told to denounce the Shia beliefs and revert back to Sunni. Interestingly, the matter was not brought to the *shari'a* court, which normally handles religious matters in Malaysia, but instead dealt through the ISA.

Between October 2000 and January 2001, six followers on Shia teachings were arrested under the ISA (Saeed and Saeed 2004, p. 128). None of them was charged under the court of law. Out of the six arrested, one was released, two were sent to restricted residence, and the rest were detained for two years. Again the same reasons were cited, essentially, that they threatened religious harmony in Malaysia, where Muslims are predominantly Sunnis. The arrests of the Shias under the ISA are not widely reported. Not much is known about the background of those being detained. Nonetheless, Marcinkowski (2006) in his paper did point out a report dated 19 July 2002, featured on Shianews.com, which revealed the identities of those who were arrested (p. 17). The report referred to the arrests made between 2000 and 2001. As reported, one of those arrested was Mr Norman Basha (then forty-two years old), a construction site worker. On the 13 October 2000, he was handcuffed back to his house and the police confiscated some of his religious books. He was detained for sixty days, sent to Kamunting Detention Centre, and sentenced to two years of detention order.

These arrests under the ISA contravene not only the principle of human rights, but also the very foundations of the Malaysian constitution that allows one to practise their faith freely. Article 11 of the Malaysian constitution affirms that every person has the right to profess and practise his or her religion; what is prohibited, nonetheless, is to propagate other religions to convert Muslims. On the other hand, Article 3 in the constitution clearly states that Islam is the religion of the Federation, but other religions may be practised in peace and harmony in any part of the Federation. Nevertheless, scholars and legal experts have interpreted this provision in the constitution as Islam being the "official" religion of the country.

More importantly, the treatment of the Shias contradicts the very foundation of the Qur'an. Islam is inherently diverse and inclusive, not only towards different faiths but also towards different views. There are many verses in the Qur'an that support the freedom of choice of one's beliefs. It also describes the diversity in languages, nations, and ethnicity, as signs of God's grace and not a cause for distinction of superiority and inferiority. Therefore, differences are divine, and societies differ in their ways of life (Syed Farid 2009, p. 13). Two of the most important verses in the Qur'an that directly speaks about pluralism are verses 27 and 28 of *Al-Faathir*.

> See you not that God sends down rain from the sky? With it We then bring out produce of various colours. And in the mountains are tracts white and red, of various shades of colour, and black intense in hue. And so amongst men and crawling creatures and cattle, are they of various colours. Those truly fear God, among His Servants, who have knowledge: for God is exalted in Might, Oft-Forgiving. (Surah *Al-Faathir* verses 27 and 28)[7]

Verse 256 of *Al-Baqarah* underlines that:

> There is no compulsion in religion: Truth stands our clear from Error: Whoever rejects evil and believes in God has grasped the most trustworthy authority handhold that never breaks. And God hears and knows all things. (Surah *Al-Baqarah* verse 256)[8]

The Qur'an also specifically stipulates freedom in finding or losing one's way in the world. According to Mohsen (2006), it has shown people the just path and leaves it them to choose or ignore it. God and the Prophet have allowed the people to choose their religion, at the same time telling them what the right path is (p. 135). *Surah An-Naml* states that:

> For me, I have been commanded to serve the Lord of this city, Him Who has sanctified it and to Whom (belong) all things: and I am commanded to be of those who bow in Islam to God's will. And to

Rehearse the *Quran*: and if any accept guidance, they do it for the good of their own souls, and if they stray, say "I am only a warner." And say "Praise be upon God, Who will soon show you his Signs, so that you shall know them": and your Lord is not unmindful of all that you do" (*Surah An-Naml* verses 91 and 92).[9]

In line with the principles of pluralism and freedom of worship, the Qur'an in *Surah Yunus* holds that: "If it had been your Lord's will, they would all have believed — all who are on earth! Will you then compel mankind, against their will, to believe!" (*Surah Yunus* verse 99)[10] Some Muslim scholars even maintain that Islam never discriminates non-Muslims from Muslims, and this is reflected in the Covenant of Medina (Asghar 2009, pp. 112–13). Some of the terms provided by the covenant include *inter alia*: Jews and Muslims are to live as one, with both communities respecting and not interfering in the affairs of each other, and that in the event of an attack on the city of Medina, both parties shall join hands to defend. Such religious differences and diversity are respected by Islam. El-Fadl (2003, p. 15) maintains that the Qur'an not only expects but accepts the reality of difference and diversity within human society: "O humankind, God has created you from male and female and made you into diverse nations and tribes so that you may come to know each other. Verily, the most honored of you in the sight of God is he who is the most righteous (*Al-Hujurat*: verse 13)". However, such views on religious pluralism and diversity are not clearly reflected in the "exclusivist" religious orientation of the religious elite in Malaysia, which subscribes to a single, absolute version of truth, based on the dogmatic adherence to selected traditions and how they are construed.

The use of legal means and detention has resulted in many Shias in Malaysia to practise their faith privately. According to Mr Kamil Zuhairi bin Abdul Aziz, leader of the *Lovers of the Prophet's Household*, "Most of the Shia is hiding because of the oppression" (sic) (*The New York Times*, 24 March 2011). Some Shias also feared that they would be discriminated when applying for jobs had the religious authorities known they were Shias. The attitude of these individuals clearly proves that draconian methods may only be counterproductive for the religious authorities if they had really wanted to promote Sunnism as the sole true Islamic doctrine. Such methods only create distrust of the Shias towards the religious authorities and hinder fruitful dialogue.

Dialogue could be seen as a softer approach in dealing with groups with different views.

CONCLUSION

The different arguments forwarded to delegitimize Shiism, conversely, deconstruct the whole notion of a homogenous ASWJ as well. Clearly, there is a diversity of views even within the group that sees themselves as ASWJ. Categories such as the "ASWJ" and "Shias", as understood in Malaysia today, are merely recent political and practical constructs, derived from the selective and ideological reading of Islamic history, texts, and opinions. While undeniably such constructs serve certain groups with interests, underlying them is an "exclusivist" Islam which resulted from greater centralization of a powerful Islamic bureaucracy, which ensures that the practice of Malaysia's official Islam — ASWJ — is adhered to by all Muslim groups through legal and even draconian means.

Nevertheless, one should not dismiss the political motivations that resulted in the treatment of the Shias as "deviant". Part of this is related to the global Islamic resurgence of the 1970s that impacted the Malay world. The Iranian Revolution, which mainly inspired many of the *dakwah* organizations (groups that spread the message of Islam) in Malaysia, posed a huge political threat to the ruling powers and traditional religious authority then. Moreover, the "petrol-dollars" offered by regimes not close to the Iranian government are too difficult to ignore.

Surprisingly, the latest arrests of the Shias in 2011 paid no heed to the international agreement signed by many Muslim nations — The Amman Message — in which Malaysia is a signatory. In 2005, King Abdullah II of Jordan sent three critical questions — (1) Who is a Muslim?, (2) Is it permissible to declare someone an apostate (*takfir*)?, and (3) Who has the right to undertake issuing *fatwas* (legal rulings)? — to 24 of the most senior religious scholars from all around the world representing all branches and schools of Islam. These senior and renowned *ulama* include great scholars from both the Sunni and Shia traditions. Amongst them are the Shaykh Al-Azhar (Sunni), Ayatollah Sistani (Shia), and the respectable Shaykh Dr Yusuf Abdallah Al-Qaradawi (Sunni). The message specifically recognized the validity of all eight Mazhhabs (legal schools) of Sunni, Shia and Ibadi Islam, of traditional Islamic theology (Ash'arism), of Islamic mysticism (Sufism), and of true Salafi thought, and came to a precise definition of who is a Muslim. Moreover, the message also forbids *takfir* (declarations of apostasy) among Muslims.[11]

Similarly, the fact that Shia states and ideology have been accepted as part of Islam in international institutions and agreements is often passed over. Both Malaysia and The Islamic Republic of Iran are members of the Organization of Islamic Conference (OIC), and both states have strong diplomatic ties. Iran is a member of this group since 1969. Iran's membership in the OIC signifies the fact that it is accepted as an Islamic country, despite being a "Shia" state. The views of the religious authority also overlooks the point that Al-Azhar University — an important religious institution and highly respected in the Sunni world for preaching moderate views on Islam — is very open to teaching all schools of thought in the Islamic world, including Shiism. By and large, Al-Azhar remains a largely popular destination for Southeast Asian students seeking tertiary religious education. Al-Azhar University teaches not only Sunni school of thought — Maliki, Syafi'I, Hanafi, and Hanbali — but also Shia schools of thought such as Jaafari, Zaidy, Adz-Zhahiri, and Al-Abaydiyyah (Quraish 2007, p. 3). This comes to show the openness other Sunni Muslims have towards Shias.

Given the negative perceptions towards the Shias in Malaysia today, pure cooperation and intra-Muslim dialogue would not be able to make headway. It must be noted that the Shias is only one of the many groups that suffer from the discriminatory practices of the religious elite in Malaysia. Other groups that do not agree with the dominant religious elite include those labelled as "liberal Muslims" and "feminist" Muslims. In exclusivist Islam, there is certainly a lack of engagement in alternative ideas and opinions. Their theological viewpoints are not only selective but also deemed absolute and complete. Exclusivist orientation is dismissive of opinions that differ from those upheld, without justification or reasoning. Hence, discussions on the Shiism remain very shallow and superficial. Labels are passed unthinkingly towards the Shias and hence dismissive towards the vast corpus of writings by both Sunni and Shia scholars on the subject. Without any discussion of new ideas and a more comprehensive understanding of an issue including problems and ramifications of views expounded, very little attempts towards reform can be initiated. It prevents the religious elite from grappling with new issues effectively and objectively. To paint a rather pessimistic view, no progress or headway can ever be made towards resolving these issues when at its foundation the religious elite have a narrow view of religious pluralism, which can impede genuine understanding needed for the well-being of the plural society in Malaysia.

Notes

1. It must be pointed out that the Islamic resurgence movement is not a homogenous group and have different conceptions of what constitute an Islamic state and society.
2. UMNO-Online, Mahathir, Khatami Minta OIC Kaji Secara Mendalam Perpecahan Antara Puak Sunnah, Syiah, available at <http://www.umno-online.my/?p=86201> (accessed 23 May 2013).
3. Portal Rasmi Fatwa Malaysia, available at <http://www.e-fatwa.gov.my> (accessed 23 May 2013).
4. See e-fatwa, Fatwa Mengenai Ajaran Islam (Kelantan), available at <http://www.e-fatwa.gov.my/fatwa-negeri/fatwa-mengenai-ajaran-syiah> (accessed 23 May 2013).
5. See for example the view of Jabatan Mufti Negeri Pulau Pinang, 3.
6. See <http://www.theedgemalaysia.com/political-news/249131-home-ministry-shia-followers-now-at-250000.html> (accessed 12 August 2013).
7. See translation of Abdullah Yusof Ali (p. 440).
8. See translation of Abdullah Yusof Ali (p. 56).
9. See translation of Abdullah Yusof Ali (p. 383).
10. See translation by Abdullah Yusuf Ali (p. 213).
11. The official website of The Amman Message, available at <http://www.ammanmessage.com/> (accessed 23 May 2013).

References

Abdul Hadi Awang. *Fahaman dan Ideologi Umat Islam* [Islamic Thought and Ideology]. Selangor: PTS Islamika Publications, 2008.

Abdullah Yusof Ali. *The Meaning of the Holy Quran*. Kuala Lumpur: Islamic Book Trust, 1996.

Ahmad Fauzi, A.H. "The Banning of Darul Arqam in Malaysia". *Review of Indonesian and Malaysian Affairs* 39, no. 1 (2005): 87–128.

Alatas, Syed Farid Alatas. "The Study of Muslim Revival: A General Framework". In *Muslim Reform in Southeast Asia*, edited by Syed Farid Alatas. Singapore: MUIS, 2009.

Allāmah Sayyid Muhammad Husayn Tabātabā'ī. *Shiite Islam*. Albany: State University of New York Press, 1975.

Asghar, Ali Engineer. "Governance and Religion — An Islamic Point of View". In *Religion and Governance*, edited by Chandra Muzaffar. Shah Alam: Arah Publications, 2009.

As-Sallaabee, Ali Muhammad. *The Biography of Abu Bakr As-Siddeeq*, translated by Faisal Shafeeq. Riyadh: Darussalam, 2007.

El-Fadl, Khaled Abou. *Speaking in God's Name: Islamic Law, Authority and Women*. England: Oneworld Publication, 2001.

———. "The Place of Tolerance in Islam". In *The Place of Tolerance in Islam*, edited by Joshua Cohen and Ian Lague. Boston: Beacon Press, 2003.

———. *The Great Theft: Wrestling Islam from the Extremist*. New York: HarperOne, 2007.

Fazlur Rahman. *Revival and Reform in Islam: A Study of Islamic Fundamentalism* Oxford: Oneworld, 2000.

Funston, John. "Malaysia". In *Voices of Islam in Southeast Asia: A Contemporary Sourcebook*, edited by Greg Fealy and Virginia Hooker. Singapore: Institute of Southeast Asian Studies, 2006.

Hamayotsu, Kikue. "Islam and Nation Building in Southeast Asia: Malaysia and Indonesia in Comparative Perspective". In *Pacific Affairs* 75, no. 3 (2002): 353–75.

"In Malaysia, Shiites Struggle to Practice Their Faith". *New York Times*, 24 March 2011.

Jabatan Mufti Negeri Pulau Pinang. *Penjelasan Ajaran-Ajaran Sesat Di Negeri Pulau Pinang*. Pulau Pinang: Jabatan Mufti Pulau Pinang, 2008.

JAKIM. *Penjelasan Terhadap Fahaman Syiah*. Kuala Lumpur: JAKIM, 1966.

Kamarulnizam Abdullah. "National Security and Malay Unity: The Issue of Radical Religious Elements in Malaysia". *Contemporary Southeast Asia* 21, no. 2 (1999): 261–83.

Liow, Joseph Chinyong. *Piety and Politics: Islamism in Contemporary Malaysia*. New York: Oxford University Press, 2009.

Mannheim, Karl. *Ideology and Utopia: An Introduction to the Sociology of Knowledge*, translated by Louis Wirth and Edward Shils. San Diego; New York; London: Harcourt INC, 1936.

Marcinkowski, Christoph. *Facets of Shi'ite Islam in Contemporary Southeast Asia (II): Malaysia and Singapore*. Singapore: Institute of Defence and Strategic Studies, 2006.

Maznah Mohamad. "The Ascendance of Bureaucratic Islam and the Secularization of the Sharia in Malaysia". *Pacific Affairs* 83, no. 3 (2010): 505–24.

Mohsen Kadivar. "Freedom of Religion and Belief in Islam". In *The New Voices of Islam: Reforming Politics and Modernity — A Reader*, edited by Mehran Kamrava. New York; London: IB Tauris, 2006.

Norani, O., A. Zainah, and M.K. Zaitun. "Malaysia: Islamization, Muslim Politics and State Authoritarianism". In *Muslim Women and the Challenges of Islamic Extremism*, edited by Norani Othman. Kuala Lumpur: Sisters in Islam, 2005.

"Pas Must Clarify Stand on Shia". *New Straits Times*, 18 May 2013.

Quraish, Shihab M. *Sunnah-Syiah: Bergandingan Tangan Mungkinkah? Kajian Atas Konsep Ajaran dan Pemikiran*. Jakarta. Lentera Hati, 2007.

Ramadan, Tariq. *Western Muslims and Future of Islam*. New York: Oxford University Press, 2004.

Saeed, A. and Saeed H. *Freedom of Religion, Apostasy and Islam*. Aldershot, UK: Ashgate, 2004.
Watt, Montgomery. "The Significance of the Early Stages of Imami Shi'ism". In *Religion and Politics in Iran: Shi'ism from Quietism to Revolution*, edited by Nikki R. Keddie. New Haven and London: Yale University Press, 1983.

Websites

Fatwa Mengenai Ajaran Islam (Kelantan). Available at <http://www.e-fatwa.gov.my/fatwa-negeri/fatwa-mengenai-ajaran-syiah> (accessed 23 May 2013).

The Official Website of the Amman Message. Available at <http://www.ammanmessage.com/> (accessed 23 May 2013).

Portal Rasmi Fatwa Malaysia. Available at <http://www.e-fatwa.gov.my> (accessed 23 May 2013).

Puak Sunnah, Syiah. Available at <http://www.umno-online.my/?p=86201> (accessed 23 May 2013).

UMNO-Online. Mahathir, Khatami Minta OIC Kaji Secara Mendalam Perpecahan Antara.

19

BEING CHRISTIANS IN MUSLIM-MAJORITY MALAYSIA
The Kelabit and Lun Bawang Experiences in Sarawak

Poline Bala

INTRODUCTION:
RELIGIOUS MINORITIES CHALLENGES IN MALAYSIA

In recent years a situation which has emerged out of Malaysia's multiculturalism and which has caught the attention of various commentators on Malaysian society is the position of religious minorities such as the Hindus, Buddhist, Taoists, Sikhs, Christians, and animists in Malaysia. This is especially within the context of freedom of belief, which is one of the fundamental rights upheld by the Federal Constitution of Malaysia. This basic right is clearly spelt out by Article 3(1): "Islam is the religion of the Federation, but other religions may be practiced in peace and harmony in any part of the Federation." Furthermore Article 11(1) indicates that, "Every person has the right to profess and practice his religion and, subject to clause 4, to propagate it." In other words, except for Article 11(4), which prohibits the propagation of any religious doctrine or belief among persons professing the religion of Islam, right to religion is protected in Malaysia.

However, procedures and processes to build non-Islamic places of worship are getting tougher, causing delays and resulting in some projects being abandoned for years before being granted approvals (see Chong in this volume). Moreover, the ban on the use of term "Allah" in all Christian publications including digital media, limitations to certain religious practices and non-Muslims being affected by Islamic Law and legal obstacles to inter-religious marriages have led to increasing concerns over rights to religion and the rise of ethnic and religious polarization in Malaysia. These circumstances (although not exclusively) have led to claims that the nation has never been so divided by race and religion as it is today. Lim and Gomes (2009) equate the contemporary situation to "a sharp crack in the cultural mosaic arising from growing ethnic, religious and cultural polarization" (p. 232). Their claims appear to affirm a long-held perspective that Malaysia is an ethnic time bomb for creating an explosive situation (Gabriel 1996, p. 3).

In other words, although Malaysia in terms of racial relationships is said to be "a model of harmony and good feeling for all the world" (Emerson 1970, p. 312 cited in Cheah 2009, p. 33) and to be "a unique model of tolerance and accommodation" (Riddel 2004, p. 67 cited in Walters 2007, p. 68), one of the main issues in Malaysia today remains the question of national unity, namely, how to create loyalty among people in a country marked by cultural, religious, and geographical heterogeneity. Although Malaysia is seen as a nation at peace with its ethnic and religious diversity where by relations are generally calm and citizens are able to get on with their lives, enjoy their rights, there are strong perceptions that while some ethnic groups are playing prominent role in politics, others are being excluded. This leads to fear of domination by one ethnic/religious group over the other. There are others who are very concerned that these situations may lead to more acute ethnic tensions, and therefore argue that the situations need to be managed skillfully by asking many difficult questions as suggested by Lim, Gomes, and Azly (2009, p. 3). In line with this are calls for the resolution of inter-religious conflict in a fair and just manner in line with the rule of law and the Federal Constitution. This is to ensure that "the spark will not become a fire" (Salfarina, Abdul Bakar, & Azeem 2009, p. 253).

Amid all this, however, little is known of the experiences of small religious minorities located at the fringe of nation-state. In particular how they grapple with the salient position of Malay culture and the increasing identification of Islamic identity with the national politics. This becomes especially significant in that Malays who follow Islam as their religion form Malaysia's majority population. The situation is compounded by the enshrining of Islam as the state religion despite a pluralistic Malaysian society.

It is in this context that this chapter turns to the experiences of the Kelabit and Lun Bawang of northeastern part of Sarawak, to highlight the ways in which "small" communities and cultures negotiate the challenges of inter-religious relations that they face in Malaysia today. This has a particular bearing on both these communities who are not only non-Malay Bumiputera but also are predominantly Christian communities. Although the Kelabit and Lun Bawang, borrowing Jomo's (1992) term have been "mute spectators" of various Islamic resurgence and movements and/or of Malay politics, there has been an increasing sense of "fear" over powerful, assertive, and intolerant Muslims and Islamic movements in Malaysia. There is a growing unease that these tendencies might be a threat to the Kelabit's and Lun Bawang's religious identity. The uncertain situation raises concerns of how to maintain a Christian-influenced identity within a Muslim-dominant culture. Yet at the same time there are ongoing debates among the Lun Bawang and Kelabit as to how, as Christian communities, they ought to respond with kindheartedness and tolerance in their everyday encounters and engagements with people of other faiths including with their Muslim friends, visitors, and relatives.

The account of their experiences in this chapter suggests that it is imperative to examine the issue of majority–minority relations and of religious freedom vis-à-vis the position of Islam in Malaysia. More importantly, the account provides an understanding of both the dilemmas and aspirations of inter-religious dealings in the public sphere and in everyday life for Christians in minority situations within Muslim-majority locales in Southeast Asia. This is important to understand in the context of growing unease over real or perceived disadvantages, exclusion and political marginalization suffered as a result of locality and numerical inferiority. As has been suggested by Li-ann Thio (2010, p. 43): "An enduring problem for constitutional design and democratic practice within the context of a plural society with ethnic, religious and linguistic religious minorities is the need to address the fears and aspirations of these groups in relation to threats to their identity and autonomy." From this perspective, the specificities of the Kelabit and Lun Bawang case provide pertinent and interesting illustrations of the interactions between religion, politics, and socio-economic factors in the growing importance of issues of religious diversity in Malaysia.

The remainder of the chapter explores these various issues in more detail and is structured as follows. The next section highlights the Kelabit and Lun Bawang situations as Christian minorities in Muslim majority Malaysia. This is followed by assessment of the impact of Islamic revivalism and ethnic-based politics upon the communities especially the ways in which an "Us vs Them syndrome" has emerged out of this situation. The chapter then moves on to highlight how the Kelabit and Lun Bawang negotiate a Christian response to Islam and to the position of Malay Muslims in Malaysia. It highlights the ongoing debates, issues, and challenges as they negotiate a way forward. The chapter concludes that today, as Christian minority groups, the Kelabit and Lun Bawang would endeavour to find the right balance in their response to Islam.

THE KELABIT AND LUN BAWANG AS CHRISTIAN COMMUNITIES

The Kelabit and the Lun Bawang traditionally inhabit the highland regions of northeastern Sarawak. Linguistically and culturally they are two closely related ethnic groups and as a result have often been viewed by some scholars as a single group. For instance, LeBar (1972, p. 153) has grouped them under the Kelabitic Murut group. In fact, although over the years the Kelabit and Lun Bawang have developed into two distinct ethnic groups as we know them today, they still maintain strong social, political, and economic ties through which each group continues to contribute to the livelihood and survival of the other (Bala 2001).

Since at the turn of the century, like many other ethnic groups of Sarawak, the Lun Bawang and the Kelabit have experienced major social transformation. Once upon a time, they were long-house-based communities in which kinship relations played dominant roles in their social and political relations, but today, with high rates of rural–urban migration, the Lun Bawang and Kelabit have adopted positions and interests that bring them in as part of Malaysia's multicultural, multi-religious, and multi-ethnic society.

This is in spite of their physical remoteness. Both homeland areas were historically cut off from the rest of the world due to the difficult physical surroundings of their homelands. The Highlands are surrounded by some of the highest and most rugged upland and mountainous terrains in Sarawak. This includes Mount Murud (the highest mountain in Sarawak) and Batu Lawih. Furthermore, and within the contemporary political geography of Malaysia, the Highlands are located at the frontier borders between Sarawak and East Kalimantan. However, today members of both communities are not only farmers but are also professionals, business persons, teachers, lawyers, engineers, policy-makers, and others engaged in the labour force and contributing to nation-building, domestically and internationally.

A social aspect, which to a certain degree distinguishes the Kelabit and Lun Bawang from many other ethnic groups in Sarawak and more generally in Malaysia, is their devotion to their Christian faith. Most writers of Kelabit and Lun Bawang life (for instance, Deegan 1973; Janowski 1991; Amster 1998; Saging 1976/1977; Bulan and Bulan-Dorai 2004; Bala 2002, 2008) allude to the effects and significance of Christianity amongst the two communities They are Kelabit and Lun Bawang themselves who claim that conversion to Christianity, more than anything else, has affected their lives and history, including their religious and ethnic identity (Amster 1998, p. 3; Saging 1976/1977, p. 244). In short, Christianity has permeated all aspects of their lives including playing significant roles in their everyday life.

At the village level, the church is of great importance to village life. As observed by Deegan of the Lun Bawang villages: "In many ways, the church was the heart of the community for a community-minded people" (Deegan 1973, p. 286). Today, each Kelabit and Lun Bawang village in the Highlands has a church.

Elsewhere I have argued at length "through the years the church and its organization have combined to become the most important focal point for organizing economic and social life in the Highlands. In fact, in certain respects the church has replaced the social and economic roles of the longhouse as a space to share and express a communal lifestyle. For example, the church today organizes almost all joint social and economic activities in the villages. These include organizing the joint work groups which are offshoots of the traditional self-help groups through which villagers provide local mutual assistance, for instance on each other's farms, on a rotation system" (Bala 2008, p. 90).

At one level, Christianity shapes the worldviews of Highlanders and their open attitudes towards change: it provides foundation and framework from which the Lun Bawang and Kelabit can consider social change, including those that come with the state's interventions in their respective Highland home areas (Bala 2009, p. 175). Their open attitudes allow both communities to embrace social changes, and at the same time to transform new ideas as important means to project their identity and position in relation to others, both in Malaysia and globally.

The significance of Christianity is so strong amongst the Lun Bawang and the Kelabit that it has become a source of identity in contemporary

Malaysia. For instance in his analysis of Christian conversion among the Kelabit, Amster (1998) concludes, "… just as Islam today is the basis for Malay identity in Malaysia, the Kelabit identity is now largely about being Christian, and that Christian practice and belief cannot be empirically separated from notions of contemporary Kelabit ethnicity" (p. 3). Similar observations were also made by Deegan (1973) amongst the Lun Bawang, whereby identity was an impetus for their conversion to Christianity.

SMALL NUMBERS AND BEING CHRISTIANS IN MUSLIM MAJORITY MALAYSIA

While the Lun Bawang and Kelabit are proud and secure about their historical experiences and conversion to Christianity, it also can be a source of dilemma. This is because it is interwoven with inter-religious, political, economic, and ethnic concerns at the national level. Within this context, their small numbers and their shared Christian identity have worked towards their peripherality within Malaysia as a nation-state. Even if they are joined as a collective in one political constituency, the Kelabit and Lun Bawang are still a minority group. In other words, because of their numerical inferiority they can feel that they are of no consequence in the wider scheme of things.

Furthermore, as mentioned earlier, their homelands are physically remote and located at the international frontier borders between Sarawak and East Kalimantan, Indonesia. In other words, they can be perceived as being far removed from the centres of powers, both at the state and national levels. In summary, they have to cope with their minority status as a small group, located at the fringe of the nation-state.

Their minority situations are compounded by the position of Malay-Muslim political cultures within Malaysia's ethnic-based political and economic system. Over the years, ethnic, cultural, and religious identities in Malaysia are topics that have received a good deal of scholarly attention (Shamsul 1986; Jomo 1985; Goh 2002). As pointed out by Jayum and King (1997) "… [the] ethnic factor become(s) the single most important consideration in political and socio-economic life in Malaysia" (p. 42). In similar vein Marger (2003, cited in Cheah 2009) suggests, "… in multiethnic societies, ethnicity serves as an extremely critical determinant of who gets what there is to get and in what amounts" (p. 36).

Of particular consequence here is the constitutional provision, which favours the numerically dominant group, the Malay Muslims. As noted by Gabriel (1996), "This is unlike normal practice logically in other places where by a majority and politically powerful group rise to support the weaker and numerically less populous sections of society" (p. 2). The positive discrimination of a majority and politically powerful group in Malaysia introduces the risk of creating imbalances in political, economical, and social spheres.

This raises a question: What are the implications for the Lun Kelabit and Lun Bawang of being a Christian religious minority? This is especially with regard to their Christian self-identity and self-expression in relation to Islam. Perhaps, more importantly how are they responding, reacting, and adapting to competing ethnic, religious, and cultural interests and the changing landscape surrounding the rights of religious minorities in Malaysia? As will be made clear, in spite of the remoteness of their traditional homelands, these situations do not escape the Kelabit and Lun Bawang of Sarawak: they require them to respond. Their responses nonetheless need to be examined within wider contexts. One is in the context of national politics and Islamic revivalism in Malaysia. The other is within the context of Sarawak as one of the Malaysian states that is located on the island of Borneo. Finally they fall within the wider Christian quest for an appropriate response to Islam and engagement with Muslims, especially post-9/11.

REVIVALISM, ETHNO-POLITICS, ENEMY IMAGE AND THE EMERGENCE OF "US VS THEM" SYNDROME

It has been argued that Christian–Muslim relations assume quite a different character in Sarawak compared to the Peninsula (Gabriel 1996). This is mainly because of Sarawak's distinct demographics and histories. Unlike Malaysia as a whole, Sarawak's demographic composition is far more complex (Shafruddin & Fadzil 1988, p. 22). The natives, who comprise many groups, collectively form the major group in the state. This is unlike in Peninsular Malaysia whereby the dominant groups are the Malays, Chinese, and Indians. Also, although constitutionally regarded as *bumiputera*, many groups do not identify themselves with the ethnic Malays, who are Muslims, while they are not.[1] Moreover, in Sarawak, the Christians make up 28.5 per cent of the state's population and a large majority are animists. This is very different to the national census which indicates that only 8.6 per cent of Malaysia's total populations are Christians which is far smaller than the Muslims who makes 60.4 per cent of the total populations. In other words, the Malay-Muslim group is not a dominant majority in Sarawak and Malay Sarawakians are often aggregated with ethnic Melanaus and their politics are always closely intertwined (Jayum and King 2004, p. 42).

Furthermore, the Federal Constitution protects the interests of Sabah and Sarawak natives. One example is Article 153(1) of the Federal Constitution, which imposed a duty on the government to safeguard their special position as natives of Sabah and Sarawak. Another example is to allow the system of justice based on native law and custom to co-exist with civil law and *syariah* law.

In short, although the population of many native groups in Sarawak is small, collectively they form a majority of the population. As a result, Sarawak's population composition to a certain degree mitigates against the vulnerability of racial and religious minorities to disadvantage, exclusion, or political marginalization which often stems from their numerical inferiority: nonetheless this is not to say that Christian–Muslim relations are free of misgivings in Sarawak. As observed by Gabriel (1996), "With regards to the privileged and dominant position of the Malay/Muslim group in Sarawak there are considerable misgivings among the Christians and other groups" (p. 3).

For the Kelabit and Lun Bawang, as part of a Christian minority, there are several dimensions to these "misgivings". One dimension is fear that their divergent cultural interests as subordinate and peripheral groups as previously described will not be given a hearing in the context of a national integration discourse, which places the Malay-Muslim *bumiputera* at the top of the hierarchy. Related to the latter are privileges provided by law to Malay Muslims as espoused through the *Ketuanan Melayu* (Malay supremacy) notion. Although *bumipuetra* status is conferred to the indigenous peoples of Sabah and Sarawak, *Ketuanan Melayu* promises a birthright for the Malays, it consequently entails differential treatments of the *bumiputera*, often at what appears to be at the expense of other ethnic groups.

For many Kelabit and Lun Bawang, the political, cultural, and social dominance of the Malay Muslims in Malaysia is made more real by their encounter with perceived privileges given to Malay Muslims, especially in terms of promotions and scholarships. It is in this context that expressions such as *Aban peh narih masuk Melayu* (unless one becomes Malay) become common, denoting "in order to have easy access to resources, promotions and positions of power one should become Malay". From this perspective, religion can become a means to get promoted especially in the public services (see also Chua in this volume). This situation led to ambivalent attitude towards the notion of *Ketuanan Melayu*.

Another important aspect to this is their experiences with issues and complications surrounding intermarriages, conversion, apostasy, and other related issues. The enforcement of Islamic laws on non-Muslims especially in cases of intermarriages can create very painful family situations. For instance, if a non-Muslim husband converts to Islam, the religion of the children becomes a contentious issue. This is because the children have to become Muslims following their father. This became a reality in Bario in 1980s when conversion of non-Muslim children by a spouse who converts to Islam against the wishes of the other parent took place. It created confusion and upheaval among families. As it is in Malaysia, the right to convert to another religion is limited to non-Muslims; a Muslim conversion to another religion is considered an apostasy. This has direct effects on those who would like to "unbecome" or stop being a Muslim for various reasons. A clear example of this involved a Kelabit mother, Raung (pseudonym) who was in her late forties when she passed away in 2006. She was divorced from her Muslim husband and soon after had contracted an incurable terminal disease. Through the turmoil of her broken marriage and disease, she reckoned to return to her Kelabit roots and Christian faith but faced fierce opposition from her former husband. Intense negotiations ensued between both families and also relevant state Islamic authority especially when she requested to be buried next to her late father at a Christian cemetery. As admitted by one of her relatives afterwards, "It was an insurmountable family trauma."[2]

Furthermore, a person who marries a Muslim is not only required to convert to Islam but also to *"me kuh lun Melayu"* (Kelabit) or *"masuk Melayu"* (to enter the Malay community). To a certain degree and in some cases, conversion to Islam entails both a change of religion and of ethnic identity. This is especially if those who convert to Islam also refuse to eat together with their families, changes the way they dress up by covering their heads, or abstain from socializing with members of the community. There have been cases where those who have become Muslims refuse to return to their villages in Ba Kelalan and Bario. These situations have led to heart wrenching experiences for some families who feel they have lost members of their family because now they have *"me kuh lun Melayu"* or become "Melayu".

This is compounded by engagements with some Malay-Muslim visitors to the Highlands who refused to eat with the people in the longhouses — at times bringing their own cooking utensils such as pots and pans, fork and spoons for cooking and eating while in the longhouses. In general, the Kelabit and Lun Bawang have good relations with those who are of other religions, but encounters such as these can be very confusing for those offering and giving food and dishes to guest is a core cultural practice — a traditional part of receiving guests in the longhouses.

For some in the Highlands, to a certain degree, these kinds of experiences have brought a perception that the privileged position of the Malay Muslim sometimes involves being rigid, guarded, unfriendly, or coercive. This does not occur all the time, but it can create a strong sense of division between "Us and Them" as far as Malay Muslims are concerned.

This latter point leads me to the other dimension of Kelabit and Lun Bawang unease or fear of the Malay Muslim group in Malaysia. This is with regard to the increasing Islamizing of institutions and processes in recent years as a result of Islamic revivalism, which has raised consciousness among the Malays for true Islam (see chapter by Chong). For minorities like the Kelabit and Lun Bawang, this raises two different kinds of concerns.

The first is the characteristics of religious revivalism in Malaysia: there is an indication of strong interconnection between Islam and the state. According to Shamsul (1986, p. 136), this is made clear through the way the *dakwah* phenomenon treats Islam and politics as one and the same in Malaysia. As such, although Islamic revival is "vast in geographical scope, affecting every single Muslim country from North Africa to Southeast Asia" (Berger 1999, p. 7 cited in Carvalho 2009, p. 1), with an aim to "return Islam to its original pure form" by cleansing Islam of all ungodly elements" (Yousif 2004, p. 30; Farouk Musa 2010, p. 252), it has become a force to be reckoned within Malaysia's religious and ethnic politics (Jomo and Cheek 1992; Shamsul 1997; Nagata 1980).

For the Kelabit and Lun Bawang, Shamsul's claims have been affirmed by range of measures taken by the governments towards conscious and concerted programmes of Islamizing Malaysia. This is quite obvious over the past few years. As a result, there is a common perception that the Malaysian government policies, for instance its education and language policies, are not intended to unify but intended to position the Malays at the top of the hierarchy.

This is made clear through calls for a legal system based on Islamic law in Malaysia. Even though the Kelabit are conscious that this is partly because of Islam position as the official religion,[3] still they are nervous and apprehensive. This is especially so when the issue of whether Malaysia is an Islamic or secular state came to the fore in the early years of 2000.⁴ The notion to a certain extent has become a considerable source of concern amongst the Kelabit and Lun Bawang as with other religious minority communities in the country.⁵ There is mistrust and fear among the people that this kind of open declaration is the beginning of coercive Islamization in the country. In this situation, many non-Muslim communities feel unsafe. A fear of Muslim dominance and creeping Islamization has developed among some Christians. A clear example of these kinds of concerns is an incident in 2010 where by the race of six natives students of Lun Bawang, Kelabit descent were changed to *Keturunan Melayu* (Malay descent) in their school report cards.⁶

This fear is also because of pressure by Islamic movements and opposition groups that aspire to transform the Malaysian society according to Islamic values and ideals.⁷ There is a common feeling, because of the government's deep commitment to Islam and the prevailing Islamic atmosphere, that greater restrictions will be imposed upon the practice of other religions. This case is well described by Ahmad Yousif (2004): "There is a general fear among non-Muslims that their religious freedom cannot be guaranteed under a situation of Islamic competition and expansionism. Some fear that the democratic system of government will eventually give way to a theocratic one, in which state and religion are one and indivisible, and that Malaysia, as a secular state, will cease to exist" (p. 38).

At another level, as mentioned earlier, are concerns that Islamic revivalism would impact the daily life, values, social relations, diet, and dress of the Kelabit and Lun Bawang, but more particularly the use of certain Malay terms and expressions in their Christian worship. As noted by Walters (2007): "With the state moving into the realm of societal values and 'Islamizing' institutions, a number of pertinent questions disturb the minds of the religious minorities. How will this affect daily life, economics, education, the legal system, the rule of law, dress, diet, etc.? What would be the implications at the practical level as they live together as individuals and communities with others of different faiths?" (p. 71).

This is especially so in Bario and Ba' Kelalan. Even though the debate whether Malaysia is an Islamic state or a secular state has not been as explicit as at the national level and in fact to a certain degree is considered a remote issue with no relevance to local surroundings, still the Kelabit and Lun Bawng have become fearful of over powerful and assertive Islamic movements in Malaysia. As suggested by Liow (2008 cited in Farouk

Musa 2010, p. 258) the discourse has moved "beyond whether Malaysia is an Islamic state towards the best ways and means to absorb Malaysian's non-Muslim minorities in a mutually acceptable *modus vivendi*." For the Kelabit and Lun Bawang, there is a feeling that they are being targeted by Islamization activities because of their Christian faiths and heritage in the Highlands. This is particularly so when on 17 November 2009 an article titled *Dakwah penduduk Bario* appeared on Kosmo Online Rencana Utama.[8] The article has bred fear, and as such a debate among members the Kelabit how best to respond to what some considered as a threat to their faith and identity. Conversely some Muslims see Christianity as part and parcel of Western imperialism and aggression and Christians are portrayed as infidels and enemies of Islam with the image of them being a threat to the local Muslim community.

Such rhetoric can be strongly divisive and unconstructive. This situation is compounded by religious claims to the exclusivity of certain words. In the 1980s legislation was passed to ban non-Muslims from using several words considered Islamic. The most prominent is the word Allah (see also discussion by Chong). The move has discriminatory effects not only on the Kelabit and Lun Bawang as Christian groups but also on other religious minorities such as Sikhs who also refer to God as "Allah". Ownership of literature carrying these terms were proscribed. This has created a great concern among the Kelabit and Lun Bawang who for years have been using the term Allah in their religious worship. The situation worsened in 2007 when the Interior Security Ministry (ISM) confiscated three boxes of religious literature imported by the Sidang Injil Borneo (SIB) from Indonesia for distribution and use by Sunday Schools in their churches.[9]

Matters came to a head in 2009 after a High Court ruling that the Catholic Church could use the term Allah in the Malay language version of their newsletter, distributed only to Catholics. There were violent attacks on churches, which saw at least ten places of worship being targeted. Furthermore, the seizing of bibles in the Malay language by the Malaysian customs authorities has raised specific concerns. In such a situation the state appears to have moved into the realm of intervening in societal values and through "Islamizing" institutions. These incidents created dilemmas for the Kelabit and Lun Bawang who in recent years have increasingly use *Bahasa Malaysia* in their church worship and prayers including the preparation of their teaching materials. An immediate impact of this situation is the formation of enemy images of the Malays in which some feel that all Muslims are against them.

There incidents and cases were highlighted by some political leaders and other opinion makers to express the fear that Muslims will grow in numbers and will introduce an Islamic state with restrictive laws in the land. This rings true for many ethnic minorities like the Kelabit and Lun Bawang who look at the future with great anxiety. This is made clear during the 10th Sarawak state election where by the confiscation of the Bible in Malay language, and the attempt to ban the use of the term Allah by Christians in Malaysia was raised as important electoral issues.

These various factors and concerns all contribute to an atmosphere of fear and mistrust among the minority groups and larger ones, who are then attracted to negative stories in the media in order to have their prejudices confirmed. In other words, a rhetoric of a protective and positively defined "We" versus a threatening and negatively defined "Them" has become more and more common leading to the cumulative effect of the same syndrome within the socio-political arenas. Based on mutual enemy images and fear, the We, or Us vs Them syndrome makes ethnic politics highly prominent in Malaysia. As it is, such mutual animosity and fear are already increasingly fueled by incidents at a global level, made possible by the Internet, radio and television. All of this has evoked negative perceptions of one another, and has affected everyday relations with each other.

AMBIVALENCE, MUTE SPECTATORS AND FORMATIONS OF COMMUNAL ASSOCIATIONS

Having said all this, when it comes to the right to religion, for a long while the Kelabit and Lun Bawang have been, in Jomo's (1992) term, "mute spectators". This is especially so with regard to Islamic revivalism in Malaysia. There are two main reasons for this. One is because of the Highlands' distance from the centre of power: they are relatively sheltered from the mêlée of Islamic politics. Second is because of certain teachings in the churches, which suggest that Christians as "good" citizens should not get entangled in politics and government. Instead Christians are to lead a quiet life as good citizens and to dutifully pray for the government of the day. It is improper to "disobey" the government and to protest. After all, the scripture such as Romans 13:1 says that God appoints all authorities.

Nonetheless, as previously mentioned, there is a growing unease over how revivalism is played out into ethnic politics in Malaysia's multi-ethnic society (Despres 1975, pp. 2–3; Nagata 1979; Shamsul 1986). Various scholars have pointed out the ways in which religious revivalism has not only raised consciousness among the Malays for true Islam, at the same time it has created a sense of Malay political, cultural, and social dominance in Malaysia (Lee 1990).

There is a concern that these tendencies might be a threat to the Kelabit's and Lun Bawang's religious identity. This is especially so in the face of self-assertion tendencies due to the Malay-Muslim position. As noted by Ahmad Yousif (2004) in response to Islam and Malays political-cultural and social dominance "non-Muslims have become more conscious of their particular ethnic-religious identity" (p. 34). His observations ring true for the Kelabit and Lun Bawang, who are concerned with ways to maintain a Christian-influenced identity within a Muslim-dominant culture. In 1998 Amster observed the significance of Christianity and formal education among the Kelabit as means to articulate and strengthen the Kelabit notions of ethnic identity and its boundaries (Barth 1969).

Others have argued similar responses amongst the Lun Bawang (Deegan 1973). As observed by Abu Bakar (2001, pp. 69–70), non-Muslims entered the fray by activating their own organizations, mobilizing their members, or forming their own societies in order to champion the cause of their co-religionists in the face of the Islamists' challenge. For the Kelabit and Lun Bawang, they have established their own communal associations, Lun Bawang Association (1977) and the Rurum Kelabit Sarawak in 1995, to shore up their own identity as minority groups and to articulate their respective economic, social, and political interests in the Malaysian state. Both become important vehicles to promote collective political agency and social status within Malaysia's economic and political terrain — as a means to negotiate and reinforce their Kelabit-ness and Lun Bawang-ness in Malaysia. At the same time, the two communities are projecting their identity in relation to others in Malaysia and globally.

FROM AMBIVALENCE AND FEAR TO THE LAW OF LOVE

Yet at the same time there are ongoing debates among the Lun Bawang and Kelabit as to how as Christian communities they ought to respond with kindheartedness and tolerance in their everyday encounters and engagements with people of other faiths including with their Muslim friends, visitors, and relatives. This includes how to respond to the ideological face of Islam in the form of Islamists conceptions of an Islamic state, Islamic/Muslim criticism, rejection, and polemics against Christian beliefs and also Islamic missionary activity — *daw'ah*. This is especially tricky given that Islam and Christianity are two faiths which have much in common.

Before I delve deeper, it is important to highlight here that there is no one standard Christian response to Islam. In fact, John Azumah (2010) has pointed out "the Christian response can be divided along the lines of 'evangelical' versus 'ecumenical', 'truth' versus 'grace', 'tough' versus 'soft', or 'confrontational' versus 'conciliatory'" (p. 83).

Among the Kelabit and Lun Bawang, there are those who say the best way to defend their Christian heritage is to be aggressive. An instance is the forbidding of *dakwah* activities, as claimed by Kosmo Online Rencana Utama, in Bario as well as in Ba Kelalan. To others this line of argument is considered not only unconstitutional but also revengeful and therefore unbiblical (Romans 12:19). They argue that Christians are commissioned as witnesses to the transforming power of the gospel (Acts 1:8), not as defenders of the faith. Furthermore, they suggest that Christians that exercising one's citizenship should not be dictated by religion but could be inspired by religious convictions. And as far as human rights in the local community is concerned, the Christians are not to ask for special privileges or protection but simply to ask not to be discriminated because of their religious and ethnic backgrounds. Instead of resorting to violence in voicing their concerns, political actions through prayer, compassion, and their vote could be used.

At another level is the notion of being salt and light (Matthew 5:13 and 1 Peter 2:9). The aim here is to correct and remove misunderstanding as far as Christians are able to and not to attack Islamic beliefs and undermine the integrity of Islam sources. In fact they are those who suggest overcoming the fear of Islamization by being welcoming, friendly, and hospitable to those who come into the Highlands. This is based on living worthy of the Gospel based on Philippians 1:27. What this means is for the Kelabit and Lun Bawang as Christians is to engage in the spirit of goodwill, respect, peaceableness, and true humility in their contacts with people of other faiths. At the same time is to engage in national life of the country and make a difference in the nation. To emphasize this point, the roles of certain Christian Kelabit such as Datuk Seri Idris Jalla and few others are highlighted — that is, how they are being channels of God's blessings and grace for the country. The notion entails contributing towards common good and public justice regardless of religious and ethnic backgrounds.

GUIDED BY THE LAW OF LOVE

The Law of Love suggests practical steps towards improved relations by using it as opposed to calls for a holy war against opponents. This entails reconciliatory approaches: being welcoming, compassionate, and friendly, but aware of your position especially of your faith. For instance, in response to Islamic revivalism and Islamization processes, there is a call for the Kelabit and Lun Bawang to develop a sound approach upon biblical understanding. A good example is the setting up the Nehemiah Ministry about three years ago. Its aims are to inculcate consciousness and awareness about their roles and positions as Christians in the nation, and the values of their Christian faith and heritage. There is an understanding that one cannot violently stop the Islamisation of the Kelabit and Lun Bawang, but there is a need to outline the legal, social, and spiritual implications of conversion. For example, it is important to explain to the Kelabit and Lun Bawang that even though a marriage between a Muslim and non-Muslim is not automatically dissolved, the *Syariah* Court will have power to end it. In such cases, the custody and guardianship of children is an issue because the non-converting spouse not only will not be eligible for inheritance but also will lose custody over the children.

CONCLUSION

What the above suggests is that as Christian minority groups like the Kelabit and Lun Bawang in general are somewhat affected by the Malay-Muslim's majority and policies related to their position in the nation. Their experiences highlight one of the main issues in Malaysia today, which is the position of religious minorities and groups. That religion is so intricately intertwined with race, culture, politics, and economics can be a blessing, when it brings industry, forbearance, and understanding; but it can also be complicated requiring careful discussion and tolerance. There is no doubt that clashes of opinions and interests in these areas have contributed to a particular polarization in the Malaysian society: majority vs minority, Malays versus non-Malays, and Muslims versus non-Muslims.

But, as noted by Ahmad Yousif (2004), "Perhaps the best recipe for accommodating religious pluralism and diversity is cultivating mutual respect and tolerance among all individuals and communities. Having said that, such mutual tolerance and respect is a two-way process. While religious minorities have rights, they also have a responsibility to respect the majority's religion" (p. 50). Li-ann Thio (2010) echoed this sentiment. She writes, "... a well-functioning civil society is not nurtured by enforced uniformity, but by tolerance and mutual respect for different racial and religious groups. If members of a politically non-dominant minority group feel protected by laws and legal processes, and if citizenship is inclusive, this will solidify their commitment to the state and enable them to focus on what is shared, rather than what divides, in cultivating a sense of common citizenship" (p. 49).

As outlined, the Kelabit and Lun Bawang are certainly facing dilemmas, yet at the same time they endeavour to find the right balance in their responses to the Malay Muslims as the majority and Islam as the official religion of the state. Since Christianity has provided a "grounding" for the Kelabit and Lun Bawang, specifically within Malaysia's multi-ethnic and religious society, they draw on the teachings of the Bible as a source of inspirations in their inter-religious dealings both in the public sphere and in everyday life. These teachings aspire to tolerance, respect, and love of others. This is important to bear, especially in situations where religion is so intricately intertwined with race, culture, politics, and economics as in Malaysia. Often in this situation the temptation to demonize one another can be strong on all sides. But this must be resisted at all cost if progress is to be made. As can be seen from the Kelabit and Lun Bawang stories, instead of using religions to exclude others which may lead to mistrust and fear of domination of one ethnic/regional/religious group by another — faith and religious teachings can be important both as an anchor and a guide to negotiate dilemmas and challenges in minority–majority situations. Conversely, it is important to assure that the constitutional and legal rights of the religious, minorities are safeguarded. This is a necessary condition to create loyalty among people to a country marked by cultural, religious, and geographical heterogeneity such as Malaysia. The improved condition of the religious minorities is important to hold Malaysia together as one nation. With compassion and mutual understanding, this diversity is something to celebrate, to be inspired by. It need not be a source of division. But this requires ongoing understanding and negotiation to a more shared and cohesive future.

Notes

1. This is also made clear through their attempts via political parties to champion the interests of their own respective groups separate from the Malay Bumiputera. An example is the former Parti Bansa Dayak Sarawak (PBDS), a Dayak-based political party of Sarawak.
2. Another example of Raung's situation, which has received wide media coverage and public commentaries, is the case of Lina Joy, a Malay-Muslim woman who had converted to Christianity (see various references to this case in this volume).
3. By adopting Islam as the religion of the Federation as stated in Article 3 of the Constitution, Islamic education and way of life can be promoted for Muslims. Islamic institutions including *Syariah* courts have been set up and Muslims are subjected to Muslim law in areas assigned by the Constitution.
4. This was a result of two statements made by the then Prime Minister, Dr Mahathir Mohamad on 29 September 2001 and in June 2002 stating that Malaysia is an Islamic state rather than the common description of Malaysia as a democratic secular federation with Islam as its official religion. This is despite the fact that Supreme Court (now Federal Court) in one case (Che Omar bin Che Soh [1988] 2 MLJ 55) had declared that although Islam is the religion of the Federation, Malaysia is a secular state.
5. Although some Malaysians have downplayed these statements as political expediency made in the context of intra-Muslim struggle between UMNO (United Malay National Organization) and PAS (Parti Islam Se-Malaysia or Pan-Malaysia) for the image of defender of the faith and Islamic correctness at certain levels, there is grave concern among both Muslim and non-Muslims alike about the effects of such pronouncements not only on religious minorities but also on Muslims themselves.
6. Chris Reubens, "Six Natives Students Race Changed to Malay, Raises Fear among Parents", *Malaysian Miror*, 30 November 2012. Available at <http://www.Malaysianmiror.Com/media-buzz-detail/139-Sarawak/50829-six-native-students-race-changed-to-Malay-raises-fear-amongparents> (Accessed 15 June 2012).
7. Albert Sundararaj Walters (2007, p. 69) argues that there is a perception among the non-Muslims that the federal government's emphasis on the inculcation of Islamic values and the PAS state governments' insistence on the implementation of Islamic law (*Syariah*) are two sides of the same coin: both represent concerted attempts at "Islamizing" Malaysia.
8. Dakwah Penduduk Bario. Available at <http:// www .my/kosmo/content.asp?y=2009 &dt=1117&pub=Kosmo&sec=Rencana_Utama&pg=ru_02.htm> (last accessed: 7 June 2013).
9. "Religious Minorities Fight Back in Malaysia", The Institute on Religion & Public Policy. 14 November 2008. Available at <http://religionandpolicy.org/cms> (accessed 8 March 2012).

References

Abu Bakar, M. "Islam, Civil Society, and Ethnic Relations in Malaysia". In *Islam and Civil Society in Southeast Asia*, edited by N. Mitsuo, S. Siddique and O.F. Bajund. Singapore: Institute of Southeast Asian Studies, 2001.

Ahmad Farouk Musa. "Political Islam: Trajectory and Discourse". In *The Road to Reform Pakatan Rakyat in Selangor*, edited by Tricia Yeoh. Petaling Jaya: Strategic Information and Research Development Centre, 2010.

Amster, Matthew. "Community, Ethnicity, and Modes of Association among the Kelabit of Sarawak, East Malaysia". Ph.D. dissertation, Department of Anthropology, Brandeis University, 1998.

Azumah, J. "Christian Responses to Islam: A Struggle for the Soul of Christianity". *Church & Society in Asia Today* 13, no. 2 (2010): 83–94.

Bala, Poline. *Desire for Progress: The Kelabit Experience with Information Communication Technologies for Rural Development in Sarawak East Malaysia*. Ph.D. dissertation, Christ's College, University of Cambridge. 2008.

———. "An Engagement with 'Modernity'? Becoming Christian in the Kelabit Highlands of Central Borneo". *Borneo Research Bulletin* 40 (2009): 173–86.

———. "Changing Borders and Identities in the Kelabit Highlands: Anthropological Reflections on Growing Up in a Kelabit Village near an International Border". *Dayak Studies Contemporary Society Series* 1. The Institute of East Asian Studies, University Malaysia Sarawak. 2002.

———. "Interethnic Ties: The Kelabit and Lun Berian in the Kelabit-Kerayan Highlands". *Borneo Research Bulletin* 32 (2001): 103–11.

Barth, Frederik. "Introduction". In *Ethnic Groups and Boundaries*. Bergen-Oslo: Universitets Forlaget. 1969.

Berger, P.L. "The Desecularization of the World: A Global Overview". In *The Desecularization of the World: Resurgent Religion and World Politics*, edited by P.L. Berger. Washington D.C.: Ethics and Public Policy Center, 1999, pp. 1–18.

Bulan, S. and L. Bulan-Dorai. *The Bario Revival*. Kuala Lumpur: HomeMatters Network, 2004.

Carvalho, Jean-Paul. "A Theory of the Islamic Revival". Department of Economics, University of Oxford, 2009. Available at <http:faculty.sites.uci.edu/jpcarv/files/2011/03/TheoryofIslamicRevival.pdf> (accessed 5 June 2012).

Cheah Boon Kheng. "Race and Ethnic Relations in Colonial Malaya during the 1920s and 1930s". In *Multiethnic Malaysia: Past, Present and Future*, edited by Lim Teck Ghee, Alberto Gomes, and Azly Rahman. Petaling Jaya: Strategic Information and Research Development Centre, 2009.

Deegan, James L. "Change among the Lun Bawang: A Borneo People". Ph.D. dissertation, Anthropology Department, University of Washington. 1973.

Despres, Leo, ed. *Ethnicity and Resource Competition in Plural Society*. The Hague and Paris: Mouton Publishers, 1975.

Emerson, Rupert. *Malaysia: A Study in Direct and Indirect Rule*. Kuala Lumpur: University of Malaya Press, 1970.

Gabriel, Theodore. *Christian-Muslim Relations: A case study of Sarawak, East Malaysia*. Aldershot: Avebury Ashgate Publishing Limit. 1996.

Goh Beng Lan. "Rethinking Modernity: State, Ethnicity, and Class in the Forging of a Modern Urban Malaysia". In *Local Cultures and the New Asia: The Society, Culture and Capitalism in Southeast Asia*, edited by C.J.W.L. Wee. Singapore: Institute of Southeast Asian Studies, 2002.

Janowski, Monica. "Rice, Work and Community Among the Kelabits in Sarawak, East Malaysia". Ph.D. dissertation, London School of Economics, University of London. 1991.

Jawan, Jayum A. and Victor T. King. "The Ibans of Sarawak: The Nature of Their Peripherality and Its Political and Economic Consequences". In *Southeast Asian Ethnography: Sociocultural Change, Development and Indigenous Peoples*, edited by Tan Chee Beng. Singapore: Board of Editors, contributions to Southeast Asian Ethnography, 1997.

———. *Ethnicity and Electoral Politics in Sarawak*. Bangi: Penerbit Universiti Kebangsaan Malaysia, 2004.

Jomo, K.S. *Malaysia's New Economic Policies: Evaluations of the Mid-term Review of the 4th MP*. Kuala Lumpur: Malaysian Economic Association, 1985.

Jomo, K.S. and A. Cheek. "Malaysia's Islamic Movements". In *Fragmented Vision, Culture and Politics in Contemporary Malaysia*, edited by Joel Kahn and Loh Kok Wah. North Sydney: Asian Studies Association of Australia, with Allen and Unwin, 1992.

LeBar, F.M. "Kelabitic Murut". In *Ethnic Groups of Insular Southeast Asia, Vol. I Indonesia, Andaman Islands and Madagascar*. New Haven, CT: Human Relations Area Files Press, 1972.

Lee, Raymond L.M. "The State, Religious Nationalism, and Ethnic Rationalization in Malaysia". *Ethnic and Racial Studies* 13, no. 4 (October 1990): 482–502.

Li-ann Thio. "Constitutional Accommodation of the Rights of Ethnic and Religious Minorities in Plural Democracies: Lessons and Cautionary Tales from South-East Asia". *Pace International Law Review* 43, vol. 22 (2010): 42–101. Available at <http://digitalcommons.pace.edu/pilr/vol22/iss1/2> (accessed 11 May 2012).

Lim, T.G. and Alberto Gomes. "Culture and Development in Malaysia". In *Multiethnic Malaysia Past, Present and Future*, edited by Lim Teck Ghee, Alberto Gomes, and Azly Rahman. Petaling Jaya: Strategic Information and Research Development Centre, 2009.

Nagata, Judith. "Religious Ideology and Social Change: The Islamic Revival in Malaysia". *Pacific Affairs* 53 (1980): 405–39.

———. *Malaysian Mosaic: Perspective from a Poly-ethnicSociety*. Vancouver, BC: University of British Columbia, 1979.

Riddell, P.G. "Islamization, civil society, and religious minorities in Malaysia". In *Islam in Southeast Asia: Political, Social and Strategic Challenges for the 21st Century*, edited by K.S. Nathan and Mohammad Hashim Kamali. Singapore: Institute of Southeast Asian Studies, 2005.

"Rights to Religious and Other Minorities in Malaysia". A paper delivered by Justice Raus Sharif, a Judge of the Federal Court of Malaysia at the 17th Commonwealth Law Conference 2011, Hyderabad, India.

Saging, R. "An Ethno-History of the Kelabit Tribe of Sarawak. A Brief Look at the Kelabit tribe before World War II and After". Graduation Exercise submitted to the Jabatan Sejarah, University of Malaya, in partial fulfilment of the requirements for the Degree of Bachelor of Arts, 1976/1977.

Salfarina A.G., M.Z. Abu Bakar, and Azeem Fazwan Ahmad Farouk. "Explaining Ethnic Relations in Malaysia through the "Concentric Circle Model": Case Studies of Perak and Kelantan, Malaysia". *European Journal of Social Sciences* 12, no. 2 (2009): 252–58.

Shafruddin, B.H. and Iftikhar A.M.Z., Fadzil, eds. *Between Centre and State: Federalism in Perspective*. Kuala Lumpur: Institute of Strategic and International Studies (ISIS), 1988.

Shamsul, Amri Baharuddin. "A Revival in the Study Of Islam in Malaysia". In *Readings in Malaysian Politics*, edited by Bruce Gale. Petaling Jaya: Pelanduk Publications, 1986.

———. "Economic Dimension of Malay Nationalism: Socioeconomic Roots of the New Economic Policy and Its Contemporary Implications". *Developing Economics* 35, no. 3 (1997): 240–61.

Snodgrass, Donald R. "Successful Economic Development in a Multi-Ethnic Society: The Malaysian Case". n.d. Available at <http://www.earthinstitute.columbia.edu/sitefiles/file/about/director/pubs/503.pdf> (accessed 24 February 2012).

Tamam, E. "Contribution of Interethnic Attitudes of Malay and Chinese-Malaysian University Students in Malaysia". *European Journal of Social Sciences* 8, no. 1 (2009): 51–61.

Walters, A.S. "Issues in Christian–Muslim Relations: A Malaysian Christian Perspective". *Islam and Christian–Muslim Relations* 18, no. 1 (2007): 67–83.

Yousif, A. "Islamic Revivalism in Malaysia: An Islamic Response to Non-Muslim Concerns". *American Journal of Islamic Social Sciences* 21, no. 4 (2004): 31–56.

Yukiko Ohashi. "The Many Faces of Islam in Malaysia". *Asia Times*, 9 July 2004. Available at <http://www.atimes.com/atimes/Southeast_Asia/FG09Ae04.html> (accessed 28 May 2012).

20

EVERYDAY RELIGIOSITY AND THE AMBIGUATION OF DEVELOPMENT IN EAST MALAYSIA
Reflections on a Dam-Construction and Resettlement Project

Liana Chua

INTRODUCTION

In December 2008, I had breakfast with an elderly Bidayuh man and his daughter in their upland village — one of four due to be resettled to make way for a new dam and reservoir. With an official land compensation ceremony[1] a few days away, the conversation meandered, as it often did, towards the project. My elderly interlocutor — a follower of the old rituals, *adat gawai* — had been reminiscing about life in the 1950s, "before [Sarawak became part of] Malaysia".[2] Back then, he said, the bus fare to Kuching was less than a dollar; food in the city came in generous portions for just ten cents, and trousers cost a few dollars. These days, however, everything was expensive because those Malays who ruled the country didn't know how to run the "economy" (English). But being Malay was difficult, added his Anglican daughter, since they were Muslim and had to live according to strict observances. Ruminating further, they began to contrast the lives of Muslims with those of Christians, who today form the bulk of the Bidayuh population.

Running through the different churches in the area, they concurred that the "strongest" of the lot was the Sidang Injil Borneo (SIB), or Borneo Evangelical Church — a non-denominational organization with a small but vocal local presence. Those people were rich, they declared, and their prayers really worked; indeed, the SIB leaders were so powerful that they were often able to tell the future. To illustrate their point, they mentioned "Pastor Henman" (pseudonym): a white preacher who visited the region regularly, and who had predicted 2004's Boxing Day tsunami. More recently, he had prophesied bad things for the dam being constructed downstream: perhaps it would collapse or just fail. But of course, this was hardly surprising, explained the old man, since the soil at the construction site was poor, prone to landslides and flooding. As I discovered later, it was also an area filled with capricious local place spirits, which might respond badly to the upheavals around them. All things considered, my interlocutors concluded that the dam would almost certainly run into problems.

As ethnographic episodes went, this was an admittedly difficult one to follow. Rather than forming a coherent narrative, our discussion drew together several topics — the economy, development, ethnicity, and religion — in a seemingly formless pastiche of associations. Here, Islam, Christianity, and the old spirit beliefs segued in and out of view; one analytical blink and a breakfast companion would have missed them. Yet their import in my acquaintances' lives cannot be overstated. In this chapter, I argue that despite the nominal a-religiosity of official discourses and policies, religious considerations play a crucial role in shaping — and ambiguating — Bidayuhs' engagements with development and the state. But rather than taking the explosive form of church-bombings or demonstrations (such as those seen during 2010's "Allah" controversy),[3] these engagements possess a far more muted, quotidian quality. By teasing out their manifestations in the context of a dam-construction and resettlement scheme, this chapter reveals how religious toleration and conflict in areas of significant ethnic plurality are not necessarily diametric states, but can exist as strands of a single tangled web. We begin, however, by situating the case study in its larger context: the developmentalist milieu of contemporary Sarawak.

THE "ANTI-POLITICS" OF SARAWAKIAN DEVELOPMENTALISM

As elsewhere in Malaysia, Sarawak's politics and economy over the last few decades have been driven by a particularly vigorous brand of "development" (*pembangunan*). A variant of the top-down, technocratic model of development that emerged in the post-World War II international order (Escobar 2012), the *pembangunan* paradigm seeks to transform Malaysia into a prosperous economic power, and eventually, a fully developed nation. Since independence, it has become Sarawak's "ultimate civil postulate, closely tied to ideas of political legitimacy" (Brosius 2000, p. 1), suffusing relations between the state and its citizens.

To a greater extent than in West Malaysia, Sarawakian developmentalism is dominated by an ideological dualism between "native rural society" and "modern society" (Bissonnette 2011, p. 350). This dichotomy feeds a powerful temporalizing discourse that depicts rural communities as impoverished and backward, needing to be incorporated into the modern, progressive mainstream of Malaysian citizenry. Decrying shifting cultivation, hunter-gathering, and other "traditional" subsistence practices as incommensurate with the nation's forward trajectory, the Sarawakian government has channelled its energy into reshaping "the practices and conceptions of rural native populations ... for the enhancement of economic production" (ibid., p. 351). This transformation is formulated in overtly economic and technological terms and visibly manifested through electricity generators, schools, and clinics in remote areas, mega-dams, and oil palm plantations. Like the "anti-politics machine" famously described in Lesotho by James Ferguson (1990), Sarawak's development apparatus appears to operate beyond ethnic, religious, and party politics. The notion of *pembangunan* as a virtuous, top-down endeavour which it enshrines, moreover, permeates the thoughts and language of Sarawak's urban elite, among them the Bidayuh politicians chiefly responsible for bringing development to their rural constituencies (e.g., Mamit, Sarok, and Amin 2003; Minos 2000).

It is within this ideological and political framework that the dam-construction and resettlement scheme discussed in this chapter has unfolded.[4] Located in the hills near the Indonesian border, several hours' walk from the nearest road, the four villages involved in this scheme are prime targets for the state's developmentalist aspirations. While by no means isolated from the "modern" world, they have not been urbanized to the same extent as their roadside counterparts, some of which are now virtually suburbs of Kuching. Most villagers are subsistence rice farmers who earn a small income by cultivating cash crops such as rubber, cocoa, and pepper, and providing irregular labour for nearby construction projects, including the dam. Many have spent some time studying or working in town, and all of them have friends and family in urban areas.

Nevertheless, their relative isolation has made it easy for the state, the media, and other Bidayuhs to portray them as "remote" (*ulu/jo*), "poor" (*miskin*), and "*not yet*" (*belum/bayuh*) developed. When the resettlement scheme was first publicized, for example, the *Borneo Post* quoted a Bidayuh politician involved in it as saying, "If we leave them there, then they are denied access to many basic infrastructure and facilities. As a leader, I feel guilty if I am unable to help these people. You know, they are too deep in the interior and their population is small. To bring major development there is not economical."

Such remarks treat the improvement of the villagers' lives as an ethical necessity — a means of making them fully Malaysian. Accordingly, the scheme has been depicted from the outset in terms of progress (*kemajuan*), modernization, and material welfare. Drawing an isomorphism between the well-being of the state and the communities, its political architects exhort the affected villagers to contribute to the greater good (averting water shortages in the capital) rather than selfishly oppose it. Their reward, so to speak, is the gift of development: a better, easier life in a planned township along the main road with free cement houses, piped water, 24-hour electricity, and access to modern amenities. In this new location, shifting agriculture will be consigned to a benighted pre-modern past; with each household being assigned just three acres of land, the villagers will be steered towards new priorities and economic opportunities such as oil palm, cash cropping, and eco-tourism.

As this brief overview reveals, the insistent futurism of Sarawak's dominant development discourse simultaneously obviates any reference to ethnicity or religion — two of the most divisive factors in Malaysian society today. Yet, as the rest of this chapter argues, the reality of development on the ground is more complex than is initially apparent. In the following pages, I shall examine the close entwinement of Islam, Christianity, and the old rituals, *adat gawai*, in rural Bidayuhs' experiences of development. My exploration centres on two interlocking themes: the politics of religion and its moral and conceptual purchase in Bidayuhs' lives. I suggest that for most Bidayuhs, development in Sarawak is inseparable from ethnic and religious politics — particularly Malay-Muslim hegemony, which they see as lying at the heart of Malaysian statehood. Rather than entering into open conflict with the government and Islam, however, many of them have found alternative means of dealing with the upheavals around them, particularly by recourse to the other two religious influences in their lives: *adat gawai* and Christianity. These responses reveal how *pembangunan* has become an arena in which religious tensions, but also strategies of accommodation, are played out in numerous small-scale, uneven ways. In this respect, the dam-construction and resettlement scheme may be seen as a microcosm of the situation in East Malaysia, where constant, daily negotiation rather than clear-cut conflict tends to characterize inter-religious relations.

FRAMING THE PROBLEM: *PEMBANGUNAN* AND MALAY-MUSLIM HEGEMONY

The Bidayuh villagers affected by the dam are not unaware of the politically charged discourses swirling around them; indeed, many are firm subscribers to the ideal of economic and material progress that underpins Sarawak's *pembangunan* paradigm. Yet their eagerness to participate in this grand enterprise is tempered by an abiding sense of marginalization by the very state that is meant to be "giving" them development. To account for this, we need to examine the peculiar relationship between development, ethnicity, and religion in Sarawak.

As elsewhere in Malaysia, Sarawak's economic and development policies have long been tempered by a form of "economic indiginism [sic]" (Siddique and Suryadinata 1981) that explicitly privileges the interests of "native" populations. Initially a post-independence measure to enable Malays to compete with other races — notably the economically dominant Chinese (Watson 1996) — the *bumiputera* (lit. "sons of the soil") system has generated a highly fraught dichotomy between Malays and non-Malays on the Peninsula (see also Yeoh, this volume). However, the situation in Sarawak and Sabah, where there are large non-Malay *bumiputera* populations, is more complex. As one of Sarawak's recognized "native" groups, Bidayuhs are theoretically entitled to the same "*bumi*" quotas, benefits, and economic incentives as Malays. But in practice, many of my acquaintances feel short-changed by the particular ethno-religious configuration of power that has dominated Sarawakian politics over the last few decades: one they associate with the government of Taib Mahmud, Sarawak's Melanau Chief Minister since 1981.

The Melanau are unusual among Sarawak's native groups in having mostly converted to Islam over centuries of contact with the Bruneian sultanate and coastal traders. Historically, such converts were assimilated into the politically dominant Malay category. Although contemporary Melanau politicians have since disentangled their ethnic identity from their religion (Boulanger 2009, pp. 72–82; Postill 2008, p. 92), the Melanau-Malay association — with Islam at its core — continues to run deep in both party politics and the eyes of most Sarawakians.⁵ In light of this, many Bidayuhs view Taib primarily as a *Muslim* whose influence stems from his collaboration with other Muslims — particularly the Malays in Kuala Lumpur who run the nation. Indeed, they routinely describe his government as "*Kirieng*" — the term for "Malay", which automatically implies "Muslim". When my acquaintances talk about the *Raja Kirieng* (the Malay *rajas*) who rule Sarawak, then, they are referring to a particular Malay/Melanau amalgam held together by their religious affiliation. Accordingly, their responses to *pembangunan*, which they also associate with Taib's government, are frequently coloured by anxieties over Malay/Melanau-Muslim dominance.

As I argue elsewhere (Chua 2007), Bidayuhs have long had an awkward relationship with Islam, which they portray as trapping its adherents in a strict religious and praxiological regime incompatible with their own modes of sociality. Since independence, these concerns have been amplified and given new shape by Malay political dominance of West Malaysia. More than being a problematic "other", *Kirieng* are now seen as having acquired a position of immense power as rulers of the nation, thereby turning Islam into a powerful means of obtaining political and economic resources. In Bidayuhs' eyes, this has generated a two-tiered *bumiputera* system, with Muslim *bumiputera* (Malays and Melanaus) monopolizing all the benefits, and non-Muslim *bumiputera* becoming "second-class indigenes" (Bala, this volume; Boulanger 2009, pp. 115–17; Postill 2008, p. 195). It is widely said, for example, that if ten civil service jobs are advertised for *bumiputera*, nine will go to Malays — even if the other candidates are better qualified. Yet it is not only ethnic Malays or Melanaus who enjoy access to these perks, for others can also buy into this world. Such was the consensus whenever my acquaintances and I drove past a nearby Bidayuh village that had converted en masse to Islam: Look at their tarred roads and brand new community hall, my interlocutors would point out; all you need to do is "enter Islam" (*mŭrŭt Islam*) to get development from this government.

Such low-level grumblings are endemic throughout Bidayuh communities, but have acquired new intensity in the context of the dam-construction project. Although the affected villagers have been split by the scheme, with some vehemently opposing resettlement, others enthusiastically supporting it and everyone else shuttling in between, all parties concur that the *Kirieng* government has a poor record of "giving" development to non-Muslim *bumiputera* like themselves. I was frequently told during fieldwork, particularly while walking past the dam construction site or

Land and Survey boundary markers, that the government only brought *kemudahan* (facilities) and *maju* (progress)[6] to its own people — Malays, Melanaus, Muslims. For my companions, this was a sore point: if the *Kirieng* could bring them to Borneo Highlands — a luxury resort and golf course built atop a nearby mountain — why could they not do so here? While the religious factor was often so self-evident as not to require exposition, it was nonetheless a resource on which people drew freely. Reflecting on different countries' economic situations, for example, an elderly man told me that Malaysia was full of poor people. When I asked if there were many poor Malay villages, however, he sniggered. "Look at what happens during their *gawai* [religious festivals, i.e., Hari Raya]", he said, "the government gives them food, drink, everything. And when it comes to our own *gawai* [i.e., Christmas and the traditional harvest festival]? Nothing."

Such remarks reveal a pervasive suspiciousness over the intentions and priorities of the Sarawakian government, even when it claims to be giving development to the people. For Bidayuhs, what sets *Kirieng* apart from other *bumiputera* is less their ethnicity than their religion, which they see as woven into the fabric of political dominance in Malaysia. While wholly endorsing official ideals of progress and prosperity, my acquaintances have less faith in a model of *pembangunan* magically emptied of ethnicity and religion. In their eyes, development — and indeed their lives in contemporary Sarawak — cannot be disassociated from Malay/Melanau-Muslim hegemony. This awareness serves as a powerful filter through which to account for recent changes while also providing a language through which to articulate their grievances.

Accordingly, what enthusiasm there is for resettlement is moderated by the nagging fear that the *Kirieng* government will renege on its promises, while objectors to the scheme cite delays and compensation-related problems as proof of the state's disinterest in non-Muslim *bumiputera*. In these moments, religious politics becomes implicated in the success or failure of government-led development, acting as one of many strands in the nexus of relations between Bidayuhs and the state.

For all their unhappiness over their perceived religious and political marginality however, Bidayuhs are aware that religion, particularly Islam, is a delicate topic in Malaysia that — as a teenage acquaintance explained with much hang-wringing — can get people into trouble with the "ISA" (Internal Security Act). This impression is reinforced through periodic reports of religious conflict in the local media, such as the Lina Joy affair, in which a Malay convert to Christianity tried unsuccessfully to obtain official recognition of her new status, and more recent protests and church-bombings over the use of the word "Allah" by Malaysian Christians (2010). Moreover, it is not uncommon for Bidayuhs — like other Sarawakians (see, for example, Bala, this volume) — to have friends and relations who have converted to Islam and "become Malay" through marriage, migration, or other reasons. In a region long characterized by such ethnic and religious fluidity, open religious conflict is thus not only politically risky, but also socially and pragmatically undesirable. In the face of all this, many Bidayuhs prefer not to rock the boat, but to find other less overt means of tapping Malaysia's *"moden"* (modern) resources. Among these, as the next section reveals, are the political affordances of their old rituals, *adat gawai*, and the religion to which nearly all of them now adhere, Christianity.

HOW TO DO THINGS WITH RELIGION

The culturalization of *"Adat Gawai"*

Until relatively recently, *adat gawai* was, like subsistence farming and remoteness, a badge of rural Bidayuhs' backwardness in the eyes of the state. Officially classified alongside other indigenous ritual complexes as a "tribal/folk religion" (*agama suku kaum/folk*), *adat gawai* occupies an implicitly inferior position to scripture-based world religions (*agama*) such as Christianity and Islam, which are associated with "modern" citizenship. As one Bidayuh politician put it in 2000:

> [M]y estimate is that less than 25 per cent of the Bidayuhs still cling to the old "adat" or religion. [...] My prediction is that, as the Bidayuhs get more educated and as the non-Christian ones meet and mix more with those already Christians [sic] in the villages or towns, one day almost 100 per cent will be Christians' (Minos 2000, p. 118).

Over the last two decades, the old rituals have indeed continued to die out, leaving behind dwindling groups of elderly practitioners in a few villages, including one affected by the dam. Interestingly, however, their decline has been inversely mirrored by *adat gawai*'s redefinition and valorization in official multiculturalist discourses as "Bidayuh culture". Since the 1990s, the preservation, promotion, and commercialization of ethnic "cultures" has become increasingly central to Sarawak's self-definition, an intrinsic part of its identity as a "modern" state. These developments have turned "culture" — reified in the Bidayuh context as *gawai*-based dances, costumes, and paraphernalia — into an important and often lucrative mediator between indigenous groups and the state (see Chua 2012*a*). For the villagers affected by the dam, this culturalized form of *gawai* has also become an increasingly useful means of negotiating with the government.

In many ways, their efforts have been stimulated by the state's own policies. "Cultural preservation" has been factored into the resettlement scheme since its commencement. Over the last few years, research teams from Sarawak's Council for Customs and Traditions have visited the area to collect "traditional" artefacts, information on *gawai* rituals, agricultural and environmental knowledge, myths and oral histories, among other things. Government funds have also been allocated for the construction of a new *baruk* (*gawai* ritual house) at the resettlement site, and for the performance of all the *gawai* rituals associated with the transition. Cumulatively, these measures have boosted the communities' awareness of the political cachet of *adat gawai* as a potential bargaining chip with the government. The elderly man mentioned at the start of this chapter, for example, told me that he and other villagers consistently reminded the government officials they met that it was the state's responsibility to provide a new *baruk* and other ritual facilities at the new site. If not, he told them forcefully, "*Gawai* will be lost. Our *culture* (*budaya*) will be lost." By transforming a developmental necessity into a moral burden, these practitioners effectively turned the state's own conceptual frameworks to their advantage.

In recent years, their case has been boosted by growing tourist interest in the four villages, particularly in the community furthest from the road, where *gawai* is still followed. Every month, small groups of backpackers, urbanites, and occasionally journalists and filmmakers, hike up to the area in search of nature and culture. Over the years, a cluster of villagers have become adept at catering to these visitors, running a number of private "homestay" programmes and offering packages that include jungle hikes, "traditional" cooking and — for a heftier sum — "cultural" dances performed by the elderly *gawai* practitioners. Such activities have brought an extra source of (non-governmental) income to the communities, but also opened the resettlement scheme to increased public scrutiny. Today, the looming prospect of moving is intrinsic to these villages' "story", winning them sympathizers and allies, widespread media coverage, and thus a modicum of leverage in their relations with the government. Over the years, newspaper clippings, photographs, and VCDs of *gawai* dances and rituals have become part of residents' engagements with the scheme: held up as proof not only of their "cultural" distinctiveness but also of their connections with influential outsiders, to whom they can (and do) report governmental missteps.

In this way, the fate of the old rituals has become a point of negotiation between some of the affected villagers and government representatives: a publicly visible platform through which the former can take the state and its developmental agenda to task. Yet they do so not by openly decrying Malay/Melanau-Muslim dominance, but by using one quintessentially Malaysian political vocabulary — that of "culture" — to critique another ("development"). In the process, they have also been able to contest earlier pejorative portrayals of their old rituals while staking their claim to *moden* benefits in a way that circumvents Sarawak's *pembangunan* apparatus.

Modernity, Munificence, and Bidayuh Christianity

Although Christianity — in the form of rudimentary mission schools and health facilities — first entered Bidayuh areas in the late-nineteenth century, it was only from the late-1960s that large-scale conversion began to take place (see Chua 2012*a*, Chapter 3). Precipitated in part by post-independence demographic and socio-economic changes, this process was largely spearheaded by educated young Bidayuhs who saw it as a religion more suited to the demands of the new, urbanizing world in which they now moved. During this period, Bidayuhs converted to Anglicanism and Catholicism in equal numbers with minimal regard for denominational specificities; as I explain elsewhere (Chua 2012*a*, p. 90), decisions on which church to "follow" (*tundak*) were often based on kin relations, friendships, rivalries, and other social considerations. Today, the vast majority of Bidayuhs belong to these two denominations, although a number of newer denominational and non-denominational churches, such as the Methodists, Seventh-Day Adventists, and SIB, have garnered smaller congregations in the area. For the most part, however, Bidayuhs tend to refer to themselves as Christians first: a cue which I shall take in the discussion that follows.

For many of my acquaintances, Christianity is a useful buffer against Muslim hegemony because of its officially recognized status as a "modern" world religion (Chua 2007, 2012*a*). This enables them to assert their modernity and parity with Malays — a difficult task for followers of *adat gawai* — without having to convert to Islam. As we have seen, however, this claim to "modernity" is no guarantee of development. Indeed, rural villagers occasionally speculate that the *Kirieng* government deliberately withholds amenities from them precisely because they are Christian. In the face of such perceived discrimination, Christianity has also come to acquire a different role: that of a benevolent provider which "gives" Bidayuhs what the state does not.

Visits from charitable outsiders are nothing new to the affected communities. Over the years, they have received clothes, toys, and medicines from the Sai Baba Council and other NGOs, funds for the upkeep of their bamboo bridges from "Chinese who go jogging in the jungle" (probably Hash House Harriers from Kuching) and occasional donations by individual politicians, particularly in the pre-Taib era. However, the longest-serving and most prominent of these beneficent parties is the Anglican church, which began providing basic healthcare and education in the region in the late-nineteenth century, well before large-scale conversion took place. Many of my acquaintances credit Anglican missionaries with teaching Bidayuhs to stop fighting and taking heads, and to live in harmony and support each other during bereavement[7] and other difficult moments (see Chua 2012*a*, pp. 82–87). In the 1990s, the Anglican Church was joined in the area by the SIB, which has also garnered a positive reputation for giving financial and other aid to its adherents.

My acquaintances roundly describe these churches and their representatives as "kind" and "generous" — characteristics which they pointedly contrast with the *Kirieng* government, whom they charge with allowing only Muslims to "*maju*". "All the *kemudahan* in this area comes from outside", a young SIB mother once told me: "But those YBs [Members of Parliament] have given us nothing." She added that whereas government officials would tell villagers to fill out endless forms in order to obtain *kemudahan*, the Christian churches and many NGOs would simply hand over the cash. Their ability to do so is sometimes linked to the transnational communities of which they are part, and whose charity and compassion have brought donations, provisions, water tanks, and even new buildings to rural areas. A blacksmith's forge built in a neighbouring village by a Singaporean church group, for instance, was sometimes held up by my informants as an exemplar of how *kemudahan* could be acquired without recourse to the government's bureaucratic, ethno-religiously biased channels.

In sum, Christianity has acquired subtle political overtones over the years as both a legible means of being modern (but not Muslim) in Malaysia and a practical route of obtaining development while circumventing the state. Like *adat gawai*, however, its capacity to do so is ultimately circumscribed by state policies and responses. I was told, for example, that although the village mentioned earlier had persuaded its "Singapore friends" to pay for a new road to replace the rocky path leading to it, the government would not permit them to undertake the project. Consequently, my acquaintances' efforts to obtain development through their own religious resources are tempered by a sense of entrapment and frustration: of being tied to and reliant on a state, which they are unwilling to trust. This is exacerbated by the widespread opinion that even when development comes, it does so at a price — in this case, the loss of their land and villages. In recent years, these sentiments have been aggravated by the widely shared expectation that the cleared area will then be gazetted as a national park, a resort built near the reservoir, and the profits shared among the politicians. It is in these moments that Christianity's limitations as a material and political resource become painfully evident. Yet, these are also the points at which it comes into its own as a theological and moral influence in Bidayuhs' lives.

DEVELOPMENT THROUGH A CHRISTIAN LENS

For most Bidayuhs, Christianity is not merely a political tool but also "a meaningful system in its own right, one capable of guiding many areas of their lives" (Robbins 2004, p. 3). In this capacity, it has become interlaced with the affected villagers' efforts to make sense of and respond to the changes caused by the dam-construction and resettlement project. Significantly, I found that Christian notions and ideals were most often invoked in the context of opposition to — or at least unease over — the scheme. Of these, three recurred with particular frequency: individual morality, communal responsibility, and the renunciation of (excessive) wealth.

As I explain elsewhere (Chua 2012*b*), a distinctive Christian addition to Bidayuh communities has been the notion of the individual self as the locus of moral agency — one involved in a direct relationship of love (*rindu*) with God. This individualist model, however, is tempered by a strong and equally Christian ethos of love for one's neighbour: of taking care of the community at large and maintaining peace and good relations. As the scheme has progressed, these motifs have grown increasingly entwined with ideas of worldly renunciation, or at least non-covetousness, in the ruminations of those who are opposed to or uncertain about resettlement. Unlike supporters of the scheme, who tend to couch it in development-oriented terms of "progress" and "modernization", these people use Christianity to muddy the situation and the power relations imbued in it. And as the following example reveals, prayer gatherings — which are the only occasions on which villagers regularly come together from their dispersed farming activities — have become sites at which the tensions between these different parties are played out.

Shortly after construction commenced, a group of affected households began working with a human rights lawyer and opposition politician to contest the legality of the scheme and obtain official recognition of their right to build their own villages on their ancestral land rather than move to the resettlement site. The leader of this group is also the sole Anglican prayer leader of his village: a talented orator who has single-handedly run its prayer gatherings for years. As matters progressed, Sunday services and fellowship meetings in his village became microcosms and barometers of its internal fissures. Just after the case went to court, several families stopped attending Sunday services in apparent protest at the prayer leader's behaviour, which they thought might jeopardize their access to government compensation. When I arrived a few months later, the strains had eased, partly because many resettlement villagers had moved out with their newfound wealth. This demographic shift altered the dynamics of church services again, turning them into less fractious arenas in which the prayer leader and his allies could discuss the situation.

During my visit, I attended a fellowship gathering at which most attendees were involved in the anti-resettlement case. Following an hour of praise and worship, the prayer leader took advantage of the largely friendly crowd and began expounding on the legal proceedings. As he spoke, he deployed an intriguing melange of language and ideas deriving from official *pembangunan* discourses, Christianity, and legal and human rights terminology (picked up from the lawyers and sympathetic NGOs). Echoing the words of earlier missionaries (Chua 2012*a*, p. 138), he exhorted his listeners not to be afraid: it was not wrong, he said, to fight for their land rights (*hak tanah*). What they needed now, he added, was for the government to acknowledge (*ngaku*) their "title" (English) to the land on which they planned to build an alternative village. Other people could take the compensation money, he pointed out, but everyone in this room was going to do the right thing. In this way, he situated his audience within a moral framework that depicted them as forgoing immediate financial gain for the sake of a righteous outcome.

The prayer leader's portrayal of the situation would have been familiar to many in attendance, for the notion of following the way of the Lord (*aran Tuhan/Tăpa*) rather than "this world" (*dunia ong*) is a common theme in sermons throughout Bidayuh communities. In recent years, it seems to have gained especial currency among opponents of resettlement as a way of accounting for their fellow villagers' co-optation into the scheme. During fieldwork, I occasionally heard morose remarks about how kin and neighbours had become greedy and waylaid by money rather than taking care of their land and community. Such actions were depicted as an abrogation of their responsibility to their fellow Christians and villagers and, by extension, their personal responsibility to God. Accordingly, such ruminations were sometimes accompanied by comments on the inner character of the people in question. When a village elder and staunch supporter of resettlement showed up at a Sunday service looking exceptionally surly, for example, the woman next to me whispered conspiratorially that perhaps his *atin* (heart, inner spirit) was troubled (*susah*) because of his recent behaviour, implying that coming to church and entering the presence of God had somehow pricked his conscience.

These examples reveal how Christian ideas, practices, and spaces have been implicated — alongside notions of indigenous rights, *pembangunan* ideals and other factors — in the affected villagers' experiences of and responses to the resettlement scheme. Crucially, I suggest, they help to mitigate a poignant problem that no amount of grumbling about Malay/Melanau-Muslim hegemony will resolve: the fact that some of the thorniest conflicts over this scheme are not between Bidayuhs and political "others", but *within* Bidayuh communities and families. On a larger scale, there is also the irrefutable but equally troubling fact that the chief engineers of state-led development projects in the area are not Malays or Melanaus, but Bidayuh politicians. Such figures are often criticized by affected villagers of all stripes for their "*nakar*" (mischief-making) behaviour: for personally profiting from state politics and development spinoffs while their fellow Bidayuhs suffer the consequences. Without recourse to an anti-Malay/Muslim critique, some rural residents have depicted their behaviour in terms of a failure to live up to Christian ideals — for not caring about their own people while chasing money and political power. Over the last few years, I have occasionally heard pronouncements to the effect of, "He [Bidayuh politician] calls himself Christian, but look at what he's doing to his own people." Similarly, a comment in English on a highly critical Sarawakian blog runs thus:

> Wonder what kind of Christians are these Bidayuh BN [Barisan Nasional, the ruling coalition] goons? Far from what Jesus teaching!

Never inside the Bible that show Jesus hang around with corrupt leaders oppressing the poor (except being cruxified [sic] for helping the poor and against evil Roman rule). [...] Bidayuh folks must get their head right this time: stop voting the BN evil looters and be a responsible Christians. Help, defend the poor Bidayuhs like what Jesus always did, not kill them for BN greed.

Whether or not the poster was from the affected area, his or her comments are an apt, if unusually eloquent, encapsulation of the sorts of sentiments I have heard in this area. Unlike the Lun Bawang and Kelabit whose responses to Malay-Muslim hegemony are framed by the "Law of Love" (Bala, this volume), my Bidayuh acquaintances' ruminations tend to focus on fairness, justice, and individual responsibility. In the process, they reconfigure their relationship to the government by holding their political representatives accountable to a different — and arguably greater — moral order than that of the state. Perhaps it was just this logic that lay behind some of my informants' grim verdict, which I heard on a few occasions, that the cancer, which later struck one of the politicians behind the scheme was a just punishment from God.

CONCLUSION

In recent decades, most scholarship on development and economic policy in Malaysia has focused on the politics of race and indigeneity on the Peninsula. If religion — usually in the form of Islam — is present in these accounts, it too is highly politicized and invariably tied to the "Malay-Muslim exceptionalism" (Yeoh, this volume) that characterizes the postcolonial state. What this chapter has attempted to do, however, is shed light on not only the politics but also the religious dimensions of *pembangunan* elsewhere in Malaysia, from the perspective of one of its ethnic minority communities.

Contrary to the resolutely "anti-political", a-religious tenor of official developmentalist discourses, *pembangunan* for my Bidayuh acquaintances is shot through with religious tensions, politics, concepts, and moral templates. By this, I do not mean to portray *adat gawai* or Christianity as all-encompassing "cultures" that invariably determine their responses to development interventions. Bidayuhs are every bit as likely to attribute the failures, problems, and indeed promises of *pembangunan* to factors such as the global economy, environmental considerations and party politics. These elements, however, are woven into their lives alongside concerns about Muslim hegemony, Christian moral responsibility, and the agency of both God and the old *gawai* spirits. Rather like the strands of a Bidayuh rattan basket, such religious influences alternate between visibility and concealment, lending shape and structure to the situation without dominating it.

In the same way that state-led development projects have become sites at which wider inter-religious tensions and concerns are played out, then, both *adat gawai* and Christianity have become means through which my acquaintances grapple with the contingencies of development. What I have tried to underscore, however, is the distinctly quotidian quality of these ongoing negotiations. Such negotiations are responses, in part, to the demographic fluidity of the region and the acknowledged riskiness of outright religious discord (see also Yeoh, this volume). However, they also reflect the suffusive nature of the different religious influences in Bidayuhs' lives. Just as my acquaintances find it impossible to disentangle Islam from contemporary Malaysian statehood and *pembangunan*, they see *adat gawai* and Christianity as intrinsic to, and not distinct from, their socio-economic and political existence (Chua 2012*a*). Consequently, I argue, they enable Bidayuhs to ambiguate rather than outwardly contest their economic, political, and religious marginality through various small-scale means: by turning "cultural" preservation into a moral duty for the state, by tapping into charitable transnational religious networks, and by morally reframing the actions of peers and political representatives through Christian tenets. Viewed in this light, religious "toleration" and "conflict" look less like dichotomous states than like intertwined strands in a tangled and ever-shifting relational bundle. And it is only by studying them from the ground up, through the prism of the everyday, that scholarly observers can do justice to their multiplicity and complexity.

Notes

[1] This was one of a series of such events at which the affected villagers were awarded compensation cheques for the land they were about to lose.

[2] Sarawak and Sabah gained independence from Britain in 1963 when they joined Malaya and Singapore to form the Federation of Malaysia.

[3] In 2010, protests and violence erupted in parts of Malaysia, including Sarawak, when the High Court ruled in favour of allowing non-Muslims to use the term "Allah" to refer to God.

[4] Owing to the controversial nature of the scheme, I refrain from describing or referencing it in detail here.

[5] Indeed, they are often grouped together as a single constituency (see, e.g., Jayum and King 1994).

[6] I cite these Malay words as they have been incorporated into everyday speech, rather than modifying them for grammatical consistency.

[7] One of the most commonly cited reasons for converting to Christianity was the fact that the old death rituals were extremely elaborate and expensive, with the bereaved family having to pay large fees (rice, jars, cash, etc.) to a ritual specialist and undertaker to dispose of the corpse. Conversion to Christianity was seen to "free" people from such expenses and encourage mutual cooperation during the mourning period.

References

Bissonnette, Jean-François. "Representations as Practices: Producing a Native Space in Sarawak, Malaysia". *Journal of Cultural Geography* 28, no. 2 (2011): 339–63.

Boulanger, Clare L. *A Sleeping Tiger: Ethnicity, Class, and New Dayak Dreams in Urban Sarawak*. Lanham, Boulder, New York, Toronto, and Plymouth: University Press of America, 2009.

Brosius, J. Peter. "Bridging the Rubicon: Development and the Project of Futurity in Sarawak". In *Borneo 2000: Politics, History and Development*, edited by Michael Leigh. Kuching: Institute of East Asian Studies, Universiti Malaysia Sarawak, 2000, pp. 1–28.

Chua, Liana. "Fixity and Flux: Bidayuh (Dis)engagements with the Malaysian Ethnic System". *Ethnos* 72, no. 2 (2007): 262–88.

———. *The Christianity of Culture: Conversion, Ethnic Citizenship and the Matter of Religion in Malaysian Borneo*. Contemporary Anthropology of Religion series. New York and Basingstoke: Palgrave Macmillan, 2012*a*.

———. "Speaking of Continuity … Religious Change and Moral Dilemmas among Christian Bidayuhs in Malaysian Borneo". *American Ethnologist* 39, no. 2 (2012*b*): 511–26.

Escobar, Arturo. *Encountering Development: The Making and Unmaking of the Third World*. Princeton NJ and Oxford: Princeton University Press, 2012 [1995].

Ferguson, James. *The Anti-Politics Machine: "Development", Depoliticization, and Bureaucratic Power in Lesotho*. Cambridge: Cambridge University Press, 1990.

Jayum, Jawan and Victor King. *Ethnicity and Electoral Politics in Sarawak*. Selangor: Penerbit Universiti Kebangsaan Malaysia, 1994.

Mamit, James D., Ahi A. Sarok, and Nicholas Amin, (eds.). *Creating a New Bidayuh Identity*. Kuching: Dayak Bidayuh National Association, 2003.

Minos, Peter. *The Future of Dayak Bidayuh in Malaysia*. Kuching: Lynch Media Services, 2000.

Postill, John. *Media and Nation building: How the Iban Became Malaysian.* New York and Oxford: Berghahn, 2008.

Robbins, Joel. *Becoming Sinners: Christianity and Moral Torment in a Papua New Guinea Society.* Berkeley, CA: University of California Press, 2004.

Siddique, Sharon and Leo Suryadinata. "Bumiputra and Pribumi: Economic Nationalism (Indiginism) in Malaysia and Indonesia". *Pacific Affairs* 54, no. 4 (1981): 662–87.

Watson, Charles W. "Reconstructing Malay Identity". *Anthropology Today* 12, no. 5 (1996): 10–14.

INDEX

A

abangan, 18
abangan-like group in *santri*
   local belief in Madura, 221–22
   origin and nature, 216–20
   religious aspects of *blater*, 223–27
   remo as ultimate *blater* characteristic, 220–21
Abbas, Farhat, 106n16
Abbas, Tan Sri Mohamed Salleh, 344
Abidin, Asri Zainul, 271
ACCIN. *See* Allied Coordinating Committee of Islamic NGOs (ACCIN)
adat, 12
   Christianity and, antagonism between, 156
   Moluccan conflict and, 158–63
   and religion, 165–68
adat gawai, culturalization of, 407–9
Adji, Mukri, 120
Adnan, Wirawan, 93
Ahlus Sunnah Wal Jamaah (ASWJ), 242, 244, 360, 369
Ahmadi communities, 76
Ahmadiyah community, 26–30, 78
Ahmadiyah movement, 59, 83
Ahmad, Mirza Ghulam, 59, 77
Alallah, Mutawakkil, 4
Al-Attas, Syed Muhammad Naquib, 254
Alex, Pak, 143–44
Alie, Marzuki, 96, 124

Ali, Muhammad, 75
Al-Islam Muhammad Cheng Hoo Mosque in Palembang, 178
Ali, Suryadharma, 27, 28, 34, 95, 96
Alkitab, 294, 295
Allied Coordinating Committee of Islamic NGOs (ACCIN), 245, 299
Amansjah, Sjam, 103
Ambonese Christians, 157
Amin, Ma'ruf, 23, 25, 187
Ang Choo Hong, 329
Annan, Kofi, 354
anti-Ahmadiyah sentiment, 26
anti-Chinese riots in 1998, 178
anti-liberalism, 23
anti-politics, of sarawakian developmentalism, 401–4
Anti-Pornography and Porno-Action Bill, 90
Anti-Pornography Law, 99
anti-pornography taskforce, 95–97
Anwar, Nurul Izzah, 271, 286n4
Appadurai, Arjun, 268
Arifinto, H., 103
Arqam, Darul, 278
Article 3(1), 379
Article 11(1), 379
Article 121(A), 351
Article 28I(1), 53
Article 28J(2), 54
Asia-Pacific Economic Cooperation Summit, 190n7

419

ASWJ. *See Ahlus Sunnah Wal Jamaah* (ASWJ)
Aziz, Imam, 24
Aziz, Mohamed Nazri Bin Abdul, 352
Azra, Azyumardi, 83, 84

B
Badawi, Abdullah Ahmad, 242, 245, 314n29, 351–52
Baharum, Johari, 294
Bahasa Indonesia, 303
Bahasa Malaysia, 302–3
   and Christian Community, 294–95
bajingan, blater as, 216, 218, 219
Bakr, Abu, 363–64
Bandung District Court, 101
Bangsa Malaysia, 276
Banyuwangi, 196
   religious history of, 197–201
   uniqueness and conformity, 208–10
Barisan Nasional (BN), 276, 344
barong, 206
Batu Caves pilgrimage shrine, 270
Bayuni, Endy, 37n1
being Muslim, 258–61
Bel Air Café, Bandung, 98–99
Beng, Kim, 324, 325
Berita NECF, 301
bersih desa, 221
Biennial National Convention, 331
Binu, Haji, 121
black-market activity, 98
Blambangan, 197–98
Blasphemy Law, 19, 22, 25, 26, 52, 55
   provisions of, 55–59
blater, 13, 214
   acts of violence, 217
   as *bajingan*, 216, 218, 219
   characteristic of *remo as*, 220–21
   charismatic *jagoan*, 218
   origin and nature, 216–20

   religious aspects of, 223–27
   religious tradition, 214
BN. *See* Barisan Nasional (BN)
Bogor Church Permit Case, 113–14, 118–24, 126, 127
Bogor Indonesian Ulama Council, 120
Bogor Ulama Forum, 121
bogus monks, 325
bomoh, 257, 258
Bräuchler, Birgit, 12
British colonial rule, 274, 283
Buddhist majority states, 321
Buddhist minority states, 321
Buddhist-society relations, 325
Bulughul Maram, 116
bumiputera system, 404, 405

C
carok, 229n4
Catholicism, 136
CCM. *See* Council of Churches Malaysia (CCM)
centralized Islam, 239–40
CFM, 297–301
charismatic churches
   in Indonesia, 134
   miracle discourses building of, 141–45
Cheng Hoo Mosque in Surabaya, 176, 177
   as cosmopolitan space, 178–80
Chinese Islam, 178
Chinese Muslims
   cultures, 189
   dakwah activities of, 183
   in Indonesia, 174–76
Chinese Muslims preachers, 180
   Handono, Irena, 182–83
   Koko Liem, 181–82
   Medan, Anton, 183
   Tan Mei Hwa, 180–81
Chinese New Year celebrations in mosques, 184–85

Index

Chinese-style mosques, 176–77
  as translocal ethno-religious imagination, 177–78
Christian communities, 121, 134, 135, 137
  Bahasa Malaysia and, 293–95
  Kelabit and Lun Bawang, 382–84
Christian Federation of Malaysia, 273, 295–96
  formation of, 296–300
Christianity
  competition between Islam and, 145
  development through, 411–14
  in Malaysia, 322
  modernity, munificence, and bidayuh, 409–11
  significance of, 383–84
Christianization, 135, 140, 142, 148, 150, 190n5
Christian minority, 150
Christian missionary
  activities, 135
  societies, 135
Christian Moluccans, 157–58
Christian–Muslim relations, in Sarawak, 386
Christians
  Ambonese Christians, 157
  changing response of, 300–8
  Dutch colonial rule, 157
  in Malaysia, 384–85
  performance of, 151
  religious field, 293–95
churches, 410
  building of, 32–36
civil Buddhism, 323
civilizational Islam. *See Islam Hadhari*
civil society, 305–8
communal associations, 391–92
community, shifting responses in, 308–11
conflicts, toleration and, 8–14

conservative Muslims, 89
constitutional-legal framework, 53–55
converts-turned-preachers, 18
cosmopolitan Islam, 180
cosmopolitanism, notion of, 175
Council of Churches Malaysia (CCM), 273, 297
Court of Judicature Act of 1964, 240
Criminal Code, 89, 91, 103, 104, 106n14
  Article 282 of, 99
culturalization, of *adat gawai*, 407–9

D

dakwah, 209
  activities of Chinese Muslims, 183
  through cultural approaches, 185–87
dakwah movement, 254, 344–45
DAP. *See* Democratic Action Party (DAP)
decentralization, 75
democracy, 34
Democratic Action Party (DAP), 345
  Islamization and, 241
democratization, process of, 75, 78
Department for the Advancement of Islam in Malaysia. *See Jabatan Kemajuan Islam Malaysia* (JAKIM)
deviance, condemnations and categorizations of, 79
deviant Muslims
  exclusivist Islam emergence, 360–63
  fatwa, 365–68
  Shias, 368–74
Dewan Perwakilan Rakyat (DPR), 90, 123
Dimas, 142
dispute resolution, 117–19
divine bureaucracy, 239
DPR. *See* Dewan Perwakilan Rakyat (DPR)

Draft Law on Inter-religious Harmony, 124–26
dukun Islami, 222
Dutch colonial rule, 157
Dutch colonization in 1767, 198
Dutch East India Company, 156

E
Eastern culture, 89–90
Effendy, Bahtiar, 25
Elucidation of Article 6, 94
Elucidation of Law, 56–57
Elucidation to Article 4(1), 107n27
emancipatory movements, 255
ethnic conflict, 237
ethno-politics, Us vs Them syndrome, 385–91
exclusivist Islam, 375
  emergence of, 360–63

F
fatwa, 23, 26, 59, 79–81, 187
  deviant Muslims, 365–68
Federal Constitution, 275, 276, 313n10
  Article 121, 279
Federal Constitution of Malaysia, 291
Federal Territory Islamic authorities, 301
Fellaz Café, Padang, 99
Festival Imlek Bantul 2007, 185
forum externum, 54, 55
forum internum, 54
Forum of Central Kalimantan, 128n4
FPI. *See* Islamic Defenders' Front (FPI)
Friday prayers, 208

G
gandrung, 206
Gaylani, Al Sheikh Afeefuddin Al, 262
general election (2008), 303–5
Ghazali, Abdul Moqsith, 25, 27–28

government funds, *adat gawai*, 408
Great Compassion Mantra, 327

H
halal/haram, 274
halalization of consumption in Malaysia, 278
Halaqah, 273
Hamzah, Fahri, 103
Handono, Irena, 182–83
haram, 175
hard-core pornography, 97–98
Hashim, Tun Mohamed Suffian, 344
Hatuhaha
  Muslim community in, 162
  unity, 161
Hatuhaha Mosque in Rohomoni, 163
Hatuhaha union, 161
Hayden, Robert, 166
Hefner, Robert, 18
Hidayati, Mbak Nur, 149–50
Hilmy, Masdar, 18
Hindraf. *See* Hindu Rights Action Force (Hindraf)
Hindu-Indian informants, 282
Hindu Rights Action Force (Hindraf), 302
  emergence of, 248
  in Malaysia, 341–57
Hindu temples, demolition of, 351–55
Hindutva movement, 284
Hindutva nationalism in India, 283
Hoffstaedter, Gerhard, 287n14
Holston, James, 268
homemade pornography, 92
home-made videos, Pornography Law, 100–3
homosexuality, 105n11
Hudud laws, 241, 332
human rights groups, 281
Human Rights Watch, 98
Hunt, Robert, 296

I

IAIN. *See* State Institute of Islamic Studies (IAIN)
Ibrahim, Anwar, 254, 271
ICCPR. *See* International Covenant on Civil and Political Rights (ICCPR)
ICG. *See* International Crisis Group (ICG)
Idul Adha, 146
Idul-Fitri, 150
ijtihad, 255
Ikatan Remaja Muhammadiyah (IRM), 22
Imami Shiism, 365
Imlek
   ceremony in the Syuhada Mosque, 185
   in Indonesia, 184
   as religious debate, 187–88
INC. *See* Indian National Congress (INC)
India, Hindutva nationalism in, 283
Indian-Hindu traders, 283
Indian National Congress (INC), 284
Indian secularism, cornerstone of, 284
Indians, marginalization of, 342
Indonesia
   Ahmadiyah, 26–30
   bi-polar, 6
   charismatic churches in, 134
   Chinese Muslims in, 174–76
   diverse majority, hybrid identities, 4–7
   freedom of religion in, 75–84
   Imlek in, 184
   Muhammadiyah. *See* Muhammadiyah
   Muslim community in, 143, 157
   Nahdlatul Ulama. *See* Nahdlatul Ulama (NU)
   pentecostalism in, 143
   pluralism in, 154
   Pornography Law, 89
   proper and improper religion, 7–8
   religions classification, 7
   religious freedom in, 53–55
   religious minorities issues, 16–19
   security, 17
   Southeast Asian Muslims, 4
   state cultural policy, 209
   state infringement, 7–8
   Syi'ah, 30–32
   tighter legal regulations, 113
   toleration and conflict, 8–14
Indonesian Christian Church, 120
Indonesian Council of Ulamas, 137
Indonesian Democratic Party of Struggle (PDI-P), 97, 123
Indonesian Islam, 77
Indonesian Muslims, 145
intellectuals, 135
Indonesian National Ombudsman, 129n18
Indonesian NGO Medical Emergency Rescue Committee, 147
Indonesian Pentecostalism, 151n9
Indonesian Protestants, 133
Indonesian Ulama Council (MUI), 58, 124, 130n29
intermarriages, non-Muslims, 387
Internal Security Act (ISA), 248, 278, 295, 359, 406
International Covenant on Civil and Political Rights (ICCPR), 51, 53–54
International Crisis Group (ICG), 83
inter-religious conflict, 4
Inter-religious Harmony Advisory Council, 114
Inter-religious Harmony Forum, 11, 113, 118, 125
inter-religious relations, challenges in, 381

IRM. *See* Ikatan Remaja
    Muhammadiyah (IRM)
ISA. *See* Internal Security Act (ISA)
Islam, 17, 21, 24–25, 256, 258–61
    blaspheming of, 58–59
    bureaucratization, 242
    centralized, 239–40
    and Christianity, competition
        between, 145
    conversion to, 245
    in Malaysia, 342–49
    and Malaysian Constitution, 240
    mystical syncretist belief, 223
    resurgence of, 239
    role in politics, 5
    secularization, 239
    self and the institutional power of,
        255–57
    Sunni, 242
    Sunni–Syiah split in, 248
    and *Syariah* Court system, 240,
        242–43
Islam Hadhari, 242, 333
*Islamic Advancement Department of
    Malaysia* (JAKIM), 270
Islamic architecture, 277
Islamic cosmopolitanism, 175
    possibilities and limitations of,
        188–89
Islamic Defenders' Front (FPI), 17,
    121
Islamic devotional pop poetry, 263
Islamic education sector, seminars to,
    261
Islamic framework, 259
Islamic fundamentalism, 292, 312n6
Islamic groups, 122
Islamic identities, 77
Islamic jurisprudence, 250n7
Islamic morality, 89
Islamic Party of Malaysia (PAS),
    362–63
Islamic praxis, multiplicity in, 262

Islamic radicalism, 277
Islamic religious sphere, 290
Islamic resurgence, 239
Islamic state, 243
    issues in, 241
Islamic theocratic polity, 269
Islamic theory, 256, 264
Islamist extremist, 151n4
Islamization, 5, 240–43
    and DAP, 241
    in Malaysia, 341–57
    of Malaysian society, 277
    and Parti Islam Se-Malaysia, 241
    policy of, 240
    process, 239
    of state, 254
    UMNO-led and PAS-led, 243
Islamization policy, 293
Islam Muhammadiyah, 201
Ismailiyah Agha group, 370

J

Jabatan Kemajuan Islam Malaysia
    (JAKIM), 240
Ja'fariyah group, 370
jago, 217
Jahja, Junus, 175
Jaringan Islam Liberal, 77
Javanese Christian Church, 137
Javanese Islam, 184
jawara, 217, 231n17
Johor Security Council's regulation,
    329
Joint Ministerial Decree, 81, 82
Joint Ministerial Regulation, 128n1
Joint Regulation, 114
    Article 13 of, 125
juru kunci, 226, 231n19

K

Kairos Research Centre (1993), 306
Karaoke, Malang, 99–100
kaum muda, 256

kaum tua, 256
Kelabit, 382–84
  communal associations, 391–92
  Law of Love, 392–94
  Us vs Them syndrome, 382, 385–91
Kelana Jaya constituency, 305
kerapan sapi, 215, 227, 228
kerukunan umat beragama, concept of, 115
Ketuanan Islam, 277
kiai, 228n3
  religious aspects, 223–27
kiai dukun, 222
kiai Islam, 201–3
Kirieng, 405, 406
Koko Liem, 181–82
Kristenisasi, 137, 140, 149
Kuala Lumpur Federal Territory of Islamic Affairs Department, 272
Kuala Lumpur, religious spaces in, 280–83

L
LAIM. *See* Lembaga Antar Iman Maluku (LAIM)
Laksono, Agung, 95
Lampion Hati, 182
Laskar Jihad, 159
law enforcement beyond Supreme Court, 122–24
Law No. 1/PNPS/1965, 55–59
  liberal Muslims and, 61–64
Law of Love, 392–94
Lebaran bernuansa budaya Tionghoa, 186
Lee, Abdul Chalim, 186
Lembaga Antar Iman Maluku (LAIM), 163, 165
Lembaga, Rekomendasi, 130n23
lesbianism, 105n11
Lia Eden community, 58–59
liberal democrats, 105n4

liberalism, 76
liberal Muslims
  and Law No. 1/PNPS/1965, 61–64
  voices, limits of, 64–66
liberal-thinking Muslims, 90
Liddle, Bill, 17
"Little India/Masjid India", 280, 282
local belief, Madura, 221–22
Lun Bawang, 382–84
  communal associations, 391–92
  Us vs Them syndrome, 382, 385–91

M
Machasin, Pak Zulfa, 147
Madjid, Nurcholish, 52
Madura, local belief, 221–22
Madurese Islam, 215
Majelis Ulama Indonesia (MUI), 23
Malay domain, 291
Malay, Islam in, 254
Malay-Muslim exceptionalism, 270, 273–80
Malay-Muslim group, 385–86
Malay-Muslim hegemony, *pembangunan* and, 404–7
Malay-Muslim identity, 291
Malay-Muslim market, 278
Malay Muslims in Kuala Lumpur, 281
Malaysia
  Christian community in, 297, 322, 384–85
  Christian federation of, 295–96
  development in, 400–16
  ethnicity and religion in, 291–92
  fatwa in, 365
  halalization of consumption in, 278
  Hindraf in, 341–57
  history of Islam in, 255
  as hybrid state, 243
  inter-religious relations challenges in, 381
  Islamization in, 341–57

non-Muslims in, 348–49
political Buddhism in, 323, 336
religious minorities challenges in, 379–82
religious revivalism in, 388
Shias in, 359–76
state-religion relationship in, 290
Malaysia National Prayer Network (MNPN) project, 307–8
Malaysian Buddhism Development Master Plan of 2002, 326
Malaysian Buddhism, politics of, 322
Malaysian Buddhist Association (MBA), 248, 322–24
  and politics, 324–28
  and YBAM, comparison of, 335
Malaysian Buddhist youth, 331
Malaysian Constitution
  Amendment 121 (1A), 242, 245–46
  Article 11, 240
  Article 121, 240
  Article 121 (1), 250n3
  Article 121(1A), 243
  Article 128, 243, 250
Malaysian Consultative Council of Buddhism, Christianity, Hinduism and Sikhism (MCCBCHS), 299–300
Malaysian Consultative Council of Buddhism, Christianity, Hinduism, Sikhism and Taoism (MCCBCHST), 245, 327
Malaysian Department of Islamic Advancement (JAKIM), 361
Malaysian education system, 254
Malaysian Indian Congress (MIC), 286n3
Malaysian Indian-Hindu rights, Hindraf for, 349–55
Malaysian society, Islamization of, 277
Malay supremacy, 271
Malay youths, 292

Maluku Reconciliation and Reconstruction Meeting 2004, 164
marriage policy, 57
Maschan, Ali, 177
Masjid Muhammad Cheng Hoo, 190n2
Mas'udi, Masdar, 35
Matta, Anis, 107n32
MBA. *See* Malaysian Buddhist Association (MBA)
MCCBCHS. *See* Malaysian Consultative Council of Buddhism, Christianity, Hinduism and Sikhism (MCCBCHS)
MCCBCHST. *See* Malaysian Consultative Council of Buddhism, Christianity, Hinduism, Sikhism and Taoism (MCCBCHST)
Medan, Anton, 178, 183
Melanau, 404–5
Membela Kebebasan Beragama, 80
MIC. *See* Malaysian Indian Congress (MIC)
The Micah Mandate (TMM), 307
minority group of Muslims, 271
MNPN project. *See* Malaysia National Prayer Network (MNPN) project
moderation, religious minorities, 21–22
modernist Muslims, 200
modus vivendi, 241
Mohamad, Mahathir, 242, 275, 277, 296, 299, 342–45
Mohamad, Maznah, 277
Moluccan archipelago, 168n3
Moluccan conflict, 158–63
Moluccan Interfaith Council, 163–64
Moluccan Muslims, long-term isolation of, 156
Moluccan society, 155

Index

cultural dichotomization of, 160
Moluccas
  Muslim community in, 161
  Protestant Church of, 156
  religious war in, 154
MONAS incident, 183, 191n9
mosques, Chinese New Year celebrations in, 184–85
Muchtar, Affandi, 33
Mufid, Ahmad Syafi'i, 33
Mufti, Perak, 270, 271
Muhammad, Ashaari, 278
Muhammadiyah, 10, 186
  contemporary views on religious minorities, 24–26
  description, 19–21, 37
  establishment of, 19
  positions on religious minorities, 21–24
Muhammadiyah Islam, 201
Muhammad, Ustaz Ashaari, 362
MUI. *See* Majelis Ulama Indonesia (MUI)
Mujani, Saiful, 17
mujizat, 142
Muktazilah, 369
Muluk, Ustadz Tajul, 30
Muslim–Christian relationships, 143, 144, 151n1
Muslim communities, 127, 135, 145, 271
  in Hatuhaha, 162
  in Moluccas, 161
Muslim groups, 91
Muslim identity, 256
Muslim-majority democracy, 78
Muslim-majority lands, 145
Muslim-majority society, 146
Muslim revitalization (*dakwah*), 209
mute spectators, 391–92
Muzadi, Hasyim, 23
Myanmar, *Saffron Revolution* in, 321
mystical syncretist belief, of Islam, 223

N
Nahdlatul Ulama (NU), 78, 201
  contemporary views on religious minorities, 24–26
  description, 19–21, 36–37
  establishment, 19
  positions on religious minorities, 21–24
nasyid groups, 263–64
National Commission on Violence Against Women, 96
National Congress on Integrity, 306
National Evangelical Christian Fellowship (NECF), 297, 301
National Fatwa Council, 273
National Film Censorship Board, 327
National Indonesian Ombudsman, 118
National Mandate Party, 103
National Registration Department (NRD), 244
NECF. *See* National Evangelical Christian Fellowship (NECF)
negeri, 161
neo-liberal urban renewal policies, 269
New Economic Policy (NEP), 275
New Malay, 276
ngaji, 202–4
non-government organizations (NGOs), 115
non-Islamic religious literature, 348
non-Islamic religious sphere, 290
non-Malay domain, 292
non-Muslim field, 292
non-Muslim minorities
  Islam in Malaysia, 342–49
  in Malaysia, 238
non-Muslim religious groups, 281
North Kluang District Council, 329
NRD. *See* National Registration Department (NRD)
NU. *See* Nahdlatul Ulama (NU)
NU Islam, 200, 206, 210, 211

O

Office of the Ombudsman, 126–27
OHMSI. *See* Oriental Hearts and Mind Institute (OHMSI)
Ombudsman, 122, 123
  role of, 117–19
Ong Ka Ting, 326
Oriental Hearts and Mind Institute (OHMSI), 306
out-Islamization, 241
  competition of, 250n5
overall Javanese syncretism, 199

P

Partai Keadilan Sejahtera (PKS), 89, 103, 104
Partai Persatuan Pembangunan (PPP), 219–20
Parti Islam Se-Malaysia (PAS), 272, 301
  Islamization and, 241
pembangunan and Malay-Muslim hegemony, 404–7
Pengadilan Tata Usaha Negara, 114
Pentecostal church, 142
Pentecostal Church of Isa-Almasih at Salatiga, 143
Pentecostal communities, 133, 134
Pentecostal congregations, 134
Pentecostalism, 133, 145
Perak constitutional crisis, 309
Perhimpunan Pengembangan Pesantren dan Masyarakat (P3M), 22
PERKIM. *See* Pertubuhan Kebajikan Islam se Malaysia (PERKIM)
permit application process, Inter-religious Harmony Forum, 114–16
Persatuan Islam Tionghoa Indonesia (PITI), 176–77
Pertubuhan Kebajikan Islam se Malaysia (PERKIM), 345

pesantren, religious aspects, 223, 224
pious Pentecostals, 144
Pious Salatiga Muslims On the Net, 138
PITI. *See* Persatuan Islam Tionghoa Indonesia (PITI)
PKS. *See* Partai Keadilan Sejahtera (PKS)
pluralism, 76, 237–39
political Buddhism
  emergence of, 247–48
  in Malaysian context, 323
pornographic act, 96
Pornography Bill, 90
Pornography Law, 89–91, 103, 104, 105n8
  Article 6 of, 107n30
  Article 7 of, 106n23
  charges under, 97–98
  decisions by constitutional court on, 91
  home-made videos, 100–3
  submissions against, 91–95
post-New Order era, 76
post-New Order liberal Muslim discourse, 60–61
Prevention of Abuse of Religion, 52
Printing Presses and Publications Act 1984, 133n14
prominent accountability mechanisms, 118
Protestant Christians, 139
Protestant Church of Moluccas, 156
Protestantism, 136
public order, 64
Puzhao Buddhist Vihara, 328

Q

Qisas law, 241
Qur'an, 372, 373
Quranic incantations, 261

Index

R
radical Islamic groups, 117
Rahman, Tunku Abdul, 324, 343, 345, 361
rahmatan lil 'alamin, concept of, 181
Rahmat, Imdadun, 24
Rajagopalan, Mrinalini, 284
Rakyat, Parti Keadilan, 271
Razak, Datuk Seri Najib, 343
Razak, Najib Abdul, 270
recognition, of minority cultures, 209
recognized religions, 56–57
Reconciliation and Mediation Centre at IAIN in 2010, 165
reformasi, 91
Reid Commission, 355–56
Religion of Java (Geertz) (1960), 199
religious atavism, 237
religious Bandung, 99
religious bureaucracies, centralization of, 362
religious communities, conflicts between, 11–12, 113
religious conflict, 239, 243–49
 ethnic, 237
religious dialogue, reintegrating society through, 163–65
religious freedom
 constitutional-legal framework of, 53–55
 modern discourse on, 67n3
 post-New Order liberal Muslim discourse on, 60–61
Religious Freedom Advocacy Team, 25, 52
religious function, 129n9
religious majority, 127
religious manifestations, 257–58
religious minorities, 85, 127
 challenges in Malaysia, 379–82
 contemporary views on, 24–26
 Law No. 1/PNPS/1965 and its challenges, 55–59
 in Malaysia, 238–39
 NU and Muhammadiyah positions on, 21–24
religious pluralism, 134, 136
religious renewal movement, 52, 68n6
religious toleration, 243–49
religious conversion, 244–46
religious values, 64
 recognition of, 54–55
remo
 as *blater* ultimate characteristic, 220–21
 consumption of alcohol, 221
 tayub performance, 221
revivalism, Us vs Them syndrome, 385–91
Ricklefs, Merle, 18
ring-fencing (ibid.) of Muslims, 244
Risman, Elly, 93
rokat festivities, 221, 228
Roy, Olivier, 5
Rukun Iman, 230n11
Rukun Islam, 229n11
rulers, law for, 103–4
Rumah Kitab, 33

S
Sabarini, Prodita, 97
sabung ayam, 215, 227, 228
Saffron Revolution in Myanmar, 321
Saint Francis Xavier church (Catholic), 306
Salatiga
 Christian character of, 148
 contesting identity of, 137–41
 Islamization of, 149
 Muslims in, 147
"Salatiga, the City of Pious Muslims" project, 138
Sangha identity, 325

Santoso, Budi, 122
santri, abangan-like group in
   local belief in Madura, 221–22
   origin and nature, 216–20
   religious aspects of *blater*, 223–27
   religious tradition, 215–16
   remo as ultimate *blater*
      characteristic, 220–21
santri Islam, 200
SARA, 154
Sarawak developmentalism, anti-politics of, 401–4
Saya Anak Bangsa Malaysia movement, 310
seblang, 206
secular state, Malaysia as, 243
"the segmentary principle" in anthropology, 160
self-actualization, 255
self-censorship, practices of, 75
Sennett, Richard, 85n3
Serang district, Banten, nude dancers in, 98
sexual deviancies, 92
A Shadow Falls (2009), 206
Shias
   as minority, 368–71
   as security threat, 371–74
Shihab, Rizieq, 183
Shiism, ban on, 366
Simone, AbdouMaliq, 269
singular Malay politics, 276
Sisters in Islam (SIS), 299
siwalima, 160
slametan, 215
socio-religious tolerance, 34, 35
STAIN. *See* State Islamic Institute (STAIN)
state-endorsed pluralism, 136
State Institute of Islamic Studies (IAIN), 165
State Islamic Institute (STAIN), 134
state-religion relationship in Malaysia, 290
State Security Council (1993), 330
Subang Jaya constituency, 305
Sufi missionaries, 253
Sufism, 253, 262–63
Sunni Islam, 215
Sunni Muslims, attack against, 3
Sunni-Shia divide, in Islamic history, 363–65
Surau, 329
Syaddzili, Mujib, 29
Syamsuddin, Din, 22–24, 28, 29, 32, 116
Syariah Court system
   change of religion, 244
   and Islam, 240, 242–44
Syariah law, 259, 277, 279
Syariah legal system, 259
Syaukanie Ong, 173
Syi'ah, 30–32
syncretism, 199
Syriah law, 255

T

Tadzkirah, 78
Taiyibi Bohra group, 370
Tangzhuang, 190n7
Tan Mei Hwa, 173, 180–81
Tan Siew Sin, 326
Tantawi, Nasrudin Hassan, 272
Tanuseputra, Abraham Alex, 143
Tanuwidjaja, Sunny, 21
taraweh prayer in mosque, 179
ten principles, 250n6
Thalib, Ali Abi, 364
three-generational households, 281
Tikaman Ahmadiyah Terhadap Islam, 85n4
TMM. *See* The Micah Mandate (TMM)
toleration, and conflict, 8–14

Tong, Stephen, 134
Town and Country Planning Act 1976, 313n10
traditionalist Islam, conformity to, 201–4
traditionalist Muslims, 200

U
UKIM. *See* University of Maluku (UKIM)
ulama, 228n3, 230n13
Ulama Association of Malaysia, 272
umat Islam, 150
UMNO. *See* United Malays National Organization (UMNO)
Undang-Undang Dasar of 1945, 82
un-Islamic rituals, 188
United Malays National Organization (UMNO), 322, 343
  Islamic legislation, 240
University of Maluku (UKIM), 165
Us vs Them syndrome, 382
  revivalism, ethno-politics, enemy image and emergence of, 385–91

V
vagrant phase, 143
Varieties of Javanese Religion (1999), 206
Vereenigde Oost-Indische Compagnie (VOC), 156
violence
  of *blater*, 217
  mob, 90

VOC. *See* Vereenigde Oost-Indische Compagnie (VOC)

W
Wahid, Abdurrahman, 22, 52, 57, 190
Walisongo, 190n1
West Java, 119, 120
White Cross, 137
worship facilities in salatiga, number and types of, 139

Y
Yasmin Church of Bogor, 46n101
YBAM. *See* Young Buddhist Association of Malaysia (YBAM)
YBAM Biennial National Convention in 1992, 332–33
YBAM National Council, 328
Young Buddhist Association of Malaysia (YBAM), 248, 322, 323, 328–31
  Fifth Six-Year Plan (2004–10) of, 333
  Islamization, 332–35
  and MBA, comparison of, 335
Yudhoyono, Kristiani, 96
Yudhoyono, Susilo Bambang, 95, 96
Yusuf, Saefullah, 31
Yusuf, Slamet Effendy, 27
Yusuf, Toni, 141, 142

Z
Zulfa, Ibu, 148

www.ingramcontent.com/pod-product-compliance
Lightning Source LLC
Chambersburg PA
CBHW052111010526
44111CB00036B/1667